T0211850

Lecture Notes in Artificial Intelligence 12776

Subseries of Lecture Notes in Computer Science

More information about this subseries at http://www.springer.com/series/1244

Dylan D. Schmorrow · Cali M. Fidopiastis (Eds.)

Augmented Cognition

15th International Conference, AC 2021
Held as Part of the 23rd HCI International Conference, HCII 2021
Virtual Event, July 24–29, 2021
Proceedings

 Springer

Editors
Dylan D. Schmorrow
Soar Technology Inc.
Orlando, FL, USA

Cali M. Fidopiastis
Design Interactive, Inc.
Orlando, FL, USA

ISSN 0302-9743   ISSN 1611-3349   (electronic)
Lecture Notes in Artificial Intelligence
ISBN 978-3-030-78113-2   ISBN 978-3-030-78114-9   (eBook)
https://doi.org/10.1007/978-3-030-78114-9

LNCS Sublibrary: SL7 – Artificial Intelligence

This Springer imprint is published by the registered company Springer Nature Switzerland AG
The registered company address is: Gewerbestrasse 11, 6330 Cham, Switzerland

Foreword

Human-Computer Interaction (HCI) is acquiring an ever-increasing scientific and industrial importance, and having more impact on people's everyday life, as an ever-growing number of human activities are progressively moving from the physical to the digital world. This process, which has been ongoing for some time now, has been dramatically accelerated by the COVID-19 pandemic. The HCI International (HCII) conference series, held yearly, aims to respond to the compelling need to advance the exchange of knowledge and research and development efforts on the human aspects of design and use of computing systems.

The 23rd International Conference on Human-Computer Interaction, HCI International 2021 (HCII 2021), was planned to be held at the Washington Hilton Hotel, Washington DC, USA, during July 24–29, 2021. Due to the COVID-19 pandemic and with everyone's health and safety in mind, HCII 2021 was organized and run as a virtual conference. It incorporated the 21 thematic areas and affiliated conferences listed on the following page.

A total of 5222 individuals from academia, research institutes, industry, and governmental agencies from 81 countries submitted contributions, and 1276 papers and 241 posters were included in the proceedings to appear just before the start of the conference. The contributions thoroughly cover the entire field of HCI, addressing major advances in knowledge and effective use of computers in a variety of application areas. These papers provide academics, researchers, engineers, scientists, practitioners, and students with state-of-the-art information on the most recent advances in HCI. The volumes constituting the set of proceedings to appear before the start of the conference are listed in the following pages.

The HCI International (HCII) conference also offers the option of 'Late Breaking Work' which applies both for papers and posters, and the corresponding volume(s) of the proceedings will appear after the conference. Full papers will be included in the 'HCII 2021 - Late Breaking Papers' volumes of the proceedings to be published in the Springer LNCS series, while 'Poster Extended Abstracts' will be included as short research papers in the 'HCII 2021 - Late Breaking Posters' volumes to be published in the Springer CCIS series.

The present volume contains papers submitted and presented in the context of the 15th International Conference on Augmented Cognition (AC 2021), an affiliated conference to HCII 2021. I would like to thank the Co-chairs, Dylan D. Schmorrow and Cali M. Fidopiastis, for their invaluable contribution to its organization and the preparation of the proceedings, as well as the members of the Program Board for their contributions and support. This year, the AC affiliated conference has focused on topics related to brain-computer interfaces and brain activity measurement, physiological measuring and human performance, modeling human cognition, and applications of the above in complex environments.

I would also like to thank the Program Board Chairs and the members of the Program Boards of all thematic areas and affiliated conferences for their contribution towards the highest scientific quality and overall success of the HCI International 2021 conference.

This conference would not have been possible without the continuous and unwavering support and advice of Gavriel Salvendy, founder, General Chair Emeritus, and Scientific Advisor. For his outstanding efforts, I would like to express my appreciation to Abbas Moallem, Communications Chair and Editor of HCI International News.

July 2021   Constantine Stephanidis

HCI International 2021 Thematic Areas and Affiliated Conferences

Thematic Areas

- HCI: Human-Computer Interaction
- HIMI: Human Interface and the Management of Information

Affiliated Conferences

- EPCE: 18th International Conference on Engineering Psychology and Cognitive Ergonomics
- UAHCI: 15th International Conference on Universal Access in Human-Computer Interaction
- VAMR: 13th International Conference on Virtual, Augmented and Mixed Reality
- CCD: 13th International Conference on Cross-Cultural Design
- SCSM: 13th International Conference on Social Computing and Social Media
- AC: 15th International Conference on Augmented Cognition
- DHM: 12th International Conference on Digital Human Modeling and Applications in Health, Safety, Ergonomics and Risk Management
- DUXU: 10th International Conference on Design, User Experience, and Usability
- DAPI: 9th International Conference on Distributed, Ambient and Pervasive Interactions
- HCIBGO: 8th International Conference on HCI in Business, Government and Organizations
- LCT: 8th International Conference on Learning and Collaboration Technologies
- ITAP: 7th International Conference on Human Aspects of IT for the Aged Population
- HCI-CPT: 3rd International Conference on HCI for Cybersecurity, Privacy and Trust
- HCI-Games: 3rd International Conference on HCI in Games
- MobiTAS: 3rd International Conference on HCI in Mobility, Transport and Automotive Systems
- AIS: 3rd International Conference on Adaptive Instructional Systems
- C&C: 9th International Conference on Culture and Computing
- MOBILE: 2nd International Conference on Design, Operation and Evaluation of Mobile Communications
- AI-HCI: 2nd International Conference on Artificial Intelligence in HCI

List of Conference Proceedings Volumes Appearing Before the Conference

1. LNCS 12762, Human-Computer Interaction: Theory, Methods and Tools (Part I), edited by Masaaki Kurosu
2. LNCS 12763, Human-Computer Interaction: Interaction Techniques and Novel Applications (Part II), edited by Masaaki Kurosu
3. LNCS 12764, Human-Computer Interaction: Design and User Experience Case Studies (Part III), edited by Masaaki Kurosu
4. LNCS 12765, Human Interface and the Management of Information: Information Presentation and Visualization (Part I), edited by Sakae Yamamoto and Hirohiko Mori
5. LNCS 12766, Human Interface and the Management of Information: Information-rich and Intelligent Environments (Part II), edited by Sakae Yamamoto and Hirohiko Mori
6. LNAI 12767, Engineering Psychology and Cognitive Ergonomics, edited by Don Harris and Wen-Chin Li
7. LNCS 12768, Universal Access in Human-Computer Interaction: Design Methods and User Experience (Part I), edited by Margherita Antona and Constantine Stephanidis
8. LNCS 12769, Universal Access in Human-Computer Interaction: Access to Media, Learning and Assistive Environments (Part II), edited by Margherita Antona and Constantine Stephanidis
9. LNCS 12770, Virtual, Augmented and Mixed Reality, edited by Jessie Y. C. Chen and Gino Fragomeni
10. LNCS 12771, Cross-Cultural Design: Experience and Product Design Across Cultures (Part I), edited by P. L. Patrick Rau
11. LNCS 12772, Cross-Cultural Design: Applications in Arts, Learning, Well-being, and Social Development (Part II), edited by P. L. Patrick Rau
12. LNCS 12773, Cross-Cultural Design: Applications in Cultural Heritage, Tourism, Autonomous Vehicles, and Intelligent Agents (Part III), edited by P. L. Patrick Rau
13. LNCS 12774, Social Computing and Social Media: Experience Design and Social Network Analysis (Part I), edited by Gabriele Meiselwitz
14. LNCS 12775, Social Computing and Social Media: Applications in Marketing, Learning, and Health (Part II), edited by Gabriele Meiselwitz
15. LNAI 12776, Augmented Cognition, edited by Dylan D. Schmorrow and Cali M. Fidopiastis
16. LNCS 12777, Digital Human Modeling and Applications in Health, Safety, Ergonomics and Risk Management: Human Body, Motion and Behavior (Part I), edited by Vincent G. Duffy
17. LNCS 12778, Digital Human Modeling and Applications in Health, Safety, Ergonomics and Risk Management: AI, Product and Service (Part II), edited by Vincent G. Duffy

http://2021.hci.international/proceedings

15th International Conference on Augmented Cognition (AC 2021)

Program Board Chairs: **Dylan D. Schmorrow,** *Soar Technology Inc., USA,* **and Cali M. Fidopiastis,** *Design Interactive, Inc., USA*

- Mehmet Emin Aksoy, Turkey
- Mark Costa, USA
- Martha Crosby, USA
- Fausto De Carvalho, Portugal
- Daniel Dolgin, USA
- Rodolphe Gentili, USA
- Ricardo Gregorio Lugo, Norway
- Monte Hancock, USA
- Robert Hubal, USA
- Kurtulus Izzetoglu, USA
- Benjamin Knox, Norway
- Chang Nam, USA
- Sarah Ostadabbas, USA
- Mannes Poel, Netherlands
- Dale Richards, UK
- Stefan Sütterlin, Norway
- Suraj Sood, USA
- Ayoung Suh, South Korea
- Ana Rita Teixeira, Portugal
- Martin Westhoven, Germany
- Ren Xu, Austria

The full list with the Program Board Chairs and the members of the Program Boards of all thematic areas and affiliated conferences is available online at:

http://www.hci.international/board-members-2021.php

HCI International 2022

The 24th International Conference on Human-Computer Interaction, HCI International 2022, will be held jointly with the affiliated conferences at the Gothia Towers Hotel and Swedish Exhibition & Congress Centre, Gothenburg, Sweden, June 26 – July 1, 2022. It will cover a broad spectrum of themes related to Human-Computer Interaction, including theoretical issues, methods, tools, processes, and case studies in HCI design, as well as novel interaction techniques, interfaces, and applications. The proceedings will be published by Springer. More information will be available on the conference website: http://2022.hci.international/:

General Chair
Prof. Constantine Stephanidis
University of Crete and ICS-FORTH
Heraklion, Crete, Greece
Email: general_chair@hcii2022.org

http://2022.hci.international/

Contents

Modelling Human Cognition

Augmented Cognition in Complex Environments

BCI and Brain Activity Measurement

Distributed Remote EEG Data Collection for NeuroIS Research: A Methodological Framework

Théophile Demazure[1]([✉]), Alexander J. Karran[1], Jared Boasen[1,2],
Pierre-Majorique Léger[1], and Sylvain Sénécal[1]

[1] HEC Montréal, Montréal, QC, Canada
theophile.demazure@hec.ca
[2] Hokkaido University, Sapporo, Hokkaido, Japan

Abstract. Remote electroencephalography (EEG) studies offers the exciting opportunity to gather data within a participants' home environment. However, remote EEG data collection trades some internal validity for ecological validity. When interacting with interfaces or other artifacts in remote settings, neurophysiological responses and behaviour may display distinct differences compared to laboratory studies. We propose a methodological approach composed of several recommendations and an iterative process framework to support this new avenue of research. The framework was developed during workshops composed of a diverse panel and a literature review of relevant research to complement our discoveries. We highlight and discuss the significant challenges associated with remote EEG data collection, and propose recommendations. We introduce the concept of self-applicability and propose a set of measures to guarantee good signal quality. Additionally, we offer specific recommendations for research design, training, and data collection strategies. We offer the iterative process framework to provide support rigorous data collection, innovative research questions, and the construction of large-scale datasets from remote EEG studies.

Keywords: Electroencephalography · Remote experiment · Real-world · Methodology · Human-computer interaction

1 Introduction

The current global pandemic has necessitated developing novel methodologies to sustain ongoing research programs relying on neurophysiological measurements, such as in the field of NeuroIS and HCI [1, 2]. The critical requirement of social distancing to reduce COVID-19 transmission severely complicates conventional neurophysiological experimental methodologies where the researcher is responsible for the installation of neuro-psychophysiological measurement tools on the research subject. A potential solution to this problem is for researchers to conduct experiments remotely. This type of solution involves using the Internet to connect with a distributed pool of experimental

© Springer Nature Switzerland AG 2021
D. D. Schmorrow and C. M. Fidopiastis (Eds.): HCII 2021, LNAI 12776, pp. 3–22, 2021.
https://doi.org/10.1007/978-3-030-78114-9_1

subjects who participate from their homes, and who are not technically trained to use neurophysiological collection tools and techniques.

In-field HCI studies offer new opportunities to observe and understand human interaction with technological artifacts in diverse environments. These studies have been shown to produce different results from lab-based experiments [3, 4] and can lead to a unique understanding of artifacts undergoing evaluation in ecologically valid contexts [5]. Likely, subjects are more at ease in their everyday environments, and the neurophysiological responses they exhibit when interacting with interfaces in these environments may be more reflective of their natural tendencies and habits. However, in-field studies suffer from several challenges, consisting of but not limited to, cost [6], time, and reproducibility [6, 7]. These problems can be further exacerbated when researchers must moderate research protocols and interact with subjects remotely.

Furthermore, collecting data in the field can become challenging when consideration is given to the environment; in laboratory studies, environmental confounds can be identified and controlled. In contrast, field environments are by their nature chaotic and in the main uncontrollable, leading to lesser quality data collection in comparison. Nowhere is this more apparent than in the case of electroencephalography (EEG) data collection, which is a challenging proposition in the field under ordinary circumstances. Add to this proposition, a global pandemic in which human touch is not indicated. Then the challenge becomes markedly increased, adding further complicating and potentially confounding factors including the self-application of an EEG headset and the need to perform experimental protocol moderation remotely. These factors alone add a host of issues concerning the reliability and consistency of data acquisition, potentially leading to artifacts and errant brain signals during the data processing. Moreover, the independence and validity of a measure can be impacted by the experimental protocol itself or natural contingencies. In these regards, the remote experimental setting differs significantly from laboratory experiments and even real-world EEG research.

The research objective presented in this manuscript is to propose a practical framework for remote EEG data collection. We aim to build upon the methodological foundation provided for the field of NeuroIS by Riedl and colleagues [8, 9], synthesis of empirically tested EEG methodologies, and further propositions from the EEG literature, to outline the challenges and highlight specific risks to remote experimental data collection methodologies caused by particular environmental factors and propose recommendations and guidelines to mitigate those risks. We narrow the scope of our proposal to focus on the research methodology - i.e., methods and experimental design, data collection and data analysis – as per [8]. The proposed framework does not cover research question development, theorizing, reviewing the literature, or interpreting the results.

2 Background

EEG is a method of monitoring and recording the brains electrical activity at the surface of the scalp, which is generated by the synchronous activity of neurons reflecting brain processes at a given point in time. EEG is non-invasive and offers a high temporal but low spatial resolution. Researchers using EEG are often interested in observing spontaneous EEG and Event-Related Potentials (ERP) [9]. Spontaneous EEG reflects ongoing brain activity, and specific frequency bands can be extracted from this signal and associated with mental states. For example, in HCI, variance in the alpha (8–13 Hz), beta (13–25 Hz) or theta (4–8 Hz) frequency bands have been used to measures engagement [10–12], workload [13, 14] or vigilance [15].

ERPs are a very weak signal present in EEG that are triggered by external and timely stimuli. These patterns are difficult to decipher from among the spontaneous EEG signal, requiring the use of repeated measurement to average the signal and increase the signal-to-noise ratio [16]. In HCI, ERPs have been used to a large degree to address a vast range of research questions such as risk-taking [17], perception processes [18], vigilance [15, 19], attention resources and age [20]. Moreover, both frequency band features and ERPs can be used simultaneously to uncover more complex cognitive phenomena, such as classifying workload in different affective contexts [21].

However, most user experience and HCI research takes place in the laboratory, with EEG research using a "neuroergonomics" approach to measure the "brain at work" only recently being embraced [19]. The study of human behaviour in naturalistic environments and motion has encouraged the development of new methods and frameworks. Using state-of-the-art light-weight clinical EEG, MobiLAB [22] combines several psychophysiological measures with EEG such as electromyography [23, 24] and motion capture [25] to study the link between a human's cognition, the physical body and the environment [24]. See [26] for a review on the link between cognitive process and natural human motion.

The recording of EEG in the field is advancing fast with the advent of light-weight wireless EEG sensor technologies. Researchers have repeatedly demonstrated the feasibility of recording in uncontrolled environments and "extreme" settings such as in classrooms [27–29], during a walk [30–32], on a bike [33], while doing sports [34, 35], and during museum visits [36]. However, these devices come with methodological challenges, such as optimizing the signal-to-noise ratio and uncontrolled motion-related artifacts [37], which lead to a consideration of the trade-off between ecological validity and data quality.

Dry electrode technology is an additional advancement that has the potential to increase EEG system usability and portability. Recent studies have shown that dry EEG system can offer good data quality while increasing ease of setup [38, 39]. Moreover, the advances in consumer-grade EEG technology has reduced associated costs significantly. While there are some divergent findings on consumer-grade EEG devices [40], there is some evidence that these devices can capture specific brain responses. For example, two studies investigating auditory stimuli and the P300 ERP while walking in the real-world were able to capture these data in high fidelity using both clinical-grade EEG [31] and consumer-grade EEG [32]. Furthermore, the popular Muse (Interaxon) consumer-grade EEG device has been shown to capture visuospatial attention N200 and p300 [41]. See [42] for a recent review of consumer-grade EEG and their signal quality.

In conclusion, EEG data collection in the real-world has created new challenges to overcome. However, even in its current nascent state, mobile EEG offers very promising possibilities to perform quality HCI research if compromises can be found to serve the ecological validity of in-field experimental studies. This manuscript proposes a set of guidelines that consider the factors associated with mobile EEG and provides a framework for completing remote neurophysiological research.

3 Method

To develop the proposed framework, we utilized a practical workshop approach to uncover challenges and threats specific to remote EEG collection. The workshop was broken into weekly sessions (# session = 5) with 9 participants. Participants all had access to a EEG system with 8 hybrid electrodes from g.Tec Neurotechnology GmbH (Unicorn, Austria) and an technological environment for stimuli presentation based on PsychoPy [43]. We identified several challenges to rigorous remote EEG collection during the workshops regarding protocol, measurements, technical components, and logistics. We then addressed the literature to substantiate our findings and uncover potential mitigation strategies.

Fig. 1. Example workshops, left a data visualization tutorial, right how to correctly configure the EEG headset

3.1 Workshop

We built our framework iteratively through collaboration with a diverse team of undergraduate, graduate students, technicians, and researchers from our host institution. Each member contributed valuable feedback concerning different aspects of the framework construction process.

The procedure we adopted to develop the workshop methodology is divided into two phases (see Fig. 1) training and iterative development. The training phase involved weekly recorded workshops to introduce, learn, and exchange information about the various hardware and software components required to perform research at a distance. The second iterative development phase involved testing various data collection methodologies. The initial testing performed in the iterative development phase were based on established experimental paradigms, and reproducible phenomena (e.g., N170 event-related potential) triggered by the neural processing of faces displayed upon participants screens using a simplified stimuli presentation paradigm developed in python.

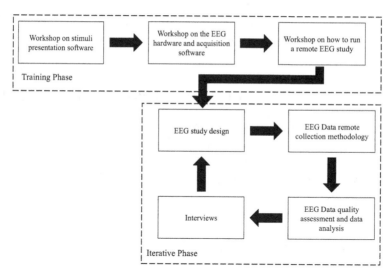

Fig. 2. Pilot study procedure.

In order to make informed decisions and validate each stage of the distributed data collection process, we collected qualitative feedback from each team member who acted as both participant and a remote actor in the data collection. This feedback was derived from the workshops during the training phase, interviews with the different actors at the end of each iterative development workshop session and general commentary throughout the framework development process. Additionally, we checked EEG data quality after each data collection, thereby permitting immediate improvement of the methodological procedure, participants' training and iterative improvement of the experimental design for subsequent data collections.

In the following sections, we generalize our findings to provide guidelines for remote EEG collection.

3.2 Literature Review

To complement our findings, we addressed the literature, using queries within Web of Science (WoS) and Google Scholar (GS) using a combination of 3 groups of keywords. To represent the context of EEG collection and we used the search terms "Real-world", "Mobile", "Uncontrolled environment", or "In-field". To limit the research to the instrument of interest, we restricted the results to "Electroencephalography" or "EEG". Finally, we limited the search to "human" subject. For WoS database, we subtracted the papers using the keywords AK = "Sensors" due to a significant amount of hardware sensor development in the search results.

This search resulted in 187 papers (GS = 100, WoS = 87). We limited our search to the first 100 papers in GS due to the high number of papers the tool commonly offers. Six papers were removed due to duplication. A first title screening was performed, resulting in 140 papers, we then completed an abstract screening using additional inclusion criteria comprised of uncommon parameters for EEG collection (e.g., outside laboratory, dry and wet electrodes, moving subjects) leaving 102 papers, which after a full reading resulted in 45 papers. Furthermore, we excluded any papers mentioning intracranial EEG and hardware development.

4 Methodological Framework for Distributed EEG Data Collection

Riedl and colleagues [8] defined six critical factors linked to the measurement of physiological states (i.e., reliability, validity, sensitivity, diagnosticity, objectivity, and intrusiveness) which are critical in NeuroIS methodologies and indeed the wider UX/HCI and ergonomics communities and can determine research quality and success. We build upon their work and identify challenges and threats to these critical factors specific to remote EEG data collection.

4.1 Instrument Related Challenges and Recommendations

Self-applicability. Contrary to traditional EEG studies, remote EEG collection implies that participants will apply and configure the EEG headset by themselves as trained research professionals are not physically but virtually present in the room. Self-applicability refers to the level at which the participant can autonomously and consistently install the EEG headset. We found that the ease in which a participant can apply and configure an EEG headset is a significant challenge requiring careful consideration when selecting an EEG system for remote data collection. Participant errors may create disparities in electrode placement, affecting measurement validity and resulting in poor signal quality.

Self-applicability Can Lead to Inter or Intra-subject Variation in Electrode Placement. Inter and intra-subject variation in electrode placement may create measurement errors both within and across subjects and present unexpected neurophysiological differences due to discrepancies in the cortical area covered by the electrodes; this can negatively impact repeated measurement and threaten a measurement's reliability and validity.

Due to the opportunity to collect data during real-world activities at home, at work and outdoors, EEG technology's self-applicability has become an important research question. Hinrichs et al. [38] asked 32 participants if they would be able to apply a dry EEG system themselves, twenty-two of which answered "yes" and eight answered, "yes, but with another person's support". Participants also found themselves more agile [39] and the installation process easier [44] with dry systems compared to wet systems. The relative-ease of installation was also found not to impact signal quality across participants significantly[45]. However, differences in electrode positions between operators and self-applied headsets were observed, particularly around the heads midline [45].

Self-application Can Induce Changes in Cognitive State. During self-application, the execution process (setting up the instruments, sensors application, calibration) can lead to unwanted changes in a participants state. This can threaten the objectivity of a study (i.e., independency of the results) [8], which can further result in replication and validity issues where the coexistence of multiple mental or emotional states can lead to misinterpretation of the results [46]. Stress, disengagement, or frustration can be adverse effects of a challenging self-application phase and "spillover" to subsequent tasks. Artifacts linked to muscle tension can be observed in anxious participants justifying the need for a non-intimidating experimental environment [47].

Recommendations. First, considering the aforementioned challenges, we propose using low-density dry electrode systems for remote EEG collection to ensure feasible self-application. High-density electrode systems have been related to higher setup times per electrodes [39], a limitation that the use of low-density systems can mitigate. Using fewer electrodes can serve to facilitate installation by reducing application time and minimize the impact of placement variability. Additionally, dry electrodes offer reduced setup time compared to wet systems [38, 45].

Secondly, based on our workshop feedback and our literature review, we propose the use of several measures for self-applicability (see Table 1). Building upon past work [39, 44, 48, 49], installation speed, comfort during preparation, and perceived application difficulty/speed offer great feedback during the first and subsequent iterations of a data collection where participants learn to apply EEG prior to beginning a study. As a comparison between EEG headsets, application time can be divided by the number of channels [39]. We also propose the measurement of perceived self-efficacy to capture participants' confidence in the process. Self-efficacy has been related to increased performance and reduced anxiety [50]. We advise that in order to observe any developing trends, multiple measurements should be taken during training phases setting a minimal quality threshold to attain before a remote experiment can begin.

Third, in the absence of an objective measure of electrode coordinates usable at a distance by layman participants, we recommend monitoring the setup and configuration through video conferencing or other virtual conferencing or experiment platforms such as lookback.io (Montréal, Québec) using a trained moderator. During initial configuration, every effort should be taken to control for user movement, and pictures of the fitted cap should be captured using multiple angles (front, back, laterals, and up). Post-hoc, these images can be used to compare variations in electrode placement across the population of participants. Additionally, the time taken to apply the headset, the quality of the EEG data, and electrode placement should be monitored in real-time to provide feedback to the participant and inform any adjustments.

Forth, we propose the use of a baseline for two reasons, the first stems from procedures already utilized in field studies such as staring at a fixed cross, standing in front of a wall for several minutes [29, 36] or passive standing in the collection environment [52]. The second reason is concerned with the return to baseline response. A consistent baseline can serve as a "reset" and help prime participant neurophysiological responses after the self-application phases. In our workshops, we observed that participants reported feeling stressed by the setup and configuration process and insecure with their ability to do so effectively. A moderator should offer direct and encouraging feedback to provide a positive environment and a return to baseline.

Finally, during the configuration and signal quality testing stage, it has been shown that actively involving the participant can improve data quality. For example, [29] introduced the participants to movement, speech, and blink artifacts in EEG data prior to the

Table 1. Questionnaire and measures proposition of self-applicability of EEG before and during an experiment

Measuring self-applicability	Measure
After headset application	
Application time of the EEG headset (taken from [45])	Time in seconds
Perceived application difficulty (adapted from [44])	How do you rate the difficulty of installing the *EEG headset* system to the head?
Perceived application speed (adapted from [44])	How do you rate the installation speed of the *EEG headset*?
Perceived self-efficacy (inspired from [50, 51])	Rate your degree of confidence by recording a number from 0 to 100 using the scale given below: - Applying the *EEG headset* - Placing the electrode correctly - Ability to apply the EEG headset again in the future - Ability to keep a consistent electrode placement in the future
After impedance and signal quality check	
Impedance process time of the EEG headset (taken from [45])	Time in seconds
Perceived impedance check difficulty	How do you rate the difficulty of adjusting the *EEG headset* system to the head?
Perceived impedance check speed	How do you rate the speed of adjusting the *EEG headset*?
Comfort after preparation (adapted from [39])	How comfortable is the *EEG headset*?
After the experiment	
Comfort after the experiment (taken from [48])	Did you feel discomfort during the experiment? Did you feel discomfort because the electrodes pinched your head? When, if at all, did the EEG cap/electrodes start to become uncomfortable?

full data collection. In HCI, Brown and Colleagues [7] echoed this idea with the concept of "participants as investigator" which proposes that in the field, participants are more than "passive subjects". They have a non-negligible role in the success of the study. In our case, following advice from [5] and [7], we adopted an approach of direct engagement with the data collection actors to foster discussion and gain a sense of their own impact on each stage of the development process. Thus, we recommend pilot sessions to ensure that the experimental technological infrastructure is working (e.g., collection instruments, stimuli presentation, synchronization) with a dummy protocol (e.g., N170 Face/Object paradigm, open-closed eyes), which will continue to train the participant and acquire futher EEG data for quality assessment.

Dry Electrodes and Mobility. Considered in the context of remote data collection, any EEG technology's mobility and consistency are essential. As discussed above, it will, by necessity, be used in an uncontrolled environment where the setup and configuration can differ due to various scenarios. Utilizing this as the operational focus, we give consideration to dry electrode EEG technologies. It is important to note, that while dry electrode EEG systems ameliorate a number of problems associated with mobility in EEG research, they come with some drawbacks, such as high impedance, highly prone to motion artifacts, and discomfort when worn for extended periods. It has been shown that increased mobility can be achieved in dry electrode EEG systems using small and wireless devices [53]. Wireless functionality facilitates swifter application and configuration by the participant and increases freedom of movement. However, wireless functionality has a significant limitation concerning data loss when used too far from the wireless receiver [36].

High Impedance Can Increase Noise Levels. High impedance can lead to an increase in low-frequency noise and distortion in the signal. High impedance has been shown to negatively affect the number of trials necessary to reach statistical significance in some ERP studies [54, 55]. Furthermore, increased power in frequencies <4 Hz has been reported compared to wet systems [38, 56]. Before moving to the field, these limitations should be acknowledged to allow informed research designs and appropriate measure selection.

Dry Electrodes Are More Prone to Motion Artifacts. Noise generated by participants' physical movements is an important challenge for dry systems [57]. ICA has been used to correct motion artifacts in a number of real-world studies [15, 16]. However, it has been recommended to use a high-density EEG system [58]. Promising but novel techniques are being developed to reduce this form of artifact are being developed for recordings involving a high level of movement such as walking [59], running [35], and more importantly for low-density EEG [60].

Comfort. The EEG cap with the electrodes should be comfortable when worn for several hours. Dry electrodes EEG systems have shown to be well accepted by subjects for long-duration tasks [38]. Repeated measurement of comfort during an experiment shows a clear reduction over time [39] for both dry and wet systems. Feelings of pressure, spiky electrodes over the scalp or other factors related to the EEG system itself can create discomfort during the experiment and lead to unwanted movement and noise.

Number of Electrodes. A practical consideration for the selection of a dry electrode system is the number of electrodes. High-density EEG headsets allow for source localization and techniques such as Independent Component Analysis (ICA) to assess the impact of artifactual components within the signal. These techniques are often used in work following the MoBi framework [25, 30, 61]. Unfortunately, high-density EEG headsets threaten self-applicability and may increase the chances of poor quality EEG data. When the number of electrodes is taken into account, the time taken to position dry electrodes correctly increases compared to wet systems due to the higher impedance levels associated with dry electrodes [39]. Considering that this process will be performed remotely, increasing electrode density can be considered a risk.

Recommendations. Firstly, the evidence suggests that low-density EEG systems are better suited for remote collection, and in this regard, consumer-grade EEG systems can be considered. However, there is concern about their ability to capture more precise patterns such as ERPs, and in this regard, empirical data shows that it is feasible (see [42] for a review). A further concern with low-density EEG systems is the use of signal processing techniques such as ICA. Applying techniques such as Artifact Subspace Reconstruction (ASR) [62] to remove short-duration high-amplitude artifacts due to motion is indicated in these cases. The approach is implemented in EEGLAB and has been shown not to distort the ERPs significantly [62]. Chang et al. [63] validated the algorithm and proposed some suggestions about parameters. ASR has been used in several field studies using EEG [36, 64, 65].

Secondly, it is essential to adapt research designs in light of the chosen mobile EEG device's limitations. The number of trials should be increased compared to laboratory experimentation for the following reasons:

- Gaining statistical significance for ERP necessitates more trials when impedance high [54, 55].
- Conservative criteria for data quality and trial rejection is required when dealing with real-world EEG recordings, which aligns with empirical work showing a rejection rate of around 50% in a similar context [29, 31].
- Some empirical evidence shows that signal features of interest can be reduced in the real-world [32] and can be further moderated by uncontrolled mental states induced by the environment [33].

With these in mind, we recommend using conservative artifact rejection thresholds and adapting experimental designs to consider the use of a signal artifact reduction method such as ASR from first principles.

Lastly, we propose that secondary measurements can be used to assess the quality of the EEG data and add convergent validity. For example, using a gyroscope embedded on the EEG cap to aid independent evaluation of movement within trials [33]. A gyroscope or accelerometer offers contextual information that can help identify when trials require rejection or categorize motion artifacts [66]. Once identified, those artifacts can be used in the analysis stage, such as using muscle artifacts as covariates within the analysis process [9].

Uncontrolled Environments. Electrical, physiological, and mechanical artifacts represent a real challenge for in-field EEG data collection. Outside of laboratory settings, unusual and unstable noise sources can reduce EEG signal quality, natural contingencies can disrupt data collection, and ambient luminosity variation recording can induce a change in the EEG signal. While some potential confound sources are impossible to control for remotely, documenting and providing minimal control during the data collection can increase the rigor of an experiment and quality of the data.

Source of Noise. In uncontrolled environments and in particular a domicile, noise sources are challenging to identify and control. Signal artifacts can be produced by light sources, electrical cables, computers, tv's etc. External noise such as ambient electrical current is habitually observed at 50 or 60 Hz and corrected via notch filters. However, each remote participants' environment will be unique, potentially leading to inconsistencies in the data. Random sources of noise can impact the reliability and validity of a measure in a remote context.

Natural Contingencies. Real-world data collection is prone to unplanned events. Researchers in the field have proposed that those events should not be considered "noise" but may contain interesting or pertinent information [67]. They are part of the study's natural context and are likely to happen during at-home remote EEG data collection. Recording video of the participant during the experiment may prove useful in this regard to annotate EEG data but also identify confounding events. However, post-hoc identification of problematic signal sections requires timestamping and synchronizing the EEG system and camera [47]. Unplanned events threaten the reliability of the EEG measures due to change in the context of data collection within and between the experiment. It also impacts negatively measures validity as it can confound the measurement of the construct of focus (e.g., attentional resources allocated to the stimuli or to external distractors).

Researchers have proposed an event-tagging framework to allow systematicity and consistency across multiple studies using Hierarchical Event Descriptors (HED) [67]. They created a standardized but rich dictionary to describe real-world events during EEG study and claim that HED facilitates the annotation of events both in real-time and post-hoc. Further research has used automated processes to annotate continuous EEG to identify unrelated stimulus responses in the signal [68]. Building on a labelled dataset consisting of 17 participants, they trained a classifier to annotate unlabeled EEG based on pattern identification. Such tools are still very nascent. However, they could provide rich insight during a field experiment.

Ambient Luminosity Changes. Changes in ambient luminosity can impact spontaneous, and stimulus-related alpha rhythms and are usually controlled in laboratory experiments [9]. A decrease in ambient luminosity can lead to an increase in spontaneous alpha amplitude [69]. During remote EEG data, collection room luminosity is challenging to control due to architectural configuration (i.e., room type, windows, type of light, the time of day). Variations in luminosity between study in a test-retest paradigm can threaten recorded EEG data reliability and quality resulting in reduced diagnosticity of the measured response.

Recommendations. Before any data collection begins, we recommend documenting the environmental factors within the participants' surroundings. Every electrical device present in the room should be documented to identify potential external noise sources in the data. These can then be subtracted during the training and practice phases. This documentation can also help with consistency and identifying noise across experimental sessions in the case of a test-retest paradigm. Furthermore, a study moderator should encourage a distraction-free environment to reduce the risk of natural or external environment perturbations through negotiation with the participant.

Additionally, a video camera such as a webcam should be used during the experimentation to help document natural or unplanned events. HCI researchers have already highlighted the importance of documenting natural contingencies and events that occur during in-field studies [7]. Similarly, transparency when reporting these events is essential to the eventual acceptance of a study within the research community. A clear statement about trial rejection for external reasons offers transparency and speaks to rigor within the methodological process. For example, [31] documented and clearly stated that they excluded more than 40% of their trials due to technical issues and unreliable data collection.

Finally, ambient luminosity can be minimally controlled by enumerating explicit experimental instructions regarding lighting placement and or type of lighting, i.e. LED lighting versus neon strip lighting, no direct sunlight, and a consistent number of lights. Another simple strategy could be to schedule experimental sessions at the same time of the day across all participants.

4.2 Technical and Logistic Challenges

In this section, we layout more pragmatic considerations such as cost, accessibility, or knowledge to apply tools necessary in remote EEG data collection. There are inherent hardware and software challenges to solve to achieve remote collection. As much as the environmental settings are different, we cannot control the computer and hardware that present and record the stimuli. A robust experimental infrastructure should be developed using the following requirements: control for computer differences, achieve time-synchronization between EEG and stimuli presentation and maintain reasonable costs. Based on these three practical requirements, we make the following recommendations.

Experimental Infrastructure. Another critical challenge with conducting remote experiments in the real world is establishing reliable time-synchronization between the EEG acquisition and the task's events. Usually, stimuli presentation software sends a TTL (transistor-transistor logic) pulse to the EEG amplifier signalling an event onset. In our context, we might have no control over the participants' computer if we do not provide any hardware other than the EEG. Inconsistency with event timestamps in the EEG data could significantly impact the reliability of the research and invalidate the study.

One solution could be to use the same computer to present the stimuli and record the EEG, allowing synchronization to the same local clock. Open-source solutions exist, such as Lab Streaming Layer[1] (LSL) developed by the Swartz Center for Computational Neuroscience, Institute for Neural Computation (University of California San Diego, USA), provides a synchronization tool with sub-milliseconds accuracy and allows data stream of different sampling rates (e.g., audio, EEG, screen-capture, events). The tool supports hardware from common EEG devices (BioSemi, g.Tec, and many others). It is part of the MobiLAB framework [22] and has been used in research [70]. The main downside is the need for an Application Programming Interface (API) for the EEG acquisition.

---

[1] https://labstreaminglayer.readthedocs.io/info/intro.html.

For stimuli presentation, Psychopy [43] is an open-source experimental stimuli presentation software compatible with LSL. The tool has been developed for behavioral sciences such as neuroscience or psychology. It has useful functions to assess the experimental settings post-hoc and can be configured to capture the computer's hardware information (e.g., operating system, processor, ram) and monitor (e.g., screen resolution, display frequency) before each experiment. In our own tests, we installed Psychopy to test the display refresh time at the start of the experiment to ensure stability. On the backend during the experiment, we recorded the number of dropped frames and the frame interval. We used this data to assess the viability of recording the home environment and identify potential synchronization issues. This functionality proved useful during the pilot phases to identify problems with a participants technological environment.

Recommendation. We recommend the use of established open-source software for stimuli presentation and synchronization. The versatility, iterative development and large communities offer the opportunity to adapt experimental infrastructure at need. In our case, the selected software was cross-platform and available in a unified programming language (i.e., Python). This allowed quick integration of different components and a simplification of installation on the participants side. Moreover, participant computer configuration and performance should be continuously monitored through each stage of a study. Undocumented changes in hardware configuration may have negative effects on reproducibility. Additionally, we recommend building an experiment utilizing a single software environment (in our case Python) to standardize the experiment and data collection process across all participant computing hardware. Furthermore, in as much as possible operating systems should remain consistent across computing hardware to enforce compatibility with EEG acquisition software. For example, we constrained our participant pool to use the Windows operating system due to the EEG acquisition software's limitations.

Costs. In-field experiments can be very costly. For remote testing, the hardware and software costs can multiply as each participant requires a functional experimental infrastructure. In line with the described experimental infrastructure, we selected free open-source software when possible (i.e., LSL and Psychopy).

For the EEG systems, we selected a consumer-grade EEG system with 8 hybrid electrodes from g.Tec neurotechnology GmbH (Unicorn, Austria). The system uses a right sensor on the mastoid for reference and left sensor on the mastoid as ground. The spiky electrodes offer direct contact with the skin and can be easily adjusted. The EEG signal is sampled at 250 Hz per channel with a 24-bit resolution. The amplifier is attached to the head at the inion and offers wireless connection via Bluetooth. G.tec provides a python API for data acquisition that fits our lab's technological infrastructure. The simple design of the cap and mobility give it high self-applicability. We believe that other low-cost consumer systems will also fit in this environment after reviewing compatibility with other infrastructure components.

Recommendations. In line with the recommendations concerning experimental infrastructure, the choice of established open-source software will reduce costs and increase compatibility. A lack of licensing issues will allow scaling the number of participants and this coupled with consumer-grade EEG devices will reduce overall costs potentially into the negligible range depending on funding sources. The probability of damage and retention of the hardware are significant factors to consider. However, some consumer-grade devices are so low cost these could potentially be classed as consumables.

5 Summary and Discussion

We leveraged the workshop methodology with a diverse panel of participants to provide a firsthand experience with remote data collection using EEG. We substantiated our findings with abundant literature related to real-world EEG research. The workshop's use case was deemed valid as there is currently a gap in the literature concerning remote EEG data collection. A number of methodological and practical challenges emerged from these workshops concerning the implementation of remote EEG studies. We generated recommendations that we categorized into five categories through our learning experience and extensive reading of the relevant literature. The summary of the recommendations is available in Table 2.

We formed an iterative process framework (IPF) for the activities necessary for a successful remote EEG study (see Fig. 2). The iterative approach ensures a satisfactory level of robustness in experimental infrastructure, self-applicability, and data quality. The IPF starts with the development of the experimental infrastructure and study design. Then, training of the participants can be performed following our recommendations (Table 2). A pretesting stage with dummy experiments follows the training phase. This stage is essential to collecting self-applicability data, EEG data, computer configuration and performance, and documenting each subject's experimental environment. This stage should be iterated using training workshops until satisfactory thresholds are achieved. This stage allows the pretesting of the entire experimental infrastructure in natural conditions, which then feeds back into the experimental design's further development. Thus, EEG data acquisition, time-synchronization, and performance issues can be identified and corrected. After all the quality conditions are met, the main experiment pretesting can be performed on a subset of participants. Data to be collected and analyzed should be planned in advance per the limitations of the remote technological infrastructure. Forethought here will allow the adjust the number of trials required based upon the estimation of issues linked to noise and trial rejections. If these pretesting phases show good results, the main experiment can begin. When this phase is launched, natural contingencies and the final environment should be carefully documented as it might not be possible to iterate backwards and control for unplanned events. This information should be explicitly present in any final manuscript to provide transparency and context (see Fig. 3).

We accept that this workshop based study contains limitations. First, remote workshops and firsthand experience were conducted with a panel of university students (from undergraduate to Ph.D.), research professionals, and professors. They are not representative of the wider population. Further testing through pilot studies of our approach is needed to validate and expand our approach. Secondly, our research is based on firsthand experience in the workshop process and discussion/interviews with the panel after the data collection phases. We will conduct further work to validate the EEG data quality and experimental paradigm using a battery of dummy experiments relevant to the HCI research (e.g., Nback, ErrP, relax-engaged task) and more complex experimental design (e.g., time-locked interaction with a technological artifact, continuous use, and longitudinal studies). Additional development and testing will ensure that we can gradually move to more applied and ecologically valid stimuli aligned with HCI and NeuroIS research in the future using the resulting framework. There is very little evidence that specific constructs of interest generalize to more complex tasks [42]. The strategy we adopted is to start with creating a methodological framework and reproducing established experimental paradigms. We will move forward to more constrained computer interactions and conclude with continuous use and longitudinal studies.

Our research is part of an ongoing effort to continue to record physiological [71] and affective data [72] remotely from our research group during a global pandemic. We

Table 2. Summary of the recommendation for remote EEG data collection

Methodological activity	Recommendation
Experimental Infrastructure (software/hardware)	Low-density consumer-grade dry EEG system help guarantee self-application and reduce risks related to damage, cost, and retention Use wireless acquisition for mobility and practicality Select an EEG system with an API for EEG data acquisition and recording to facilitate the integration with other components Use open-source software for time-synchronization and stimuli presentation (e.g., LSL + Psychopy) to reduce scaling cost and enable reproducibility Monitor participants computer configuration and performance before and during an experiment
Training	Measure self-applicability and comfort during training and pretesting phases Monitor and provide feedback during self-application Engage the participant in the setup and adjustment of the electrodes to attain high data quality Assess data quality and experimental infrastructure with dummy experiments
Study design	Research questions and analysis should be informed by the limitations of the selected EEG system Increase the number of trials to to account for remote setting and attain statistical significance Produce long baselines for neurophysiological responses to reduce the impact of self-application of EEG sensors Rely upon neurophysiological indices that produce robust brain responses capturable by the selected EEG system
Data collection	Document the participants' environment Use strategies to reduce potential ambient luminosity variation in the environment Measure self-applicability before each data collection Capture the self-applied EEG montage with front, lateral, back, and top images of the head Measure comfort after the setup phases and at the end of the experiment Create a distraction-free environment Document the occurrence of natural contingencies using a camera Use secondary measurements for independent assessments of data quality (e.g., gyroscope, accelerometer)

(continued)

Table 2. (*continued*)

Methodological activity	Recommendation
Data analysis	Use conservative rejection thresholds and quality conditions to guarantee good signal quality (study design should reflect this recommendation)
	Use adapted data reconstruction algorithm for low-density EEG (e.g., ASR)

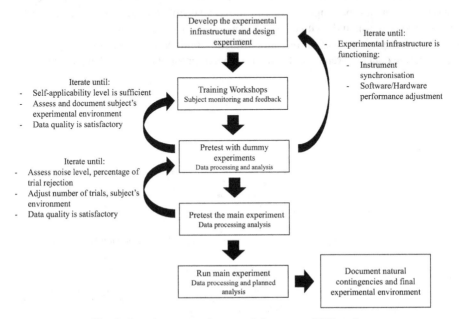

Fig. 3. Iterative process framework for remote EEG study.

believe that our iterative process framework will facilitate creating a rigorous environment for remote EEG data collection. The ability to reach large sample sizes is limited due to feasibility constraints. However, remote experiments offer the ability to collect for long periods and conduct longitudinal research. As Ladouce [37] proposed, it can enable the creation of large datasets of single participants and could lead to innovative research questions and methods.

References

1. Riedl, R., Léger, P.-M.: Fundamentals of NeuroIS. SNPBE, Springer, Heidelberg (2016). https://doi.org/10.1007/978-3-662-45091-8
2. Krout, K., Carrascal, J.P., Lowdermilk, T.: Lean UX research at scale: a case study. In: Proceedings of the Conference on Mensch und Computer, pp. 53–59 (2020)
3. Nielsen, C.M., Overgaard, M., Pedersen, M.B., Stage, J., Stenild, S.: It's worth the hassle! the added value of evaluating the usability of mobile systems in the field. In: Proceedings of

the 4th Nordic Conference on Human-Computer Interaction: Changing Roles, pp. 272–280 (2006)

4. Voit, A., Mayer, S., Schwind, V., Henze, N.: Online, VR, AR, Lab, and In-Situ: comparison of research methods to evaluate smart artifacts. In: Proceedings of the 2019 CHI Conference on Human Factors in Computing Systems, pp. 1–12 (2019)

5. Rogers, Y., et al.: Why it's worth the hassle: the value of in-situ studies when designing ubicomp. In: Krumm, J., Abowd, G.D., Seneviratne, A., Strang, T. (eds.) UbiComp 2007. LNCS, vol. 4717, pp. 336–353. Springer, Heidelberg (2007). https://doi.org/10.1007/978-3-540-74853-3_20

6. Kjeldskov, J., Skov, M.B.: Was it worth the hassle? Ten years of mobile HCI research discussions on lab and field evaluations. In: Proceedings of the 16th International Conference on Human-Computer Interaction with Mobile Devices & Services, pp. 43–52 (2014)

7. Brown, B., Reeves, S., Sherwood, S.: Into the wild: challenges and opportunities for field trial methods. In: Proceedings of the SIGCHI Conference on Human Factors in Computing Systems, pp. 1657–1666 (2011)

8. Riedl, R., Davis, F.D., Hevner, A.R.: Towards a NeuroIS research methodology: intensifying the discussion on methods, tools, and measurement. J. Assoc. Inf. Syst. **15**, 4 (2014)

9. Müller-Putz, G.R., Riedl, R., Wriessnegger, S.C.: Electroencephalography (EEG) as a research tool in the information systems discipline: foundations, measurement, and applications. CAIS **37**, 46 (2015)

10. Tezza, D., Caprio, D., Pinto, B., Mantilla, I., Andujar, M.: An analysis of engagement levels while playing brain-controlled games. In: Fang, X. (ed.) HCII 2020. LNCS, vol. 12211, pp. 361–372. Springer, Cham (2020). https://doi.org/10.1007/978-3-030-50164-8_26

11. Ewing, K.C., Fairclough, S.H., Gilleade, K.: Evaluation of an adaptive game that uses EEG measures validated during the design process as inputs to a biocybernetic loop. Front. Hum. Neurosci. **10**, 223 (2016). https://doi.org/10.3389/fnhum.2016.00223

12. Hassib, M., Schneegass, S., Eiglsperger, P., Henze, N., Schmidt, A., Alt, F.: EngageMeter: a system for implicit audience engagement sensing using electroencephalography. In: Proceedings of the 2017 CHI Conference on Human Factors in Computing Systems, pp. 5114–5119 (2017)

13. Smith, M.E., Gevins, A., Brown, H., Karnik, A., Du, R.: Monitoring task loading with multivariate EEG measures during complex forms of human-computer interaction. Hum. Factors **43**, 366–380 (2001)

14. Di Flumeri, G., et al.: EEG-based mental workload neurometric to evaluate the impact of different traffic and road conditions in real driving settings. Front. Hum. Neurosci. **12**, 509 (2018). https://doi.org/10.3389/fnhum.2018.00509

15. Van Benthem, K.D., Cebulski, S., Herdman, C.M., Keillor, J.: An EEG brain-computer interface approach for classifying vigilance states in humans: a gamma band focus supports low misclassification rates. Int. J. Hum.-Comput. Interact. **34**, 226–237 (2018). https://doi.org/10.1080/10447318.2017.1342942

16. Luck, S.J.: An introduction to the event-related potential technique (2014)

17. Vance, A., Anderson, B.B., Kirwan, C.B., Eargle, D.: Using measures of risk perception to predict information security behavior: Insights from electroencephalography (EEG). J. Assoc. Inf. Syst. **15**, 2 (2014)

18. Putze, F., et al.: Hybrid fNIRS-EEG based classification of auditory and visual perception processes. Front. Neurosci. **8**, 373 (2014)

19. Karran, A.J., et al.: Towards a hybrid passive BCI for the modulation of sustained attention using EEG and fNIRS. Front. Hum. Neurosci. (2018). https://doi.org/10.3389/conf.fnhum.2018.227.00115

20. Turabian, M., Van Benthem, K., Herdman, C.M.: Impairments in early auditory detection coincide with substandard visual-spatial task performance in older age: an ERP study. In: Stephanidis, C., Antona, M., Ntoa, S. (eds.) HCII 2020. CCIS, vol. 1294, pp. 110–118. Springer, Cham (2020). https://doi.org/10.1007/978-3-030-60703-6_14

21. Mühl, C., Jeunet, C., Lotte, F.: EEG-based workload estimation across affective contexts. Front. Neurosci. **8**, 114 (2014)

22. Ojeda, A., Bigdely-Shamlo, N., Makeig, S.: MoBILAB: an open source toolbox for analysis and visualization of mobile brain/body imaging data. Front. Hum. Neurosci. **8**, 121 (2014). https://doi.org/10.3389/fnhum.2014.00121

23. Gennaro, F., de Bruin, E.D.: Assessing brain-muscle connectivity in human locomotion through mobile brain/body imaging: opportunities, pitfalls, and future directions. Front. Public Health **6**, 39 (2018). https://doi.org/10.3389/fpubh.2018.00039

24. Gramann, K., Ferris, D.P., Gwin, J., Makeig, S.: Imaging natural cognition in action. Int. J. Psychophysiol. **91**, 22–29 (2014). https://doi.org/10.1016/j.ijpsycho.2013.09.003

25. Jungnickel, E., Gramann, K.: Mobile brain/body imaging (MoBI) of physical interaction with dynamically moving objects. Front. Hum. Neurosci. **10**, 306 (2016). https://doi.org/10.3389/fnhum.2016.00306

26. Gramann, K., et al.: Cognition in action: imaging brain/body dynamics in mobile humans. Rev. Neurosci. **22**, 593–608 (2011). https://doi.org/10.1515/RNS.2011.047

27. Ko, L.W., Komarov, O., Hairston, W.D., Jung, T.P., Lin, C.T.: Sustained attention in real classroom settings: an EEG study. Front. Hum. Neurosci. **11**, 388 (2017). https://doi.org/10.3389/fnhum.2017.00388

28. Dikker, S., et al.: Brain-to-brain synchrony tracks real-world dynamic group interactions in the classroom. Curr. Biol. **27**, 1375–1380 (2017). https://doi.org/10.1016/j.cub.2017.04.002

29. Bevilacqua, D., et al.: Brain-to-brain synchrony and learning outcomes vary by student-teacher dynamics: evidence from a real-world classroom electroencephalography study. J. Cogn. Neurosci. **31**, 401–411 (2019). https://doi.org/10.1162/jocn_a_01274

30. Pizzamiglio, S., Naeem, U., Abdalla, H., Turner, D.L.: Neural correlates of single- and dual-task walking in the real world. Front. Hum. Neurosci. **11**, 460 (2017). https://doi.org/10.3389/fnhum.2017.00460

31. Ladouce, S., Donaldson, D.I., Dudchenko, P.A., Ietswaart, M.: Mobile EEG identifies the re-allocation of attention during real-world activity. Sci. Rep. **9**, 15851 (2019). https://doi.org/10.1038/s41598-019-51996-y

32. Debener, S., Minow, F., Emkes, R., Gandras, K., De Vos, M.: How about taking a low-cost, small, and wireless EEG for a walk? Psychophysiology **49**, 1617–1621 (2012)

33. Zink, R., Hunyadi, B., Huffel, S.V., Vos, M.D.: Mobile EEG on the bike: disentangling attentional and physical contributions to auditory attention tasks. J. Neural Eng. **13**, 046017 (2016). https://doi.org/10.1088/1741-2560/13/4/046017

34. Wang, C.H., Moreau, D., Kao, S.C.: From the lab to the field: potential applications of dry EEG systems to understand the brain-behavior relationship in sports. Front. Neurosci. **13**, 893 (2019). https://doi.org/10.3389/fnins.2019.00893

35. Butkeviciute, E., et al.: Removal of movement artefact for mobile EEG analysis in sports exercises. IEEE Access **7**, 7206–7217 (2019). https://doi.org/10.1109/access.2018.2890335

36. Cruz-Garza, J.G., et al.: Deployment of mobile EEG technology in an art museum setting: evaluation of signal quality and usability. Front. Hum. Neurosci. **11**, 527 (2017). https://doi.org/10.3389/fnhum.2017.00527

37. Ladouce, S., Donaldson, D.I., Dudchenko, P.A., Ietswaart, M.: Understanding minds in real-world environments: toward a mobile cognition approach. Front. Hum. Neurosci. **10**, 694 (2016). https://doi.org/10.3389/fnhum.2016.00694

38. Hinrichs, H., Scholz, M., Baum, A.K., Kam, J.W., Knight, R.T., Heinze, H.-J.: Comparison between a wireless dry electrode EEG system with a conventional wired wet electrode EEG system for clinical applications. Sci. Rep. **10**, 1–14 (2020)
39. Kam, J.W., et al.: Systematic comparison between a wireless EEG system with dry electrodes and a wired EEG system with wet electrodes. Neuroimage **184**, 119–129 (2019)
40. Maskeliunas, R., Damasevicius, R., Martisius, I., Vasiljevas, M.: Consumer-grade EEG devices: are they usable for control tasks? PeerJ **4**, e1746 (2016)
41. Krigolson, O., Williams, C., Colino, F.: Using portable EEG to assess human visual attention. In: Schmorrow, D.D., Fidopiastis, C.M. (eds.) AC 2017. LNCS (LNAI), vol. 10284, pp. 56–65. Springer, Cham (2017). https://doi.org/10.1007/978-3-319-58628-1_5
42. Riedl, R., Minas, R.K., Dennis, A.R., Müller-Putz, G.R.: Consumer-grade EEG instruments: insights on the measurement quality based on a literature review and implications for NeuroIS research. In: Davis, F.D., Riedl, R., vom Brocke, J., Léger, P.-M., Randolph, A.B., Fischer, T. (eds.) NeuroIS 2020. LNISO, vol. 43, pp. 350–361. Springer, Cham (2020). https://doi.org/10.1007/978-3-030-60073-0_41
43. Peirce, J.W.: PsychoPy—psychophysics software in Python. J. Neurosci. Methods **162**, 8–13 (2007)
44. Tsiara, A., Mikropoulos, T.A., Chalki, P.: EEG systems for educational neuroscience. In: Antona, M., Stephanidis, C. (eds.) HCII 2019. LNCS, vol. 11573, pp. 575–586. Springer, Cham (2019). https://doi.org/10.1007/978-3-030-23563-5_45
45. Zander, T.O., et al.: Evaluation of a Dry EEG system for application of passive brain-computer interfaces in autonomous driving. Front. Hum. Neurosci. **11**, 78 (2017). https://doi.org/10.3389/fnhum.2017.00078
46. Aricò, P., Borghini, G., Di Flumeri, G., Sciaraffa, N., Babiloni, F.: Passive BCI beyond the lab: current trends and future directions. Physiol. Meas. **39**(8), 08TR02 (2018). https://doi.org/10.1088/1361-6579/aad57e
47. Puce, A., Hamalainen, M.S.: A review of issues related to data acquisition and analysis in EEG/MEG studies. Brain Sci. **7**, 58 (2017). https://doi.org/10.3390/brainsci7060058
48. Oliveira, A.S., Schlink, B.R., Hairston, W.D., Konig, P., Ferris, D.P.: Proposing metrics for benchmarking novel EEG technologies towards real-world measurements. Front. Hum. Neurosci. **10**, 188 (2016). https://doi.org/10.3389/fnhum.2016.00188
49. Hairston, W.D., et al.: Usability of four commercially-oriented EEG systems. J. Neural Eng. **11**, 046018 (2014)
50. Bandura, A.: Perceived self-efficacy in cognitive development and functioning. Educ. Psychol. **28**, 117–148 (1993)
51. Bandura, A.: Guide for constructing self-efficacy scales. Self-efficacy Beliefs Adolescents **5**, 307–337 (2006)
52. Toppi, J., et al.: Investigating cooperative behavior in ecological settings: an EEG hyperscanning study. PLoS ONE **11**, e0154236 (2016). https://doi.org/10.1371/journal.pone.0154236
53. Miralles, F., et al.: Brain computer interface on track to home. Sci. World J. **2015**, 623896 (2015). https://doi.org/10.1155/2015/623896
54. Kappenman, E.S., Luck, S.J.: The effects of electrode impedance on data quality and statistical significance in ERP recordings. Psychophysiology **47**, 888–904 (2010)
55. Mathewson, K.E., Harrison, T.J., Kizuk, S.A.: High and dry? Comparing active dry EEG electrodes to active and passive wet electrodes. Psychophysiology **54**, 74–82 (2017). https://doi.org/10.1111/psyp.12536
56. Halford, J.J., et al.: Comparison of a novel dry electrode headset to standard routine EEG in veterans. J. Clin. Neurophysiol. **33**, 530–537 (2016)
57. Popescu, F., Blankertz, B., Mueller, K.-R.: Computational challenges for noninvasive brain computer interfaces (2008)

58. Park, J.L., Dudchenko, P.A., Donaldson, D.I.: Navigation in real-world environments: new opportunities afforded by advances in mobile brain imaging. Front. Hum. Neurosci. **12**, 361 (2018). https://doi.org/10.3389/fnhum.2018.00361

59. Oliveira, A.S., Schlink, B.R., Hairston, W.D., Konig, P., Ferris, D.P.: A channel rejection method for attenuating motion-related artifacts in EEG recordings during walking. Front. Neurosci. **11**, 225 (2017). https://doi.org/10.3389/fnins.2017.00225

60. Soler, A., Muñoz-Gutiérrez, P.A., Bueno-López, M., Giraldo, E., Molinas, M.: Low-density EEG for neural activity reconstruction using multivariate empirical mode decomposition. Front. Neurosci. **14**, 175 (2020)

61. Banaei, M., Hatami, J., Yazdanfar, A., Gramann, K.: Walking through architectural spaces: the impact of interior forms on human brain dynamics. Front. Hum. Neurosci. **11**, 477 (2017). https://doi.org/10.3389/fnhum.2017.00477

62. Mullen, T.R., et al.: Real-time neuroimaging and cognitive monitoring using wearable dry EEG. IEEE Trans. Biomed. Eng. **62**, 2553–2567 (2015)

63. Chang, C.-Y., Hsu, S.-H., Pion-Tonachini, L., Jung, T.-P.: Evaluation of artifact subspace reconstruction for automatic EEG artifact removal. In: 2018 40th Annual International Conference of the IEEE Engineering in Medicine and Biology Society (EMBC), pp. 1242–1245. IEEE (2018)

64. Dehais, F., et al.: Monitoring pilot's mental workload using ERPs and spectral power with a six-dry-electrode EEG system in real flight conditions. Sensors **19**, 1324 (2019)

65. Bulea, T.C., Prasad, S., Kilicarslan, A., Contreras-Vidal, J.L.: Sitting and standing intention can be decoded from scalp EEG recorded prior to movement execution. Front. Neurosci. **8**, 376 (2014). https://doi.org/10.3389/fnins.2014.00376

66. Mihajlović, V., Grundlehner, B., Vullers, R., Penders, J.: Wearable, wireless EEG solutions in daily life applications: what are we missing? IEEE J. Biomed. Health Inform. **19**, 6–21 (2014)

67. Bigdely-Shamlo, N., et al.: Hierarchical event descriptors (HED): semi-structured tagging for real-world events in large-scale EEG. Front. Neuroinform. **10**, 42 (2016). https://doi.org/10.3389/fninf.2016.00042

68. Su, K.M., Hairston, W.D., Robbins, K.: EEG-annotate: automated identification and labeling of events in continuous signals with applications to EEG. J. Neurosci. Methods **293**, 359–374 (2018). https://doi.org/10.1016/j.jneumeth.2017.10.011

69. Benedetto, A., Lozano-Soldevilla, D., VanRullen, R.: Different responses of spontaneous and stimulus-related alpha activity to ambient luminance changes. Eur. J. Neurosci. **48**, 2599–2608 (2018). https://doi.org/10.1111/ejn.13791

70. Sburlea, A.I., Müller-Putz, G.R.: Exploring representations of human grasping in neural, muscle and kinematic signals. Sci. Rep. **8**, 1–14 (2018)

71. Vasseur, A., et al.: Distributed remote psychophysiological data collection for UX evaluation: a pilot project. In: International Conference on Human-Computer Interaction. Springer, Heidelberg (2021)

72. Giroux, F., et al.: Guidelines for collecting automatic facial expression detection data synchronized with a dynamic stimulus in remote moderated user tests. In: International Conference on Human-Computer Interaction. Springer, Heidelberg (2021)

Neurochat: Artistic Affective State Facial Filters in Online Video Communication

Sarah Garcia$^{(\boxtimes)}$ and Marvin Andujar

University of South Florida, Tampa, FL 33620, USA
{sarahgarcia,andujar1}@usf.edu

Abstract. This paper describes "Neurochat", a novel artistic Brain Computer Interface (aBCI) application that allows users to explore the combination of art and brain activity in a live online chat experience. This new interaction method enables users to video-chat online while expressing themselves using artistic facial filters that represent their real-time affective state, generated from electroencephalogram (EEG) brain activity from a mobile EEG headset. This paper discusses motivations for creating such an application by giving an overview of the current state of the art in aBCI. It also discusses the architecture of the created system, including the associated application components, application flow, design of facial filters with the descriptions of their associated affective state, and classification method that was used. Additionally, a preliminary user study was conducted to investigate the effect of the application combined with an existing online video-chatting method, Google Hangouts, to gain insight on user perspective towards the system.

Keywords: Brain Computer Interfaces · Affective state · EEG · Self expression · Video chat · Artistic Brain Computer Interfaces · Facial filters

1 Introduction

Art is frequently used as a means of expression that often has the goal of communicating emotions, feelings, or thoughts to others. Brain Computer Interfaces (BCI) can be used to enhance user's self expression and augment video communication by selecting artistic facial filters in real time based on the user's brain activity measured from electroencephalogram (EEG) signals. In this way, communication and user experience can potentially be enhanced through the displaying of the user's current affective state through art. Artistic BCI is a subset of BCI that is used for self expression of the user [1]. This self expression can be in the form of affective state, emotion classification, or depiction of brain activity in an artistic way. Artistic BCI has been used to allow users to express themselves through brain data seen in contemporary art, where increase in mobility and user friendliness of BCI devices in recent years has encouraged several artists to create artworks using EEG activity [7]. Another form of artistic BCI, Brain

© Springer Nature Switzerland AG 2021
D. D. Schmorrow and C. M. Fidopiastis (Eds.): HCII 2021, LNAI 12776, pp. 23–32, 2021.
https://doi.org/10.1007/978-3-030-78114-9_2

Painting, allows ALS patients to create digital pictures using their brain waves. Brain painting has been further extended to virtual and 3D environments for able-bodied users with positive reception from study participants [5,6]. These examples showcase that there is interest in self expression through physiological means such as brain activity. Similarly, the proposed Neurochat application is an extension of the user's physiology and has the potential to allow users to express themselves while engaging in conversation with others. This can be potentially useful for those who have trouble expressing their emotions, such as those who are diagnosed with autism or have social anxiety.

One important work to be noted is the development of the application called NeuroSnap [3], a BCI application based on SnapChat's facial filters. The application applied one of three different facial filters to the user by classifying their affective state. The application discussed in this paper builds upon NeuroSnap's use of real-time facial filters. This work differs from [3] in that it will be applied to a two-person communication application. Therefore, this project allows for the sharing of user's self expression with another individual to create a new aBCI interaction that allows the generated filters to be incorporated as part of the users online chat experience and conversation. The created application, titled Neurochat, allows users to use facial filters to express their affective state during online communication. The application in use can be seen in Fig. 1. In this paper a preliminary usability study is discussed regarding the application using the System Usability Scale (SUS) [2].

Fig. 1. Two users online using the Neurochat application along with Google Hangouts. Each user can be seen with generated facial filters based on their individual brain data in real time.

2   Neurochat Architecture

Neurochat allows the user to view various facial filters superimposed on themselves while video chatting, based on the affective state of the user. Neurochat makes use of the Emotiv Insight mobile BCI headset device to continuously read user brain signals in the form of EEG data. This data is then used to classify the users current affective state, and a corresponding facial filter is chosen. Therefore, Neurochat continuously generates facial filters associated with the affective state in real time at a specific time. Neurochat is implemented as a virtual camera device for Windows that can be used with any video chat application that uses Directshow filters [4]. This allows for integration with many popular platforms. In this particular user study, it is integrated with Google Hangouts. The implemented architecture splits functionalities into two components: 1) A filter selection process and 2) a Directshow virtual camera device. The overall architecture can be observed in Fig. 2. The filter selection process encapsulates all tasks related to the use of the BCI device and classification of the data. The process receives information from the EEG headset and then uses it to classify the user's affective state in real-time. The latest classification results are provided as output for the virtual camera device by writing them on a fixed position in shared memory. Similarly, the virtual camera device encapsulates all computer vision related tasks. The device is implemented as a Directshow capture filter, using OpenCV to capture frames from a real camera, perform face detection, and overlay the current facial filter being used. When a frame is requested by the video chat application, the virtual camera reads the face filter id from shared memory and applies the respective filter to the last detected face.

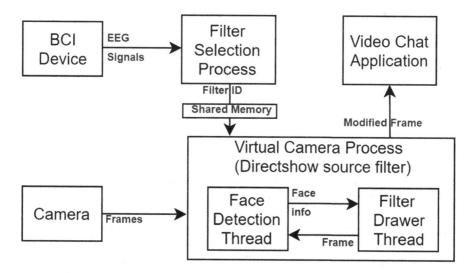

Fig. 2. Visual depiction of the implemented architecture.

3   Methodology

3.1   Participants

A total of six participants were recruited from the University of South Florida. Four were male and two were female with age ranges from 18–34. Education between participants varied. Two participants had some college credit, two had a bachelor's degree, and two had a master's degree.

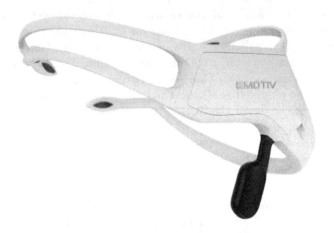

Fig. 3. The Emotiv insight brain computer interface headset.

3.2   Equipment

The Emotiv Insight is a non-invasive, mobile EEG headset. It uses semi-dry electrodes to read electrical activity from the user's scalp, as shown in Fig. 3. This headset has five EEG channels which are located at the AF3, AF4, T7, T8, and Pz locations according to the 10–20 International System shown in Fig. 4.

3.3   Face Detection and Filters

User face detection is performed using Haar Cascades, with OpenCV's default training files and configuration used to position and scale face filters when applied. Neurochat uses three different affective state facial filters available, similar to the facial filters used in the previous "NeuroSnap" application [3]: Highly Focused (High Beta), Lightly Focused (Low Beta), and Relaxed (Alpha). The images are depicted in Figs. 5, 6, and 7. The current facial filters available are as follows: alpha depicted as meditation hands placed below the user's face, low beta depicted as gears turning in the mind placed on the user's forehead (right), and high beta as question marks coming out of the top of the user's head (left).

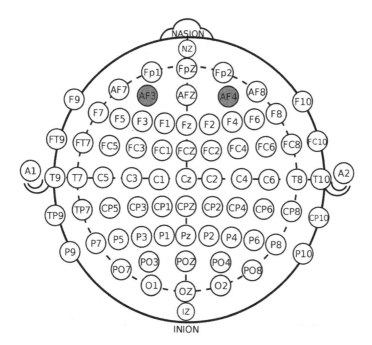

Fig. 4. 10–20 International System with used channels highlighted. (Color figure online)

These three filters represent relaxation, low focus, and high focus, respectively. Facial filters were created in Photoshop to represent the three affective states in the form of an artistic depiction. The filters were designed to fit on or around the face of a user during conversation, and were subjectively created. Filters were designed to give the other user in the chat a visual cue of the persons mental state. Therefore symbols such as gears turning for critical thinking, and meditation hands for relaxation were used.

3.4   Affective State Classification

Based on the previously published NeuroSnap [3], classification is performed by finding the waves with highest power between Alpha, Low Beta and High Beta within a given time window. Table 1 shows the EEG wave frequencies used in the application, along with their associated affective meanings. Wave power information is obtained from channels AF3 and AF4 using the Emotiv Insight, a mobile non-invasive EEG headset. Channels AF3 and AF4, highlighted in Fig. 4, are located in the frontal lobes of the brain, which are sufficient for collecting data regarding Alpha and Beta waves [8]. The Emotiv Insight provides information of Alpha and Beta by calculating a moving average of the last two seconds.

Fig. 5. Alpha Depiction of two hands meditating.

Fig. 6. Low Beta depiction of gears turning in a brain.

Fig. 7. High Beta depiction of many question marks leaving a head.

Table 1. EEG wave frequencies used along with their respective associated affective meanings.

Affective representation	EEG waves	Frequency range
Relaxed	Alpha	8–12 Hz
Lightly focused	Low beta	12–16 Hz
Highly focused	High beta	16–25 Hz

3.5   Study Design

A user study was conducted to investigate and explore the effects of BCI technology for communication between two people using the application prototype. The authors hypothesized that generation of affective state facial filters through classification of measured EEG brain data from a mobile BCI device during online video chat would improve video chat communication. First, the participant completed a pre-survey with questions related to demographics. Following, participants used the Neurochat prototype. For the experiment, participants were paired up with another participant, whom they had never met, as their conversation partner. The tasks required each pair to video chat online using the developed prototype. Participants were given the following two prompts:

1. Discuss the weather recently.
2. Discuss what you enjoy doing during your spare time.

During conversations, participants were required to wear the Emotiv Insight to acquire the EEG brain signals that were used to classify the affective state in real-time. To evaluate the experiment, after interacting with the system, subjects were given a post-experiment survey with questions regarding what they thought about the application. This post-survey included using the System Usability Scale (SUS) quest [2], allowing us to gain insights about the usability of the prototype. Each participant attended one session, which lasted approximately 30 min.

3.6   Procedures

Participants were scheduled in groups of two to participate in the study. Beginning each session, a member of the research team explained the experiment and acquired inform consent from both participants to take part in the study. Following, participants filled out a pre-survey using Qualtrics Survey software on a provided laptop computer. Following, study personnel assisted the users in fitment of the BCI device on their scalp, in order to ensure proper placement. Using the Emotiv official software suite, study personnel then verified that the headset had successful contact with the scalp and proper signal quality was achieved. Figure 8 illustrates the study setup used. Both users were placed on opposite sides of the room where they could not see each other, facing opposite directions, and wearing noise-cancelling headphones. Groups were then given the two conversation starter prompts, one at a time. After giving each prompt, subjects talked freely for exactly two minutes. A member of the research team alerted participants when the two minutes was complete and gave them the next prompt. The order of the prompts alternated between pairs of subjects to reduce bias. Lastly, each participant was asked to complete a post-survey experiment questionnaire and respond to the SUS questionnaire through the Qualtrics Survey.

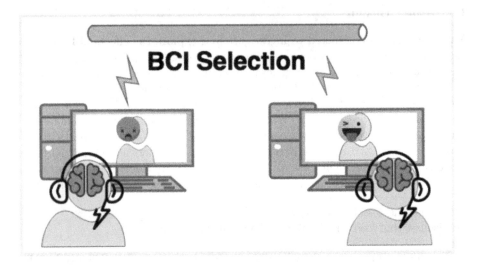

Fig. 8. Depiction of users during user study conversations.

4   Results

4.1   System Usability Scale

The survey taken by participants included the System Usability Scale (SUS). The average calculated SUS score from the six participants was 49.167, which is considered low. Several factors may have affected this, and survey answers from participants as described in the following section may give insight into improvements that could increase the SUS score.

4.2   Participant Feedback

In the provided survey, participants were asked if there was anything that could be improved about the application. Some answers included better face tracking capabilities and better hardware accuracy. Users also mentioned that the headset was uncomfortable for the duration of use and noted that it was time-consuming to set it up. Comments regarding comfort suggest that the BCI headset itself had a negative impact on usability. Low accuracy could potentially be due to the participant's inability to be relaxed enough for relaxation to appear, as the study was conducted during finals week at their University.

Participants were asked to rate the following statements on a scale from 1 to 10, with 1 being very unlikely and 10 being very likely:

- Q1 - "I would use an application such as this"
- Q2 - "I believe that an application such as this could improve my video chat communication"

Table 2. All scores provided by study participants for Q1 and Q2 in the post experiment survey.

Likeliness	1	2	3	4	5	6	7	8	9	10
Q1	0	0	0	0	2	1	1	0	1	1
Q2	0	0	0	1	1	1	0	1	1	1

This data can be seen in Table 2, where most participants rated these statements positively. The four participants who indicated that they liked the idea of facial filters a "great deal", also rated the application high on statements Q1 and Q2. This suggests that those who enjoy facial filters may enjoy this application. Four out of six participants agree that they want to use this system frequently. Though more than 50% of the participants thought that the system was not easy to use, and they would need support of a technical person to use the system. Four out of six participants found the system well integrated. More than 50% found the system cumbersome and did not feel confident using it. Two out of three participants of the age range 25 to 34 years disliked the application, and all three participants of the age range 18 to 24 years liked the application. However, it is difficult to predict any pattern based on age with such small number of participants.

5   Conclusion and Future Work

This article presented Neurochat, a new artistic BCI interaction that generates filter selection while video chatting, along with user study experiment to gain insight on user perspectives and usability. The user study showed that although users show positive interest towards Neurochat, the difficulties using the system (in particular, using the Emotiv Insight) and the low accuracy suggest that the application requires usability improvement. A significant improvement in BCI headset hardware will be needed before an application such as this can become viable. Overall, the created application has the potential to improve public perceptions of BCI by providing a fun way for users to use brain computer interfaces in everyday conversation. In addition, exploring the effects that artistic representations of affective states have on improving conversations between users can be useful in today's world, where online video chat has become a common form of communication between people. For example, this application could eventually help express and understand emotions to people with empathy disorders such as people with autism or those with social anxiety. Additionally, it can be used for users who are diagnosed with ALS and have limited facial mobility, allowing them to express their emotions. This application also has the ability to scale upwards, as future development of the application can include the addition of new facial filters, such as the affective state of valence to potentially result in more engaging filters. Additionally, further studies to test accuracy with other BCI headsets can be conducted. As online communication puts distance between users physically, the discussed application can give insight into the possible use cases that this technology can provide to impact communication between users.

References

1. Andujar, M., Crawford, C.S., Nijholt, A., Jackson, F., Gilbert, J.E.: Artistic brain-computer interfaces: the expression and stimulation of the user's affective state. Brain-Comput. Interfaces **2–3**, 60–69 (2015)
2. Brooke, J.: Sus: A "quick and dirty" usability. Usability Evaluation in Industry (1996)
3. Lieblein, R., Hunter, C., Garcia, S., Andujar, M., Crawford, C.S., Gilbert, J.E.: NeuroSnap: expressing the user's affective state with facial filters. In: Schmorrow, D.D., Fidopiastis, C.M. (eds.) AC 2017. LNCS (LNAI), vol. 10285, pp. 345–353. Springer, Cham (2017). https://doi.org/10.1007/978-3-319-58625-0_25
4. Magazine, M.: Directshow: core media technology in windows XP empowers you to create custom audio/video processing components (2002)
5. McClinton, W., Caprio, D., Laesker, D., Pinto, B., Garcia, S., Andujar, M.: P300-based 3D brain painting in virtual reality. In: Extended Abstracts of the 2019 CHI Conference on Human Factors in Computing Systems, pp. 1–6 (2019)
6. McClinton, W., Garcia, S., Andujar, M.: An immersive brain painting: the effects of brain painting in a virtual reality environment. In: Schmorrow, D.D., Fidopiastis, C.M. (eds.) HCII 2019. LNCS (LNAI), vol. 11580, pp. 436–445. Springer, Cham (2019). https://doi.org/10.1007/978-3-030-22419-6_31
7. Prpa, M., Pasquier, P.: Brain-computer interfaces in contemporary art: a state of the art and taxonomy. In: Nijholt, A. (ed.) Brain Art, pp. 65–115. Springer, Cham (2019). https://doi.org/10.1007/978-3-030-14323-7_3
8. Reuderink, B., Mühl, C., Poel, M.: Valence, arousal and dominance in the EEG during game play. Int. J. Auton. Adaptive Commun. Syst. **1**, 45–62 (2013)

A New Methodology to Learn Loops: Validation through Brain Computer Interaction

Anabela Gomes[1,2(✉)] , Ana Rita Teixeira[3,4] , and António José Mendes[2]

[1] Coimbra Polytechnic - ISEC, Coimbra, Portugal
anabela@isec.pt
[2] CISUC—Department of Informatics Engineering, University of Coimbra, Coimbra, Portugal
toze@dei.uc.pt
[3] Coimbra Polytechnic - ESEC, Coimbra, Portugal
ateixeira@ua.pt
[4] Institute of Electronics and Informatics Engineering of Aveiro,
University of Aveiro, Aveiro, Portugal

Abstract. Learning to program is a difficult process for many students anywhere in the world. Our experience indicates that the greatest difficulties start when the concept of loops is introduced. Since this is a difficult concept to learn, we think of an activity that, in our perspective, could lead to a better understanding of that concept. To do this, we created a visual representation of the loop control structure, through cards. In order to collect some indicators on the effectiveness of this methodology, we carried out an experiment using 2 groups. In one group the concept of the loop was explained in the traditional way and in the other a new methodology was applied. At the end, tests were performed on paper with exercises on loops and linked loops. An activity was also carried out using a Brain Computer Interface, the Mindwave device, in which students had to answer a set of questions about loops and linked loops. The results indicate that the students who were submitted to the new card methodology obtained better results, indicating that the methodology had some effectiveness.

Keywords: CS1 · Programming learning · Computer programming education · Programming loops · Visual representations

1 Introduction

There are many difficulties that students face when programming for the first time, often resulting in failures. There are reports in the literature on the failure and dropout rates in the introductory programming courses, a phenomenon that happens all over the world [1, 2]. The causes pointed out for this failure are also very diverse [3, 6].

It is also possible to find in the literature many proposals for solving this problem, some of which appear to have some effectiveness. However, the problem remains unresolved in most situations [7–14].

We believe that the best solution to try to solve the problem will be, first, to understand the real difficulties students have and later propose specific methodologies for each of the

© Springer Nature Switzerland AG 2021
D. D. Schmorrow and C. M. Fidopiastis (Eds.): HCII 2021, LNAI 12776, pp. 33–48, 2021.
https://doi.org/10.1007/978-3-030-78114-9_3

difficulties identified. This approach should be followed for topics or concepts identified as being particularly difficult. Our experience indicates that the difficulties begin, or are strongly accentuated, when the loops are introduced. Thus, in this study we focus on understanding the difficulties that students face when understanding and applying them. To this end, we developed a visual methodology to represent this control structure and all the elements that comprise it. This methodology used cards that students could manipulate to simulate the behaviour of a loop they were working on.

Section 2 of this paper presents some related work. Section 3 describes the proposed methodology. Section 4 describes the experimental setup of our study. In Sect. 5 the results of our study are analyzed, and Sect. 6 ends with some conclusions.

2   Related Work

There are reports in the literature, indicated by several authors, about the difficulties that students present in understanding and applying loops [15–17] and also several approaches to try to better deal with this problem. We can mention, for example, using a game-like module or approach to help visualize loops [16–19], using a sub goal learning model and worked examples [20–22], using methods that teach recursion before loops [23], using systems that automatically analyze the structure of a loop [24] or using web tools for deducing and implementing loop patterns [25].

The next section describes the proposed methodology for understanding loops, focusing especially on the for control structure. We consider this structure to be more difficult to understand than the while, since it is a very compact structure and although things happen at different times, everything is represented in the same line. Therefore, an emphasis is given to this specific loop.

3   The Proposed Methodology

The proposed methodology consists in an unplugged approach using a paper-based card to illustrate the for loop instruction (Fig. 1). In this card we can observe three distinct parts, to represent the three usual elements of the for, the initialization, the condition to be evaluated and the iteration statement (afterthought).

To represent the different components of the for we designed areas of different sizes and different but related colours. We decided to highlight the first component, to indicate that it is the first to be executed and that it occurs only once. To visually transmit this idea, we reduced the size of this component to also give the idea of separation from the other components. For that, we used a smaller dark brown rectangle. After that component, there are the other components of the repetitive structure of the same size indicating that if one is executed the others are also executed and in equal number of times. The different intensities of the colours serve to indicate the different moments and actions.

The main idea of this methodology is to be played like a game, having external boxes to represent variables and several small cards with several values to represent the values that the variables are assuming. The idea of this metaphor is to communicate that the variable is a content that can store a value. However, the length, width and height of the cards that contain values is enough for a box to fit only one value and convey the idea that a variable can only assume one value at a time. There are also small cards corresponding to several instructions belonging to the repetitive structure, that can be glued to the area reserved for it.

The idea of the arrow coming from the last component to the condition is to show that after the execution of one iteration of the loop a new evaluation of the condition is performed. To note that to emphasize the evaluation of the condition there is a set of "?" drawn like a watermark in a smoother colour. As the instruction of a loop can be another loop, we have the possibility to represent a chained loop (Fig. 2). For that inner loop, we have exactly the same visual representation of the external loop but with different colours and in a proportional smaller size.

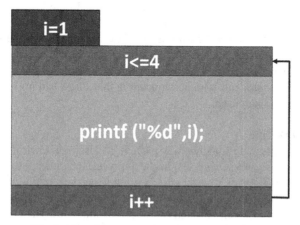

Fig. 1. Visual representation of a simple **for** loop

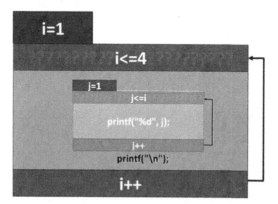

Fig. 2. Visual representation of a nested **for** loop

4 The Study

The main objective of this study is to test the card-based strategy created to help students understand loops, particularly the **for** loop.

A. Students Involved
Eigtheen students (8 males and 10 females), between 19 and 20 years old, from the second year of the Design and Multimedia course from Polytechnic Institute of Coimbra participated voluntarily in this study. The students had never programmed in any programming language, not knowing the semantics behind the for loops. The study was conducted in the curricular unit called Web Programming. The curricular plan is divided into three parts, HTML5, CSS3 and javascript language. In the last one, the students learnt the main concepts of the programming language.

All students provided informed consent prior to participating in the study. At the beginning of the experiment, a questionnaire was made to each participant in order to obtain a more detailed characterization: age, gender and knowledge of any programming language. Note that all students who participated in this study, had not had any contact with any programming language.

B. Experimental Design
The experimental study with students took place in a classroom environment, during a period of 3 consecutive weeks (Fig. 3). In the 1st week the concept of the loops was presented, in the second week it was carried out on paper test and in the third week a digital test with the collection of the EEG signal was done. The methodology adopted for teaching loops to students, went through two different strategies. The class was divided into two groups, Group A and Group B. The Group A was presented with loops using the traditional methodology: presentation of theoretical semantics and examples on the board and on slides. The same teacher taught Group B that was presented with loops using the innovative described card methodology.

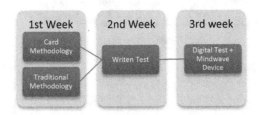

Fig. 3. The experimental study along the three weeks.

It is important to note that the time used to explain loops in each class for both groups was the same (1 h). After that, in the following week, 2nd week, all students were submitted to two written tests. The purpose of the tests was to see if the students understood the information given in the previous class about the **for** loops considering the two methodologies.

There were two written tests: Test1 and Test2. Test1 had 4 questions where students selected the code corresponding to the output presented. Test2 had 7 questions where students chose the correct option corresponding to the output after analyzing the presented code.

In the last week, 3rd week, of the experimental study, the students took another test, a digital test, about loops, considering two stages, Stage1 with questions corresponding to Test2 and Stage2 with questions corresponding to Test1, but during the execution of these activities the students used a BCI device, the Mindwave, that collected the EEG signal. The division of this activity into two distinct stages aims to understand what the main difficulties of the students were, when viewing the code and choosing its output or when viewing the output and choosing the corresponding code.

In Test1, there were 2 questions about simple loops and 2 questions about chained loops. In each of these questions, students were provided with an output plus four code options and they had to indicate which of the 4 encodings produced that output.

In Test2, there were 2 questions about simple loops and 5 questions about chained loops. In each question a code was given, and students had to select which of the 4 output possibilities were generated by that piece of code.

In some questions, only the limit value of the condition and the element to be printed changed. In other questions a decreasing control variable was used, with or without changing the program output. So, each question contained small variations that produced different outputs.

The following figures illustrate the type of questions given in both test papers (Test1 and Test2) and using BCI device (Stage2 and Stage1). In Fig. 4 for each one of the questions (Q1 to Q4) the students had one output, having to choose which one of the 4 presented codifications could produce that shown output. Figure 5 corresponds to the Second Stage of BCI experiment where students had to do similar activities to Test1 but using the BCI device.

Q1	Q2
5432	2
Q3	Q4
&&$	%%%
&&&$	$%%$

Fig. 4. Questions of paper Test1

Q1	Q2
5*	4
4*	
3*	
2*	
Q3	Q4
1	1111
12	222
123	33
1234	4

Fig. 5. Questions of second stage

In Fig. 6 for each one of the questions (Q1 to Q7) the students had 4 code options, having to choose which one produced the output presented. Figure 7 corresponds to the First Stage of BCI experiment where students had to do similar activities but using the BCI device.

In this experiment we introduced an innovative aspect, the use of Brain Computer Interfaces (BCIs). BCIs are direct functional interactions between a human brain and an external device. They measure the brain activity by detecting minute voltage changes in specific areas of the brain making it possible to extract information about the user and infer his/her mental states (e.g. workload, attention) [26].

In this work to ensure that students did not answer by guesswork, we analysed brain activity, while students answered questions. Therefore, one week after these activities, the students were submitted to a set of activities (digital test), focusing on loops and nested loops. These activities were similar to the others made on paper tests, but in this case, students had BCIs. The digital test was composed of 4 questions in the first stage and 4 questions in the second stage. These activities had two phases/stages. In one phase for each of these questions, students were provided with one codification and four outputs, they had to choose which one of the outputs were produced by the presented codification. In the other phase, in each of the 4 questions, students were provided with an output and four code options and they had to indicate which of the 4 encodings produced that output. The idea was to analyse the complex ERD/ERS on alfa band, as described in the next section.

DataSet Acquisition and Parameters

During the digital test, the brain activity of students was measured simultaneously, by the Neurosky's Mindwave device [27]. The raw signal, sampled at 512 Hz was used to compute the energy in theta band, [4–8] Hz, and in alfa band [8–12] Hz. The attention parameters provided by the device was also used to better understand the students' performance throughout the test. The study of the EEG signal focused particularly in the alpha band activity. The complex ERD/ERS is computed on alfa band, through the formula $ERD\% = (A-R)/R$, where A is the interval analysed and R is the interval of the base line reference [28]. In the literature, alpha band activity can be seen as a correlation of deactivated cortical networks, that represents the ERS, a synchronization state, where positive power increases. On the other hand, activated state with enhanced processing

Q1	Q2

var 6exto = "";
var i;
for (i = 3; i < 7; i++) {
  text += + i;
}
	var 6exto = "";
	var i;
	for (i = 9; i > 7; i--) {
	  text += + i ;
	}

Q3	**Q4**

for (var x=4;x<5;x++) {
  for(var i = 3;i<=x;i++){
    document.write(i);
  }
  document.write('
');
}
	for (var x=4;x<6;x++) {
	  for(var i = 9;i>=x;i--){
	    document.write(i);
	  }
	  document.write('
	');
	}

Q5	**Q6**

for (var x=10;x>8;x--) {
  for(var i = 7;i<x;i++){
    document.write('&');
  }
  document.write('@');
}
	for (var x=4;x<8;x++) {
	  for(var i = 3;i<=x;i++){
	    document.write('*');
	  }
	  document.write('
	');
	}

Q7	

</script><script>
for (var x=4;x<6;x++) {
  for(var i = 9;i>=x;i--){
  }
  document.write(i);
  document.write('
');
}	

Fig. 6. Questions of paper Test2

of information in a specific system, increased excitability of cortical neurons, represents the ERD, a desynchronization state, where negative power decreases.

To clarify the experiment done, the timing diagram represented in Fig. 8, shows the procedure performed in the digital test where the EEG signal was kept. The number of intervals analysed to compute the ERD/ERS complex was 4 in each stage.

Q1

``
<script>
var text = "";
var i;
for (i = 2; i < 5; i++) {
    text += + i + "
";
}
document.getElementById("demo").innerHTML = text;
</script>
``

Q2

``
<script>
var text = "";
var i;
for (i =5; i < 2; i--) {
    text += + i + "
";
}
document.getElementById("demo").innerHTML = text;
</script>
``

Q3

``
<script>
var text = "";
var i,j;
for (i =2; i <5; i++) {
    for (j=2; j<=i; j++){
        text += + j + "
";
    }
}
document.getElementById("demo").innerHTML = text;
</script>
``

Q4

``
<script>
var text = "";
var i,j;
for (i =2; i <5; i++) {
    for (j=2; j<=i; j++){
        text += + j + "
";
    }
}
document.getElementById("demo").innerHTML = text;
</script>
``

Fig. 7. Questions of first stage

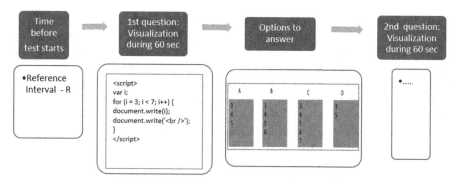

Fig. 8. The timing diagram of the experiment.

5 Results Analysis

In this section we present the main findings resulting from the described activities.

A. Analysis and Discussion of Test Results

In paper Test1, the grades were all extremely high and there were no significant differences in results between students submitted to different methodologies.

In paper Test2, in question Q1 (increasing simple loop) the grades were all extremely high and there were no significant differences in the results, among students submitted to different methodologies. In paper Test2, in questions Q3 and Q6 (increasing chained loops) there were differences between groups but not significant ones, noting that the card methodology group obtained slightly better results. Questions Q1, Q3 and Q6 of Test2 make us confirm that, in general, the students obtained better results in the responses with a single loop and in the increment exercises even when having chained loops, as would be expected.

In questions Q2, Q4, Q5 and Q7 of paper Test2, students submitted to the card methodology obtained much better results, so we analysed what characterizes these questions. Question Q2 consisted of a simple decreasing loop. We think that this difference did not happen in the corresponding questions of Test1 because in paper Test2 the students had to discover the output of a coding and in paper Test1 they had to indicate which coding corresponded to a given output, seeming to reveal more easily in this type of exercise.

Questions Q5 and Q7 (decreasing chained loop) of paper Test2 were those in which the results were significantly accentuated among the samples, with the answers obtained by the group submitted to the card methodology having a duplication of positive results in relation to the group submitted to the traditional method. These questions were the most difficult of the tests, since not only did they have chained loops, but in one loop the variable controlling it had an increasing behaviour and the one controlling the other loop had a decreasing behaviour. This aspect was allied to the fact already evidenced previously that students have more difficulties to discover what the output of a given code is than the other way around. Q4 was a similar question to Q5 and Q7, however the difference between samples was not confirmed, perhaps students answered by guesswork in this question.

The small number of students in each group did not allow to verify if there were significant differences in relation to the errors produced by each group submitted to the different strategies. Analysing the set of wrong answers from all the students, the main reasoning errors corresponding to the choices made seems to be the following. Even though many students appeared to understand simple loops their weaknesses appear when they have to understand chained loops. A common mistake, when they look for a written for, is to think that all its components are executed in each iteration. This doesn't happen when they recur to the cards' methodology. Even though, this methodology seems to help students to understand simple loops when chained loops appear, some students continue to have difficulties.

It is usually easy to understand what happens in each for. However, when they have to simulate the chained execution, they start to have problems, from the 2nd iteration of the external loop, especially when they have to start the execution of the internal loop. The confusion between the interaction of the different variables that control each of the loops is another element that confuses students.

B. Analysis and Discussion of the Results Obtained in Activities with BCIs

The results presented are divided considering the first stage (Stage1) and the second stage (Stage2) of the digital test. The EEG raw data was analysed in frequency.

We consider that there is a correspondence between the questions in Test1 and Stage2 from one to one, that is, questions Q1, Q2, Q3 and Q4 are equivalent in Test1 and Stage2.

Regarding Test2 and Stage1, there is a correspondence between Q1 (a simple increasing for) and Q2 (a simple decreasing for). However, to confirm our results we arranged 2 questions corresponding to Q3 of the digital test, Q3 and Q6 of paper Test2 (chained for loops, all increasing). We also had for Q4 of the digital test, Q4, Q5 and Q7 in the paper Test2 (chained for loops, one increasing and other decreasing).

First Stage

The ERS/ERD complex was computed, Fig. 9, where the reference interval considered was the time before the test started. The results show that for questions Q2 and Q4

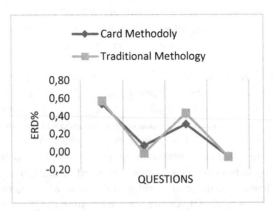

Fig. 9. ERD% of the Alpha band, considering the digital test in first stage: Card and Traditional Methodology

there is a desynchronization (ERD) being more accentuated in the traditional method. Questions Q1 and Q3, present a synchronization and is more evident in the card method. To note that question Q1 was about a simple increasing loop and question Q3 about chained increasing loops. Note that question Q2 was about a decreasing simple loop and question Q4 decreasing chained loops, more difficult questions for students, with more desynchronization meaning more difficulties for students submitted to the traditional method. The attention level provided by the Mindwave device also reflects the ERD% results. The traditional methodology needs more attention, except in questions Q1 and Q3, Fig. 10.

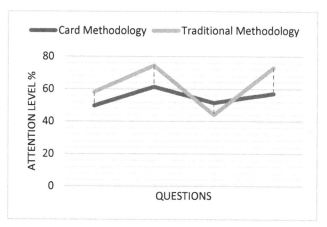

Fig. 10. Attention Level considering the digital test in first stage: Card and Traditional Methodology

Second Stage

In this case, questions Q1 (decreasing simple loop) and Q4 (decreasing chained loops) presents a desyncronization (ERD) and questions Q2 (increasing simple loop) and Q3

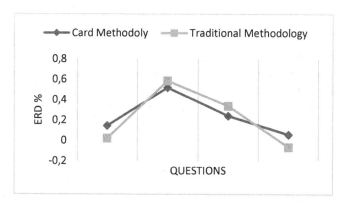

Fig. 11. ERD% of the Alpha band, considering the digital test in second stage: Card and Traditional Methodology

(increasing chained loops) a syncronization (ERS), Fig. 11. This can be explained by the already confirmed difficulty associated to the understanding of a loop with a decreasing variable and worsens in a chained loop.

The attention level provided by the Mindwave device also shows that the attention level is always higher for cards' methodology. This confirms that the traditional methodology needs more attention and effort for the comprehension of the questions (Fig. 12).

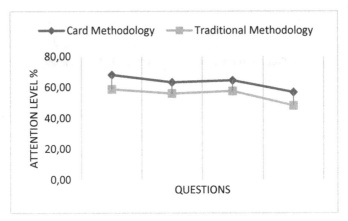

Fig. 12. Attention Level considering the digital test in second stage: Card and Traditional Methodology

The results using BCI confirmed the results students obtained in the paper-based tests. In exercises with decreasing simple loop and exercises with decreasing chained loop, when more difficult questions were presented for students, more desynchronization occurred, meaning more difficulties for students, happening mainly in students submitted to the traditional method. This gives some indication that the most difficult exercises were even more difficult for the students submitted to the traditional method, indicating the efficacy of the cards' method.

The following graphs (Fig. 13, Fig. 14, Fig. 15 and Fig. 16) allow us to compare the ERS levels for attention corresponding to Stage1 and Stage2. Remember that in Stage1 a codification is given, and the student has to choose the output and in Stage2 the output is given, and the student has to choose the code. The results on paper show that students find it easier to answer questions in Test1 (corresponding to Stage2) in which the output is given and choosing the code, than in Test2 (corresponding to Stage1) in which the code is given and they had to choose the output. The following figures confirm this trend.

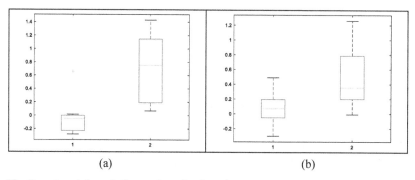

Fig. 13. Stage1 and Stage2 Comparison for Question1: (a) – Traditional methodology and b) Cards' methodology

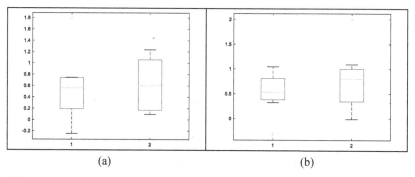

Fig. 14. Stage1 and Stage2 Comparison for Question2: (a) – Traditional methodology and b) Cards methodology

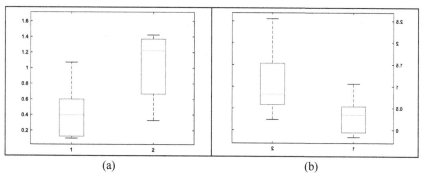

Fig. 15. Stage1 and Stage2 Comparison for Question3: (a) – Traditional methodology and b) Cards methodology

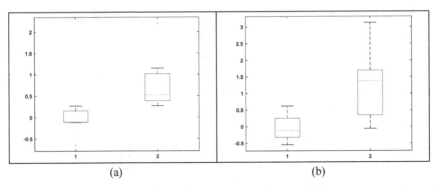

(a)   (b)

Fig. 16. Stage1 and Stage2 Comparison for Question4: (a) – Traditional methodology and b) Cards methodology

6 Conclusions

The problems related to students' difficulties when they start to program are well-known. Although various initiatives have appeared over the years to try to solve the problem, it remains unresolved, so we present another approach with this purpose.

This time, a proposal that helps better understand the repetitive structure "for" through a visual representation is used. Two different instruments were used to access this methodology, a paper-based test and a digital test done simultaneously with a BCI.

This approach has already been done, where students using this visual methodology showed small improvements concerning the understanding and application of loops relatively to students using a traditional approach. This time we added a BCI while students were doing the assessment activities to guarantee that the results of the students were not done by guesswork.

Even though we can not say explicitly that the initiative proves the efficacy of the new methodology there were indicators that it is a good approach. Therefore, we want to continue experimenting the use of visualizations and concrete manipulation in order to better understand the students' mental models and their misconceptions.

Acknowledgment. The authors would like to thank all students that participated in the experiment.

References

1. Hawi, N.: Causal attributions of success and failure made by undergraduate students in an introductory-level computer programming course. Comput. Educ. **54**(4), 1127–1136 (2010). https://doi.org/10.1016/j.compedu.2009.10.020
2. Watson, C., Li, F.W.B.: Failure rates in introductory programming revisited. In: Proceedings of the 2014 Conference on Innovation and Technology in Computer Science Education, ITiCSE 2014 (2014). https://doi.org/10.1145/2591708.2591749
3. Jenkins, T.: On the Difficulty of Learning to Program. Language (Baltim) (2002)

4. Robins, A., Rountree, J., Rountree, N.: Learning and teaching programming: a review and discussion. Comput. Sci. Educ. (2003). https://doi.org/10.1076/csed.13.2.137.14200
5. Lahtinen, E., Ala-Mutka, K., Järvinen, H.-M.: A study of the difficulties of novice programmers. ACM SIGCSE Bull. (2006). https://doi.org/10.1145/1151954.1067453
6. Gray, S.A., Goldberg, W.D., Byrnes, N.C.: Novices and programming: merely a difficult subject (why?) or a means to mastering metacognitive skills? [Review of the book Studying the Novice Programmer]. J. Educ. Res. Comput. (2007)
7. Pattis, R.: Karel the Robot: A Gentle Introduction to the Art of Programming. Wiley, Hoboken (1981)
8. Naps, T.L., Eagan, J.R., Norton, L.L.: JHAVÉ—an environment to actively engage students in Web-based algorithm visualizations. ACM SIGCSE Bull. (2004). https://doi.org/10.1145/331795.331829
9. Roberts, E.: An overview of MiniJava. ACM SIGCSE Bull. (2004)
10. Ben-Bassat Levy, R., Ben-Ari, M., Uronen, P.A.: The Jeliot 2000 program animation system. Comput. Educ. **40**, 1–15 (2003)
11. Kölling, M., Quig, B., Patterson, A., Rosenberg, J.: The BlueJ system and its pedagogy. Comput. Sci. Educ. (2003). https://doi.org/10.1076/csed.13.4.249.17496
12. Pears, A., et al.: A survey of literature on the teaching of introductory programming. In: Working Group Reports on ITiCSE on Innovation and Technology in Computer Science Education, ITiCSE-WGR 2007 (2007). https://doi.org/10.1145/1345443.1345441
13. Rajala, T., Laakso, M.-J., Kaila, E., Salakoski, T.: VILLE – a language-independent program visualization tool. In: Seventh Baltic Sea Conference on Computing Education Research (Koli Call. 2007) (2007)
14. Santos, Á., Gomes, A., Mendes, A.J.: Integrating new technologies and existing tools to promote programming learning. Algorithms (2010). https://doi.org/10.3390/a3020183
15. Dale, N.B.: Most difficult topics in CS1: results of an online survey of educators. ACM SIGCSE Bull. **38**(2), 49–53 (2006). https://doi.org/10.1145/1138403.1138432
16. Zhang, J., Atay, M., Caldwell, E.R., Jones, E.J.: Visualizing loops using a game-like instructional module. In: Proceedings - 2013 IEEE 13th International Conference on Advanced Learning Technologies, ICALT 2013 (2013). https://doi.org/10.1109/ICALT.2013.137
17. Grover, S., Basu, S.: Measuring student learning in introductory block-based programming: examining misconceptions of loops, variables, and Boolean logic. In: Proceedings of the 2017 ACM SIGCSE Technical Symposium on Computer Science Education, SIGCSE 2017 (2017). https://doi.org/10.1145/3017680.3017723
18. Rudder, A., Bernard, M., Mohammed, S.: Teaching programming using visualization. In: Proceedings of the Sixth IASTED International Conference on Web-Based Education, WBED 2007, vol. 2 (2007)
19. Eagle, M., Barnes, T.: Wu's castle: teaching arrays and loops in a game. In: Proceedings of the 13th Annual Conference on Innovation and Technology in Computer Science Education, ITiCSE 2008 (2008). https://doi.org/10.1145/1384271.1384337
20. Catrambone, R.: The subgoal learning model: creating better examples so that students can solve novel problems. J. Exp. Psychol. Gen. (1998). https://doi.org/10.1037/0096-3445.127.4.355
21. Morrison, B.B., Decker, A., Margulieux, L.E.: Learning loops: a replication study illuminates impact of HS courses. In: Proceedings of the 2016 ACM Conference on International Computing Education Research, ICER 2016 (2016). https://doi.org/10.1145/2960310.2960330
22. Morrison, B.B., Margulieux, L.E., Guzdial, M.: Subgoals, context, and worked examples in learning computing problem solving. In: Proceedings of the 2015 ACM Conference on International Conference on International Computing Education Research, ICER 2015 (2015). https://doi.org/10.1145/2787622.2787733

23. Turbak, F., Royden, C., Stephan, J., Herbst, J.: Teaching recursion before loops in CS1. Appear. J. Comput. Small Coll. **14**, 86–101 (1999)
24. Waters, R.C.: A method for analyzing loop programs. IEEE Trans. Softw. Eng. **5**(3), 237–247 (1979). https://doi.org/10.1109/TSE.1979.234185
25. Fernández Alemán, J.L., Oufaska, Y.: SAMtool, a tool for deducing and implementing loop patterns. In: Proceedings of the Fifteenth Annual Conference on Innovation and Technology in Computer Science Education, ITiCSE 2010 (2010). https://doi.org/10.1145/1822090.182 2111
26. Spüler, M., Krumpe, T., Walter, C., Scharinger, C., Rosenstiel, W., Gerjets, P.: Brain-computer interfaces for educational applications. In: Buder, J., Hesse, F.W. (eds.) Informational Environments, pp. 177–201. Springer, Cham (2017). https://doi.org/10.1007/978-3-319-64274-1_8
27. Neurosky Mindwave User Guide: Neurosky Mindwave User Guide (2018)
28. Pfurtscheller, G.: Functional brain imaging based on ERD/ERS. Vis. Res. **41**(10–11), 1257–1260 (2001). https://doi.org/10.1016/S0042-6989(00)00235-2

Individual Differences in fNIRS Measures of Cognitive Workload During a UAS Mission

Jaime Kerr[1]($\boxtimes$), Cooper Molloy[1], Pratusha Reddy[1], Patricia A. Shewokis[1,2], and Kurtulus Izzetoglu[1]

[1] School of Biomedical Engineering, Science and Health Systems, Drexel University, Philadelphia, PA 19104, USA
jkk57@drexel.edu
[2] Nutrition Sciences Department, College of Nursing and Health Professions, Drexel University, Philadelphia, PA 19104, USA

Abstract. Unmanned aerial system (UAS) sensor operators continue to experience increasing levels of workload due to progressively complex systems, yet few studies have effectively recreated realistic transitional workload conditions. Human operators experience a variety of challenges during execution of tasks (e.g., visibility changes, object prevalence, sustained alertness), often becoming disengaged and hindering performance. Many studies have examined group-wise changes but exploring subject-dependent changes is critical to improving operator training efficacy, through personalization and enhancing engagement. This study sought to examine individual differences in human operator's task performance observed via behavioral and neurophysiological measures during various workload conditions. Functional near infrared spectroscopy (fNIRS) is a commonly used non-invasive functional neuroimaging technique to obtain neurophysiological measures for detecting changes in mental workload in real-world settings. This protocol captured data from 13 novice participants who completed complex realistic tasks implemented using a high-fidelity simulator, with varying workload conditions resulting from changes in time-of-day. Participants' behavioral performance and prefrontal cortex activation indicated higher levels of training were necessary to avoid overloading or disengagement from the workload condition.

Keywords: Functional near infrared spectroscopy · fNIRS · Mental workload · Individual performance · Unmanned systems · UAS

1 Introduction

Unmanned aerial systems (UASs) have continued to increase in complexity as adoption of the technology grows; consequently, this directly impacts sensor operators (SOs) navigating these increasingly complex systems and expanding data. In a simplified capacity, SO tasks primarily involve area scanning, target find, and a range of intelligence gathering assignments [1]. However, these tasks can become progressively more difficult depending on the speed and altitude of the flight path, visibility changes, object prevalence [2, 3], and removal of the SO from the task environment [4]. In attempting to

© Springer Nature Switzerland AG 2021
D. D. Schmorrow and C. M. Fidopiastis (Eds.): HCII 2021, LNAI 12776, pp. 49–62, 2021.
https://doi.org/10.1007/978-3-030-78114-9_4

overcome or compensate for these challenges, it is probable that SOs may become over-loaded. Alternatively, serving in a monitoring or search capacity from a remote location for long periods of time can increase the likelihood of operators experiencing boredom and disengagement as a result of vigilance error [3]. Furthermore, human error in aviation, health and automotive industries can often be attributed to lacking awareness, perception, and comprehension of elements within observable environments in a timely manner [5]. However, the same tasks and situations can become increasingly manageable via operator preparedness, technique, and ability.

In evaluating operator preparedness and ability, one approach employed in previous studies [1, 4, 6, 7] includes monitoring aspects of cognitive workload, referring to a multidimensional construct and multimodal load placed on operators during task execution [8, 9]. Specifically monitoring attentional control and working memory, allows for insight into the cognitive systems important for learning, visuospatial reasoning, task execution and completion [10]. This approach was used in previous studies assessing cognitive workload in UAS applications, as increases in cognitive workload can drastically affect UAS mission outcomes via increased human error [6]. Overloading the working memory system has been shown to cause disengagement from the task and lower task performance [11].

Previous literature has noted the presence of individual differences in working memory but indicate competing theories regarding the source of these differences, such as age, domain-specificity, or domain generality [12]. Extensive reviews on potential sources for individual variation in working memory have attributed similar sources with support of various theories, including executive attention, attentional inhibition, and proactive control [11]. Therefore, it is especially important to examine how working memory is affected in individual SOs, as they use attentional resources to maintain flight systems and complete their task objectives.

Functional brain activity monitoring has been shown to give insight into working memory and attentional resources being used during task completion, with the most common measures being functional magnetic resonance imaging (fMRI), electroencephalography (EEG) and functional near infrared spectroscopy (fNIRS). Despite higher spatial resolution, limitations placed on subject movement have prevented employment of fMRI in monitoring cortical activation during task completion outside of lab settings. EEG has moderately lower spatial resolution and portability, but higher temporal resolution than fNIRS; however, fNIRS balances portability and cost with similar performance to EEG, which allow for greater potential for in-field applications [13]. fNIRS has become a valuable tool for monitoring prefrontal cortex (PFC) areas associated with working memory, and attentional resources in both lab and field conditions. Particularly it has shown immense potential in assessing cognitive workload during SO task performance [6, 7, 14].

Previous studies utilizing fNIRS during SO task performance assessed groupwise differences [1, 4, 6, 15] and general trends [7] in behavioral performance and hemodynamic response during task completion. This study sought to analyze individual differences in comparison to subject groupings from order of conditions (a priori) and behavioral performance (ad hoc), following task completion using a high-fidelity simulator. By analyzing individual differences, insights can be drawn regarding how those subjects responded to their condition, and their overall improvement between conditions can be factored in when assessing operator preparedness. Additional insight can be drawn from understanding how subject variability factors into the assessment of groupwise differences.

2 Methods

2.1 Participants

This study reports analyses of data collected from a sample of 13 subjects between the ages of 19 and 40, with a mean age of 22.9 ± 5.9 years, consisting of 9 males and 4 females. Each participant provided written informed consent before participating in the study. The experimental protocol was approved by the Drexel University Institutional Review Board (IRB). Overall, trainees self-reported 43 h of 3D gaming, 26 h of first-person 3D gaming and no flight simulator experience prior to participating in this study. All participants had vision correctable to 20/20. To properly assess the experimental objective, exclusion criteria included: people who experience migraines; people who have color blindness; those with a history of head injuries, seizures, or neurological dysfunction; people who have a diagnosed reading disability; and those taking medication shown to affect alertness or brain activity.

2.2 Experimental Protocol and UAS Simulator

The protocol used Simlat's C-STAR GCS, a high-fidelity flight simulator, to represent UAS SO task scenarios. C-STAR is a training simulation program used in various studies [1, 4, 7, 15] to train individuals in search and rescue, maritime exploration, mining, and counter-UAS scenarios [16]. Participants were instructed to operate the UAS sensor camera to scan six consecutive map-defined regions of interest (ROIs) along the automated flight path; see Fig. 1 for an example route. During ROI scanning, participants were directed to identify, track, and lock targets in each ROI indicated by a red bus. All formal simulation sessions lasted approximately 12.5 min. Task load changes were implemented through simulated visibility changes from changing the time of day. Specifically, five sessions were implemented with three being easy (11:00–11:12), one being medium (20:00–20:12), and one being hard (06:00–06:12). All participants began experimentation with three easy condition followed by either medium then hard or hard then medium. For the purposes of this paper only the last easy session and hard sessions will be analyzed.

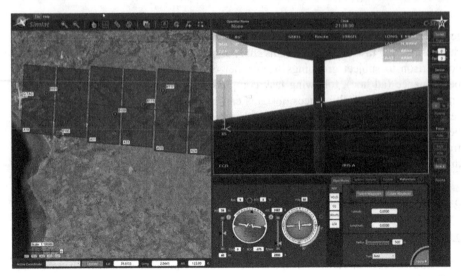

Fig. 1. A) Example of participant screen, with route information and sensor camera window. For ease of understanding, targets in this example are marked with a waypoint and denoted (B101, B105, B109, B113 and B117), which were not available to participants during simulations.

2.3 Measurements

Behavioral task performance throughout flight sessions were captured using the C-STAR integrated Performance Analysis and Evaluation Module (PANEL) logs. PANEL data tracks SO scanning by recording scan polygons from the camera's field of view (FOV) throughout the task in nano-second increments. Raw polygon data exists as a list of polygons with vertices recorded as a series of Latitude/Longitude points. These polygon coordinates are used to calculate SO behavioral patterns, efficiency, and performance. PANEL enables the use of internal filters that limit acceptable FOV polygon sizes, such as: the maximum length of the bottom line between vertices (FOV Bottom Max Size), and the maximal ratio between FOV polygon area and task ROI area (FOV Area Ratio). All measures used in this analysis were filtered by standard parameters of 750 FOV Bottom Max Size and 0.5 FOV Area Ratio, limiting polygons that are too large to be informative. Following filtering, various summary measures were computed that illustrate SO performance for each scan task (ROI), including: the total number of FOV scan polygons (Number of Polygons); scan polygons contained within the task ROI borders and the percent of the ROI area that participants scanned (Scan); and scan polygons touching or extending past the ROI border (OverScan). Within the limited scope of this paper, operator behavioral performance was analyzed using only scan and overscan measures.

For this study, an 18-channel fNIRS device with a sampling frequency of 10 Hz was used to maintain consistency with previous experiments [1, 7]; see Fig. 2. The fNIRS device was complete with 16 long channels and two short separation channels for measuring cortical activity and superficial brain layer information, respectively. Pre-processing techniques were applied to tease out extraneous instrument and physiological noise, including a high-pass filter with a cutoff frequency of 0.005 Hz, and a finite impulse response low-pass filter with cutoff frequency of 0.09 Hz. Saturation and noise level governed signal quality and channel rejection analysis. Following signal quality analysis, a modified Beer-Lambert Law (MBLL) was applied to calculate channel-specific measures of oxygenated hemoglobin (HbO) and deoxygenated hemoglobin (HbR). Grouping of spatially relevant channels was performed to assess cerebral oxygenation in four areas of the prefrontal cortex (PFC): left dorsolateral PFC (Left DLPFC), left anterior medial PFC (Left AMPFC), right anterior medial PFC (Right AMPFC) and right dorsolateral PFC (Right DLPFC).

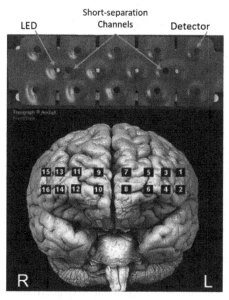

Fig. 2. 18-channel fNIRS sensor, documented with identified LEDs, detectors, short-separation channels, and node locations overlayed on participant PFC areas. Left Dorsolateral PFC (Left DLPFC: optodes 3–4). Left Anterior Medial PFC (Left AMPFC: optodes 5–6). Right Anterior Medial PFC (Right AMPFC: optodes 11–12). Right Dorsolateral PFC (Right DLPFC: optodes 13–14).

2.4 Data Analysis

This protocol focuses on variability from individual subjects; therefore, all subjects were pooled and grouped according to behavioral performance during the final easy and hard conditions. Initial grouping was performed in Matlab 2020a$^©$, with subsequent analysis taking place in R [17]. Subjects who were able to maintain or improve performance during the transition from easy to hard conditions were categorized as well-adjusted (n = 8); well-adjusted participants recorded equal or greater scan behavior during the transition to the hard condition, as well as lower overscan following the easy condition. Subjects with reduced behavioral performance during the transition from easy to hard conditions were categorized as mal-adjusted (n = 5); mal-adjusted participants recorded lower scan and higher overscan during the hard condition when compared to the easy condition. Univariate statistics were calculated for each participant and group overall to compare subject-dependent results between conditions and against the performance of the group, provided as (median, 95% confidence interval (CI)).

3 Results

3.1 Behavioral Performance

Prior to grouping participant scan results according to behavioral performance, we observed median scan and overscan across all participants, according to condition. Across all participants, Scan was lower during the easy condition (0.22, CI [0.21, 0.24]) than in the hard condition (0.25, CI [0.22, 0.26]). OverScan was equivalent between the easy condition (0.71, CI [0.69, 0.74]), and hard condition (0.71, CI [0.67, 0.73]). From this, a general assumption could be that all participants behaved similarly; however, this only provide differences for the conditions.

To analyze how participants performed, subjects were assigned groups based on scan and overscan performance. Scan and overscan performance for well-adjusted and mal-adjusted groups are shown in Fig. 3 by condition. Well-adjusted (WA) indicates scan performance was equal or greater during the hard condition and overscan was less than that of the easy condition. WA participants (n = 8) demonstrated increases in median scan from the easy condition (0.22, CI [0.19, 0.23]) to the hard condition (0.26, CI [0.23, 0.27]) and decreases in median overscan from the easy condition (0.74, CI [0.71, 0.77]) to the hard condition (0.72, CI [0.67, 0.74]). Mal-adjusted (MA) indicated scan decreased and overscan was equal or greater during the hard condition when compared to the easy condition. MA participants (n = 5) demonstrated decreases in median scan from the easy condition (0.25, CI [0.21, 0.28]) to the hard condition (0.23, CI [0.20, 0.27]) and increases in median overscan from the easy condition (0.64, CI [0.61, 0.70]) to the hard condition (0.69, CI [0.66, 0.74]).

From the performance groups, we cannot directly understand sources of variability or average performance levels, and we can only make general estimations of how participants in each group adjusted to the hard condition. To understand potential sources of variability or deviations from group trends, median scan and overscan measures were calculated for each participant; see Fig. 4.

Figure 4 demonstrates inconsistencies in performance across both well-adjusted and mal-adjusted participants. From the WA group, subject 16's scan marginally decreases from the easy to hard condition, demonstrating that rounding errors may have affected the outcome during group selection, as could be using median instead of mean. Albeit, subject 16's overscan decreased from easy to hard conditions, despite overscan in both the easy (0.77, CI [0.74, 0.82]) and hard condition (0.75, CI [0.48, 0.82]) at the upper limit of the group median. Subject 17 exhibited similarly elevated overscan that was equivalent between the two conditions (0.77) and moderate changes in confidence interval. Subject 18 likely contributed to the low well-adjusted group scan estimate for the easy condition, exhibited by extraordinarily low scan (0.03, CI [0.00, 0.28]); however, biomarker data can help inform whether this was disengagement, fatigue, or ability.

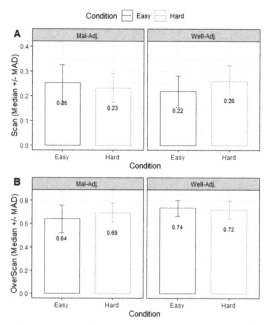

Fig. 3. Behavioral performance group summary by condition, with median absolute deviation (MAD) error bars. A) Median Scan for mal-adjusted and well-adjusted groups during easy and hard conditions. Group trends suggest proper grouping, as scan decreased from easy to hard conditions for the mal-adjusted group, and the opposite being true for the well-adjusted group. B) Median OverScan for mal-adjusted and well-adjusted groups during easy and hard conditions. Group trends are further supported by overscan increasing from easy to hard conditions for the mal-adjusted group, with the opposite being true for the well-adjusted group.

From the MA group, all participants demonstrated scan changes consistent with group trends except for participants 15 and 26. Subject 15 was unique in comparison to both group trends since scan measures improved from easy (0.19, CI [0.17, 0.23]) to hard conditions (0.28, CI [0.21, 0.34]), with a similar increase in overscan from the easy (0.52, CI [0.40, 0.66]) to hard conditions (0.66, CI [0.53, 0.73]). Subject 26 demonstrated a similar trend as subject 26; however, the increases in both scan and overscan were less drastic.

3.2 Hemodynamic Response

The same top-down approach demonstrated with the behavioral results is repeated for biomarker data. Figure 5 exhibits the overall variability for the relative concentration of HbO during easy and hard conditions from each performance group, in dorsolateral and anterior medial PFC areas.

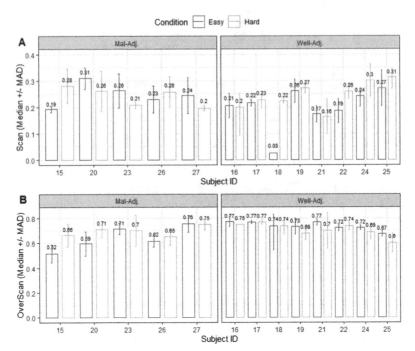

Fig. 4. Median behavioral performance for each subject during the easy and hard condition, organized by performance group, with median absolute deviation error bars. A) Median scan for each participant in mal-adjusted and well-adjusted groups during easy and hard conditions. B) Median overscan for each participant in mal-adjusted and well-adjusted groups during easy and hard conditions.

Similar trends of increasing relative concentrations of HbR from easy to hard conditions are demonstrated in Fig. 6. Variability is extremely high across plots from both figures, which was a concern for categorizing biomarker results according to performance group. Group relative concentrations can be informative for assessing movement and providing concentrations for which individuals can be compared to the group. To assess whether assumptions about participants from behavioral analysis are supported, it is necessary to analyze individual concentrations, as each person can have their own baseline. Relative concentrations of HbO and HbR across all four PFC regions for each participant are demonstrated in Fig. 7 and Fig. 8, respectively.

Well-Adjusted

As behavioral performance results were discussed more in-depth specifically for WA participants 16, 17, and 18, biomarker levels for those participants were examined more thoroughly. Relative HbO and HbR concentrations for subject 16 decreased in the left DLPFC, right AMPFC, and right DLPFC from easy to hard conditions; however, there was a large increase in HbO in the left AMPFC, with a similar increase of half the magnitude in left AMPFC HbR levels. This suggests that there may have been relaxation of attentional resources and the subject may have disengaged for some, or all, of the tasks during the hard condition. Subject 17 demonstrated a large increase in HbO from easy

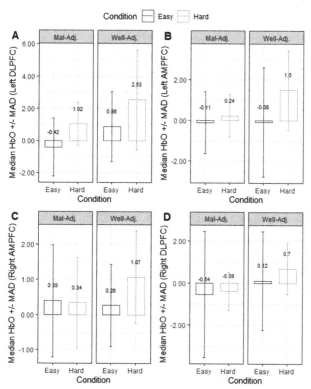

Fig. 5. Median oxygenated hemoglobin levels during each condition, grouped by performance, with median absolute deviation (MAD) error bars. A) Median relative concentration of oxygenated hemoglobin in the left dorsolateral prefrontal cortex, for mal-adjusted and well-adjusted groups. B) Median relative concentration of oxygenated hemoglobin in the left anterior medial prefrontal cortex, for mal-adjusted and well-adjusted groups. C) Median relative concentration of oxygenated hemoglobin in the right anterior medial prefrontal cortex, for mal-adjusted and well-adjusted groups. D) Median relative concentration of oxygenated hemoglobin in the right dorsolateral prefrontal cortex, for mal-adjusted and well-adjusted groups.

to hard conditions for all PFC regions, as well as increases in HbR of similar magnitude in the right AMPFC regions and half the magnitude from easy to hard conditions in all remaining PFC regions. Greater concentrations of oxygenated hemoglobin across all regions may indicate that the subject remained engaged, and in combination with behavioral results, suggests the hard condition was particularly challenging but did not overload the participant. Subject 18 exhibited reductions of relative concentrations in HbO in all PFC regions. Marginal increases in HbR concentrations were observed in left DLPFC and left AMPFC regions of subject 18, with large reduction in right AMPFC and marginal reduction in right DLPFC areas from easy to hard conditions. Biomarker

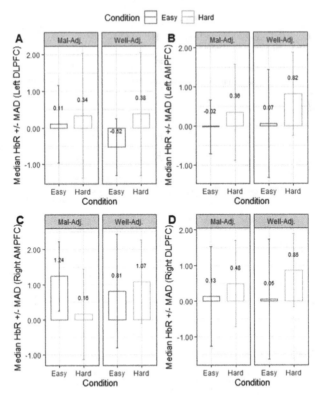

Fig. 6. Median deoxygenated hemoglobin levels during each condition, grouped by performance, with median absolute deviation (MAD) error bars. A) Median relative concentration of deoxygenated hemoglobin in the left dorsolateral prefrontal cortex, for mal-adjusted and well-adjusted groups. B) Median relative concentration of deoxygenated hemoglobin in the left anterior medial prefrontal cortex, for mal-adjusted and well-adjusted groups. C) Median relative concentration of deoxygenated hemoglobin in the right anterior medial prefrontal cortex, for mal-adjusted and well-adjusted groups. D) Median relative concentration of deoxygenated hemoglobin in the right dorsolateral prefrontal cortex, for mal-adjusted and well-adjusted groups.

results for subject 18 indicate that the subject was engaged but overloaded during the hard condition, and therefore may call for further training.

Mal-Adjusted

Since behavioral performance results were discussed more in-depth specifically for MA participants 15 and 26, biomarker levels for those participants were examined more thoroughly. Subject 15 demonstrated minor reduction in relative HbO concentrations in the left DLPFC, left AMPFC and right AMPFC regions, and a marginal increase in right DLPFC from easy to hard condition. Similarly, low reductions in relative concentration of HbR were exhibited in left DLPFC, right AMPFC and right DLPFC areas, with a minor increase in HbR in the left AMPFC region. Biomarker and behavioral results for subject 15 suggest that the participant was increasing attentional resources during the hard condition, and potentially employed a scan methodology that led to more scan

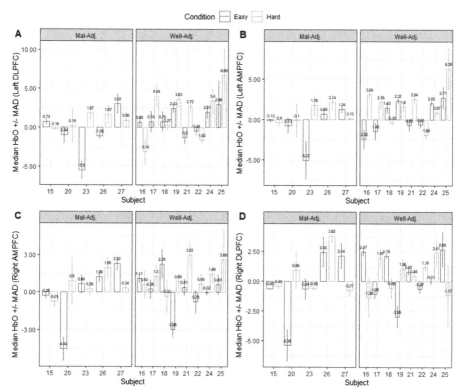

Fig. 7. Median oxygenated hemoglobin levels during each condition for all participants, grouped by performance, with median absolute deviation (MAD) error bars. A) Median relative concentration of oxygenated hemoglobin in the left dorsolateral prefrontal cortex, for each participant in mal-adjusted and well-adjusted groups. B) Median relative concentration of oxygenated hemoglobin in the left anterior medial prefrontal cortex, for each participant in mal-adjusted and well-adjusted groups. C) Median relative concentration of oxygenated hemoglobin in the right anterior medial prefrontal cortex, for each participant in mal-adjusted and well-adjusted groups. D) Median relative concentration of oxygenated hemoglobin in the right dorsolateral prefrontal cortex, for each participant in mal-adjusted and well-adjusted groups.

polygons infringing on task ROI boundaries, indicating the hard condition may be been too challenging for their level of training or current skill level. For subject 26, increases in median relative HbO concentrations were observed in all PFC areas from easy to hard conditions, with the largest increase occurring in the left DLPFC region. Moderate increases in median relative HbR concentration were observed in the left and right DLPFC regions, a large increase in the left AMPFC area, and a marginal decrease in the right AMPFC region. Biomarker and behavioral results for subject 26 suggest that the hard condition may have been too difficult for their current skill level and were overloaded, despite remaining engaged with the tasks.

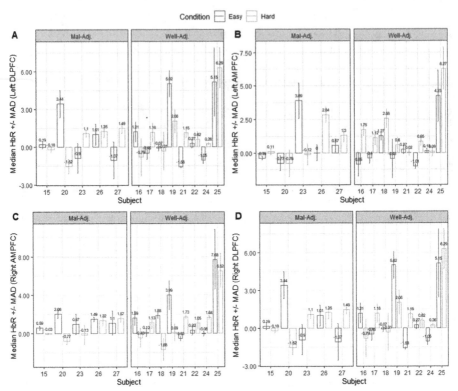

Fig. 8. Median oxygenated hemoglobin levels during each condition for all participants, grouped by performance, with median absolute deviation (MAD) error bars. A) Median relative concentration of deoxygenated hemoglobin in the left dorsolateral prefrontal cortex, for each participant in mal-adjusted and well-adjusted groups. B) Median relative concentration of deoxygenated hemoglobin in the left anterior medial prefrontal cortex, for each participant in mal-adjusted and well-adjusted groups. C) Median relative concentration of deoxygenated hemoglobin in the right anterior medial prefrontal cortex, for each participant in mal-adjusted and well-adjusted groups. D) Median relative concentration of deoxygenated hemoglobin in the right dorsolateral prefrontal cortex, for each participant in mal-adjusted and well-adjusted groups.

4 Discussion

Operators experience high levels of mental workload as they devote cognitive resources to the tasks at hand to maximize their performance and avoid the introduction of human error. For instance, UAS SOs are prone to disengagement from both under- and overloading their mental resources, thereby decreasing performance metrics. However, proper training and assessments of operator readiness can be implemented to minimize operator error in the field [1]. One method explored in this paper for personalized training and performance assessments for participants beyond typical group analysis or comparisons, is to monitor and assess individual behavioral metrics and cortical hemodynamic measures during task completion.

In a minority of well-adjusted participants, the hard condition was too challenging, and participants disengaged for part of the hard condition. Others from the well-adjusted group demonstrated that the hard condition was challenging but not overloading, while others were overloaded. Taken with behavioral measures and that participants were novice SOs, these results indicate that further training was required prior to environmental shifts exhibited during the hard condition [14]. Within the mal-adjusted group, the hard condition shifted some subjects' scanning strategy to a more disordered approach, suggesting that the condition was too difficult for their current skill level, and may have been overloaded rather than disengaged.

Similar trends between behavioral performance and relative concentrations of oxygenated hemoglobin across dorsolateral and anterior medial PFC areas were identified in previous studies [4, 7], as well as the interpretation of anterior medial PFC activation and deactivation regarding attentional resources [18]. Further exploration of this area of study may benefit from multi-day sessions, to assist participants' training and prevent undue disengagement or fatigue during the introduction of higher workload condition.

Acknowledgements. The authors would like to thank Shahar Kosti and Simlat, Inc., of Miamisburg, Ohio, USA, for providing access and data extraction from the C-STAR simulator.

References

1. Richards, D., Izzetoglu, K.: Human performance assessment: evaluation of wearable sensors for monitoring brain activity. In: Vidulich, M.A., Tsang, P.S. (eds.) Improving Aviation Performance through Applying Engineering Psychology: Advances in Aviation Psychology, 1st edn, pp. 163–180. CRC Press, London (2019)
2. Schwark, J., Sandry, J., Dolgov, I.: Evidence for a positive relationship between working-memory capacity and detection of low-prevalence targets in visual search. Perception **42**(1), 112–114 (2013). https://doi.org/10.1068/p7386
3. Wolfe, J.M., Horowitz, T.S., Van Wert, M.J., Kenner, N.M., Place, S.S., Kibbi, N.: Low target prevalence is a stubborn source of errors in visual search tasks. J. Exp. Psychol. Gen. **136**(4), 623–638 (2007). https://doi.org/10.1037/0096-3445.136.4.623
4. Richards, D., Izzetoglu, K., Shelton-Rayner, G.: UAV operator mental workload - a neurophysiological comparison of mental workload and vigilance. In: AIAA Modeling and Simulation Technologies Conference, (AIAA AVIATION Forum: American Institute of Aeronautics and Astronautics) (2017)
5. Bhavsar, P., Srinivasan, B., Srinivasan, R.: Pupillometry based real-time monitoring of operator's cognitive workload to prevent human error during abnormal situations. Ind. Eng. Chem. Res. **55**(12), 3372–3382 (2016). https://doi.org/10.1021/acs.iecr.5b03685
6. Izzetoglu, K., et al.: UAV operators workload assessment by optical brain imaging technology (fNIR). In: Valavanis, K.P., Vachtsevanos, G.J. (eds.) Handbook of Unmanned Aerial Vehicles, pp. 2475–2500. Springer, Dordrecht (2015). https://doi.org/10.1007/978-90-481-9707-1_22
7. Kerr, J., Reddy, P., Kosti, S., Izzetoglu, K.: UAS operator workload assessment during search and surveillance tasks through simulated fluctuations in environmental visibility. In: Schmorrow, D.D., Fidopiastis, C.M. (eds.) HCII 2019. LNCS (LNAI), vol. 11580, pp. 394–406. Springer, Cham (2019). https://doi.org/10.1007/978-3-030-22419-6_28
8. Curtin, A., Ayaz, H.: The age of neuroergonomics: towards ubiquitous and continuous measurement of brain function with fNIRS: the age of neuroergonomics and fNIRS. Jpn. Psychol. Res. **60**(4), 374–386 (2018). https://doi.org/10.1111/jpr.12227

9. Paas, F., Tuovinen, J., Tabbers, H., Van Gerven, P.W.M.: Cognitive load measurement as a means to advance cognitive load theory. Educ. Psychol. **38**(1), 63–71 (2003). https://doi.org/10.1207/S15326985EP3801_8

10. Cowan, N.: Working memory underpins cognitive development, learning, and education. Educ. Psychol. Rev. **26**(2), 197–223 (2013). https://doi.org/10.1007/s10648-013-9246-y

11. Yun, R.J., Krystal, J.H., Mathalon, D.H.: Working memory overload: fronto-limbic interactions and effects on subsequent working memory function. Brain Imaging Behav. **4**(1), 96–108 (2010). https://doi.org/10.1007/s11682-010-9089-9

12. Miyake, A.: Individual differences in working memory: introduction to the special section. J. Exp. Psychol. Gen. **130**(2), 163–168 (2001). https://doi.org/10.1037/0096-3445.130.2.163

13. Mehta, R., Parasuraman, R.: Neuroergonomics: a review of applications to physical and cognitive work. Front. Hum. Neurosci. **7**, 889 (2013). https://doi.org/10.3389/fnhum.2013.00889. https://www.frontiersin.org/article/10.3389/fnhum.2013.00889

14. Ayaz, H., Shewokis, P., Bunce, S., Izzetoglu, K., Willems, B., Onaral, B.: Optical brain monitoring for operator training and mental workload assessment. NeuroImage **59**(1), 36–47 (2012). https://doi.org/10.1016/j.neuroimage.2011.06.023

15. Armstrong, J., Izzetoglu, K., Richards, D.: Using functional near infrared spectroscopy to assess cognitive performance of UAV sensor operators during route scanning. In: 11th International Joint Conference on Biomedical Engineering Systems and Technologies, vol. 3, pp. 286–293. SCITEPRESS - Science and Technology Publications (2018). https://doi.org/10.5220/0006731502860293. https://www.scitepress.org/Link.aspx?doi=10.5220%2f0006731502860293

16. Products | Simlat. https://www.simlat.com/products

17. R: A language and environment for statistical computing (2020). R Foundation for Statistical Computing, Vienna, Austria. http://www.R-project.org/

18. Koshino, H., Minamoto, T., Ikeda, T., Osaka, M., Otsuka, Y., Osaka, N.: Anterior medial prefrontal cortex exhibits activation during task preparation but deactivation during task execution (in English). PLoS ONE **6**(8), e22909–e22909 (2011). https://doi.org/10.1371/journal.pone.0022909

Brain Activity Changes Elicited Through Multi-session Training Assessment in the Prefrontal Cortex by fNIRS

Pratusha Reddy[1]($\boxtimes$), Jaime Kerr[1], Patricia A. Shewokis[1,2], and Kurtulus Izzetoglu[1]

[1] School of Biomedical Engineering, Science and Health Systems, Drexel University, Philadelphia, PA 19104, USA
ylr26@drexel.edu

[2] Nutrition Science Department, College of Nursing and Health Professions, Drexel University, Philadelphia, PA 19104, USA

Abstract. This study aims to utilize a non-invasive and portable neuroimaging modality – functional near infrared spectroscopy (fNIRS) to investigate training and transfer of skills in unmanned aerial system (UAS) sensor operators (SOs). To achieve this objective, we recruited 13 novice participants and exposed them to three similar training sessions followed by a testing session on a UAS simulator. The training sessions occurred at 11 AM (high visibility), while the testing session occurred at 6 AM or 8 PM (low visibility). Regardless of the session, the participants were asked to scan pre-defined areas to best of their abilities and identify targets (red bus). Behavioral results from training sessions indicated that some participants improved their scan performance, while others did not. No significant changes in target find performance were observed within and between groups. Associated average oxyhemoglobin (HbO) changes significantly decreased in right prefrontal cortex (PFC) regions for high performers and in left PFC regions for low performers. During the transfer task, scan performance was maintained by both groups, while average HbO significantly increased in left dorsolateral PFC of high performers and left and right anterior medial PFC of low performers. In conclusion, we demonstrated intraindividual differences in expertise development during multi-session training.

Keywords: Functional near infrared spectroscopy · fNIRS · Training · Expertise development · Aviation · UAS

1 Introduction

Although utility of unmanned aerial systems (UAS) in military and civilian operations has exponentially grown within the last decade, their use has been limited by a shortage of qualified operators [1]. This shortage is further exacerbated with respect to payload or sensor operators (SOs), whose responsibilities vary from manipulating sensors to maintaining flight operations and disseminating information. To ensure that such missions are successfully accomplished, it is reasonable to assume that a SO must undergo an

© Springer Nature Switzerland AG 2021
D. D. Schmorrow and C. M. Fidopiastis (Eds.): HCII 2021, LNAI 12776, pp. 63–73, 2021.
https://doi.org/10.1007/978-3-030-78114-9_5

effective training program that ensures successful transfer of acquired skills to novel situations, while efficiently using capacity- and duration-limited executive processes such as working memory and attention.

Developing such programs requires evaluation of changes in cognitive workload as one learns a complex cognitive task. Cognitive workload can be evaluated by assessing the effect of the interaction between task and individual characteristics on performance and mental effort executed by the particular individual [2]. Performance is defined as a measure of learner's achievements, while mental effort is a measure of cognitive resources allocated for completion of the task. While performance is an easier aspect to measure, the objective measurement of mental effort has been a challenge. The most common methods of evaluating mental effort have been to utilize primary or secondary task performances or subjective rating methods. However, such methods do not enable direct assessment into an individual's mental state or are after-the-fact.

A growing trend in literature indicates the use of noninvasive neuroimaging techniques to objectively measure mental effort. Specifically, techniques such as functional magnetic resonance imaging (fMRI) have allowed us to gain insights into the structure and dynamic mechanisms of the brain during skill acquisition [3]. A prominent finding of this research has been the involvement of prefrontal cortex (PFC) in higher order functioning. While these findings have made a substantial contribution to what we know about the brain now, the technical limitations posed by the modality has constrained the findings to laboratory settings [4].

Functional near infrared spectroscopy (fNIRS) is a portable, neuroimaging modality capable of measuring correlates of brain activity in ecologically valid environments, simulation settings and laboratories. Specifically, fNIRS allows for continuous measurements of changes in oxyhemoglobin (HbO) and deoxy-hemoglobin (HbR) concentrations within the PFC as elicited by metabolic demands imposed by cognitive activation [5]. Research over the last decade has repeatedly indicated the potential of fNIRS in assessing cognitive workload, and expertise development in natural environment and everyday settings [6].

Our lab has been utilizing fNIRS to assess the aforementioned phenomenon in UAS operators and air traffic controllers [7–13]. These studies have indicated considerable activation in the right medial and left dorsolateral prefrontal cortices in both novice and expert operators as they engaged in sustained attention and working memory tasks. We have also quantitatively demonstrated transfer by reporting substantial decreases in activity with training and increases in activity upon introduction of novel tasks or environments, with performance maintenances [14–16].

This study is a continuation of this line of research. In this investigation, we aim to examine training and transfer of human operator skills as measured by behavioral metrics and neurophysiological data collected using fNIRS. We are primarily interested in surveillance and reconnaissance missions, which constitute the majority of SO missions. During such missions, a SO is tasked to manipulate a camera to search a targeted area and identify any threats. In line with previous studies, we hypothesize that individuals will strategize differently while conducting sensor operators' tasks and that these changes will be reflected in their behavioral performance data. Furthermore, we hypothesize that those who improve their behavioral performances with training, will show decreased brain activity in PFC and positive transfer or generalizability of skills during the transfer task.

2 Materials and Methods

2.1 Participants

Thirteen right-handed participants ranging from 19 to 40 years consisting of nine males and four females volunteered to participate in this study. Prior to the experimentation, all participants signed informed written consent forms approved by the Drexel University Human Subjects Institution Review Board. All participants had no prior UAS simulator experience and had corrected to normal vision.

2.2 UAS Simulator

A commercially available Simlat C-STAR (Simlat Inc., Miamisburg, Ohio) simulation system was used to generate SO task scenarios. This simulator has not only been widely used by researchers but is also currently being used to support over 80 UAS training centers across 30 countries. In this study, the simulator was used in a single instructor and trainee configuration (see Fig. 1). Both instructor and trainee screens were split into map and payload portions. The map portion displayed the flight path, the location of the aircraft on the flight path, area that needs to be scanned and the scan polygon associated with the camera's field of view (FOV). The payload portion displayed cameras FOV and zoom angle associated with the FOV. The trainee used a joystick to move the camera position and a lever on the joystick to zoom in and out to complete assigned tasks. The primary differences between the instructor and trainee screens were based on the fact that the instructor had the ability to take back flight or sensor controls, see marked target locations on the map screen and have additional controls (changing weather conditions, assigning engine failure, etc.).

The simulator also consists of a Performance Analysis & Evaluation module (PANEL), which collects, evaluates and summarizes trainee's performance. Specifically, the module outputs the cameras FOV zoom angle, logical index representing whether target was in FOV and the coordinates of the scan polygon associated with FOV every nano second.

Fig. 1. Simulator setup on the left and trainee's screen on the right

2.3 Functional Near Infrared Spectroscopy Sensor

A continuous wave fNIRS device (fNIRS Imager 1200; fNIR Devices LLC, Potomac, MD) was used to measure hemodynamic changes from the PFC of the trainees. The sensor emits light at peak wavelengths of 730 and 850 nm, samples every 100 ms, has 12 detectors and 4 light sources. The detector and light source combination result in a total of 16 cerebral and 2 extracerebral measurement locations (see Fig. 2).

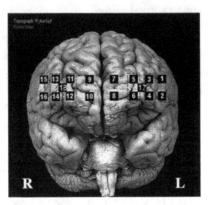

Fig. 2. Location of fNIRS channels on the prefrontal cortex (PFC). Channels highlighted by yellow boxes indicate anterior medial PFC, while orange boxes reflect dorsolateral PFC. (Color figure online)

2.4 Experimental Protocol

Each trainee underwent a five-minute introductory period, followed by three unique 12-min-long training scenarios and two 12-min-long testing scenarios. The introductory period allowed trainees to familiarize themselves with task objectives, program-specific classification of proper area scanning and target locking execution during task completion. The training scenarios occurred at a simulation time of 11AM, while the testing scenarios occurred at 6AM or 8 PM. The scenarios were randomly presented within each scenario type. Since the scope of this study is to show training and transfer, only training and first of the two testing scenarios will be discussed in the rest of this paper.

Each scenario consisted of six consecutive areas. Of the six areas, only five areas had a target – a red civilian bus. The area, which had no target was randomly assigned and trainees were not informed of this fact or that there was only one target per area. The aircraft took approximately two minutes to pass each area and a voice command was given every time the aircraft entered the subsequent area.

2.5 Pre-processing and Feature Extraction

Performance Analysis and Evaluation Module (PANEL) classifies each scan polygon into twenty different groups, based on a combination of five FOV Bottom Max Sizes (the maximum bottom line size of FOV polygons from one vertex to the other - 1500, 1250, 750, 500, and 250) and four FOV Area Ratios (maximal ratio between a FOV polygon area and the area of the applicable task region - 1.00, 0.75, 0.50, and 0.25). After classifying the polygons into their respective groups, scanned ratio was calculated using Eq. 1, where P_i is a scan polygon within the task area A. Based on industry standard and previously reported studies, scanned ratio related to FOV Bottom Max Size of 750 and FOV Area Ratio of 0.5 was extracted for following analysis [9–11]. For the target find task, the module outputs time points at which the trigger was pressed, the zoom angle at which the scan was being conducted and whether target was in FOV or not. Based on previous studies and instructions given to the trainee related to proper find (when zoom angle is lower than 15 and target is tracked for 3 s) a logical index indicating whether target was found or not was assigned to each session-subarea per subject. Then accuracy using Eq. 2, where F_i is true find or true no find (when no target was found in area that had no target) was extracted per session.

$$scanned = \left(\bigcup_i P_i \right) \bigcap A \tag{1}$$

$$accuracy = \sum_i F_i / 6 \tag{2}$$

fNIRS signals are often confounded by the factors such as head movement, systemic physiological changes, instrumentation, and environment noises. To extract neural-activity related signals, the following methods were applied. First, the visual inspection was employed, and saturated channels or corrupted signals due to bad contacts or misplacements and/or device failures during experimental session were removed [17, 18]. Second, wavelet-based motion artifact removal (the tuning parameter was set to 0.1) was applied to remove abrupt spikes [19]. Third, finite impulse response high and low pass filters with cut-off frequencies of 0.005 and 0.9 Hz, respectively were used to remove high frequency noise associated with motion, respiration and cardiac functions [5]. Optical density data was then converted into the relative concentration changes of oxy-hemoglobin (HbO) and deoxy-hemoglobin using modified beer lambert law, with the baseline period defined as ten seconds prior to the onset of tasks [20]. Average HbO per subarea were extracted from left dorsolateral (LDlPFC – channels 3 and 4), left anterior medial PFC (LAMPFC – channels 5 and 6), right anterior medial PFC (RAMPFC – channels 11 and 12), and right dorsolateral PFC (RDlPFC – channels 13 and 14) (see Fig. 2).

2.6 Statistical Analysis

Similar to previous studies, trainees were grouped based on their scanned performance across the training sessions [11]. Specifically, trainees who displayed improvements in scan performance were labelled high performers, and other were labelled low performers. This grouping variable was then marked as a between-subject factor for further analysis.

A mixed model ANOVA with performance group as a between-subject factor and session as a within-subject factor was used to evaluate the effect of training and transfer on scan performance, and mental effort as represented by average HbO (LDlPFC,

LAMPFC, RAMPFC, and RDlPFC). Post hoc analysis for main and interaction effects was conducted using Tukey's multiple comparison tests. Specifically, comparisons were planned, with four tests comparing groups per session (E.g., high performers vs low performers for training session 1), and six tests comparing training sessions per group (E.g., training session 1 vs training session 2 in high-performance group) and two tests comparing the training session 3 against the testing session per group.

Prior to conducting the statistical test, data was checked for normality, homogeneity of variance and homogeneity of covariance assumptions. If data did not meet the assumptions, then the regular aligned rank and Wilcoxon tests were used to conduct non-parametric mixed ANOVAs and one sample t-tests, respectively. For all statistical analyses, the level of significance was set at $\alpha = 0.05$. Adjustments using false discovery rate was made on p-values to account for Type I error inflation. Partial eta-squared (η_p^2) was calculated to examine main and interaction effect sizes, while Cohen's d was used to examine post hoc effects [21]. For η_p^2, 0.01 reflects a small effect, while 0.06 and > 0.14 reflect medium and large effects, respectively. Alternatively, d of 0.2 is considered small effect, while 0.5 and 0.8 represent medium and large effects, respectively. All statistical analyses were conducted in R (R Core Team, 2019). ARTool package was used to conduct the non-parametric tests [22].

3   Results

A significant interaction effect between session and performance group was observed for scan ($F(3, 293) = 10.75, p < 0.001, \eta_p^2 = 0.10$) and target find ($F(3, 33) = 3.92, p = 0.017, \eta_p^2 = 0.26$) performance measures (see Fig. 3). No post hoc comparisons were significant for target find performance. Post hoc comparisons between performance groups per session revealed significant differences in training session 1 ($p < 0.001, d = -1.01$) and training session 3 ($p = 0.010, d = 0.64$), with scan performance being greater in low-performance group for session 1 and high-performance group for session 3, respectively. Pairwise comparisons between sessions within the high-performance group indicated significant increases in scan performance between session 1 and session 3 ($p = 0.034, d = 0.69$). Comparisons within low-performance group indicated significant decreases in performance between session 1 and session 2 ($p = 0.021, d = -0.68$) and session 1 and session 3 ($p < 0.001, d = -0.96$).

Significant interaction effect between session and group was observed for average HbO measures taken from LAMPFC ($F(3, 293) = 3.49, p = 0.016, \eta_p^2 = 0.03$), RAMPFC ($F(3, 293) = 4.52, p = 0.004, \eta_p^2 = 0.04$) and RDlPFC ($F(3, 293) = 3.47, p = 0.017, \eta_p^2 = 0.03$) regions. Pairwise comparisons investigating differences between sessions per performance group and performance groups per session are shown in Table 1. Firstly, results indicate significant large decreases in activity from training sessions 3 to 1 in right PFC regions for high performers (RAMPFC: $p = 0.018, d = -0.74$, RDlPFC: $p < 0.001, d = -1.11$) and left PFC regions for low performers (LAMPFC: $p < 0.001, d = -0.92$, LDlPFC: $p = 0.030, d = -0.65$). Furthermore, significant large decreases in activity from training session 1 to 2 were observed in RDlPFC of high performers ($p = 0.003, d = -0.88$) and left regions for low performers (LAMPFC: $p < 0.001, d = -0.96$, LDlPFC: $p = 0.035, d = -0.64$). Secondly, comparing activity from training session 3 and testing

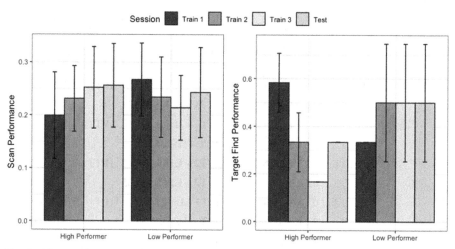

Fig. 3. Changes in scan and target find performance across training and testing sessions per performance group. High performers (n = 6), and Low Performers (n = 7). Bars on the graphs reflect median and median absolute deviation.

session indicated significant increases in LDlPFC for both performance groups (High: $p = 0.029$, $d = 0.72$, Low: $p < 0.001$, $d = 1.06$), LAMPFC for low performers ($p < 0.001$, $d = 0.91$) and RAMPFC ($p < 0.001$, $d = 1.00$) for low performers. Lastly, comparison between the performance groups indicated significant differences in only in right PFC (RAMPFC: $p < 0.001$, $d = -1.27$, RDlPFC: $p = 0.007$, $d = -0.78$) regions for testing session. Specifically, activity was larger in low performance group than high performance group for all comparisons.

4 Discussion

Cognitive demands placed on the human operators play a crucial role not only within the context of aviation, but also have the potential to offer important insight into training methodology needed to improve the success rate of the safety-critical tasks. Apart from taking into account the different cognitive styles of operators during training, it is important to consider the role of working memory and sustained attention during SO tasks. An individual's cognitive aptitude for the task will often determine how they guide and control attentional resources in the face of changing demands during the course of a complex task. In this work we explored the evolving relationship between performance and mental effort placed on a novice SO as they undergo multi-session training.

Behavioral results indicated that some participants largely improved their scan performance (Cohen's d for Training 3 vs 1: 0.69), while others deteriorated (Cohen's d for Training 3 vs 1: −0.96). Such intra individual differences in scan performance is similar to what we have reported previously in a different group of novice SOs who underwent three sessions of training on the same UAS simulator with different scenarios [11]. Analysis of target find performance based on scan performance grouping revealed large significant interaction term. However, post hoc comparisons revealed no significant differences between groups per session and between session per group. These 'target find'

Table 1. Effect of session and group on average HbO measures for each region of the PFC.

Regions	G	S	Value (M ± Mad)	Post hoc between S per G (d)	Post hoc between G per S (d)
Left DlPFC	H	T1	0.66 ± 1.25	H:T2 – H:T1: −0.33	H:T1 – L:T1: −0.44
		T2	−0.22 ± 1.02	H:T3 – H:T1: -0.37	
		T3	0.15 ± 2.29	H:T3 – H:T2: −0.02	H:T2 – L:T2: −0.15
		T	1.53 ± 1.62	**H:T – H:T3: 0.72**	
	L	T1	1.23 ± 2.56	**L:T2 – L:T1: −0.64**	H:T3 – L:T3: −0.15
		T2	0.50 ± 1.58	**L:T3 – L:T1: −0.65**	
		T3	0.54 ± 1.94	L:T3 – L:T2: −0.02	H:T – L:T: −0.49
		T	2.11 ± 1.52	**L:T – L:T3: 1.06**	
Left AMPFC	H	T1	0.03 ± 0.96	H:T2 – H:T1: −0.38	**H:T1 – L:T1: −0.72**
		T2	−0.54 ± 1.56	H:T3 – H:T1: −0.12	
		T3	0.14 ± 1.65	H:T3 – H:T2: 0.26	H:T2 – L:T2: −0.14
		T	0.40 ± 1.19	H:T – H:T3: 0.21	
	L	T1	1.32 ± 1.70	**L:T2 – L:T1: −0.96**	H:T3 – L:T3: 0.08
		T2	0.27 ± 2.02	**L:T3 – L:T1: −0.92**	
		T3	−0.36 ± 2.52	L:T3 – L:T2: 0.04	H:T – L:T: −0.62
		T	2.10 ± 2.45	**L:T – L:T3: 0.91**	
Right AMPFC	H	T1	1.36 ± 1.44	H:T2 – H:T1: −0.61	H:T1 – L:T1: −0.10
		T2	−0.24 ± 2.64	**H:T3 – H:T1: −0.74**	
		T3	−0.12 ± 2.37	H:T3 – H:T2: −0.13	H:T2 – L:T2: −0.35
		T	0.19 ± 0.99	H:T – H:T3: 0.03	
	L	T1	1.64 ± 2.53	L:T2 – L:T1: −0.36	H:T3 – L:T3: −0.30
		T2	0.65 ± 2.37	L:T3 – L:T1: −0.54	
		T3	0.45 ± 0.85	L:T3 – L:T2: −0.18	**H:T – L:T: −1.27**
		T	2.28 ± 2.05	**L:T – L:T3: 1.00**	
Right DlPFC	H	T1	1.87 ± 1.74	**H:T2 – H:T1: −0.88**	H:T1 – L:T1: 0.25
		T2	−0.21 ± 3.55	**H:T3 – H:T1: −1.11**	
		T3	−0.62 ± 3.16	H:T3 – H:T2: −0.24	H:T2 – L:T2: −0.13
		T	−0.40 ± 0.97	H:T – H:T3: −0.02	
	L	T1	1.27 ± 2.86	L:T2 – L:T1: −0.49	H:T3 – L:T3: −0.43

(*continued*)

Table 1. (*continued*)

Regions	G	S	Value (M ± Mad)	Post hoc between S per G (d)	Post hoc between G per S (d)
		T2	0.67 ± 2.78	L:T3 – L:T1: −0.43	
		T3	0.64 ± 2.17	L:T3 – L:T2: 0.06	**H:T – L:T: −0.78**
		T	0.97 ± 1.25	L:T – L:T3: 0.33	

G – group; S – session; η_p^2 – Partial eta squared; M – Median; Mad – Median absolute deviation; d – Cohen's d; HbO – oxygenated hemoglobin; DlPFC – dorsolateral prefrontal cortex, AMPFC – anterior medial prefrontal cortex; H – high-performance group; L – low-performance group; T1 – training session 1; T2 – training session 2; T3 – training session 3; T – testing session. Bolded values were significant at an α of 0.05 after correcting for false discovery rate. Positive d in post hoc comparisons between session per group imply higher activity in the first term. For example, for the following comparison "H:T2 – H:T1: 0.33", activity is greater in H:T2 than H:T1. Positive d in post hoc comparisons between group per session imply higher activity in the high-performance group for that session.

results are not align with our previously reported results [10]. This incongruency may likely be due to the fact that trainees were engaging in a dual task, therefore indicating that the classification of performance may not be binary (i.e., low scan performers and high scan performers), but quaternary (e.g., low scan and target find performers, high scan and low target find performers). However, due to limited sample size such detailed classification was not performed in this study. Furthermore, since scanning is considered a primary task for SOs and target find is a by-product of good scanning, choice of using scan metrics to classify subjects is appropriate.

Large and important decreases in average HbO were observed in right PFC regions for high performers (Cohen's d for Training 3 vs 1: −0.74 to −1.11) and left PFC regions for low performers (Cohen's d for Training 3 vs 1: −0.65 to −0.92). fMRI studies have reported that activity in right PFC is associated with sustained attention, while the left PFC is associated with spatial working memory [3]. Training and development of expertise is known to involve decreased activation across attentional and control areas, freeing neural resources to attend to other incoming stimuli or task demands. However, these changes in relation to SO tasks, indicate that groups may have possibly prioritized different tasks. Specifically, high performers have focused on scanning the area, while low performers focused on finding target (see Fig. 3). Such results have been observed when assessing expertise development in simple and complex environments and reflect task strategy consolidation [8, 14, 15].

Scanned performance was maintained during the transfer task in both groups. Average HbO increased in LDlPFC in both performance groups (Cohen's d: 0.72 to 1.06) and LAMPFC and RAMPFC regions in low performers (Cohen's d: 0.91 to 1.06). These results are consistent with cognitive workload and transfer literature that states that mental effort increases to maintain the same or better performance in novel situations [4, 6, 9]. However, significant increased activity in more regions of the PFC and higher mental effort (Cohen's d between high and low performance group in testing session: −0.78 to

−1.27) indicates that the low-performance group may require more training than high performance group to achieve similar status.

Although the behavioral and neurophysiological measures are in line with previous reports and add to the previous findings, cognitive workload as assessed by efficiency and involvement needs to be conducted to validate the reported findings. Furthermore, the results presented here are limited to HbO average measures only. The choice of using HbO was due to its higher signal to noise ratio. However studies have reported that HbR devoid of artifacts is a more sensitive measure of mental effort [23]. Therefore, mental effort defined by changes in HbR need to be evaluated. Lastly, since SOs typically engage in more than one task at a time, performance and mental effort as defined by dual tasking needs to be further evaluated.

In conclusion, this study showcases the interaction effects of task, individual and practice on performance and mental effort and provides a method of evaluating expertise during multiple training sessions. In addition, the investigation further highlights sensitivity of fNIRS measures as a biomarker for assessing mental effort and expertise development.

Acknowledgements. The authors would like to thank Shahar Kosti and Simlat, Inc., of Miamisburg, Ohio, USA, for providing access, licensing, and data extraction from the C-STAR simulator.

References

1. Jevglevskaja, N., Galliott, J.: Airmen and unmanned aerial vehicles: the danger of generalization (2015)
2. Sweller, J., Van Merrienboer, J.J.G., Paas, F.G.W.C.: Cognitive architecture and instructional design. Educ. Psychol. Rev. **10**(3), 251–296 (1998). https://doi.org/10.1023/A:1022193728205
3. Cabeza, R., Nyberg, L.: Imaging cognition II: an emperical review of 275 PET and fMRI Studies. J. Cogn. Neurosci. **12**(1), 1–47 (2000)
4. Pinti, P., et al.: The present and future use of functional near-infrared spectroscopy (fNIRS) for cognitive neuroscience. Ann. N. Y. Acad. Sci. **1464**(1), 5–29 (2020). https://doi.org/10.1111/nyas.13948
5. Izzetoglu, M., Bunce, S.C., Izzetoglu, K., Onaral, B., Pourrezaei, K.: Functional brain imaging using near-infrared technology. IEEE Eng. Med. Biol. Mag. **26**(4), 38–46 (2007)
6. Curtin, A., Ayaz, H.: The age of neuroergonomics: towards ubiquitous and continuous measurement of brain function with fNIRS. Jpn. Psychol. Res. **60**(4), 374–386 (2018). https://doi.org/10.1111/jpr.12227
7. Menda, J., et al.: Optical brain imaging to enhance UAV operator training, evaluation, and interface development. J. Intell. Robot. Syst. Theory Appl. **61**(1–4), 423–443 (2011). https://doi.org/10.1007/s10846-010-9507-7
8. Ayaz, H., Shewokis, P.A., Bunce, S., Izzetoglu, K., Willems, B., Onaral, B.: Optical brain monitoring for operator training and mental workload assessment. Neuroimage **59**, 36–47 (2012). https://doi.org/10.1016/j.neuroimage.2011.06.023
9. Kerr, J., Reddy, P., Kosti, S., Izzetoglu, K.: UAS operator workload assessment during search and surveillance tasks through simulated fluctuations in environmental visibility. In: Schmorrow, D.D., Fidopiastis, C.M. (eds.) HCII 2019. LNCS (LNAI), vol. 11580, pp. 394–406. Springer, Cham (2019). https://doi.org/10.1007/978-3-030-22419-6_28

10. Reddy, P., Richards, D., Izzetoglu, K.: Evaluation of UAS operator training during search and surveillance tasks. In: 20th International Symposium on Aviation Psychology (2019)
11. Izzetoglu, K., Richards, D.: Human performance assessment: evaluation of wearable sensors for monitoring brain activity. In: Vidulich, M.A., Tsang, P.S. (eds.) Improving Aviation Performance through Applying Engineering Psychology. Advances in Aviation Psychology, 1st ed, pp. 163–180. CRC Press, London (2019). https://doi.org/10.4324/9780429492181-8
12. Reddy, P., Richards, D., Izzetoglu, K.: Cognitive performance assessment of UAS sensor operators via neurophysiological measures. In: 2nd International Neuroergonomics Conference (2018)
13. Palma Fraga, R., Reddy, P., Kang, Z., Izzetoglu, K.: Multimodal analysis using neuroimaging and eye movements to assess cognitive workload. In: Schmorrow, D.D., Fidopiastis, C.M. (eds.) HCII 2020. LNCS (LNAI), vol. 12196, pp. 50–63. Springer, Cham (2020). https://doi.org/10.1007/978-3-030-50353-6_4
14. Shewokis, P.A., Shariff, F.U., Liu, Y., Ayaz, H., Castellanos, A., Lind, D.S.: Acquisition, retention and transfer of simulated laparoscopic tasks using fNIR and a contextual interference paradigm. Am. J. Surg. **213**(2), 336–345 (2017). https://doi.org/10.1016/j.amjsurg.2016.11.043
15. Galoyan, T., Betts, K., Abramian, H., Reddy, P., Izzetoglu, K., Shewokis, P.A.: Examining mental workload in a spatial navigation transfer game via functional near infrared spectroscopy. Brain Sci. **11**(1), 45 (2021). https://doi.org/10.3390/brainsci11010045
16. Shewokis, P.A., et al.: Brain-in-the-Loop Learning using fNIR and simulated virtual reality surgical tasks: hemodynamic and behavioral effects. In: Schmorrow, D.D., Fidopiastis, C.M. (eds.) AC 2015. LNCS (LNAI), vol. 9183, pp. 324–335. Springer, Cham (2015). https://doi.org/10.1007/978-3-319-20816-9_31
17. Ayaz, H., Shewokis, P.A., Curtin, A., Izzetoglu, M., Izzetoglu, K., Onaral, B.: Using MazeSuite and functional near infrared spectroscopy to study learning in spatial navigation. J. Vis. Exp. **8**(56), 3443 (2011). https://doi.org/10.3791/3443
18. Izzetoglu, M., Izzetoglu, K.: Real time artifact removal. US 2014/0372081 A1, 18 December 2014
19. Molavi, B., Dumont, G.A.: Wavelet-based motion artifact removal for functional near-infrared spectroscopy. Physiol. Meas. **33**(2), 259–270 (2012). https://doi.org/10.1088/0967-3334/33/2/259
20. Villringer, A., Chance, B.: Non invasive optical spectroscopy and imaging of human brain function. Trends Neurosci. **20**(10), 435–442 (1997). https://doi.org/10.1016/S0166-2236(97)01132-6
21. Westfall, J., Kenny, D.A., Judd, C.M.: Statistical Power And Optimal Design In Experiments In Which Samples Of Participants Respond To Samples Of Stimuli. J. Exp. Psychol. Gen. **143**(5), 2020–2045 (2014). https://doi.org/10.1037/xge0000014
22. Wobbrock, J.O., Findlater, L., Gergle, D., Higgins, J.J.: The aligned rank transform for non-parametric factorial analyses using only ANOVA procedures. In: Conference on Human Factors in Computing Systems - Proceedings, pp. 143–146 (2011). https://doi.org/10.1145/1978942.1978963
23. Kirilina, E., et al.: The physiological origin of task-evoked systemic artefacts in functional near infrared spectroscopy. Neuroimage **61**(1), 70–81 (2012). https://doi.org/10.1016/j.neuroimage.2012.02.074

Using Brain Computer Interaction to Evaluate Problem Solving Abilities

Ana Rita Teixeira[1]([envelope]) [iD], Igor Rodrigues[2], Anabela Gomes[3] [iD], Pedro Abreu[2] [iD],
and Germán Rodríguez-Bermúdez[4] [iD]

[1] Coimbra Polytechnic – ESEC UNICID and IEETA -Institute of Electronics and Informatics
Engineering of Aveiro, Coimbra, Portugal
ateixeira@ua.pt
[2] CISUC—Department of Informatics Engineering, University of Coimbra, Coimbra, Portugal
igor@student.dei.uc.pt, pha@dei.uc.pt
[3] Coimbra Polytechnic – ISEC and CISUC—Department of Informatics Engineering,
University of Coimbra, Coimbra, Portugal
anabela@isec.pt
[4] University Centre of Defence at the Spanish Air Force Academy, UPCT-MDE Calle Coronel
Lopez Pena, s/n, Santiago de La Ribera, 30720 Murcia, Spain
german.rodriguez@cud.upct.es

Abstract. The ability to solve problems is increasingly important in today's world, not only for good school performance but also to be successful in today's world, being one of the most desired skills for the XXI century. However, the existence of tasks with an inadequate cognitive load may discourage the individuals involved in it. Thus, we believe that the effective monitoring of this capacity must be well monitored. To this end, we started an experiment made up of 2 different samples to assess the ability to solve logical problems through the testing of Raven's Progressive Matrices. The research project developed and presented in this paper sought to assess differences in the ability to solve logical problems considering brain activity when solving them. Therefore, EEG was used to infer the cognitive workload of individuals. Our main interest was to identify specific ERP waveforms, namely the feedback-related negativity (FRN) component about the correctness of the students answers to each question.

The analysis presented in this work shows that it is possible to find the FRN potential associated to a greater negativity meaning a greater astonishment for an unconsciousness of the wrong answer. Therefore, this aspect is related with the performance of the participant based on their knowledge of the abstract principle underlying the task. Despite having only 2 samples with few students, these data indicate that our findings demonstrate that cognitive load can be predicted using these features, even using a low number of channels.

Keywords: Raven matrices · Enobio · Feedback-related negativity (FRN)

1 Introduction

Cognitive ability, or fluid intelligence, has been commonly used to help predict an individual's capacity and ability for academic learning [1–3]. Measuring and assessing the

© Springer Nature Switzerland AG 2021
D. D. Schmorrow and C. M. Fidopiastis (Eds.): HCII 2021, LNAI 12776, pp. 74–83, 2021.
https://doi.org/10.1007/978-3-030-78114-9_6

cognitive load associated with different tasks is crucial for many applications in several fields namely in design [4], in health [5], or in education [6]. We are particularly interested in problem solving. The problem-solving ability of students has gained an interest on the part of the scientific community, as this is increasingly important for their school progress and their careers. Given this importance, it is necessary to monitor this capacity, in order to better supervise students and identify their failures at this level. The research project developed sought to assess differences in the ability to solve logical problems considering brain activity when solving them. Therefore, the goal of this paper is to utilize EEG to infer the cognitive workload of individuals during the Raven's Progressive Matrices (RPM) test [7–10]. The RPM test paradigm was chosen as an ideal framework because it presents problems at increasing levels of difficulty and has been rigorously validated in past experiments [7]. The RPM test paradigm is intended to measure the logical reasoning ability and the ability to extract and process information from a novel situation. There are some studies in the literature that evaluate human intelligence using Electroencephalogram (EEG), [11–14]. Although RPM is a test widely studied in the literature, the study of the evoked potentials associated with this test is practically unknown, representing a gap that we consider interesting to study.

The main objective of this work was to demonstrate the possibility of meaningfully recording, analyzing and interpreting event-related potentials associated with performance on the RPM test. To the best of our knowledge, this has never been done before. The main question addressed in this paper is whether it is possible to identify specific ERP waveforms, namely the feedback-related negativity (FRN) component after feedback, which should be able to differentiate between right and wrong answers.

In EEG, which is well known for its high temporal resolution, FRN has been suggested to reflect surprise. It is known that negative (i.e., wrong) feedback signals generate the FRN. The FRN is evident as a negative deflection that accompanies feedback indicating negative performance outcomes, typically at frontocentral scalp sites [15]. In the present study it is expected a more negative, FRN-like ERP deflection for incorrect compared to correct classification outcome feedback signals.

In [16] is shown that it is possible to find the FRN Potential at single-trial level and relate its characteristics with the performance of the participant based on their knowledge of the abstract principle underlying the task.

The analysis done in this work shows that it is possible to find the FRN potential and relate its characteristics with the performance of the participant based on their knowledge of the abstract principle underlying the task. Preliminary results showed a significant difference for correct versus incorrect answers in the training phase considering the two subsets. Our findings demonstrate that cognitive load can be well predicted using these features, even for a low number of channels. Moreover, error potentials such as the FRN have clear potential as input features for cognitive or passive BCI paradigms, as discussed in [17].

The paper is organized as follows: Sect. 2 describes the subject, the participants and task, the signal acquisition protocol and the data analysis; Sect. 3 presents the results which are followed by the discussion and conclusion in Sect. 4.

2   Material and Methods

2.1   Subjects

Raven matrices tests have widespread practical use as a measure of intelligence in the general population for both adults and children, for job applicants as a psychometric test, for applicants to the armed forces, and for assessing clinical (e.g. Autism) populations. The advanced form [7] of the matrices has 48 items, presented as one set of 12 (set I), and another of 36 (set II). Items are presented in black and white background similar to the standard version. All of the questions consist of visual geometric design with a missing piece. The test taker is given six to eight choices to pick from and fill in the missing piece (Fig. 1). Each successive set is generally interpreted to be more difficult than the prior set. In our experiment the feedback event in set I (training phase) is introduced.

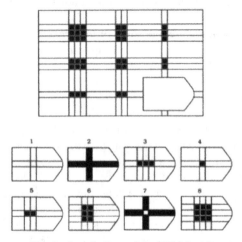

Fig. 1. Sample item of the RPM (set 1)

The idea is to understand if the performance should be adjusted based on feedback after each trial. For this purpose, the volunteer students were asked to solve a computerized version of the Raven Advanced Progressive Matrix test, divided into two phases: training and testing.

2.2   Participants and Task

In this study the Advanced Progressive Matrices (RAPM) with 48 problems were applied to two populations:

Subset I - 21 students of Design and Multimedia
Subset II - 24 students of Engineering Informatics.

These subsets correspond to degrees that attract students with different characteristics, but whose entry conditions are similar, requiring admission conditions, such as exams of mathematics or descriptive geometry, focusing on mathematical aspects, problem solving and a high capacity of abstraction.

EEG signals were recorded while the participants perform the tasks of the test. The 48 problems that form the test are divided into two phases: the first 12 where the participant receive a feedback about their answers and the last 36 where no feedback is given. The score of the test is the number of correct answers of the second part. The Fig. 2 illustrates the time evolution and the relevant marks for each.

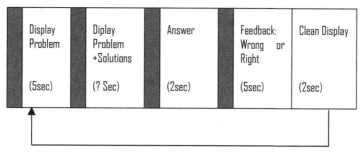

Fig. 2. The signal acquisition protocol while participants answer the problems. The first 12 problems include the feedback while the last 36 do not. The red bars represent the time markers (triggers) stored with the signals

Visual feedback is provided after each response, to indicate if the participant's response was Right or Wrong. The information is presented 2000 ms after the response and remains on the screen for 5000 ms and after it the display cleans during 2000 ms. Based on this feedback, the participants must maintain or change their response strategy accordingly.

2.3 EEG Acquisition

The EEG data was recorded from 8 electrodes mounted on a wave guard cap according to the 10–20 system at a sampling rate of 512 Hz. The channel locations are displayed in Fig. 3 (left). The EOG was also recorded to serve as reference for ocular correction algorithms. The ocular artifacts in the EEG signals were then eliminated using an eye-movement correction algorithm and the resulting data was re-referenced to the average of the left and right mastoid electrodes. The signals were registered using Enobio 8 EEG recording headset [18], Fig. 3 (right).

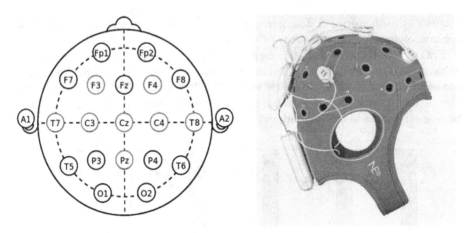

Fig. 3. Left: Schematic representation of electrode placement; Right: Enobio 8 headset

2.4 Data Analysis

Data was analyzed using a combination of the EEGLAB Matlab plug-in [19] routines and custom code. Data was first high-pass filtered (cut-off 1 Hz), then a customized adaptive filter was applied to suppress line-noise.

The dataset is read in sequence of the cognitive operations that are happening and mapped on peaks. These peaks are the dominant way of data gathering and when they are extracted from an epoch-averaged signal they are traditionally called Event-Related Potential (ERP) [20]. They are basically brain neuron activities stimulated by a given response. An ERP waveform is a series of positive and negative voltage deflections related to a set of underlying components [21]. In this study the chosen event-related potentials were FRN. Feedback related negativity is a front-central negative potential related to a subject's choices. It arises in response to passively observed products 200–300 ms after the presentation of unfavorable versus favorable products. This paper is focused considering the feedback information. Note that only 12 questions for all participants were analyzed (the ones corresponding to the training phase). The idea is applying supervised machine learning methods to study the following problems:

a) Are the two subsets different considering the FRN?
b) What is different in right and wrong answers for each subset?

ERP analyses were conducted using ERPLAB [19]. In line with previous research, FRN amplitudes were calculated for each condition as the mean amplitude from 200 to 350 ms post-stimulus at the fronto-central channels F3, F4, Cz, C3 and C4. These five channels are located above the medial frontal cortex, a candidate generator for the FRN [22]. Although the 5 channels mentioned above have been studied, only the channel Cz results are present and discussed in this work. The decision to use a 200–350 ms analysis window was motivated by identification of the FRN with this time period in several recent studies [22].

3 Results

Observing the sequence of responses, in general, the participants provide more frequently Wrong answers in subtest II than in subtest I, as shown in Fig. 4. Anyway, note that the number of Wrong answers in a total of 12 trials is small.

The number of participants giving a higher number of Wrong answers is larger on subset I. It has to be noticed that, in subtest II, more than half of the participants gave 0 or 1 Wrong answers.

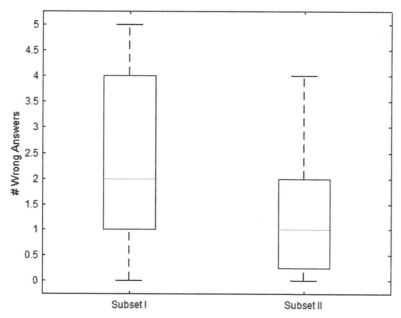

Fig. 4. Number of Wrong answers in subtest I and subset II for all participants.

Considering the first research question "Are the two subsets different considering the FRN?", the amplitude and latency of the FRN wave in all participants for each subset considering the mean of Wrong answer is computed. Figure 5 (left side) shows the amplitude of the FRN for the subset I and subset II which have different values in both subtests. The same figure (right side) also illustrates the range of latencies of the wave. It has to be noticed that, although the range values are similar in both subtests, the median value is different. The test was computed with 95% of confidence between the amplitudes and latencies of the two subsets with ($p = 0.074$) and ($p = 0.0804$), respectively. So, the amplitude values are statically different.

Figure 6 shows the grand-average waveform in channel Cz time-locked to onset of feedback stimuli considering the subset I and subset II. Note that the FRN wave is more prominent in subset I, which is the subset with more wrong answers.

Considering the second research question "What is different in right and wrong answers for each subset?", the wave of wrong and right answers is compared in both subsets, Fig. 7. Thus, results indicate, as expected, that errors elicited significantly more negative FRN amplitudes than correct responses. Furthermore, there were no significant differences in peak latency.

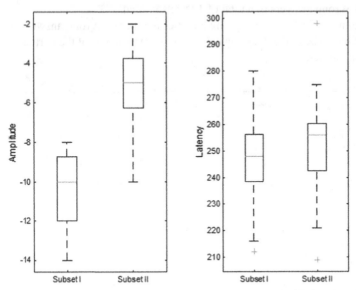

Fig. 5. Amplitude and Latency of the FRN wave in all participants considering the subset I and subset II.

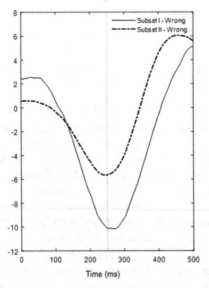

Fig. 6. Grand- average waveform in channel Cz time-locked to onset of feedback stimuli considering the subset I and subset II.

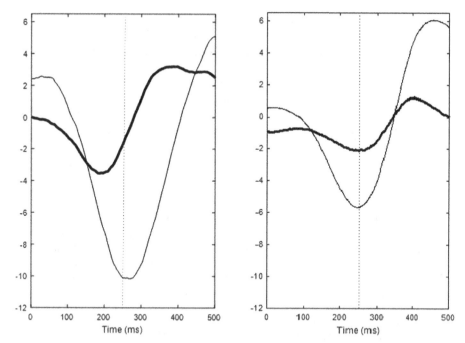

Fig. 7. Grand-average waveform in channel Cz for subset I (left) and subset II (right), considering Wrong answers (solid line) versus Right answers (**bold line**).

4   Discussion and Conclusion

The present work aimed to demonstrate that is possible to study event-related potentials during the performance of Raven's Progressive Matrices (RPM) test [7], an Intelligent Quotient (IQ) test. The possibility of coupling the brain activity recorded simultaneously with the performance of the test can usefully increase the potential of the test, allowing for a higher specificity in detecting brain patterns in the field of physiological study of human intelligence. The study shows that it is possible to find FRN wave after feedback onset considering two subsets with different characteristics.

The analysis shows that it is possible to find the FRN potential and relate its characteristics with the performance of the participant based on their knowledge of the abstract principle underlying the task. Preliminary results showed a significant difference for correct versus incorrect answers in the training phase considering the two subsets. Results show a larger negative amplitude for negative feedback (wrong answers) compared to positive feedback (right answers) in the FRN component during performance on the RPM.

Moreover, the results show a difference in wrong answers considering the subset I and the subset II. Note that the number of wrong answers in the two subsets are distinct.

Our findings demonstrate that cognitive load can be well predicted using these features, even for a low number of channels. Note that BCI's are prone to errors in the recognition of subject's intent. An elegant approach to improve the accuracy of BCIs consists in a verification procedure directly based on the presence of error-related potentials in the EEG recorded right after the occurrence of an error [23]. Further developments of this work are to study the dynamics of the signals detected and to relate them with the participants' performance.

Furthermore, studying the signal considering other stimulis can be another way, namely studying the P100, P300 and some patters like immersion, attention, and alfa lateralization. Studying the synchronizations and desynchronizations is also another topic that will be studied and deepened with these dataset.

References

1. Koczwara, A., Patterson, F., Zibarras, L., Kerrin, M., Irish, B., Wilkinson, M.: Evaluating cognitive ability, knowledge tests and situational judgement tests for postgraduate selection. Med Educ. **46**, 399–408 (2012). https://doi.org/10.1111/j.1365-2923.2011.04195.x
2. Rindermann, H., Neubauer, A.: Processing speed, intelligence, creativity, and school performance: testing of causal hypotheses using structural equation models. Intelligence **32**, 573–589 (2004). https://doi.org/10.1016/j.intell.2004.06.005
3. Wang, T., Ren, X., Altmeyer, M., Schweizer, K.: An account of the relationship between fluid intelligence and complex learning in considering storage capacity and executive attention. Intelligence **41**, 537–545 (2013). https://doi.org/10.1016/j.intell.2013.07.008
4. Kumar, N., Kumar, J.: Measurement of cognitive load in HCI systems using EEG power spectrum: an experimental study. Procedia Comput. Sci. **84**, 70–78 (2016). https://doi.org/10.1016/j.procs.2016.04.068. ISSN 1877-0509
5. Young, J.Q., Irby, D.M., Barilla-LaBarca, M.-L., et al.: Measuring cognitive load: mixed results from a handover simulation for medical students. Perspect. Med. Educ. **5**(1), 24–32 (2015). https://doi.org/10.1007/s40037-015-0240-6
6. Gomes, A., Assuncao Teixeira, A.R.A., Eloy, J., Mendes, A.J.: An Exploratory study of brain computer interfaces in computer science education. IEEE Revista Iberoamericana De Tecnologias Del Aprendizaje-Ieee Rita, **14**(4), 152–161 (2019). https://doi.org/10.1109/rita.2019.2952273
7. Penrose, L.S., Raven, J.C.: A new series of perceptual tests: preliminary communication. Br. J. Med. Psychol. **16**(2), 97–104 (1936)
8. Raven, J.: The raven progressive matrices tests: their theoretical basis and measurement model, chapter 1 (2016)
9. Raven, J.: The raven's progressive matrices: change and stability over culture and time. Cogn. Psychol. **41**, 1–48 (2000)
10. Spearman, C.: "General intelligence," objectively determined and measured. Am. J. Psychol. **15**(2), 201 (1904)
11. Binet, A.: New methods for the diagnosis of the intellectual level of subnormals. L'Annee Psychologique **12**, 191–244 (1905)
12. Thatcher, R.W., North, D., Biver, C.: EEG and intelligence: relations between EEG coherence, EEG phase delay and power. Clin. Neurophysiol. **116**, 2129–2141 (2005)
13. Neubauer, A.C., Grabner, R.H., Fink, A., Neuper, C.: Intelligence and neural efficiency: further evidence of the influence of task content and sex on the brain-IQ relationship. Cogn. Brain Res. **25**, 217–225 (2005)
14. Fink, A., Neubauer, A.: EEG alpha oscillations during the performance of verbal creativity tasks: differential effects of sex and verbal intelligence. Int. J. Psychophysiol. **62**(1), 46–53 (2006)

15. Miltner, W.H.R., Braun, C.H., Coles, M.G.H.: Event-related brain potentials following incorrect feedback in a time-estimation task: evidence for a 'generic' neural system for error detection. Cogn. Neurosci. **9**(6), 788–798 (1997)
16. Santos, I.M., et al.: ERP correlates of error processing during performance on the Halstead category test. Int. J. Psychophysiol. **106**, 97–105 (2016). https://doi.org/10.1016/j.ijpsycho.2016.06.010
17. Ferrez, W., Millán, J.D.R.: Error-related EEG potentials generated during simulated brain-computer interaction. IEEE Trans. Biomed. Eng. **55**(3), 923–929 (2008)
18. Emotiv   (2021).   https://www.emotiv.com/product/emotiv-epoc-14-channel-mobileeeg/. Accessed 25 Jan 2021
19. Delorme, A., Makeig, S.: EEGLAB: an open source toolbox for analysis of single-trial EEG dynamics including independent component analysis. J. Neurosci. Methods **134**, 9–2 (2004)
20. Sanei, S., Chambers, J.A.: EEG Signal Processing (2013). ISBN 9780470025819. https://doi.org/10.1002/9780470511923
21. Kappenman, E.S., Luck, S.J.: The Oxford Handbook of Event-Related Potential Components (2012). ISBN 9780199940356. https://doi.org/10.1093/oxfordhb/9780195374148.001.0001
22. Walsh, M.M., Anderson, J.R.: Learning from experience: event-related potential correlates of reward processing, neural adaptation, and behavioral choice. Neurosci. Biobehav. Rev. **36**, 1870–1884 (2012)
23. Zander, T.O., Kothe, C.: Towards passive brain-computer interfaces: applying brain-computer interface technology to human-machine systems in general. J. Neural Eng. **8**(2) (2011). https://doi.org/10.1088/1741-2560/8/2/025005.025005

Analysis of Effect of RSVP Speller BCI Paradigm Along with CNN to Analysis P300 Signals

M. Uma[1] (ID), S. Prabhu[2] (ID), Murali Subramaniyam[2](✉) (ID), and Seung Nam Min[3](✉) (ID)

[1] Department of Software Engineering, S.R.M. Institute of Science and Technology, Potheri, Chengalpattu District, Kattankulathur 603203, Tamilnadu, India

[2] Department of Mechanical Engineering, S.R.M. Institute of Science and Technology, Potheri, Chengalpattu District, Kattankulathur 603203, Tamilnadu, India
murali.subramaniyam@gmail.com

[3] Department of Drone and Industrial Safety Engineering, Shinsung University, Dangjin, Republic of Korea
msnijn12@hanmail.net

Abstract. People suffering from neurological disorders, including spinal cord injury (S.C.I.), stroke, Parkinson's disease may be severely paralyzed and incapable of performing any motor functions. However, they may still have some cognitive abilities, and that can be accessed through brain-computer interaction (BCI). Electroencephalography (E.E.G.) pattern classification is attractive for many researchers in the field of BCI. P300 may be a style of ERP signal which is employed by the BCI system. P300, well known as a prominent component of event-related potential (ERP) from E.E.G. signal. It's also elicited in an oddball paradigm. In some cases, patients get completely locked in until losing control of their ocular movements. Researchers have shifted toward the BCI system because of these people, which will work without the eye movement. Hence the proposed approach is attempting to implement the BCI system without using oculomotor movements. The traditional methods/algorithms such as the hidden Markov model, support vector machine (SVM), and Linear discriminant analysis (LDA) may not perform well for cross-subject variations with extreme variations. Hence, in recent years, deep neural networks, particularly the conventional neural networks (CNN) widely used, have shown high performance compared to the traditional approach for various applications. CNN can extract data from raw data as well as give us unknown information about the data. Most of the research work related to P300 and various speller system involved the gaze of the subject. However, these systems are not suitable for the patient having problems in oculomotor control. The proposed convolution neural network (CNN) has been used for high-level feature extraction and improves the performance of P300 classification to predict target and non-target character. Along with CNN to analyze P300 signals, this study used gaze independent BCI speller paradigm called rapid serial visual presentation (RSVP). We have selected/formed the letters intuitively by attending target letters in the stream of visual stimuli. A vocabulary of 30 symbols was presented one by one in a pseudo-random sequence at the same display location. We applied the CNN on the RSVP Dataset which gave us an average accuracy of 97% which is

D. D. Schmorrow and C. M. Fidopiastis (Eds.): HCII 2021, LNAI 12776, pp. 84–96, 2021.
https://doi.org/10.1007/978-3-030-78114-9_7

better than the previously implemented on the BCI competition dataset II without channel selection before the classification, i.e. 95.5%.

Keywords: Brain-computer interface (BCI) · Rapid serial visual presentation (RSVP) · Convolutional neural network (CNN) · Electroencephalograph (E.E.G.)

1 Introduction

In today's world, some patients who have suffered brain disease, a brainstem stroke, or that are diagnosed with a nervous disorder like Amyotrophic Lateral Sclerosis (A.L.S.) face severe motor impairments. Sometimes, they'll even enter into a locked-in state, where, they lose control on their muscular activities. A brain-computer interface came into the picture to help these patients to interact with the outer world. In the past several decades, the brain-computer interface (BCI) came into popularity. BCI may be a computer-based technology that is employed by patients who lost their ocular movement, it converts the user's intent into the corresponding control command then send it to an external device that can do what the user wants to try and do like interacting with another person, surfing the web, employing a robotic chair, etc. The signal is largely an Electroencephalographic (E.E.G.) activity that exists in humans all the time. E.E.G. was recorded by externally attaching several electrodes on the human scalp. E.E.G. may be a technique used for recording the brain's electrical potentials, which are accustomed study the dynamics of neural I.P. within the brain and diagnose processes and brain disorders cognitively. Large data of E.E.G. signals are obtained, and it's unfeasible to investigate E.E.G. recordings visually. Therefore, there's a robust demand to extract information from E.E.G. data for correct evaluation and classification to determine cognitive processes. The steps involved in extracting relevant information from E.E.G. data include signal acquisition, pre-processing, feature extraction and classification.

The event-related potential is that the brain signal style chosen to drive a BCI depends on the particular application. These ERP are brain responses phase and time-locked to an inside or external event. P300 may be a style of ERP signal which is employed by the BCI system. It's also elicited in an oddball paradigm. In some cases, patients get completely locked in until losing control of their eye movements. Because of these people, researchers have shifted toward the BCI system which will work without eye movements. Researchers are attempting to implement the BCI system without using oculomotor movements. The new Rapid Visual Speller Paradigm (RSVP) takes care of the problem to assist the patients because it is independent of gaze shift.

Ye Ma researched BCI in which classification and feature extraction for P300 are covered. This literature discusses P300's less signal to noise ratio (SNR) and classification. They had proposed independent or separate component analysis and Support Vector Machine (SVM). First, P300 signal made to superposition averaging, in accordance to I.C.A. algorithm. Then the superimposed average signal is de-averaged and whitened. After this Fast I.C.A. is used to extract the feature vector of the P300 signal. The extracted feature vector is then supplied to the support vector machine (SVM) for classification. This paper is conducted on Dataset II of the International BCI Contest III. The SVM algorithm yields the highest classification accuracy is 90.12% [1].

Shunying Guo researched E.E.G. signals and proposed Discrete Wavelet Transform (DWT) with the fisher criterion. The DWT converts the signal data into wavelet form. Then, by the means of the fisher criterion method the feature space where best differentiated between two types of E.E.G. signal found. Finally, the features extracted are stored into a feature vector. The proposed technique was tested on E.E.G. data which was obtained by BCI2000. It gives average accuracy of 238 runs [2]. Fa-jiang T.A.N. conducted research for BCI which consists of feature extraction algorithm analysis. This literature discusses feature extraction of E.E.G. signals for the BCI system. The paper examines the representative algorithms including Fast Fourier Transform (FFT), Wavelet Transform (W.T.), and Independent Component Analysis (I.C.A.). These algorithms are effective to identify the target characters. Feature Extraction phase is a crucial phase BCI system to get maximum efficiency [3].

José L. Sirvent conducted research for BCI's P300 signals which provides a computer interface for surfing on the internet. This literature discusses a system which allows the user to control the internet browsing through E.E.G. signal for physically able patients who cannot communicate like normal people and cannot move their hand and even fingers. The system gives a virtual keyboard and mouse to browse the internet. The system was developed under BCI2000 [4]. Margrit Betke conducted research for BCI in which it allows people with severe motor disabilities like A.L.S. to access computing features. This literature discusses above a system that severely disabled people can use to provide computer access using eye movements using a camera module. The paper proposed a device that tracks the computer user movement details with a video camera and translates or converts them into commands. The system uses a visual tracking algorithm [5].

Lucia Rita Quitadamo researched BCI using a different approach i.e. using UML implementation. This literature proposed UML diagrams for Brain-Computer Interface. Paper discusses diagrams like a Class diagram, Sequence Diagram, etc. The paper's main aim was to define Unified Modeling Language (UML) implementation of BCI system that anyone can use according to their requirements. The models also include some definitions related to the BCI system like a trail, session, etc. [6]. Lucia Rita Quitadamo researched BCI using UML for different systems. This literature discusses the lack of a universal descriptive language among the Brain-Computer Interface (BCI). This paper proposes Unified Model Language (UML) implementation that can use by any experiment with any requirements. This paper also defines some important terminologies which are part of this field. These UML help people to compare the performance of different models smoothly and correctly [7].

Laura Acqualagna researched BCI using a different approach for recording signals for the symbols which makes it more reliable. This literature proposed a new paradigm for Brain-Computer Interface (BCI) which is Independent of Gaze shift. The Paradigm is known as Rapid Serial Visual Presentation (RSVP). In this paper, they discuss a new way to help patients who are suffering from a severe disability that can't even move their eyes. This system yields good results while experimenting. This paradigm has overcome the flaws of the previous paradigm like the oddball paradigm which requires gaze shift [8]. Hubert Cecotti researched BCI in which different classifier is used i.e. CNN for better accuracy and results. This literature proposed a Neural Network for P300 EEG signals for classification. The model is Convolutional Neural Network (CNN). This paper discusses two classification problems associated with P300 signals. The main problem with the efficiency of the model depends upon the feature extraction phase. The CNN model helps with this by extracting the feature itself during the training period. The CNN model was used on Dataset II of the Competition, which accuracy was 95.5% [9]. The paper helps in giving directions for future work [10].

Xiang suggested instead of using machine learning; many researchers started to use the convolutional neural network (CNN) to classify target and non-target P300 EEG signals for better information transfer rate and accuracy [11]. Donchin et al. have described a complete Dataset of P300 evoked potentials recorded with BCI2000 using a paradigm. In these experiments, a user-focused on one out of 36 different characters. This contest aims to predict the correct character in each of the provided character selection epochs [12]. Vaibhav et al. has proposed a real-time implementation of a novel iAUI design for a mobile robot control task. The major advantage with the iAUI is the user-centric graphical user interface design that presents all the control options to the BCI user at all times. This system, including the R.Q.N.N. technique for E.E.G. filtering and the user-centric iAUI for enhancing the bandwidth, was implemented for the robot control task in the physical environment. Authors claimed that, the research output shown with the 100% BCI accuracy assumption can be achieved with more training on the paradigm [13].

Chandra et al. have developed an algorithm that would automatically determine the necessary amount of data to collect during operation. Dynamic data collection was controlled by a threshold on the probabilities that each possible character was the target character, and these probabilities were continually updated with each additional measurement. This Bayesian technique differs from other dynamic data collection techniques by relying on a participant-independent, probability-based metric as the stopping criterion. The accuracy and communication rate for dynamic and static data collection in P300 spellers were compared for 26 users. Dynamic data collection resulted in a significant increase in accuracy and communication rate [14]. The approach can be especially useful in mental fatigue analysis where the relative variability of P300 subcomponents is the key factor in detecting the level of fatigue [15].

This paper proposed a new approach that combines convolution neural network (CNN) and gaze independent BCI speller paradigm called rapid serial visual presentation (RSVP). The convolution neural network (CNN) has been used for high-level feature extraction and improves the performance of P300 classification to predict target and non-target character. Along with CNN to analyze P300 signals, RSVP used as a gaze independent BCI speller paradigm.

2 Proposed Methodology - RSVP and P300 Speller Paradigm

Rapid Serial Visual Presentation (RSVP) is a paradigm in which the subject does not require gaze movement. The data set is taken from the B.N.C.I. Horizon site and E.E.G. signals were collected using the RSVP paradigm as most of the other paradigm require gaze shift to perform successfully. Researchers have found that the oddball paradigm has some disadvantages like gaze shift, color, and capitalization. These problems have been overcome in the RSVP paradigm. The paradigm is also very easy to understand for first-time users [1]. RSVP speller system depicts in Fig. 1.

The dataset consists of 11 subjects. The subjects are fat, gcb, gcc, gcd, gce, gcf, gcg, gch, iay, icn, icr, pia. The experiment was conducted for each subject separately with the same setting. The study was conducted with 30 alphabets and symbols. All the alphabets and two punctuation marks '.', '!', underscore used to separate to words and ' <' for backspace. Signals are required using equipment with 55 channels except for Fp1, Fp2, AF3, AF4, F9, F10, FT7, FT8 from 64 channels. In total, 20000 samples for each subject from 1/30 samples contains P300 target. The total number of features is 55 * 25 = 1375 features.

In the P300 speller system depicted in Fig. 1B, subjects were asked to focus a 6 × 6 matrix which consists of letters (A-Z), digits (1–9), and spaces (_), as depicted in Fig. 1B. Each sequence contains 12 flashes (six columns and six rows) with a 125 ms flash duration followed by a 62.5 ms inter-stimulus interval (I.S.I.). The experiment was performed with fifteen occurrences (trials) per sequence to focus on a target character.

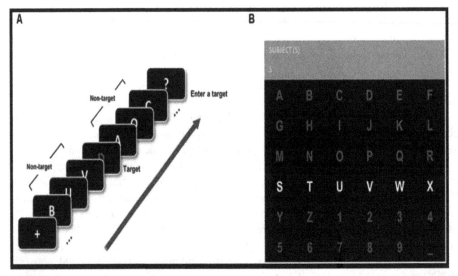

Fig. 1. (A) RSVP and P300 speller system; (B) The conventional 6x6 matrix speller of BCI2000.

The overall architecture of RSVP is shown in Fig. 2. The data creation part consisted of computer, interface, and subject and data acquisition system. The data set module stores acquired data. The utility module do the data extraction from the stored files and do the down sampling for further analysis. There is a model module where feature extraction and classification took place on the down sampled data. The final module called "run_multi_subject_experiment" is the system's main module through which other modules are called. This module finally prints the accuracy, precision, recall, f1-score, and confusion matrix on the command line.

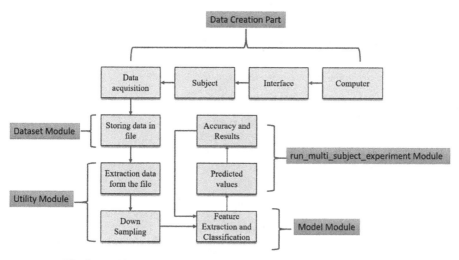

Fig. 2. Architecture diagram of RSVP paradigm using CNN algorithm

3 Feature Extraction and Classification for Predicting Target and Non-target Character

A convolutional neural network (CNN) is a sub class of deep learning or deep neural networks. This neural network has been widely used for image classification, handwritten recognition, and signal processing application. To predict the target and non-target P300 signals, the CNN based classification is used. It allows extracting the features automatically.

In the proposed system the CNN model has five layers. The first layer comprises 10 spatial filters each of size 55 * 1 – number of channels. The second layer is composed of 13 temporal filters with the size of 1 * 5. The third and fourth layer is fully connected layers with each other. The fifth layer is a single neuron consisting of the sigmoid function. Figure 3 depicts the CNN layered model.

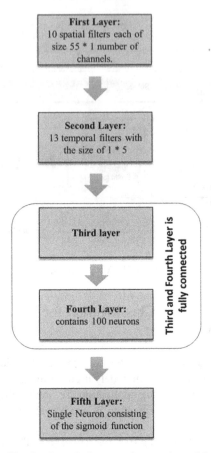

Fig. 3. Convolution neural network model

4   Experiment Results and Analysis

CNN classification applied for Rapid Serial Visual Presentation (RSVP) data set and BCI completion dataset. After combining these two results, it produced an average accuracy of 97% for the classification. We split the dataset into two parts. The first part, with 192000 samples for training. The second part, with 23100 samples for testing. Finally, the experiment result shows 97% accuracy. The CNN model was previously applied to P300 dataset II of the competition [2] which gave 95.5% whereas the RSVP paradigm's dataset gave 97%. Python has been used for implementation. The result of different iteration and average accuracy is depicted in Fig. 4, 5 and 6.

4.1   Confusion Matrix for Performance Measure

A confusion matrix is a summary of prediction results on a classification problem. The number of correct and incorrect predictions are summarized with count values and broken down by each class. This is the key to the confusion matrix.

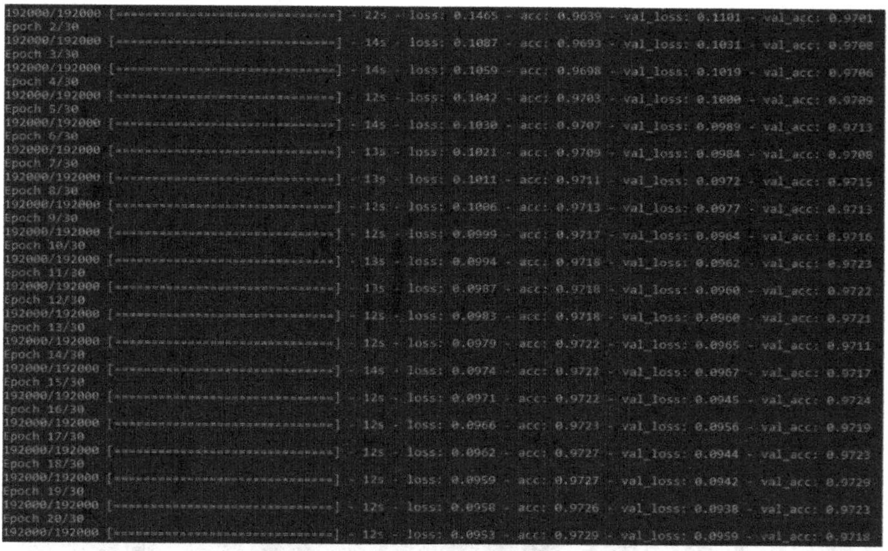

Fig. 4. Screenshot of epochs 1–20

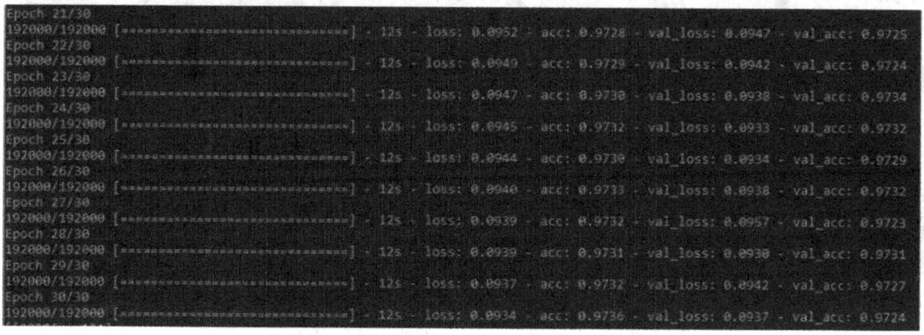

Fig. 5. Screenshot of epochs 21–30

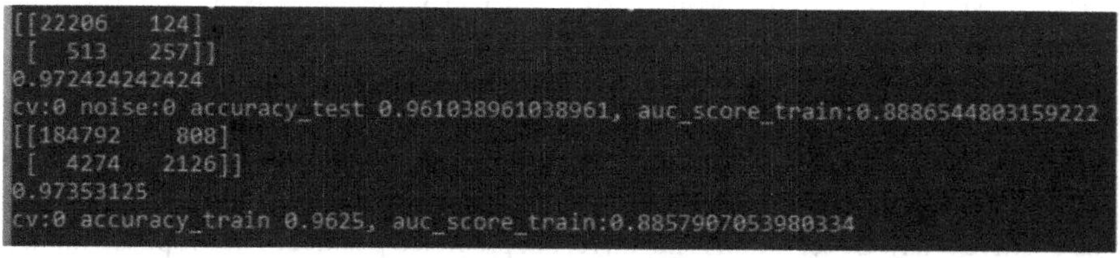

Fig. 6. Screenshot of results

The confusion matrix (Table 1) shows how your classification model is confused when it makes predictions. It gives us insight into the errors being made by a classifier and the types of errors that are being made. Figure 7 and Table 2 shown the precision, recall, f1 - score, and support with the average accuracy.

Table 1. Confusion matrix

TP	FN
FP	TN

Table 2. The formula for the confusion matrix

Parameter	Formula
Precision	TP/(TP + FP)
Recall	TP/(TP + FP)
F1-score	(2 * Recall * Precision)/(Recall + Precision)
Accuracy	(TP + TN)/(TP + FP + TN + FN)

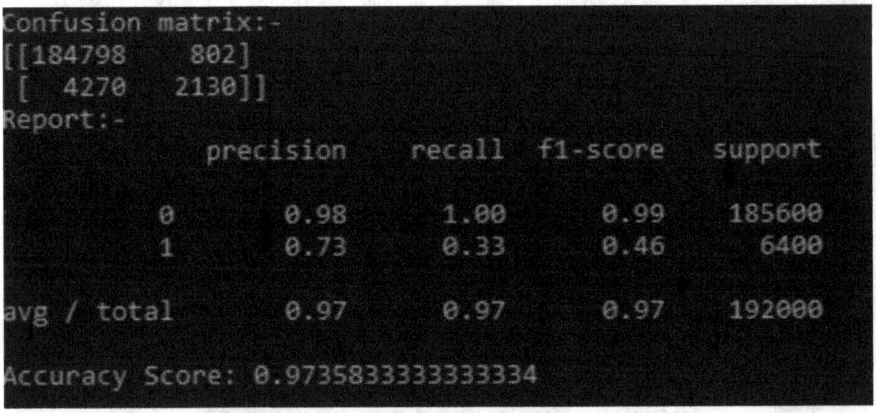

```
Confusion matrix:-
[[184798    802]
 [  4270   2130]]
Report:-
              precision    recall  f1-score   support

           0       0.98      1.00      0.99    185600
           1       0.73      0.33      0.46      6400

avg / total       0.97      0.97      0.97    192000

Accuracy Score: 0.9735833333333334
```

Fig. 7. Screenshot of result for train dataset

Positive (P): Observation is positive, Negative (N): Observation is not positive, True Positive (T.P.): Observation is positive, and predicted to be positive. In the proposed model it was successfully predicted for 184792 samples. False Negative (F.N.): Observation is positive, but predicted negative. Falsely predicted 4274 samples, while samples were incorrect. True Negative (T.N.): Observation is negative, and predicted to be negative. The proposed model predicted false for 2126 samples while samples were correct. False Positive (F.P.): Observation is negative, but predicted positive. The proposed model falsely predicted 808 samples while samples were correct.

4.2   Comparison CNN Model on a Different Dataset

The comparison between CNN models with test dataset of 23100 samples gives the following result. The bar graph in Fig. 8, depicts the comparison of the same CNN model on P300 dataset II of the competition and RSVP paradigm dataset.

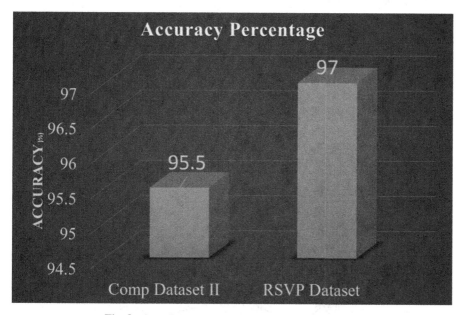

Fig. 8. Comparison CNN model on a different dataset

4.3   Comparison of Neural Network, CNN Model on a Different Dataset

NEURAL NETWORK FOR PREDICTING P300 TARGET IMAGE/CHARACTER

The datasets were taken from http://mmspg.epfl.ch/BCI_datasets, 4 electrodes (Fz, Cz, Pz, Oz) were consider and placed at the standard positions of 10–20 international system as in [16, 17] and from two mastoid electrode with a sampling rate of 2048 Hz. Speller paradigm involves six images depicted in Fig. 9, placed in the order. Instead of character, images were flashed into the random sequences and asked the subject to focus on images. Features like Mean, variance Welch's power spectrum density and wavelet packet transform have been extracted [18] and applied neural network classifiers to predict the P300 component. To classify p300 target and non-target character by obtaining a feature vector to achieve accuracy up to 84%. Neural network structure as depicted in Fig. 10. In this work, the feature vector was given as input data, and target vector was given as target data. The dataset is divided into three parts: training data - 70%, testing data - 15%, validation data - 15%. The mean square error denotes the performance of Neural Network training [18]. In this context, deep learning (DL) could significantly improve the accuracy; comparison result were shown in Table 3.

Fig. 9. Single character paradigm

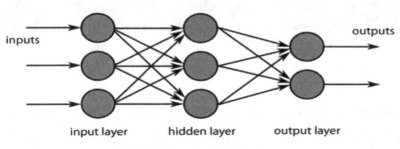

Fig. 10. Neural network structure

Table 3. Comparison of Machine Learning (N.N.) with proposed Deep Learning (CNN) Model

Algorithm	Dataset	Accuracy
Machine Learning (Neural Network) with 4 channel	BCI -Dataset-II	84%
Deep Learning (CNN) without channel selection	BCI -Dataset-II	95.5%
Deep Learning (CNN) without channel selection	RSVP	97%

5 Conclusion

P300 RSVP speller paradigm easily understands by the patients and can communicate with an external world. This model was constructed using Convolutional Neural Network where a hidden layer can extract the features automatically. Feature extraction performs a predominant role for better classification with good accuracy. In the proposed work, 55 channels were used invoked for classification. In the future, channels can be optimized for better results. Finally, the results were compared with the neural network classifier in the BCI dataset with 4 channels (electrodes) that produced less accuracy than without channel selection of the deep learning model. In future, P300 RSVP optimized channel selection with the CNN model could give better results.

Acknowledgement. This work was supported by the National Research Council of Science & Technology (N.S.T.) grant by the Korean government (M.S.I.P.) (No. CRC-15–05-ETRI).

References

1. Acqualagna, L., Blankertz, B.: Gaze-independent BCI-spelling using rapid serial visual presentation (RSVP). Clin. Neurophysiol. **124**(5), 901–908 (2013)
2. Cecotti, H., Graser, A.: Convolutional neural networks for P300 detection with application to brain-computer interfaces. IEEE Trans. Pattern Anal. Mach. Intell. **33**(3), 433–445 (2011)
3. Tan, F.-J: Analysis of feature extraction algorithms used in brain-computer interfaces. DEStech Trans. Eng. Technol. Res. (AMEME) (2016)
4. Sirvent, J., Azorín, J., Iáñez, E., Úbeda, A., Fernández, E.: P300-based brain-computer interface for internet browsing. In: Demazeau, Y., et al. (eds.) Trends in Practical Applications of Agents and Multiagent Systems: 8th International Conference on Practical Applications of Agents and Multiagent Systems, pp. 615–622. Springer Berlin Heidelberg, Berlin, Heidelberg (2010). https://doi.org/10.1007/978-3-642-12433-4_72
5. Betke, M., Gips, J., Fleming, P.: The camera mouse: visual tracking of body features to provide computer access for people with severe disabilities. IEEE Trans. Neural Syst. Rehabil. Eng. **10**(1), 1–10 (2002)
6. Quitadamo, L.R., Marciani, M.G., Cardarilli, G., Bianchi, L.: Describing different brain computer interface systems through a unique model: a UML implementation. Neuroinformatics **6**(2), 81–96 (2008). https://doi.org/10.1007/s12021-008-9015-0
7. Quitadamo, L.R., Abbafati, M., Saggio, G., Marciani, M.G., Cardarilli, G.C., Bianchi, L.: A UML model for the description of different brain-computer interface systems. In: 30th Annual International Conference of the IEEE Engineering in Medicine and Biology Society, pp. 1363–1366. IEEE (2008)
8. Ma, Y., Jiang, G., Chang, T., Guo, L.: Research on feature extraction and classification of P300 EEG signals. In: 2nd International Conference on Electrical, Automation and Mechanical Engineering (E.A.M.E. 2017), pp. 26–30. Atlantis Press (2017)
9. Guo, S., Lin, S., Huang, Z.: Feature extraction of P300s in E.E.G. signal with discrete wavelet transform and fisher criterion. In: 8th International Conference on Biomedical Engineering and Informatics (B.M.E.I.), pp. 200–204. IEEE (2015)
10. Zhang, X., Yao, L., Wang, X., Monaghan, J., Mcalpine, D., Zhang, Y.: A survey on deep learning based brain computer interface: recent advances and new frontiers. arXiv preprint arXiv:1905.04149 (2019)

11. Xiang, L., Guo, G., Jingming, Y., Sheng, V.S., Yang, P.: A convolutional neural network-based linguistic steganalysis for synonym substitution steganography. Math. Biosci. Eng. **17**(2), 1041–1058 (2020)
12. Rrusienski, D., Schalk, G.: Documentation Wadsworth BCI Dataset (P300 Evoked Potentials) Data Acquired Using BCI2000's P3 Speller Paradigm. BCI Competition III Challenge, pp. 1–8 (2004)
13. Gandhi, V., Prasad, G., Coyle, D., Behera, L., McGinnity, T.: EEG-based mobile robot control through an adaptive brain–robot interface. IEEE Tran. Syst. Man Cybern.: Syst. **44**(9), 1278–1285 (2014)
14. Throckmorton, C.S., Colwell, K.A., Ryan, D.B., Sellers, E.W., Collins, L.M.: Bayesian approach to dynamically controlling data collection in P300 spellers. IEEE Trans. Neural Syst. Rehabil. Eng. **21**(3), 508–517 (2013)
15. Jarchi, D., Sanei, S., Principe, J., Makkiabadi, B.: A new spatiotemporal filtering method for single-trial estimation of correlated ERP subcomponents. IEEE Trans. Biomed. Eng. **58**(1), 132–143 (2011)
16. Hoffmann, U.: Bayesian machine learning applied in a brain-computer interface for disabled users, E.P.F.L., Lausanne (2007)
17. Sharbrough, F., Chatrian, G.-E., Lesser, R.P., Lüders, H., Nuwer, M., Picton, T.W.: American electroencephalographic society guidelines for standard electrode position nomenclature. J. Clin. Neurophysiol. **8**, 200–202 (1991)
18. Carlos, T.S.C.L., Uma, M., Prabhu, S.: Analysis of P300 detection with different configuration electrodes based on offline dataset. J. Chem. Pharm. Sci. **9**(3), 1730–1734 (2016)

A Literature Review on a Neuro-Psychological Approach to Immersive Technology Research

Guan Wang[1] and Ayoung Suh[2(✉)] (iD)

[1] BBK Education Electronics, Shenzhen, China
wangguan@bbkedu.com
[2] Business School, Sungkyunkwan University, Seoul, Korea
aysuh@skku.edu

Abstract. One of the challenges of immersive technology research is that its increasing system complexity makes evaluating the user experience difficult. The use of an electroencephalogram (EEG) has been suggested as a promising approach to understanding the user's cognitive, emotional, and behavioral responses to immersive technology. However, the translation of this method into clear applications for user research remains challenging. To address this challenge, this paper outlines a systematic literature review to identify the applications of EEG measures currently adopted in immersive technology research. The full range of journal articles and major conference proceedings that reference the adoption of EEG measures to address immersive technology usage issues were searched. Based on rigorous inclusion and exclusion criteria, 84 relevant papers were identified and reviewed in the study. This literature review involves analysis of bibliometric data, research contexts, EEG analysis methods, and EEG stimuli. Presented in this paper are research gaps identified and opportunities for future research recommended based on the analysis results. This study contributes to advancing our knowledge about how to collect and analyze EEG data in immersive technology research.

Keywords: Immersive technology · User experience · Electroencephalogram · Neuropsychological response · Literature review

1 Introduction

Immersive technology is the technology that immerses users in a synthesized environment, blurring the line between the physical and digital worlds [52], which encompasses virtual reality (VR), augmented reality (AR), and mixed reality (MR). Using immersive technology, people can coordinate multiple spaces (virtual and real) while moving fluidly between different environments. Researchers have reported that, due to the complexity of immersive technology and its unique system features, measures of user responses to the technology are limited by traditional data collection methods (e.g., self-reported evaluation).

To overcome this challenge, a neurophysiological approach has been widely adopted in research to detect the user's mental state and the quality of the user's experience. Neurophysiological methods can provide precise information and alternative theories that

© Springer Nature Switzerland AG 2021
D. D. Schmorrow and C. M. Fidopiastis (Eds.): HCII 2021, LNAI 12776, pp. 97–115, 2021.
https://doi.org/10.1007/978-3-030-78114-9_8

complement traditional research methods. Particularly, electroencephalography (EEG) is found to dominate neuro-information systems (neuroIS) research because of its advantages, such as spatial resolution, temporal resolution, cost and available knowledge base [61].

Despite the increasing scholarly attention being paid to EEG as a neuropsychological approach to immersive technology research, little research has been conducted to understand how to apply this method to measure user experiences in the immersive environment. Motivated by this lack of understanding of the neuropsychological approach using EEG in immersive technology, this investigation was designed to systematically review relevant studies in which EEG measures have been adopted to examine user experiences in using immersive technology; analysis of research trends, topics, and methods related to these studies are included. The goal of the present study is to identify research gaps through analysis of the literature on immersive technology research involving the use of EEG and recommend future research directions based on the findings. Specifically, this review is guided by the following questions:

1. What are the trends and topics of immersive technology studies that have employed EEG measures?
2. What are the EEG measures and EEG stimuli that appear in previous immersive technology studies that employed EEG measures?
3. What are the research gaps existing on EEG use in immersive technology?

The paper is organized as follows. First, we provide a brief introduction to the EEG method and its utility in immersive technology research. Next, the procedure of the systematic review is described. Third, a detailed description of our results is presented. Lastly, we discuss the current state of research and challenges to conducting such research and offer recommendations for future studies.

2 Background

EEG is "a recording of the summed electrical activity of populations of neurons," which can be captured by electrodes placed at assigned positions on the scalp (we only discuss scalp- recorded EEG in this review) [9, 70]. EEG has been applied to immersive technology research due to its several advantages over other data collection methods. First, neurophysiological data are not susceptible to the subjectivity bias, social desirability bias, and common method bias that usually challenge self-reported data [24]. For example, data on immersive technology's impact on cognitive load, one of the most important constructs in immersive technology research, has been elusive due to self-reported evaluations. However, researchers have found that EEG data enhance the validity of cognitive load measures [73].

Second, EEG is instrumental to understanding the subconscious processes involved in the use of immersive technology [24]. Researchers have suggested that EEG can measure a user's cognitive and emotional state in a more precise manner than other methods, thus assisting researchers in identifying causal relationships between the stimuli and their associated responses [61]. For example, researchers have shown how EEG measures are related to active cognitive processing and arousal during the use of immersive technology [79].

Third, EEG allows for the continuous monitoring of brain function [or] collection of continuous data in a certain period. Continuous data recording enables researchers to understand how users respond to immersive technology over time. For instance, researchers can keep track of presence [98] or motion sickness [30, 43] during exposure to an immersive environment. It is difficult for researchers to obtain multiple measures of responses from users who are actively engaged in the technology without interrupting them in both survey and experimental studies. However, EEG helps to overcome such limitations by recording user responses without interruptions.

Nevertheless, researchers have also identified disadvantages associated with using EEG measures in research, including poor spatial resolution, lengthy preparation time, and discomfort-induced distraction [9]. Indeed, one of the major concerns is that EEG tools often cause research participants discomfort because of the sensors attached to their heads in experimental settings. Additionally, previous studies have pointed out that some EEG studies failed to ensure data quality during data collection procedures, leading to incorrect data analysis and misinterpretations of the results [37].

In summary, despite increasing scholarly and practical attention to a neuropsychological approach to immersive technology research, the use of EEG measures in research is in its early stages and many methodological issues have yet to be fully discussed.

3   Search Strategy

We began this literature review by identifying articles that reported on the use of EEGs as measures in the context of immersive technology. A two-stage approach was adopted to reduce potential biases [11]. In the first stage, a keyword search was conducted to identify articles. In the second stage, we applied a rigorous inclusion and exclusion process to select relevant articles.

We chose the Scopus database to search for peer-reviewed journal articles and conference proceedings to ensure the quality of the source materials. To identify relevant publications in the database, we conducted a keyword search. In the literature, several terms are used synonymously for what we call EEG. Therefore, we applied the terms "EEG," "electroencephalogram," "electrophysiology," and "electroencephalography" to search the titles, abstracts, and keywords of the sources. To identify sources related to immersive technology, several keywords and phrases were used: "virtual reality," "augmented reality," "mixed reality," and "immersive technology." The initial search yielded 731 papers.

In the second stage, we excluded papers that reported on immersive technology used for clinical purposes, such as treatments for mental or physical diseases. We conjectured that those with disabilities and functional impairments may exhibit different patterns from ordinary users of immersive technology. We also excluded papers that documented the use of the EEG as a tool for brain-computer interface (BCI), which is a communication system that recognizes user's commands from their brainwaves only and reacts accordingly [100]. Although BCI studies are important for applying EEG responses to develop assistive devices and input controls [79], BCI studies do not focus on applying EEG responses as measures of user experiences. Therefore, we excluded BCI research from our review. We also excluded papers on studies in which non-human objects, such as animals, were the research targets. To summarize, papers focusing on topics such as BIC, animals, and disease/disorder were excluded from this review. Then, two researchers discussed and reached an agreement on the inclusion and exclusion of the remaining articles. This procedure led to the final selection of 84 papers that served as the basis for our subsequent analysis.

To conduct the literature review, we developed a coding scheme that involved a set of categories, and the selected papers were coded based on this scheme, which included publication period, number of study participants, research context, and EEG measures for variables of interest in research.

4   Bibliometric Analysis

Figure 1 shows the publication years of the relevant literature. Our results indicate that the number of publications on this topic has increased continuously since 2010. Although only seven papers from 2001 to 2009 were included in our review, the number of relevant sources peaked in 2014–2015. The period 2016–2017 showed a slight setback, which can be explained by the fact that our filtering criteria excluded BCI and rehabilitation papers published during that time period. Overall, the increased number of results since 2010 illustrates an increasing interest in employing EEG measures for immersive technology research.

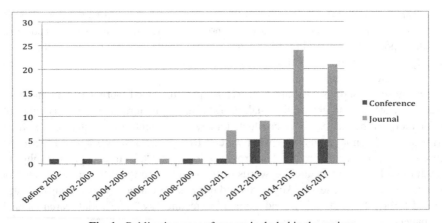

Fig. 1. Publication year of papers included in the review

4.1   Research Context

Immersive technologies have many kinds of implications in entertainment, health, business, education, and other fields. Based on the core service or an activity with the application of immersive technology, we identified the specific contexts in our reviewed papers as education (n = 8, 9.5%), transportation (n = 5, 6%), healthcare (n = 6, 4.8%), workplace (n = 3, 3.6%), crime (n = 3, 3.6%), entertainment (n = 3, 3.6%), and architecture (n = 3, 3.6%). The rest of the papers did not have specific contexts (n = 53, 63.1%). In these 53 studies, EEG correlates were identified to understand overall user experiences in the immersive environment and to provide suggestions for tuning applications for specific purposes during their development.

4.2 Types of EEG Analysis Methods

Researchers have adopted different types of EEG analysis methods to understand users' perceptual, emotional, and cognitive states while engaged in the use of immersive technology. Certain EEG signals reflecting the momentary informational content of the immersive environment are called event-related potential (ERP). Other signals documented were correlates of more durable psychophysiological states, such as cognitive reactions or emotional reactions during an exposure to an immersive environment, which are called continuous EEG. ERP and continuous EEG are the two major brain wave types captured in these reviewed papers.

Table 1 summarizes the studies presented in papers in which the ERP technique was adopted as the major measure. An ERP component typically refers to averaged EEG responses that are time-locked and phase-locked to a specific stimulus [60]. It involves the experimental manipulation of the stimulus, such as the presentation of a word, an image, a user interface, or a sound. Researchers name an ERP component by using "P/N" (i.e., positive/negative peak according to the polarity) and "a number" (i.e., the appearing time after the presentation of the stimulus, in milliseconds). For example, P1 or P100 means there is a positive peak appearing around 100 ms after the onset of a stimulus [9].

Early components in ERP research, such as P1 and N1, have been linked primarily to attentional processes that allocate perceptual resources and encode elementary stimulus features [5]. Specifically, the P1 component is a sensitive index of visuospatial attention [13, 56]. The N1 component shows links to a person's attention and auditory stimuli [49, 76].

A sensory-obligatory component of the visual system, referred to as N170, is widely adopted to capture facial processing [26]. Most studies that addressed this topic in our review set demonstrated that the face-sensitive N170 component is an important neural response for processing different facial stimuli [93]. It is noteworthy that N170 is also responsible for the spatial location of reward-related stimuli, which is specified as "topographical N170" (NT170) [2].

The component N2 is associated with object recognition and categorization, which ultimately signals that a perceptual representation is formed [78]. Three subcomponents comprise N2: N2a, known as mismatch negativity (MMN), N2b, and N2c. It has been argued that MMN is related to an infrequent change in a repetitive sequence of stimuli, such as auditory or visual mismatch [62].

The most studied ERP is the P3, which is associated with allocation of perceptual and central resources [49]. The central processes are assumed to involve controlled processing and activation of working memory [50]. Thus, P3 has been regarded as a sign of memory access processes evoked by evaluation of stimuli in tasks that require a response [50]. The P3 component can be divided into two subcomponents: P3a (related to the engagement of attention and novelty processing) and P3b (related to cognitive processes). Several studies reviewed reported that P3 was associated with cognitive processing [36, 107], deception detection [66], visual recognition [101], and tactile illusion [53].

Oftentimes, N2 and P3 are sensitive to similar stimuli and studied together, because they represent a connection of mental mechanisms that work together [107]. For example, motion- related visual evoked potential (M-VEP) is an objective estimate of the time properties of the visual system [21]. According to the type of motion, the M-VEP is typically composed of three main components—P1, N2, and P3 [21, 36].

The N4 component has been linked to meaning processing of various stimuli (e.g., words, sounds, and objects), especially semantic incongruence across written, spoken, and signed language. The component can also be evoked by observation of erroneous actions. For example, our literature review revealed that N400 was correlated with mismatches such as those between visual and auditory information [102] and embodied error detection [75]. Additionally, successive neurocognitive stages of spatial cognitive mapping were associated with N4 [77].

It has been suggested that late negative-going slow waves (SW) are associated with central cognitive processing and allocation of attentional resources [49] and Burns and Fairclough [13] provided evidence that an increased presence and immersion experience were associated with decreased late negative SW amplitudes. Other studies have indicated that an error-related negativity (ERN, or Ne) [64, 75] or error positivity (Pe) [75] is elicited after the occurrence of an erroneous response or observing erroneous actions in others. The remaining ERPs identified in the literature review include N3 for motor imagery [16], P350 for joint attention [14, 15], and P450 for body ownership [13] and target-distractor detection [39].

Using continuous EEG in immersive technology research is based on the fact that the composition of the EEG can change in response to human mental states. Continuous EEGs have several frequency bands associated with specific mental states, including delta waves (1–4 Hz, deep sleep), theta waves (4–8 Hz, mediation), alpha waves (8–13 Hz, relaxation), beta waves (13–25 Hz, attention) and gamma waves (25–200 Hz, arousal).

Table 1. Summary of EEG correlates of continuous EEG

Construct	EEG measure	Ref.
Attention	P1	[13, 56]
Attention, Auditory stimuli	N1	[49, 76]
Face recognition (e.g., facial expressions, gaze processing)	N170	[2, 14, 88, 93]
Self-face recognition	P2	[32]
Cognitive processing, Cognitive conflict in decision, Mismatch detector, Control of movement responses	N2	[21, 62, 76, 107]
Perceptual attention, Embodied cognition, Cognitive processing, Motion-related VEP, Deception detection, Visual recognition, Tactile illusion	P3	[21, 36, 53, 66, 71, 101, 107]
Motor imagery	N3	[16]
Joint attention (i.e., a common focus of attention with a partner)	P350	[14, 15]
Central cognitive processing, Mismatches between visual and auditory information, Embodied error detection, Spatial cognitive mapping, Language processing	N4	[75, 77, 102]
Body ownership, Target-distractor detection	P450	[31, 39]
Presence, Sensory immersion	SW	[13, 49]
Error detection	ERN	[64, 75]

5 Thematic Analysis

5.1 Mental Load

Research has investigated the effects of technology, stimuli, tasks and user factors on changes in EEG patterns correlated with mental load (also known as workload, memory load, or cognitive load). Studies have reported that the theta power increase in the frontal lobe and the alpha power decrease in the frontal and parietal lobe are correlated with a high mental load [7, 38, 44, 82, 118]. Zacharis et al. [117] found that stronger alpha power in the occipital lobe indicated less mental effort and attentional demands. Investigating fatigue-related EEG changes, Gharagozlou et al. [29] reported that the increase in alpha power indicated a decrease in the level of alertness and attention and the onset of fatigue. Dan and Reiner [22] adopted a ratio between theta frontal and alpha parietal to capture cognitive load, both of which are well-established approaches for estimating mental load. Researchers have also found that increased frontal theta power indicates higher focused attention and that higher alpha power is inversely associated with the quantity of sensory information processing [38]. As another correlate, measuring a beta wave in the frontal lobe was found to be a useful approach to estimate mental load [115, 117].

5.2 Embodiment

Our literature review reveals that one of the major themes appearing in immersive technology research is to assessing how users are engaged in practices of the body in a virtual environment. The first important component of embodiment is body ownership—the feeling that an artificial agent is part of one's body. The second component of embodiment is a sense of agency—the feeling that users are responsible for the movement)—which is essential for distinguishing self-generated from other-produced actions. Research has found that sensorimotor and multisensory integration may play a fundamental role in embodiment in an immersive environment [55]. Previous studies have found that alpha waves in the sensorimotor cortex are associated with the perception of human bodies and motor/somatosensory activities, reflecting changes in embodiment. For example, González-Franco et al. [31] argued that alpha band activity in the motor cortex is important in the generation of body ownership. Senkowski et al. [87] found that gamma waves were correlated to integration across different sensory modalities into a coherent perception. Lee et al. [54] found that beta and gamma waves in the frontal lobe were correlated with a sense of agency during cross-modal sensory processing.

5.3 Spatial Navigation

Spatial navigation is a task influenced by visual features, such as spatial cues and landmarks in an immersive environment. The theta band during landmark processing has been frequently reported in previous studies because theta waves coordinate sensory information with a motor plan to direct wayfinding behavior to known goal locations [48]. Researchers have found that frontal- midline theta is correlated to landmark and route processing [48, 69, 89, 95].

Spatial navigation requires maintaining a correct spatial representation of the environment for users to determine direction and orientation. The studies we reviewed were consistent in the viewpoint that the parietal lobe is involved in generating an egocentric view, the function of which is to integrate information from different sensory modalities and form a coherent representation of space. Specifically, researchers have found that spatial navigation based on an egocentric reference frame engenders a network of the alpha wave in motor, parietal, and occipital cortices and theta wave in the frontal cortex [58], whereas an allocentric spatial reference frame involves alpha waves and beta waves in the retrosplenial cortex [47].

5.4 Presence

Our literature review reveals that although one of the most important experiences relevant to immersive technology is presence, the EEG correlates of presence vary depending on how researchers define presence. For example, Jeon and Park [40] defined presence as a psychological and physiological reaction related to the individual emotions. Correspondingly, presence was measured by EEG correlates of emotions in this study. The other studies mainly adopted the definition that presence is "the extent to which a user feels that he or she is in a particular place, even while physically situated in another place" [112], which is also known as spatial presence. Considering presence is one type of egocentric spatial experience in immersive environments, it activates similar brain areas involved in spatial navigation, such as the parietal and frontal lobes. Most studies in our literature review found that presence is associated with the activation of the frontal-midline theta, which can be caused by the involvement of sensorimotor integration mechanisms [8, 34, 47, 49, 104]. According to Clemente et al. [19] and Wiederhold and Riva [111], the insula activation is related to stimulus attention and self-awareness processes, thus related to presence. Moreover, an increased task- related power decrease (TRPD) in the alpha band at parietal electrode sites is associated with presence [8, 34, 47]. It is also worth noting that several studies suggest that certain ERPs (e.g., N200, SW) are also relative to presence [13, 49, 107].

5.5 Emotion

Another stream of research concerns how EEG correlates capture user emotions. Researchers have suggested that emotion recognition accuracy obtained for emotion valence outperforms that obtained for emotion arousal [65]. Davidson [23] argued that positive emotions are related to left hemisphere activation and negative emotions are related to right hemisphere activation, especially in the frontal region of the brain. Our reviewed papers provide evidence that both positive and negative emotions can be predicted by EEG data. For instance, sadness can be detected if there is a significant increase in brain activation in the right inferior frontal gyrus and the right middle frontal gyrus for the alpha band [81]. Multiple studies empirically found that left hemisphere activation was dominant for positive emotions [35, 56]. Researchers have also found that positive or negative emotions could be reflected in prefrontal alpha asymmetry [57]. Researchers have measured asymmetry values by comparing the frontal alpha power in two hemispheres [12, 57]. Banaei [4] measured changes in theta activity originating in or near the anterior cingulate cortex to capture the ratings of two distinct emotions, such as arousal and pleasure during aesthetic experiences [4]. Wrzesien et al. [113] measured the activation in the cingulate gyrus and postcentral gyrus to capture a user's negative emotion (i.e., frustration).

5.6 Postural Control

Immersive technology utilizes optic flow to provoke self-motion illusion and presence, which is often accompanied by the loss of postural control and cybersickness. Several studies suggested EEG correlates of postural stability and balance could be frontal–central theta activity, which might relate to cortical control of body balance [17, 95, 96]. Stronger frontal– central theta band activity reflected increased efforts to control balance [96]. Moreover, alpha waves in the parietal and occipital lobes were also used to evaluate cortical responses to dynamic visual stimulation [17, 20]. Researchers suggest that instability in the control of body orientation is a sufficient condition that causes cybersickness [80]. The studies we reviewed confirmed similar brain responses between postural control and cybersickness. Researchers have found that alpha and gamma waves in the parietal and occipital lobes are the EEG correlates of cybersickness [45, 59, 110]. Table 2 presents important constructs measurable with the continuous EEG and related brain areas.

Table 2. Summary of EEG correlates of continuous EEG.

Construct	Sample brain areas	Ref.
Mental load	Alpha in frontal and parietal lobe, theta in frontal lobe, the ratio of the average power of frontal theta and parietal alpha, beta in frontal lobe	[1, 7, 22, 29, 38, 44, 82, 115, 117, 118]
Embodiment	Alpha wave in the sensorimotor cortex, gamma wave in frontal lobe	[31, 41, 53–55, 74, 88, 94]
Spatial navigation	Theta wave in frontal midline, alpha wave in parietal lobe	[48, 58, 69, 89, 116]
Presence	Theta wave in frontal midline, alpha wave in parietal lobe	[8, 19, 34, 40, 47, 49, 104]
Emotion	Alpha wave in frontal lobe, theta wave in anterior cingulate cortex, prefrontal alpha asymmetry, theta wave in cingulate gyrus, postcentral gyrus	[4, 12, 57, 81, 113]
Postural control	Theta wave in frontal-central alpha and gamma waves in parietal and occipital lobes	[17, 20, 45, 59, 95, 96, 110]

6   Discussion

Our literature review reveals that EEG is a valid method for collecting data from immersive technology users to evaluate their mental states and quality of experience. In the following section, future research directions and contributions of this study are discussed.

6.1   Future Research Direction

EEG Complements Subjective Measurement. By providing precise information and alternative theories that complement traditional research methods, continuous EEG patterns allow researchers to precisely measure a user's mental load, embodiment, presence, cybersickness, and emotion responses. For example, researchers can measure the extent of mental load a user experiences while using an immersive technology via his or her brainwaves, which is much objective than data collected through subjective assessments such as self-administered questionnaires. The EEG method also allows researchers to measure the extent of embodiment by capturing sensorimotor and multisensory integration [87]. Furthermore, the EEG method enables researchers to measure a user's affective responses to immersive environments beyond the conscious reflection of affective processes [4].

EEG Tests Various Immersive Technology Designs. For immersive technology research, it is important to study the effects of various design features on the quality of user experience. However, there has been limited investigation about this topic. Previous studies have limited their examination to the effects of general interface features (e.g., 2D/3D, screen size, interactivity and image quality) on users' brain activation. Interface features unique in immersive technology have yet to be empirically explored. For example, researchers can use EEG to capture user brain responses of wayfinding during an AR-facilitated navigation. The adoption of EEG to study immersive technology is still at its early developing stage, and more diverse design features unique to immersive technology need to be tested in the future via the EEG method.

Testing Various Task Designs with EEG. The EEG method can be applied to developing more effective virtual tasks. Researchers found that first-person perspective was correlated with better user experience due to higher spatial presence, sense of agency, and embodiment of an avatar [34, 54, 75, 90]. It has also been found that difficult tasks require greater cognitive load than easy tasks [22]. Therefore, the EEG method enables immersive technology developers to balance task difficulty and user skill levels in a more effective manner by tuning task design in various contexts, such as learning, training, health, and marketing.

EEG Can Examine Individual Differences. Our literature analysis indicates that the use of psychophysiological correlates can further demonstrate individual differences in reaction and adaptation to a given combination of stimulus variables in immersive technology. For example, different demographic groups (e.g., age and gender) may have different brain activation patterns. Additionally, brain activation patterns can be influenced by individual differences, such as psychological strain, physical state, ability, preference, and technology use experiences. The existence of individual differences in EEG correlates brings both opportunities and challenges to immersive technology research. First, by checking the EEG features among different user groups, the EEG method provides opportunities to better understand the mechanism by which users have different immersive experiences and performances. However, it also challenges the generalization of the research findings, considering that current immersive technology studies have limited samples. The researchers need to be cautious about whether the existence of individual differences has an influence on their findings.

EEG Capabilities in Verifying Measurement Validify. Our literature review indicates that various types of EEG measures for a specific construct coexist. Specifically, presence, emotions, and cognition load were measured by different locations and patterns of EEG signals in our selected papers. Some papers failed to explain why EEG responses occurred in these areas. In some studies, certain EEG measures could be linked to several theoretical constructs. For example, Jeon and Park [40] interpreted the left hemisphere's beta value as pleasant emotions, attention, and ultimately presence. Researchers need to precisely define the constructs and make sure that the EEG measures capture the investigated theoretical constructs as opposed to other constructs.

Most of our reviewed studies have identified the activation of brain regions inferred from EEG data. By exposing participants to different scenarios to study the immersive experience, activation of a particular brain region can be detected during the process. However, most studies offered no explanation of the correlational relationship between activation in a brain region and a certain behavior or experience. These brain activities should match the psychological concepts used by researchers. Thus, we suggest that the interpretation methods of EEG data and research design strategies should be carefully selected with relevant justifications in future research. The solution is to directly manipulate the predicted underlying psychological process based on the theory. The interpretation of findings can be bases on the function of a brain region on the basis of prior studies. For example, our literature review finds that the researchers identified distinguished EEG measures of presence because of different definitions or mechanisms applied. Vecchiato et al. [104] suggested that a higher degree of presence could be revealed by frontal midline theta power based on the hypothesis of sensorimotor integration mechanisms. According to Clemente et al. [19] and Wiederhold and Riva [111], the insula activation is related to stimulus attention and self-awareness processes, directly related to presence. As a higher sense of presence can elicit positive emotions, some studies measured presence by identifying specific EEG correlates of emotions [40].

The Possibility of Mobile EEG Studies. The compatibility of immersive technologies with psychophysiological recording equipment is an important issue. When subjects move with their head or whole body in experimental paradigms involving EEG, various types of motion artifacts can be induced, which may pose a serious problem to any measurement [67]. To reduce the artifacts, various methods have been applied during the EEG recording processes. Some papers proposed a fixed setting in which participants were required to sit still while their head was restrained to prevent head motion [92]. Participants are not required to turn their head fast or look up or down abruptly. However, user experiences in immersive technology will lack naturalness if users' movements are restricted. The omission of important aspects of sensory feedback under natural conditions by stationary experiments has been demonstrated [25].

Another line of studies agreed that natural movement is the best way to investigate brain responses during an experiment [4]. Recent technological developments have made it possible to study EEG during movement [96]. Some of our reviewed papers investigated how users' performance in navigation tasks successfully handles the issue. As an example, Banaei et al. [4] allowed participants to actively walk and explore wearing a head-mounted display.

It is challenging to perform EEG experiments where subjects are allowed to move and perform complex behaviors [33]. A mobile EEG setup can enable participants to move with their head or whole body and actively explore the environments, which is beneficial for the investigation of the user experience during the active interaction with the immersive technology. There is a trend in immersive technology from stationary setup to more interactive and movable ones, which requires an improvement of EEG devices, from being static and sensitive to mobile and noise-resistant.

6.2 Contribution to Research

This study contributes to academia from several perspectives. First, the systematic review can help researchers understand the current state of EEG studies in immersive technology. The bibliometric information shows that EEG was a relevant method for IS research. There is a growing trend of EEG applicability in multiple research themes and contexts, including system design, health, education, and the workplace. Second, we summarized the various constructs of interest in immersive technology research that could be measured by EEG data. The summary is a valuable resource to the research community because researchers can apply the EEG method to initiate their studies from a new angle. Third, we summarized the stimuli in immersive technology as well as the connections between the stimuli and brain responses. Fourth, selected opportunities for future research and challenges related to EEG and immersive technology were discussed in this study. Studies considering EEG and immersive technologies could be conducted in many domains in the future.

References

1. Anopas, D., Wongsawat, Y.: Virtual reality game for memory skills enhancement based on QEEG. In: 2014 7th Biomedical Engineering International Conference (BMEiCON), pp. 1–5. IEEE (2014)
2. Baker, T.E., Holroyd, C.B.: The topographical N170: electrophysiological evidence of a neural mechanism for human spatial navigation. Biol. Psychol. **94**(1), 90–105 (2013)
3. Baltatzis, V., Bintsi, K.-M., Apostolidis, G.K., Hadjileontiadis, L.J.: Bullying incidences identification within an immersive environment using HD EEG-based analysis: a swarm decomposition and deep learning approach. Sci. Rep. **7**(1), 17292 (2017)
4. Banaei, M., Hatami, J., Yazdanfar, A., Gramann, K.: Walking through architectural spaces: the impact of interior forms on human brain dynamics. Front. Hum. Neurosci. **11**, 477 (2017)
5. Bartholow, B.D., Amodio, D.M.: Brain potentials in social psychological research. Methods in social neuroscience, vol. 198 (2009)
6. Bauman, B., Seeling, P.: Visual interface evaluation for wearables datasets: predicting the subjective augmented vision image QoE and QoS. Fut. Internet **9**(3), 40 (2017)
7. Baumeister, J., Reinecke, K., Cordes, M., Lerch, C., Weiß, M.: Brain activity in goal-directed movements in a real compared to a virtual environment using the nintendo WII. Neurosci. Lett. **481**(1), 47–50 (2010)
8. Baumgartner, T., Valko, L., Esslen, M., Jäncke, L.: Neural correlate of spatial presence in an arousing and noninteractive virtual reality: an EEG and psychophysiology study. Cyberpsychol. Behav. **9**(1), 30–45 (2006)
9. Beres, A.M.: Time is of the essence: a review of electroencephalography (EEG) and event-related brain potentials (ERPs) in language research. Appl. Psychophysiol. Biofeedback **42**(4), 247–255 (2017)
10. Bischof, W.F., Boulanger, P.: Spatial navigation in virtual reality environments: an EEG analysis. Cyberpsychol. Behav. **6**(5), 487–495 (2003)
11. Boell, S.K., Cecez-Kecmanovic, D.: On being 'systematic' in literature reviews in IS. J. Inf. Technol. **30**(2), 161–173 (2015)
12. Brouwer, A.-M., Neerincx, M.A., Kallen, V., van der Leer, L., ten Brinke, M.: EEG alpha asymmetry, heart rate variability and cortisol in response to virtual reality induced stress. J. Cyberther. Rehabil. **4**(1), 21–34 (2011)

13. Burns, C.G., Fairclough, S.H.: Use of auditory event-related potentials to measure immersion during a computer game. Int. J. Hum Comput. Stud. **73**, 107–114 (2015)
14. Caruana, N., de Lissa, P., McArthur, G.: Beliefs about human agency influence the neural processing of gaze during joint attention. Soc. Neurosci. **12**(2), 194–206 (2017)
15. Caruana, N., de Lissa, P., McArthur, G.: The neural time course of evaluating self-initiated joint attention bids. Brain Cognit. **98**, 43–52 (2015)
16. Cebolla, A.M., Petieau, M., Cevallos, C., Leroy, A., Dan, B., Cheron, G.: Long-lasting cortical reorganization as the result of motor imagery of throwing a ball in a virtual tennis court. Front. Psychol. **6**, 1869 (2015)
17. Chang, C.-J., Yang, T.-F., Yang, S.-W., Chern, J.-S.: Cortical modulation of motor control biofeedback among the elderly with high fall risk during a posture perturbation task with augmented rality. Front. Aging Neurosci. **8**, 80 (2016)
18. Chun, J., Kaongoen, N., Jo, S.: EEG signal analysis for measuring the quality of virtual reality. In: 2015 15th International Conference on Control, Automation and Systems (ICCAS), pp. 1801–1804. IEEE (2015)
19. Clemente, M., Rodríguez, A., Rey, B., Alcañiz, M.: Assessment of the influence of navigation control and screen size on the sense of presence in virtual reality using EEG. Exp. Syst. Appl. Int. J. **41**(4), 1584–1592 (2014)
20. Da-Silva, P., Infantosi, A., Nadal, J.: Event-related synchronization/desynchronization for evaluating cortical response detection induced by dynamic visual stimuli. In: XII Mediterranean Conference on Medical and Biological Engineering and Computing 2010, pp. 37–40. Springer (2010). https://doi.org/10.1007/978-3-642-13039-7_10
21. Da Silva, P., Rosa, B., Cagy, M., Infantosi, A.: Motion-related VEPs elicited by dynamic virtual stimulation. In: XIII Mediterranean Conference on Medical and Biological Engineering and Computing 2013, pp. 1809–1812. Springer (2014). https://doi.org/10.1007/978-3-319-00846-2_446
22. Dan, A., Reiner, M.: EEG-based cognitive load of processing events in 3D virtual worlds is lower than processing events in 2D displays. Int. J. Psychophysiol. **122**, 75–84 (2017)
23. Davidson, R.J.: Cerebral asymmetry and emotion: conceptual and methodological conundrums. Cogn. Emot. **7**(1), 115–138 (1993)
24. Dimoka, A., et al.: On the use of neurophysiological tools in IS research: developing a research agenda for NeuroIS. MIS Q. **36**(3), 679–702 (2012)
25. Ehinger, B.V., et al.: Kinesthetic and vestibular information modulate alpha activity during spatial navigation: a mobile EEG study. Front. Hum. Neurosci. **8**, 71 (2014)
26. Eimer, M.: The face-sensitivity of the n170 component. Front. Hum. Neurosci. **5**, 119 (2011)
27. Frömer, R., Hafner, V., Sommer, W.: Aiming for the bull's eye: preparing for throwing investigated with event-related brain potentials. Psychophysiology **49**(3), 335–344 (2012)
28. Gerjets, P., Walter, C., Rosenstiel, W., Bogdan, M., Zander, T.O.: Cognitive state monitoring and the design of adaptive instruction in digital environments: lessons learned from cognitive workload assessment using a passive brain-computer interface approach. Front. Neurosci. **8**, 385 (2014)
29. Gharagozlou, F., et al.: Detecting driver mental fatigue based on EEG alpha power changes during simulated driving. Iran. J. Publ. Health **44**(12), 1693 (2015)
30. Golding, J.F.: Motion sickness susceptibility. Auton. Neurosci.: Basic Clin. **129**(1), 67–76 (2006)
31. González-Franco, M., Peck, T.C., Rodríguez-Fornells, A., Slater, M.: A threat to a virtual hand elicits motor cortex activation. Exp. Brain Res. **232**(3), 875–887 (2014)
32. Gonzalez-Franco, M., Bellido, A.I., Blom, K.J., Slater, M., Rodriguez-Fornells, A.: The neurological traces of look-alike avatars. Front. Hum. Neurosci. **10**, 392 (2016)
33. Gramann, K., et al.: Cognition in action: imaging brain/body dynamics in mobile humans. Rev. Neurosci. **22**(6), 593–608 (2011)

34. Havranek, M., Langer, N., Cheetham, M., Jäncke, L.: Perspective and agency during video gaming influences spatial presence experience and brain activation patterns. Behav. Brain Funct. **8**(1), 34 (2012)
35. Hubbard, R., Sipolins, A., Zhou, L.: Enhancing learning through virtual reality and neuro-feedback: a first step. In: Proceedings of the Seventh International Learning Analytics & Knowledge Conference, pp. 398–403. ACM (2017)
36. Invitto, S., Spada, I., De Paolis, L.T.: Augmented reality, embodied cognition and learning. In: De Paolis, L.T., Mongelli, A. (eds.) AVR 2015. LNCS, vol. 9254, pp. 125–134. Springer, Cham (2015). https://doi.org/10.1007/978-3-319-22888-4_10
37. Jackson, A.F., Bolger, D.J.: The neurophysiological bases of EEG and EEG measurement: a review for the rest of us. Psychophysiology **51**(11), 1061–1071 (2014)
38. Jaiswal, N., Ray, W., Slobounov, S.: Encoding of visual–spatial information in working memory requires more cerebral efforts than retrieval: evidence from an EEG and virtual reality study. Brain Res. **1347**, 80–89 (2010)
39. Jangraw, D.C., Sajda, P.: Feature selection for gaze, pupillary, and EEG signals evoked in a 3D environment. In: Proceedings of the 6th Workshop on Eye gaze in Intelligent Human Machine Interaction: Gaze in Multimodal Interaction, pp. 45–50. ACM (2013)
40. Jeon, S., Park, W.: Computing presence in nonfigurative virtual environment under color and motion stimulus. In: Proceedings of the Future Technologies Conference, pp. 1100–1106. IEEE (2016)
41. Kang, S.Y., et al.: Brain networks responsible for sense of agency: an EEG study. PLoS ONE **10**(8), e0135261 (2015)
42. Kastner, A.K., Pauli, P., Wieser, M.J.: Sustained attention in context conditioning: evidence from steady-state VEPs. Int. J. Psychophysiol. **98**(3), 546–556 (2015)
43. Kennedy, R.S., Stanney, K.M., Dunlap, W.P.: Duration and exposure to virtual environments: sickness curves during and across sessions. Presence: Teleoper. Virtual Environ. **9**(5), 463–472 (2000)
44. Kim, S.-P., et al.: Modulation of theta phase synchronization in the human electroencephalogram during a recognition memory task. NeuroReport **23**(11), 637–641 (2012)
45. Kim, Y., Kim, H., Ko, H., Kim, H.: Psychophysiological changes by navigation in a virtual reality. In: Proceedings of the 23rd Annual International Conference of the IEEE Engineering in Medicine and Biology Society, 2001, pp. 3773–3776. IEEE (2001)
46. Klatzky, R.L.: Allocentric and egocentric spatial representations: Definitions, distinctions, and interconnections. In: Spatial Cognition, pp. 1–17. Springer (1998). https://doi.org/10.1007/3-540-69342-4_1
47. Kober, S.E., Kurzmann, J., Neuper, C.: Cortical correlate of spatial presence in 2D and 3D interactive virtual reality: an EEG study. Int. J. Psychophysiol. **83**(3), 365–374 (2012)
48. Kober, S.E., Neuper, C.: Sex differences in human EEG theta oscillations during spatial navigation in virtual reality. Int. J. Psychophysiol. **79**(3), 347–355 (2011)
49. Kober, S.E., Neuper, C.: Using auditory event-related EEG potentials to assess presence in virtual reality. Int. J. Hum. Comput. Stud. **70**(9), 577–587 (2012)
50. Kok, A.: Event-related-potential (ERP) reflections of mental resources: a review and synthesis. Biol. Psychol. **45**(1–3), 19–56 (1997)
51. LaViola Jr., J.J.: A discussion of cybersickness in virtual environments. ACM SIGCHI Bull. **32**(1), 47–56 (2000)
52. Lee, H.-G., Chung, S., Lee, W.-H.: Presence in virtual golf simulators: the effects of presence on perceived enjoyment, perceived value, and behavioral intention. New Med. Soc. **15**(6), 930–946 (2013)
53. Lee, H.J., Lee, J., Kim, C.J., Kim, G.J., Kim, E.-S., Whang, M.: Brain process for perception of the "Out of The Body" tactile illusion for virtual object interaction. Sensors **15**(4), 7913–7932 (2015)

54. Lee, J., Moon, S.-E., Cheon, M., Lee, J.-S.: EEG analysis on 3D navigation in virtual realty with different perspectives. In: Proceedings of the 3rd International Conference on Human-Agent Interaction, pp. 227–229. ACM (2015)

55. Lenggenhager, B., Halje, P., Blanke, O.: Alpha band oscillations correlate with illusory self-location induced by virtual reality. Eur. J. Neurosci. **33**(10), 1935–1943 (2011)

56. Leroy, A., Cevallos, C., Cebolla, A.-M., Caharel, S., Dan, B., Cheron, G.: Short-term EEG dynamics and neural generators evoked by navigational images. PLoS ONE **12**(6), e0178817 (2017)

57. Li, M., Jiang, Q., Tan, C.-H., Wei, K.-K.: Enhancing user-game engagement through software gaming elements. J. Manage. Inf. Syst. **30**(4), 115–150 (2014)

58. Lin, C.-T., Chiu, T.-C., Gramann, K.: EEG correlates of spatial orientation in the human retrosplenial complex. Neuroimage **120**, 123–132 (2015)

59. Lin, C.-T., Tsai, S.-F., Ko, L.-W.: EEG-based learning system for online motion sickness level estimation in a dynamic vehicle environment. IEEE Trans. Neural Netw. Learn. Syst. **24**(10), 1689–1700 (2013)

60. Luck, S.J., Kappenman, E.S.: ERP components and selective attention. In: The Oxford Handbook of Event-Related Potential Components, pp. 295–327 (2012)

61. Müller-Putz, G.R., Riedl, R., Wriessnegger, S.C.: Electroencephalography (EEG) as a research tool in the information systems discipline: foundations, measurement, and applications. CAIS **37**, 46 (2015)

62. Mager, R., et al.: Neurophysiological age differences during task- performance in a stereoscopic virtual environment. Appl. Psychophysiol. Biofeedback **30**(3), 233–238 (2005)

63. Maguire, E.A., Burke, T., Phillips, J., Staunton, H.: Topographical disorientation following unilateral temporal lobe lesions in humans. Neuropsychologia **34**(10), 993–1001 (1996)

64. Maurer, L.K., Maurer, H., Müller, H.: Neural correlates of error prediction in a complex motor task. Front. Behav. Neurosci. **9**, 209 (2015)

65. Menezes, M., et al.: Towards emotion recognition for virtual environments: an evaluation of EEG features on benchmark dataset. Pers. Ubiquit. Comput. **21**(6), 1003–1013 (2017)

66. Mertens, R., Allen, J.J.: The role of psychophysiology in forensic assessments: deception detection, ERPs, and virtual reality mock crime scenarios. Psychophysiology **45**(2), 286–298 (2008)

67. Neubauer, A.C., Bergner, S., Schatz, M.: Two-vs. three-dimensional presentation of mental rotation tasks: sex differences and effects of training on performance and brain activation. Intelligence **38**(5), 529–539 (2010)

68. Nguyen, H.M., Matsumoto, J., Tran, A.H., Ono, T., Nishijo, H.: sLORETA current source density analysis of evoked potentials for spatial updating in a virtual navigation task. Front. Behav. Neurosci. **8**, 66 (2014)

69. Nishiyama, N., Mizuhara, H., Miwakeichi, F., Yamaguchi, Y.: Theta episodes observed in human scalp EEG during virtual navigation-spatial distribution and task dependence. In: Proceedings of the 9th International Conference on Neural Information Processing, 2002. ICONIP 2002, pp. 428–432. IEEE (2002)

70. Nunez, P.L., Srinivasan, R.: Electric Fields of the Brain: The Neurophysics of EEG. Oxford University Press, USA (2006)

71. Occhialini, M., Bernardini, G., Ferracuti, F., Iarlori, S., D'Orazio, M., Longhi, S.: Fire exit signs: the use of neurological activity analysis for quantitative evaluations on their perceptiveness in a virtual environment. Fire Saf. J. **82**, 63–75 (2016)

72. Pacheco, T.B.F., Oliveira Rego, I.A., Campos, T.F., Cavalcanti, F.A.D.C.: Brain activity during a lower limb functional task in a real and virtual environment: a comparative study. NeuroRehabilitation **40**(3), 391–400 (2017)

73. Parasuraman, R., Sheridan, T.B., Wickens, C.D.: Situation awareness, mental workload, and trust in automation: viable, empirically supported cognitive engineering constructs. J. Cognit. Eng. Decis. Making **2**(2), 140–160 (2008)

74. Park, H.-D., Bernasconi, F., Bello-Ruiz, J., Pfeiffer, C., Salomon, R., Blanke, O.: Transient modulations of neural responses to heartbeats covary with bodily self-consciousness. J. Neurosci. **36**(32), 8453–8460 (2016)

75. Pavone, E.F., Tieri, G., Rizza, G., Tidoni, E., Grisoni, L., Aglioti, S.M.: Embodying others in immersive virtual reality: electro-cortical signatures of monitoring the errors in the actions of an avatar seen from a first-person perspective. J. Neurosci. **36**(2), 268–279 (2016)

76. Petras, K., ten Oever, S., Jansma, B.M.: The effect of distance on moral engagement: event related potentials and alpha power are sensitive to perspective in a virtual shooting task. Front. Psychol. **6**, 2008 (2016)

77. Plank, M., Snider, J., Kaestner, E., Halgren, E., Poizner, H.: neurocognitive stages of spatial cognitive mapping measured during free exploration of a large-scale virtual environment. J. Neurophysiol. **113**(3), 740–753 (2014)

78. Potts, G.F., Patel, S.H., Azzam, P.N.: Impact of instructed relevance on the visual ERP. Int. J. Psychophysiol. **52**(2), 197–209 (2004)

79. Pugnetti, L., Meehan, M., Mendozzi, L.: Psychophysiological correlates of virtual reality: a review. Presence: Teleoper. Virtual Environ. **10**(4), 384–400 (2001)

80. Riccio, G.E., Stoffregen, T.A.: An ecological theory of motion sickness and postural instability. Ecol. Psychol. **3**(3), 195–240 (1991)

81. Rodríguez, A., Rey, B., Clemente, M., Wrzesien, M., Alcañiz, M.: Assessing brain activations associated with emotional regulation during virtual reality mood induction procedures. Exp. Syst. Appl. **42**(3), 1699–1709 (2015)

82. Saproo, S., Shih, V., Jangraw, D.C., Sajda, P.: Neural mechanisms underlying catastrophic failure in human–machine interaction during aerial navigation. J. Neural Eng. **13**(6), 066005 (2016)

83. Saravanamoorthi, A., Banu, R.W.: EEG spectrum analysis of various electrodes from sleep stages of detection and drowsiness with monitoring driving performance of estimation control system. Asian J. Inf. Technol. **13**(10), 618–626 (2014)

84. Schultze, U.: Embodiment and presence in virtual worlds: a review. J. Inf. Technol. **25**(4), 434–449 (2010)

85. Seeling, P.: Image quality in augmented binocular vision: QoE approximations with QoS and EEG. Periodica Polytechnica. Electr. Eng. Comput. Sci. **61**(4), 327 (2017)

86. Sella, I., Reiner, M., Pratt, H.: Natural stimuli from three coherent modalities enhance behavioral responses and electrophysiological cortical activity in humans. Int. J. Psychophysiol. **93**(1), 45–55 (2014)

87. Senkowski, D., Talsma, D., Grigutsch, M., Herrmann, C.S., Woldorff, M.G.: Good times for multisensory integration: effects of the precision of temporal synchrony as revealed by gamma- band oscillations. Neuropsychologia **45**(3), 561–571 (2007)

88. Serino, A., et al.: Tuning of temporo-occipital activity by frontal oscillations during virtual mirror exposure causes erroneous self-recognition. Eur. J. Neurosci. **42**(8), 2515–2526 (2015)

89. Sharma, G., Kaushal, Y., Chandra, S., Singh, V., Mittal, A.P., Dutt, V.: Influence of landmarks on wayfinding and brain connectivity in immersive virtual reality environment. Front. Psychol. **8**, 1220 (2017)

90. Sharma, G., Salam, A.A., Chandra, S., Singh, V., Mittal, A.: Influence of spatial learning perspectives on navigation through virtual reality environment. In: Ascoli, G.A., Hawrylycz, M., Ali, H., Khazanchi, D., Shi, Y. (eds.) BIH 2016. LNCS (LNAI), vol. 9919, pp. 346–354. Springer, Cham (2016). https://doi.org/10.1007/978-3-319-47103-7_34

91. Sharma, G., Singh, V., Daniel, R.V., Mittal, A.P., Chandra, S.: Brain connectivity in spatial orientation task. In: Proceedings of the International Conference on Emerging Trends in Communication Technologies, pp. 1–4. IEEE (2016)
92. Shemesh, A., Talmon, R., Karp, O., Amir, I., Bar, M., Grobman, Y.J.: Affective response to architecture-investigating human reaction to spaces with different geometry. Archit. Sci. Rev. **60**(2), 116–125 (2017)
93. Simões, M., Amaral, C., Carvalho, P., Castelo-Branco, M.: Specific EEG/ERP responses to dynamic facial expressions in virtual reality environments. In: The International Conference on Health Informatics, pp. 331–334. Springer (2014). https://doi.org/10.1007/978-3-319-03005-0_84
94. Škola, F., Liarokapis, F.: Examining the effect of body ownership in immersive virtual and augmented reality environments. Vis. Comput. **32**(6–8), 761–770 (2016). https://doi.org/10.1007/s00371-016-1246-8
95. Slobounov, S.M., Ray, W., Johnson, B., Slobounov, E., Newell, K.M.: Modulation of cortical activity in 2D versus 3D virtual reality environments: an EEG study. Int. J. Psychophysiol. **95**(3), 254–260 (2015)
96. Slobounov, S.M., Teel, E., Newell, K.M.: Modulation of cortical activity in response to visually induced postural perturbation: combined VR and EEG study. Neurosci. Lett. **547**, 6–9 (2013)
97. Snider, J., Ahmed, O.J., Halgren, E., Poizner, H., Cash, S.S.: Human intracranial recordings during spatial exploration of a 3D virtual environment. In: 2013 6th International IEEE/EMBS Conference on Neural Engineering (NER), pp. 464–467. IEEE (2013)
98. Stanney, K.M., Kingdon, K.S., Graeber, D., Kennedy, R.S.: Human performance in immersive virtual environments: effects of exposure duration, user control, and scene complexity. Hum. Perform. **15**(4), 339–366 (2002)
99. Steed, A., Pan, Y., Zisch, F., Steptoe, W.: The impact of a self-avatar on cognitive load in immersive virtual reality. In: 2016 IEEE Virtual Reality Conference (Vr), pp. 67–76. IEEE (2016)
100. Teplan, M.: Fundamentals of EEG measurement. Meas. Sci. Rev. **2**(2), 1–11 (2002)
101. de Tommaso, M., et al.: Testing a novel method for improving wayfinding by means of a P3b virtual reality visual paradigm in normal aging. Springerplus **5**(1), 1–12 (2016). https://doi.org/10.1186/s40064-016-2978-7
102. Tromp, J., Peeters, D., Meyer, A.S., Hagoort, P.: The combined use of virtual reality and EEG to study language processing in naturalistic environments. Behav. Res. Methods **50**(2), 862–869 (2018)
103. Vavrečka, M., Gerla, V., Lhotska, L., Brunovský, M.: Frames of reference and their neural correlates within navigation in a 3D environment. Vis. Neurosci. **29**(3), 183–191 (2012)
104. Vecchiato, G., Tieri, G., Jelic, A., De Matteis, F., Maglione, A.G., Babiloni, F.: Electroencephalographic correlates of sensorimotor integration and embodiment during the appreciation of virtual architectural environments. Front. Psychol. **6**, 1944 (2015)
105. Vidugiriene, A., Vaskevicius, E., Kaminskas, V.: Modeling of affective state response to a virtual 3D face. In: Modelling Symposium (EMS), 2013 European, pp. 175–180. IEEE (2013)
106. Vogt, T., Herpers, R., Askew, C.D., Scherfgen, D., Strüder, H.K., Schneider, S.: Effects of exercise in immersive virtual environments on cortical neural oscillations and mental state. Neural Plasticity **2015** (2015)
107. Vogt, T., Herpers, R., Scherfgen, D., Strüder, H.K., Schneider, S.: Neuroelectric adaptations to cognitive processing in virtual environments: an exercise-related approach. Exp. Brain Res. **233**(4), 1321–1329 (2015)
108. Wamain, Y., Gabrielli, F., Coello, Y.: EEG μ rhythm in virtual reality reveals that motor coding of visual objects in peripersonal space is task dependent. Cortex **74**, 20–30 (2016)

109. Webster, J., Watson, R.T.: Analyzing the past to prepare for the future: writing a literature review. MIS Q. **26**(2), 13–23 (2002)
110. White, D.J., Congedo, M., Ciorciari, J., Silberstein, R.B.: Brain oscillatory activity during spatial navigation: theta and gamma activity link medial temporal and parietal regions. J. Cogn. Neurosci. **24**(3), 686–697 (2012)
111. Wiederhold, B., Riva, G.: Measuring presence during the navigation in a virtual environment using EEG. Ann. Rev. Cyberther. Telemed. **191**, 136–140 (2013)
112. Witmer, B.G., Singer, M.J.: Measuring presence in virtual environments: a presence questionnaire. Presence **7**(3), 225–240 (1998)
113. Wrzesien, M., Rodríguez, A., Rey, B., Alcañiz, M., Baños, R.M., Vara, M.D.: How the physical similarity of avatars can influence the learning of emotion regulation strategies in teenagers. Comput. Hum. Behav. **43**, 101–111 (2015)
114. Xu, J., Zhong, B.: Review on portable EEG technology in educational research. Comput. Hum. Behav. **81**, 340–349 (2018)
115. Yamamoto, S., Miyashita, H., Miyata, A., Hayashi, M., Okada, K.: Basic experiment for switching difficulty in virtual environment. In: Proceedings of the 3rd International Conference on Human Computer Interaction, pp. 49–56. ACTA Press (2008)
116. Yang, S.-R., Chen, S.-A., Tsai, S.-F., Lin, C.-T.: Transcutaneous electrical nerve stimulation system for improvement of flight orientation in a VR-based motion environment. In: 2012 IEEE International Symposium on Circuits and Systems (ISCAS), pp. 2055–2058. IEEE (2012)
117. Zacharis, G.K., Mikropoulos, T.A., Kalyvioti, K.: Cognitive load and attentional demands during objects' position change in real and digital environments. Themes Sci. Technol. Educ. **9**(2), 83–91 (2017)
118. Zhang, S., Zhang, Y., Sun, Y., Thakor, N., Bezerianos, A.: Graph theoretical analysis of EEG functional network during multi-workload flight simulation experiment in virtual reality environment. In: 2017 39th Annual International Conference of the IEEE Engineering in Medicine and Biology Society (EMBC), pp. 3957–3960. IEEE (2017)

Physiological Measuring and Human Performance

Cognitive Workload Quantified by Physiological Sensors in Realistic Immersive Settings

Ashley Bishop, Emma MacNeil, and Kurtulus Izzetoglu[✉]

School of Biomedical Engineering, Science and Health Systems, Drexel University, Philadelphia, USA
{amb688,ki25}@drexel.edu

Abstract. Cognitive workload changes have been studied and utilized as a means of assessment for engagement and learner's performance during training. Yet, it is unclear how varying levels of simulator immersion affect learner cognitive workload. Wearable sensors allow us to monitor direct physiological changes associated with cognitive workload in real time. This study seeks to utilize multiple physiological and neurological measures: functional near-infrared spectroscopy (fNIRS), eye-tracking, electrodermal activity (EDA), heart rate, and respiratory rate; in order to assess cognitive workload changes during different training conditions. The National Aeronautics and Space Administration's (NASA) Task Load Index (TLX) and flow state scale questionnaires were additionally used to record self-reported cognitive workload and subjective experience. Nine law enforcement trainees participated in different immersions conditions in a law enforcement use-of-force (UOF) simulator. Results from a low immersion condition were compared to results from a high immersion condition. Preliminary comparison between these two conditions suggests that the Index of Cognitive Activity (ICA) and respiration rate were greater in the low immersion condition. However, a notable increase in the oxygenated hemoglobin of the right anterior medial prefrontal cortex was detected via fNIRS. Heart rate also increased between the two conditions. Traditional questionnaires used to measure cognitive load showed no significance between conditions. Compared to self-report subjective metrics, biometrics such as fNIRS were operationally more effective at smaller sample sizes. Not only do these results show that features associated with trainees' workload can viably be collected in realistic simulator settings, but they also suggest that increased immersion in law enforcement simulators may have a measurable effect on biometrics associated with cognitive workload.

Keywords: Human performance · Training · Cognitive workload · Biometrics · fNIRS · Eye-tracking · Electrodermal activity · EDA · Heart rate · Respiratory rate

© Springer Nature Switzerland AG 2021
D. D. Schmorrow and C. M. Fidopiastis (Eds.): HCII 2021, LNAI 12776, pp. 119–133, 2021.
https://doi.org/10.1007/978-3-030-78114-9_9

1 Introduction

1.1 Background

A fundamental part of law enforcement training involves the use of force commensurate with the totality of the circumstances faced by the officer or agent. The decisions surrounding the use of force can be complex and must often be made quickly in suboptimal settings. To train and facilitate UOF decision making skills (including de-escalation) – both for novice trainees in basic programs and active officers in specialized or in-service training – many law enforcement training organizations employ video-based simulators capable of presenting realistic scenarios to which trainees respond. These simulators vary in degrees of convenience and portability as well as in sophistication and realistic immersion. At one end of the spectrum are portable systems projecting video scenarios onto a single live-sized screen; at the other end are "theater" styled systems that immerse trainees with up to 300° of both visual and auditory environments. Besides the initial cost differences between simpler and more complex systems, the latter often require not only a greater physical space but also additional sound isolation when multiple systems are installed in close proximity. While the cost of a training system is a significant factor for all law enforcement organizations, it must be balanced against training needs, such as the intended outcomes of the training, training efficacy and required throughput of trainees. One critical, high-level decision point then becomes whether an investment in larger, immersive systems is warranted for a particular training mission. Financial and logistic cost-benefit analyses can typically be carried out using pre-existing agency information. However, assessment of the efficacy of a training system should consider not only traditional measures of training outcomes but should also account for method-specific advantages a particular mode of training may offer.

Advances in the measurement of physiological and neurological phenomena, such as EDA, pupil dilation, and local oxygenation changes in the brain bring promising new assessment alternatives within reach for traditional training operations. For example, constructs such as cognitive workload during the execution of learned skills may be added to both formative and summative assessments in practical training programs leading to operational readiness. It is also reasonable to explore practical means of measurement of workload that can, not only be implemented into existing training paradigms, but also be used to more objectively evaluate alternatives in training systems or methods. Our study investigates the feasibility and efficacy of multiple objective physiological and neurological measures to detect differences in workload between two extreme levels of UOF simulator immersion.

Law enforcement officers engage in various training courses including the use of a wide range of simulators. Simulators allow law enforcement training providers to create realistic and repeatable scenarios, while minimizing costs and resource utilization over time. However, traditional assessment methods for tracking training progress may not fully capitalize on the benefits that new training methods and technologies may offer. Measurement of cognitive workload changes during training could offer additional insight to the monitoring of trainees' expertise development toward operational readiness.

One way to define cognitive workload is as an interaction between task requirements and human capabilities or resources [1, 2]. In this interaction, workload involves the objective effects of task difficulty on the participant, and the participant's effort while engaged in maintaining performance. That is, workload can be defined in terms of some objective criteria for task difficulty (e.g., an air traffic controller managing 6 versus 12 planes), or in terms of the participant's capability to perform the identified task. Another perspective of cognitive workload is a conglomeration of demands placed on cognitive, perceptual, and neurophysiological processes [3]. Such demands elicit activation of these neurophysiological pathways that can then be measured. Objective criteria for task difficulty and task demand also call for reliable assessment of the performance that is required to execute a particular mission. Measurement of mental load or neural reserve is key in such an objective assessment as simply observed performance may not reflect the true cognitive workload. For instance, two operators can complete the same task with similar observed performance. However, one of them may have utilized significant cognitive resources to reach that level of performance and has no further resources to allocate, compared to the other operator who may have a greater reserve cognitive capacity. When a dynamic situation demands processing new information and alteration of a chosen action strategy, the former operator would have to reallocate cognitive efforts, increasing the likelihood of mission failure, while the latter operator could maintain skill performance while simultaneously processing the new information.

A common method for assessing cognitive load is through psychometric instruments such as the NASA TLX [4]. This and other psychometric tools have been used to show varying levels of cognitive workload between novice and expert groups [5]. Psychometric instruments for measuring cognitive workload primarily capture the participants' subjective experience through recall and post hoc self-reflection with some degree of lag between the performance event and the completion of the questionnaire. Though commonly used for medical training, these types of psychometric tools could also be leveraged in law enforcement UOF training to determine cognitive load of the trainees. They tend to be relatively easy to administer and score and require little specialized equipment beyond paper and a pencil. It is reasonable to include these types of metrics to attempt to differentiate cognitive load under different UOF training conditions, where cognitive load is altered, for example by increasing the audiovisual information presented to trainees.

1.2 Physiological Biomarkers of Cognitive Workload

Advances in functional brain activity monitoring techniques have taken place over the last two decades, and in particular their deployment in simulation-based training and real-world field studies to support performance assessment metrics in both aerospace and medical domains [6–8]. In general, increased brain activity raises the metabolic demand of neurons, leading to local increases in oxygenated hemoglobin. Near-infrared light can be utilized to measure concentration changes in oxygenated and deoxygenated blood hemoglobin levels by applying a modified Beer-Lambert Law [9]. The modified Beer-Lambert law provides an empirical description of how light propagates differentially in tissue, depending on relative hemoglobin concentrations. These principles are applied when using a continuous wave fNIRS device to quantify brain activity in the prefrontal cortex (PFC). Studies have utilized fNIRS to demonstrate hemodynamic responses in the PFC due to cognitive workload in multitasking environments, such as unmanned aerial pilot training or medical personnel training [7, 10].

Studies have similarly shown a connection between the sympathetic nervous system (SNS), the system responsible for a body's "flight or fight" response, and EDA of the skin. This connection exists because the neurons that control the sweat glands in the skin are part of the SNS; when the SNS becomes active, these innervating neurons are activated and cause changes in the conductivity of the skin [11]. Studies have also shown that continuous mental activity, such as solving arithmetic problems, increase the frequency of skin conductance responses (SCR). SCRs are measured as phasic increases in skin conductance and can be measured by two electrodes placed on the skin [11].

A third candidate for measuring cognitive load focuses on fluctuations in pupil size. Pupillometry has been used for many years as a measure of cognitive load because cognitive load can be reflected in pupil size [12]. Because levels of ambient light are also reflected in pupil size, a reliable inference of cognitive workload from this measure can be challenging. However, the ICA measures the small, rapid changes in pupil size that are attributed to cognitive load, while simultaneously accounting for the pupil dilations that occur from the light reflex, which are larger and slower [13]. Various studies have suggested that ICA is sensitive to facets of cognitive load, such as language processing, mental demands of a task, and overlapping tasks [14].

Heart rate (HR), and more specifically heart rate variability (HRV), has been implicated as an indicator of psychological and emotional stress [15]. While more research needs to be conducted to further explore and explain the use of HRV as a measure of cognitive load, Thayer et al. [16] report the possibility of measurable HR changes as a result of PFC activation.

Extensive research has also been conducted on the effects that cognitive load has on respiration-based biomarkers such as respiration rate (RR). For example, a review paper reported 54 journal articles containing some component linking cognitive workload to respiration factors [17]. The consensus of the reviewed papers showed that respiration rate tended to rise with increasing cognitive workload.

Combining these biomarkers in the form of wearable sensors could give an in-depth analysis of the cognitive load of trainees' experience during training, such as when practicing UOF scenarios. Given that measures of most of the suggested biomarkers appear to increase in magnitude during informationally dense tasks, it can be hypothesized here that the same relationship will occur in UOF situations that presumably increase mental effort by increasing audiovisual immersion.

2 Methodology

2.1 Participants

Nine law enforcement trainees between the ages of 21 to 31 volunteered to participate in the study. These trainees were recruited with the help of the Federal Law Enforcement Training Centers.

2.2   Sensors and Simulators Used

The UOF training task was displayed to participants using the MILORange Theater 300 system (FAAC Incorporated, Ann Arbor, Michigan). UOF scenarios were pre-recorded, branching videos streamed on HD screens. The scenarios are included with the MILO-Range Theater system. Participants were equipped with a duty belt holding a holstered laser-emitting pistol and were instructed to respond to the scenarios according to their training as if in real life. Depending on the scenario, they could engage verbally to deescalate the situation, give commands, or respond to sudden threats using the simulation pistol. The simulation pistol emits a coded infrared laser pulse when fired. Shots, including locations, are tracked by sensors calibrated to each screen. An instructor was present to operate the simulator and control the scenario branching depending on each participant's actions. Two screening conditions were used to maximize the difference in the amount of audiovisual immersion and information presented to the participants. The first screening configuration consisted of a singular screen in front of the participant with a single hidden speaker behind the screen. The second arrangement entailed the use of five screens, each with its own hidden speaker and audio channel, as shown in Fig. 1.

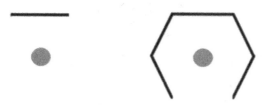

Fig. 1. Diagram of the screen layout for one screen (left) and five screen (right) conditions. The red circle indicates the location of the subject relative to the UOF simulator screen(s). (Color figure online)

Four wearable sensors were used for physiological data collection. Neurological data, monitoring oxygenation in the prefrontal cortex, was captured by an 18-optode fNIR Devices 2000M (fNIR Devices LLC, Potomac, MD) headband operated with LED wavelengths at 730 nm and 850 nm and a sampling frequency of 10 Hz. A pair of Dikablis 3 glasses (Ergoneers, Portland, OR) recorded pupil dilation at 60 Hz. The pupil dilation data was streamed to WorkloadRT software (EyeTracking Inc., San Diego, CA) to calculate ICA. ICA values were computed on a scale from 0 to 1 by a proprietary wavelet analysis [18, 19]. This wavelet analysis accounts for natural light reflexes of the pupil when measuring changes. The eye tracking system reported the ICA wavelet coefficients as a moving average in both the left and right eye at 1 Hz. EDA was measured as micro-Siemens by an E4 wristband (Empatica Inc., Boston, MA) at a frequency of 4 Hz. The wristband was placed on the participant's non-dominant hand just below the wrist and positioned so that two silver (Ag) electrodes aligned between the index and middle finger [20]. Lastly, a Hexoskin wearable garment measured both heart rate and respiration at 1 Hz. Prior to use, the textile electrodes found on the shirt were moistened with a water-based gel. Participants were instructed to wear the garment snug so that the electrodes had close skin contact. Figure 2 displays the collection of sensors used.

124 A. Bishop et al.

Participants were given two questionnaires after each screening condition to gauge subjective measures of cognitive load and feeling of psychological flow. The NASA TLX questionnaire was used to address self-reported cognitive load and produced an overall score based on six scoring factors: mental demand, physical demand, temporal demand, performance, effort, and frustration [21]. Participants were also instructed to fill out a flow state scale [22] to measure subjective feelings of psychological flow for potential use as a discriminant measure.

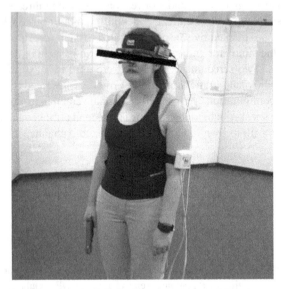

Fig. 2. Example of how the physiological sensors were positioned on each participant.

2.3 Scenarios and Protocol

Figure 3 shows the approximate timeline for the experimental protocol of each subject. Prior to each screening condition, a baseline recording of at least two minutes was acquired to attenuate the effects of the previous condition and for initial sensor calibration. During the screening conditions, participants responded to three or four UOF scenarios to interact with by verbally responding to live action prompts or through engagement with an simulation pistol. The scenarios ranged from simple trespassing to persons in crisis to homicide and were grouped to provide similar total session lengths. The scenarios were not repeated for any participant, ensuring novelty of content regardless of screening condition. The order of screening conditions was counterbalanced among participants. The simulator was operated in a darkened environment to control ambient light conditions and increase salience of the simulator environment. After each screening condition, participants were instructed to complete a series of self-report questionnaires to subjectively report sense of immersion.

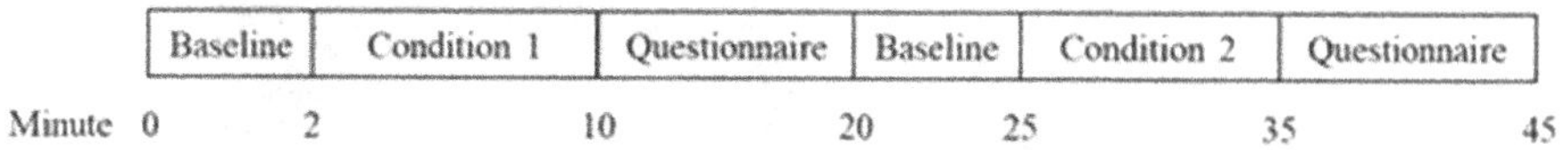

Baseline	Condition 1	Questionnaire	Baseline	Condition 2	Questionnaire

Minute 0   2   10   20   25   35   45

Fig. 3. Timeline of the experimental protocol. Condition 1 corresponds to one screen, and Condition 2 corresponds to the five-screen trial.

2.4 Data Analysis

HR and RR averages were calculated for each timestamp among subjects for each screening condition. The outliers due to instrumentation and/or errors in sensor placement were teased out across subjects using a simple approach in this preliminary study, that is to calculate levels by using 2.5 times of standard deviations.

Analysis of the EDA data was conducted using a MATLAB software package called Ledalab [23], to extract the frequency of non-specific skin conductance responses (NS-SCRs) during each screen condition recording. Before calculating the frequency of NS-SCRs, major artifacts that could have resulted from loose electrode contact or significant movement were removed manually [24]. Signals were then subjected to a discrete decomposition analysis utilizing nonnegative devolution as outlined by Benedek & Kaernback [25] to find the number of NS-SCRs. A threshold of 0.05 μS was used to determine NS-SCRs [26]. Frequency of NS-SCRs was calculated by dividing the number of NS-SCRs in a recording by the recording time.

The level of ICA in both the left and right eyes were determined independently by recording the median value at each sampling point across the participants. The median of the average ICA values was used to account for possible skewness in the data. The average of the medians was then calculated to obtain the ICA magnitude across participants for each screening condition.

fNIRS measures are susceptible to motion artifacts, and physiological and instrument noise. Hence, multiple signal pre-processing techniques for artifact removal were applied: First, the signal was corrected for ambient light leakage by simply subtracting dark current signal (also known as a reference signal for measures of artifact) from the other raw light intensity measures acquired for two light sources (730 nm, and 850 nm). The signals were then filtered with a cutoff frequency of 0.09 Hz to remove instrument noise and physiological noise, such as cardiac output and respiration [27, 28]. Using the modified Beer-Lambert Law, the oxygenated (HbO) and deoxygenated-hemoglobin (Hb) changes at each channel were calculated [29]. Finally, oxygenation (HbO-Hb) changes and total hemoglobin (HbT = HbO + Hb) were calculated. Oxygenation changes were calculated for each quadrant of the PFC from left to right: left dorsolateral PFC (DLPFC), left anterior medial PFC (AMPFC), right AMPFC, right DLPFC (see Fig. 4).

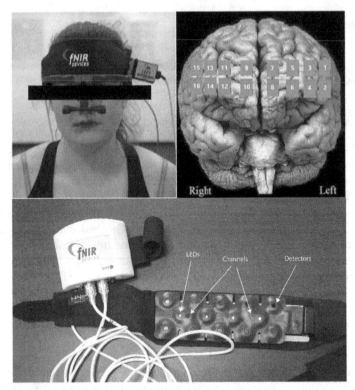

Fig. 4. 18-channel fNIRS sensor with sensor placement of LEDs, detectors, and optode locations on participant PFC areas. Left Dorsolateral PFC (Left DLPFC: optodes 1–4). Left Anterior Medial PFC (Left AMPFC: optodes 5–8). Right Anterior Medial PFC (Right AMPFC: optodes 9–12). Right Dorsolateral PFC (Right DLPFC: optodes 13–16). Image of optode locations (1–16; top right) is adapted from [36].

3   Results

Data for each analysis were evaluated for assumptions underlying typical statistical inference tests. Adjustments to the analyses resulting from violation of such assumptions are noted below.

3.1   Self-report Questionnaires

Mean total scores for NASA TLX and the Flow State Scale were compared across immersion levels (see Table 1). No statistically significant differences were found.

3.2   Functional Near-Infrared Spectroscopy

The Shapiro-Wilk test was used to test our sample data for normality. This test was chosen for having the best power for small samples [30]. The test indicated the focal fNIRS value distributions were non-normal. For this reason and given the low sample size,

Table 1. Sample descriptives and means comparison (t-test) for questionnaires.

	n	1 Screen		2 Screens		df	t
		Mean	SD	Mean	SD		
NASA TLX	9	10.89	2.26	11.22	3.38	8	−.236[1]
Flow state	9	134.78	17.25	133.11	18.88	8	.414[1]

[1]Not significant

the Wilcoxon Signed-Rank test was chosen to evaluate differences between immersion levels. The tests indicated statistically significantly higher levels of oxygenation in 3 of the 4 focal areas of the PFC when participants trained in the high immersion/5-screen condition as compared to the low immersion/1-screen condition (see Table 2).

Table 2. Wilcoxon Signed-Rank tests for PFC oxygenation across levels of immersion.

	Negative ranks			Positive ranks			Ties	Z
	n	Mean rank	Sum of ranks	n	Mean rank	Sum of ranks		
Left DLPFC (1–5 screens)	12	6.5	78	0	0	0	0	−3.09**
Right DLPFC (1–5 screens)	10	7.5	75	2	1.5	3	0	−2.85**
Left AMPFC (1–5 screens)	4	6.5	26	4	2.5	10	0	−1.14
Right AMPFC (1–5 screens)	6	5.5	33	2	1.5	3	0	−2.13*

* p<.05
**p<.01

3.3   Other Physiological Measures

Heart rate differences between the two screening conditions were found to be statistically significant, increasing from the one-screen condition to the five-screen condition. On the other hand, respiration decreased significantly from the one-screen condition to the five-screen condition.

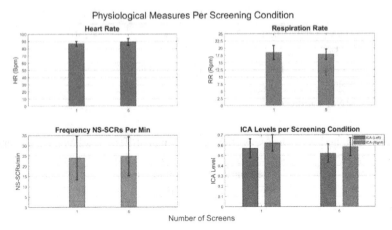

Fig. 5. Relationship of four physiological biomarkers across the multiple screening conditions: heart rate (top left), respiration rate (top right), frequency of NS-SCRs per min (bottom left), and ICA (bottom right). ICA represent both the left (blue) and right (red) eyes. Error bars represent one standard deviation from the mean reported in Table 3. (Color figure online)

Table 3. Sample descriptives and means comparison (t-test) for physiological data.

Biomarker		n	1 Screen		5 Screens		df	t
			Mean	SD	Mean	SD		
HR		446	86.70	3.26	87.66	4.59	445	2.305[**]
RR		442	18.49	2.42	17.84	1.76	441	5.734[**]
NS-SCRs†		6	23.89	10.59	24.81	9.44	5	−0.264
ICA	Left	85	0.57	0.09	0.52	0.09	84	3.476[**]
	Right	82	0.62	0.08	0.58	0.09	81	2.687[**]

† Samples per min.
** p < 0.01.

Although average frequency of NS-SCRs appeared to increase between the one screen and five screen conditions (see Fig. 5), this difference was not statistically significant, as noted in Table 3. The frequencies of NS-SCRs are, however, in the expected range of more than 20 NS-SCRs per min for arousal, as suggested by Visnovcova, et al. [31].

Analysis of ICA showed a statistically significant decrease in both the left and right eyes from the one screen condition to the five-screen condition, as depicted in Fig. 5 and reported in Table 3.

4 Discussion

Training efficacy is an important factor in cost-benefit analyses for training programs. The organizations, such as law enforcement training or military training centers often use UOF and other simulators to engage trainees through realistic immersion. Trainees are sometimes evaluated using checklists and rubrics but may also undergo simulator training to gain repeated experiences in situations that may be challenging or prohibitively resource intensive to re-create in real life. However, the current metrics for operational readiness, if used, do not appear to incorporate cognitive workload. Further attempts to use measures of cognitive workload to evaluate instructional methods or technologies in an operational (for training organizations) environment are also needed. While our data collection was paused due to unforeseen external restrictions (related to the COVID-19 pandemic), similarly sized samples may be all that modest training operations can provide. Our preliminary study with small sample size shows that despite limitations, measurement of constructs like cognitive workload is feasible in operational contexts using commercially available, wearable sensors.

4.1 Cognitive Load via Self-report Questionnaires

Results from comparisons of the total scores for both the NASA TLX and the Flow State Scale indicated no statistically discernible change in cognitive workload or subjective experience between the one-screen and five-screen UOF conditions. A plausible explanation for this is the lack of statistical power given the small sample size. The NASA TLX has been shown to be a valid and sensitive instrument for measuring subjective cognitive workload [32]. As such, it is appropriate for numerous purposes. However, when only small samples may be obtained, it may lack the power to detect small to moderate effects.

The Flow State Scale was included here in an exploratory fashion for evaluation as a possible measure in future validation studies. It too appears to have suffered from a low sample size. However, unlike our measurement of cognitive workload which yielded some statistically significant results with other measures, the Flow State Scale was the only measurement of that construct in our study. It is possible that altering the level of audiovisual immersion simply has no meaningful effect on flow. Any studies of effects on psychological flow in similar settings, and the implications thereof, should strive to substantially increase the sample size. While psychometrically sound, measures of flow still aim to quantify highly subjective experiences which may have complex and unexpected relationships with more traditional evaluation constructs [22, 33]. Operationally, it may become difficult to acquire sample sizes that are sufficient to provide enough statistical power to have meaningful results. Thus, physiological metrics such, as fNIRS and HR, were also analyzed in this study to observe changes in cognitive load as a function of audiovisual immersion.

4.2 Cognitive Load via Biometrics

We observed statistically significantly increased oxygenation between the one-screen and five-screen conditions in three of the four PFC quadrants acquired by the fNIRS.

Caution is warranted in interpreting any regional differentiation based on our limited data. However, any change in PFC activation as a result of altering a training parameter should be of interest to training providers. With additional data, further validation of operational fNIRS measurement coupled with findings from functional differentiation by spatial analysis, such as attention or decision making [34], may offer training professionals insights on training and higher-order skills previously not attainable.

Compared to self-report questionnaires, we were able to use fNIRS to detect changes in cognitive load with only a small number of participants. Further experimentation with a larger sample size should be conducted to confirm these preliminary findings. However, it appears feasible to use fNIRS to collect sufficient data from even a small sample in a realistic training setting to evaluate the effect that different delivery methods or systems may have on the cognitive workload of trainees – even when the trained task remains the same.

Indications of cognitive workload varied among the physiological biomarkers between the two levels of audiovisual immersion analyzed. The reported statistically significant changes in HR supported the hypothesis that more information presented to the trainee would lead to a higher HR. Other studies have also showed increasing heart rate in response to cognitive tasks, such as in various Stroop tests [35]. HR monitors are relatively inexpensive and easy to use. More stringent evaluations are warranted of this finding, of what would constitute a meaningful effect size, and whether HR adds incremental value to measurements like fNIRS. However, it again appears feasible to incorporate HR as a practical measurement beyond its traditional use in areas, such as exercise science.

The difference in RR was statistically significant, but also had averages across subjects decrease when comparing the one-screen condition to the five-screen condition. This direction contradicted our expectations and hypothesis, as well as other studies [17] where the expected change for RR is an increase during periods where the participant is expected to experience higher cognitive workload. It is important to note, however, that in this literature review, papers that allowed participants to speak or move were excluded due to possible confounding factors. During UOF training, trainees are expected to engage with the scenario to deescalate a situation. They are also allowed, and expected, to move to a certain degree. Further data collection and studies may facilitate a better understanding of the small, but unexpected difference between conditions. However, the negligible practical differences in RR, despite the number of data points, suggest that this biomarker, even if reliably measured, may not be sensitive enough for inferences of cognitive workload changes due to training parameters.

We expected to see a difference in EDA across conditions, but our results were not statistically significant. One explanation for the lack of significance between the two conditions for this biometric is a possibly modest effect size where the difference between the information presented between the conditions simply did not elicit a differential electrodermal response. Another study experienced similar effects when comparing electrodermal responses between mental activity during a Stroop task and mental arithmetic [31]. Though the frequencies were not found to be statistically significant between the mental tests, a noticeable difference was anecdotally observed between periods of rest and during task performance, warranting further investigation. The obtained standard deviations within conditions are also encouraging for further inclusion in future studies.

The ICA data showed a statistically significant difference between the one-screen and five-screen conditions. However, this difference occurred in the opposite direction from our hypothesis. As the ICA has been successfully used to measure cognitive workload [13, 14], additional research, both in terms of increasing sample size and testing other paradigms, is recommended before any attempts are made to explain our findings.

Several limitations were encountered during this study. Besides the small sample size, one of the most prominent difficulties was that the one-screen and five-screen conditions could not be run on the same simulator. Ideally, using the same simulator throughout the study would control some external factors not accounted for here. However, the simulator used for the five-screen condition was unable to run the scenarios on only one screen. Thus, a separate MILORange simulator had to be used which necessitated physically moving participants to a separate room in the same building between conditions.

References

1. Hancock, P.A., Chignell, M.H.: Toward a theory of mental workload: stress and adaptability in human-machine systems. In: Proceedings of the International IEEE Conference on Systems, Man and Cybernetics, pp. 378–383 (1986)
2. Welford, A.T.: Forty years of experimental psychology in relation to age: retrospect and prospect. Exp. Gerontol. **21**, 469–481 (1986)
3. Baldwin, C.L., Coyne, J.T.: Mental Workload as a Function of Traffic Density: Comparison of Physiological, Behavioral, and Subjective Indices (2003)
4. Hart, S.G., Staveland, L.E.: Development of NASA-TLX (task load index): results of empirical and theoretical research. In: Hancock, P.A., Meshkati, N. (eds.) Advances in Psychology, Human Mental Workload, North-Holland, vol. 52, pp. 139–183 (1988). https://doi.org/10.1016/S0166-4115(08)62386-9
5. Szulewski, A., Gegenfurtner, A., Howes, D.W., Sivilotti, M.L.A., van Merriënboer, J.J.G.: Measuring physician cognitive load: validity evidence for a physiologic and a psychometric tool. Adv. Health Sci. Educ. **22**(4), 951–968 (2016). https://doi.org/10.1007/s10459-016-9725-2
6. Aksoy, E., Izzetoglu, K., Baysoy, E., Agrali, A., Kitapcioglu, D., Onaral, B.: Performance monitoring via functional near infrared spectroscopy for virtual reality based basic life support training. Front. Neurosci. **13**, 1336 (2019). https://doi.org/10.3389/fnins.2019.01336
7. Shewokis, P.A., Shariff, F.U., Liu, Y., Ayaz, H., Castellanos, A., Lind, D.S.: Acquisition, retention and transfer of simulated laparoscopic tasks using fNIR and a contextual interference paradigm. Am. J. Surg. **213**(2), 336–345 (2017). https://doi.org/10.1016/j.amjsurg.2016.11.043
8. Izzetoglu, K., et al.: The evolution of field deployable fNIR spectroscopy from bench to clinical settings. J. Innov. Opt. Health Sci. **4**(3), 239–250 (2011). https://doi.org/10.1142/S1793545811001587
9. Strangman, G., Boas, D., Sutton, J.: Non-invasive neuroimaging using near-infrared light. Biol. Psychiat. **52**(7), 679–693 (2002)
10. Izzetoglu, K., et al.: UAV operators workload assessment by optical brain imaging technology (fNIR). In: Valavanis, K.P., Vachtsevanos, G.J. (eds.) Handbook of Unmanned Aerial Vehicles, pp. 2475–2500. Springer, Dordrecht (2015). https://doi.org/10.1007/978-90-481-9707-1_22

11. Dawson, M.E., Schell, A.M., Filion, D.L.: The electrodermal system. In: Cacioppo, J.T., Tassinary, L.G., Berntson, G.G. (eds.) Cambridge Handbooks in Psychology, pp. 200–223. Cambridge University Press, Handbook of psychophysiology (2000)

12. Hess, E.H., Polt, J.M.: Pupil size in relation to mental activity during simple problem-solving. Science **143**(3611), 1190–1192 (1964)

13. Demberg, V., Sayeed, A.: The frequency of rapid pupil dilations as a measure of linguistic processing difficulty. PLoS ONE **11**(1), 1–30 (2016)

14. Vogels, J., Demberg, V., Kray, J.: The index of cognitive activity as a measure of cognitive processing load in dual task settings. Front. Psychol. **9**, 1–19 (2018). https://doi.org/10.3389/fpsyg.2018.02276

15. Thayer, J.F., Åhs, F., Fredrikson, M., Sollers, J.J., Wager, T.D.: A meta-analysis of heart rate variability and neuroimaging studies: implications for heart rate variability as a marker of stress and health. Neurosci. Biobehav. Rev. **36**(2), 747–756 (2012). https://doi.org/10.1016/j.neubiorev.2011.11.009

16. Thayer, J.F., Hansen, A.L., Saus-Rose, E., Johnsen, B.H.: Heart rate variability, prefrontal neural function, and cognitive performance: the neurovisceral integration perspective on self-regulation, adaptation, and health. Ann. Behav. Med. **37**(2), 141–153 (2009)

17. Grassmann, M., Vlemincx, E., Von Leupoldt, A., Mittelstädt, J., Den Bergh, O.: Respiratory Changes in Response to Cognitive Load: A Systematic Review. Hindawi Publishing Corporation (2016)

18. Marshall, S.P.: The index of cognitive activity: measuring cognitive workload. In: Proceedings of the IEEE 7th Conference on Human Factors and Power Plants, Scottsdale, AZ, USA, p. 7 (2002)

19. Devos, H., Gustafson, K., Ahmadnezhad, P., Liao, K., Mahnken, J., Brooks, W., Burns, J.: Psychometric properties of NASA-TLX and index of cognitive activity as measures of cognitive workload in older adults. Brain Sci. **10**(12):994 (2020). https://doi.org/10.3390/brainsci10120994

20. Fowles, D., Christie, M., Edelberg, R., Grings, W., Lykken, D., Venables, P.: Publication recommendations for electrodermal measurements. Psychophysiology **18**(3), 232–239 (1981)

21. National Aeronautics and Space Administration. https://humansystems.arc.nasa.gov/groups/tlx/

22. Jackson, S.A., Marsh, H.W.: Development and validation of a scale to measure optimal experience: the flow state scale. J. Sport Exerc. Psychol. **18**(1), 17–35 (1996). https://doi.org/10.1123/jsep.18.1.17

23. Ledalab. http://www.ledalab.de/

24. Boucsein, W.: Electrodermal Activity, 2nd edn. Springer, New York (2012)

25. Benedek, M., Kaernbach, C.: Decomposition of skin conductance data by means of nonnegative deconvolution. Psychophysiology (2010). https://doi.org/10.1111/j.1469-8986.2009.00972.x

26. Boucsein, W., et al.: Publication recommendations for electrodermal measurements. Psychophysiology **49**(8), 1017–1034 (2012). https://doi.org/10.1111/j.1469-8986.2012.01384.x

27. Reddy, P., Richards, D., Izzetoglu, K.: Cognitive performance assessment of UAS sensor operators via neurophysiological measures. Front. Hum. Neurosci. 12 (2018). https://doi.org/10.3389/conf.fnhum.2018.227.00032

28. Kerr, J., Reddy, P., Kosti, S., Izzetoglu, K.: UAS operator workload assessment during search and surveillance tasks through simulated fluctuations in environmental visibility. In: Schmorrow, D.D., Fidopiastis, C.M. (eds.) HCII 2019. LNCS (LNAI), vol. 11580, pp. 394–406. Springer, Cham (2019). https://doi.org/10.1007/978-3-030-22419-6_28

29. Izzetoglu, K., Bunce, S., Onaral, B., Pourrezaei, K., Chance, B.: Functional optical brain imaging using near-infrared during cognitive tasks. Int. J. Hum.-Comput. Interact. **17**(2), 211–227 (2010). https://doi.org/10.1207/s15327590ijhc1702_6

30. Razali, N.M., Wah, Y.B.: Power comparisons of shapiro-wilk, kolmogorov-smirnov, lilliefors and anderson-darling tests. J. Statist. Model. Analyt. **2**(1), 21–33 (2011)
31. Visnovcova, Z., Mestanik, M., Gala, M., Mestanikova, A., Tonhajzerova, I.: The complexity of electrodermal activity is altered in mental cognitive stressors. Comput. Biol. Med. **79**, 123–129 (2016). https://doi.org/10.1016/j.compbiomed.2016.10.014
32. Hill, S., Iavecchia, H., Byers, J., Bittner, A., Zaklad, A., Christ, R.: Comparison of four subjective workload rating scales. Hum. Factors **34**(4), 429–439 (1992). https://doi.org/10.1177/001872089203400405
33. Yoshida, K., et al.: The flow state scale for occupational tasks: development, reliability, and validity. Hong Kong J. Occup. Ther. **23**(2), 54–61 (2013). https://doi.org/10.1016/j.hkjot.2013.09.002
34. Schmitz, T., Johnson, S.: Self-appraisal decisions evoke dissociated dorsal—ventral aMPFC networks. NeuroImage Orlando Fla. **30**(3), 1050–1058 (2006). https://doi.org/10.1016/j.neuroimage.2005.10.030
35. Boutcher, Y.N., Boutcher, S.H.: Cardiovascular response to stroop: effect of verbal response and task difficulty. Biol. Psychol. **73**(3), 235–241 (2006). https://doi.org/10.1016/j.biopsycho.2006.04.005
36. Izzetoglu, K., et al.: Applications of functional near infrared imaging: case study on UAV ground controller. In: Schmorrow, D.D., Fidopiastis, C.M. (eds.) FAC 2011. LNCS (LNAI), vol. 6780, pp. 608–617. Springer, Heidelberg (2011). https://doi.org/10.1007/978-3-642-21852-1_70

Pressure Analysis in Dynamic Handwriting for Forgery Detection

Mariam Doliashvili[1,2,3]([✉]), Dwayne Jeffrey[1,2,3], Michael-Brian C. Ogawa[1,2,3], and Martha E. Crosby[1,2,3]

[1] Microsoft, Honolulu, HI 96822, USA
{mariamd,ogawam,crosby}@hawaii.edu
[2] SEEQR, Honolulu, HI 96822, USA
[3] University of Hawai'i at Mānoa, Honolulu, HI 96822, USA

Abstract. Handwritten signatures are extensively used over many fields for processing transactions and contracts. Online (dynamic) handwritten signatures have been used as a way of identification and there has also been intensive research done on distinguishing genuine signatures from forgeries for over past 40 years. However, dealing with high-skilled forgeries still remains a challenge. Therefore, handwritten signatures have not been used for authentication in electronic systems. Unlike static signatures, online handwritten signatures contain dynamic features and are able to identify individuals with more precision. The pressure value recorded during the online signature process has been a crucial information for automatic signature verification systems. In addition, the pressure an individual applies to mouse is also shown to enable continuous authentication. This paper focuses on the analysis of the pressure patterns during the process of dynamic signature. Comparing the pressure values for genuine signatures and skilled forgeries allows us to detect forgery while having the minimal information about the genuine signature. This fact significantly decreases the need of storing very sensitive biometric information with the potential to make the process writer independent.

Keywords: Online signature · Handwriting · Signature · Verification · Authentication · Biometrics · Preprocessing · Pressure

1 Introduction

A handwriting signature is a behavioural biometric characterized by behavioural traits that a person learns and adapts over a period of time. Handwriting is one of the accepted biometric traits for the identification of a person, which means that we expect each handwritten signature to be unique to a person. The assumption is proved to be true and widely used in forensic studies. Hence, in everyday scenarios (transactions, marriages, employment, healthcare, ID security, etc.) that need an authentication of a person, handwritten signatures have been used as an identity marker for quite a long time. In fact, the use of signatures is recorded in the Talmud [1] (fourth century), as a security procedure to prevent the alteration of documents after they are signed. The use of Dynamic Biometric

© Springer Nature Switzerland AG 2021
D. D. Schmorrow and C. M. Fidopiastis (Eds.): HCII 2021, LNAI 12776, pp. 134–146, 2021.
https://doi.org/10.1007/978-3-030-78114-9_10

Signatures is now an important alternative to traditional electronic signatures based on or used in conjunction with cryptographic methods.

Different writers do not write in the same way, according to forensic handwriting examiners (FHEs). The variations of the intrawriter and interwriter affect each single signature. Therefore, it is necessary to establish a degree of variation for a genuine signature. Based on the past observations, FHEs divide signatures into the following categories [2, 3]:

1. The genuine signature, written by the original writer in their own style.
2. The forged signature (a simulation), unnaturally written by some writer other than the specimen writer.
3. The signature is written by a person in his or her own style but falsely claims to be some other individual.
4. When the author attempts to make his or her signatures seem like a forgery attempt, the signature is not authentic, unnaturally written by the writer of the specimen. The intention may be to subsequently deny writing the signature, in which case it is also referred to as "auto-simulation." The author of the specimen writes both genuine and disguised signatures, but with different intentions.
5. The signature is unnaturally written by the specimen writer under the influence of internal or external factors like illness or alcohol.

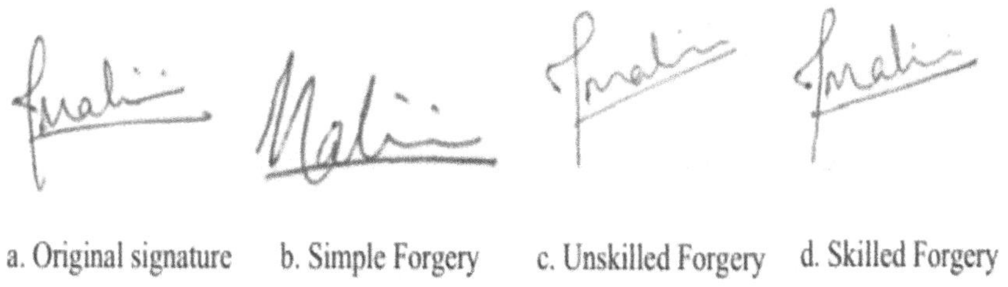

a. Original signature   b. Simple Forgery   c. Unskilled Forgery   d. Skilled Forgery

Fig. 1. Types of forgeries in case of offline signatures [4]

Based on the feature characteristics that we are taking into account while analysing handwriting, the signatures are online (dynamic) and offline (Static). After adapting the usage of handwritten signatures for signing electronic documents, many technologies have been developed in this field. Given that electronic handwriting process captures each person's characteristics and behaviour while writing, there are dynamic features (vertical inclination, pace of writing, Sequence of writing moves, etc.) that could give more identifying information about the person other than just the overall outline of the same offline writing. These characteristics in combination are impossible to reproduce by any forger, even if the visual writing of signatures are visually similar [5] (Fig. 3).

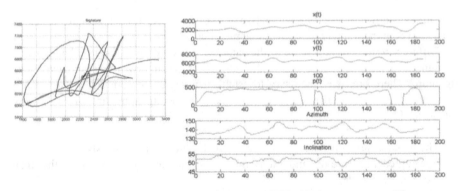

Fig. 2. A sample online signature from the MCYT-100 signature corpus [6]

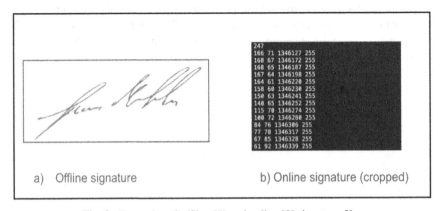

| a) Offline signature | b) Online signature (cropped) |

Fig. 3. Examples of offline [7] and online [8] signature files

Therefore, dynamic online signature verification systems usage of dynamic features such as pressure and stylus inclination, in addition to static features used in offline systems makes them more reliable. However, it is obviously requiring more biometric information from the individual. Storing large volumes of sensitive data leads to privacy concerns.

The interest towards researching electronic handwritten signature verification systems has been growing over the past 40 years. There are numerous studies on automatic signature verification (ASV). However, there is a room for improvement in detecting high-skilled forgeries (Fig. 4).

The amount of publicly accessible data remains limited when it comes to checking handwritten signatures or sequences of characters, as it is difficult to collect data due to the delicate nature regarding the user privacy issue. Training sophisticated neural networks have a high demand for the amount of data, quality of data and diversity of samples. Therefore, methods based on the feature engineering and classical algorithms are used to improve the results of these systems.

To address the above issues, it is necessary to develop methods minimizing the necessary information for user identification and maximizing the accuracy for detecting

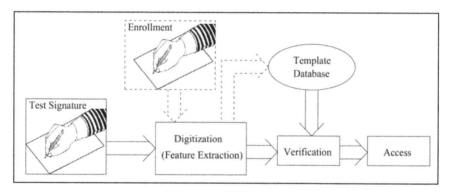

Fig. 4. Phases of automatic signature verification system [9]

high skilled forgeries. Hence, in this study we focused on the common characteristics of behaviour of the original writer of the signature and a skilled forger during the signature process described by the dynamic features. That can lead to the task towards detecting a person with the intention of forging a signature. Which decreases the information about the characteristics of original writer and potentially making the solution writer independent. Our aim is to use pen pressure, pen-ups and other pen dynamics that reflect the internal variations of the writers for distinguishing a genuine signature from a skilled forgery.

2 Background

A particular tool such as a stylus or mouse is used to perform online handwriting. A stylus has a pressure sensor for detecting the pressure applied and can determine the pen-up and pen-down motions. Some factors that affect the acquired features as the online signature capturing devices can pick up on the outside environment. The size of the tool used to sign can be different; same is true for the posture of the individual and other environmental changes. The signature may also be influenced by internal variables such as tiredness or emotional state. These variations are dealt with during preprocessing of the online handwriting to remove irrelevant information for the verification task and standardize the samples. Dynamic handwritten signature characteristics are grouped into two key categories: function features and parameter features. Parameter features are represented as a vector of a local feature or a global feature. Some of these features are component-oriented, extracted at the level of each component. For example, positions of the strokes, stroke orientation, stroke trajectory, etc. (Fig. 5).

The global features describe characteristics of the entire signature. Typical global features are the total time taken to write a signature, number of pen-ups, the orientation of the signature, the number of components/characters of the signature, etc. The global features are extracted in the feature-based approach and local features are extracted in the function-based approach.

S.No:	Description
1	Coordinate x(t)
2	Coordinate y(t)
3	Pressure p(t)
4	Time stamp
5	Absolute Position, $r(t) = \sqrt{x^2(t) + y^2(t)}$
6	Velocity in x $\nu_x(t)$
7	Velocity in y $\nu_y(t)$
8	Absolute Velocity $v(t) = \sqrt{\nu_x^2(t) + \nu_y^2(t)}$
9	Velocity of r(t) $\nu_r(t)$
10	Acceleration in x $a_x(t)$
11	Acceleration in y $a_y(t)$
12	Absolute Acceleration, $a(t) = \sqrt{x^2(t) + y^2(t)}$

Fig. 5. List of common features

3 Pressure

Studies done by the forensic experts give an indication to observe the way pressure is applied by the original writer compared to the forger. Genuine signatures are written naturally, since that are created by a writer as a personal identifier and performed over many years. It is a combination of strokes or characters written in natural conditions. The speed of their hand movement is consistent and fast. The authentic writing is done carelessly without much deliberation and effort put into it.

Forgery is an attempt to recreate another person's identity characteristic, modifying one's natural behaviour. Skilled forgers train themselves in order to mimic others and the act of forgery itself could be viewed as the examination of their learned skill. They need to be careful to not make any mistakes. Therefore, their internal state is completely different from the authentic writer. The forgers take longer time to perform the signature. This can be result in odd/unnatural appearance of the handwriting since they attentively write each character. Most importantly while they write a stroke or a character they will do so with the same diligence during the process. The later can affect the pressure applied during the writing. Writing naturally people tend to apply more pressure in the beginning of the stroke and gradually (almost linearly) decreases until the end of the stroke. The study for writer-independent handwriting recognition for Japanese Kanji used this fact about the pressure value to detect the trajectory of a stroke and improve the recognition of handwriting [10]. It is also studied that acceleration of handwriting results in decrease of the pressure. Identifying the writing moves is also important since it has been studied that sequence of moves is almost never repeated in the same order by the forgers [5].

Therefore, the variation of pressure value and the time required for the signature can be significant signs of a forgery. Since each individual's authentic handwriting has some variability, these differences are often removed during the preprocessing step to normalize the data for making further comparisons easier with less accompanying noise.

However, during preprocessing it is possible to avoid removing the important information and instead research stability regions of signatures. Stability regions can be identified as the longest similar stroke sequences between a pair of genuine signatures. [11]. Additionally, one of the online handwritten signature competitions winners during 2004 conference only used pressure for achieving a good result.

4 Motivation

The spread of low-cost technologies allowing online handwriting (PDAs, tablets, smartphones, etc.) lead to the high acceptability for daily use of the biometric traits for authentication. The identity of an individual can be determined using pattern recognition on various biometric traits such as palm print, iris, fingerprint, retina, face, signature, voice recognition, etc. (Fig. 6).

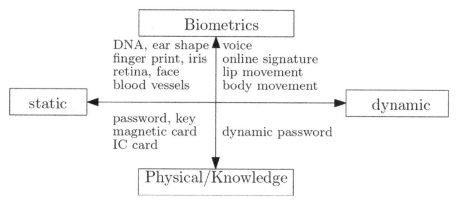

Fig. 6. Means for authentication

It is important to note that biometric characteristics can be physical (such as face, iris, fingerprint) or behavioural (such as handwriting or signature). While storing biometric data for user authentication is always associated with the risk of exposure for unauthorized individuals, behavioural traits pose less damage for the users' identity. In case they are needed for future authentication attempts behavioural traits can be changed much easier compared to the physical traits.

On the other hand, it is a more sensitive issue to process the genuine signatures of individuals and store them as their identification than to store passwords. The security of biometric templates is a major concern among researchers, as attacks that expose biometric traits threaten users by potentially exposing their identity. Other authentication mechanisms such as using passwords cannot reveal a person's identity, but biometric traits are capable of doing so and exposing it can lead to the privacy loss of a person. In addition, it does not require much effort to change a password, however changing a biometric trait can be extremely difficult. n the scope of authentication based on a biometric feature, there is no need to remember or store keys for the user. Additionally, biometric traits cannot be stolen or forgotten. Generally, it is more difficult to forge a signature than copy a password.

Out of the numerous applications of online handwritten signature verification, we reckon that the one that can have a significant impact on increasing user security online is its properties to be used instead of a password and/or an additional security layer during user authentication i. e. for two-factor authentication. BioTouch2 [12] paper describes a scenario where handwritten digits are used as a two-factor authentication method. The person receiving a security code through text/voice is supposed to write the digits by hand instead of typing them, that adds another layer of protection in case the device used for two-factor authentication is compromised. Therefore, it is quite promising to use handwriting for authentication and it certainly improves reliability of an authentication system especially for the scenarios when a physical layer of security fails i. e. when a user's phone or other physical device used for authentication is stolen, etc.

The fact that we can use dynamic features for verification also take care of the issues associated with multiscript signatures. By eliminating the necessity to study the scripts separately or retain any additional information about the multiscript signature. Hence, decreasing the amount of data/computation is needed and protecting the person's identity at the same time.

Furthermore, the pressure value can be used for continues authentication after signing in. It is researched [13] that when continuously measuring the pressure applied to the mouse button each individual had their own unique pattern and it was possible to identify a person after a few clicks with high accuracy - 95%. Another paper [14] researched continuous identity authentication based on biometric features.

Therefore, we believe there is enough ground for believing that having a lightweight system that can perform dynamic signature verification with limited data and computing requirements would serve as a significant improvement for user authentication tasks.

Despite its necessity in commercial transactions and applications, the random forgery scenario has become of low interest in many of the latest competitions, which focus mainly on skilled forgeries.

5   Implementation/Analysis

The variations in authentic author's writing are dealt with during preprocessing of the online handwriting. Preprocessing is done to remove irrelevant information for the verification task and in some cases to standardize the samples. This step includes resampling, resizing, normalization, and filtering. In the verification step the task is to determine whether a given signature belongs to the individual or not. We used publicly available DeepSign [8] dataset for the experiments. The DeepSign database is created through the combination of some of the best-known databases, and a novel dataset. It comprises more than 70K signatures acquired using both stylus and finger inputs from a total 1526 users. Two acquisition scenarios are considered, office and mobile, with a total of 8 different devices. Additionally, different types of impostors and numbers of acquisition sessions are considered.

The DeepSign database comprises a total of 1526 users from four different popular databases (i.e., MCYT [6], Boise-curID, Biosecure DS2, and e-BioSign DS1) and a novel signature database not presented yet, named e-BioSign DS2.

In order to analyse the dataset for the influence of the pressure feature we had to:

Remove the incomplete entries from the dataset and filter any additional noise (i.e. removing empty or out of scale values). Remove the data that was recorded using a finger, since it does not contain pressure as a feature.

We also limited the dataset to the subset that was collected using the devices that allowed to record exactly six features adequately. The result contains 11500 signatures from 230 users (50 ~ signatures per user).

The features included in the dataset are:

- COLUMN 1: represents the X coordinate.
- COLUMN 2: represents the Y coordinate.
- COLUMN 3: represents the timestamp.

4th and the following columns/features are not sorted in the same order.

For different sub-datasets in DeepSign, the pressure information is recorded at different columns. The MCYT dataset has the pressure information stored at column 6, BiosecureDS2 at column 7, BiosecurID at column 7, e_bioSign_DS1 and e_bioSign_DS2 at column 4.

Therefore, the current dataset has the following structure:

- COLUMN 1: represents the X coordinate.
- COLUMN 2: represents the Y coordinate.
- COLUMN 3: represents the timestamp.
- COLUMN 4: represents the pressure.

The remaining of the columns could provide other information acquired by the sensor (e.g., azimuth and altitude angles). However, we did not include them in the experimental dataset to avoid mixing the different feature values. It is also notable that there are signatures with only the above four features (X, Y, timestamp, pressure). Therefore, increasing the feature set size will decrease the number of signatures available for training.

The graphs for the genuine signatures display different patterns of applying the pressure to the stylus compared to the skilled forgeries.

The range for the pressure value is (0, 1024). However, in the recorded dataset the range for each signature is not close to each other i.e. there are signatures with the pressure value reaching 1000 ~ level and there are also signatures not exceeding level 100. Therefore scaling/standardizing features is necessary during the preprocessing (Fig. 7).

5.1 Results

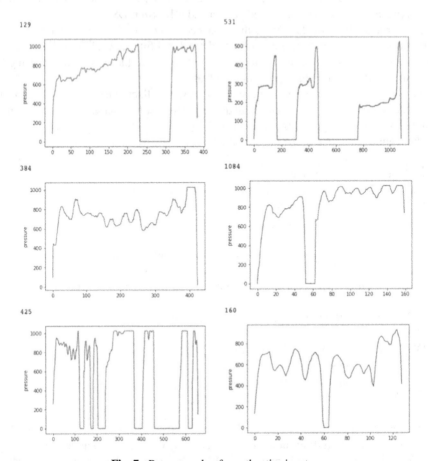

Fig. 7. Pressure value for authentic signature

The above graphs are the pressure value change over time for authentic hand-written signatures. As we previously discussed, it seems that pressure gradually increases/decreases during the writing, likely caused by starting a new stroke or a character.

As for the forged handwriting the following graphs show the odd behaviour because of being attentive while repeating a recently learned signature (Fig. 8).

Uniqueness of signature is ensured by focusing on the unique set of parameters during the process of writing. We can Observation of the Fig. 1 and Fig. 2 it became apparent that a person's behaviour, whether it is for an interview, lie detector test or forging handwriting, internal factors affected on the behaviour and made it unnatural.

We developed a method of analysing the amount of "stops" made when the pressure value changes from the local minimums to local maximums. The "stops" refer to constant value of the pressure over the time change. Analysing the data showed that the skilled

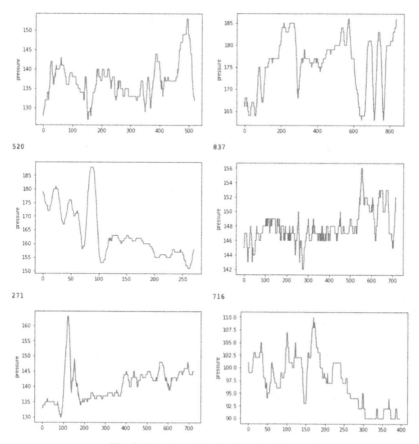

Fig. 8. Pressure value for forged signature

forgeries contained more than 25 such "stops" for every single entry, the same value was on average 3 and not exceeding 14 for the genuine signatures. Additionally, based on our observations, skilled forgers do not use pen-ups and downs often. The forgers pen up/down behaviour is very short and does not happen many times during the signature. Taking these two observations into account we can detect the forgery; therefore we do not actually need to have any information about the original writer.

6 Conclusion

The verification of dynamic handwriting is ensured by focusing on the unique set of parameters during the process of writing. Existing automatic online signature verification systems need the authentic writer's biometric data and numerous features associated with it. By doing so, posing potential threat for the individuals' privacy if the database is exposed to unauthorized access. The ASV's perform with nearly 100% accuracy on random signatures, comparably they find the skilled forgeries challenging to predict. Therefore, we focused on decreasing the need of storing the authentic writer's biometric information in a database and shifted the importance on the general characteristics of forged signatures. We can identify the authentic author and the forger based on their intrawriter variations that can be seen through the pressure applied to stylus in the process. We described the ways a forger's behaviour differs from the authentic writer during the dynamic writing process. The drawback of the method is its focus on the behaviour of skilled forger that might not generalize for a random forgery attempt. However, detecting random forgeries is a less complex task and there are numerous methods tackling it with high accuracy. There is also potential for combining the minimal information requirements for detecting a random signature (i.e. global features) with proposed method without compromising privacy.

References

1. Ketubot (The Talmud): In Tractate Ketubot (with commentary by Rabbi Adin Steinsalz), vol. VIII, Section 18B, p. 57. Random House, New York (1992)
2. E. Participation: Statute of Frauds (1677). https://www.legislation.gov.uk/aep/Cha2/29/3/contents. Accessed 12 Aug 2020
3. Mohammed, L.A., Found, B., Caligiuri, M., Rogers, D.: The dynamic character of disguise behavior for text-based, mixed, and stylized signatures. J. Forensic Sci. **56**(Suppl 1), S136-141 (2011). https://doi.org/10.1111/j.1556-4029.2010.01584.x
4. Harrison, D., Seiger, D.P.: Meeting the Daubert Challenge: A Bibliography of Handwriting Articles for the Forensic Document Examiner, FBI.https://www.fbi.gov/about-us/lab/forensic-science-communications/fsc/jan2003/seiger.htm. Accessed 12 Aug 2020
5. Ooi, S.Y., Teoh, A.B.J., Pang, Y., Hiew, B.Y.: Image-based handwritten signature verification using hybrid methods of discrete radon transform, principal component analysis and probabilistic neural network. Appl. Soft Comput. (2016). https://doi.org/10.1016/j.asoc.2015.11.039
6. Ortega-Garcia, J., et al.: MCYT baseline corpus: a bimodal biometric database. In: IEE Proceedings - Vision Image Signal Processing, vol. 150, no. 6, pp. 395–401, December 2003. https://doi.org/10.1049/ip-vis:20031078
7. Parmar, P., Mehta, J., Sharma, S., Patel, K., Singh, P.: A Survey of Handwritten Signature Verification System Methodologies, vol. 6, no. 5, p. 6 (2019)
8. Tolosana, R., Vera-Rodriguez, R., Fierrez, J., Ortega-Garcia, J.: DeepSign: Deep On-Line Signature Verification, ArXiv200210119 Cs, February 2020. Accessed 12 Aug 2020, http://arxiv.org/abs/2002.10119
9. Sanda, S., Amirisetti, S.: Online Handwritten Signature Verification System, p. 50
10. Diaz, M., Ferrer, M.A., Eskander, G.S., Sabourin, R.: Generation of duplicated off-line signature images for verification systems. IEEE Trans. Pattern Anal. Mach. Intell. **39**(5), 951–964 (2017). https://doi.org/10.1109/TPAMI.2016.2560810
11. Diaz, M., Fischer, A., Ferrer, M.A., Plamondon, R.: Dynamic signature verification system based on one real signature. IEEE Trans. Cybern. **48**(1), 228–239 (2018). https://doi.org/10.1109/TCYB.2016.2630419
12. Pirlo, G., Cuccovillo, V., Diaz-Cabrera, M., Impedovo, D., Mignone, P.: Multidomain Verification of Dynamic Signatures Using Local Stability Analysis. IEEE Trans Hum.-Mach. Syst. **45**(6), 805–810 (2015). https://doi.org/10.1109/THMS.2015.2443050
13. Offline signature verification and quality characterization using poset-oriented grid features|Pattern Recognition. https://doi.org/10.1016/j.patcog.2016.01.009. Accessed 12 Aug 2020

14. Fischer, A., Diaz, M., Plamondon, R., Ferrer, M.A.: Robust score normalization for DTW-based on-line signature verification. In: 2015 13th International Conference on Document Analysis and Recognition (ICDAR), August 2015, pp. 241–245 (2015). https://doi.org/10.1109/ICDAR.2015.7333760.
15. Farimani, S.A., Jahan, M.V.: An HMM for online signature verification based on velocity and hand movement directions. In: IEEE Conference Publication (2018). https://ieeexplore.ieee.org/abstract/document/8336639. Accessed 12 Aug 2020
16. Fahmy, M.M.M.: Online handwritten signature verification system based on DWT features extraction and neural network classification. Ain Shams Eng. J. 1(1), 59–70 (2010). https://doi.org/10.1016/j.asej.2010.09.007
17. Maiorana, E., Campisi, P., Neri, A.: Bioconvolving: cancelable templates for a multi-biometrics signature recognition system. In: 2011 IEEE International Systems Conference, April 2011, pp. 495–500 (2011). https://doi.org/10.1109/SYSCON.2011.5929064
18. Nanni, L., Maiorana, E., Lumini, A., Campisi, P.: Combining local, regional and global matchers for a template protected on-line signature verification system. Exp. Syst. Appl.: Int. J. (2010). https://doi.org/10.1016/j.eswa.2009.10.023. Accessed 12 Aug 2020
19. Blumenstein, M., Ferrer, M.A., Vargas, J.F.: The 4NSigComp2010 off-line signature verification competition: scenario 2. In: 2010 12th International Conference on Frontiers in Handwriting Recognition, November 2010, pp. 721–726 (2010). https://doi.org/10.1109/ICFHR.2010.117
20. Deep Learning for Biometrics|Bir Bhanu|Springer. https://www.springer.com/gp/book/9783319616568. Accessed 12 Aug 2020
21. Ahrabian, K., BabaAli, B.: Usage of autoencoders and siamese networks for online handwritten signature verification. Neural Comput. Appl. 31(12), 9321–9334 (2018). https://doi.org/10.1007/s00521-018-3844-z
22. Mutlu Yapici, M., Tekerek, A., Topaloglu, N.: Convolutional neural network based offline signature verification application. In: 2018 International Congress on Big Data, Deep Learning and Fighting Cyber Terrorism (IBIGDELFT), December 2018, pp. 30–34 (2018). https://doi.org/10.1109/IBIGDELFT.2018.8625290
23. Hafemann, L.G., Sabourin, R., Oliveira, L.S.: Writer-independent feature learning for offline signature verification using deep convolutional neural networks. In: 2016 International Joint Conference on Neural Networks (IJCNN), July 2016, pp. 2576–2583 (2016). https://doi.org/10.1109/IJCNN.2016.7727521
24. Soleimani, A., Araabi, B.N., Fouladi, K.: Deep Multitask Metric Learning for Offline Signature Verification. Pattern Recognit. Lett. 80, 84–90 (2016). https://doi.org/10.1016/j.patrec.2016.05.023
25. Wang, D., Zhang, Y., Yao, C., Wu, J., Jiao, H., Liu, M.: Toward force-based signature verification: a pen-type sensor and preliminary validation. IEEE Trans. Instrum. Meas. 59(4), 752–762 (2010). https://doi.org/10.1109/TIM.2009.2037871
26. Houmani, N., Garcia-Salicetti, S., Dorizzi, B.: On assessing the robustness of pen coordinates, pen pressure and pen inclination to time variability with personal entropy. In: 2009 IEEE 3rd International Conference on Biometrics: Theory, Applications, and Systems, September 2009, pp. 1–6 (2009). https://doi.org/10.1109/BTAS.2009.5339074
27. Rantzsch, H., Yang, H., Meinel, C.: Signature embedding: writer independent offline signature verification with deep metric learning. In: Bebis, G., et al. (eds.) ISVC 2016. LNCS, vol. 10073, pp. 616–625. Springer, Cham (2016). https://doi.org/10.1007/978-3-319-50832-0_60
28. Barkoula, K., Economou, G., Fotopoulos, S.: Online signature verification based on signatures turning angle representation using longest common subsequence matching. Int. J. Doc. Anal. Recognit. IJDAR (2012). https://doi.org/10.1007/s10032-012-0193-9

29. Ibrahim, M.T., Kyan, M.J., Khan, M.A., Guan, L.: On-line signature verification using 1-D velocity-based directional analysis. In: 2010 20th International Conference on Pattern Recognition (2010).https://doi.org/10.1109/ICPR.2010.933

30. Liu, Y., Yang, Z., Yang, L.: Online signature verification based on dct and sparse representation. IEEE Trans. Cybern. **45**(11), 2498–2511 (2015). https://doi.org/10.1109/TCYB.2014.2375959

31. Impedovo, D., Pirlo, G.: On-line signature verification by stroke-dependent representation domains. In: 2010 12th International Conference on Frontiers in Handwriting Recognition, November 2010, pp. 623–627 (2010). https://doi.org/10.1109/ICFHR.2010.102

32. Fierrez-Aguilar, J., Alonso-Hermira, N., Moreno-Marquez, G., Ortega-Garcia, J.: An off-line signature verification system based on fusion of local and global information. In: Maltoni, D., Jain, A.K. (eds.) BioAW 2004. LNCS, vol. 3087, pp. 295–306. Springer, Heidelberg (2004). https://doi.org/10.1007/978-3-540-25976-3_27

33. Martinez-Diaz, M., Fierrez, J., Krish, R.P., Galbally, J.: Mobile signature verification: feature robustness and performance comparison. IET Biom. **3**(4), 267–277 (2014). https://doi.org/10.1049/iet-bmt.2013.0081

34. Galbally, J., Diaz-Cabrera, M., Ferrer, M.A., Gomez-Barrero, M., Morales, A., Fierrez, J.: On-line signature recognition through the combination of real dynamic data and synthetically generated static data. Pattern Recognit. **48**(9), 2921–2934 (2015). https://doi.org/10.1016/j.patcog.2015.03.019

35. Sharma, A., Sundaram, S.: On the exploration of information from the DTW cost matrix for online signature verification. IEEE Trans. Cybern. **48**(2), 611–624 (2018). https://doi.org/10.1109/TCYB.2017.2647826

36. Tolosana, R., Vera-Rodriguez, R., Ortega-Garcia, J., Fierrez, J.: Preprocessing and feature selection for improved sensor interoperability in online biometric signature verification. IEEE Access **3**, 478–489 (2015). https://doi.org/10.1109/ACCESS.2015.2431493

37. Gruber, C., Gruber, T., Krinninger, S., Sick, B.: Online signature verification with support vector machines based on LCSS kernel functions. IEEE Trans syst. Man Cybern. Part B Cybern. **40**(4), 1088–1100 (2010). https://doi.org/10.1109/TSMCB.2009.2034382

38. Meng, M., Xi, X., Luo, Z.: On-line signature verification based on support vector data description and genetic algorithm. In: 2008 7th World Congress on Intelligent Control and Automation, June 2008, pp. 3778–3782 (2008). https://doi.org/10.1109/WCICA.2008.4593531.

39. Guru, D.S., Prakash, H.N.: Online signature verification and recognition: an approach based on symbolic representation. IEEE Trans. Pattern Anal. Mach. Intell. **31**(6), 1059–1073 (2009). https://doi.org/10.1109/TPAMI.2008.302

40. Maiorana, E., Campisi, P., Fierrez, J., Ortega-Garcia, J., Neri, A.: Cancelable templates for sequence-based biometrics with application to on-line signature recognition. IEEE Trans. Syst. Man Cybern. - Part Syst. Hum. **40**(3), 525–538 (2010). https://doi.org/10.1109/TSMCA.2010.2041653

41. Sae-Bae, N., Memon, N.: Online signature verification on mobile devices. IEEE Trans. Inf. Forensics Secur. **9**(6), 933–947 (2014). https://doi.org/10.1109/TIFS.2014.2316472

42. Djioua, M., Plamondon, R.: Studying the variability of handwriting patterns using the kinematic theory. Hum. Mov. Sci. **28**(5), 588–601 (2009). https://doi.org/10.1016/j.humov.2009.01.005.doi:10.1109/ICFHR.2012.217

Goal Orientation in Human Computer Interaction Tasks: An Experimental Investigation of User Engagement and Interaction Modalities

Mehmetcan Fal[1,2] and Cengiz Acartürk[1(✉)]

[1] Institute of Informatics, Department of Cognitive Science, Middle East Technical University, Ankara, Turkey
acarturk@metu.edu.tr
[2] TAI, Turkish Aerospace Industries, Ankara, Turkey
mehmetcan.fal@tai.com.tr

Abstract. Developing natural and intuitive Human Computer Interaction is a primary target of interaction design. The analysis of a user's engagement to the task is an essential component for the assessment of the interaction for design efficiency. The investigation of task engagement requires considering users' goal orientation since performance-oriented and learning-oriented individuals exhibit motivational differences. Learning-oriented individuals focus on progress and mastery, whereas performance-oriented individuals focus on their ability. We present an experimental investigation of users' task engagement and its interaction with modalities to study the role of goal orientation in Human Computer Interaction tasks. Twenty-five participants participated in the study. They performed the same task with three alternative interaction modalities: a mouse, an eye tracker, and a Microsoft Kinect v2 sensor. The participants also filled in a goal orientation questionnaire and user engagement questionnaire. The findings revealed that different modalities resulted in different task completion times. The completion time was then used as a factor for the analysis of the efficiency of the interaction. Further analyses showed significant interactions among the participants' goal orientation, their engagement scores, and the interaction modalities.

Keywords: Goal-orientation · Task engagement · Human computer interaction modalities · Eye tracking · Microsoft kinect remote sensing

1 Introduction

The current methods of Human Computer Interaction (HCI) employ various modalities and sensors. Novel HCI methods have been developed for several decades, including verbal interaction modalities that utilize speech perception and generation, and non-verbal interaction modalities that employ sensors that process physical characteristics provided by the user, such as motion. The surprising fact about the development of novel interaction modalities is that they have been integrated into our daily life settings

D. D. Schmorrow and C. M. Fidopiastis (Eds.): HCII 2021, LNAI 12776, pp. 147–157, 2021.
https://doi.org/10.1007/978-3-030-78114-9_11

quickly. Why are we so efficient in using novel HCI interfaces? What are the factors that influence the efficiency of using an interface? The present study aims at contributing to addressing those long-standing research questions for relatively novel methods of HCI.

The classical conception of HCI is that an interface between a human and a computer is a border between the physical, real-world, and virtual environments. That border is designed for reducing the complexity of the virtual environment [1]. The recent debates about the concept of *reality* present alternative conceptualizations of reality. From the perspective of the human perceptual and cognitive systems, the *physical* is a concept under debate [2]. Therefore, it is likely that we perceive the virtual as the real, in a similar way that we perceive the real as the virtual. This may explain why we are so efficient in using novel HCI interfaces, which we did not experience before. Nevertheless, the efficiency of the use of HCI interfaces is influenced by numerous factors, including the modality of the interaction, the quality of the interaction (i.e., the capability and congruency of the interaction device), the contextual environment that the interaction takes place, and the users' traits, such as their motivation, engagement, and experience.

Finding the methods of developing intuitively understandable input-output devices has been a challenge of HCI since its establishment as a research field in the 1980s [3]. For example, humans were conceived as active processors that interacted with a virtual environment via the perceptual-sensory system, the motor system, and the cognitive system. Therefore, the key to creating efficient interaction modalities was to analyze the relationship between those three subsystems [4].

On top of all the methods that would increase the interaction's efficiency, *user's task engagement* is an essential part of the integration of HCI interfaces in daily life settings, such as gaming. In particular, task engagement may be employed as a predictor for investigating the user perception of the usefulness of an interaction modality. In the present study, we aim to investigate the relationship between the users' perception of engagement and the interaction modalities for three methods of interaction. The three modalities are the mouse, eye tracking, and remote sensing by Microsoft Kinect v2. We also address the users' role of goal orientation since it was reported as a significant factor that influences user experience. For this, we used two questionnaires, namely the User Engagement Scale [5] and the Goal Orientation Scale [6]. In the following sections, we first present the components of the study within the framework of the relevant literature and the background for the interaction modalities. We then introduce the software that was developed for the study. Finally, we present the results and the findings of the study.

1.1   User Engagement Scale and Goal Orientation Scale

The User Engagement Scale (UES) was developed by [7] for measuring the online shopping experiences of users. The primary goal of the UES is to investigate the implications of the hedonic and utilitarian motivation on user engagement. The scale has been used as an indicator of the efficiency of the interaction In various HCI domains, including video games and mobile interaction [5, 8].

The previous studies on user motivation provide a basis for understanding users' engagement in task performance. It was specified as a particular motivational behavior

[7]. According to [9], the motivational intensity increases with the difficulty of instrumental behavior; however, the motivational arousal decreases when the task requirements overrun the individual skills and abilities. Several factors influence the relationship between task difficulty and motivation [10–14]. In particular, from the learners' perspective, learners may lose motivation to perform a task if the task's challenge is too simple or too complex. Therefore, a task must be designed by taking into account the cut off point of task difficulty [9, 15]. Another factor that influences user motivation is their goal orientation.

Although early goal orientation studies were applied to children, the findings can be extended to adults [16]. Accordingly, the studies on user orientation have well-established literature. The previous studies show that user orientation may be classified into two broad types: performance orientation and learning orientation. Individuals with a different type of orientation exhibit differences in their motivational behavior [17]. In particular, performance-oriented children focus on their ability level, whereas learning-oriented children focus on their mastery and progress about the task. For instance, if a person has a learning-oriented personality, then the person will tend to show a mastery-oriented behavioral pattern. [18].

In educational environments, goal orientation has been studied as a predictor of performance [18–21]. In addition to the two main types of orientation, namely performance orientation and learning orientation, performance-avoidance was also used as a performance predictor. In particular, a performance-oriented person evaluates their performance among others and avoid a task if a likely failure is the expected outcome. On the other hand, if the person assumes that they have the relevant ability to accomplish the task, they exhibit mastery-oriented behavior. Contrary to performance orientation, a learning-oriented person conceives competence as an event where an improvement is a possibility [17, 18]. Those patterns on the relationship between specific types of orientation and task performance allow making predictions in various domains in daily settings. For instance, measuring the goal orientation of employees in a work environment provides a way to understand and predict employees' behaviors and interests since goal orientation is closely related to a person's performance [6]. In the present study, we employed Vanderwalle's Goal Orientation Scale since it shows a close resemblance to the context of the HCI environment. It is applied to adult persons for assessing their goal orientation. In the following section, we present the interaction methodologies investigated in the present study.

1.2 Research Questions and Design

The primary goal of the present study is to investigate the relationship between user motivation and task difficulty within the context of specific interaction modalities. If a task is too easy, then they may exhibit poor motivational behavior towards the task. On the other hand, if a task needs a higher capacity than a person's skills, then the person's motivation drops [9]. One of the motivation related factors is goal orientation. Different orientations lead users to show various task performances. For example, complex tasks may not drop their motivation since learning-oriented people consider competence a source of mastery.

On the other hand, the difference between the user's required skills and their available skills has to be kept under control. Contrary to a learning-oriented person, a performance-oriented person may not show a motivational drop for an easy task [17]. In the present study, we employed a modified version of the original User Engagement Scale, which was adopted for measuring user engagement in video-games [5, 7]. For measuring goal orientation, we employed the Goal Orientation Scale by [6].

We designed the study and identified the relevant variables within the framework of a set of research questions listed below.

- Do different modalities of interaction result in different task accomplishment times?
- Do different interaction modalities provides intrinsic training option?
- Does user engagement result in task efficiency differences among different modalities?
- Does the efficiency of the interaction modality differ from the engagement scores of the participants concerning their goal orientation?

We identified the interaction modalities, the users' goal orientation, and task difficulty as the independent variables of the study. The user engagement scores and task accomplishment times were identified as dependent variables. We hypotesized that users' engagement scores would be influenced by their specific type of goal orientation since a person's goal orientation is an influential factor for motivational behavior. We predicted that different task accomplishment times due to modalities' kinematic requirements, which might also be perceived as a mastery opportunity for the participants. In particular, performance-oriented participants' engagement scores might be higher for the modalities that enable users to have faster task accomplishment time since task accomplishment times indicate the level of difficulty. Finally, learning-oriented participants' engagement scores would be higher for the modalities with slower task accomplishment times due to the modalities' high kinematic demand.

In the following section, we present the background for the Human Computer Interaction modalities employed in the present study.

1.3 Human Computer Interaction Modalities

We investigated three HCI methods in their relation to user engagement and orientation, namely mouse, eye tracking, and remote sensing by Microsoft Kinect v2.

The mouse is the most frequently used input device in Human Computer Interfaces since its development in the 1980s. It allows specific interaction methods that the user can accomplish several tasks, such as pointing, dragging, dropping, and selecting. In the present study, we used mouse control for controlling a cursor on the screen, as it has been typically used in user interfaces.

Interactive use of an eye tracker as a pointing device is a technique that provides a method of manipulating a user interface by gaze [22]. Eye tracking is a high-speed pointing device. Gaze-controlled interfaces have been employed as advanced user interfaces for the past several decades [23–29], among others.

Although the high speed of gaze interaction is a promising potential for eye tracking as an efficient interaction modality, the method is also subject to a set of problems, including the so-called Midas Touch Problem [28]. The problem is about the difficulty of detecting intentional visual commands during the interaction. Therefore, it is difficult to make predictions about the user experience of the interaction without empirical results. In the present study, we used eye tracking for controlling the mouse cursor by gaze.

Microsoft Kinect is a remote-sensing sensor that provides information about tracked users' body limbs position in a three-dimensional coordinate system. In the present study, we used Kinect v2 to record joints' coordinates of the participants' tracked bodies. We analyzed the right-hand tip since it was used for controlling the cursor at the interface.

2   Methodology

2.1   Participants

Twenty-five university students and staff participated in the study (five male). Their ages ranged from 20 to 42. None of the participants used glasses or contact lenses during the experiment. The majority of the participants were right-handed ($N = 23$). Participants were asked to filled informed consent form and demographic data form and the goal orientation scale.

2.2   Materials

A standard desktop computer was used for presenting the environment of the experiment. The screen resolution of the computer was 1600 x 1200 pixels. The left-upper corner of the screen represents the first pixel of the resolution (x = 0, y = 0 in screen coordinates). As for the interaction modalities, we used an EyeTribe eye tracker (Sampling Rate: 60 Hz, Accuracy: $0.5° - 1°$, Latency: < 20ms, Calibration: 9 points) for recording gaze screen coordinates of the participants during task performance. An A4Tech desktop mouse was the device for mouse interaction. The final equipment was Microsoft Kinect v2 that provided three-dimensional locations of the participants' body parts. We developed a software application for the interface, by C#, an object-oriented programming language. The application stands for performing an identical task with different types of modality. During the task performance, only the right-hand tip's Kinect's joint was used for manipulating the cursor location. Note that the 3D right-hand tip's coordinate transformed into a 2D screen coordinate with the coordinate mapper supported by Microsoft Kinect's SDK. For the eye tracker, the right eye's raw screen coordinate was used. And for the mouse, screen coordinate received from the System.Forms.Inputs library of C# resources. A chin rest was used for collecting eye movements' data.

The 12-item Goal Orientation Scale [6] was translated into Turkish by an expert translator, and two experts checked it for clarity of the expressions. The first five items in the questionnaire are related to learning orientation. The following four items are related to performance orientation, and the last three items are related to performance-avoidance. The last three items were not taken into account since the study focused on learning and performance orientation. Principal Component Analyses and Confirmatory Factor Analyses were conducted to reveal the instrument's applicability for the workers in Turkey. The alpha values for items were .85, .75, and .71 for learning, performance performance-provenance avoidance orientations. Moreover, a Confirmatory

Factor Analysis was conducted to investigate if the items' loading was in line with the original, three-factor model. Comparative and goodness of fit values were found as satisfactory, with the values .94 and .92, respectively [30].

2.3 Procedure

The experiment session had three phases, and each phase had its practice session. In each phase, users were exposed to 10 practice trials and 50 experiment trials with a particular interaction modality. The participants performed the experiment trials in five different starting locations of the cursor on the screen (10 trials per location). The order of the presentation of the modality was randomized. After each phase, the participants filled in the User Engagement Scale. Therefore, the participants reported their engagement for the task for each modality separately. Since all the participants were exposed to all the modalities, the experiment's design can be summarized as a 3 x 5 repeated measure design.

The task of the participant was to move the mouse cursor between two stimuli. These stimuli can be named as *the starting point* and *the target point*. At the beginning of each phase, in the practice session, ten trials had to be performed by the participants. To avoid familiarization within the practice sessions, the targets' location was assigned randomly on the screen. After the practice session, the participants were presented with 50 trials to finish each phase.

For each trial, the participants located the cursor at the starting point first to trigger the target's appearance. Then they located the cursor on the target to make it disappear. We call the former even the *triggering event* and the latter the *hit event*. There was no chance to trigger a new event before the previously triggered one hit by the participants. Therefore, each trial had its timing, and they were in consecutive order. When the participants located the cursor at the starting position, there were five different possible locations that the target would appear. More specifically, the target's horizontal location could be x = {500, 700, 900, 1100, 1300}px, and the vertical location of the target was always y = 600 px (pixel). To establish a proper interaction, a set of procedural adjustments were made. For instance, the click event was not used in eye tracking and interaction with Kinect. Instead, a conditional click simulation algorithm was designed and implemented. The simulation was based on applying a rule, which stated that the cursor must be located in the same spatial range of a predetermined frame number. This click simulation function initialized for each collision of the cursor and the start or target stimuli. The click simulation function's pseudocode is presented below.

In Fig. 1, the function `ClickSimulation()` was called by the application if the cursor collided with a stimulus in the application. The first condition checks whether the cursor was in the boundary or not. Since CXL, CXR, CYD, and CYU were not initiated, the algorithm goes on its process with the `else` branch, where the counter is 0 and CXL, CXR, CYD, and CYU were substituted with the cursor axis values. The axis values are then increased with a `bip` pixel more and a `bip` pixel less. If the cursor still collides with the stimuli in an iterative process, the function is called by the application again. If the cursor falls within the range of CXL, CXR, CYD, and CYU then the counter was incremented by 1, and the condition was checked if the counter was equal to the variable `sib` or not. If that is true, then the `click()` function is simulated, and it is used for

```
Variable: CXL, CXR, CYU, CYD //the variables for defining the boundaries.
Variable: counter //counts conditionally true frames.
Variable: sib //(still in the border) predetermined frame amount.
Variable: bip // (boundary in pixels) predetermined pixel amount for a boundary.
Input: RCX, RCW //real-time cursor x, and y location.
funtion ClickSimulation()
{
   Start
   if((RCX < CXR) & (RCX > CXL) & (RCY < CYU) & (RCY > CYD))
   {
      counter++;
      if(counter==sib)
         click();
   {
   else
   {
      counter =0;
      CXL=RCX - bip;
      CXR=RCX + bip;
      CYU=RCY - bip;
      CYD=RCY + bip;
   }
}
```

Fig. 1. Alternative face morphologies utilized in the virtual reality environment.

triggering an event for the start stimuli or a hit event for the target stimuli. The click() function, which is the part of the ClickSimulation() is the original function from the C# library.

The stimuli on the screen consisted of a gray bull eye (the starting position) and a white bull eye (the target position) with identical size. To minimize the differences between the participants in the initial locations, invisible boundaries were used for the stimuli rather than their visible boundaries. This procedure allowed us to guarantee an equal distance in each experimental trial. For the eye tracking, we used the click simulation with the sib values reduced to 5 frames. In the following section, we present the results of the experiment.

3   Results

The statistical analyses were conducted with JASP 0.7.5.6, an open-source statistics software. The participants were divided into two groups according to their goal orientation scores: Learning oriented ($N = 12$) and performance oriented ($N = 13$).

3.1   Task Completion Times

To analyze the relationship between the modality of the interaction and task completion time (henceforth, the movement time of the cursor), we conducted a repeated measures ANOVA analysis. The results showed that the movement time was significantly different among the conditions, $F(2,8) = 1390.6, p < .001$. The interaction between the distance and the movement time was also significant, $F(2,8) = 45.1, p < .001$. A post hoc comparison using Tukey HSD indicated that the movement time in the eye tracking condition was shorter than the movement times in the other two conditions ($p < .001$), Moreover, the movement time with Kinect was longer than the movement time with the mouse ($p < .001$).

Figure 2 shows the task completion results obtained in the experiment.

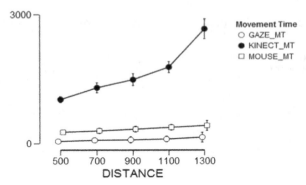

Fig. 2. Task completion times (movement times). GAZE_MT is the eye tracking condition, KINECT_MT is the Kinect condition, MOUSE_MET is the mouse condition.

To understand whether any of the modalities resulted in an undesired training effect, we conducted a learning curve prediction analysis for each target location, for each modality. The calculation of a learning curve was first described by Ebbinghaus in 1885. Wright (1936) published a theory, which was based on a repetitive production. According to the theory, any task completion would decrease by a constant percentage when the output's quantity doubled. Since our task sequence included ten trials for each target location, the most folded production point was the 8th trial for each target location. Our analyses revealed no learning opportunities provided by any modalities, except the mouse condition for the target appeared at x = 1300 screen coordinates (%94). This trial was the most challenging task within the experiment.

3.2 User Engagement Scores

To analyze the effect of modalities on users' engagement scores, a repeated measures ANOVA analysis was employed. As the repeated measure factors, eye tracker, Kinect, and mouse engagement scores were defined. The orientation goal types were given as between-subject factors. The analysis revealed that the engagement scores were statistically different among the interaction modalities, $F(2,246) = 94.48$, $p < .001$. The interaction of the type of orientation type and the modality was also statistically significant, $F(2, 246) = 5.179, p < .006$. Post Hoc comparisons using Tukey HSD showed that the mean Gaze engagement score was higher than the other two engagement scores ($p < .001$). The difference between the mean scores of the Kinect condition and the Mouse condition was also significant ($p < .001$).

Figure 3 shows the results for the User Engagement Scores.

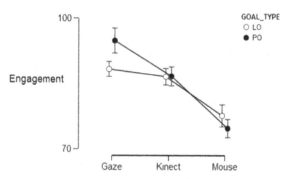

Fig. 3. User Engagement Scores. LO is the learning-oriented group, PO is the performance-oriented group.

4 Discussion and Conclusion

The main goal of the study was to investigate the role of interaction modalities on users' engagement while they interacted with a simple cursor movement task. The second aim was to understand whether users' goal orientation types influence their task engagement. Besides, we aimed at understanding the time and distance relationship for each interaction modality.

The results of the experiment revealed significant differences in task completion time among the interaction modalities (mouse, Kinect, eye tracking). A major source of those differences might be due to the kinematic requirements of the specific interaction devices. Another major finding of the present study was the significant time-distance relationship between the order of trial and the task completion time for the target located at x = 1300 px, which was the longest distance between the starting point and target point in the experiment. It likely influenced participants' familiarization with the task. The participants might have become more competent to complete the task. Another finding of the experiment was that the interaction's modality had a significant impact on participants' engagement scores. In particular, the eye tracker returned the highest engagement scores, whereas the mouse returned the lowest engagement scores. Finally, we found a limited influence of goal orientation type on user engagement scores only for eye tracking.

Several factors have been proposed to assess the quality of service and the quality of experiences between a human and a machine, such as aesthetics, input and output quality, joy and ease of use, utility, and learnability [31]. In the present study, we addressed some of those experience related factors by employing the User Engagement Scale [5]. Further research is needed to evaluate the modalities' kinematic patterns and users' efforts under similar task performances.

We found partial evidence for the influence of goal orientation type on user engagement. It was only when the participants used eye tracking, the orientation type influenced the engagement scores. Learning-oriented participants likely conceived the progress and mastery opportunities of the task, whereas performance-oriented individuals focused on their ability in eye tracking. A possible explanation of the finding may be the lack of a chance to improve task accomplishment times in eye tracking,

In conclusion, the present study contributes to the existing literature by reporting the effect of interaction modalities on user engagement. It also proposes that users' goal orientation may have limited user engagement effects under specific interaction modalities. Our findings also show that task completion time may not always predict the efficiency of the interaction. In particular, the Microsoft Kinect sensor was the slowest interaction modality in our study, whereas its engagement score was higher than the mouse with a faster timing.

Future research should expand the task types by including smooth pursuit in eye tracking and relevant movements in the other modalities. This may increase the task's difficulty for the eye tracker while decreasing it in the other modalities. The study can also be extended for diagonal movements rather than cardinal directions to further analyze task difficulty under different interaction modalities.

The study has a set of limitations that should be addressed by future research. A major limitation is the low number of participants in the experiment ($N = 25$), given the richness and complexity of the interaction modalities. Another limitation of the present study was the relatively low quality of the eye tracking equipment. Gaze interaction with a higher resolution eye tracker may influence the reported results. Moreover, the reliability and validity of the translated questionnaires are necessary since they were validated only in their original language.

References

1. Dix, A., Dix, A., Finlay, J., Abowd, G.D., Beale, R.: Human-computer interaction. Pearson (2003)
2. Hoffman, D.D.: Did we evolve to see reality, or are spacetime and objects just our user interface? Ann. N. Y. Acad. Sci. **1458**(1), 65–69 (2019)
3. Wachsmuth, I., Fröhlich, M. (Eds.): Gesture and Sign Language in Human-Computer Interaction: International Gesture Workshop, Bielefeld, Germany, 17–19 September 1997. In: Proceedings (vol. 1371). Springer Science & Business Media (1998) https://doi.org/10.1007/BFb0052983
4. Card, S.K., Moran, T.P., Newell, A.: The Psychology of Human-Computer Interaction. L. Erlbaum Associates, Hillsdale (1983)
5. Wiebe, E.N., Lamb, A., Hardy, M., Sharek, D.: Measuring engagement in video game-based environments: investigation of the user engagement scale. Comput. Hum. Behav. **32**, 123–132 (2014)
6. Vandewalle, D.: Development and validation of a work domain goal orientation instrument. Educ. Psychol. Measur. **57**(6), 995–1015 (1997)
7. O'Brien, H.L., Toms, E.G.: The development and evaluation of a survey to measure user engagement. J. Am. Soc. Inform. Sci. Technol. **61**(1), 50–69 (2010)
8. Oh, J., Kang, H.: User engagement with smart wearables: four defining factors and a process model. Mob. Media Commun. (2020). https://doi.org/10.1177/2050157920958440
9. Brehm, J.W., Self, E.A.: The intensity of motivation. Annu. Rev. Psychol. **40**(1), 109–131 (1989)
10. Broadhurst, P.L.: The interaction of task difficulty and motivation: The Yerkes Dodson law revived. Acta Psychologica, Amsterdam (1959)
11. Schunk, D.H.: Sequential attributional feedback and children's achievement behaviors. J. Educ. Psychol. **76**(6), 1159 (1984)

12. Capa, R.L., Audiffren, M., Ragot, S.: The effects of achievement motivation, task difficulty, and goal difficulty on physiological, behavioural, and subjective effort. Psychophysiology **45**(5), 859–868 (2008)
13. Nicholls, J.G.: Achievement motivation: conceptions of ability, subjective experience, task choice, and performance. Psychol. Rev. **91**(3), 328 (1984)
14. Lomas, J.D., Koedinger, K., Patel, N., Shodhan, S., Poonwala, N., Forlizzi, J.L.: Is difficulty overrated? The effects of choice, novelty and suspense on intrinsic motivation in educational games. In: Proceedings of the 2017 CHI conference on human factors in computing systems, pp. 1028–1039 (2017)
15. Wang, S.K., Reeves, T.C.: The effects of a web-based learning environment on student motivation in a high school earth science course. Educ. Tech. Res. Dev. **55**(2), 169–192 (2007)
16. Colquitt, J.A., Simmering, M.J.: Conscientiousness, goal orientation, and motivation to learn during the learning process: a longitudinal study. J. Appl. Psychol. **83**(4), 654 (1998)
17. Steele-Johnson, D., Beauregard, R.S., Hoover, P.B., Schmidt, A.M.: Goal orientation and task demand effects on motivation, affect, and performance. J. Appl. Psychol. **85**(5), 724 (2000)
18. Dweck, C.S., Leggett, E.L.: A social-cognitive approach to motivation and personality. Psychol. Rev. **95**(2), 256 (1988)
19. Dweck, C.S.:Self-theories: Their role in motivation, personality, and development. Psychology Press (2000)
20. Koul, R., Roy, L., Lerdpornkulrat, T.: Motivational goal orientation, perceptions of biology and physics classroom learning environments, and gender. Learning Environ. Res. **15**(2), 217–229 (2012)
21. Feyzioğlu, B.: The role of inquiry-based self-efficacy, achievement goal orientation, and learning strategies on secondary-school students' inquiry skills. Res. Sci. Technol. Educ. **37**(3), 366–392 (2019)
22. Stellmach, S., Dachselt, R.: Look & touch: gaze-supported target acquisition. In: Proceedings of the SIGCHI conference on human factors in computing systems, pp. 2981–2990 (2012)
23. Zhai, S., Morimoto, C., Ihde, S.: Manual and gaze input cascaded (MAGIC) pointing. In: Proceedings of the SIGCHI conference on Human factors in computing systems, pp. 246–253 (1999)
24. Hutchinson, T.E., White, K.P., Martin, W.N., Reichert, K.C., Frey, L.A.: Human-computer interaction using eye-gaze input. IEEE Trans. Syst. Man Cybern. **19**(6), 1527–1534 (1989)
25. Tecce, J.J., Gips, J., Olivieri, C.P., Pok, L.J., Consiglio, M.R.: Eye movement control of computer functions. Int. J. Psychophysiol. **29**(3), 319–325 (1998)
26. Hansen, J.P., Andersen, A.W., Roed, P.: Eye-gaze control of multimedia systems. Adv. Hum. Factors Ergon. **20**, 37–42 (1995)
27. Kaufman, A.E., Bandopadhay, A., Shaviv, B.D.: An eye tracking computer user interface. In: Virtual Reality, 1993. Proceedings of the IEEE 1993 Symposium on Research Frontiers in Virtual Reality, pp. 120–121. IEEE (1993)
28. Jacob, R.J., Karn, K.S.: Eye tracking in human-computer interaction and usability research: ready to deliver the promises. Mind **2**(3), 4 (2003)
29. Kumar, C., Menges, R., Staab, S.: Eye-controlled interfaces for multimedia interaction. IEEE Multimedia **23**(4), 6–13 (2016)
30. Tayfur, Ö.: Antecedents of feedback seeking behaviors. Unpublished master's thesis. Middle East Technical University, Turkey (2006)
31. Moller, S., Engelbrecht, K.P., Kuhnel, C., Wechsung, I., Weiss, B.: A taxonomy of quality of service and quality of experience of multimodal human-machine interaction. In: 2009 International Workshop on Quality of Multimedia Experience, pp. 7–12. IEEE (2009)

Repurposing the Quality Adjusted Life Year: Inferring and Navigating Wellness Cliques from High Sample Rate Multi-factor QALY

Monte Hancock[1], Ben Bowles[2(✉)], Robert Hanlon[2], and Joshua Wiser[2]

[1] 4Digital, Los Angeles, CA, USA
[2] Living Centerline Institute, Morristown, USA

Abstract. Modern medical technology provides a wide range of treatment options, each having a corresponding cost. There are established accounting procedures for quantifying costs, but a principled cost-benefit analysis for a treatment option cannot be performed without corresponding procedures for quantifying treatment benefits. Can the "quality" of lives lived under different treatment outcomes be objectively quantified?

This is the purpose of the QALY (Quality Adjusted Life Year), an internationally recognized metric designed to make possible consistent cost-benefit analyses in support of medical, pharmacological, and actuarial decision-making [Whitehead, et. al.]. Viewing health as a function of both length of life and quality of life, life quality might be mathematically summarized as the numeric product of a "life quality" measure and the time duration over which it obtains. For the QALY, the duration is one year.

A person's life (the "subject") can be modeled as a sequence of state vectors through time. This sequence defines a trajectory through a state space. In this work, the state vector components are values of wellness measures of various types. The resulting state space is called the Wellness Space, and the trajectory through this space we call the subject's lifeline.

We extend the single-quality, large time-step QALY to an EQALY, a multi-factor, variable-step model using vector calculus in a scalar field. Most importantly, we describe how, given an appropriate measuring methodology whereby the EQALY can be repurposed. Instead of serving as a general population metric for informing public policy, the EQALY supports a personalized tool for monitoring and optimizing individual wellness. To achieve this personalization, the EQALY:

- Generalizes the time-sampling scheme for data collection
- Supports the introduction of arbitrary numeric wellness measures into the QALY
- Improves the fidelity and utility of the QALY so that it can serve as a multi-factor, integrated, comprehensive wellness metric for a wide range of wellness applications, including:
- Monitoring current wellness as a process
- Predicting future wellness
- Determining subject behaviors that will optimize the quality of life over a subject's lifeline

© Springer Nature Switzerland AG 2021
D. D. Schmorrow and C. M. Fidopiastis (Eds.): HCII 2021, LNAI 12776, pp. 158–177, 2021.
https://doi.org/10.1007/978-3-030-78114-9_12

The authors implemented software prototypes of these features. Feasibility and fidelity have been demonstrated on a population of simulants (simulated subjects), with a human trial using members of the U.S. Winter Olympic Team as subjects beginning in spring, 2021.

The psychological import of such an integrated personalized QALY is clear. "Eat right, exercise, learn to relax, live within your means" are all good suggestions. But without specificity, quantification, and assessment of relative costs and effects, they are easily disregarded platitudes. In short, what cannot be measured cannot be managed. The EQALY enables objective, proactive management of every facet of wellness.

Keywords: QALY · Quality-adjusted life year · Data fusion · Wellness

1   Background

Objective numeric "quality of life" metrics can be combined with the associated treatment costs to carry out a principled cost-benefit analysis for assessing and comparing treatments. Such metrics can also be repurposed using advanced analytic methods (e.g., machine learning) to build personalized recommender systems to help individuals assess and optimize their wellness as a life process. One such metric is the Quality Adjusted Life Year (QALY), which we here refine and extend to the Extended Quality of Life Year (EQALY).

1.1   Purpose and Definitions

A subject's life can be modeled as a sequence of state vectors through time. The components of these state vectors are measures of wellness in different areas (e.g., psychological, physical, and financial metrics). These we call <u>wellness vectors</u>. The space of all such vectors is a Euclidean space we call <u>wellness space</u>. A time sequence of wellness vectors constitutes a <u>trajectory</u> through wellness space that we call the subject's <u>lifeline</u>.

Projecting lifeline vectors onto their components yields <u>component lifelines</u>: separate trajectories for each wellness component. A time sequence of Component lifelines can be combined to produce a single numeric measure summarizing a subject's wellness along the corresponding component lifeline. This is a data fusion operation we call <u>adjudication</u>.

1.2   Standard QALY

The standard QALY model employs a single quality value over a time interval measured in years. This gives a numeric rating for the quality of an individual's life over that interval (typically one year). The QALY can be regarded as a quantitative measure of disease burden, including both the quality and quantity of life. As such, the QALY is often used in healthcare to assess the economic value of medical interventions. One QALY equates to one year lived in perfect health [Haraldstad, et. al].

To generalize the standard QALY, let Q denote a numeric measure of the subject's quality of life that is constant for a period of time T (in years). If T is one year, then the standard QALY equals Q. By allowing T to assume arbitrary values, it is possible to aggregate quality-of-life over arbitrary periods.

Q = quality-of-life,
T = duration of life (in years),

And the total accumulated quality of a life, or QALY, is Q x T. Essentially, the existing QALY method uses Riemann sums to infer the curve of wellness trajectories.

Fig. 1. The standard QALY calculates a wellness estimation as a uniform block, akin to a coarse Riemann sum.

The QALY is an innovative insurance standard for measuring the human quality of life. However, the QALY suffers from low fidelity due to the twists and turns inherent in human lives and its low number of samples. A high-fidelity, objective QALY based on data collected from wearable technology and psychological self-reported data could summarize psychological, physical, and financial wellness. This QALY parameterizes a subject's path through wellness and helps to inform optimal fitness decisions.

In the real world, life circumstances and wellness vary over time. With a small sample size, random noise can mask the true quality of life and misinform readings. This coarse approach to the QALY could drastically misinterpret a single bad day. For example, it might fail to differentiate between a subject who struggles with chronic depression and one who went through a difficult breakup that week.

Following the geometric approach in Fig. 1, the EQALY can accommodate both arbitrary sampling rates and variable quality measures by viewing the aggregate summary EQALY as a Riemann Integral (see Fig. 2).

Of course, in the "real world", quality of life tends to vary relatively smoothly rather than remaining constant between large jumps. QALY as currently practiced does not model this high-fidelity situation because this can only be accomplished with when "quality" is measured frequently.

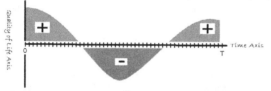

LCI's sampling methodology uses frequent manual and instrumented feedback to determine many Q-values close in time for essentially continuous estimation of the quality of life.

In this way, Q becomes, not a discrete sequence of constants, but a piecewise-continuous function of time, Q(t).

Using the QALY-as-an-Area paradigm, The LCI QALY model is moved from discrete, "chunky" sums to a Calculus-based Riemann Integral model:

$$QALY = \int_0^T Q(t)\, dt$$

Fig. 2. The definition of the QALY can be extended to support arbitrary sampling rates over arbitrary durations employing the obvious geometric analogy.

1.3 Wellness Features

The authors have previously used three categories to evaluate wellness: psychological, physical, and financial [Hanlon, et. al.] Different wellness components can interact in complex ways that affect overall wellness. For example, increased stress from physical problems can decrease job performance and damage financial stability, creating a deleterious feedback loop. Alternatively, new financial security could bolster psychological wellness and decrease stress on physical systems. The thirty wellness components constituting the dimensions of our wellness space are (Table 1):

Table 1. Wellness components listed in the three wellness categories: psychological, physical, and financial ("Mind, Body, and Balance Sheet")

Psychological	Physical	Financial
Positivity	BMI	Annual income
Engagement with life	Systolic blood pressure	Credit score
Relationship satisfaction	Diastolic blood pressure	short-term savings
Meaning in Life	Blood sugar	Long-term savings
Accomplishment	Resting heart rate	Health insurance
Emotional stability	Active heart rate	Life insurance
Optimism	Age	Budgeting
Resilience	Sleep/Night	Mortgage
Self esteem	Total calories	College debt
Vitality	Carbohydrate calories	Unsecured debt

1.4 Assessing Wellness Features

At each point in their life trajectory, an individual will make choices that tend to increase or decrease their wellness in one or more wellness components; the aggregate effect of these choices is reflected in their EQALY over the resulting trajectory through wellness space.

To separately quantify the impact of each of the thirty wellness features used for quality assessment, we have formulated four parameterizable weighting functions (see Sect. 2.3). Each wellness component has its quality weighting function and parameters established by expert judgment. These weighting functions establish a scalar field for each corresponding wellness component. That is, each wellness value has an associated numeric weight. The quality-weighted time sequence of wellness values can then be aggregated as contour integrals along each projected component lifeline.

As an example, consider one of the wellness components in our model, Body Mass Index (BMI). Let a subject have a sequence of BMI values at time samples T_i (not necessarily a uniform mesh):

$$(BMI(T_1), BMI(T_2), \ldots, BMI(T_m))$$

This time sequence of BMI values is the projected lifeline for this subject's BMI over the time interval $[T_1, T_m]$.

We express wellness values as z-scores concerning a reasonable BMI demographic for the subject, registering the optimal BMI for the demographic at a z-score of zero. Thus, a BMI score of 1 would be one standard deviation above the optimal z-score of 0, a score of -1 one standard deviation below, and so forth. This process can be applied to any number of wellness components.

Plotting the pairs $\{BMI(T_i), T_i)\}$ shows the wellness lifeline for the subject in the wellness component Body Mass Index (Fig. 3, left panel). Notice that the subject falls into the Low BMI region, which, once the weighting is applied, will result in a lower QALY value for the BMI component of the wellness vector (Fig. 3, right panel).

The weighting function for the BMI example is roughly normal. The highest quality is at z-score $= 0$, while wellness quality is lower as the BMI falls below or rises above the optimum.

The same quality weighting function is used for all time samples. This establishes a scalar field in the BMI x Time-space. Weighting is applied to each BMI sample by evaluating the weighting function at the corresponding BMI value, giving the component quality $Q_k = G_k(BMI)$. The line integral along this trajectory through the scalar field sums the BMI quality over the entire lifeline.

$$Q_k = \oint G_k ds = \oint G_k(r_k(t)) ds = \oint G_k(r_k(t)) \left| r_k'(t) \right| dt \qquad (1)$$

The trajectory is the piecewise linear path parametrized by $r_k(t)$, and G_k is the quality weighting function for this wellness component. In our work, a quality model has been selected for each of the thirty wellness components. Q_k is the trajectory QALY for the kth wellness component, where k ranges from one to thirty. Parameterizations have been created for sixteen subject demographics (described in Sect. 3.1), establishing

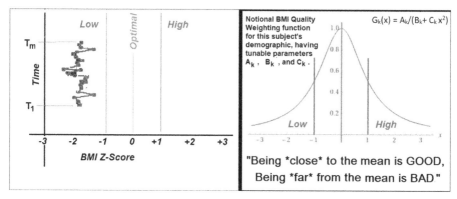

Fig. 3. This subject's low BMI rating will result in a decreased EQALY.

demographic cliques. These cliques can be used as collections of examples for supervised and unsupervised learning, collaborative filtering, and more.

The sixteen high-fidelity simulant demographics are being defined in recognition of the fact that separate weighting models will be required for different subject demographics. Tuning for a demographic is accomplished by adjusting the weighting function parameters. Work to date uses eight demographics, splitting on age group, gender, and marital status.

In this way, separate quality models with their associated weighting schemes are established in each wellness area. Each wellness component (e.g., separately for Heart Rate Variance Stress Level, Body Mass Index, Total Unsecured Debt, etc.) has a corresponding time sequence of wellness values. Arranging these in an ordered array gives rise to a time sequence of wellness vectors in an N-dimensional (Euclidean) wellness space. Application of the weighting functions (by contour integration) obtains a vector of QALY's in each wellness component for the entire time sequence.

2 Repurposing the QALY

Our multi-factor QALY expects life to vary over time (see Fig. 4). The total accumulated quality over the entire period is the sum of the accumulated qualities at each measurement. In the simple example below, generally high wellness balances out a difficult patch in the middle of the subject's life. Moreover, smart technology could allow an even more granular approach, perhaps collecting data weekly.

We extend the QALY to a multi-factor model by translating wellness into multiple numeric components and computing a time sequence of qualities for each. We transform the resulting time sequence of QALY vectors to obtain an Extended Quality Adjusted Life Year or EQALY.

The EQALY Model generalizes the time-sampling scheme for data collection and supports the introduction of arbitrary wellness measures into the QALY. This allows it to improve the fidelity and utility of the QALY so it can serve as a multi-factor, comprehensive wellness metric for a wide range of applications, including monitoring of current fitness, and prediction of future health risks.

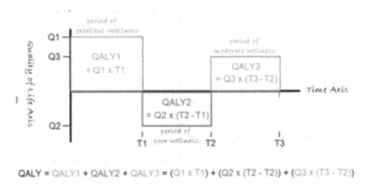

QALY = QALY1 + QALY2 + QALY3 = (Q1 x T1) + (Q2 x (T2 - T2)) + (Q3 x (T3 - T2))

Fig. 4. Granular assessments provide a nuanced view of life's fortunes.

While the standard QALY is computed as the product of a single quality metric and time duration, the EQALY is obtained by calculating a time sequence of QALY's in many wellness areas and adjudicating the resulting vector of QALY's to obtain a single numeric EQALY for the entire time sequence of wellness measurements (lifeline).

2.1 Quality Space

The inherent correlation and causal linkages among the indicators and metrics for the three wellness domains ("Mind, Body, and Balance Sheet") suggest the application of data fusion methods to formalize an integrated EQALY as a holistic wellness assessment for the subject. Using high-sample rate data collection methods described below, this EQALY can provide not just occasional point estimates, but high sample-rate lifelines of the subject through a Quality Space, **Q**.

In our software implementation, **Q** is a 30-dimensional Euclidean Space. The EQALY is computed as a high-fidelity fitness estimate using a contour integral along the lifeline of the subject through **Q**.

Through periodic first-person checklists, advisor interviews, and bio-measurements from wearable devices, we can obtain psychological, physical, and financial high sample-rate measurements.

The figure below shows how the EQALY for a particular one of the thirty wellness features (Body Mass Index) is computed along the subject's lifeline as a contour integral. The portion of the contour used for this computation can be adjusted to suit applications. For example, a retrospective integral may be useful for hospital analysis (Fig. 5).

2.2 Multi-factor EQALY Process

The Multi-factor EQALY Process allows us to integrate an arbitrary number of features into a single metric (see Fig. 6). The time sequence of vectors constitutes a health trajectory through the N-dimensional wellness space. The weighting function for each wellness component is established by demographic norms, expert knowledge, and human trials. Additionally, these weighting functions' parameters can modulate the relative impact of each wellness component. A graphical depiction of the EQALY process follows.

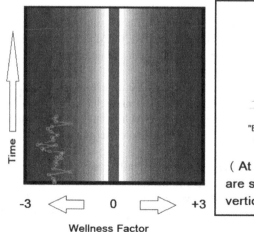
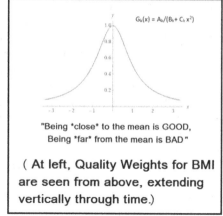

$G_k(x) = A_k/(B_k + C_k x^2)$

"Being *close* to the mean is GOOD,
Being *far* from the mean is BAD"

(At left, Quality Weights for BMI
are seen from above, extending
vertically through time.)

Time

-3   ⟵   0   ⟹   +3

Wellness Factor
(e.g., BMI) as a z-score

The weighted Quality contribution for BMI is the contour
integral of the trajectory through time ("lifeline") :

$$Q(\text{BMI}) = \int_C G \, ds = \int_a^b G(\mathbf{r}(t)) |\mathbf{r}'(t)| \, dt$$

Fig. 5. A contour integral describes each subject's path through all thirty wellness areas.

The vector $(B_1, B_2, ..., B_m)$ is the vector of importance values for each wellness
component for this demographic. A Q-vector which is similar in direction to B_m will
have a large EQALY value, and vice versa.

$$Q_k = \oint G_k \, ds = \oint G_k(r_k(t)) \, ds = \oint G_k(r_k(t)) \, |r'_k(t)| \, dt$$

Time -----   T1 T2 T3 ——— Tm

Instrumentation
Daily Checklist
Periodic Interviews

Metric Normalization
(z-scores viz. user
demographic norms)

⟹ Psychological $r_1(Tk)$→   → $\oint G_1 \, ds =$
                    $r_2(Tk)$→

⟹ Physiological

⟹ Financial $r_n(Tk)$→   → $\oint G_n \, ds =$

$$\text{EQALY}(\tau) = \text{ArcCos}\left(\frac{(Q1, Q2, ..., Qn) \bullet (B1, B2, ..., Bn)}{|(Q1, Q2, ..., Qn)| \, |(B1, B2, ..., Bn)|} \right)$$

Fig. 6. The EQALY integrates separate measurements from the three wellness areas into a single
measurement. The vectors of wellness components at the sample times are vertical tri-color bars
(for the three wellness areas). The contour integrations are performed *horizontally* through time
for each wellness component.

With its weighting, each component of the aggregate quality-of-life along a given trajectory can be computed as a line integral of the scalar field given by the weighting function for that component. This yields N component QALY's (one in each wellness component), giving an N component vector of QALY's for the entire time sequence ("trajectory") in the N-dimensional wellness space.

A metric transform is applied to the vector of QALY's to create an adjudicated EQALY for the entire trajectory. Our approach to adjudicating the QALY vectors for a trajectory is to compute the cosine distance between the QALY vector and a benchmark vector of optimum values for each wellness component. The closer the cosine distance is to 1, the higher the assigned EQALY.

The EQALY benchmark vectors can be assigned differently based on demographic data. This is important because optimum wellness values and their associated weighting must be tuned for the demographics to which they are applied. In this way, the EQALY quantifies the aggregate wellness of the individual along a trajectory through the EQALY wellness space.

2.3   The Weighting Functions

The figure below is a depiction of the scalar field that arises from each of the four notional quality weighting schemes. The horizontal axis is the z-score for the wellness component, and the vertical axis is time (Fig. 7).

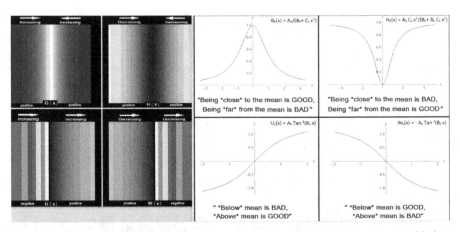

Fig. 7. The right panel shows the four quality weighting functions. These do not vary with time; seen "from above", they establish a scalar field in the BMI x Time-space. Positive values are in grayscale, negative values are in color (brown is most negative) (Color figure Online)

3   The Human Trial

3.1   Experimentation

Since this new EQALY is experimental, future work should verify its helpfulness in improving wellness. Human trials to evaluate these concepts are described briefly in

Sect. 3.3. They are scheduled to begin in the spring of 2021 as the subjects of the trial are members of the U.S. Winter Olympic Team. Due to a delay in real-world data, life-like simulated data was provided to allow theoretical progress to continue.

3.2 Avatar Simulation

To test the improved QALY on realistic subjects, we generated data from simulants. These sixteen "avatars" describe specific types of people and their key traits. We generated several subjects from each type of avatar and followed them throughout their projected lives. Each avatar has customized parameters in our wellness features, corresponding to their demographics. Avatars are distributed normally around a population mean, allowing each instance of an avatar to bear nuanced differences from the rest. Avatars also have programmed in random noise, which simulates the randomness in real health data. Below are biographical descriptions of selected avatars:

> Darrel is a millennial male in his late twenties to early thirties with type one diabetes. He graduated from Johns Hopkins University with a Biomedical Sciences degree and has begun working in his field.

> Oliver is a millennial male in his late twenties to early thirties with Obsessive-Compulsive Disorder. He did not attend a post-secondary institution, though he does have plans to do so soon. He has instead been working, trying to earn enough money to cover his college fees, and has climbed the ranks of the IT company he works for. He hopes to get his degree to climb even higher in his field.

> Amelia is a millennial female in her late twenties to early thirties with asthma. She is currently enrolled at the University of Central Florida, on track to receive her degree in Astrophysics.

> Blaze is a millennial male in his late twenties to early thirties who volunteers at a soup kitchen in his spare time. He is currently enrolled at the University of Central Los Angeles to earn his bachelor's degree in Computer Science.

> Perry is a generation x male in his late forties to early fifties who has been paralyzed from the waist down since he was nineteen. He was in the military, serving in the Gulf War when this happened, and received an honorable discharge from the military. He later got a job in accounting.

> Andrew is a Baby Boomer male in his late fifties to early sixties with Antisocial Personality Disorder. He worked at his local Department of Motor Vehicles for the past 30 years and plans to retire when he turns seventy. He has never been married and plans to live in solitude until he dies.

To simulate the progress of these avatars, we used Python to assign a life trajectory in each field, based on their parameters and a normal random distribution. This gives each person a thirty-dimensional path through Q-Space which charts their physical, psychological, and financial health. Then, the outcomes from the lives of these avatars were passed to our EQALY model as a substitute for real data.

3.3 Human Trials with Members of the U. S. Winter Olympic Team

The authors are preparing a study to assess and optimize the Wellness Recommender System involving volunteers from the U.S. Winter Olympic Team. The study will collect information to assess and refine the performance of the system. The study will last three months, with onboarding in the first week of each month.

3.4 The Study Architecture

Purpose:

- Collect information to assess and refine the performance of the Centerline Wellness system
- Collect empirical data to support the completion of a scientific paper to be presented at an international technical conference.

Duration of Study: 3 months

- Onboarding can occur in Week 1 of any month.
- In-Brief includes a survey instrument
- Subjects will complete the psychological assessment(s) online and report the results within the week of their In-Brief.
- Subjects will interact with Financial Counselors at the beginning, middle, and end of each month.

  - Subjects will be advised using recommendations created by the Centerline Wellness system.
  - It is anticipated that all Financial Counselors will be Ph.D. Students/Candidates acting under the direction of one of the study Principal authors.

Out-Brief includes a summary interview.

The figure below characterizes the study architecture (Fig. 8).

On-Boarding of subjects will include a Study Pre-Test Information will be collected during the In-Brief (Fig. 9).

The information being collected is only that which is required for the operation of the Centerline Wellness System.

Some physical information will be collected using a wearable device that subjects will wear throughout the study. Other data will be collected during Check-ins with Financial Counselors or in a post-study survey completed by subjects. Further data will be self-reported in surveys.

Subjects will complete a checklist once a day upon rising (see Fig. 10). These will be collected at the Financial Counselor Check-ins and/or monthly recaps. The information being collected is only that which is required for the operation of the Centerline Wellness System.

After the study, subjects will complete a Summary Interview. The Summary Interview includes a survey about the study experience. The Out-brief Survey has not yet been developed.

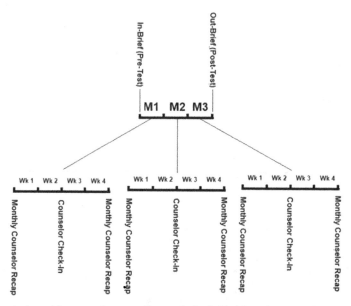

Fig. 8. The study architecture: the centerline study is divided into three month-long intervals to allow onboarding.

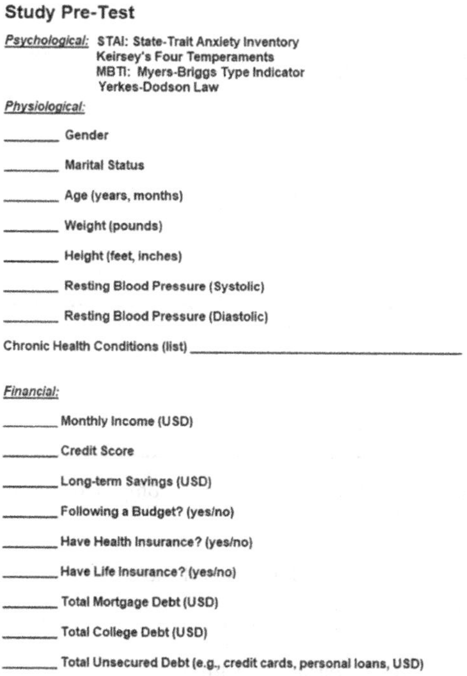

Study Pre-Test

Psychological: STAI: State-Trait Anxiety Inventory
Keirsey's Four Temperaments
MBTI: Myers-Briggs Type Indicator
Yerkes-Dodson Law

Physiological:

_____ Gender

_____ Marital Status

_____ Age (years, months)

_____ Weight (pounds)

_____ Height (feet, inches)

_____ Resting Blood Pressure (Systolic)

_____ Resting Blood Pressure (Diastolic)

Chronic Health Conditions (list) _____

Financial:

_____ Monthly Income (USD)

_____ Credit Score

_____ Long-term Savings (USD)

_____ Following a Budget? (yes/no)

_____ Have Health Insurance? (yes/no)

_____ Have Life Insurance? (yes/no)

_____ Total Mortgage Debt (USD)

_____ Total College Debt (USD)

_____ Total Unsecured Debt (e.g., credit cards, personal loans, USD)

Fig. 9. Prototype of the pre-test questionnaire.

Applicants will be surveyed to establish a baseline for the wellness features. The study will assess the following psychological profiles to contextualize daily wellness:

- STAI: State-Trait Anxiety Inventory
- Keirsey's Four Temperaments
- MBTI: Myers-Briggs Type Indicator

Name: **Date:**   ☐ Morning   Evening ☐

Psychological Twice-Daily Checklist Items

(Check a box in each row, or leave blank...)
(- means more negative feeling, + means more positive feeling, leave blank if "just OK")

−   +

OK	Positivity:	I think today is a GOOD day!
OK	Engagement:	I feel like I am part what is going on around me today.
OK	Relationships:	I am satisfied with my relationships with others today.
OK	Meaning:	I believe that what I am doing today matters.
OK	Accomplishment:	I feel GOOD about this week's plans and accomplishments.
OK	Emo_Stability:	My emotions are steady and under control today.
OK	Optimism:	I am looking forward to the rest of this week.
OK	Resilience:	I am overcoming today's challenges.
OK	Self_Esteem:	I feel GOOD about myself today.
OK	Vitality:	I have plenty of energy today.

In at most three words: Best thing about today   ⇨ [_____]

In at most three words: Worst thing about today ⇨ [_____]

Physiological Twice-Daily Checklist Items

[_____] ⇦ Hours of Sleep in the last 12 hours (write in box)

[_____] ⇦ Blood Sugar (if measured) (write in box)   ☐YES   NO☐   Menstruating?

Total Calories consumed since waking up today: (check one box)
☐ 0 - 1000   ☐ 1000 - 2000   ☐ 2000 - 3000   ☐ Over 3000

Total Colories of Carbohydrates consumed since waking up today: (check one box)
☐ 0 - 1000   ☐ 1000 - 2000   ☐ 2000 - 3000   ☐ Over 3000

Financial Twice-Daily Checklist Items

(check one box in each row)
☐YES   NO☐   Short-term Savings: I have more than enough money to meet this month's expenses.
☐YES   NO☐   Budgeting: I am sticking to a budget today.

Fig. 10. Quick-checklist survey to be completed by subjects.

Some of the data provided by the devices and the checklist will be calculated into z scores:

- Heart Rate Variability (Mean, Variance, Sigma)
- Resting Heart Rate (-0.5 Z)
- Active Heart Rate (1.0 Z)
- Minutes of inactivity in last 24 h (minutes $Z < -0.5$)

- Minutes of elevated activity in last 24 h (minutes Z > 1)

This data goes directly to the Centerline Wellness Recommender System to facilitate immediate feedback. Additional information will be collected during Check-ins with Financial Counselors and a post-study survey completed by subjects.

3.5 Sample Report Generated by the Recommender Expert System

A sample report generated automatically follows. This report corresponds to a simulant input by our prototype Wellness Recommender System. It combines machine learning with EQALY data to facilitate improved wellness (Table 2).

Table 2. The wellness recommender system absorbs a subject's Z-scores in all of the wellness areas.

ANTONE MCMAHON is a 31-year-old single male					
Evaluation Report **Financial State** ANTONE MCMAHON's overall financial wellness level is 0.004, which is at the Centerline for his demographic He has reached or exceeded Centerline Financial Wellness in 8 out of 10 areas The Financial Wellness factors that meet or exceed the centerline for his demographic are:					
Assessment	Value	Z-Score	Set Point	Importance	Compliance
A medium level of annual income is fine:	31.1	−0.485	35.002	0.848	0.881
A medium level of short save is fine:	0.057	0.337	0.05	0.681	0.796
A medium level of long save is fine:	0.461	−0.173	0.496	0.257	0.235
A medium level of college debt is fine:	28.875	−0.383	31.786	0.876	0.812
A medium level of unsec debt is fine:	5.785	0.086	5.218	0.544	0.248
A medium level of credit score is fine:	603.143	−0.282	610.03	0.671	0.151
A medium level of life insure is fine:	0.995	−0.022	1.003	0.501	0.758
A low level of mortgage debt is good:	11.517	−1.293	100.995	0.539	0.222

(*continued*)

Table 2. (*continued*)

ANTONE MCMAHON is a 31-year-old single male

Evaluation Report
Financial State
ANTONE MCMAHON's overall financial wellness level is 0.004, which is at the Centerline for his demographic
He has reached or exceeded Centerline Financial Wellness in 8 out of 10 areas
The Financial Wellness factors that meet or exceed the centerline for his demographic are:

Assessment	Value	Z-Score	Set Point	Importance	Compliance
His Financial Wellness factors that need improvement are:					
A low level of health insure is not healthy:	0.751	−0.612	1.0	0.325	0.793
A low level of budgeting is not healthy:	0.411	−1.444	1.011	0.682	0.756

Physical State
ANTONE MCMAHON's overall physical wellness level is −0.112, which is under the Centerline for his demographic
He has reached or exceeded Centerline Physical Wellness in 9 out of 10 areas
The Physical Wellness factors that meet or exceed the centerline for his demographic are:

A medium level of bmi is fine:	22.07	0.087	21.554	0.178	0.783
A medium level of wb sugar is fine:	92.474	0.914	84.864	0.605	0.963
A medium level of act hr is fine:	128.178	−0.112	129.594	0.199	0.766
A medium level of age is fine:	31.588	−0.203	31.588	0.171	0.216
A medium level of tot cals is fine:	2711.334	0.971	2395.075	0.484	0.177
A medium level of carb cals is fine:	497.583	0.593	402.509	0.563	0.202
A very high level of bp diastolic is quite unhealthy:	97.501	2.131	79.816	0.171	0.765
A very low level of resting hr is quite unhealthy:	45.935	−3.184	71.723	0.207	0.248
A very low level of sleep is quite unhealthy:	3.775	−2.574	8.009	0.698	0.753
His Physical Wellness factors that need improvement are:					
A high level of bp systolic is not healthy:	137.864	1.095	119.667	0.507	0.22

Psychological State
ANTONE MCMAHON's overall psychological wellness level is −0.067, which is under the Centerline for his demographic
He has reached or exceeded Centerline Psychological Wellness in 6 out of 10 areas
The Psychological Wellness factors that meet or exceed the centerline for his demographic are:

(*continued*)

Table 2. (*continued*)

ANTONE MCMAHON is a 31-year-old single male

Evaluation Report
Financial State
ANTONE MCMAHON's overall financial wellness level is 0.004, which is at the Centerline for his demographic
He has reached or exceeded Centerline Financial Wellness in 8 out of 10 areas
The Financial Wellness factors that meet or exceed the centerline for his demographic are:

Assessment	Value	Z-Score	Set Point	Importance	Compliance
A medium level of positivity is fine:	0.325	0.159	0.308	0.436	0.196
A medium level of engagement is fine:	0.585	−0.105	0.61	0.397	0.784
A medium level of meaning is fine:	0.679	0.328	0.618	0.739	0.951
A medium level of emo stability is fine:	0.38	−0.148	0.412	0.547	0.889
A medium level of optimism is fine:	0.368	0.258	0.323	0.411	0.17
A medium level of resilience is fine:	0.594	−0.042	0.617	0.663	0.804

His Psychological Wellness factors that need improvement are:

A low level of relationships is not healthy:	0.291	−0.89	0.513	0.408	0.842
A low level of accomplishment is not healthy:	0.011	−1.873	0.309	0.463	0.155
A low level of self-esteem is not healthy:	0.572	−0.783	0.708	0.563	0.755
A low level of vitality is not healthy:	0.503	−1.21	0.725	0.899	0.237

3.6 Wellness Recommender System Application

Subjects will interact with Financial Counselors three times each month, who will be Ph.D. students or candidates acting under the direction of the study's authors. Check-ins will provide advice to guide subjects through optimal financial wellness. These recommendations will be created by the Wellness Recommender System, as informed by the EQALY model. More generally, the EQALY and wellness history can be used to create an <u>automated</u>, personalized wellness advisor.

The wellness time-history and the associated sequence of EQALY values can be used by an intelligent system (e.g., a knowledge-based expert system) to construct an automated advisor to the individual subject, performing life tracking and goal-aware planning and advisory functions.

3.7 Recommendation and Forecast Sample Report

The Forecast is generated automatically by a knowledge-based expert system using wellness quality data. Each subject is provided a recommendation report based on the information in their evaluation report (Figs. 11, 12, 13).

For domain financial, the significant issue area is budgeting:
Significance Score: 0.409

Importance to the subject:	0.682
subject Compliance:	75.6 %
Centerline Deviation:	-0.6

Recommendations:
Increase: Plan! Develop weekly monthly and annual budgets you can live with. Be realistic but hold your resolve.

If essential expenses overshoot 50 percent of your income you may need to dip into the wants portion of your budget for a while. It is not the end of the world, but you will have to adjust your spending. Even if your necessities fall under the 50 percent cap revisiting these fixed expenses occasionally is smart. You may find a better cell phone plan an opportunity to refinance your mortgage or less expensive car insurance. That leaves you more to work with elsewhere.

Forecast:
If he follows the recommendation above, he may expect an 82.343% improvement in 5 weeks.

Fig. 11. The wellness recommender system makes recommendations to improve financial wellness, tailored to the needs of individual subjects.

This information will be used for the Wellness Recommender System, which integrates the EQALY with smart technology and expert advice to aid in optimal wellness. Based on the wealth of wellness data, the system will be able to advise on which areas could lead to a most dramatic improvement and what measures should be taken. Subjects can then work with these guidelines to improve their quality of life. This granular, advice-based EQALY provides a more high-fidelity picture of wellness and also works to leave a positive impact on subjects' health.

3.8 Gradient-Descent Lifeline Optimization

The ability to assess lifelines using the EQALY naturally facilitates the automated formulation of optimized behavior plans by which the subject can explicitly and specifically steer their multi-factor wellness trajectory, subject to their goals and abilities. The subject can see where they are in Q-Space and where they might wish to be. Our intelligent system determines the specific elements and cost of an actionable, real-world, multi-factor plan to approach the subject's chosen wellness destination.

The EQALY facilitates automated selection of an optimal lifeline. This can be done through the Calculus of Variations, Monte Carlo optimization, or gradient descent on

For domain physical, the significant issue area is bp_systolic:

Significance Score:	9.228
Importance to the subject:	0.507
subject Compliance:	22.0 %
Centerline Deviation:	18.197

Recommendations:

Decrease: Enroll in a gym for weekly exercise. Take an afternoon and evening walk. Spend less time on sedentary activities.

When it comes to resting heart rate, lower is better. It usually means your heart muscle is in better condition and doesn't have to work as hard to maintain a steady beat. Studies have found that a higher resting heart rate is linked with lower physical fitness and higher blood pressure and body weight.

Forecast:

If he follows the recommendation above, he may expect a 92.892% improvement in 5 weeks.

Fig. 12. The wellness recommender system makes recommendations to improve financial wellness, tailored to the needs of individual subjects.

For domain psychological, the significant issue area is relationships:

Significance Score:	0.09
Importance to the subject:	0.408
subject Compliance:	84.2 %
Centerline Deviation:	-0.221

Recommendations:

Increase: Discuss relationships with someone who cares about you. Positive physical contact can help release oxytocin and lower cortisol. This can help lower blood pressure and heart rate both of which are physical symptoms of stress. Interestingly, humans aren't the only animals who cuddle for stress relief. Chimpanzees also cuddle friends who are stressed.

Forecast:

If he follows the recommendation above, he may expect a 73.517% improvement in 5 weeks.

Fig. 13. The wellness recommender system creates psychological recommendations based on metrics the subject provides.

the value of the contour integral itself. As a confirmation that this application of the EQALY is feasible, Fig. 14 depicts the result of using gradient descent to find a lifeline that minimizes a contour integral through a scalar field.

The left panel is a scalar field having a central local minimum; the left panel is a scalar field having a central local maximum. As expected, with a central minimum, the contour attempts to flow perpendicular to the gradient, while minimizing length. With a central maximum, the contour attempts to flow parallel to low-value arcs.

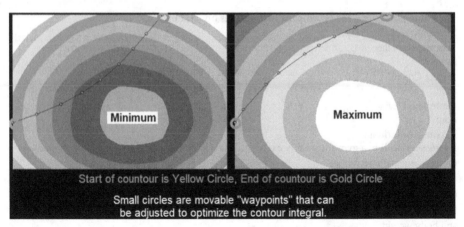

Fig. 14. Using gradient descent for positioning lifeline waypoints to find a contour that minimizes the line integral. For both treatments, waypoints were initialized on the straight-line path from the start location to the end location; both x and y coordinates of the waypoints could vary. The figure depicts the contours after 2,000 epochs.

4 Conclusion

The psychological import of such an integrated personalized QALY is clear. Advising to eat right, exercise, learn to relax, and live within their means provides insufficient direction. The high-fidelity EQALY provides specificity, quantification, and assessment of relative costs and effects, which can help to facilitate optimal wellness paths.

The EQALY is an innovative tool for quantifying and optimizing wellness. The EQALY's assessment of relative health can aid subjects' everyday decision-making. With further experimentation, the EQALY and supporting Wellness Recommender System have the potential to bolster self-improvement efforts. This system's nuanced representations of trajectories and instantaneous course corrections can empower people to improve their well-being.

Acknowledgement. This research was supported by the Living Centerline Institute.

References

1. Grable, J.E.: Psychophysical economics: introducing an emerging field of study. J. Financ. Serv. Prof. **67**(5), 16–18 (2013)
2. Hancock, M.: Non-monotonic bias-based reasoning under uncertainty. In: Proceedings of the 14th International Conference on Augmented Cognition, Copenhagen, Denmark, July 2020
3. Hanlon, B., et. al.: Feedback control for optimizing human wellness. In: Proceedings of the 14th International Conference on Augmented Cognition, Copenhagen, Denmark, July 2020
4. Haraldstad, K., et al.: A systematic review of quality of life research in medicine and health sciences. Qual. Life Res. **28**(10), 2641–2650 (2019). https://doi.org/10.1007/s11136-019-022 14-9

5. Thayer, J., Abs, F., Fredrikson, M., Sollers, J., Wager, D.: A meta-analysis of heart rate variability and neuroimaging studies: implications for heart rate variability as a marker of stress and health. Neurosci. Biobehav. Rev. **36**(2), 747–756 (2012)
6. Whitehead, S.J., Ali, S.: Health outcomes in economic evaluation: the QALY and utilities. British Med. Bull. **96**(1), 5–21 (2010)

Comparison Study of Attention Between Training in a Simulator vs. Live-Fire Range

Gregory P. Krätzig[✉], Chet C. Hembroff[✉], and Billea Ahlgrim[✉]

University of Regina, 3737 Wascana Parkway, Regina, Saskatchewan, Canada
Greg.kratzig@uregina.ca

Abstract. This study was designed to measure if simulation can be used beyond basic marksmanship training. The results provide evidence that the training environment (i.e., live; Group One, vs. synthetic; Group Two) does not affect overall learning and dynamic and tactical skills learned are transferable in situ, supporting earlier research that simulation training can be used for novice candidates [2, 9, 10, 12].

Following discussions with both training candidates and instructors, it was thought that participants who were trained in the synthetic environment would experience greater physiological arousal (i.e., stress) because they felt their training would not have properly prepared them for the final test. However, the results did not support this assumption, and that the design of the course produced high levels of stress during each of the two tests regardless of training environment.

We found that cognitive load was increased during training on Day 2 and Day 3 but during the final day (i.e., Final Test, Day 4) that cognitive effort appeared to decrease. These results suggest considerable resources were expended to learn new skills, and that the frequency of training resulted in a level of confidence and automaticity by the final test.

These results are important for law enforcement as it provides some initial evidence that learning tactical shooting skills can be acquired without live-fire practice. The course was designed to challenge the end-user both physically and psychologically, which we were able to validate using functional near-infrared spectroscopy (fNIR's) and electrocardiograph (ECG) recording devices. These findings support utilizing simulation technology for training, as it results in similar training outcomes, while reducing costs, mitigating health concerns (e.g., lead exposure, noise reduction), and it addresses access needs for a limited number of live-firearms ranges.

Keywords: fNIR · ECG · Firearms · Performance

1 Introduction

There are many factors known to affect police performance in both training and operational settings (e.g., decision-making during firearms practice or during the use of force); however, a growing area of research has focused on how stress, cognitive effort,

© Springer Nature Switzerland AG 2021
D. D. Schmorrow and C. M. Fidopiastis (Eds.): HCII 2021, LNAI 12776, pp. 178–197, 2021.
https://doi.org/10.1007/978-3-030-78114-9_13

and fatigue affect performance in the field. To-date there is still relatively little literature on the effects of stress and cognitive effort on training performance. Nieuwenhuys and Oudejans [11] found that police officers participating in both low- and high-anxiety shooting tests were able to counteract the negative effects of stress by increasing their cognitive effort and attention onto task relevant information. They argued that while increases in cognitive effort were initially ineffective, once participants gained more experience shooting under emotionally arousing situations, the increased cognitive effort was more effective at combating the negative effects of stress. However, due to the realities of policing, eliminating cognitive demand and stress from an officer's daily duties is not possible, but introducing and controlling for these factors within a training environment could provide solutions to mitigate the effects of cognitive load and stress and improve overall performance, ultimately improving public safety.

Cognitive load and stress in training can be increased safely; however, until recently this type of training typically occurred in live settings. The advancement of simulation technology has become an essential part of training in professions such as medicine, aviation, and more recently in policing. The addition of this technology allows the student to experience situations that they can expect to encounter in the field, without having to expose students to unnecessary risks or harm. Although the value of simulation technology has been recognized in aviation4 and medical1 training programs, it is less accepted as a training tool for pistol marksmanship training [2, 9, 10, 12].

This study was designed to determine if simulation training could be used beyond basic marksmanship training and if high-intensity courses that elicited emotional arousal and increased cognitive load could be replicated in a simulated environment. These findings could allow organizations that have limited range access, who have health and safety concerns, or budgetary challenges, to leverage simulation as a viable means in which to deliver training while increasing student throughput. In an effort to address some of these issues, this twofold study examined whether using a synthetic environment elicited similar physiological responses during an advanced, dynamic training course compared to a live counterpart, and second, is this technology a viable solution for training advanced firearms skills [2, 9, 10, 12].

2 Procedure

2.1 Method

Participants. Eleven experienced police officers (males = 11) with advanced firearms training were recruited for this study from across Canada. Advanced skills required included being part of Emergency Response Teams (ERT), Air Marshalls, or advanced firearms instructors. Six of the participants completed the study training course in a live-fire environment and five completed it in a synthetic environment. One participant from the live-fire condition was not included in some analyses due to an injury that prohibited them from participating in the final test.

Materials. The study training course was a reactive shooter course designed to respond to an active shooter threat while increasing the physical and psychological limits of the student. The training occurs over four days and takes approximately 30 h to complete.

The course consists of classroom instruction (i.e., primarily course description and range-safety), dry-fire practice (i.e., firing a pistol without ammunition), and live-fire training sessions. For security reasons the details of the participants and agencies are excluded.

Physiological measurements were recorded using smart shirt technology developed by Carre®. The Carre® Hexoskin® [5] shirt records continuous electrocardiograph (ECG) and breathing rate [5, 13]. This non-invasive system uses three heart sensors and two respiratory sensors embedded into the garment, which provide low variability and error, and good consistency [13].

Cognitive load was measured using an ambulatory functional near-infrared spectroscopy (fNIR) device. This non-invasive system places light emitting diodes (LEDs) directly on the participant's forehead that measure changes in oxygenated and deoxygenated hemoglobin concentrations in the dorsolateral prefrontal cortex (DLPFC). The fNIR measures hemoglobin concentration across four regions of the DLPFC each of which are responsible for unique aspects of executive control. While Regions 1 and 2 have been shown to be associated with attention, Region 3 has been found to be associated with problem solving, and Region 4 has been shown to be associated with working memory [6, 7].

Brief Psychomotor Vigilance Task. PVT-B [2] The brief Psychomotor Vigilance Task (PVT-B) [3] is the most commonly used metric to measure alertness and vigilance during sleep loss [3, 8]. The PVT-B measures sustained and vigilant attention by recording response times (RTs) to stimuli that appear on a screen at random inter-stimulus intervals (ISIs[2]). When an individual is fatigued, performance on the PVT-B is associated with slower RTs, increased errors of omission (i.e., lapses; failing to hit the response button within 355ms), and increased errors of commission (i.e., false starts; hitting the response button before a stimulus is present).

Synthetic Range. A computerized system projects a digital firearms range in units of 122cm wide lanes or shooting stalls. The targets are computer generated and can be presented at different distances (e.g., 3 to 25m). A double action only 9mm pistol was used for the simulation portion of the research, but the pistol was deactivated and a laser (used for interacting with the simulation equipment) was inserted into the barrel. All safety protocols required in a live-fire range were also adhered to in the synthetic range.

Training
Group One (Live Environment). Participants completed four 7.5 - hour days. Each participant completed the PVT-B on the mornings of training days 1, 3, and 4, and each participant wore a Hexoskin® [5] shirt for the entirety of each training day and two participants wore the fNIR device for the entirety of the training course. The fNIR devices were removed during the lunch breaks and placed back on the participants when they had returned in the afternoon.

Training Day 1. The day began with safety briefings and an introduction to the training course. This was followed by a dry-fire session in establishing grip and trigger control. Once complete the participants and instructors transitioned to a live-fire test to establish base-line skills (i.e., Test 1), and performance differences were measured against this score.

Training Day 2. This day consisted of both dry-fire and live-fire training, and approximately 650 rounds were fired.

Training Day 3. This day also consisted of dry-fire and live-fire training; however, some training drills required participants to complete tasks such as walk/run while shooting, shoot while off-balance, shoot while being distracted by the instructor, and rapid close range shooting. Each participant shot approximately 650 rounds.

Training Day 4. The time spent on the final day was about 5 h long and involved both dry-fire and live-fire instruction. The day ended with each participant being re-tested (i.e., Test 2).

Group 2 (Synthetic Environment). The participants for this group completed the same training as Group One; however, all training exercises occurred using dry-fire, non-recoil pistols in a computerized range. In order to measure skill transferability from the synthetic environment to a live-fire setting, the participants completed Test 1 and Test 2 in a live-fire range on day one and four, respectively.

Each participant completed the PVT-B the mornings of each training day. Each participant wore a Hexoskin® [5] shirt and three participants wore the fNIR device for the entirety of the training course. The participants removed the fNIR device during lunch breaks and they were placed back on when they returned for the remainder of the training.

3   Results

3.1   Fatigue

PVT-B scores are calculated four ways; mean reciprocal response time (RT), false starts, lapses, and combined errors (i.e., number of false starts and lapses). Mean reciprocal RT is a measure of the participant's response speed [3] and is calculated by dividing each RT by 1000, reciprocally transforming the number, and calculating an average and demonstrates that it is an optimal outcome metric for the PVT-B [3]. False starts were calculated as any response before a stimulus was shown and lapses were calculated as any response after the 355ms threshold [3].

One-Way ANOVAs were conducted to investigate differences between Group One and Group Two. These data revealed no differences in mean reciprocal RT between the live-fire and synthetic conditions for any of the PVT-B administrations (Table 1).

An analysis of combined errors found significant differences with a large effect size between Groups on the Day 1 PVT-B administration, $F(1,8) = 8.53, p = .019, \eta^2 = .52$. These data indicate that the participants in Group One had more combined errors than the participants in Group Two during the first administration (Table 2). Further analyses found that the difference in errors between the two Groups was due to a combination of false starts and lapses, as there were no differences for false starts or lapses when examined separately (Table 3).

182 G. P. Krätzig et al.

Table 1. PVT-B mean reciprocal RT

Administration	F	η^2	Group one			Group two		
			N	M	SE	N	M	SE
1	.550	.06	5	4.39	.58	5	3.95	.15
2	.182	.02	5	3.96	.11	5	3.81	.34
3	.596	.07	5	3.80	.16	5	3.44	.44

Note. Administration 1 occurred on Day 1 for both Groups, Administration 2 occurred on Day 3 for Group One and Day 2 for Group Two, and Administration 3 occurred on Day 5 for Group One and Day 3 for Group Two.

Table 2. PVT-B combined errors

Administration	F	η^2	Group one			Group two		
			N	M	SE	N	M	SE
1	8.53*	.52	5	3.4	.40	5	1.8	.37
2	.397	.05	5	2.4	.68	5	3.4	1.44
3	1.109	.11	6	2.83	1.08	5	4.8	1.59

Note. Administration 1 occurred on Day 1 for both Groups, Administration 2 occurred on Day 3 for Group One and Day 2 for Group Two, and Administration 3 occurred on Day 5 for Group One and Day 3 for Group Two.
*$p < .05$; **$p < .01$

Table 3. PVT-B errors

	Administration	F	η^2	Group one			Group two		
				N	M	SE	N	M	SE
False starts	1	7.2	.08	5	1.40	.60	5	.80	.37
	2	.00	.00	5	1.00	.45	5	.71	.32
	3	.021	.00	5	2.20	1.02	5	2.12	.96
Lapses	1	1.67	.17	5	2.00	.55	5	1.23	.55
	2	.25	.03	5	1.40	.60	5	2.20	1.50
	3	1.29	.14	5	1.20	.50	5	2.80	1.32

Note. Administration 1 occurred on Day 1 for both Groups, Administration 2 occurred on Day 3 for Group One and Day 2 for Group Two, and Administration 3 occurred on Day 5 for Group One and Day 3 for Group Two.
*$p < .05$; **$p < .01$

Repeated Measures analyses with training condition as the between subjects factor were conducted on PVT-B metrics over the week of training. There were no differences in reciprocal mean RT, combined errors, false starts, or lapses over the course of the week in either training condition, suggesting that fatigue was similar across training days (Fig. 1, Fig. 2, Fig. 3).

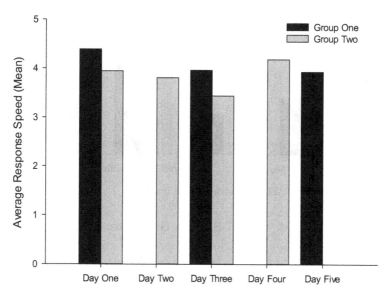

Fig. 1. Average response speed on each PVT-B administration by condition

3.2 Firearms Performance

Firearms performance is scored using three metrics: target score, time penalty, and final score. Target score is calculated by totaling the number of rounds inside the target multiplied by two. A time penalty is calculated by totalling the number of rounds shot after the prescribed time limit and is represented by a negative number. Final scores are calculated by using the target score minus the time penalty. A One-Way ANOVA was used and no differences in performance (i.e., Test 1 and Test 2) was found between Groups.

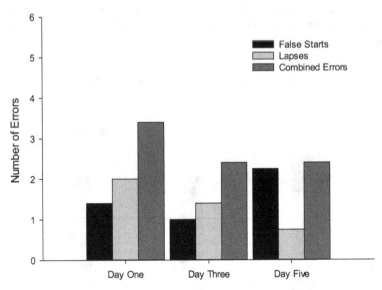

Fig. 2. Average errors group one

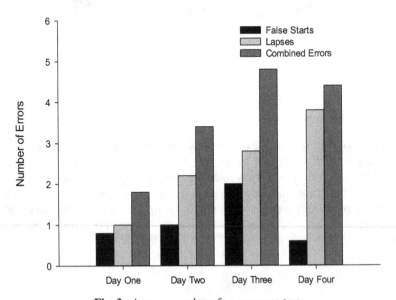

Fig. 3. Average number of errors group two

Although there were no differences in performance between training conditions, there were differences between time penalties and final scores between Test 1 and Test 2. These results suggest performance improved between tests, regardless of the training condition (Group One and Group Two). Although participants' target scores were nominally lower on Test 2, the benefit of training was evidenced in significantly increasing speed, decreasing time penalties, and improving final scores (Table 4, Fig. 4, Fig. 5).

Table 4. Participant performance

	F	η^2	Test 1			Test 2		
			N	M	SE	N	M	SE
Target score	1.59	.08	10	96.00	1.52	10	93.70	1.01
Time penalty	23.67**	.57	10	−19.10	2.28	10	−6.3	1.31
Final score	10.20**	.36	10	76.90	3.06	10	87.90	1.57

$*p < .05; **p < .01$

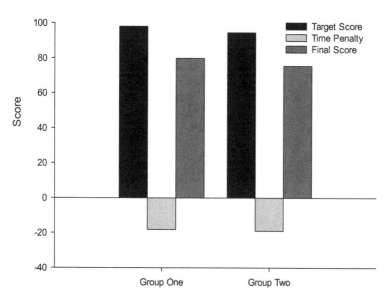

Test 1 Firearms Performance

Fig. 4. Firearms performance for Test 1 by group.

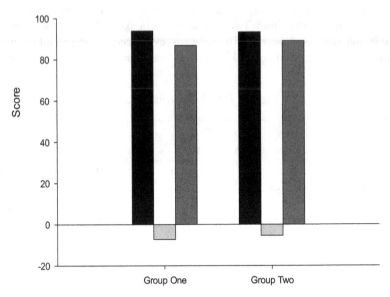

Fig.5. Firearms performance for Test 2 by group.

There were no correlations between PVT-B metrics and Test 1. Correlations between PVT-B metrics and Test 2 could only be conducted with Group Two, as the PVT-B was not administered on the day of Test 2 for Group Two. However, there were still no correlations found between PVT-B and performance metrics (Table 5 and Table 6).

Table 5. PVT-B and Test 1 correlations

	Mean reciprocal RT	Combined errors	False starts	Lapses
Mean reciprocal RT	–			
Combined errors	.26	–		
False starts	.14	.38	–	
Lapses	.12	.60	−.52	–
Test 1 target score	.29	−.12	.11	−.21
Test 1 time penalty	.27	−.03	−.54	.44
Test 1 final score	.34	−.08	−.34	.22

$*p < .05; **p < .01$

Table 6. PVT-B and Test 2 correlations

	Mean reciprocal RT	Combined errors	False starts	Lapses
Mean reciprocal RT	–			
Combined errors	−.86	–		
False starts	−.31	.39	–	
Lapses	-.82	.94*	.07	–
Test 2 target score	.17	−.30	.26	−.42
Test 2 time penalty	.44	−.50	−.64	−.32
Test 2 final score	.07	−.21	−.95*	.12

*$p < .05$; **$p < .01$

3.3 Physiology

Heart Rate. Physiological measurements included resting heart rate (HR) taken at the beginning of the test day, maximum HR during the test, average HR during the test, and recovery rate taken at the end of the testing period. One-Way ANOVAs were conducted to determine if there were differences in HR between Test 1 and Test 2. There were no differences between participant resting rates, maximum HR, average HR, and recovery rates (Table 7).

Table 7. Participant physiological measurements (Hexoskin®)

HR Metrics	F	η^2	Test 1			Test 2		
			N	M	SE	N	M	SE
Resting rate	.01	.00	10	91.40	4.99	10	90.86	4.49
Maximum HR	2.86	.14	10	127.40	4.89	10	113.96	6.26
Average HR	2.18	.11	10	99.13	4.74	10	110.00	5.64
Recovery rate	.03	.00	10	95.60	4.00	10	96.57	3.81

*$p < .05$; **$p < .01$

Paired t-tests were conducted to investigate differences in resting, testing, and recovery HR measures. Although no HR differences were found between the two tests, there were differences between the average resting rates and some HR metrics during testing. There were significant differences between the average resting HR and maximum Test 1 h, $p < .001$; between the average resting rate and the average Test 1 h, $p = .03$; and between the average resting rate and the maximum Test 2 h, $p < .001$ (Table 8). These results suggest that experiences of stress were increased during testing periods.

Table 8. Paired t-test HR metrics test 1 and 2

	Test 1			Test 2		
	t	M	SD	t	M	SD
Resting rate	−12.97**	91.40	15.79	−5.84**	96.30	17.98
Maximum HR (During Test)		127.40	15.47		126.90	12.63
Resting rate	−2.57*	91.40	15.79	−1.12	96.30	17.98
Average HR (During Test)		99.13	14.98		102.56	14.60
Resting rate	−1.29	91.40	15.79	−2.22	96.30	17.98
Recovery rate		95.60	12.64		105.60	18.03

$*p < .05; **p < .01$

Paired t-tests within Group One revealed differences between the average resting rate and maximum Test 1 h and between the average resting rate and the average Test 1 recovery rate. Comparably in Group Two, significant differences were observed between average resting rate and the maximum HR for Test 1, but not between the average resting rate and the average Test 1 recovery rate. These results suggest that participants experienced an increase in stress during Test 1, regardless of the training condition (Table 9).

Table 9. Paired t-test HR metrics test 1

	Group One			Group Two		
	t	M	SD	t	M	SD
Resting rate	−15.78**	94.60	10.45	−6.54*	88.20	20.64
Maximum HR (During Test)		132.40	11.91		122.40	18.28
Resting rate	−2.01	94.60	10.45	−1.65	88.20	20.64
Average HR (During Test)		101.09	11.20		97.16	19.23
Resting rate	−3.03*	94.60	10.45	.30	88.20	20.64
Recovery rate		104.40	6.88		86.80	10.89

$*p < .05; **p < .01$

Within Test 2, Group One paired t-tests revealed significant differences in average resting rate and maximum HR in Test 2 ($p = .002$) and between average resting rate and recovery HR in Test 2 ($p = .03$). The Group 2, Test 2 analyses revealed significant differences between average resting rate and maximum Test 2 h ($p = .001$), between average resting rate and average Test 2 h ($p = .01$), and between average resting rate and Test 2 recovery HR ($p = .04$; Table 10).

Table 10. Paired t-test HR metrics test 2

	Group one			Group two		
	t	*M*	*SD*	*t*	*M*	*SD*
Resting rate	−7.59*	110	11.47	−8.23*	82.60	11.24
Maximum HR (During Test)		127.20	8.76		126.60	16.79
Resting rate	3.21*	110	11.47	−4.60*	82.60	11.24
Average HR (During Test)		101.33	14.15		103.80	16.61
Resting rate	−.81	110	11.47	−3.13*	82.60	11.24
Recovery rate		116.20	18.53		95.00	10.37

*$p < .05$; **$p < .01$

One-Way ANOVAs investigating HR metrics for Test 1 found differences between conditions for recovery rates only, $F(1,8) = 9.33, p = .016, \eta^2 = .54$ (Table 11). For Test 2, these analyses found differences between conditions for maximum HR only, $F(1,8) = 6.628, p = .033, \eta^2 = .45$ (Table 12).

Table 11. Test 1 physiological measurements (ECG)

	F	η^2	Group one			Group two		
			N	*M*	*SE*	*N*	*M*	*SE*
Resting rate	.38	.05	5	94.60	4.68	5	88.20	9.23
Maximum HR	1.05	.12	5	132.40	5.33	5	122.40	8.18
Average HR	.46	.02	5	101.09	5.01	5	97.16	8.60
Recovery rate	9.33*	.54	5	104.40	3.08	5	86.80	4.87

*$p < .05$; **$p < .01$

Table 12. Test 2 physiological measurements (ECG)

	F	η^2	Group one			Group two		
			N	*M*	*SE*	*N*	*M*	*SE*
Resting rate	4.81	.38	5	99.11	5.60	5	82.60	5.03
Maximum HR	6.63*	.45	5	101.33	6.33	5	126.60	7.51
Average HR	1.24	.13	5	116.20	8.28	5	103.80	7.43
Recovery rate	.15	.02	5	98.14	6.53	5	95.00	4.64

*$p < .05$; **$p < .01$

Blood Oxygenation. Differences in oxygenation within each region of the brain were analyzed for changes between each training day and test. Due to signal interference, the sample size for fNIR was limited. It was believed that the "handshake" between the computer and the recording device was unable to manage the constraints placed on it within a controlled firing range, resulting in substantial losses in data. While there were issues with data collection, some individual data was able to be reported.

Repeated measures ANOVAs were used to evaluate individual oxygenation changes between training days (i.e., the difference in oxygenated and deoxygenated hemoglobin concentrations). Data for Participant 4, 6, and 9 revealed linear decreases in oxygenation from Training Day 1 to Day 4, demonstrating a straight-line pattern for oxygenation changes. Conversely, Participant 11 had significant quadratic changes across days, in which oxygenation was low during Day 1, significantly higher during Day 2 and 3, and then significantly lower during Day 4, demonstrating a curved pattern for oxygenation changes. Participants 4 and 7 also demonstrated a significant quadratic relationship; however, these were only observed in Regions 3 and 4 for thee participants. These data demonstrate that oxygenation was highest during the days in which training was most concentrated (i.e., Day 2 and 3), and a significant decrease in oxygenation is consistently observed during Day 4 (i.e., when participants are being tested on the learned material; Table 13; Fig. 6).

A series of independent samples t-tests were used to evaluate oxygenation changes that occurred in each region of the brain during Test 1 and Test 2 within Group One and Group Two. During Test 1, these analyses revealed that there were no significant differences between Group One and Group Two. During Test 2, there were no significant differences between conditions in Regions 1, 2, and 4; however, there was a significant difference observed in Region 3, $t(2) = 5.041$, $p = .037$. These data suggest that participants who performed Test 2 in Group Two had significantly less oxygenation in this region of the brain compared to those in Group One, indicating that Test 2 required less problem solving effort for those who completed the test in the synthetic environment (Fig. 7).

A series of correlations were conducted to examine the impact of blood oxygenation on firearms performance. These analyses revealed that Region 3 and 4 oxygenation was significantly correlated with time penalties during Test 1 ($r = .99$, $p = .033$; $r = .99$, $p = .023$, respectively). Participants who allocated more mental resources to problem solving and working memory had significantly fewer time penalties during Test 1. There were no significant correlations between blood oxygenation and Test 1 target score or final score or with any of the Test 2 performance metrics (Table 14 and Table 15).

Table 13. Repeated measures within-subjects contrasts of blood oxygenation across days

Participant	Region	Direction	F	df	η^2
P4	1	Linear	26943.02	1,22108	.549**
	2	Linear	9300.09	1,6225	.599**
	3	Quadratic	8540.54	1,7949	.518**
	4	Linear	26768.41	1,23934	.450**
P6	1	Linear	46535.89	1,39340	.542**
	2	Linear	10786.09	1,2013	.843**
	3	Linear	34210.51	1,22402	.604**
	4	Linear	61644.49	1,41190	.599**
P7	1	Linear	1351.07	1,5990	.184**
	2	–	–	–	–
	3	–	–	–	–
	4	Quadratic	20410.50	1,7954	.720**
P9	1	Linear	27953.16	1,15159	.648**
	2	Linear	11211.54	1,13400	.456**
	3	Linear	49481.78	1,13727	.783**
	4	Linear	8911.15	1,17772	.334**
P11	1	Quadratic	43122.42	1,9842	.814**
	2	Quadratic	28106.34	1,8899	.760**
	3	Quadratic	22279.67	1,10642	.677**
	4	Quadratic	6539.66	1,9659	.404**

$*p < .05; **p < .01$

Activation. While there was not enough fNIR data to aggregate, we were able to plot the moment that the shot clock was activated (Fig. 8 vs. Fig. 9). This image shows the increased oxygen that was required in the DLPFC that was needed to perform the task of accurately hitting the target before the allotted time had elapsed.

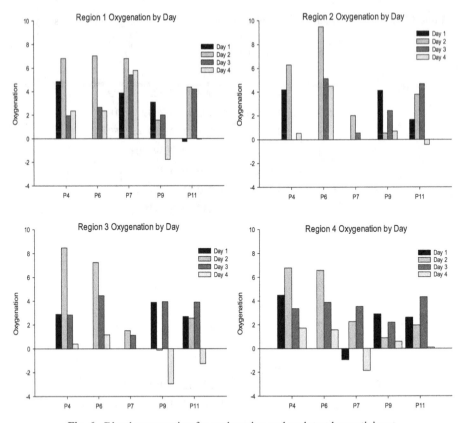

Fig. 6. Blood oxygenation for each region and each test by participant.

4   Discussion

Results indicated there were no differences on any of the performance measures between conditions for Test 1 or Test 2. There was improvement in performance between Test 1 and Test 2 with lower time penalties and higher final scores, regardless of the training condition. These results provide evidence that the training environment does not affect overall learning, and that the dynamic and tactical skills learned in a dry-fire non-recoil synthetic range environment transfer to a live-fire setting. These results build on existing literature by [2, 9, 10, 12].

Results suggest that the participants in the live-fire condition had more PVT-B combined errors the morning of Training Day 1 than those participants in the synthetic condition. This may have been due to the earlier start time for the participants in the live-fire condition (i.e., 06:00) compared to those who were trained in the synthetic condition (i.e., 12:00). There were no differences in PVT-B score over the training week for either the live-fire or the synthetic conditions. Despite verbal reports of fatigue, it appears vigilance was stable, and any differences on PVT-B were due to training condition and not fatigue.

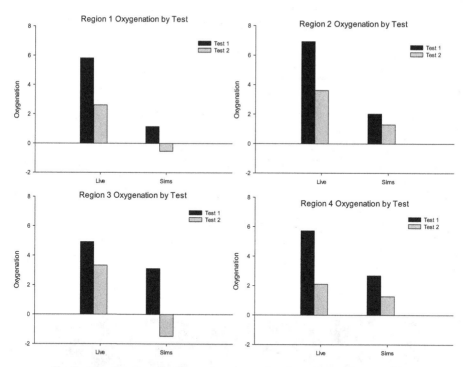

Fig. 7. Blood oxygenation for each region and each test by training condition.

Table 14. Correlations of Test 1 blood oxygenation and performance

	Region 1	Region 2	Region 3	Region 4	Test 1 target score	Test 1 time penalty	Test 1 final score
Region 1	–						
Region 2	.99	–					
Region 3	.98	.97	–				
Region 4	.99	.99*	.95	–			
Test 1 target score	.82	.77	.91	.73	–		
Test 1 time penalty	.99*	.99*	.98	.99	.32	–	
Test 1 final score	.96	.93	.99	.90	.72*	.89**	–

$*p < .05; **p < .01$

Table 15. Correlations of Test 2 blood oxygenation and performance

	Region 1	Region 2	Region 3	Region 4	Test 1 target score	Test 1 time penalty	Test 1 final score
Region 1	–						
Region 2	.88	–					
Region 3	.97*	.92	–				
Region 4	.72	.93	.74	–			
Test 2 target score	−.19	−.45	−.11	−.62	–		
Test 2 time penalty	.07	.29	−.09	.54	−.30	–	
Test 2 final score	−.36	−.06	−.43	.25	.37	.73*	–

$*p < .05; **p < .01$

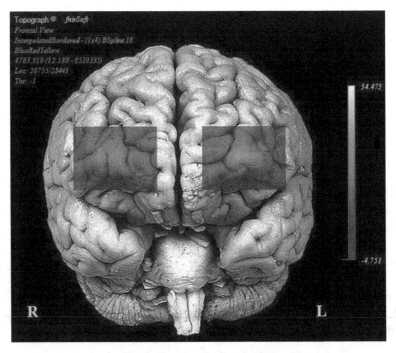

Fig. 8. Pre-shot clock activation

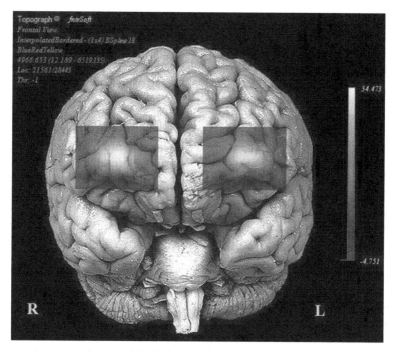

Fig. 9. Shot clock activation

Results indicate there were no differences in HR metrics between Test 1 and Test 2, which suggests that the participants were able to manage their stress levels during high-stress situations. This effect was expected due to their previous policing experience and expertise in the domain. However, there were differences in resting HR and average and maximum HR during Test 1 and Test 2 for both conditions, which suggests that all participants were experiencing similar and increased levels of stress during both tests. These results provide further evidence that the training environment does not affect learning. Anecdotally, it was argued that those who were trained in the dry-fire, non-recoil synthetic environment would experience greater physiological arousal because they would have felt unprepared for a live-fire test; however, these results were contrary to those ideas.

The participants in Group One had higher recovery HRs for Test 1 than those who were in Group Two; however, these differences could be attributed to the smaller sample size as training for Group Two had not yet started training in the simulated environment. Alternatively, the participants in Group Two had higher maximum HR for Test 2 than Group One. It is possible that the higher maximum HRs were the result of training without recoil, and the auditory feedback that results from shooting a live weapon. Perhaps, due to the absence of recoil and noise during training in the synthetic environment and the presence of it in the live environment during the tests. However, there were no significant correlations between any HR metrics and any Test performance metric, which indicates that even if HR metrics are higher for specific tests, it is not enough to affect performance.

This effect was observed regardless of training condition, recoil, and/or noise factors being present.

Participants' blood oxygenation changed significantly across their training days. Although participants' oxygenation varied during Day 1, the majority of participants experienced the highest increase in oxygenation during training focused days (i.e., Days 2 and 3) and significantly less when being tested during Day 4. This finding would suggest that participants require most of their cognitive resources when they are learning and practicing new skills. When participants are required to perform the skills they are experienced in, it requires fewer cognitive resources. Furthermore, the changes in oxygenation were similar in each region of the brain, suggesting that these skills require similar levels of attention, problem solving, and working memory to learn and perform them.

Although there appeared to be minor differences in oxygenation between training conditions, there was only one significant difference between groups, which occurred within Region 3, the region involved in problem solving, during Test 2. This finding suggests that the overall cognitive resources required were similar for both training conditions. Lastly, oxygenation was associated only with time penalties during Test 1. Oxygenation of Regions 1 and 2 were correlated with time penalties, indicating that participants who were applying more attention to Test 1 were experiencing fewer time penalties; however, additional participants would re-enforce the results.

These results are important for training as it provides evidence for the first time, that learning dynamic tactical shooting skills can be acquired without live-fire practice. The results of this study can provide support to training programs designed to elicit physiological arousal through elevated heart rate (HR) and increased cognitive load. Lastly, these findings support incorporating technology into firearms training programs, especially when access to live-ranges is limited. This technology can help reduce costs by reducing ammunition needs, paper target use, range maintenance, health risks (e.g., lead exposure, noise reduction) and can improve overall safety (i.e., use of non-lethal weapons) and training accessibility. Through the use of technology, the training could be brought to the students, resulting in significant cost savings by having two or three instructors travel to the students, instead of 12 students traveling to a central location.

References

1. Abrahamson, S., Denson, J.S., Wolf, R.M.: Effectiveness of a simulator in training anesthesiology residents. Qual. Safe Health Care **13**, 395–397 (2004). https://doi.org/10.1136/qhc.13.5.395
2. Band, D., Dragota, D., Sizemore, E.: Virtual firearms ranges. Fed. Law Enforc. Train. Cent. J. **16**, 21–26 (2016)
3. Basner, M., Mollicone, D., Dinges, D.F.: Validity and sensitivity of a brief psychomotor vigilance test (PVT-B) to total and partial sleep deprivation. Acta Astronaut. **69**, 949–959 (2011). https://doi.org/10.1016/j.actaastro.2011.07.015
4. Bürke-Cohen, J., Go, T.H., Longridge, T.: Flight simulator fidelity considerations for total air line pilot training and evaluation. In: Proceedings of the AIAA Modeling and Simulation Technologies Conference, Montreal, Canada (2001). http://www.raa.org/Portals/0/CommitteePages/FlightTraining/10-12_AIAA2001-4425final_header.pdf

5. Hexoskin®: Hexoskin® Wearable Body Metrics (2017)
6. http://www.hexoskin.com/
7. Izzetoglu, M., Bunce, S.C., Izzetoglu, K., Onaral, B., Pourrezaei, K.: Functional brain imaging using near-infrared technology: Assessing cognitive activity in real-life situations. IEEE Eng. Med. Biol. Mag. **26**(4), 38 (2007)
8. Izzetoglu, K., Bunce, S., Onaral, B., Pourrezaei, K., Chance, B.: Functional optical brain imagining using near-infrared during cognitive tasks. Int. J. Hum. Comput. Interact. **17**, 211–227 (2004). https://doi.org/10.1207/s15327590ijhc1702_6
9. Killgore, W.D.S.: Effects of sleep deprivation on cognition. Prog. Brain Res. **185**, 105–129 (2010). https://doi.org/10.1016/B978-0-444-53702-7.00007-5
10. Krätzig, G.P.: Pistol skill acquisition and retention: a 3-year longitudinal study. (Paper No. 14042). In: Interservice/Industry Training, Simulation, and Education Conference (2014)
11. Krätzig, G.P., Bell, G., Groff, R., Ford, C.: Simulator Emergency Police Vehicle Operation: Efficiencies and skill transfer. (Paper No. 10115). In: Interservice/Industry Training, Simulation, and Education Conference (2010)
12. Nieuwenhuys, A., Oudejans, R.R.D.: Training with anxiety: short- and long-term effects on police officers' shooting behavior under pressure. Cogn. Process. **12**, 277–288 (2011). https://doi.org/10.1007/s10339-011-0396-x
13. Sizemore, E.: A continuing story of firearms simulation. Fed. Law Enforc. Train. Cent. J. **11**, 8–10 (2013)
14. Villar, R., Beltrame, T., Hughson, R.L.: Validation of the Hexoskin wearable vest during lying, sitting, standing, and walking activities. Appl. Physiol. Nutr. Metab. **40**, 1019–1024 (2015). https://doi.org/10.1139/apnm-2015-0140

Passphrase Authentication and Individual Physiological Differences

Lila A. Loos[✉], Randall K. Minas[✉], Michael-Brian C. Ogawa[✉],
and Martha E. Crosby[✉]

University of Hawai'i at Mānoa, Honolulu, HI 96822, USA
{lila7194,rminas,ogawam,crosby}@hawaii.edu

Abstract. Computer passphrase authentication designed with usability consideration encourages memorability. This passphrase study suggests successful recollection using an assembly of meaningful word groups evidenced by individual physiological performance measurements. Participant data collected at the Hawai'i Interdisciplinary Neurobehavioral and Technology Lab (HINT) demonstrate physiological responses to passphrase decision making. The results from university students indicate psychophysiological influences predict passphrase characteristics. The repeated measures investigation of user-created and system-imposed passphrases contribute understanding toward user authentication selection that supports encoding and recalling a secret, unlike the current traditional password composed of alphanumeric and special characters. Passphrases constructed with usability considerations support security compliance requirements. This explanatory study employs pilot-tested passphrases designed to reveal predictive psychophysiological behavior. Overall results indicate user-created passphrases produce less cognitive load stressors on working memory than system-imposed passphrases. However, physiological measurements from heart rate, skin conductance, and the facial corrugator supercilii muscle signify a mixture of passphrase types that imply memorability. Study results suggest a platform for future passphrase design research of longer passwords that inform security access, improve memorability, and enhance usability evaluated by human-centered performance.

Keywords: Passphrase authentication · Physiological factors · Psychophysiology · Memorability · Usability · Cognitive load

1 Introduction

Computer authentication using passphrases consisting of multiple words suggest security endurance and memorability [12]. Therefore, it is proposed that 64 characters support a memorized secret of user-generated word groups; passphrases remain valid until a user requests a change or if evidence of a compromise exists [11]. The current complex password is based on a dissimilar formula to this study's passphrases that compose a lengthier authentication secret. To obtain physiological data, electrical measurements were collected as participants responded to various passphrase rule sets.

© Springer Nature Switzerland AG 2021
D. D. Schmorrow and C. M. Fidopiastis (Eds.): HCII 2021, LNAI 12776, pp. 198–209, 2021.
https://doi.org/10.1007/978-3-030-78114-9_14

The main goal is to evaluate the physiological impact of passphrase usability and improve the security mechanism of authenticating to secure resources. Specifically, this study addresses the following questions:

1. Which physiological responses can be measured during passphrase recall?
2. How are physiological responses evidenced in passphrase selection?
3. Which physiological outcomes predict passphrase memorability?

Contributions of this study identify the following: (a) an understanding of physiological responses to specific passphrases, (b) a repeated measures research of passphrase conditions that manifest objective phenomena of personified characteristics as opposed to a universal mechanism, and (c) predictive passphrases indicated by physiological factors. As of this writing, physiological investigations of computer passphrase selection were unfounded. Therefore, this study informs psychophysiological examination, the communication of cognitive processes measured by physiological expressions [16], in the inquiry of behavior to passphrase authentication events.

2 Theoretical Background: Psychophysiological Factors

Physiological factors embody discrete elements of the autonomic nervous system (ANS), evidenced by psychophysiological factors. This regulatory partition controls heart rate, skin conductance, and facial muscle activity [16]. Emotion is defined as a "conscious mental reaction (such as anger or fear) subjectively experienced as a strong feeling usually directed toward a specific object and typically accompanied by physiological and behavioral changes in the body" [15]. Physiological responses to cognitive tasks result in heart rate variability, skin conductance, and facial corrugator supercilii muscle activity. Capturing these psychophysiological expressions allow for behavioral illumination of passphrase selection.

Physiological experiences are recordable as data values in response to an event [5]. Emotional expression to varied passphrase types provides a theoretical basis of psychophysiological representation captured during the cognitive processing of passphrase stimuli. The examination of physiological reactions to cognitive load during working memory was collected from electrodermal (EDA), electrocardiography or heart rate variability (HRV), and facial electromyography (fEMG) as manifestations of emotion [3]. The collection of reactive variances produced during the memory processing of passphrases articulate recall performance of working memory [3].

Although working memory studies employ physiological functions wherein skin conductance and heart rate produce correlated studies on working memory; negative reactions of anger, fear, and sadness are evident in heart rate and skin conductance increases, unlike continuous measurement associated with happiness [9]. Additionally, individual responses from the autonomic nervous system span 122 years suggesting physiological illustrations of emotion [8].

Traversing from the autonomic nervous system are sympathetic nervous system (SNS) behaviors that increase arousal in the heart and skin conductance. Parasympathetic nervous system (PNS) portrays satisfaction with a decrease in heart rate [16]. Individual responses of blood flow and electrodermal skin conductance react to stimuli by increasing arousal in the SNS and decreasing arousal in the PNS. Impulses generated from the facial supercilii muscle fibers respond to cognitive stressors by activating a non-reflective physiological state [17]. These discrete behaviors convey negative or positive affective states related to emotional response [18]. fEMG decreases when arousal is combined with positive valence and increases with negative valence. Psychophysiological inferences of emotion derived from a one-to-one relationship with physiological reactions [6] were applied to this study's passphrase proficiency performance of personified cognition (see Fig. 1).

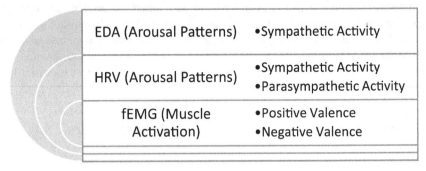

Fig. 1. Psychophysiological inferences

3   Methodology

This inquiry is based on a repeated measures methodology to collect electrophysiological data from the skin, heart, and corrugator supercilii facial muscle. It is designed for all participants to be exposed to fixed variables for replication under the same circumstances. Approval for this study (which included identifying the locus of control personality traits and cognitive load measurements are not discussed in this writing) was granted by the University of Hawai'i's Institutional Review Board. Individual participant data from the passphrase survey was collected during individual 90-min visits over three weeks at the HINT laboratory.

3.1   Population Sample Description

The population consisted of 58 adult students attending the University of Hawai'i at Mānoa who authenticate and manage passwords of various online accounts. This finite group of subjects adhere to homogeneity as they share similar demographics, including education standing and academic concentrations [7]. The majority (77.6%) listed a business field as their major (accounting, entrepreneurship, finance, or management) with (65.5%) ranging in age from 19 to 21 years old, and (44.8%) maintained 4 to 10 password protected online accounts followed by (43.1%) who maintained 14 to 57 accounts.

3.2 Passphrase Rules for the Survey Instrument

Grounded on a literature review, the survey instrument was designed with cognitive load and working memorability considerations. It was pre-tested and revised based on the three pilot study results. The same rule sets used for system-imposed passphrases were applied to user-generated passphrases. Eight rules were structured to contain four words with a minimum of five characters per word. Subjects were either provided a passphrase or instructed to create a passphrase based on each rule set (see Table 1).

Table 1. Passphrase rule sets

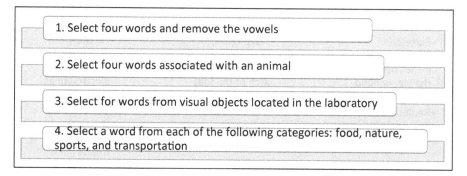

1. Select four words and remove the vowels

2. Select four words associated with an animal

3. Select for words from visual objects located in the laboratory

4. Select a word from each of the following categories: food, nature, sports, and transportation

Participants were prompted to recall each passphrase sixteen times while random distractions from the Stroop [20] word and color test appeared throughout the survey to compete for attention. Cognitive load is tasked with overcoming working memory challenges as participants were prompted to enter the ink color–even if the word is mismatched to its color–while maintaining processing capacity [14]. Therefore, reading the word BLUE displayed with red ink suggests interference with the automatic response to identifying the word.

3.3 Electrophysiological Data Collection Procedure

This study collected anonymized data and did not include photographing or video taping of the sample. Therefore, personally indentifiable information such as name, address, birthdate, or student identification was unknown to the researcher. In an area adjacent to the subjects, the researcher recorded each participant's session as separate monitors displayed the passphrase survey and the electrophysiological activity. To ensure data security, the researcher and participant computers were password protected. The University of Hawai'i at Mānoa maintained user licenses for the Internet-based Qualtrics survey, BIOPAC physiological data acquisition system, and AcqKnowledge physiological graphical data simulation software. Session notes were taken to log unexpected occurrences such as survey activity, participant artifacts, observations, annotations, and technical difficulties.

The HINT laboratory is equipped with the BIOPAC System that is compliant with the International Organization for Standardization for electrophysiological test centers. Physiological data were recorded using sensors for heart rate, skin conductance, and the facial corrugator muscle. The electrodes connect to the corresponding channels on the bioamplifier that transforms and transfers the physiological data waveform signals to the computer for recording. A simultaneous collection of physiological responses to the passphrase survey was performed for each subject. The data collection procedure for the subjects adhered to the following process: (a) prepare skin with electrode cleaning pad, (b) connect the electrode led to the adhesive patch, and (c) continue with Fig. 2.

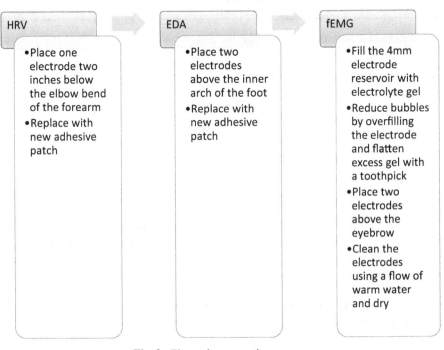

Fig. 2. Electrode preparation process

3.4 Data Analysis

The physiological measurements were analyzed using the AcqKnowledge data acquisition and analysis software. Physiological data was time sequenced with the Qualtrics survey and manually scored. IBM's statistical package for the social sciences (SPSS) was used to perform statistical analysis to compare the probability in significance testing of the stimuli effects on physiological changes. A repeated measures analysis of variance provided statistical results on the measured variables' main effect and interactions using alpha .05. The false discovery rate (FDR) was applied to the physiological data to address type one error when executing probabilistic tests using multiple regression, correlation, t-tests, and Cohen's d effect size [2]. Prior use of the FDR statistical adjustment has been applied to large data sets produced by functional magnetic resonance physiological data collection experiments [10].

4   Results

This section illustrates the passphrase memorability results and addresses the study's research questions. First, Sect. 4.1 describes the overall statistical test results without factoring in the physiological scores. Second, physiological passphrase results are reported in Sect. 4.2. Including both types of results provides dual comparison data.

4.1   Passphrase Recall: Overall Scores

Passphrase recall suggests a significant effect of the eight passphrase types: Wilks' Lambda = .414, $F(1, 57) = 80.66$, $p < .01$. Figure 3 represents the contrast between the recall of system-imposed (mean = .66 to 8.19) and user-generated (mean = 9.5 to 12.43) passphrases. Overall results suggest higher recollection for created passphrases.

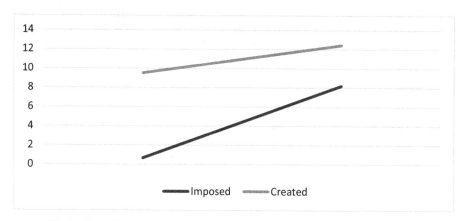

Fig. 3. Overall user-created and system-imposed passphrase recall mean results

The overall recollection mean scores rank the list of passphrase types as shown below in Table 2.

The results suggest that participants remembered more passphrases from the user-created passphrase group.

Table 2. Passphrase recall mean results

Passphrase type	Mean
Imposed no vowels	.66
Imposed animal associations	5.66
Imposed room objects	6.98
Imposed 4 categories	8.19
Created 4 categories	9.59
Created animal associations	10.62
Created room objects	11.90
Created no vowels	12.43

4.2 Passphrase Recall: Physiological Responses

This section details the results from participant physiological responses that examine cognitive behavior when interacting with various passphrases. An examination from the simultaneous collection of physiological arousal and affect measurements are detailed in this section.

RQ1. Which physiological responses can be measured during passphrase recall?
Wavelength data was successfully collected from heart rate variability, skin conductance, and the facial corrugator muscle supercilii. A repeated measures ANOVA test on the physiological factors shown in Table 3 produced a significant effect on heart rate and skin conductance. However, the corrugator supercilii muscle was not significant during passphrase recall.

Table 3. Multivariate test results for passphrase recall of physiological events

Physiological event	Wilks' Lambda	F	Hypothesis df	Error df	Sig.
HRV	.671	3.57	7	51	.003
EDA	.715	2.906	7	51	.012
fEMG	.840	1.388	7	51	.230

Computed using alpha = .05

RQ2. How are physiological responses evidenced in passphrase selection?
Based on the physiological arousal levels demonstrated by heart rate and skin conductance, a lower score indicates a decrease in activation when comparing specific types of passphrase responses. As illustrated in Table 4, the heart rate and skin conductance levels decreased when recalling the user-created passphrase group. Unlike HRV and EDA, a comparison of the fEMG mean scores with the overall sample mean score (−.00176) revealed positive affect, a response decrease in the corrugator supercilii muscle, with imposed passphrases and negative affect, increased muscle activity, with the created passphrase group.

Table 4. Overall mean and standard deviation results for passphrase recall of physiological events

Physiological event	Imposed M, SD	Created M, SD
HRV	81.89	**81.55**
	10.71	10.84
EDA	2.78	**2.75**
	3.45	3.55
fEMG*	**−.00216***	−.00140
	.0041	.0004

Mean (M), Standard Deviation (SD)
*fEMG overall sample mean score (−.00176)
(−.00176) < −.00216 = positive affect*
(−.00176) > −.00140 = negative affect

A paired samples t-test resulted in a significant effect on the first pair of passphrases for the facial corrugator muscle; the second pair suggests correlation (see Table 5).

Table 5. fEMG paired samples t-test for passphrase recall

Passphrase pairs	Sig.	Cohen's d	Effect size
Created 4 categories	.028	.295	$d \geq 0.2$
Created animal associations			
Imposed animal associations	.056*	.296	$d \geq 0.2$
Created animal associations			

Computed using alpha = .05
FDR Adjustment
*Pearson correlation is significant at the .05 level (2-tailed) p = .014

Heart rate decreased when remembering the following user-created passphrase types: 4 categories, no vowels, and animal associations, as well as the system-imposed room objects passphrase. Skin conductance was reduced when recalling user-created 4 categories and room objects passphrases, including system-imposed no vowels and animal associations phrases (see Table 6).

Table 6. HRV and EDA mean and standard deviation results for passphrase recall

Passphrase type	HRV M, SD	EDA M, SD
Created 4 categories	**80.36**	**2.34**
	11.25	3.10
Imposed 4 categories	81.84	3.00
	10.41	3.96
Created no vowels	**81.81**	2.76
	10.58	3.86
Imposed no vowels	82.34	**2.50**
	11.48	**2.50**
Created animal associations	**81.97**	3.00
	11.54	4.00
Imposed animal associations	82.40	**2.70**
	12.00	3.70
Created room objects	82.06	**2.91**
	11.41	3.83
Imposed room objects	**80.97**	2.93
	11.04	3.70

Mean (M), Standard Deviation (SD)

RQ3. Which physiological outcomes predict passphrase memorability?

The user-created 4 categories passphrase ranked the highest in all physiological events. A decrease in heart rate activation, skin conductance arousal signals, and corrugator muscle engagement was indicated during passphrase recall. The specific passphrase types for recalling user-created and system-imposed passphrases are listed below by physiological response (see Fig. 4).

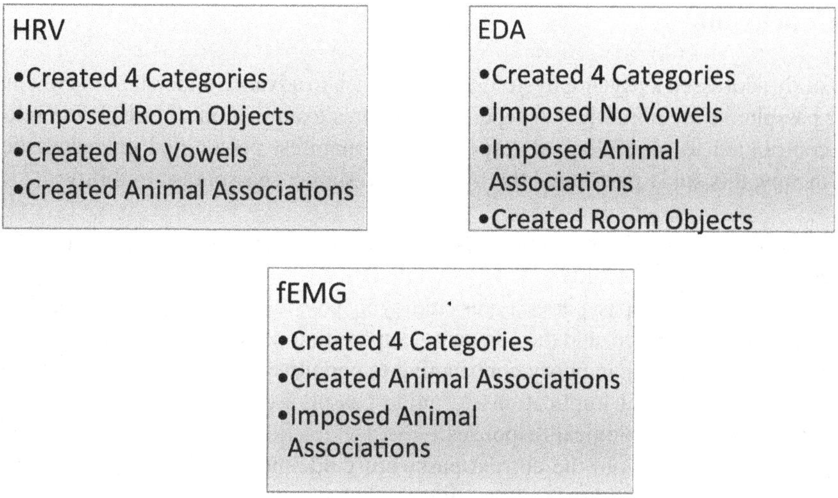

HRV

- •Created 4 Categories
- •Imposed Room Objects
- •Created No Vowels
- •Created Animal Associations

EDA

- •Created 4 Categories
- •Imposed No Vowels
- •Imposed Animal Associations
- •Created Room Objects

fEMG

- •Created 4 Categories
- •Created Animal Associations
- •Imposed Animal Associations

Fig. 4. Passphrase recall based on physiological responses

5   Discussion

An explanation of HRV, EDA, and fEMG physiological findings is discussed in subsequent sections. Overall results showed a high recall for user-created passphrases compared to system-imposed passphrases. Additionally, the lowest scores indicate increased cognitive load on working memory were the system-imposed no vowels and animal associations passphrases. Psychological states of working memory processing specify the cognitive demands of passphrase memorability as represented in the autonomic nervous system's manifestation of physiological responses.

5.1   HRV Heart Rate Variability and EDA Electrodermal/Skin Conductance Activity

Heart rate and skin conductance studies reveal a correlation with cognitive processing and emotion [9, 13]. In accordance with literature, HRV and EDA passphrase memorability were correlated with the highest recall of the user-created 4 categories phrase. Therefore, arousal activation placed the least demand on cognitive load during working memory processing for this passphrase. A decrease in heart rate variability favored user-created passphrases, although the system-imposed room objects phrase ranked second.

Additionally, skin conductance decreased with the system-imposed animal associations phrase, which correlates with fEMG.

5.2   fEMG Facial Electromyography/Corrugator Supercilii Muscle

The non-reflective expression from the corrugator supercilii muscle showed decreased activation, positive affect, for the overall system-imposed passphrase group. However, fEMG was significant on the user-created 4 categories and system-imposed animal association phrases.

6 Conclusion

This study addressed a psychophysiological approach to advance understanding of computer passphrase memorability. A repeated-measures examination of passphrase selection contributed to physiological responses that manifest personified characteristics. Specifically, this study performed the following to support passphrase usability:

1. Tested user-created and system-imposed passphrase types by exploring behavior responsive to memorability.
2. Produced predictive passphrase types employing physiological inferences from heart rate, skin conductance, and the corrugator supercilii muscle activation that increases or decreases working memory contributing to cognitive load.
3. Determined practical implications to guide passphrase authentication design that yield positive physiological responses.
4. Presented challenges to the current password guidelines and encourage a human-centric approach considerate of emotion and behavior.

Although autonomic nervous systems studies extending over a hundred years suggest psychophysiological associations support multivariate theory-based investigations [8], the lack of causal evidence from the ANS or physiological research categorizes the study results as subjective measurable outcomes [1]. Therefore, continued passphrase formulation is essential to advance human computer interaction and effective password management. Future personified studies can positively influence authentication design policies that increase global computer security.

References

1. Barrett, L.F.: Are emotions natural kinds? Perspect. Psychol. Sci. **1**(1), 28–58 (2006)
2. Benjamini, Y., Hochberg, Y.: Controlling the false discovery rate: a practical and powerful approach to multiple testing. J. Roy. Stat. Soc.: Ser. B (Methodol.) **57**(1), 289–300 (1995)
3. Berntson, G.G., Cacioppo, J.T., Tassinary, L.G. (eds.): Handbook of Psychophysiology. Cambridge University Press, Cambridge (2017)
4. Boucsein, W., et al.: Publication recommendations for electrodermal measurements: publication standards for EDA. Psychophysiology **49**(8), 1017–1034 (2012). https://doi.org/10.1111/j.1469-8986.2012.01384.x
5. Cacioppo, J.T., Tassinary, L.G.: Inferring psychological significance from physiological signals. Am. Psychol. **45**(1), 16 (1990)
6. Cacioppo, J.T., Tassinary, L.G., Berntson, G.G.: Psychophysiological science: Interdisciplinary approaches to classic questions about the mind. Handb. Psychophysiol. **3**, 1–16 (2007)
7. Etikan, I., Musa, S.A., Alkassim, R.S.: Comparison of convenience sampling and purposive sampling. Am. J. Theor. Appl. Stat. **5**(1), 1–4 (2016)
8. Friedman, B.H.: Feelings and the body: the Jamesian perspective on autonomic specificity of emotion. Biol. Psychol. **84**(3), 383–393 (2010)
9. Garcia, A., Uribe, C.E., Tavares, M.C., Tomaz, C.: EEG and autonomic responses during performance of matching and non-matching to sample working memory tasks with emotional content. Front. Behav. Neurosci. **5**, 82 (2011)

10. Genovese, C.R., Lazar, N.A., Nichols, T.: Thresholding of statistical maps in functional neuroimaging using the false discovery rate. Neuroimage **15**(4), 870–878 (2002)
11. Grassi, P.A., Garcia, M.E., Fenton, J.L.: DRAFT NIST special publication 800-63-3 digital identity guidelines. National Institute of Standards and Technology, Los Altos, CA (2017)
12. Keith, M., Shao, B., Steinbart, P.: A behavioral analysis of passphrase design and effectiveness. J. Assoc. Inf. Syst. **10**(2), 2 (2009)
13. Kreibig, S.D.: Autonomic nervous system activity in emotion: a review. Biol. Psychol. **84**(3), 394–421 (2010). https://doi.org/10.1016/j.biopsycho.2010.03.010
14. Lavie, N.: Distracted and confused?: selective attention under load. Trends Cogn. Sci. **9**(2), 75–82 (2005)
15. Merriam-Webster. Emotion. Merriam-Webster.com dictionary (n.d.). https://www.merriam-webster.com/dictionary/emotion. Accessed 9 Feb 2021
16. Potter, R.F., Bolls, P.: Psychophysiological Measurement and Meaning: Cognitive and Emotional Processing of Media. Routledge, London (2012)
17. Russell, J.A.: Core affect and the psychological construction of emotion. Psychol. Rev. **110**(1), 145 (2003)
18. Sander, D., Scherer, K. (eds.): Oxford Companion to Emotion and the Affective Sciences. OUP, Oxford (2014)
19. Scarpina, F., Tagini, S.: The stroop color and word test. Front. Psychol. **8**, 557 (2017)
20. Stroop, J.R.: Studies of interference in serial verbal reactions. J. Exp. Psychol. **18**, 643–662 (1935)

Visual Hierarchy and Communication Effectiveness in Medical Decision Tools for Surrogate-Decision-Makers of Critically Ill Traumatic Brain Injury Patients

Javad Norouzi Nia[1]([✉]), Fatima Varzgani[1], Soussan Djamasbi[1], Bengisu Tulu[1], Christopher Lee[2], and Susanne Muehlschlegel[2]

[1] Worcester Polytechnic Institute, Worcester, MA, USA
{jnorouzinia,fvarzgani,djamasbi,bengisu}@wpi.edu
[2] University of Massachusetts Medical School, Worcester, USA
Christopher.Lee@umassmed.edu,
Susanne.Muehlschlegel@umassmemorial.org

Abstract. A major goal of decision support tools (decision aids [DAs]) is to help people make informed decisions; hence, they often provide users with important information. This is particularly true for medical shared decision-making tools (decision aids [DAs]) for surrogate-decision-makers. These tools are designed to help individuals make crucial life-or-death decisions for loved ones who, due to a severe illness, are unable to make their own decisions. Making such decisions on behalf of a loved one often requires the processing of a great deal of medical information, typically in a short period of time, while respecting the patient's values and preferences. Hence, it is particularly important to design such DAs in a way to communicate provided information effectively. In this study, we examined the impact of visual hierarchy on the communication effectiveness of a DA designed for surrogate decision-makers of critically ill traumatic brain injury patients. We compared users' viewing behavior between two prototypes with different visual hierarchy levels. We also examined the impact of visual hierarchy that was created through images on engagement with the content. Our results show that creating distinct visual hierarchies can have a notable impact on how effectively provided information is communicated to users. The results also show that creating visual hierarchies via images can improve user engagement with textual information in medical tools designed for surrogate-decision-makers.

Keywords: User experience · Decision making · Decision support tool · Decision aid · Eye tracking · Navigation · Visual hierarchy

1 Introduction

One way to improve the communication effectiveness of a system is by making its visual hierarchy more distinct [1]. Visual hierarchy refers to how perceptual elements are arranged on a visual stimulus to guide a user viewing behavior with the goal of

© Springer Nature Switzerland AG 2021
D. D. Schmorrow and C. M. Fidopiastis (Eds.): HCII 2021, LNAI 12776, pp. 210–220, 2021.
https://doi.org/10.1007/978-3-030-78114-9_15

helping them understand the provided material more easily [1]. A user's encounter with a computerized tool is a subjective experience; hence, the user's experience of visual hierarchy (and thus the system's communication effectiveness) may be different from what designers envisioned [2, 3]. Eye-tracking is an excellent method for assessing the effectiveness of a designed visual hierarchy as it allows us to visualize how users process visual information. Our eyes constantly scan visual fields to select information and send it to our brain for processing. Eye-tracking allows us to capture the information that a user's eyes have identified as relevant and important for the brain to process [4]. Hence eye-tracking is increasingly useful in user experience research [5], and it is argued that eye-tracking will eventually become an industry standard for system developments [6].

In this study, we used eye-tracking to examine how visual hierarchy of a medical shared decision-making tool (decision aid [DA]) for surrogate-decision-making affects users' viewing patterns, which could impact their ability to understand the provided content. DAs play an increasingly important role in helping people make informed decisions, especially in time-sensitive contexts. This is particularly true for surrogate-decision-making tools for patients with traumatic brain injury (TBI), a leading cause of death and disability in American adults [7]. We recently developed a DA prototype for surrogates of patients with TBI, which is designed to help individuals, who often lack medical knowledge, make decisions on life-support interventions for their loved ones. Effective communication of relevant information in DAs is of utmost importance. The user of such a system must rely on this information to make a life-or-death decision on behalf of his/her loved one who, due to a severe illness, is incapacitated and non-responsive.

1.1 Visual Hierarchy and Navigation Design

One of the most important perceptual elements of a system is its navigation bar. A strategically designed navigation bar not only gives users direct access to the content placed across many different pages but also serves as a map for revealing the overall structure of a collection [8]. Not surprisingly, research shows that people often prefer to use navigation (vs. the search feature) to view the content of a multi-page system such as a website [9].

In this study, we examined the impact of visual hierarchy of two different navigation designs on guiding user viewing behavior. The system used in our study was designed for surrogate-decision-makers of TBI patients to help them make a life-support decision for their loved one [10].

A major communication design goal for this system was to encourage users to view the provided material in a specific order. We designed two different navigation styles: top navigation and left navigation. Because English language has a left-to-right and top-to-bottom writing system, information is naturally processed by English readers in the same directions. Therefore, both the navigation styles in our study were designed in a way to naturally prime users to view content in the intended order. Both navigation styles require a prime location on a visual display (top and left locations on a screen); hence, both navigation styles prime users to pay attention to them.

The top navigation bar provided a simple visual hierarchy, which is typical of this type of navigation style. To minimize clutter, the top navigation bar was designed with

8 tabs, each covering a major topic for the provided content. The left navigation bar was designed to create a more distinct visual hierarchy, which: 1) occupied a larger portion of the screen, 2) provided a top-down list of links, 3) provided a more comprehensive map of the provided content through an expanded list of links, and 4) used a check mark to highlight content that was already viewed by a user. As can be seen in Fig. 1, the left navigation bar design (Fig. 1a) compared to the top navigation bar design (Fig. 1b) provides a more distinct visual hierarchy.

1.2   Visual Hierarchy and Images

Important information is often communicated via text [11]. Given the importance of the information they provide, medical decision tools for surrogate-decision-making tend to be text heavy. Research, however, shows that textual information is less effective in sustaining user attention. For example, eye-tracking studies show that 80% of textual information on webpages is ignored, and when people view textual information, they don't read it carefully [1, 12].

The lack of engagement with content can be improved by enhancing the visual hierarchy of a display, particularly by using images to create distinct visual hierarchies [1, 13]. Users often look around for an entry point on a visual display. Images tend to easily attract user attention; hence, they can serve as effective entry points on a visual stimulus [1].

The current version of the TBI DA relies heavily on text to communicate information. In a handful of its pages, however, the TBI DA uses relevant images. To examine the effectiveness of relevant images on enhancing the visual hierarchy of the content, we compared users' engagement with textual information that included images with those that did not.

2   Eye Tracking Experiment

Sixteen graduate and undergraduate students from a university in the northeastern part of the United States participated in this study. Participants were randomly assigned to two groups: Top Nav and Left Nav groups. In each group, participants were required to read a scenario based on which they had to make a decision on continuation or withdrawal of life-support. All participants were provided with the same scenario describing the condition of their loved one [14].

We used Tobii X300 eye-tracking device to capture user eye movements. The eye tracker was calibrated for each participant. This calibration process was brief (about 15 s) and took place before starting the task. Because Tobii X300 eye tracker does not require the removal of glasses or contacts, it provided a natural environment for studying user viewing behavior. The eye tracker functions remotely from the user (it is attached to the screen looking much like a regular monitor); hence, it can capture user gaze unobtrusively. As was observed in this study as well as many other studies conducted by our team, after initial calibration, participants often forget that their eyes are being tracked.

2.1 Prototypes

To study the impact of the visual hierarchy of navigation design on information processing behavior, we developed two different prototypes. In one prototype (Left Nav), we used a left navigation bar, and in the other prototype (Top Nav), we used a top navigation bar. The left navigation bar used a larger space than the top navigation bar; hence, it created a more prominent visual hierarchy. Because of its larger available space, this navigation style facilitated providing more information about the overall content structure without creating visual clutter (Fig. 1). Related content on the left navigation bar was grouped in 6 clusters to create a more distinct visual hierarchy for guiding users viewing behavior within the navigation bar. The Left Nav prototype also provided a check mark next to links to content in the DA that were visited by the user. The checkmark was designed to help a user have a better sense of his/her viewing process.

The information needed for decision-making in both prototypes was organized across 18 pages, which were expected to be read in order (1 to 18). To encourage linearity in reading order, clearly visible "Next" buttons were provided on the top and bottom of each page. Naturally, a "Previous" button was provided on each page as well (Fig. 1).

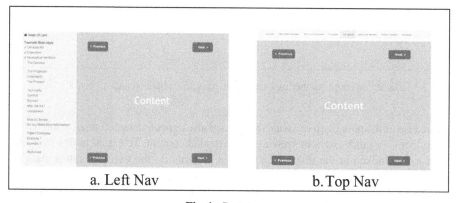

a. Left Nav   b. Top Nav

Fig. 1. Prototypes

3 Results

We used Tobii Studio version 3.4.8 to process the collected gaze data. We utilized I-VT filter with $30°/\text{sec}$ saccadic velocity threshold to delineate between saccades and fixations and used fixations that were 100 ms or longer in our analysis [15, 16].

3.1 Navigation Design

Both navigation bars occupied prime locations on the screen; hence, we expected that they both attract user attention. However, because of its more distinct visual hierarchy, we expected the Left Nav prototype to receive more attention. To test this possibility, we compared the average number of fixations on the two navigation bars. As shown in Fig. 2, on average, there were more fixations on the left navigation bar (Left Nav = 3.85, Top Nav = 2.57). There was a statistically significant difference in average frequency of fixations between the two designs ($p = 0.012$).

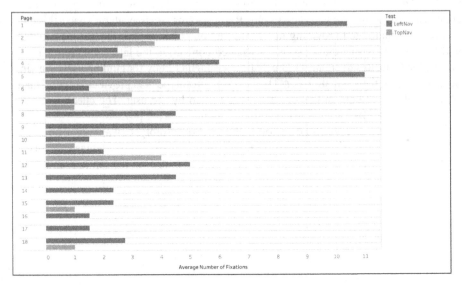

Fig. 2. Average number of fixations on navigation bars on pages 1 to 18

Because of its more distinct visual design, we also expected the left navigation bar to more effectively guide users in viewing the provided content. To examine this possible behavior, we looked at the dispersion of gaze patterns on the two navigation bars to inspect how navigation bar items were processed. The gaze maps in Fig. 3 show that the navigation bar on the first page in both conditions received the most attention. The attention on the navigation bar on the first page in both conditions was dispersed over all items. This behavior indicates the natural tendency to get an overall sense of content structure when starting to use the decision tool. The results showed that regardless of prototype, participants went through the content in the expected order (page 1 through page 18). As participants progressed through the content, the gaze maps for the Left Nav condition showed a more organized viewing behavior. As shown in Fig. 3a, as participants went through the DA, their fixations tended to fall on links to content that was ahead rather than on those that were already viewed. On the Top Nav condition, however, fixations tended to be scattered through all tabs.

During interviews where participants reflected on their experience, those in the Left Nav group provided more positive comments about the navigation design than those in the Top Nav group. Comments such as "the nav bar on the left lets you track performance" and "I could easily tell what I already read and how to get back to those places" showed that the left navigation bar was perceived and used exactly as intended.

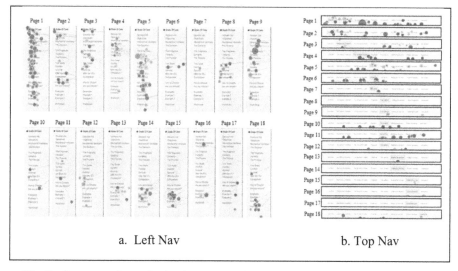

a. Left Nav   b. Top Nav

Fig. 3. Gaze maps for navigation bars (a. on left side: left Nav, b. on right side: top Nav)

3.1.1 Perceived Decision Readiness

A major objective of shared decision-making tools is to help their users get ready to make difficult decisions. A navigation design that is more effective in guiding users' viewing of the content is likely to be more effective in communicating the needed information for decision making. Hence, the more effective the navigation design of a DA, the more likely its users feel ready to make a decision. To test this possibility, we included a question on the last page of the decision tool, which asked users to express how sure they felt about making a life-support decision after reading the content that was provided by the DA. The analysis of responses to this question, displayed in Fig. 4, showed that 43% of participants in the Left Nav condition felt ready to make a life-support decision, while only 25% of their counterparts in the Top Nav condition felt ready to do the same. Fewer participants in the Left Nav condition (29%) compared to the Top Nav condition (38%) felt unsure about decision making. While nobody in the Left Nav condition selected the *not ready at all* option, 13% of participants in the Top Nav condition reported that they were not ready to make a decision. These results, which show that people in the Left Nav condition felt more confident about making a life-support decision, suggests that the left navigation bar facilitated a more effective communication of the content.

Next, we looked at the aggregated heatmaps of gaze patterns when users were responding to the decision-making readiness question on the last page of the decision tool (Fig. 5). The analysis of heatmaps can provide information about how participants in the two conditions went about processing the question and responding to it. The gaze patterns of the participants in the Top Nav groups showed a more dispersed pattern covering all the provided options (from "not ready at all" to "ready"), while the gaze patterns of participants in the Left Nav condition were more focused on the latter part of the scale. Both groups exhibited similar gaze intensity for the item "unsure." The similarity between the gaze pattern of the two groups suggests that participants in both

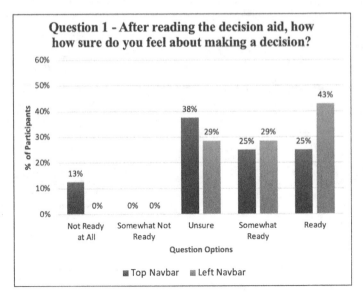

Fig. 4. The effects of navigation design on perceived decision-making readiness

groups paid equal attention to the "unsure" (similar, yellow-colored circle). The difference in viewing pattern between the two groups suggests that participants in the Top Nav group thought about all the available options while the participants in the Left Nav condition considered "unsure", "somewhat ready", and "ready" options. The gaze on items "somewhat ready" and "ready" is more intense in the Left Nav condition than in the Top Nav condition. These patterns together suggest that after reading the provided material, participants in the Left Nav group felt more prepared to make a life-support decision compared to their counterparts in the Top Nav group.

Fig. 5. Heatmaps for responses to perceived decision-making readiness question (red color in the heatmaps indicates the most intense fixation, followed by yellow and green) (Color figure online)

3.2 Visual Hierarchy Through Images

Viewing a stimulus consists of two major activities: 1) finding an entry point and 2) using the entry point as an anchor to scan for information [17]. Because images tend to serve as excellent entry points to visual displays, they provide an effective way to create distinct visual hierarchies, with which we can guide users' viewing behavior to process the provided information [1].

To explore the effects of visual hierarchy, designed with images, on processing the provided information, we compared attention to text on pages that included images with those that did not. To measure information processing behavior, as in prior research, we examined users' total fixation duration on provided content [6]. Because textual content on different pages varied in length, we adjusted total fixation durations for text length on each page (total fixation duration on text/number of words in the text) for each user [18]. Our results showed that, on average, participants exhibited significantly longer fixation durations on textual information when a page contained an image (p-value: 0.044, average of pages with images: 0.226 s, average of pages without images: 0.188 s) (Table 1). In other words, participants spent more time reading text when visual hierarchy was created with images. Furthermore, our analysis showed that the effect of images on attention to content was independent of navigation style; participants paid more attention to textual information on pages that contained images regardless whether they were in the Left Nav or Top Nav condition.

Table 1. Comparing attention* to text between pages with and without images

	Mean (SD)
With image	0.226 (0.085)
Without image	0.188 (0.046)
	t Stat = 2.234, df = 13, p = 0.044

*Attention was measured as total fixation duration adjusted for text length

Because faces are invaluable sources of information in social communication people are naturally drawn to them. Hence, images that include faces can serve as particularly effective entry points on visual displays. The analysis of heatmaps in our study, consistent with prior research [6, 19], revealed intense focus on faces when they were visible in pictures (Fig. 6). This analysis suggests that including faces in images, when appropriate, may be particularly helpful in guiding users' viewing of the provided content in medical decision tools for surrogate decision-making.

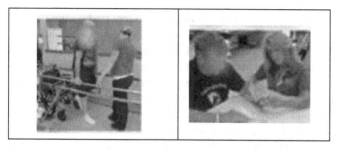

Fig. 6. Heatmaps showing attention to faces

3.3 Discussion

In this paper, we examined the impact of visual hierarchy created through navigation design (left navigation vs. top navigation style) on effective communication of information for a DA. As expected, the results showed that the design with a more distinct visual hierarchy, namely the left navigation bar design, attracted more attention to the navigation bar. As a result, the left navigation bar was more successful in guiding users' viewing behavior; hence, more effective in communicating the provided content. For example, the analysis of gaze patterns revealed that participants in the Left Nav group, compared to those in the Top Nav group, showed a more organized viewing pattern when using the navigation bar. Because a main objective of the navigation bar is to guide users in viewing the provided content, the more organized viewing behavior on the left navigation bar indicated a more effective communication of the provided information. The analysis of responses to a question on the last page of the decision aid that gauged decision-making readiness supported this interpretation. This analysis showed that more people in the left navigation bar condition felt *ready* or *somewhat ready* to make a decision, and fewer people in the left navigation bar condition felt *unsure* about decision making; no participant in the left navigation bar chose the option *not ready at all*. The analysis of heatmaps capturing user gaze patterns when choosing an option ranging from *not ready at all* to *ready*, showed that people in the Left Nav condition exhibited more decisiveness when providing responses to the decision-making readiness question. While people in top navigation bar condition exhibited a more diffused gaze pattern covering all provided options, people in the left navigation bar condition exhibited a more focused gaze pattern covering the options *unsure, somewhat ready*, and *ready* (with the most intense focus on *somewhat ready*). The effectiveness of the left navigation bar in guiding users' viewing of the provided content was also supported by post-task interviews. The analysis of these unstructured interviews revealed that more participants in the left navigation bar condition reported positive feedback about communication effectiveness of the decision tool.

Improving attention to content is particularly important for medical DAs, such as the one used in our study, because the provided textual information is crucial for making informed decisions. Hence, in this paper, we also examined the impact of visual hierarchy, created through images, on attention to textual content. People tend to skim through a stimulus to find an entry point, which then they use as an anchor to help them scan for information [17]. Research shows that images, particularly faces, can serve as effective entry points on visual displays [6, 19]. Our results supported prior research by showing that using images to create distinct visual hierarchies improved attention to content. The analysis of gaze patterns on textual information between pages that had images and those that did not, showed that attention to textual information was significantly heightened when pictures accompanied text. These results suggest that medical proxy decision tools, which require their users to carefully process provided textual information, are likely to benefit from visual hierarchies that are created via images and/or other multi-media components. Supporting previous research, our results showed that faces in images received intense attention [6, 20]. This viewing pattern suggests that using images that include faces may prove more effective in designing visual hierarchy for medical proxy decision tools.

3.4   Limitations and Future Research

The results of this study are limited by its setting (laboratory environment) and population (graduate and undergraduate students) from which its participants were selected. Typical to eye-tracking studies, this study had a small sample size. Future research using surrogates of different ages, health-literacy, computer literacy, and education levels in the real environment of the ICU are needed to address the limitations of this study and extend the generalizability of its results. A larger sample size is likely to provide more insight into users' viewing patterns and information processing behavior.

4   Conclusion

Critical decisions about the continuation or withdrawal of life-support of a family member require the processing of a great deal of medical information in a relatively short period of time. It is then of utmost importance for medical DAs to effectively communicate the information that is needed for decision making. The results of our study show that this objective can be achieved by creating distinct visual hierarchies through navigation design.

Our analysis also showed that creating distinct visual hierarchies by including images is likely to improve the communication of medical information that tends to be cognitively complex and emotionally taxing for most users. Including faces in images is likely to create an even more distinct visual hierarchy, which in turn, is likely to help guide information processing behavior in a more effective way.

Finally, our results highlight the value of eye-tracking in HCI research, particularly when examining communication effectiveness [6]. Our heatmaps and gaze maps help to view the dispersion of user attention which provides insight, directly and unobtrusively from a user point of view, about how effectively information is communicated to them. Capturing gaze data in a continuous manner allows us to gain a more nuanced understanding of user behavior by allowing us to observe changes in attention moment by moment. As such, both qualitative and quantitative analyses of eye-tracking data allow us to gain a more comprehensive view of user information processing and decision behavior.

References

1. Djamasbi, S., Siegel, M., Tullis, T.: Visual hierarchy and viewing behavior: an eye tracking study. In: Jacko, J.A. (ed.) HCI 2011. LNCS, vol. 6761, pp. 331–340. Springer, Heidelberg (2011). https://doi.org/10.1007/978-3-642-21602-2_36
2. Hassenzahl, M.: The thing and i: understanding the relationship between user and product. In: Blythe, M.A., et al. (eds.) Funology: From Usability to Enjoyment, pp. 31–42. Springer, Dordrecht (2004). https://doi.org/10.1007/1-4020-2967-5_4
3. Hassenzahl, M., et al.: Experience-oriented and product-oriented evaluation: psychological need fulfillment, positive affect, and product perception. Int. J. Hum.-Comput. Interact. **31**(8), 530–544 (2015)
4. Andrzejewska, M., Stolińska, A.: Comparing the difficulty of tasks using eye tracking combined with subjective and behavioural criteria. J. Eye Move. Res. **9**(3), 1–16 (2016)

5. Jacob, R.J.K., Karn, K.S.: Commentary on section 4 - eye tracking in human-computer interaction and usability research: ready to deliver the promises. In: Hyönä, J., Radach, R., Deubel, H. (eds.) The Mind's Eye. Amsterdam, North-Holland, pp. 573–605 (2003)
6. Djamasbi, S.: Eye Tracking and Web Experience. AIS Trans. Hum.-Comput. Interact. 6(2), 37–54 (2014)
7. Traumatic Brain Injury: Hope Through Research. 2018 Fri, 2018-09-07 15:51; National Institute of Neurological Disorders and Stroke. https://www.ninds.nih.gov/Disorders/Patient-Caregiver-Education/Hope-Through-Research/Traumatic-Brain-Injury-Hope-Through
8. Nielsen, J.: Search and you may find (1997). https://www.nngroup.com/articles/search-and-you-may-find/. Accessed 5 Jan 2021
9. Katz, M.A., Byrne, M.D.: Effects of scent and breadth on use of site-specific search on e-commerce Web sites. ACM Trans. Comput.-Hum. Interact. 10(3), 198–220 (2003)
10. Muehlschlegel, S., et al.: Goals-of-care decision aid for critically ill patients with TBI: development and feasibility testing. Neurology. 95(2) (2020). https://doi.org/10.1212/wnl.0000000000009770
11. Djamasbi, S., et al.: Text simplification and generation Y: an eye tracking study (2016)
12. Nielsen, J.: How little do users read? (2008). https://www.nngroup.com/articles/how-little-do-users-read/. Accessed 5 Jan 2021
13. Djamasbi, S., Siegel, M., Tullis, T.: Generation Y, web design, and eye tracking. Int. J. Hum.-Comput. Stud. 68(5), 307–323 (2010)
14. Khan, M.W., Muehlschlegel, S.: Shared decision making in neurocritical care. Neurol. Clin. 35(4), 825–834 (2017)
15. Shojaeizadeh, M., Djamasbi, S., Chen, P., Rochford, J.: Text simplification and pupillometry: an exploratory study. In: Schmorrow, Dylan D., Fidopiastis, Cali M. (eds.) AC 2017. LNCS (LNAI), vol. 10285, pp. 65–77. Springer, Cham (2017). https://doi.org/10.1007/978-3-319-58625-0_5
16. Shojaeizadeh, M., et al.: Task condition and pupillometry (2017)
17. Djamasbi, S., Hall-Phillips, A.: Visual search (2014)
18. Poole, A., Ball, L.: Eye tracking in human-computer interaction and usability research: current status and future prospects, pp. 211–219 (2006)
19. Djamasbi, S., Siegel, M., Tullis, T.: Faces and viewing behavior: an exploratory investigation. AIS Trans. Hum.-Comput. Interact. 4(3), 190–211 (2012)
20. Cyr, D., et al.: Exploring human images in website design: a multi-method approach. MIS Q. 33(3), 539–566 (2009)

Stepwise Evaluation Methodology for Smart Watch Sensor Function and Usability

Blaine Reeder[1,2(✉)], Malaika Gallimore[1], Chelsea Howland[1], Chuka Emezue[1], Katrina Boles[2], Allison Anbari[1], and Jo-Ana D. Chase[1]

[1] University of Missouri Sinclair School of Nursing, Columbia, MO, USA
{blaine.reeder,malaika.gallimore,chelsea.howland,cnec65,anbaria,
chasej}@missouri.edu
[2] Institute for Data Science and Informatics, University of Missouri, Columbia, MO, USA
koubak@missouri.edu

Abstract. Physiological and behavioral sensors on consumer-grade wearable devices have great potential to inform augmented cognition applications in everyday living. However, lack of understanding of usability and function of new devices when embedded within larger technical systems is a barrier to their implementation in translational research. Practical evaluation methods are needed to overcome this fundamental barrier in a rapidly changing consumer-grade device landscape. We describe a stepwise evaluation methodology developed in our lab that is designed to rapidly evaluate and position consumer-grade sensors for use in larger studies.

Keyword: Smart watch · Sensors · Digital health · Usability · Evaluation

1 Introduction

Consumer-grade wearable devices hold great potential to enable and support augmented cognition applications for health and wellness in everyday living [1]. However, interdisciplinary researchers seeking to integrate these technologies in their studies must navigate a wide range of devices and data formats, variable maturity and availability of devices, and rapid technology change due to short industry product release cycles. These factors represent barriers to successful implementation of these devices in augmented cognition research.

The Precision Smart Technologies and Applications for Rapid Translation (START) Laboratory was established in 2019 to address challenges in the timely use of consumer-grade "smart technologies" (e.g., mobile and wearable devices, smart home sensors, software, apps) in translational research. We have developed a stepwise, systematic evaluation methodology informed by an informatics study typology [2] and the concepts of technical proof-of-concept and clinical proof-of-concept tests [3]. The goal of the Precision START methodology is to generate evidence of smart technology usability and function that moves from device selection to readiness for larger study implementation within an optimized timeline.

© Springer Nature Switzerland AG 2021
D. D. Schmorrow and C. M. Fidopiastis (Eds.): HCII 2021, LNAI 12776, pp. 221–233, 2021.
https://doi.org/10.1007/978-3-030-78114-9_16

The objective of this paper is to describe the Precision START lab methodology and provide a report of a current evaluation of the Amazfit Bip S smart watch that illustrates application of the methodology. We briefly review the literature on augmented cognition and the use of sensors in health research. We then provide an overview of current smart watch devices that are likely candidates to support augmented cognition applications in real-world settings after evaluation. Next, we describe the approach and steps of the Precision START methodology followed by an evaluation report of the Amazfit Bip S smart watch. We conclude with next steps for our lab and recommendations for future smart watch research.

2   Background

2.1   Augmented Cognition and Wearable Devices

Consumer-grade wearable devices increasingly incorporate onboard sensors that capture physiological measures and can enable the *Cognitive State Assessment* [4–6] required by any augmented cognition system. Wearable sensors can capture direct measurements of physiological processes such as heart rate, skin temperature, electrocardiogram (ECG), pulse oximetry, and respiration. Other measures are imputed such as step counts, activity levels, sleep quality, and stress levels. These sensor-based measures can be combined with alerts in a closed loop system consisting of the wearer, the wearable device, and computing processes that inform *Mitigation Strategies* to help the wearer achieve a desired state or behavior change [5, 6]. For example, a person experiencing a sleep disorder could leverage an augmented cognition system enabled by a wearable device that monitors sleep quality as part of an automatically tailored technology-supported intervention to improve sleep. Other computing processes comprise the *Robust Controllers (RC)* required to monitor augmented cognition system operations that maintain operational resilience [5, 6] in the face of the unpredictable real-world circumstances in everyday living.

2.2   Consumer-Grade Smart Watches

Consumer-grade smart watches are a component of the rapidly expanding health and lifestyle marketplace characterized by frequent innovations, rapid technology change, and availability of devices to consumers. Interventions using consumer-grade smart watches have the potential to support health and wellness. Smart watches in health research have been used to detect and monitor activity levels, eating behaviors, medication adherence, heart rate and temperature, seizures, Parkinsonian tremors and speech therapy progress, scratching, emotional states, diabetes self-management behaviors, and cardiopulmonary resuscitation and nursing work performance [7]. Due to the rapid technological innovations and availability of devices in the marketplace, new device features are released to consumers that typically have seen limited testing to determine device usability and functionality. Features such as electrocardiography, skin temperature monitoring, respiration rate, and pulse oximetry are now commonly available on consumer-grade smart watches. Table 1 provides a summary of advertised device features for selected consumer-grade wearable devices that may support augmented cognition applications. However, manufacturers do not typically test their devices to determine their fitness for health-related or augmented cognition applications.

Table 1. Consumer-grade smart watch sensors and features

Feature	Fitbit versa 3	Apple Watch S6	Garmin Vivoactive 4	Samsung Galaxy watch active2	Casio G-shock move GBDH1000	Withings scanwatch	Letscome ID205G	Polar grit X
Heart rate	√	√	√	√	√	√	√	√
Step counts	√	√	√	√	√	√	√	√
Activity	√	√	√	√	√	√	√	√
Sleep	√	√	√	√	–	√	√	√
Skin temperature	√	–	–	–	–	–	–	–
Electrocardiogram	√	√	–	√	–	√	–	–
Pulse oximetry	√	√	√	–	–	√	–	–
Breath rate	√	–	√	–	–	√	–	–
Stress level	–	–	√	√	–	–	–	–

2.3 Technology Acceptance

Adoption and acceptance of technology are required before commencing research on the effectiveness of smart watch sensors. Therefore, some assessment of how users perceive new technologies is a necessary step in evaluating devices for use in technology-supported research. The concepts of perceived usefulness and perceived ease of use from the Technology Acceptance Model (TAM), can explain why users adopt or reject a technology [8, 9]. Perceived usefulness is the concept that defines how well a technology will help a user perform a task or behavior [8]. When a technology has high perceived usefulness, the user has a positive belief that the technology enables them to perform their desired task [8]. Perceived ease of use is the effort that the user believes is needed to use a technology [8]. If a user finds the technology too difficult to use, then usefulness of the technology suffers [9].

3 Evaluation Methodology

3.1 Stepwise Approach

Our methodology relies on a set of steps that progress from device selection based on project needs, team testing of usability and functionality as part of technical proof-concept tests [3], lab-based participant testing of usability and functionality, and field-based participant testing in real-world settings as clinical proof-of-concept tests [3]. Each iteration employs small samples and a mixed-methods approach using research-grade devices as comparison controls for technical function. Example research-grade devices are the Actigraph w3GTX-BT [10] or Actigraph 9GTX-LINK [11]. Usability testing relies on heuristic evaluations [12–17], a smart wearable device evaluation framework from our previous research [18], cognitive walk-throughs with think-aloud protocols [19, 20], interviews, surveys to identify user perceptions of ease of use and usefulness such as the System Usability Scale (SUS) [21, 22], technology acceptability and appropriateness, and implementation factors. Figure 1 shows an overview of our stepwise evaluation methodology.

DEVICE CANDIDATES   TEAM TESTS   LAB USER TESTS   FIELD USER TESTS

Fig. 1. Stepwise device and mobile app evaluation methodology from the Precision START lab

3.2 Device Selection

Consumer-grade devices are selected based on multiple criteria and informed by project needs, such as characteristics of the target population, the conditions they manage daily, and behaviors they may want to change. Advertised features are used to identify smart watch candidates with similar feature sets that allow for device comparisons. Physiologic and behavioral sensors available on consumer-grade smart watches vary by device. Common features include: heart rate, steps, activity, and sleep pattern monitoring. Devices are also selected based on cost, availability, consumer reports, and device model release cycles. Table 1 provides an example of descriptions of smart watch physiologic and behavioral sensor features based on advertised features.

3.3 Team Tests

Technical proof-of-concept tests [3] are conducted by team members in preparation for participant engagements after selecting devices based on initial criteria. These tests occur in lab and field settings, using the same protocol that participants will follow in participant lab and field testing. Our laboratory has adopted completely digital processes such that "lab" activities within our group connote any controlled or scripted circumstances, regardless of physical location. All lab meetings are conducted virtually via videoconference. Team members live in six different states, so physical materials are managed by a centrally located research technology manager, and devices are shipped to evaluators. Team tests are conducted with 3–5 evaluators based on sample sizes drawn from the usability testing literature [23, 24]. Team tests include feature availability documentation, usability tests based on scenarios of use that exemplify potential uses by participants [25], and function tests for comparing consumer-grade device data to research-grade device data. Testing involves stepping through scenarios of use based on scripted workflows to validate features and function. Instruments include the SUS [21, 22], feature evaluation checklists, heuristic evaluations [12–17], and subjective documentation of lab team members' user experiences. Evaluators test technical function by wearing test devices and research-grade devices as control comparisons, performing sets of scripted activities and logging daily activities to compare the relative performance of device measurements. Team tests also evaluate protocols for engagement with participants and use of specific devices by piloting all study instruments in the order they will be used. In addition, we assess potential complications that may occur during participant studies such as issues with charging of devices or configuring apps after devices are mailed to participants.

3.4 Lab User Tests

Lab user tests engage participants in scripted device usage and physical movement activities to evaluate usability and function of devices. As with team tests, participants are asked to wear the test device(s) and control device(s). All devices are configured, sanitized and shipped to participants after they enroll. All data collection is conducted remotely and includes video interviews. Participants are asked to verbally describe their self-perceived technology proficiency or to complete technical proficiency self-assessments such as the Computer Proficiency Questionnaire (CPQ-12) [26] or the Mobile Device Proficiency Questionnaire (MDPQ-16) [27] in the case of older adults. The CPQ-12 is a six-item questionnaire measuring the participant's ability to perform tasks with a computer on a Likert scale [26]. The MDPQ-16 is an eight-item questionnaire measuring the participant's ability to perform tasks with a mobile device on a Likert scale [27].

Usability tests include cognitive walk-throughs with think-aloud sessions where participants step through scripted tasks or scenarios and "think aloud" about their experiences of use [19, 20]. Lab user tests also include individual interviews to evaluate visual displays and application interfaces or solicit perceptions of and preferences for devices and apps. Lab user tests involve 6–12 participants to determine usability, usefulness and acceptability of devices. Sample size is derived from the usability test literature [24] and interview research that shows this number is sufficient to achieve code saturation within a homogeneous sample of participants [28]. Participants wear the same test and research-grade devices and perform the same sets of scripted activities as those worn and performed during technical proof-of-concept testing. Sensor data from test devices and control devices are compared for relative accuracy.

3.5 Field User Tests

Field user tests engage participants with use of devices and apps in everyday living (AKA "in the wild" or "in situ"). Participants are asked to simultaneously wear test and control devices for a predetermined period (a week) to capture targeted activities. Participants also wear control devices for function comparison with test devices. Field user tests include individual interviews to evaluate visual displays and application interfaces or solicit perceptions of and preferences for devices and apps. Instruments are the same as those employed for lab user tests with interviews for subjective documentation of participant user experiences and administration of the SUS [21, 22] at the end of the test period. Ideally, field user tests may be scheduled immediately following lab user tests within a contiguous timeline. As in the previous tests, sensor data from test devices and control devices are compared for relative accuracy. All devices are configured, sanitized and shipped to participants. All data collection is conducted through remote video interviews and remote data capture.

3.6 Data Analysis Considerations

Research using data output from smart watch sensors have been used in a variety of health and wellness studies [7]. In addition to published studies, data-inquisitive users are able to download and analyze data captured by their own smart watches. Some of these users, such as Alexander Junge, a data scientist, and blogger Mark Koester, share their processes and experiences for others [29, 30], but since the methods require coding and technical background, it is likely the majority of users rely on dashboards provided by device manufacturers. We will follow three avenues of data analysis, which include: 1) assessment of device performance with between-device comparison of data output from both smart watch sensors worn concurrently to determine if there is significant variation in sensor-based measures; 2) comparison of usefulness of granular data obtained and generated from devices with aggregate information displayed in dashboards provided by manufacturers; 3) developing methods of prediction of future activity (forecasting) and identifying ways to implement alert triggers if behaviors change.

4   Amazfit Bip S Smart Watch Evaluation

4.1   Overview

We present the initial validation of our methodology with team tests for evaluation of the Amazfit Bip S smart watch (Amazfit, Huami Inc., New York, USA) and its supporting Mi Fit mobile app. The Amazfit was chosen as a likely candidate for research with older adults based on its advertised feature set (step counts, GPS and heart rate) and low cost ($79.99 USD). The five-member evaluation team were members of the Precision START lab. Four of the evaluators conducted usability testing and comparisons of the Amazfit using their personal smart watches. For the function test comparison of the Amazfit with a research-grade device as control, one of the four evaluators was replaced with the fifth evaluation team member. Each evaluator was a daily user of wearable and mobile devices and used their personal smart phones during testing (three Android and two iOS phones). All evaluators are co-authors of this manuscript and were not enrolled as study participants. Thus, an institutional review board approval was neither required nor sought.

4.2   Methods

Usability Test Methods. The lead evaluator conducted usability training as part of lab procedures and prior to the evaluation study. Four of the five evaluators began the first test period on the same day and wore the watch for a 7-day period, taking notes about their experiences. Evaluators wore the Amazfit smart watch straight from the box. The assessment protocol was adapted from a wearable evaluation framework [18]. Each of the four evaluators completed a nine-item checklist (five items for smart watch, four items for mobile app) to assess user experience of common features ranked on a scale of 1–5 (1 is lowest and 5 is highest) and a 24-item checklist of perceived availability of common features with yes/no ratings. Evaluators documented comments for features where appropriate or desired. The System Usability Scale (SUS) is a 10-item question- naire measuring global usability from a subjective viewpoint on a Likert scale [21, 22] and was used to assess usability for both the Amazfit Bip S interface and the supporting Mi Fit mobile app.

Function Test Methods. Evaluators completed a set of scripted activities for walking using their personal consumer-grade smart watches as comparators and research-grade devices as controls. For the walking activity protocol, evaluators walk a straight path with 0% incline at three self-rated exertion levels for 8-min, followed by a 2-min rest period between activities. Evaluators walked with a normal arm swing and stood motionless during rest periods. Walking paces were self-selected for *very light*, *light*, and *moderately hard* levels of perceived exertion using Borg's Rate of Perceived Exertion Scale (RPE) [31]. See Table 2 for full scripted walking protocol.

Table 2. Walking activity protocol

Walking activity	Minutes	Additional information
Rest	2	Standing motionless. Record steps counted by devices
Very light	8	With normal arm swing, corresponding to RPE* of 9–10
Rest	2	Standing motionless. Record steps counted by devices
Light	8	With normal arm swing, corresponding to RPE* of 11–12
Rest	2	Standing motionless. Record steps counted by devices
Moderately Hard	8	With normal arm swing, corresponding to RPE* of 13–14
Rest	2	Standing motionless. Record steps counted by devices

*RPE (Rate of Perceived Exertion) [31]

4.3 Amazfit Results

Amazfit Usability Test Results. User experience checklists indicated high usability for both watch (five items) and mobile app (four items) features. However, there was a divergence in usability perceptions for the watch and mobile app usability from the SUS. Average SUS usability score for the Amazfit smart watch was 83.1 (77.5, 82.5, 82.5, 90) or *excellent* usability. In contrast, the average SUS usability score for the Mi Fit mobile app was 44.4 (22.5, 35, 60, 60) or *poor* usability.

Smart watch user experience item average scores were:

- Ease of Physical Controls: 3.5/5
- Wearability: 3.75/5
- Aesthetics: 4.75/5
- Display Viewability: 4.25/5
- Display Interpretability: 4/5

Mobile app user experience item averages were:

- Ease of Setup: 4.25/5
- Syncing: 4.75/5
- Mobile Battery: 4.5/5
- Mobile App Ease of Use: 4/5

For the perceived feature availability checklist, there was 100% agreement about availability of 10 common features that aligned with ground truth. There was disagreement between evaluators about the availability of 14 other features, 10 of which actually existed and four of which did not. This disagreement about perceived availability of features indicates low discoverability for features of the smart watch.

Summaries of evaluation comments indicated that two evaluators downloaded an app labeled "Amazfit" from the app store but the app not associated with this Amazfit Bip S smart watch. This caused confusion until resolved when both evaluators learned the supporting app is labeled "Mi Fit" after further search. Set up and pairing of the Mi Fit mobile app with the Amazfit Bip S was uniformly perceived as straightforward though required an unexpected 20–25-min software update. In addition, GPS activation was required during set up and location was automatically captured, presenting a privacy concern. Design of the interface of the mobile app was idiosyncratic and did not follow a uniform navigation scheme. In addition, the app had no help feature but, fortunately, was easily learned by the evaluators. Features for "Behavior Tagging", "Body Analysis" and message alerts did not function correctly. Ability to configure the watch was limited on the device itself and was enabled primarily through mobile app. However, the app sometimes froze when communicating with the watch and configuration was not always successful. The watch itself provided only basic data about current steps, heart rate, distance, and the number of hour-long sedentary periods.

Amazfit Function Test Results. Four evaluators (E01, E02, E03, and E04) wore their personal smart watches during scripted walk activities (see Table 2) to capture step counts for function comparison with the Amazfit Bip S smart watch. These devices were the Pebble Time, Fitbit Blaze, Fitbit Versa 2, and Fitbit Alta HR (Fitbit Inc., California, USA). Table 3 shows step count comparisons with Amazfit percentage error in relation to the comparison device for scripted walk activities where "E01" stands for "Evaluator 1", "E02" stands for "Evaluator 2", etc. Notably, evaluators who wore Fitbit devices (Alta HR, Blaze, Versa 2) observed apparent step undercounts by the Amazfit Bip S during daily use.

In a subsequent iteration of the scripted walk activities, four evaluators (E02, E03, E04, and E05) wore the Actigraph wGT3X-BT (Actigraph Inc., Florida, USA) research-grade activity monitor as a control device to capture step counts during scripted walk activities (see Table 2) for function comparison with the Amazfit Bip S. Table 4 shows step count comparisons with Amazfit percentage error in relation to the Actigraph control device for scripted walk activities where "E02" stands for "Evaluator 2", "E03" stands for "Evaluator 3", etc. Activity data were accessed by the study team through the ActiLife analysis software (Actigraph, LLC). Percent error calculated as absolute value of difference between control and test devices divided by control, multiplied by 100. The data for Evaluator 5's moderately hard walking activity could not be reconciled and were not included in the table. Of note, the Actigraph control device did not capture walking speed for evaluator E03 for very light exertion walking. Accelerometers are known to be less reliable at slow walking speeds [32]. This measurement error may have occurred because the evaluator's perceived very light exertion walk speed fell below the control device's ability to count steps at that speed. In sum, the Amazfit Bip S varied in error (both step over- and undercounts) when compared to consumer devices. In contrast, the Amazfit Bip S demonstrated consistent step overcounts compared to the control device.

Table 3. Step count comparison of Amazfit Bip S and other smart watches

Walk activity	Device	Steps			
		E01	E02	E03	E04
Very light	Amazfit smart watch	760	412	818	553
	Comparison device*	755	325	820	616
	Amazfit % error	**0.7**	**26.8**	**0.2**	**10.2**
Light	Amazfit smart watch	791	552	882	708
	Comparison device*	827	564	858	717
	Amazfit % error	**4.4**	**2.1**	**2.8**	**1.3**
Moderately hard	Amazfit smart watch	988	668	920	730
	Comparison device*	922	540	889	748
	Amazfit % error	**7.2**	**23.7**	**3.5**	**2.4**

*Devices: E01- Pebble Time, E02 - Fitbit Blaze, E03 - Fitbit Versa 2, E04 - Fitbit Alta HR

Table 4. Step count comparison of Amazfit Bip S and actigraph wGT3X-BT control

Walk activity	Device	Steps			
		E02	E03	E04	E05
Very light	Amazfit smart watch	541	382	485	574
	Actigraph control	335	4	311	310
	Amazfit % error	**61.5**	**9450.0**	**55.9**	**85.2**
Light	Amazfit smart watch	760	667	738	706
	Actigraph control	656	558	419	359
	Amazfit % error	**15.9**	**19.5**	**76.1**	**96.7**
Moderately hard	Amazfit smart watch	824	769	816	– *
	Actigraph control	703	850	791	– *
	Amazfit % error	**17.2**	**9.5**	**3.2**	– *

*Data could not be reconciled between test and control devices for comparison

4.4 Amazfit Evaluation Implications

Failures in pairing, usability and navigation challenges for the Mi Fit app, and small screen size for the smart watch make the Amazfit Bip S better suited for studies with older adults who have a high degree of technical proficiency. For those with little technical experience or high disease burden, training materials and dedicated training with support may be required. In addition, posts on public web forums suggest that the Amazfit Bip S may have an application programming interface (API) that could facilitate automated data collection for larger scale research studies. However, API documentation was not easily discoverable by our team so API utility could not be evaluated. Given results of the team test, we discontinued plans for testing with older adult participants.

5 Conclusion

We have formulated a stepwise evaluation methodology for usability and function testing of consumer-grade smart watches based on our prior technology design, evaluation, and clinical research experience. The aim of this paper was to demonstrate how this methodology can be used to test and prepare consumer-grade devices for deployment in support of augmented cognition research. Results of our initial test case using the Amazfit Bip S watch show the feasibility of the test protocol designed for both research team and participant testing. Team test results ruled out the Amazfit Bip S, prior to participant testing, as a feasible option for inclusion in research with older adults who have low technical proficiency.

We are currently engaged in usability and function evaluation of the Fitbit Versa 3 (Fitbit Inc., California, USA) and the Oura ring (Oura, Oula, Finland) as promising candidates to support larger research studies, particularly with older adult participants. Team tests of device function have been completed, and we have received Institutional Review Board (IRB) approval from the University of Missouri to begin lab- and field-based testing with older adult participants (>65 years of age).

For this next round of evaluations, we will report on expanded activities from our test protocol. For example, during team tests of the Fitbit Versa 3 and Oura ring, evaluators completed scripted stair climbing activities using available flights of stairs. Stair climbing began with standing motionless for 2 min, then ascending the flight of stairs with normal arm swing, standing motionless for another 2 min, and descending the flight of stairs with a normal arm swing. Evaluators logged step counts after ascending and descending. Each evaluator completed three stair climbing repetitions. In addition, we plan to evaluate the Fitbit Versa 3 and the Oura ring against research-grade control devices for features such as heart rate and skin temperature as well as testing performance of device APIs for data collection. Usability testing will additionally include evaluation with the Mobile Application Rating Scale [33]. Lastly, we have piloted the protocol for logging daily activities during team testing. During participant testing, participants will document daily activities on an average weekday and weekend day during the 7-day field testing duration. Participants will be asked to document the start and stop time of activities, a general description of the activity performed (ex. Cooking dinner, riding a bicycle, walking the dog), and provide additional comments to clarify the activity description.

References

1. Reeder, B., Cook, P.F., Meek, P.M., Ozkaynak, M.: Smart watch potential to support augmented cognition for health-related decision making. In: Schmorrow, D.D., Fidopiastis, C.M. (eds.) AC 2017. LNCS (LNAI), vol. 10284, pp. 372–382. Springer, Cham (2017). https://doi.org/10.1007/978-3-319-58628-1_29
2. Friedman, C.P., Wyatt, J.C., Owens, D.K.: Evaluation and technology assessment. In: Shortliffe, E.H., Cimino, J.J. (eds.) Biomedical Informatics: Computer Applications in Health Care and Biomedicine, pp. 403–443. Springer, New York (2006). https://doi.org/10.1007/0-387-36278-9_11
3. Bardram, J.E.: Pervasive healthcare as a scientific discipline. Methods Inf. Med. **47**, 178–185 (2008)
4. Schmorrow, D., Kruse, A.A.: DARPA's augmented cognition program-tomorrow's human computer interaction from vision to reality: building cognitively aware computational systems. In: 2002 Proceedings of the 2002 IEEE 7th Conference on Human Factors and Power Plants, p. 7. IEEE (2002)
5. Fuchs, S., Hale, K.S., Axelsson, P.: Augmented cognition can increase human performance in the control room. In: 2007 IEEE 8th Human Factors and Power Plants and HPRCT 13th Annual Meeting, pp. 128–132. IEEE (2007)

6. Reeves, L.M., Schmorrow, D.D., Stanney, K.M.: Augmented cognition and cognitive state assessment technology – near-term, mid-term, and long-term research objectives. In: Schmorrow, D.D., Reeves, L.M. (eds.) FAC 2007. LNCS (LNAI), vol. 4565, pp. 220–228. Springer, Heidelberg (2007). https://doi.org/10.1007/978-3-540-73216-7_25

7. Reeder, B., David, A.: Health at hand: a systematic review of smart watch uses for health and wellness. J. Biomed. Inform. **63**, 269–276 (2016)

8. Davis, F.D., Bagozzi, R.P., Warshaw, P.R.: User acceptance of computer technology: a comparison of two theoretical models. Manage. Sci. **35**, 982–1003 (1989)

9. Ammenwerth, E.: Technology acceptance models in health informatics: TAM and UTAUT. Stud Health Technol Inform **263**, 64–71 (2019)

10. https://actigraphcorp.com/actigraph-wgt3x-bt/

11. https://actigraphcorp.com/support/activity-monitors/gt9x-link/

12. Alexander, G.L., et al.: Passive sensor technology interface to assess elder activity in independent living. Nurs. Res. **60**, 318–325 (2011)

13. Lai, T.Y., Bakken, S.: Heuristic evaluation of HIV-TIDES - tailored interventions for management of DEpressive symptoms in HIV-infected individuals. In: AMIA ... Annual Symposium proceedings/AMIA Symposium. AMIA Symposium, p. 996 (2006)

14. Kneale, L., Mikles, S., Choi, Y.K., Thompson, H., Demiris, G.: Using scenarios and personas to enhance the effectiveness of heuristic usability evaluations for older adults and their care team. J. Biomed. Inform. **73**, 43–50 (2017)

15. Pierotti, D.: Heuristic evaluation-a system checklist. Xerox Corporation (1995)

16. Sharp, H., Rogers, Y., Preece, J.J.: Interactive heuristic evaluation toolkit. Interaction Design: Beyond Human-Computer Interaction Web site (2007)

17. Chisnell, D.E., Redish, J.C.G., Lee, A.: New heuristics for understanding older adults as web users. Tech. Commun. **53**, 39–59 (2006)

18. Connelly, K., et al.: Evaluation framework for selecting wearable activity monitors for research. mHealth **7**, 1–13 (2021)

19. Kaufman, D.R., et al.: Usability in the real world: assessing medical information technologies in patients' homes. J. Biomed. Inf. **36**, 45–60 (2003)

20. Jaspers, M.W.M., Steen, T., Bos, C.V.D., Geenen, M.: The think aloud method: a guide to user interface design. Int. J. Med. Inform. **73**, 781–795 (2004)

21. Sauro, J.: A practical guide to the system usability scale: Background, benchmarks & best practices. Measuring Usability LLC Denver, CO (2011)

22. Brooke, J.: SUS: a retrospective. J. Usability Stud. **8**, 29–40 (2013)

23. Nielsen, J., Molich, R.: Heuristic evaluation of user interfaces. In: Proceedings of the SIGCHI Conference on Human Factors in Computing Systems, pp. 249–256. ACM (1990)

24. Turner, C.W., Lewis, J.R., Nielsen, J.: Determining usability test sample size. Int. Encycl. Ergon. Hum. Factors **3**, 3084–3088 (2006)

25. Zayas-Cabán, T., Marquard, J.L., Radhakrishnan, K., Duffey, N., Evernden, D.L.: Scenario-based user testing to guide consumer health informatics design. In: AMIA ... Annual Symposium proceedings/AMIA Symposium. AMIA Symposium 2009, pp. 719–723 (2009)

26. Boot, W.R., et al.: Computer proficiency questionnaire: assessing low and high computer proficient seniors. Gerontologist **55**, 404–411 (2013)

27. Roque, N.A., Boot, W.R.: A new tool for assessing mobile device proficiency in older adults: the mobile device proficiency questionnaire. J. Appl. Gerontol. **37**, 131–156 (2016)

28. Guest, G., Bunce, A., Johnson, L.: How many interviews are enough? Field Methods **18**, 59–82 (2006)

29. https://www.alexanderjunge.net/blog/fitbit-data-01/

30. http://www.markwk.com/data-analysis-for-apple-health.html

31. Borg, G.A.: Psychophysical bases of perceived exertion. Med. Sci. Sports Exerc. **14**, 377–381 (1982)

32. Reeder, B., Whitehouse, K.: Sensor-based detection of gait speed in older adults: an integrative review. Res. Gerontol. Nurs. **8**, 12–27 (2015)
33. Stoyanov, S.R., Hides, L., Kavanagh, D.J., Zelenko, O., Tjondronegoro, D., Mani, M.: Mobile app rating scale: a new tool for assessing the quality of health mobile apps. JMIR Mhealth Uhealth **3**, e27 (2015)

Modelling Human Cognition

Kantian Computational Linguistics

Karina Ionkina[1], Suraj Sood[2(✉)], Monte Hancock[3], Charlotte Walker[4],
and Raman Kannan[5]

[1] Hunter College, City University of New York, 695 Park Ave, New York, NY 10065, USA
karina.ionkina58@myhunter.cuny.edu
[2] PCH Mexican Grill and Seafood, El Segundo, USA
ssood2@my.westga.edu
[3] 4Digital, Los Angeles, USA
[4] The Sirius Project, Sacramento, USA
charlotte@charlottewalker.com
[5] New York University, New York, USA
rk1750@nyu.edu

Abstract. Language is a defining characteristic of higher order species—particularly of us, *homo sapiens*. For that reason, it is only appropriate to conclude that linguistic capability—the ability to understand and generate natural language—is essential in any tools that we build for cognitive assistance. Fast and superior automated solutions exist in most other competencies, including numeracy and vision, but parity in linguistic skills remains elusive [1] for many reasons. In this chapter, we seek to identify why we find ourselves here and propose an alternative approach to overcome identified deficiencies. We do not know yet if this approach is useful or effective, but we proceed to share our thoughts because the biggest risk is doing nothing.

First, we review seminal work on linguistics and the structure of language. We then examine the most popular contemporary solutions, identify their drawbacks and propose alternatives to address them.

Keywords: Computational linguistics · Deep structure · Kant's categories

1 Linguistics

1.1 Structure of Language

Language consists of two parts: spoken and written words, and the two differ only in their input modes. Therefore, understanding these formats is a reasonable place to start. Plausible components for spoken and written language include visual and auditory activation, lexical selection, lemma activation, lemma, and conceptual activation (see Fig. 1). As shown, the last two steps—i.e., lemma and conceptual activation–are likely shared in processing both auditory and visual word forms.

© Springer Nature Switzerland AG 2021
D. D. Schmorrow and C. M. Fidopiastis (Eds.): HCII 2021, LNAI 12776, pp. 237–249, 2021.
https://doi.org/10.1007/978-3-030-78114-9_17

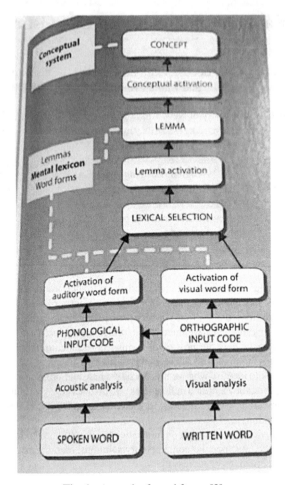

Fig. 1. A graph of word forms [2].

- Linguistics is broken into Phonology
- Morphology
- Syntax
- Semantics
- Pragmatics

Our focus is Syntax and Semantics, the central concepts in word representation, mental lexicon [2]. In this paper, we are not concerned about representational issues addressed by [3–6] many decades before or knowledge graphs [7, 8].

1.2 Structure of Language

Chomsky (and Russell before him) agreed that logical methods of formal language analysis do not apply to natural languages. Chomsky [9] proposed two structures—deep and surface structure—where the semantic component is derived from the deep structure while the phonological component is derived from surface structure. These deep and surface structure lead directly to semantics and surface, respectively. The difficulty in comprehending following statements.

- "The little old lady bites the gigantic dog" [2],
- "The tall man planted a tree on the bank" [2],
- "The spy saw the cop with binoculars" [2]

without semantics and context, such as using syntax alone, is well documented. Processing such statements from PoS (Verb/Noun etc.), while important, is not sufficient.

1.3 Syntax and Semantics

Word order, Parts of Speech, Types of sentences, etc. are studied in Syntax and syntactic analysis of a sentence reveals its structure, actor, action, and subject. On the other hand, semantics studies the more ambiguous relationship between words and sentences based on meaning. Context is critical for semantics [10] and syntax is independent of context. A syntactically correct sentence is not necessarily a meaningful sentence. A semantically correct sentence is necessarily syntactically correct. For example, "The little old lady bites the gigantic dog" [2]. Though syntactically correct this is not consistent with our world experience. To illustrate that grammar is independent of meaning, Chomsky used the sentence "Colorless green ideas sleep furiously." While grammatically correct, it is not semantically plausible.

1.4 Grammatical Structure

Grammatical Structure is best viewed as a tree structure (see Fig. 2).

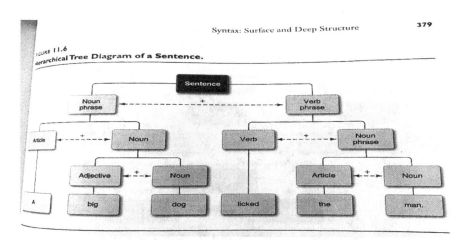

Fig. 2. Hierarchical tree diagram of a sentence [11].

Grammatical Structure is easily extracted using standard libraries [12–15] and working code is included below.

```
library('magrittr')
library(sqldf)
library(spacyr)
# change the next two lines for your environment
mypyexe<- "/home/rkannan/anaconda3/bin/python"
textfile<-'/home/rkannan/ML/NLP/corpus/01032021/tayos.txt'
rm(list=ls())
spacy_initialize(python_executable = mypyexe)
spacy_initialize(model = "en_core_web_sm")
#on windows
wiki<-readLines(textfile)
parsedtxt<-spacy_parse(wiki,depend-
ency=TRUE,lemma=FALSE,tag=TRUE,nounphrase=TRUE)
who_isit<-function(ptxt) {
    if (class(ptxt)[[1]]=="spacyr_parsed")
    {
    persons<-ptxt[ptxt$pos=="PROPN",4:9]
    sqldf::sqldf('select * from persons where entity LIKE "PERSON%"')
    }
}
where_about<-function(ptxt) {
if (class(ptxt)[[1]]=="spacyr_parsed")
{
sqldf::sqldf('select token,pos,tag,entity from ptxt where entity LIKE "GPE%" or entity
LIKE "LOC%"')
}
}
```
Proper Nouns can be extracted from any text corpus using
who_isit(parsedtxt)
where_about(parsedtxt)

```
> who_isit(parsedtxt)
        token    pos tag head_token_id    dep_rel    entity
1        Stan  PROPN NNP             3   compound  PERSON_B
2        Hall  PROPN NNP             4      nsubj  PERSON_I
3        Neil  PROPN NNP            24   compound  PERSON_B
4   Armstrong  PROPN NNP            22       pobj  PERSON_I
5        Moon  PROPN NNP            37       pobj  PERSON_B
6        Hall  PROPN NNP            44       pobj  PERSON_B
7         Weh  PROPN NNP            30       pobj  PERSON_B
8     Hoffman  PROPN NNP             3      nsubj  PERSON_B
9       Jaime  PROPN NNP             5      nsubj  PERSON_B
10      Jaime  PROPN NNP             2       pobj  PERSON_B
11      Jaime  PROPN NNP             9      nsubj  PERSON_B
12      Erich  PROPN NNP             9   compound  PERSON_B
13        von  PROPN NNP            10   compound  PERSON_I
14    Däniken  PROPN NNP             5       pobj  PERSON_I
15        Von  PROPN NNP             2   compound  PERSON_B
16    Däniken  PROPN NNP             5      nsubj  PERSON_I
```

By default each token within a multi-token entities are resolved as separate tokens and it can be resolved as shown below [14].

```
> content<-nounphrase_consolidate(parsedtxt)
Note: removing head_token_id, dep_rel for nounphrases
> content%>% head
   doc_id sentence_id token_id     token        pos        tag
1   text1           1        1   Journey nounphrase nounphrase
2   text1           1        2        to        ADP         IN
3   text1           1        3 the_Center nounphrase nounphrase
4   text1           1        4        of        ADP         IN
5   text1           1        5 the_Earth nounphrase nounphrase
```

Location (named entities: persons, locations, dates) can be extracted from any text corpus using utilities for NER.

```
> where_about(parsedtxt)
          token   pos tag entity
1          A.M. PROPN NNP  GPE_B
2         Jaime PROPN NNP  GPE_B
3         Jaime PROPN NNP  GPE_B
4         Jaime PROPN NNP  GPE_B
5         Wells PROPN NNP  GPE_B
6    California PROPN NNP  GPE_B
7        Desert PROPN NNP  GPE_B
8       Ecuador PROPN NNP  GPE_B
9        London PROPN NNP  GPE_B
10      Kuankus PROPN NNP  GPE_B
11        Andes PROPN NNP  LOC_B
12       London PROPN NNP  GPE_B
13       Arutam PROPN NNP  GPE_B
14         Mera PROPN NNP  GPE_B
15        Andes PROPN NNP  LOC_B
16           UK PROPN NNP  GPE_B
17      Ecuador PROPN NNP  GPE_B
18       Dunbar PROPN NNP  GPE_B
19    Edinburgh PROPN NNP  GPE_B
20        Quito PROPN NNP  GPE_B
21    Ecuadoran PROPN NNP  GPE_B
```

1.5 Elements of Cognitive Equity

Chomsky proposed two structures—deep and surface structure—where the semantic component is derived from the deep structure while the phonological component is derived from surface structure. Frege is credited with the principle of compositionality, i.e. the meaning of complex expression is a function of the meanings of its parts and of the way they are syntactically combined.

Chomsky's Deep Structure can then be transformed into negation and question as shown below. These capabilities to negate or enquire relating to a given assertion is essential to achieve cognitive compatibility. We posit for a machine to achieve cognitive equity with a human, the machine must exhibit all these elements. To paraphrase Langer [17] "to understand language and to employ linguistic capability is to appreciate the analogy between the syntactic structure (Chomsky's Surface structure) and the complex of ideas (the deep structure) such that the surface structure functions as a representation of the deep (logical picture)" (Fig. 3).

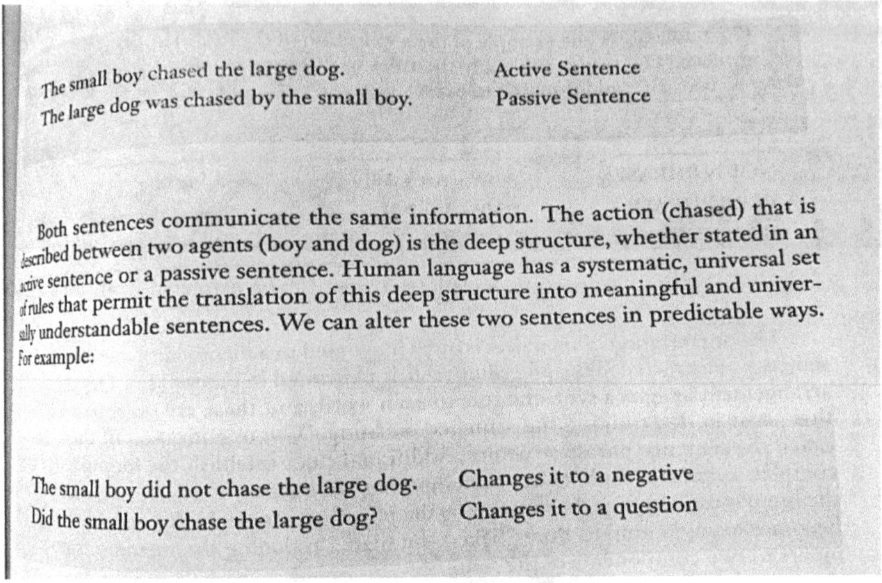

The small boy chased the large dog.   Active Sentence
The large dog was chased by the small boy.   Passive Sentence

Both sentences communicate the same information. The action (chased) that is described between two agents (boy and dog) is the deep structure, whether stated in an active sentence or a passive sentence. Human language has a systematic, universal set of rules that permit the translation of this deep structure into meaningful and universally understandable sentences. We can alter these two sentences in predictable ways. For example:

The small boy did not chase the large dog.   Changes it to a negative
Did the small boy chase the large dog?   Changes it to a question

Fig. 3. An example of deep structure [11]

1.6 Semantic Equivalence

There has been a concerted effort to incorporate semantics and context, both at a word level and sentence level. Merely focusing on syntactic correctness leads us to implausible assertions like the one Chomsky made up or a statement like "The little old lady bites the gigantic dog". Context is critical. At a world level, most recent strategy is vector representation of word [16]. Word embeddings (word2vec) definitely aid in getting to the underlying meaning. Here we show how to compute the embeddings using many available open software packages [12–15].

```
library(text2vec)
text8_file<-'~/ML/NLP/GloVE.mahonny.net/text8'
wiki = readLines(text8_file, n = 1, warn = FALSE)
tokens <- space_tokenizer(wiki)
it = itoken(tokens, progressbar = FALSE)
vocab <- create_vocabulary(it)
vocab <- prune_vocabulary(vocab, term_count_min = 5L)
vectorizer <- vocab_vectorizer(vocab)
tcm <- create_tcm(it, vectorizer, skip_grams_window = 5L)
glove = GlobalVectors$new(rank = 50, x_max = 10)
gft<-glove$fit_transform(tcm, n_iter = 20)
gft_context<-glove$components
gft_vectors<-gft+t(gft_context)
berlin7<-gft_vectors["paris",,drop=FALSE]-
 gft_vectors["france",,drop=FALSE]+
 gft_vectors["germany",,drop=FALSE]
cos_gft=sim2(x=gft_vectors,y=berlin7, method = "cosine", norm = "l2")
head(sort(cos_gft[,1], decreasing = TRUE), 5)

berlin9<-gft_vectors["france",,drop=FALSE]+
gft_vectors["germany",,drop=FALSE]
cos_gft9=sim2(x=gft_vectors,y=berlin9, method = "cosine", norm = "l2")
head(sort(cos_gft9[,1], decreasing = TRUE), 5)

berlin6<-gft_vectors["germany",,drop=FALSE]
cos_gft6=sim2(x=gft_vectors,y=berlin6, method = "cosine", norm = "l2")
head(sort(cos_gft9[,1], decreasing = TRUE), 5)
related_terms<-function(glovevector,term, nn=5) {
 elements<-glovevector[term,,drop=FALSE]
 cos_dist<-sim2(x=glovevector,y=elements,method='cosine', norm='l2')
 head(sort(cos_dist[,1],decreasing=TRUE),nn)
 }
```

```
> related_terms(gft_vectors,'professor',5)
  professor university   editor   harvard  emeritus
  1.0000000  0.6401693  0.6122829  0.5999861  0.5896451
> related_terms(gft_vectors,'divine',5)
  divine essence     god  spirit  liturgy
  1.0000000 0.6836824 0.6422958 0.6411167 0.6373955
> related_terms(gft_vectors,'demon',5)
  demon uranium    glory    seed   spirit
  1.0000000 0.6357948 0.5834405 0.5582620 0.5532927
> related_terms(gft_vectors,'uranium',5)
  uranium    ore manganese    zinc   demon
  1.0000000 0.6934426 0.6643776 0.6410305 0.6357948
> related_terms(gft_vectors,'river',5)
  river   valley   basin   nile   lake
  1.0000000 0.7822934 0.7047691 0.6801703 0.6774941
> related_terms(gft_vectors,'river')
  river   valley   basin   nile   lake
  1.0000000 0.7822934 0.7047691 0.6801703 0.6774941
> related_terms(gft_vectors,'human')
  human individual  behavior   animal biological
  1.0000000  0.7532117  0.7407295  0.7371031  0.7055417
> related_terms(gft_vectors,'moon')
  moon    earth    sun    orbit   lunar
  1.0        0.7991328 0.7862749 0.7535682 0.7450282
```

We tabulate below related terms we retrieved using GloVe [16] above, and at the least for the corpus we analyzed, these results are encouraging.

GloVe [16]				
Search term	RT-01	RT-02	RT-03	RT-04
Professor	University	Editor	Harvard	emeritus
Divine	Essence	God	Spirit	liturgy
Demon	Uranium	Glory	Seed	Spirit
Uranium	Ore	Manganese	Zinc	Demon
River	Valley	Basic	Nile	Lake
Human	Individual	Behavior	Animal	Biological
Moon	Earth	Sun	Orbit	lunar

It should be noted that GloVe [16] employs vectorization whereas WordNet [18] is based on human curated lexical database.

2   Need for a New Approach

2.1   Integrating WordNet

Undeniable progress has been made and readily usable software is available in the public domain, including GloVe [16] and WordNet [18] at word level. A conversational agent that can read all my emails, on my behalf, prioritize and carry on a meaningful conversation is still a dream. Filtering emails based on spam-word dictionary, or predicting most probable word sequences are significant but fall short of conversational (sentence level or Chomsky's Deep Structure) comprehension. Therefore, we have arrived at a critical point. Study of language is not a recent effort and the meager results are not due to lack of effort. It is well established that extracting and perfecting semantics is much harder than perfecting syntactic issues, at both the level of a word and sentences. "The problem of resolving semantic ambiguity is generally known as word sense disambiguation and has proved to be more difficult than syntactic disambiguation" [19–21]. We just have to rethink, retool and pursue a different approach.

The GloVe [16] Embeddings and WordNet do appear to bear significant utility to find related terms but making sense of entire sentence remains elusive.

2.2   Other Approaches

Whitman [22] enumerates why a Rule-Based approach does not handle categorization processes well.

Recall the sentences we referred earlier, from [2]

- The little old lady bites the gigantic dog
- The tall man planted a tree on the bank
- The spy saw the cop with binoculars

Correctly sensing the semantics in these cases remains elusive. There are many such sentences, which currently are easily disambiguated by the human cognition apparatus but remains elusive to automated solutions. Interested readers are referred to earlier work reported in [23–26] for several other sentences which pose similar challenges.

To quote [23] "To discover the general principles of natural-language communication, we must study how people transfer information by talking to people. Extracting information from books, or translating books, or proving mathematical theorems, or interacting with computers, constitute highly specialized forms of communication". Who better than early philosophers who critically evaluated human understanding from every possible perspective and so we turn to Kant's *Critique of Pure Reason* [30] for guidance, Locke's *Essay Concerning Human Understanding* [31] and David Hume's *An Enquiry Concerning Human Understanding* [29].

2.3   Opportunity: Seat at the Philosopher's Table

Immanuel Kant is not alone, John Locke and David Hume have made original and impactful inquiry into comprehension.

2.4   David Hume: An Enquiry Concerning Human Understanding

David Hume stipulates "All the objects of human reason or enquiry may naturally be divided into two kinds, to wit, *Relations of Ideas* and *Matters of Fact*" ([29], p. 108). ([27] offers a helpful, fully-modernized translation of this stipulation.) Hume further divides relations of ideas into *resemblance, cause and effect* and *contiguity.*

2.5   John Locke: Essay Concerning Human Understanding

John Locke stipulates that knowledge is perception of the agreement, or disagreement, between two or more ideas ([31], p. 93). Agreement is then reduced to four different types:

- Identify or diversity.
- Relation
- Coexistence or necessary connection, and
- Real existence.

2.6   Kant's Categories

According to [28], "Kant distinguishes between three mental capacities that are relevant for knowing objects: *sensibility, understanding,* and *reason*".

   First of all, *any* judgment, irrespective of where the data in it comes, has:

- A quantity: whether it says something of *all, some,* or *one* entity,
- A quality: whether it *affirms* or *negates,* or affirms a negation (infinite judgment*), of it,
- A relation: whether it is of the form "A is B", "if A, then B", or "A or B or C...", and
- A modality: whether it is asserted as *possibly, actually,* or *necessarily* true.

   These are then *pure* forms of judgment, arising from understanding alone. They correspond basically to traditional Aristotelian logic. In other words, constructing judgments using these forms does not require sensible data: we do not according to Kant get the concepts of *affirmation* or *negation,* among others, from the senses.

   Second, *any* concept of an object, irrespective of whether the data for that object comes from, has to have the following properties:

- A quantity: whether it is a *unity*, a *plurality*, or a *totality*, and
- A quality: whether it is a *positive, negative,* or a *limiting* thing (light vs. darkness vs. shadow),
- A relation: first within itself, where there is a thing (*substance*) and its properties (*accidents*), then to other objects as *causes* and *effects*.
- A modality: whether it exists *possibly, actually,* or *necessarily*".

   A picture, also from [27] and [28], is worth 1000 words (Fig. 4).

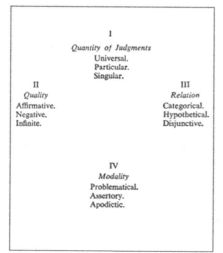
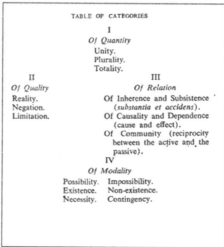

Fig. 4. Properties of an object [27, 28].

3   Proposal

We propose to address these problems by incorporating these ideas from Hume, Locke and Kant.

Having tried widely available software tools, at a word level the results are promising but at a sentence level, achieving cognitive equity, with human linguistic capabilities, continues to be elusive. Can Kant's categories aid in making better sense?. Does it help to know a proposition is a matter of fact, as Hume proposed? Or that a proposition is in relation to another proposition as Locke posited?

Thus, per our proposal, we must seek to overcome semantic deficiencies with:

- Annotate each sentence with Kant's category
- And with the four sorts proposed by Locke
- And with Hume's relations of ideas or matters of fact.

Given any sentence or proposition, we wish to know if it is a matter of fact for example and use these generic annotations to further analyze text corpus. We do not know at this time everything that needs to be maintained tracked. Project is work in progress. We intend to integrate, the Deep Structure propounded by early philosophers in addition to surface structure (PoS elements), embeddings and wordnet, at the level of words.

Acknowledgements. IBM Power Systems Academic Initiative IBM PSAI for their generous support for all my courses. Charlotte Walker and Monte Hancock for their encouragement and guidance.

References

1. https://www.forbes.com/sites/cognitiveworld/2019/02/18/not-good-as-gold-todays-ais-are-dangerously-lacking-in-au-artificial-understanding/
2. Gazzaniga, M.S., Ivry, R.B., Mangun, G.R., Steven, M.S.: Cognitive Nueroscience; The Biology of the Mind, 3rd edn., Chapter 10: language, pp. 388–444
3. Bobrow, R.J.: Semantic interpretation in PSI-KLONE. In: Research in Natural Language Understanding. Annual report (Report No. 4274). Bolt Beranek and Newman, Cambridge (1979b)
4. Brachman, R.J.: What's in a concept: structural foundations for semantic networks. Int. J. Man-Mach. Stud. **9**, 127–152 (1977)
5. Brachman, R.J.: On the epistemological status of semantic networks. In: Findler, N.V. (ed.) Associative Networks: Representation and Use of Knowledge by Computers. Academic, New York (1979)
6. Lenat, D., Feigenbaum, E.A.: On the thresholds of knowledge (1987)
7. Wang, C., Liu, X., Song, D.: Language models are open knowledge graphs. https://arxiv.org/pdf/2010.11967.pdf
8. Hogan, A., et al.: Knowledge graph. https://arxiv.org/pdf/2003.02320v2.pdf,
9. Chomsky, N.: Aspects of the Theory of Syntax (1965)
10. https://philosophynow.org/issues/106/Wittgenstein_Frege_and_The_Context_Principle
11. The Description and overview of Language, Cognition, Douglas Whitman, Chapter 11
12. https://code.google.com/archive/p/word2vec/ and https://code.google.com/p/word2vec/
13. https://quanteda.io/articles/pkgdown/replication/text2vec.html
14. https://spacyr.quanteda.io/reference/nounphrase_extract.html
15. http://nlp.stanford.edu/projects/glove/
16. Pennington, J., Socher, R., Manning, C.D.: Glove: global vectors for word representation. In: EMNLP, pp. 1532–1543 (2014)
17. Langer, S.K.: An Introduction to Symbolic Logic
18. Fellbaum, C.: WordNet: An Electronic Lexical Database. MIT Press, Cambridge (1998)
19. Navigli, R.: Word sense disambiguation: a survey. ACM Comput. Surv. **41**(2), Article 10 (2009)
20. Voorhees, E.M.: Using wordnet to disambiguate word senses for text retrieval. In: SIGIR 1993, pp. 171–180 (1993)
21. Liu, Y.: Using WordNet to disambiguate word senses. http://users.ece.northwestern.edu/~yingliu/papers/master_thesis.pdf
22. Whitman, D.: Categories and Semantic Networks; The classical Rule-Based Approach, Cognition, Chapter 9
23. Hausser, R.: Computation of Language. An Essay on Syntax, Semantics and Pragmatics in Natural Man-Machine Communication. Springer, Heidelberg. https://lagrammar.net/monographs/1989/cl-input.pdf
24. Jacobs, P.S.: Integrating language and meaning in structured inheritance networks
25. Angeli, G., et al.: Leveraging linguistic structure for open domain information extraction. http://nlp.stanford.edu/pubs/2015angeli-openie.pdf
26. Wang, P.: Natural language processing by reasoning and learning. In: Kühnberger, K.-U., Rudolph, S., Wang, P. (eds.) AGI 2013. LNCS (LNAI), vol. 7999, pp. 160–169. Springer, Heidelberg (2013). https://doi.org/10.1007/978-3-642-39521-5_17
27. Ariew, R., Watkins, E.: Modern Philosophy: An Anthology of Primary Sources
28. Kannisto, T.: A summary on the categories. https://qr.ae/pNzSgQ. https://www.quora.com/q/physicsandphilosophy. Accessed 2 Feb 2021

29. Hume, D.: An Enquiry Concerning Human Understanding. Oxford University Press, Oxford (1999)
30. Kant, I: Critique of Pure Reason
31. Locke, J.: An essay concerning human understanding. https://books.googleusercontent.com/books/content?req=AKW5Qadxd7jPy-dS-wbPtX6EDX3apaNzb0m-4S9rmIy6UNJq z2V-DqWLIncr_2WNrbf5nGcGd9wp4orA1JtBbtjKk_aebg8L2eMpI2Q9kK8b4m2_L92 wAwZawsU8XmUY_ODeYCz2S8GIVlZtNhpbUeo3cwe2BJmeoiRpdmIul7MSc6n4V5 cYi4pKUvNOkLvi0zbObVaASpqCTchSH0Zbwn3JwyhH2gWEV2mx6Ml-f1p8UKxB4 dsYoq8SYR6k-jA3hIkR0q8JVIDeslPsOqCgGrd8Ktdr9B5Dir9BBloE_LLF0BSFANGr8dI. Accessed 2 Feb 2021

Exploring Relationship Between Driver's Behavior and Cognitive Measures Observed by fNIRS in a Driving Simulator

Meltem Izzetoglu[1] and Seri Park[2(✉)]

[1] Electrical and Computer Engineering, Villanova University, Villanova, PA 19085, USA
[2] Civil and Environmental Engineering, Villanova University, Villanova, PA 19085, USA
seri.park@villanova.edu

Abstract. The data from World Health Organization and the National Highway Safety Administration show that traffic crash is the leading cause of death. In particular, the distracted driving behavior of young drivers (15–20 age) is identified as the main contributor to fatal crashes. Proper driving behaviors (e.g., keeping the vehicle within the lane, observing traffic signs) are regarded as complex activities that involve diverse cognitive processes such as attention, memory, vision, spatial orientation, and decision making. Therefore, it is imperative to explore how the cognitive processes related to the driving to understand the underpinnings of the driving behavior and ultimately develop various countermeasures to reduce fatal crashes. The advances in technology allowing the design of high-fidelity driving simulators and the wearable neuroimaging modalities have offered possibilities for the investigation of cognitive mechanisms of driving behavior in naturalistic settings, safely and effectively. This preliminary study examines an innovative approach to analyze the underlying cognitive activity changes among the young drivers while performing the driving task with and without a secondary task. In this study, the emerging sensing technologies, functional near infrared spectroscopy (fNIRS) and the state-of-art driving simulator were applied. Our initial results suggest that the driving and the chosen cognitive task conditions performed separately did not generate brain activations in prefrontal cortex (PFC) in young drivers. On the contrary, increased PFC activations were observed when driving and cognitive interference task were performed simultaneously. Furthermore, our study findings indicate that additional neural resources are required in the PFC during high speeds driving condition compared to the lower speeds case during dual task driving.

Keywords: Functional near infrared spectroscopy (fNIRS) · Young driver · Driving simulator · Brain activity · Speed · Dual task

1 Introduction

Motor vehicle crashes are the leading cause of death for adolescents and young adults. The latest statistics of World Health Organization (WHO) shows that worldwide every year approximately 1.35 million people die due to the traffic crashes and road traffic

© Springer Nature Switzerland AG 2021
D. D. Schmorrow and C. M. Fidopiastis (Eds.): HCII 2021, LNAI 12776, pp. 250–263, 2021.
https://doi.org/10.1007/978-3-030-78114-9_18

injuries are the primary cause of death for the population aged 5 to 29 year-old (WHO 2018). In addition, National Highway Traffic Safety Administration (NHTSA) data indicates that approximately 1,830 young drivers (15–20 age) are involved in fatal crashes (NHTSA 2019). Especially noted is the distracted driving behavior that claimed 2,841 lives (NHTSA 2020a) where approximately 7% of the distraction-affected fatal crashes were due to the teenagers' driving, ages 15–19 (NHTSA 2020b). These facts underline the research urgency regarding younger drivers. In order to address the listed issues, NHTSA is actively exploring various approaches in identifying effective countermeasures to implement (NHTSA 2010). While it is imperative to research countermeasure identification, it is equally essential to investigate how the cognitive processes related to the driving to understand the underpinnings of the driving behavior. Specifically, as the research on adolescent drivers indicates that brain development and mastery of driving tasks lag behind the increased responsibility that teens experience as they learn to drive, study of cognitive processing during driving specifically in young drivers can help in identifying the basis of differences in their driving performance outcomes and to identify effective counter measures to improve it.

Considering all of the several different tasks associated with driving such as speed control, maintaining safe distance, lane keeping, and response to hazards that has to be performed simultaneously and continually, driving is well acknowledged as a complex activity (Haghani et al. 2020; Choi et al. 2017; Calhoun et al. 2002; Walter et al. 2001). It requires coordination between range of physical as well as mental cognitive efforts involving attention, memory, decision-making, problem solving, planning, visuo-motor and auditory skills (Haghani et al. 2020; Calhoun et al. 2002; Walter et al. 2001). Moreover, driving a car is influenced not only by a variety of neurocognitive capacities but also with social and contextual factors (i.e. peer influence) that can produce more or less risky driving. Hence, there is a growing interest and application of neuroimaging methods to driving and road safety research to understand human factors and uncover the underlying mental and neural processes of driving behavior.

The advances in technology allowing the design of high-fidelity driving simulators and the wearable neuroimaging modalities have offered possibilities for the investigation of cognitive mechanisms of driving behavior in naturalistic settings, safely and effectively. Neuroimaging methods used in driving research including the functional magnetic resonance imaging (fMRI), electroencephalography (EEG), magnetoencephalogram (MEG) and recently functional near infrared spectroscopy (fNIRS) have increased our knowledge on drivers' cognitive processing (Walter et al. 2001; Schweiser et al. 2013; Nosrati et al. 2016; Choi et al. 2017; Calhoun et al. 2002; Haghani et al. 2020). Specifically, drivers' mental state and fatigue, tactical and operational decision-making and intentions and various driving activities such as emergency braking, turning, lane changing, and acceleration/deceleration have been studied. Prior work not only focused on the general driving behavior such as steering, turning, lane changing, etc. under normal healthy conditions but also on distracted, risky, intoxicated, neurologically impaired, fatigued or drowsy driving behavior or in semi-automated settings (Walter et al. 2001; Calhoun et al. 2002; Haghani et al. 2020). fMRI studies showed that driving involves coordinated activations in occipital, parietal and motor areas of the brain which can be modulated with driving speed. In fact, there were negative correlations between driving speed and activity in areas associated with error monitoring and inhibition and vigilance (Calhoun et al. 2002). Some of the other findings specifically in distracted driving with multi-tasking conditions indicated that with the addition of a secondary task (auditory task with sentence comprehension), brain activation associated with spatial processing during driving decreased while the activity in the temporal and prefrontal areas increased (Walter et al. 2001; Schweiser et al. 2013, Nosrati et al. 2016; Choi et al. 2017). It was discussed that engaging in an auditory task may result in sacrifices of mental resources in cognitive domains required for driving and recruitment of more resources in others to perform the secondary task resulting in the observed deterioration in driving performance. Even though underlying behavioral factors associated with driving is extensively studied, there is still not much known about the brain mechanisms involved in the execution of this complex task.

Among the existing neuroimaging modalities, fNIRS holds great potential in providing information on the neural underpinnings of driving behavior in many realistic setting, simulation environments, field conditions in healthy and diseased populations of all age groups. Due to its non-invasive, safe, portable, easy to use and low-cost characteristics together with its relative immunity to movement artifacts, it has been used in various cognitive activity monitoring studies including simulated and real driving tasks recently. (Izzetoglu M et al. 2020a; Holtzer et al. 2019; Izzetoglu et al. 2011; Ayaz et al. 2012; Foy et al. 2016; Izzetoglu et al. 2021). fNIRS is an optics based neuroimaging modality measuring relative changes in hemoglobin response related to neural activity using light in the near infrared range (650–950 nm). fNIRS results in driving research implementing driving simulators complemented prior fMRI and EEG findings (Foy et al. 2016; Ahn et al. 2016; Xu et al. 2017; Seraglia et al. 2011; Tsunashigma et al. 2009; Khan et al. 2015; Oka et al. 2015; Liu et al. 2012; Izzetoglu et al. 2021). Moreover, due to its wearability and immunity to movement artifacts, it was also used actual driving and semi-autonomous driving settings (Yoshino et al. 2013; Yamamoto et al. 2018).

This preliminary study explores young drivers' driving behavior and the underlying cognitive activity changes as measured by fNIRS while driving in a simulator with and without a secondary task at low (start of the driving) and higher (cruising) individual speeds. The summarized outcomes here are the initial findings of an ongoing study where different driving activities (turning, lane changing, acceleration/deceleration), under various conditions (distracted, fatigued, drowsy) in different age groups (young, middle aged and older drivers) will be studied in the future. Our preliminary findings suggest that the driving and the selected cognitive task conditions performed separately did not generate brain activations in prefrontal cortex (PFC) in young individuals. However, brain oxygenation levels were found to increase in PFC bilaterally while driving and performing the secondary cognitive task simultaneously in line with prior fMRI findings on distracted driving with the inclusion of secondary tasks. Furthermore, our initial findings suggested that driving speed modulated the increase in oxygenation levels in dual-task driving where positive correlations were observed. These findings suggested that more neural resources were required in the PFC related with the increased attentional need and mental workload in driving higher speeds as compared to lower ones under distracted driving conditions. The study findings will help support various initiatives that transportation engineers, policy and law makers are promoting to enhance a safe driving culture, especially for the young drivers.

2   Materials and Method

2.1   Participants

A total of n = 10 undergraduate students, four males and six females, were recruited for this study. Participation in this study was voluntary and the study was approved by the Institutional Review Board (IRB) at Villanova University (IRB-FY2021–56). All the participants signed the informed consent before starting the test procedures.

2.2   Procedure

Overall task procedures are shown in Fig. 1. The study started with the regular consenting process of obtaining written informed consent and enrolling the participants to the study. A pre-survey was administered to gather each participant's socio demographic information as well as self-stated driving behavior and experience. Once the pre-survey was completed, for one minute, participant tested the driving simulator to get familiar with the test setting. This process also allowed the team to screen any potential motion sickness incident. After the driving simulator testing, participants were asked to perform cognitive task and driving task separately and simultaneously with the fNIRS mounted on the participants' forehead. To minimize task order effects on the outcome measures, the order of the conducted task was counterbalanced using a Latin-square design. Overall, the procedure lasted to an average 30-min per participant. Details of each test step are presented in the following sections.

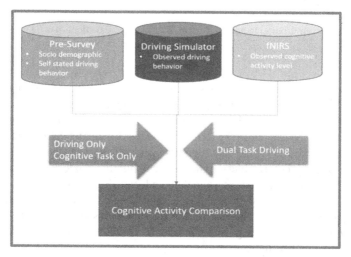

Fig. 1. Overall task protocol and procedures.

Pre-survey. A pre-survey was administered one the signed consent form was collected. The age distribution shows six 19-year old, three 21-year old, and one 22-year old with all of them having at least three years of driving experience. To further understand each participant's stated driving behavior, questions about participant's comfortable driving speed, their own tendency in taking risks while driving, stress level behind the wheel, as well as their own driving behavior adaption to the weather conditions were asked. Survey results indicated that none of the participants was issued speeding tickets and most of the participants do not enjoy risk taking while driving. Majority of the participants rated themselves as "good drivers" in general. With the open-ended question regarding their driving speeds on the highway, an average of 76.5 mile-per-hour (mph) with a standard deviation (STD) of 13.6 was observed among the participant. Survey results demonstrated that a homogenous population was recruited in this study. Table 1 summarizes the collected participants' driving behaviors.

Table 1. Participant's driving behavior questions and answers

Questions	Answer distribution
Number of speeding tickets issued in the last two years from today	None (n = 10)
How fast can you drive on the highway (Open ended)	Average = 76.5 (mph), STD = 13.6
Do you enjoy taking the risks when driving?	Never (n = 2), Not really (n = 7), Maybe (n = 1)
In general, are you stressed when driving?	Never (n = 1), Not really (n = 7), Maybe (n = 2)
Do you adapt your driving to the weather driving?	Often (n = 7), always (n = 3)
How do you rate your driving, in general?	Good (n = 9), Excellent (n = 1)

Driving Simulation Setting. In this study, the state-of-art RDS-1000 driving simulator is used. The RDS-1000 represents a real-vehicle equipment, including a real steering wheel with control, loaded steering, real accelerator, and brake pedals along with a fully customizable virtual dashboard. The RDS-1000 features a quarter cab design with three large-panel monitors. RDS-1000 also supports visual effects such as fog, rain, dynamic shadows, headlights, deformable terrain, ambient lighting models, and pre-rendered light maps. Furthermore, an audio system that renders realistic traffic and environmental sounds (e.g., high wind) is also integrated into the RDS-1000 that allows mimicking the fully immersive driving case. A typical urban network with signalized intersections and various roadway geometrics (e.g., sharp horizontal curve) at a moderate traffic volume level was applied in this study.

fNIRS Setting. After the trial run in the driving simulator, fNIRS sensor was mounted on the participant's forehead using the predefined sensor montage procedures. During the data collection, each participant conducted three tasks, driving only (DO), cognitive task (Alpha) only and dual task driving (DC) in a randomized order which was counter-balanced using a Latin-square design. Note that a proximal baseline was collected for 10-s before each task where participants were asked to rest and relax while looking at the frontal view of the driving simulator while the vehicle was at park. Figure 2 represents the study setting with a sample participant wearing fNIRS and performing driving task.

The task conditions that the participants performed while being monitored with fNIRS were as follows:

- Driving only (DO): In this single task driving condition, participants were asked to drive in an urban setting during daytime under normal weather conditions for around 1 min. Participants were instructed that they can select their driving course freely but need to abide by the traffic rules.
- Cognitive Task (Alpha): Participants were instructed to recite alternate letters of the alphabet (e.g., A, C, E) for around 30 s out loud while sitting in the simulator and not driving If they reached the end of the alphabet before the task period was over, they were given another letter to start with.
- Dual task Driving (DC): Under this dual task condition, participants were instructed to drive in the same urban scenario as in DO while reciting alternate letters of the alphabet (Alpha task) at the same time for around 1 min. In order to reduce task prioritization effects, participants were specifically asked to pay equal attention to both tasks.

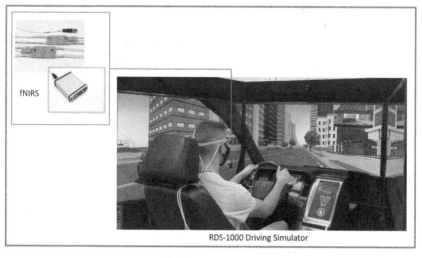

Fig. 2. Study setting.

Data Acquisition

Driving Behavior Measurements. Each participant's driving speed trajectory, longitudinal and lateral accelerations, lane offset status, and brake setting were collected as to represent driving behavior measurements. The sampling interval of data collection was set at an average of 0.02-s corresponding to 50 Hz sampling frequency.

Hemodynamic Response Measurements via fNIRS. Hemodynamic responses from the PFC were collected using fNIR Imager, 1200W (fNIR Devices, LLC. Photomac, MD). The fNIRS system consisted of two identical sensors to be placed on the participant's forehead bilaterally (Fig. 3) connected to a control box for data acquisition that is wirelessly communicating with a computer for data collection and storage. Each of the identical fNIRS sensors were built on a flexible circuit board covered with a silicone material for comfort, sealing and hygiene. Each sensor housed 1 light source in the middle with three built in LEDs at peak wavelengths of 730, 805 and 850 nm and 2 photodetectors on each side of it arranged in a linear form with a source-detector separation of 2.5 cm. With this sensor configuration and its standard placement procedures (Izzetoglu et al. 2021; Izzetoglu et al. 2020a), fNIRS system collected data from leftmost, left middle, right middle and rightmost forehead locations in its channels 1, 2, 3 and 4, respectively as shown in Fig. 3. Cognitive Optical Brain Imaging (COBI) studio data collection software of the fNIRS system was used on a Windows 10 laptop computer to collect the fNIRS data at the sampling rate of ~4.43 Hz.

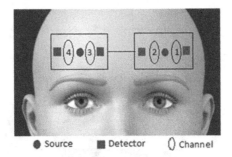

Fig. 3. fNIRS sensor placement on the forehead with corresponding channel recording locations.

2.3 Data Analysis and Statistics

Out of the 10 participant recordings, one participant's fNIRS data was not recorded for the full procedure and one other participant's driving speed data was not generated. Therefore, two participants were excluded from further analysis. Hence, fNIRS analysis was based on available n = 8 participant data. In addition, for a detailed analysis of the relationship between driving speeds and oxygenation levels, data from the participants without any full stop due to the red-light signal was reviewed (n = 6).

fNIRS Data Processing. Initially, data from each of the four fNIRS channels were visually inspected. The channels having saturation, dark current or extreme noise levels due to incorrect sensor placement were eliminated from further analysis. Then, we applied wavelet denoising to the remaining raw intensity measurements at 730 and 850 nm wavelengths for spiky noise suppression (Molavi et al. 2014). Changes in oxygenated hemoglobin ($HbO2$) and deoxygenated hemoglobin (Hb) were calculated from those artifact-removed raw intensity measurements relative to the resting baseline collected in the beginning of the task using modified Beer-Lambert law with select parameters as previously described (Izzetoglu et al. 2020b). To remove possible baseline shifts and to suppress physiological artifacts such as respiration and Mayer waves, we first applied Spline filtering (Scholkmann et al. 2010) followed by a finite impulse response low-pass filter with cut-off frequency at 0.08 Hz (Izzetoglu et al. 2020b). In this study, we focused on $HbO2$ measurements in all comparisons, as it was shown to be a good indicator of cognitive activations in driving studies using fNIRS technology.

Statistical Analysis. With the main goal of assessing potential relationship between driving behavior and oxygenation levels, we had to use small dataset (n = 6). Therefore, a rigorous statistical analysis was not feasible at this stage. Even though an in-depth statistical analysis was not performed, the correlation analysis between oxygenation levels and driving behavior was conducted using the Pearson correlation with the significance criterion ($\alpha = 0.05$) approach.

3   Results and Discussion

In this preliminary study, we investigated participants' brain oxygenation level in PFC under different driving conditions (single and dual task driving) in relation to their driving behavior, e.g. speed. Here we will summarize our initial findings with discussions.

3.1   Cognitive Activity at Different Driving Conditions

First, we evaluated changes in oxygenation levels in PFC for each three task condition, driving only (DO), cognitive task only (Alpha), driving while performing cognitive task (DC). As the task lengths were different for driving tasks (~1min for DO and DC) and the Alpha condition (30 s), we used the first 30 s of data epochs for all task conditions. We applied baseline correction to each data epoch to obtain task related changes in oxygenation relative to the start of the task by subtracting the average of 2 s of data immediately preceding the task start from the data epochs. To reduce dimensionality, we averaged the data epochs for the channels 1 and 2 for left hemisphere and 3 and 4 for right hemisphere.

Since the participants could select their driving course freely, we observed that some participants reached a traffic light that tuned red and hence stopped the car fully within the first 30 s of their driving period. Initially, we wanted to analyze oxygenation differences in different task conditions (e.g. dual task driving to driving only). However, stopping fully for a period of time could have affected the nature of the intended task condition (dual task driving will be Alpha during stopped intervals). Hence, we separated the participants who did not encounter red lights and stopped (n = 6) and the ones who did (n = 2) during the first 30 s of the driving tasks.

In Fig. 4, we present example participant's 30 s data epochs for HbO2 (in blue line) and their driving speed (orange line) for conditions, DO (dashed line), Alpha (dotted line), and DC (solid line). Note that, for Alpha, no speed line is generated. In Fig. 4(a) the recordings of an example participant who did not fully stop and in Fig. 4(b) an example participant who stopped are shown for left and right hemispheres. It can be observed that patterns in the HbO2 signal specifically the increase in oxygenation in dual-task driving, DC condition in comparison to single task conditions, DO and Alpha were different in the participant with no stop and the one with a stop.

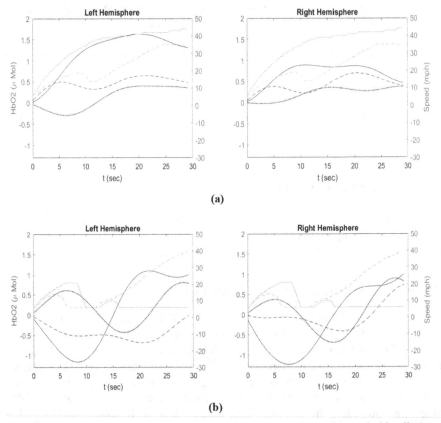

Fig. 4. HbO2 epochs on left and right hemispheres in three task conditions (in blue line) and the corresponding driving speed (orange line) for conditions, DO (dashed line), Alpha (dotted line), and DC (solid line). (a) Participant #7, Participant without full STOP. (b) Participant #1, Participant with full STOP due to the red signal (Color figure online)

For an in-depth comparison across single and dual tasks, the data of participants without full stop during driving conditions (n = 6) were further analyzed. The average

HbO2 values within the 30 s data epochs for DO, Alpha and DC conditions in the left and right hemisphere (in blue bars) is shown in Fig. 5. For the single task condition (DO and Alpha), it was observed that the oxygenation levels in the PFC did not increase. This result may suggest that these tasks did not require higher order cognitive processing subserved by PFC in this healthy young adult population and were more like automatic processes. Our results do not rule out any possible oxygenation changes in other brain areas in language or visuo-spatial domains as we were not able to monitor them with the fNIRS device used in this study.

In contrast, results show that dual tasking in DC condition required more activation in PFC bilaterally during continual driving activity with the added cognitive interference task. Since none of the single tasks DO and Alpha generated an increase in PFC oxygenation, we can assume that simultaneously combined tasks in DC condition contributed to the increase in activation of frontal cortex and not due to a specific single task. Since dual tasking is a more cognitively taxing activity as shown in prior fMRI studies on driving and fNIRS studies in walking (Holtzer et al. 2019; Schweiser et al. 2013), the increase in oxygenation during DC as observed in this study was in line with prior findings and reflects the higher mental workload in PFC. Moreover, prior fMRI studies showed that during distracted driving the activity moved to frontal areas (Walter et al. 2001; Schweiser et al. 2013; Nosrati et al. 2016; Choi et al. 2017) requiring the recruitment of mental resources in PFC subserving attention, memory, decision making and problems solving domains as also found in this study. Note that, for the participants with the full stop due to the red signal (n = 2), this increase in PFC activation in DC condition was not present (Fig. 5 orange bars). This could be due to the fact when participants stopped driving during DC, the dual task condition becomes as single task only as in Alpha condition without the driving load.

3.2 Cognitive Activity at Different Speed Under Dual-Tasking

In the next step, we explored the relationship between driving speed and oxygenation levels. In this analysis, we selected the participants who did not experience a full STOP (n = 6) and their recordings in DC condition since that task generated increased activations in PFC. Figure 6(a) and (b) show HbO2 vs speed averaged for the first 15-s and the last 15-s of the recordings during DC task in left and right PFC, respectively. The task started from 0 speed and usually reached a cruising speed within the task epoch by 30 s (Fig. 4(a)). Hence, the first and last 15 s of data provided low and high speed regions. The results as shown in Fig. 6, indicated that high speed driving during dual task driving resulted in higher oxygenation levels in PFC. Moreover, Pearson correlation analysis using all data points in recordings showed statistically significant, strong positive correlation between driving speed and HbO2 bilaterally (Left hemisphere $R(127) = 0.86 \pm 0.14$, and Right hemisphere $R(127) = 0.79 \pm 0.25$, in all participant $p < 0.001$). These finding suggested that as driving speed increased during dual tasking, more neural resources were needed to perform the task, especially at higher speeds. This is a significant finding in supporting the needs of young driver education focusing on the traffic safety regulation such as texting banning while driving.

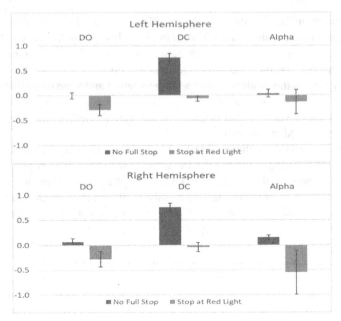

Fig. 5. Average HbO2 across three task conditions on left and right hemispheres (error bars represent standard error of the mean)

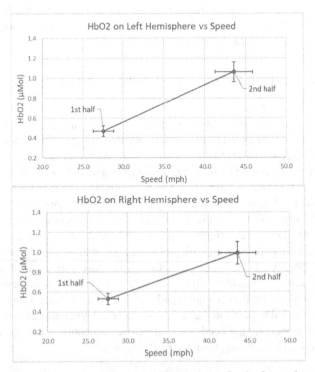

Fig. 6. Average HbO2 vs speed on left and right hemispheres for the first and second half of the epochs (error bars represent standard error of the mean)

3.3 Limitations of the Study

There were several limitations to the study. As this is a preliminary study, the sample size is very small and hence statistical comparisons could not be performed. Future studies need to include larger sample size. Here, we only tested healthy young drivers. Diverse age ranges inexperienced adolescents, middle and older age drivers can be tested and brain activation levels in single and dual task driving conditions can be evaluated. In this study we only tested driving in urban areas under normal driving conditions. Various roadway scenarios in different settings including highways and rural areas during daytime and nighttime, under rainy and snowy conditions should be evaluated. Brain activation during different driving tasks (left and right turn, lane change, acceleration/deceleration) and for various human factors (fatigue, drowsiness, risky behavior, etc.) can also be studied in future work. Finally, we have used a wireless fNIRS system with only four channels to monitor the PFC and hence activations in other brain areas such as temporal, parietal and occipital areas could not be monitored.

4 Conclusion

In this study, we investigated young drivers' underlying cognitive activation levels while driving inside a state-of-art driving simulator with and without a cognitive task (i.e., reciting the alphabet). The brain oxygenation level in the PFC was measured as the criterion to explore its relationship with driving speeds. While we acknowledge the limited dataset is used, the results were promising. Overall, our preliminary results demonstrated that driving speed affected the increase in oxygenation levels in dual-task driving where positive correlations were observed. Moreover, our study findings indicate that additional neural resources are required in the PFC during high speeds driving conditions compared to the lower speeds ones. The findings herein also provide a basis in supporting various initiatives that promote a safe driving culture by presenting the potential danger of distractive driving behavior that requires additional neural resources.

References

Ahn, S., Nguyen, T., Jang, H., Kim, J.G., Jun, S.C.: Exploring neuro-physiological correlates of drivers' mental fatigue caused by sleep deprivation using simultaneous EEG, ECG, and fNIRS data. Front. Hum. Neurosci. **10**, 219 (2016)

Ayaz, H., Shewokis, P.A., Bunce, S., Izzetoglu, K., Willems, B., Onaral, B.: Optical brain monitoring for operator training and mental workload assessment. Neuroimage **59**(1), 36–47 (2012). https://doi.org/10.1016/j.neuroimage.2011.06.023

Calhoun, V.D., Pekar, J.J., McGinty, V.B., Adali, T., Watson, T.D., Pearlson, G.D.: Different activation dynamics in multiple neural systems during simulated driving. Hum. Brain Mapp. **16**(3), 158–167 (2002)

Choi, M.H., et al.: Increase in brain activation due to sub-tasks during driving: fMRI study using new MR-compatible driving simulator. J. Physiol. Anthropol. **36**(1), 1–12 (2017)

Foy, H.J., Runham, P., Chapman, P.: Prefrontal cortex activation and young driver behaviour: a fNIRS study. PLoS ONE **11**(5) (2016). https://doi.org/10.1371/journal.pone.0156512

Haghani, M., et al.: Applications of brain imaging methods in driving behaviour research. arXiv preprint arXiv:2007.09341 (2020)

Holtzer, R., Izzetoglu, M., Chen, M., Wang, C.: Distinct FNIRS-Derived HbO2 trajectories during the course and over repeated walking trials under single-and dual-task conditions: implications for within session learning and prefrontal cortex efficiency in older adults. J. Gerontol.: Ser. A **74**(7), 1076–1083 (2019). https://doi.org/10.1093/gerona/gly181

Izzetoglu, K., et al.: The evolution of field deployable fNIR spectroscopy from bench to clinical settings. J. Innov. Opt. Health Sci. **4**(03), 239–250 (2011)

Izzetoglu, M., Shewokis, P.A., Tsai, K., Dantoin, P., Sparango, K., Min, K.: Short-term effects of meditation on sustained attention as measured by fNIRS. Brain Sci. **10**(9), 608 (2020). https://doi.org/10.3390/brainsci10090608

Izzetoglu, M., Holtzer, R.: Effects of processing methods on fNIRS signals assessed during active walking tasks in older adults. IEEE Trans. Neural Syst. Rehabil. Eng. **28**(3), 699–709 (2020). https://doi.org/10.1109/TNSRE.2020.2970407

Izzetoglu, M., Jiao, X., Park, S.: Understanding driving behavior using fNIRS and machine learning. Accepted for presentation and publication for ASCE International Conference on Transportation & Development, June 8–10, 2021, Virtual Event

Khan, M.J., Hong, K.S.: Passive BCI based on drowsiness detection: an fNIRS study. Biomed. Opt. Express **6**(10), 4063–4078 (2015)

Liu, T., Saito, H., Oi, M.: Distinctive activation patterns under intrinsically versus extrinsically driven cognitive loads in prefrontal cortex: a near-infrared spectroscopy study using a driving video game. Neurosci. Lett. **506**(2), 220–224 (2012). https://doi.org/10.1016/j.neulet.2011.11.009

Molavi, B., Dumont, G.A.: Wavelet-based motion artifact removal for functional near-infrared spectroscopy. Physiol. Meas. **33**(2), 259 (2012)

National Highway Traffic Safety Administration (NHTSA). "Young Drivers" (2019). https://crashstats.nhtsa.dot.gov/Api/Public/ViewPublication/812753. Accessed 1 November 2020

National Highway Traffic Safety Administration (NHTSA). 2020a. "Distracted Driving." https://www.nhtsa.gov/risky-driving/distracted-driving. Accessed 10 October 2020

National Highway Traffic Safety Administration (NHTSA). Teens and Distracted Driving (2020b). Accessed 1 November 2020. https://crashstats.nhtsa.dot.gov/Api/Public/ViewPublication/812667

National Highway Traffic Safety Administration (NHTSA). "Driver Distraction Program" (2010). https://www.nhtsa.gov/sites/nhtsa.dot.gov/files/811299.pdf. Accessed 1 October 2020

Nosrati, R., Vesely, K., Schweizer, T.A., Toronov, V.: Event-related changes of the prefrontal cortex oxygen delivery and metabolism during driving measured by hyperspectral fNIRS. Biomed. Opt. Express **7**(4), 1323–1335 (2016). https://doi.org/10.1364/BOE.7.001323

Oka, N., et al.: Greater activity in the frontal cortex on left curves: a vector-based fNIRS study of left and right curve driving. PLoS ONE **10**(5), e0127594 (2015)

Scholkmann, F., Spichtig, S., Muehlemann, T., Wolf, M.: How to detect and reduce movement artifacts in near-infrared imaging using moving standard deviation and spline interpolation. Physiol. Meas. **31**(5), 649 (2010)

Schweizer, T.A., Kan, K., Hung, Y., Tam, F., Naglie, G., Graham, S.: Brain activity during driving with distraction: an immersive fMRI study. Front. Hum. Neurosci. **7**, 53 (2013). https://doi.org/10.3389/fnhum.2013.00053

Seraglia, B., Gamberini, L., Priftis, K., Scatturin, P., Martinelli, M., Cutini, S.: An exploratory fNIRS study with immersive virtual reality: a new method for technical implementation. Front. Hum. Neurosci. **5**, 176 (2011)

Tsunashima, H., Yanagisawa, K.: Measurement of brain function of car driver using functional near-infrared spectroscopy (fNIRS). Comput. Intell. Neurosci. (2009)

Walter, H., Vetter, S.C., Grothe, J.O., Wunderlich, A.P., Hahn, S., Spitzer, M.: The neural correlates of driving. NeuroReport **12**(8), 1763–1767 (2001)

World Health Organization (WHO). Road Traffic Injuries (2018). https://www.who.int/newsroom/fact-sheets/detail/road-traffic-injuries. Accessed 1 October 2020

Xu, G., et al.: Functional connectivity analysis of distracted drivers based on the wavelet phase coherence of functional near-infrared spectroscopy signals. PLoS ONE **12**(11), e0188329 (2017)

Yoshino, K., Oka, N., Yamamoto, K., Takahashi, H., Kato, T.: Functional brain imaging using near-infrared spectroscopy during actual driving on an expressway. Front. Hum. Neurosci. **7**, 882 (2013). https://doi.org/10.3389/fnhum.2013.00882

Yamamoto, K., Takahashi, H., Sugimachi, T., Suda, Y.: The study of driver's reaction for traffic information on actual driving and DS using fNIRS. In: 2018 IEEE International Conference on Computational Intelligence and Virtual Environments for Measurement Systems and Applications (CIVEMSA), pp. 1–6. IEEE, June 2018

Automatic Engagement Recognition for Distance Learning Systems: A Literature Study of Engagement Datasets and Methods

Shofiyati Nur Karimah[(✉)] and Shinobu Hasegawa

Japan Advanced Institute of Science and Technology (JAIST), Nomi 923-1211, Japan
{karimah,hasegawa}@jaist.ac.jp

Abstract. With the paradigm shift of learning processes from traditional classroom to distance learning systems, the recent success of artificial intelligent research and applications, including machine learning and deep neural networks, have increasingly been leveraged to learn how to include engagement state analysis into the distance learning process. Recent automatic engagement estimations employ several modalities, such as, video, audio, and biological signals or neuro-sensing information as source input to be analyzed. In this paper, we provide a literature review of engagement estimation, including dataset, algorithms as well as the discussion and evaluation. First of all, we present the engagement datasets, including publicly available and proprietary sources built for some specific concerns. We then describe the methodology of engagement measurements that are widely used in literature and state-of-the-art algorithms to automate the estimation. The advantages and limitations of the algorithms are briefly discussed and summarized in benchmark of the used modalities and datasets. Additionally, we extend this literature review to the insight for the practical use of automatic engagement estimation in a real education process that is crucial to distance learning improvement. Finally, we review the remaining challenges for robust engagement estimation as part of attempts in improving distance learning quality and performance by taking personalized engagement into account.

Keywords: Engagement estimation · Distance learning · Machine learning · Deep learning

1 Introduction

Engagement is a complex state which includes affective, cognitive, behavioral and agentic factors [58] as well as intention and emotion or a task. In learning processes, learners' engagement involves their attention and emotion such as curiosity, interest, optimism, and passion for what they learn or are being taught, which extends to the level of motivation to pursue the learning and

© Springer Nature Switzerland AG 2021
D. D. Schmorrow and C. M. Fidopiastis (Eds.): HCII 2021, LNAI 12776, pp. 264–276, 2021.
https://doi.org/10.1007/978-3-030-78114-9_19

make progress. Therefore, engagement is an essential component in a learning process to reduce the dropout rates [2], increase productivity and learning, and provoke insights to improve course content and lecture plans [20,46,68].

In recent years, even prior to the outbreak of the Severe Acute Respiratory Syndrome coronavirus 2 (SARS-CoV-2) which causes the coronavirus disease 2019 (COVID-19) necessitating social distancing and often mandatory remote learning, a paradigm shift of learning processes from the traditional classroom environment to distance learning systems such as Massive Open Online Courses (MOOCs) could be observed. Furthermore, the recent success of artificial intelligent research and applications, including machine learning and deep neural networks, have increasingly been leveraged to learn how to include engagement state analysis into the distance learning process. Recognizing learners' engagement level with the system(s) they are interacting with will not only improve engagement with the system but also pave the way for better human-computer interaction [63].

Recent improvements of computational hardware and software are supporting traditional machine learning and deep neural networks with respect to computer vision tasks, studies analyzing facial features through automatic recognition and subsequent artificial intelligence analysis have been proposed as a highly promising approach. [15,27]. Similarly, the current development on bio-signal hardware such as electroencephalograms (EEG) received considerable attention from engagement researchers, since it is getting cheaper, portable and can provide a simple, and easy-to-use solution [1] for identification of some biological signal which can be used in engagement analysis.

There are two ways to measure learners' engagement, namely, internal measurements by using self-reporting and externally observable factors such as facial features, posture, speech and action [18,68]. In traditional classrooms, the external examination of learners' engagement can be done by the educator using observational checklists and rating scales. In contrast, in distance learning settings, computer vision can be utilized to automate the engagement estimation, in which facial expression is the most popular to be analyzed because it offers an assessment process similar to the classroom situation where the teacher observes the learners without interrupting their activities.

Dewan et al. [21] has reviewed engagement detection in online learning, where they categorized the detection methods into automatic, semi-automatic, and manual. In this paper, we provide a literature review specifically for automatic engagement estimation, where the summary of dataset, the algorithms and their performances are the point of topic. We aim to give an overview of primary requirements and current trends of methods used for this particular field based on the research studies published between 2010 to 2019.

First of all, we present the publicly available datasets. These are comprised of some including both engagement state labels and facial expression datasets, such as DAiSEE [63] and EmotiW 2019 [22], and datasets only containing facial expressions without prior engagement labeling. Additionally, specialized datasets gathered for specific engagement recognition experiments are discussed. A brief overview of these datasets, including the data gathering methods, number of subjects, number of images or video captures, will be compared and evaluated in the following discussion regarding their reliability and feasibility.

We then describe the methodologies of the engagement measurement that are widely used in the literature and the state-of-the-art algorithms to automate the estimation. We examine the advantages and limitations of the state-of-the-art algorithms as well as the results of works published between 2010–2020 which to our knowledge have not been reviewed in previous engagement estimation studies. The brief discussion of the used modalities, datasets, algorithms and performances is summarized in a benchmark table to give an easy overview of the systematic frameworks.

Furthermore, we extend this literature review with an insight into the practical use of automatic engagement estimation in a real education process that is crucial to distance learning improvement. Finally, we review the remaining challenges for robust engagement estimation by taking personalized engagement into account.

2 Engagement Datasets

Unlike emotion recognition where the dataset is based on six or seven basic expressions e.g., anger, disgust, fear, happiness, sadness, surprise, and neutral. There are only few publicly available datasets which includes engagement on their labelling, e.g., DAiSEE [63] and EmotiW2018 [23]. Therefore, most of engagement studies build their own custom engagement dataset. Table 1 provides an overview of datasets, including the references, collection environment, publicity of the dataset, number of subjects, samples, data grouping, and the label description.

2.1 Public Available Engagement Datasets

The term public here means that the dataset is available for public either directly by download or through a prior request or registration process.

Bosphorus [61], ***SEMAINE*** [44], *and* ***Youtube Faces*** [71] Bosphorus and SEMAINE are not directly used for the engagement estimation, instead they sometimes used in pre-processing to extract the face landmark information and face action coding system (FACS) a popular method proposed by Ekman and Friesen [24] to describe facial muscle Action Units (AUs) and corresponding expressions.

The Bosphorus dataset consists of 105 subjects, which most of the subjects are Caucasian, in a lab environment with predefined poses, expressions and occlusion conditions identical for each subject. The total 4,652 3D face scans are manually labelled for 24 facial landmark points and defined into multi-expressions (happiness, surprise, fear, sadness, anger, disgust) and multi-poses (head pose, Action Units combinations, occlutions).

Table 1. Summary of dataset for engagement estimation tables.

Dataset	Collection Env.	Publicity	N of Subjects	Samples	Data Group	Label Description
Bosphorus [61]	Lab (posed)	✓	105 (45f, 60m)	4,652 face scans	-	Multi-expressions and multi-poses 3D face
SEMAINE [44]	Lab	✓	150 (93f, 57m)	959 character interactions (± 5 min)	Train,Dev.,Test	Basic emotions, Epistemic states, Interaction Process Analysis, Validity
Youtube Faces [71]	In-the-wild	✓	1,595	3,425 clips	10-fold	Similarity description
DAiSEE [28]	in-the-wild	✓	112 (32f, 80m)	9,068 clips (10 sec)	Train:Val.:Test (60:20:20)	Boredom, Confusion, Engagement, Frustation
EmotiW2018 [23,36]	in-the-wild	✓	91 (27f, 64m)	264 clips (5 min)	Train,Val.,Test (149,48,67)	*Engagement ({0,1,2,3})
Kamath et al. [34]	in-the-wild	✓	23	4,408 images	3-fold	Engaged, Not-Engaged, Very Engaged
HBCU & UC [68]	Lab (in task)	✗	34 (25f, 9m)	60 clips (60sec) 505 clips (10 sec)	v4-fold	Engagement ({1,2,3,4})
Monkaresi et al. [46]	Lab (in task)	✗	23 (9f, 14 m)	1,325 clips (± 9.78 sec)	10-fold	Engaged, Not-Engaged (self-report)
Sanghvi et al. [60]	Lab (with robot interaction)	✗	5 (3m, 2f)	4 clips (7 sec)	10-fold	Engaged, Not-Engaged
Booth [8]	Lab	✗	12	3,365 images	5-fold	Engaged, Not-Engaged Highly-Engaged
Bosch [9]	Lab (in task)	✗	98	3,272 clips (12 sec)	Dev. set, Evaluation set	Engaged, Not-Engaged
Bosch et al.[10]	Lab (group interaction)	✗	137 (80f, 57m)	20 groups (55 min)	Train and Test set	Boredom, Confusion, Delight, Engagement Frustation
Grafsgaard et al. [26]	Lab (1-on-1 interaction)	✗	67	650,000 frames, 7 sessions	-	FACS-annotation
Alkabbany et al. [3]	Lab (in task and watch)	✗	14	109,325 frames	-	Engagement ({0,1,2,3})
Nezami et al. [45,51]	Lab (in task)	✗	20 (11f, 9m)	1,000 frames	Train,Val.,Test (3224,715,688)	Engaged, Not-Engaged
Psaltis et al. [55,56]	Classroom (in Group)	✗	72 (11f, 38m)	750 clips (3 sec)	4-fold	Engaged, Not-Engaged
Thomas et al. [64]	Lab (in Group)	✗	10 (7f, 3m)	30 videos (12 min)	10-fold	Engaged, Not-Engaged
Chauoachi et al. [15]	Lab (in task)	✗	35 (13f, 22m)	Data of 8 sensors, 2 videos	-	4 quadrants of the 2D affective space (Q1-Q4)

The SEMAINE dataset consists of recordings of 150 subjects in conversation with an individual Sensitive Artificial Listener (SAL) agent, for a total of 959 character interactions in approximately 5 min each.

The Youtube Faces dataset is comprised of 3,425 youtube clips from 1,595 subjects. The data is labeled with the names of the subjects in each video allowing similarity and identity checks on the dataset. Ramya et al. use this dataset for their engagement estimation along with the Bosphorus dataset.

Other datasets used for similar purposes include DISFA [43] and BP4D [73], which utilized in training OpenFace [6,7] and OpenFace2.0 [5], a tool widely used by engagement estimation researcher to extract facial landmark detection, head pose estimation, facial action unit recognition, and eye-gaze estimation. For OpenFace2.0, other dataset, namely, UNBC-McMaster [42], and FERA2011 [66] are also used in training for better recognizing action units (AUs).

DAiSEE [28,63]. Gupta et al. introduce Dataset for Affective States in E-Environment (DAiSEE) which includes 112 Asian-Indian participants. The approximately 13 min videos are split into 10 s clips, resulting in a total of 9,068 clips from all subjects combined. The dataset is divided into three parts: training, validation, and testing sets with the division ratio 60 : 20 : 20.

The dataset was collected in-the-wild enviroment where the subject join the experiment by watching learning video from anywhere, such as at a computer laboratory, dormitory rooms, or outside, via Skype. Therefore, the term in-the-wild refers to settings typically seen in the real-world where students may shows any behavior in distane learning and there is a wide variety of different backgrounds, occlusion, and illumination in the dataset samples.

The annotation was done by a crowd with votes from 10 different annotators from crowdFlower for each clip. They classified the dataset into four affective labels: boredom, confusion, engagement and frustration, with a point value regarding their applicability ranging from 0 to 3.

EmotiW2018 [23,36]. The 6th Emotion Recognition in the Wild Challenge (EmotiW2018) provides a database containing the face videos of subjects watching an educational video (MOOC). The dataset consists of 264 videos captured from 91 subjects with an average duration of the video of 5 min. The dataset is grouped in three parts: training, validation and testing, which contain 149, 48 and 67 videos, respectively.

The recordings are from in-the-wild environments and graded based on engagement level, with a grade of 0 indicating complete disengagement, and 3 signalling highly engaged subjects. The annotation was done by five annotators for every five minute video.

Kamath et al. [34]. Kamath et al. used a crowd-sourced approach to create database for engagement estimation taking into account Hawthorne effect, i.e., subject awareness of experiment objectives during the capture. It consists of 4,708 images from 23 subjects, which is relatively small compared to other publicly available datasets. There are at least 25 annotations for each image, by a total of 76 different annotators on Crowdflower.

2.2 Non-public Engagement Datasets

Compare to facial expression dataset, where basic expression annotations are presented, there are few datasets available publicly that can be used for engagement detection [21] specifically for distance learning purpose. Moreover, some public datasets are not in accordance with the need. Hence, some studies build their own dataset as shown in Table 1.

3 Automatic Engagement Estimation

In this section, we briefly summarize the existing algorithms widely used in best practice implementations according to literature. We summarize the algorithms

Table 2. Summary of automatic engagement estimation research (2010–2020) tables.

Year	Name	Modalities	Pre-proccesses	Exracted Features	Methods	Dataset	Performance Evaluation
2010	Chauoachi et al. [15]	Brain signals, Videos HR, GSR	EEG, Fast Fourier Transform (FFT)	Engagement index [25,54]	one way ANNOVA, LR	35 (13f, 22m)	-
	Nakano et al. [49]	Videos, Audio	Julius-4.0.2, Tobii X-120	Eye gaze, Speech	Clustering technique	$N = 9$ (6m, 3f)	$\approx 17\%$
2011	Sanghvi et al. [60]	Videos	ANIVIL [37], CAMShift OpenCV [12]	Body postures (BLA, SF QoM, CI)	WEKA	$N = 5$ (3m, 2f)	≥ 0.70
	Cocea et al. [19]	Log-files	HTML-Tutor	30 log attributes	WEKA	$N = 48$	85-91%
2013	Grafsgaard et al. [26]	Videos	CERT	AUs	CERT (Regression)	$N = 65$	RMSE = 8.50%
2014	Whitehill et al. [68]	Videos / Images	CERT	BF, Gabor, 3D face pose, AUs	CERT (Regression)	HBCU & UC	2AFC $\approx$ 0.69
2016	Bosch et al. [10]	Videos	FACET, RELIEF-F [38]	AUs, head pose & orient., body motion	WEKA	$N = 137$ (80f, 57m)	64% (AUC = 0.679)
	Bosch [9]	Videos	EmotionSDK	LBP-TOP,AUs	SVM	$N = 98$	-
	Tofighi et al. [65]	Biometric data	Depth camera & NiTE SDK	3D points sequence	SVM	$N = 5$	86.3%
	Kamath et al. [34]	Videos / Images	V & J	HoG	MKL SVM	$N = 23$	50.77%
2017	Booth [8]	Videos	KinectV2, OpenCV lib.[11], feature detector [47]	Face landmarks, AUs, Eye codes, Head pose	k-means clustering	$N = 12$	F-score = 0.369
	Monkaresi et al. [46]	Videos, HR	MKFT ECG	animation units, LBP -TOP, & Heart rates	WEKA	$N = 23$ (9f, 14 m)	AUC = 0.758
	Thomas et al. [64]	Videos	CMT [50], OpenFace	Eye gaze, AUs, Head pose	SVM, LR	$N = 10$ (7f, 3m)	90%, 87%
	Nezami et al. [51]	Videos	OpenFace [6,7]	AUs	S4VM	$N = 19$	AUC = 0.733
2018	Kaur et al. [36]	Videos	OpenFace	LBP-TOP[74], head pose, eye gaze	RF, SVR, LSTM [30], DNN	EmotiW2018	MSE = 0.05, 0.09 0.06, 0.08
	Niu et al. [52]	Videos	OpenFace 2.0	Eye gaze, AUs, Head pose	GRU [17]	EmotiW2018	MSE = 0.0724
	Chang et.al. [14]	Videos	OpenFace, OpenPose [13]	Eye gaze, AUs, & Head, Body, and Hand pose	AdaBoost regressor	EmotiW2018	MSE = 0.081
	Zhang et.al. [72]	Videos	BRFV4 JavaScript Lib.	Head pose, Face landmarks	RNN [14]	EmotiW2018	-
	Gupta et al. [28]	Videos/ Images	Bi-linear interpolation	Image pixels	CNN	DAiSEE	57.9%
	Dewan et al. [20]	Videos / Images	V & J [67], IVT [59]	LDP [32]	DBN [29]	DAiSEE	2 classes: 90.89% 3 classes: 87.25%
	Aung et al. [4]	Images	CERT	48 × 48 grayscale pixel values	Gabor + Log. Regression	HBCU [68] ($N = 20$)	57.522 %
	Ramya et al. [57]	Videos / Images	MATLAB	Facial landmark points	SVM, PNN	Bosphorus [61], Youtube [71]	3 classes: 97.36%, 94.73%
	Psaltis et al. [55]	Videos	MKFT	AU, body motion (e.g. kinematics)	ANN	$N = 72$ (38m, 34f)	85%
	Lee et al. [39]	Text, Video	LIWC	Clout, Authentic, Emotional tone	LIWC2015 [53]	$N = 49$	-
2019	Mursheed et al. [48]	Videos / Images	V & J [67] IVT [59]	Image pixels	CNN	DAiSEE	3 classes: 92.33%
	Kaur et al. [35]	Videos	OpenFace	Head pose&orient.,AUs, Eye gaze&prob.	AdaBoost regressor	EmotiW2018 DAiSEE	MSE = 0.07
	Alkabbany at el. [3]	Videos	V&J, features detector [47]	AU, Pose angles, eye gaze	SVM	$N = 14$	70%
2020	Nezami et al. [45]	Images	CNN	Image pixels	CNN	$N = 20$ (9m, 11f)	77.6 %

regarding their modalities, pre-processes, extracted features, methods to recognize the engagement, dataset they use and what metic is used to evaluate the performance as shown in Table 2.

The term of modalities refers to the type of input source to be analysed for the engagement recognition such as videos, images, log files [19], audio [49], text [39], brain signals [15], heart rate (HR) [15], galvanic skin response (GSR) [15], or biometric data [65]. Videos and images are, by far, the most popular modalities due simplicity in obtaining raw data.

For the pre-processing of image or video data, OpenFace, including the first version and 2.0 version, is the mostly used for feature extraction [8,14,35,36,52,64] due to its capability of real-time performance and not require additional hardware. Similar to OpenFace, OpenPose is used to extract body pose and orientation [14]. Other popular tools to track and extract facial features are Microsoft Kinect Face Tracker (MKFT) [8,9,46] and Computer Expression Recognition Toolbox (CERT) [41], which also can be used for classification/regression. Other modalities require specific processing tools, which are often built in to the monitoring devices providing the raw data, such as for physiological signals like a heart rate extracted from an Electrocardiogram (EEG) or the different types of brainwaves, such as Delta, Theta, Alpha, and Gamma brain waves, from an Electroencephalogram (ECG) [1].

The existing studies on engagement estimation extracted various features including high-level features, e.g., eye gaze, head pose and action units (AUs), and low-level features, e.g., Local Binary Patterns in Three Orthogonal Planes (LBP-TOP), Gabor features, and Box Filter (BF). The Body Lean Angle (BLA), Slouch Factor (SF), Quantity of Motion (QoM), or Contraction Index (CI), which can be extracted for example using CAMShift OpenCV library [12].

In early 2010, the trend of engagement estimation was utilizing machine learning methods including Support Vector Machine (SVM) and its variations, Logistic Regression (LR), clustering techniques (e.g., K-nearest neighbor (KNN)), Support Vector Regression (SVR), or RandomForest (RF), which are available and conveniently used in machine learning toolboxes such as Waikato Environment for Knowledge Analysis (WEKA) [31,69,70] and CERT [41]. Starting from 2018, Neural Network methods including Convolutional Neural Network (CNN) family, Deep Believe Network (DBN), and Gated Recurrent Unit (GRU) are included for automatic engagement estimation. Furthermore, time series-based engagement estimation that has been tried in [36] and [72] remain the challenging.

The performance evaluation of the engagement estimation are shown in the last column on Table 2. To evaluate the performance, researchers uses different metrics such as Mean Squared Error (MSE), area under the receiver operating characteristic (AUC) or accuracy (recognition rate). The AUC is preferably used for skwed data and also able to handle imbalanced data to find true classifier performance [33].

One of the challenges in the evaluation of the performance of engagement estimation is data imbalanced. Imbalanced datasets in training may lead to biased models and misrepresent the minority classes [3,36,40]. To handle the data imbalance on training data, Monkaresi [46] used Synthetic Minority Over-sampling Technique (SMOTE [16]), while Singh used Clustering Based Oversampling (CBOS [62]). In contrast, Alkabanny et al. [3] used downsampling which involves the removal of part of the majority classes data by using every tenth frame only for each category. Meanwhile, Bosch et al. [10] used both majority-class downsampling and synthetic oversampling.

4   Discussion

From the Table 1, there are few number of publicly available dataset intentionally for engagement. We see one of the reasons the public datasets are not in accordance with the need is due to the individual different that is not included in a certain dataset. For example, in DAiSEE dataset that the participants are Asian-Indian, there is possibility of different feature in Caucasian participant. Furthermore, different time of sample collection as well as the gender and age participant may not be generalized. Therefore, designing dataset collection with taking into account the individual different is a challenge for future engagement estimation.

Furthermore, including individual different in engagement estimation not only considered from only dataset point of view but also from the algorithm and methodology in developing the engagement estimation system, for example, by use multiple modalities in the estimation or considering time-series based estimation. As shown in Table 2, from 2018, various deep learning method are explored, which most of them are non-sequential based analysis. Therefore, the time-series based engagement estimation can be one of the future direction to improve quality of distance learning systems.

Moreover, there are some research questions left for future work such as detail discussion of how good is the performance? How fast can stuff be analyzed? How available are the resources for analysis? How large do the datasets need to be? How easy is it to get datasets?.

5   Conclusion

In this paper we explored the literature review of engagement estimation from the references published in between 2010-2020 as summarized in Table 1 and 2. We aim to give an easy brief overview to newcomers to engagement estimation research especially targeting to improve distance learning systems.

There are some limitations in terms of collection criteria and the discussion. The terms used to find related articles are only in English and have the engagement keyword on their title. Therefore, some contributions might not get covered in this literature review. Finally, this literature review is mainly summarizing the current research on engagement estimation, which is the first state of further discussion as described in Sect. 4.

References

1. Alarcão, S.M., Fonseca, M.J.: Emotions recognition using EEG signals: a survey. IEEE Trans. Affect. Comput. **10**(3), 374–393 (2019). https://doi.org/10.1109/TAFFC.2017.2714671
2. Alexander, K.L., Entwisle, D.R., Horsey, C.S.: From first grade forward: early foundations of high school dropout. Sociol. Educ. **70**(2), 87–107 (1997). http://www.jstor.org/stable/2673158
3. Alkabbany, I., Ali, A., Farag, A., Bennett, I., Ghanoum, M., Farag, A.: Measuring student engagement level using facial information. In: 2019 IEEE International Conference on Image Processing (ICIP), pp. 3337–3341 (2019). https://doi.org/10.1109/ICIP.2019.8803590
4. Aung, A.M., Whitehill, J.: Harnessing label uncertainty to improve modeling: an application to student engagement recognition. In: 2018 13th IEEE International Conference on Automatic Face Gesture Recognition (FG 2018), pp. 166–170, May 2018. https://doi.org/10.1109/FG.2018.00033
5. Baltrusaitis, T., Zadeh, A., Lim, Y.C., Morency, L.: Openface 2.0: facial behavior analysis toolkit. In: 2018 13th IEEE International Conference on Automatic Face Gesture Recognition (FG 2018), pp. 59–66 (2018). https://doi.org/10.1109/FG.2018.00019
6. Baltrušaitis, T., Mahmoud, M., Robinson, P.: Cross-dataset learning and person-specific normalisation for automatic action unit detection. In: 2015 11th IEEE International Conference and Workshops on Automatic Face and Gesture Recognition (FG), vol. 06, pp. 1–6 (2015). https://doi.org/10.1109/FG.2015.7284869
7. Baltrušaitis, T., Robinson, P., Morency, L.: Openface: an open source facial behavior analysis toolkit. In: 2016 IEEE Winter Conference on Applications of Computer Vision (WACV), pp. 1–10, March 2016. https://doi.org/10.1109/WACV.2016.7477553
8. Booth, B.M., Ali, A.M., Narayanan, S.S., Bennett, I., Farag, A.A.: Toward active and unobtrusive engagement assessment of distance learners. In: 2017 Seventh International Conference on Affective Computing and Intelligent Interaction (ACII), pp. 470–476 (2017). https://doi.org/10.1109/ACII.2017.8273641
9. Bosch, N.: Detecting student engagement: human versus machine. In: UMAP 2016: Proceedings of the 2016 Conference on User Modeling Adaptation and Personalization, pp. 317–320, July 2016. https://doi.org/10.1145/2930238.2930371
10. Bosch, N., et al.: Detecting student emotions in computer-enabled classrooms. In: Proceedings of the Twenty-Fifth International Joint Conference on Artificial Intelligence, IJCAI 2016, pp. 4125–4129. AAAI Press (2016)
11. Bradski, G.: The opencv library. Dr. Dobb's J. Softw. Tools (2000)
12. Bradski, G., Kaehler, A.: Learning OpenCV: Computer vision with the OpenCV library. O'Reilly (2008)
13. Cao, Z., Simon, T., Wei, S., Sheikh, Y.: Realtime multi-person 2D pose estimation using part affinity fields. In: 2017 IEEE Conference on Computer Vision and Pattern Recognition (CVPR), pp. 1302–1310 (2017). https://doi.org/10.1109/CVPR.2017.143
14. Chang, C., Zhang, C., Chen, L., Liu, Y.: An ensemble model using face and body tracking for engagement detection. In: Proceedings of the 20th ACM International Conference on Multimodal Interaction, ICMI 2018, pp. 616–622. Association for Computing Machinery, New York (2018). https://doi.org/10.1145/3242969.3264986

15. Chaouachi, M., Chalfoun, P., Jraidi, I., Frasson, C.: Affect and mental engagement: Towards adaptability for intelligent. In: Proceedings of the Twenty-Third International Florida Artificial Intelligence Research Society Conference (FLAIRS 2010), pp. 355–360, January 2010
16. Chawla, N.V., Bowyer, K.W., Hall, L.O., Kegelmeyer, W.P.: Smote: synthetic minority over-sampling technique. J. Artif. Int. Res. **16**(1), 321–357 (2002)
17. Cho, K., et al.: Learning phrase representations using RNN encoder-decoder for statistical machine translation. In: Proceedings of the 2014 Conference on Empirical Methods in Natural Language Processing (EMNLP), pp. 1724–1734. Association for Computational Linguistics, Doha, October 2014. https://doi.org/10.3115/v1/D14-1179, https://www.aclweb.org/anthology/D14-1179
18. Christenson, S.L., Reschly, A.L., Wylie, C.: Handbook of Research on Student Engagement. Springer, New York (2012). https://doi.org/10.1007/978-1-4614-2018-7
19. Cocea, M., Weibelzahl, S.: Disengagement detection in online learning: validation studies and perspectives. IEEE Trans. Learn. Technol. **4**(2), 114–124 (2011). https://doi.org/10.1109/TLT.2010.14
20. Dewan, M.A.A., Lin, F., Wen, D., Murshed, M., Uddin, Z.: A deep learning approach to detecting engagement of online learners. In: 2018 IEEE SmartWorld, Ubiquitous Intelligence Computing, Advanced Trusted Computing, Scalable Computing Communications, Cloud Big Data Computing, Internet of People and Smart City Innovation (SmartWorld/SCALCOM/UIC/ATC/CBDCom/IOP/SCI), pp. 1895–1902, October 2018. https://doi.org/10.1109/SmartWorld.2018.00318
21. Dewan, M.A.A., Murshed, M., Lin, F.: Engagement detection in online learning: a review. Smart Learn. Environ. **6**(1) (2019). https://doi.org/10.1186/s40561-018-0080-z
22. Dhall, A.: Emotiw 2019: automatic emotion, engagement and cohesion prediction tasks. In: 2019 International Conference on Multimodal Interaction, ICMI 2019, pp. 546–550. Association for Computing Machinery, New York (2019). https://doi.org/10.1145/3340555.3355710
23. Dhall, A., Kaur, A., Goecke, R., Gedeon, T.: Emotiw 2018: audio-video, student engagement and group-level affect prediction. In: Proceedings of the 20th ACM International Conference on Multimodal Interaction, ICMI 2018, pp. 653–656. Association for Computing Machinery, New York (2018). https://doi.org/10.1145/3242969.3264993
24. Ekman, P., Friesen, W.V.: Facial Action Coding System. Consulting Psychologists Press, Palo Alto (1978)
25. Freeman, F.G., Mikulka, P.J., Prinzel, L.J., Scerbo, M.W.: Evaluation of an adaptive automation system using three EEG indices with a visual tracking task. Biol. Psychol. **50**(1), 61–76 (1999). https://doi.org/10.1016/S0301-0511(99)00002-2, http://www.sciencedirect.com/science/article/pii/S0301051199000022
26. Grafsgaard, J.F., Wiggins, J.B., Boyer, K.E., Wiebe, E.N., Lester, J.C.: Automatically recognizing facial expression: Predicting engagement and frustration. In: Proceedings of the 6th International Conference on Educational Data Mining. Memphis, Tennessee (2013)
27. Gudi, A., Tasli, H.E., den Uyl, T.M., Maroulis, A.: Deep learning based facs action unit occurrence and intensity estimation. In: 2015 11th IEEE International Conference and Workshops on Automatic Face and Gesture Recognition, vol. 06, pp. 1–5, May 2015. https://doi.org/10.1109/FG.2015.7284873
28. Gupta, A., D'Cunha, A., Awasthi, K., Balasubramanian, V.: DAiSEE: Towards user engagement recognition in the wild. arXiv preprint arXiv:1609.01885 (2018)

29. Hinton, G.E., Osindero, S., Teh, Y.W.: A fast learning algorithm for deep belief nets. Neural Comput. **18**(7), 1527–1554 (2006). https://doi.org/10.1162/neco. 2006.18.7.1527

30. Hochreiter, S., Schmidhuber, J.: Long short-term memory. Neural Comput. **9**(8), 1735–1780 (1997). https://doi.org/10.1162/neco.1997.9.8.1735

31. Holmes, G., Donkin, A., Witten, I.H.: WEKA: a machine learning workbench. In: Proceedings of ANZIIS '94 - Australian New Zealand Intelligent Information Systems Conference, pp. 357–361 (1994)

32. Jabid, T., Kabir, M., Chae, O.: Robust facial expression recognition based on local directional pattern. ETRI J. **32** (2010). https://doi.org/10.4218/etrij.10.1510.0132

33. Jeni, L.A., Cohn, J.F., De La Torre, F.: Facing imbalanced data-recommendations for the use of performance metrics. In: 2013 Humaine Association Conference on Affective Computing and Intelligent Interaction, pp. 245–251 (2013). https://doi. org/10.1109/ACII.2013.47

34. Kamath, A., Biswas, A., Balasubramanian, V.: A crowdsourced approach to student engagement recognition in e-learning environments. In: 2016 IEEE Winter Conference on Applications of Computer Vision (WACV), pp. 1–9, March 2016. https://doi.org/10.1109/WACV.2016.7477618

35. Kaur, A., Ghosh, B., Singh, N.D., Dhall, A.: Domain adaptation based topic modeling techniques for engagement estimation in the wild. In: 2019 14th IEEE International Conference on Automatic Face Gesture Recognition (FG 2019), pp. 1–6, May 2019. https://doi.org/10.1109/FG.2019.8756511

36. Kaur, A., Mustafa, A., Mehta, L., Dhall, A.: Prediction and localization of student engagement in the wild. In: 2018 Digital Image Computing: Techniques and Applications (DICTA), pp. 1–8 (2018). https://doi.org/10.1109/DICTA.2018.8615851

37. Kipp, M.: Spatiotemporal coding in anvil. In: Proceedings of the 6th International Conference on Language Resources and Evaluation. International Conference on Language Resources and Evaluation (LREC-2008), 6th, May 28–30, Marrakech, Morocco. ELRA (2008)

38. Kononenko, I.: Estimating attributes: analysis and extensions of relief. In: Bergadano, F., De Raedt, L. (eds.) Machine Learning: ECML-94, pp. 171–182. Springer, Heidelberg (1994). https://doi.org/10.1007/3-540-57868-4_57

39. Lee, S.P., Perez, M.R., Worsley, M.B., Burgess, B.D.: Utilizing natural language processing (NLP) to evaluate engagement in project-based learning. In: 2018 IEEE International Conference on Teaching, Assessment, and Learning for Engineering (TALE), pp. 1146–1149 (2018). https://doi.org/10.1109/TALE.2018.8615395

40. Li, S., Deng, W.: Deep facial expression recognition: a survey. IEEE Trans. Affective Comput. 1 (2020)

41. Littlewort, G., et al.: The computer expression recognition toolbox (CERT). Face Gesture **2011**, 298–305 (2011). https://doi.org/10.1109/FG.2011.5771414

42. Lucey, P., Cohn, J.F., Prkachin, K.M., Solomon, P.E., Matthews, I.: Painful data: the UNBC-McMaster shoulder pain expression archive database. In: 2011 IEEE International Conference on Automatic Face Gesture Recognition (FG), pp. 57–64 (2011). https://doi.org/10.1109/FG.2011.5771462

43. Mavadati, S.M., Mahoor, M.H., Bartlett, K., Trinh, P., Cohn, J.F.: DISFA: a spontaneous facial action intensity database. IEEE Trans. Affect. Comput. **4**(2), 151–160 (2013). https://doi.org/10.1109/T-AFFC.2013.4

44. McKeown, G., Valstar, M., Cowie, R., Pantic, M., Schroder, M.: The semaine database: annotated multimodal records of emotionally colored conversations between a person and a limited agent. IEEE Trans. Affect. Comput. **3**(1), 5–17 (2012). https://doi.org/10.1109/T-AFFC.2011.20

45. Mohamad Nezami, O., Dras, M., Hamey, L., Richards, D., Wan, S., Paris, C.: Automatic recognition of student engagement using deep learning and facial expression. In: Brefeld, U., Fromont, E., Hotho, A., Knobbe, A., Maathuis, M., Robardet, C. (eds.) Machine Learning and Knowledge Discovery in Databases, vol. 11908, pp. 273–289. Springer International Publishing, Cham (2020). https://doi.org/10.1007/978-3-030-46133-1_17

46. Monkaresi, H., Bosch, N., Calvo, R.A., D'Mello, S.K.: Automated detection of engagement using video-based estimation of facial expressions and heart rate. IEEE Trans. Affect. Comput. 8(1), 15–28 (2017). https://doi.org/10.1109/TAFFC.2016.2515084

47. Mostafa, E., Ali, A.A., Shalaby, A., Farag, A.: A facial features detector integrating holistic facial information and part-based model. In: 2015 IEEE Conference on Computer Vision and Pattern Recognition Workshops (CVPRW), pp. 93–99 (2015). https://doi.org/10.1109/CVPRW.2015.7301324

48. Murshed, M., Dewan, M.A.A., Lin, F., Wen, D.: Engagement detection in e-learning environments using convolutional neural networks. In: 2019 IEEE International Conference on Dependable, Autonomic and Secure Computing, International Conference on Pervasive Intelligence and Computing, International Conference on Cloud and Big Data Computing, International Conference on Cyber Science and Technology Congress (DASC/PiCom/CBDCom/CyberSciTech), pp. 80–86 (2019). https://doi.org/10.1109/DASC/PiCom/CBDCom/CyberSciTech.2019.00028

49. Nakano, Y.I., Ishii, R.: Estimating user's engagement from eye-gaze behaviors in human-agent conversations. In: Proceedings of the 15th International Conference on Intelligent User Interfaces, IUI 2010, pp. 139–148. Association for Computing Machinery, New York (2010). https://doi.org/10.1145/1719970.1719990

50. Nebehay, G., Pflugfelder, R.: Clustering of static-adaptive correspondences for deformable object tracking. In: 2015 IEEE Conference on Computer Vision and Pattern Recognition (CVPR), pp. 2784–2791 (2015). https://doi.org/10.1109/CVPR.2015.7298895

51. Nezami, O.M., Richards, D., Hamey, L.: Semi-supervised detection of student engagement. In: PACIS 2017 Proceedings, p. 157 (2017)

52. Niu, X., et al.: Automatic engagement prediction with GAP feature. In: Proceedings of the 20th ACM International Conference on Multimodal Interaction, ICMI 2018, pp. 599–603. Association for Computing Machinery, New York (2018). https://doi.org/10.1145/3242969.3264982

53. Pennebaker, J., Booth, R.J., Boyd, R.L., Francis, M.E.: Linguistic inquiry and word count. http://liwc.wpengine.com

54. Pope, A.T., Bogart, E.H., Bartolome, D.S.: Biocybernetic system evaluates indices of operator engagement in automated task. Biol. Psychol. 40(1), 187–195 (1995). https://doi.org/10.1016/0301-0511(95)05116-3, http://www.sciencedirect.com/science/article/pii/0301051195051163, eEG in Basic and Applied Settings

55. Psaltis, A., Apostolakis, K.C., Dimitropoulos, K., Daras, P.: Multimodal student engagement recognition in prosocial games. IEEE Trans. Games 10(3), 292–303 (2018). https://doi.org/10.1109/TCIAIG.2017.2743341

56. Psaltis, A., et al.: Multimodal affective state recognition in serious games applications. In: 2016 IEEE International Conference on Imaging Systems and Techniques (IST), pp. 435–439 (2016). https://doi.org/10.1109/IST.2016.7738265

57. Ramya, R., Mala, K., Sindhuja, C.: Student engagement identification based on facial expression analysis using 3D video/image of students. TAGA J. 14, 2446–2454 (2018)

58. Reeve, J., Tseng, C.M.: Agency as fourth aspect of students' engagement during learning activities. Contemp. Educ. Psychol. **36**(4), 257–267 (2011)
59. Ross, D.A., Lim, J., Lin, R.S., Yang, M.H.: Incremental learning for robust visual tracking. Int. J. Comput. Vision **77**, 125–141 (2008)
60. Sanghvi, J., Castellano, G., Leite, I., Pereira, A., McOwan, P.W., Paiva, A.: Automatic analysis of affective postures and body motion to detect engagement with a game companion. In: 2011 6th ACM/IEEE International Conference on Human-Robot Interaction (HRI), pp. 305–311, March 2011. https://doi.org/10.1145/1957656.1957781
61. Savran, A., et al.: Bosphorus database for 3D face analysis. In: Schouten, B., Juul, N.C., Drygajlo, A., Tistarelli, M. (eds.) Biometrics and Identity Management, pp. 47–56. Springer, Heidelberg (2008)
62. Singh, N.D., Dhall, A.: Clustering and learning from imbalanced data. arXiv:1811.00972v2 (2018)
63. Team, D.: About DAiSEE. https://iith.ac.in/~daisee-dataset/
64. Thomas, C., Jayagopi, D.B.: Predicting student engagement in classrooms using facial behavioral cues. In: Proceedings of the 1st ACM SIGCHI International Workshop on Multimodal Interaction for Education, MIE 2017, pp. 33–40. Association for Computing Machinery, New York (2017). https://doi.org/10.1145/3139513.3139514
65. Tofighi, G., Gu, H., Raahemifar, K.: Vision-based engagement detection in virtual reality. In: 2016 Digital Media Industry Academic Forum (DMIAF), pp. 202–206 (2016). https://doi.org/10.1109/DMIAF.2016.7574933
66. Valstar, M.F., Jiang, B., Mehu, M., Pantic, M., Scherer, K.: The first facial expression recognition and analysis challenge. In: 2011 IEEE International Conference on Automatic Face Gesture Recognition (FG), pp. 921–926 (2011). https://doi.org/10.1109/FG.2011.5771374
67. Viola, P., Jones, M.J.: Robust real-time face detection. Int. J. Comput. Vision **57**(2), 137–154 (2004). https://doi.org/10.1023/B:VISI.0000013087.49260.fb
68. Whitehill, J., Serpell, Z., Lin, Y., Foster, A., Movellan, J.R.: The faces of engagement: automatic recognition of student engagement from facial expressions. IEEE Trans. Affect. Comput. **5**(1), 86–98 (2014). https://doi.org/10.1109/TAFFC.2014.2316163
69. Witten, I., Frank, E.: Morgan Kaufmann/Elsevier, New York (2000)
70. Witten, I., Frank, E.: Morgan Kaufmann/Elsevier, New York, USA (2005)
71. Wolf, L., Hassner, T., Maoz, I.: Face recognition in unconstrained videos with matched background similarity. CVPR **2011**, 529–534 (2011). https://doi.org/10.1109/CVPR.2011.5995566
72. Zhang, C., Chang, C., Chen, L., Liu, Y.: Online privacy-safe engagement tracking system. In: Proceedings of the 20th ACM International Conference on Multimodal Interaction, ICMI 2018, pp. 553–554. Association for Computing Machinery, New York (2018). https://doi.org/10.1145/3242969.3266295
73. Zhang, X., et al.: BP4D-spontaneous: a high-resolution spontaneous 3D dynamic facial expression database. Image Vis. Comput. **32**(10), 692–706 (2014). https://doi.org/10.1016/j.imavis.2014.06.002, http://www.sciencedirect.com/science/article/pii/S0262885614001012, best of Automatic Face and Gesture Recognition 2013
74. Zhao, G., Pietikainen, M.: Dynamic texture recognition using local binary patterns with an application to facial expressions. IEEE Trans. Pattern Anal. Mach. Intell. **29**(6), 915–928 (2007). https://doi.org/10.1109/TPAMI.2007.1110

The Impact of Auditory Based Immersive Virtual Travel Experience on Mental Health of the Visually Impaired

Linghong Li[✉]

Soochow University, Suzhou, China
lilinghongchina@hotmail.com

Abstract. There are extremely limited chances for the visually impaired go travel in China due to lack of effective public facilities and services for the disabled. According to statistics, there are up to 30% of visually impaired population in China never go outdoors per year. Depressed emotions are raging along with different degrees of mental health problems. Virtual reality systems have potential to provide users with an engaging and realistic valid environment in which to get an experience similar to activities in the real world. The purposes of this study were to (1) determine the feasibility in using auditory based immersive virtual travel in individuals with the visually impaired, and (2) evaluate the impact of the auditory based immersive virtual travel experience on mental health of the visually impaired. To that end, a novel VR task, the auditory based Immersive Virtual Reality of travel would be used as one treatment of mental health problems of the visually impaired.

Keywords: Auditory based · Immersive virtual travel · Mental health · Visually impaired

1 Introduction

According to the China Disabled Persons' Federation (CDPF) statistics report in 2016, the Chinese visually impaired population is around 17.31 million [1]. It is a very largest population. However, due to various reasons, such as lacking enough public facilities and public services for the disabled, there are extremely limited chances for the Chinese visually impaired to travel. Even the chances for outdoor activities are also scarce in China. It is most common to see that the blind sidewalks stop at the street crossing (Fig. 1 and Fig. 2), which is one of the reasons that the visually impaired cannot go outdoors independently. They are, somehow, as trapped indoor. According to statistics, there are up to 30% of visually impaired people in China never go outdoors in per year [2].

In addition, great majority of the visually impaired live on the national subsistence allowance which means their income is lower than the national average. Their inadequate inadequate incomes are not enough for travel. Depressed emotions are raging along with different degrees of mental health problems of them.

© Springer Nature Switzerland AG 2021
D. D. Schmorrow and C. M. Fidopiastis (Eds.): HCII 2021, LNAI 12776, pp. 277–287, 2021.
https://doi.org/10.1007/978-3-030-78114-9_20

Fig. 1. The blind sidewalks stop at the street crossing.

Fig. 2. There are no blind sidewalks when the visually impaired cross the street.

The study in this paper was part of our research on travel for the visually impaired. In our surveys, the visually impaired expressed their eagerness for travel but lack such opportunities. Because in reality, their wish to travel is most difficult to realize. They took travel as the way to get pleasure.

In our study, the visually impaired were very good at using hearing as the main ways to keep social connections, such as using hearing to "browse" websites and communicating by voice by using WeChat APP. Hearing was their most important way for social activities in common. They were very sensitive to changes in sound. Therefore, we used the sound and tested their experience on auditory based immersive virtual travel.

Meanwhile the fact that must be considered was that the inadequate incomes of the visually impaired in China were general, and the not optimistic current circumstances of tourism for the visually impaired in China. All these factors were considered in the research.

The purposes of this study were to (1) determine the feasibility in using auditory based immersive virtual travel in individuals with the visually impaired, and (2) evaluate the impact of the auditory based immersive virtual travel experience on mental health of the visually impaired. To that end, under the premise of combining various factors, a novel VR task, the auditory based Immersive Virtual Reality of travel would be used as one treatment of mental health problems of the visually impaired.

2 Methodology

2.1 Symptom Checklist-90 Revised (SCL-90-R)

The Symptom Checklist-90 Revised (SCL-90-R) instrument helps evaluate a broad range of psychological problems and symptoms of psychopathology. To determine the mental health of the visually impaired impacted by the immersive virtual Travel experience, the Symptom Checklist-90 Revised (SCL-90-R) was distributed to 30 visually impaired located in Shanghai. The questionnaire was read out in Chinese by the interviewers. The interviewers ticked each option on the questionnaire instead of the visually impaired.

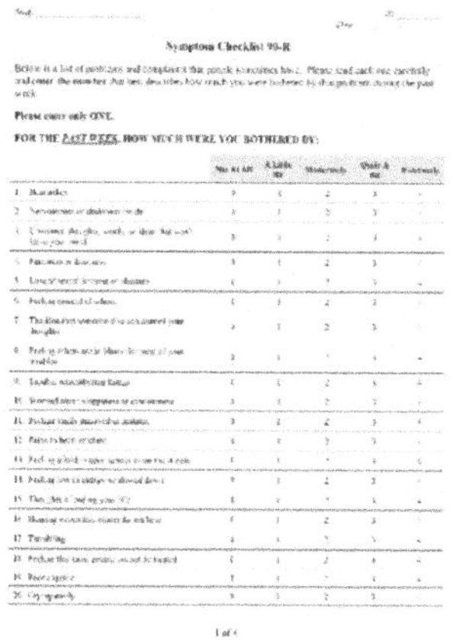

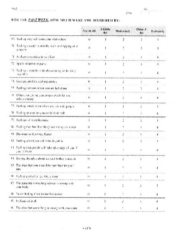

Fig. 3. The Symptom Checklist-90 Revised used in this paper, part I

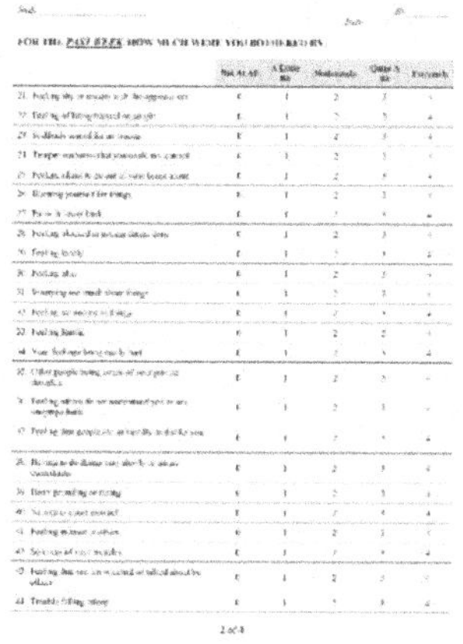

Fig. 4. The Symptom Checklist-90 Revised used in this paper, part II

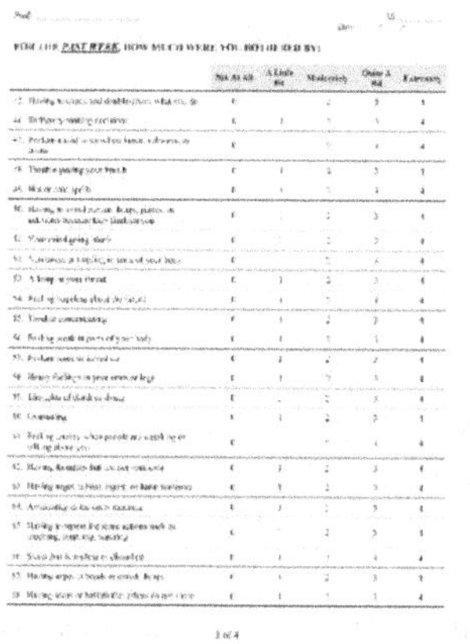

Fig. 5. The Symptom Checklist-90 Revised used in this paper, part III

Fig. 6. The Symptom Checklist-90 Revised used in this paper, part IV

In this study, the English version of the Symptom Checklist-90 Revised (SCL-90-R) was used (Fig. 3, Fig. 4, Fig. 5 and Fig. 6), which was very closely related to the original SCL-90-R questionnaire of University of Pennsylvania Department of Psychiatry [3]. Due to the respondents who spoke Chinese did not fill in the questionnaire themselves, and the interviewers asked questions in Chinese, so the English version did not cause obstacles to the questionnaire survey. The English version questionnaire facilitates comparison with other international documents for this study.

Each item in the SCL-90-R questionnaire is rated on a five-point scale ranging from 0 (= not at all) to 4 (= extremely). The interviewees were asked to answer the items to indicate the extent to which the symptoms of the SCL-90-R were manifest during the week preceding the day of answering [4]. In the study, there are 30 SCL-90-R questionnaires for the mental health before the auditory based immersive virtual travel tests. A total of 30 SCL-90-R questionnaires were collected.

2.2 Other Surveys

In addition to the SCL-90-R questionnaire, the participants' basic demographic information, the general health information, the travel experience and their subjective description and feedback of feeling were surveyed. One another questionnaire was answered by the participants.

2.3 Participants

Ten females and twenty males with age ranging from 21 to 45 years (Mean = 31.5 yrs) took part in the study. The participants were visually impaired who were willing to participate. The participants were not recruited by special selection. The participants were selected in a random manner.

2.4 The Play Tools for Auditory Based Immersive Virtual Travel Experience Tests

The laptops and mobile phones were used as play tools. The wired earbuds were connected to laptops and mobile phones (Fig. 7 and Fig. 8). In order to avoid unpredictable connection interruption, the Bluetooth wireless earphone and wireless headsets were not used in the tests.

During the tests, the room should be quiet. All participants should sit down indoors and wear the wired earbuds to listen to the audio files played by the computers or mobile phones. Each participant should listen to three audio files. Each audio file was set to 15 min, and the playing interval between every two audio files was 10 min. In order to make the observation time of the three tests consistent, a 10-min interval was still set after the last audio file was end. The tests stopped after the third 10-min interval was over. The test time for each participant was 75 min.

In the 10-min interval after each audio file was played, participants may choose to be silent or engage in some relaxing activities as they wished or chat with the researchers. If a conversation occurred, the content of the conversation would not be used as research references.

In order to avoid uncontrollable interference factors, there were only researchers in each participant's room.

2.5 The Audio Files for Auditory Based Immersive Virtual Travel Experience Tests

Tests. A total of three audio files were used for testing. The names of all the virtual reality soundscapes used in the study were familiar to the participants. In order to create the feeling of immersive virtual reality, the sounds in these audio files simulated as much as possible the real tourist sights. Each audio file was synthetic sound that was

Fig. 7. The laptops with wired earbuds were used as play tools.

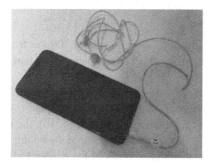

Fig. 8. The mobile phones were used as play tools, to which the wired earbuds were connected.

composed of real sounds sampled from the real travel scenes with artificial simulation tour guide commentary. The three audio files worked as the testing files for auditory based immersive virtual travel. The three audio files were played in the prescribed order.

The first audio file used for testing was synthetic sound expressed the most well-known night view of the Bund in Shanghai where the city the participants located. The pictures showed the scenes when the sounds were sampled (Fig. 9).

In the first audio file, two types of sounds were synthesized to create auditory-based virtual reality. One type of sounds was the real sound sampled, including the sound of Huangpu River in Fig. 9, the sound of cruise ships, the sound of tourists sightseeing in Shanghai Bund, and the sound of the surrounding environment. Another type of sounds was the voice artificially simulated of the tour guide, which was used to "guide" the participants to the Shanghai Bund tour as immersive virtual travel based on auditory. The necessary tour guide commentaries were contained in the artificially simulated voice.

The second audio file used for testing was synthetic sound expressed the most world-famous views of classical gardens of Suzhou and the water village in Suzhou where the city was called the Venice of the East. The pictures showed the scenes when the sounds were sampled (Fig. 10).

(a)   (b)

Fig. 9. The scenes when the sounds of the first audio file were sampled.

Suzhou is adjacent to Shanghai which is about 100 km from Shanghai. This audio file was used to test virtual reality travel experiences of the participants on the sceneries near where they located.

In the second audio file, two types of sounds were synthesized to create auditory-based virtual reality too. The real sounds were also sampled in this audio file, including the sound of the boater shaking the long oar (b of Fig. 10), the sound of rolling the boat in the water (b of Fig. 10), the singing and talking of the boater (b of Fig. 10), the sound of tourists (b of Fig. 10), the sound of birds in the garden (a of Fig. 10), the sound of flowing streams (a of Fig. 10), the sound of wind (a of Fig. 10), the sound of tourists (a of Fig. 10), and the sounds of all the surroundings (a and b of Fig. 10).

(a)   (b)

Fig. 10. The scenes when the sounds of the second audio file were sampled.

The artificially simulated tour guide voices were also created, which were used to "guide" participants to the scenic tour shown in Fig. 10 to produce an immersive feeling, thereby acted as an immersive virtual tour based on hearing too. The artificially simulated voice contained necessary tour guide comments too.

The third audio file used for testing was synthetic sound expressed the views of sea. The pictures showed the scenes when the sounds were sampled (Fig. 11). The participants were told this audio file was a distant sea tour. This audio file was used to test virtual reality travel experiences of the participants on the sceneries far from where they located.

Fig. 11. The scenes when the sounds of the third audio file were sampled.

In the third audio file, in order to create auditory-based virtual reality, the sounds synthesized also contained two types of sounds. The real sounds sampled in this audio file included the sound of waves, the sound of waves hitting the beach, the sound of surrounding tourists, and the sound of the surrounding environment.

Similar to the first and second audio files, the artificially simulated tour guide voices were created, which were also used to "guide" participants to the scenic tour shown in Fig. 11 to produce an immersive feeling, thereby acted as an immersive virtual tour based on hearing. The artificially simulated voice contained necessary tour guide comments.

3   Results and Discussion

Thirty visually impaired as participants were studied, who located in Shanghai. The participants consisted of ten females (33.3%) and twenty males (66.7%) with age ranging from 21 to 45 years with mean age 31.5 yrs. The descriptive characteristics and physical illnesses information of study participants are presented in Table 1.

Table 1. Descriptive characteristics statistics of the 30 participants

Variable	Number, %
Gender	
Female	10, 33.3%
Male	20, 66.7%
Age (mean)	31.5 yrs
In physical illness (number, percentage of total)	0, 0%

As to acceptability, all tests received a positive value: all participants were able to accomplish the auditory-based virtual reality travel tests within the time limits. None of the participants reported negative senses or physiological uncomfortable. During each test, the participants were fully absorbed in. All participants were enthusiastic to participate to the tests. In each interval of immersive virtual travel based on auditory, participants were keen to express their feelings about the test to the researchers (100%), and all participants showed varying degrees of pleasure throughout the process. Table 2 gave the participants' performance statistics in each test interval. The two items "in relaxing activities as they wish" and "chat" could be counted repeatedly.

Table 2. Participants' performance statistics in each test interval

Variable	Number, %
During the first interval	
Keep quiet	0, 0%
In relaxing activities as they wish	4, 13.3%
Chat	30, 100%
During the second interval	
Keep quiet	0, 0%
In relaxing activities as they wish	19, 63.3%
Chat	30, 100%
During the third interval	
Keep quiet	0, 0%
In relaxing activities as they wish	26, 86.7%
Chat	30, 100%

It was obvious to view the participants' performance were in a clearly excited and happy state during and after the tests. The contents in the auditory-based immersive virtual reality travel promoted their willingness to communicate. The ratio of the communications (100% per interval) showed positive and optimistic characteristics.

This auditory-based immersive virtual reality travel did be accepted by them and did stimulate their positive emotions.

Table 3 gave the travel experience statistics of the visually impaired participants in this study. The proportion of participants with overseas travel experience was 0%. The proportion of participants with domestic travel experience was 23.3%. None of the participants had frequent travel experience (0% per item). However, in their small amount of domestic travel experience, the tourist destination limited to the city jurisdiction where they located. The proportion of lacking outdoor activities (43.3%) did not distinguishably differ from the proportion of national average (up to 30%).

It could be identified from Table 2 and Table 3 the positive feedback of visually impaired participants on auditory based immersive virtual travel did not necessarily related to their travel experience.

Table 3. Travel experience statistics of the participants

Variable	Number, %
Travel experience (domestic)	
Frequent travel (number, percentage of total)	0, 0%
Sometimes travel (number, percentage of total)	7, 23.3%
Never (number, percentage of total)	23, 76.7%
Travel experience (overseas)	
Frequent travel (number, percentage of total)	0, 0%
Sometimes travel (number, percentage of total)	0, 0%
Never (number, percentage of total)	30, 100%
Travel experience (within the city of residence)	
Frequent travel (number, percentage of total)	0, 0%
Sometimes travel (number, percentage of total)	7, 23.3%
Never (number, percentage of total)	23, 76.7%
Outdoors activities experience (during the week preceding the tests)	
Frequent (number, percentage of total)	0, 0%
Sometimes (number, percentage of total)	17, 56.7%
Never (number, percentage of total)	13, 43.3%

The above phenomena and Tables reflected the feasibility in using auditory based immersive virtual travel in individuals with the visually impaired: it was feasible to and effective for the visually impaired with or without travel experience.

Before the auditory based immersive virtual travel experience tests, the participants were asked about their overall emotional feelings during the week preceding. The following results were collected:

- Feel happy: 23.30%
- Feel unhappy: 46.67%
- Feel sad: 6.67%
- Feel depressed: 13.33%
- Other feeling: 10%

Meanwhile the participants were asked to score their mental states they felt during the week preceding according to the nine scoring items of SCL-90-R questionnaire. They should use 1–5 to score each item (Not at All = 0, A Little Bit = 1, Moderately = 2, Quite A Bit = 3, Extremely = 4). Different from SCL-90-R questionnaire, they only scored nine main category items but not each sub-item. Table 4 gave the scores statistics.

The score of "Phobic anxiety" was rather high (mean = 3.17), the high scores of "Obsessive-compulsive" (mean = 2.10), "Interpersonal sensitivity" (mean = 2.30), "Depression" (mean = 2.13) and "Hostility" (mean = 2.03) indicated serious degree in these

Table 4. Nine main category item scores before tests

Item	Total (n = 30)	Mean (n = 30)
Somatization	41	1.37
Obsessive-compulsive	63	2.10
Interpersonal sensitivity	69	2.30
Depression	64	2.13
Anxiety	53	1.77
Hostility	61	2.03
Phobic anxiety	95	3.17
Paranoid ideation	54	1.80
Psychoticism	43	1.43

mental health statuses. These scores helped to infer the causes that the participants' unhappy feeling of everyday living in common before the test.

After the auditory based immersive virtual travel experience tests, the participants were asked to answer the Symptom Checklist-90 Revised (SCL-90-R). Table 5 gave the SCL-90-R scores statistics of the participants in this study. They should use 1–5 to score each item (Not at All = 0, A Little Bit = 1, Moderately = 2, Quite A Bit = 3, Extremely = 4).

Table 5. SCL-90-R scores

Item	National normal (n = 1388) [5]	Participant (n = 30)
Somatization	1.37 ± 0.48	1.34
Obsessive-compulsive	1.62 ± 0.58	2.03
Interpersonal sensitivity	1.65 ± 0.61	1.97
Depression	1.50 ± 0.59	1.94
Anxiety	1.39 ± 0.43	1.71
Hostility	1.48 ± 0.56	1.62
Phobic anxiety	1.23 ± 0.41	1.87
Paranoid ideation	1.43 ± 0.57	1.69
Psychoticism	1.29 ± 0.42	1.33

Compare scores before (Table 4) and after (Table 5) the auditory based immersive virtual travel experience tests, the scores of each item dropped slightly, especially in the scores of "Phobic anxiety", "Interpersonal sensitivity" and "Hostility", which could be understood as signs to prove the positive impacts of the 75-min test on the mental health of the participants.

But the mental health problems of the participants were obvious, which was a problem that requires intervention.

4   Conclusion

Actually, for the visually impaired individuals, the everyday living is particularly depressive because they have lost vision to see the colorful world. Furthermore, due to the limitation of going out, they are limited in social interaction. After all these causes have accumulated over a long period of time, it caused their mental problems in varied degrees of mental problems.

The study in this paper focused on the problem of their going out limitations, selected one of their most yearning outdoor activities "travel" as the achievable aim. This study managed to applicate auditory based immersive virtual reality for the visually impaired, on the premise that it would adapt to the current state of their lives such as going out restrictions and even the financial income of them.

To our knowledge, there are a lot of research on visual and tactile VR devices for the visually impaired. The study of this paper supposed a novel VR task, the auditory based immersive virtual reality of travel as one treatment of mental health problems of the visually impaired. The feasibility in using auditory based immersive virtual travel in individuals with the visually impaired were determined in this study: it was feasible to and effective for the visually impaired with or without travel experience.

The results in this study could represent the foundations for a novel VR task, with respect to potential application, the auditory based Immersive Virtual Reality of travel could be used as one treatment of mental health problems of the visually impaired.

Acknowledgments. Thank all the visually impaired who involved in the study, and all the volunteer assistants for their support during the research.

References

1. The Visually Impaired Population in China Is About 17.31 Million, Young People Under 30 Account for 23.5%. https://china.huanqiu.com/article
2. China Internet Visually Impaired Users Basic Situation Report. http://www.199it.com/
3. Symptom Checklist 90-R. https://dmu.trc.upenn.edu
4. van der Laan, L., van Spaendonck, K., Horstink, M.W.I.M., Goris, R.J.A.: The symptom checklist-90 revised questionnaire: no psychological profiles in complex regional pain syndrome-dystonia. J. Pain Symptom Manag. **17**(5), 357–362 (1999)
5. Hao, Y.J.: Analysis of SCL-90 sampling survey results of female students in our college. J. Mudanjiang Med. Coll. **29**(2), 78–79 (2008)

New Methods for Metastimuli: Architecture, Embeddings, and Neural Network Optimization

Rico A. R. Picone[1,2]([✉]) [iD], Dane Webb[1] [iD], Finbarr Obierefu[3] [iD],
and Jotham Lentz[2] [iD]

[1] Saint Martin's University, Lacey, WA 98503, USA
rpicone@stmartin.edu
[2] Dialectica LLC, Olympia, WA 98501, USA
rico@dialectica.io
[3] Université Bourgogne Franche-Comté, Besançon, France
http://www.stmartin.edu, http://dialectica.io, http://www.ubfc.fr

Abstract. Six significant new methodological developments of the
previously-presented "metastimuli architecture" for human learning
through machine learning of spatially correlated structural position
within a user's personal information management system (PIMS), providing the basis for haptic metastimuli, are presented. These include
architectural innovation, recurrent (RNN) artificial neural network
(ANN) application, a variety of atom embedding techniques (including
a novel technique we call "∇" embedding inspired by linguistics), ANN
hyper-parameter (one that affects the network but is not trained, e.g. the
learning rate) optimization, and meta-parameter (one that determines
the system performance but is not trained and not a hyper-parameter,
e.g. the atom embedding technique) optimization for exploring the large
design space. A technique for using the system for automatic atom categorization in a user's PIMS is outlined. ANN training and hyper- and
meta-parameter optimization results are presented and discussed in service of methodological recommendations.

Keywords: Design · Human centered design and user centered
design · Design · Information design · Technology: Augmented reality
and environments · Technology: Haptic user interface · Technology:
Intelligent and agent systems · Technology: Natural user interfaces
(NUI)

1 Objective and Significance

We present six significant developments in the metastimuli architecture introduced by [22]. The goal of the architecture remains: to improve human learning
of textual source material (i.e. text, audio, video with dialog) by presenting
a user with, in addition to their direct experience of the material, correlated

D. D. Schmorrow and C. M. Fidopiastis (Eds.): HCII 2021, LNAI 12776, pp. 288–304, 2021.
https://doi.org/10.1007/978-3-030-78114-9_21

metastimuli that represent (through time) the structural "position" the source material has in their own personal information management system (PIMS). Some of the methods of the original architecture [22] are augmented in the architecture presented here, illustrated in Fig. 1. In particular, the *classification* of atoms of information, which was a discrete process in the original architecture, is here integrated into the training of the primary artificial neural network (ANN) of the system. In fact, explicit classification has been circumvented altogether. Furthermore, the original method of *atom embedding*, which is similar to sentence embedding with its basis in word embedding, is compared to several newer techniques. Two variations of PIMS-trained artificial neural network (ANN) are compared: a feedforward is compared with a recurrent neural network (RNN). Finally, the atom embedder and PIMS-trained ANN can be straightforwardly adopted as a standalone *classifier* in its own right; however, since explicit classification is not strictly required for metastimuli, its presentation is limited to a structural exposition.

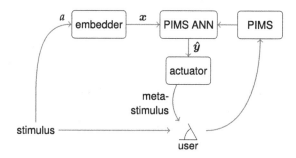

Fig. 1. The metastimuli system architecture. An atom a of stimulus, experienced directly by the user, is, in textual form, also directed through an embedder block that embeds the atom as a vector x, which is the input to an artificial neural network (ANN) pre-trained on the user's structured personal information management system (PIMS). The output of the ANN $\hat{y}$ is a low-dimension real vector representing the structural "location" of the atom a, which is converted by an actuator into a metastimulus (e.g. haptic stimulus) [21].

2   Methods

The six methodological innovations are presented below.

2.1   Integrated PIMS Classification

Figure 2 illustrates the new training loop for the PIMS ANN. A key innovation here is that the projected PIMS representation is trained-into the ANN such that a separate classification process is circumvented altogether.

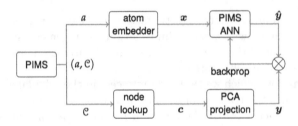

Fig. 2. Training of the PIMS ANN. An atom a with category label $\mathcal{C}$ (corresponding to the structural "location" of a) from a training set of the user's PIMS is directed to two paths, the upper for the atom and the lower for the category label. The atom embedder encodes the atom a as vector x, which is the input to the PIMS ANN. The category $\mathcal{C}$ is first given a high-dimensional one-hot vector representation c, then projected via principal component analysis (PCA) projection to low-dimensional y, which is the numerical label of the atom. The difference between this and the ANN output $\hat{y}$ is then backpropagated [19].

2.2   Recurrent PIMS-trained ANN

We compare the performance of a FFNN and a RNN for the PIMS ANN object in Fig. 2 and Fig. 4. FFNNs are a simple form of neural networks with a lot of general utility. Connections in FFNNs do not loop and the information always moves "forward", (input layer to hidden layer to output layer). RNNs are excellent for natural language processing tasks. RNNs are able to use the sequential nature of natural language in the neural network architecture.

2.3   Null Set Validation

One of the conventionally presented results of an ANN training is a plot of training and (sometimes) testing loss versus training epoch. A downward trend of training loss signifies learning, whereas the downward trend of testing loss signifies the generality of that learning beyond the training set. Overfitting occurs when the ANN learns to predict the testing data to the detriment of generality therebeyond. In the context of natural language processing (NLP), overfitting is the learning of specific semantic (meaning) constructions to the detriment of recognizing similar constructions, observable when the training loss continues to decrease while the testing loss begins to increase. Mitigation techniques for overfitting include the familiar "dropout" method in which certain data is ignored during parts of training.

A question remains, however: how significant is the learning, really? The magnitude of loss is not easily compared between data sets and learning methods, and there is no readily available "baseline" for comparison. Now consider an ANN's prediction performance on a set of testing data that is randomly labeled, meaning its semantic content is as unrelated to its labels as possible. Such a testing set should show, on average, no learning (reduced loss) and can be thought

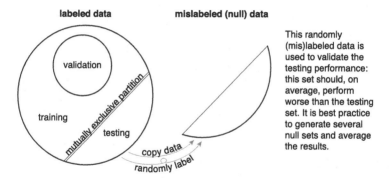

Fig. 3. An illustration of the data partitions, including the null partition, a copy of the testing data labeled randomly. This technique is derived from the experimental and statistical validation method of the same name. Despite the significant computational overhead, computing the loss for several null sets and averaging them for comparison to training loss (which should be lower) is recommended at least during early development of a new model [18].

of as representing a sort of contextually relevant "random guess" of predictions. We call this data a *null set*; this is illustrated in Fig. 3.

It is difficult in practice to construct a null set that is truly unrelated to the content, however, given that the content and labels, despite their random assignment, are always already somewhat related. Therefore, a small amount of learning does in fact occur, but it represents a contextual "baseline" for training and testing loss. The null loss baseline places a lower-bound on performance metrics.

It is best to generate several randomly labeled copies of the testing data, test the network on all of them and averaging the loss (to mitigate any "luck" in the randomly assigned labels). This does increase computational cost, especially if undertaken at every training epoch, so its use should be limited to early development and final testing of an ANN model.

The term "null" is used to draw attention to the similarity of this technique with the *null hypothesis testing* of statistics and "null sample" measurement in experimental physics, in which the results of a challenging experiment are considered well-validated when the only difference between two measurements is the sample, one of which is of interest and the other of which yields a baseline, zero, or null result.

2.4   Atom Embeddings

Word embeddings are representations of words in a real vector space that maintains word context and relations thereamong. Embeddings can be learned via a neural network from training data that includes many examples of natural-language usage of the words in question [5]. Embeddings of words that, in the training set, appear in similar contexts, drift toward each other over the course of training.

Sentence embeddings are similar to word embeddings in that they encode a sentence as a vector that represents the semantics of each sentence. Sentence embeddings are typically mapped or learned from component word embeddings. Good embeddings filter some of the sharper contrasts in sentences and help convey the context, intention, and subtleties in the text.

Sentence embedding techniques can be adapted to word sequences of different length. Our application calls for approximately paragraph-length sequences we call *atoms*.

Embedding Atoms. In both the training loop, Fig. 2, and in application, Fig. 4, the atom embedder converts atoms to vector representations that the PIMS ANN can process. The atom embedder contains a word embedder that encodes each word into its word embedding vector. An atom a of word embedding vectors is then encoded into an atom embedding x.

Two word embedders are evaluated. The first is trained with a relatively small custom corpus and the second is trained with a large publicly available corpus. The custom corpus contains a mechatronics textbook and a dynamic systems textbook written by one of the authors. The large dataset is from TensorFlow Datasets, the "scientific-papers" corpus [6], which contains over 200,000 scientific papers from https://ArXiv.org.

Quality of embeddings depends on the specificity of the dataset to the use-case and on the size of the dataset. We compare the performance of the small but specific custom corpus and the large but less-specific corpus.

There are several sentence embedding methods that can be applied to atoms. We evaluate the relative performance of several of these methods.

Four candidate methods are described below.

Bag of Words (BOW) sums or averages component word embedding vectors. While surprisingly accurate for its simplicity, word order, distance between words, and semantics are lost [13].

Distributed Memory "Paragraph" Vector (PVDM) assigns each sentence ("paragraph") in an atom a trained identification (ID) vector. This ID vector and its sentence's word vectors are trained together [13].

Smooth Inverse Frequency (SIF) computes sentence embeddings as a weighted average of word vectors [1].

Universal Sentence Encoders Averages all the words of a sentence before feeding into multi-layered ANN [4].

The results of Sect. 3 include the first two above, and the novel ∇-embeddings presented below.

∇ Embeddings. The father of linguistics, Ferdinand de Saussure introduced the concept of the *differential* value of meanings and words. First considering the signifier or word.

The important thing in the word is not the sound alone but the phonic differences that make it possible to distinguish this word from all others, for differences carry signification. This may seem surprising, but how indeed could the reverse be possible? Since one vocal image is no better suited than the next for what it is commissioned to express, it is evident, even *a priori*, that a segment of language can never in the final analysis be based on anything except its noncoincidence with the rest. *Arbitrary* and *differential* are two correlative qualities. [28, p. 118]

So the "vocal image" or word is itself *arbitrary* and only takes on meaning in its *difference* from others. Consider the following with regard to meaning.

Instead of pre-existing ideas then, we find [...] values emanating from the system. When they are said to correspond to concepts, it is understood that the concepts are purely differential and defined not by their positive content but negatively by their relations with the other terms of the system. Their most precise characteristic is in being what the others are not. [28, p. 117]

This differentiality holds for both the word and its meaning.

Word embeddings differentially (usually via recurrence) embed word meanings. Therefore, when considering a sentence or paragraph embedding—for us, an *atom* embedding—it is worth considering differentiality. For instance, consider the sentence *She opens tonight*. Not until the final word do the preceding words take on their proper meaning: *She opens . . .* could go a different way, such as *She opens presents*. So *tonight* actually fixes the meaning of *opens*, in this case in the sense: she is the opening act.

There is much nuance, here. The bag-of-words methods of sentence embedding that sum or average the word embeddings in a sentence retain some differentiality of meaning left over from the word embeddings, but they ignore *order*, which impacts the differential meanings. Several newer methods, including those listed above, encode in some way the ordering of words, but increase (system and computational) complexity significantly.

We introduce a simple approach we call ∇-*embeddings*. Consider atom a and the difference between two sequential word embedding vectors $\boldsymbol{e}_i$ and $\boldsymbol{e}_{i+1}$,

$$\nabla_i^1 = \boldsymbol{e}_{i+1} - \boldsymbol{e}_i. \tag{1}$$

Furthermore, consider the next-level of difference of differences

$$\nabla_i^2 = \nabla_{i+1}^2 - \nabla_i^2 \tag{2}$$

such that ∇_i^j signifies the ith difference at the jth level. Proceeding in an array over an atom with ν words, we obtain the following inverted Pascal's triangle, standing on its head if you will.

$$
\begin{array}{ccccccc}
\boldsymbol{e}_1 & \boldsymbol{e}_2 & \boldsymbol{e}_3 & \cdots & \boldsymbol{e}_{\nu-2} & \boldsymbol{e}_{\nu-1} & \boldsymbol{e}_\nu \\
 & \nabla^1_1 & \nabla^1_2 & \cdots & & \nabla^1_{\nu-2} & \nabla^1_{\nu-1} \\
 & & \nabla^2_1 & \cdots & & \nabla^2_{\nu-1} & \\
 & & \ddots & \vdots & \ddots & & \\
 & & \ddots & \vdots & \ddots & & \\
 & & & \nabla^{\nu-1}_1 & & &
\end{array}
$$

Furthermore, consider a sum $\boldsymbol{x}^j$ over a level j,

$$
\boldsymbol{x}^j = \sum_i \nabla^j_i. \tag{3}
$$

This is a ∇^j-*embedding* of the atom a. Note that even a ∇^1-embedding retains some differential information.

This new embedding method is applicable to atoms, paragraphs, and sentences. It is included among the established atom embedding methods in the results of Sect. 3.

Keyword Weighting. Artificial neural networks encode a large range of subtle and crude characteristics/representation of text. We expect that much correct categorization could be achieved with simple keyword[1] identification (e.g. the category *voltage* likely applies to an atom containing the word *volts*), so the ANN should include similar functionality.

This functionality is trained into the network by multiplying keyword vectors by a keyword weighting factor that scales the corresponding embedding vectors inflate atom vectors, effectively expressing the greater importance of keywords in an atom embedding.

A concern with weighting the keywords is that the ANN may ignore semantic content and rely too much on simple keyword recognition. Dropout that simply removes random atoms from each training cycle, already used to reduce general overfitting, is one method to counter this concern. Another is to include the keyword scaling factor as meta-parameter to be optimized, as described below. In this way, if semantic content is undervalued, the optimizer will adjust accordingly.

2.5 Meta- and Hyper-parameter Optimization

Optimization weights and biases of a ANN, are commonly optimized by gradient descent algorithms. Gradient descent algorithms are fast and are guaranteed to

---

[1] Using available machine learning natural language libraries, such as the popular NLTK used here [2], it is straightforward to lemmatize a category name in order to generate relevant keywords automatically.

reach a minimum. ANN training space is not plagued by large numbers of local minimum. Instead, vanishing gradients and saddle points are issues.

Alternatively, the meta-parameters and the remaining hyper-parameters do present a plane with many local minima. The hyper-parameters are tuned using keras-tuner. Keras-tuner includes three, not including sklearn, derivative-free optimizers. Random search, bayesian, and hyperband are included within the keras-tuner module.

Meta-parameters are optimized with a pattern search algorithm. Any derivative free algorithm could be substituted that works well with integer objective variables, scales search range near minimum, and is quick.

Table 1. A list of hyper-parameters optimized via keras-tuner and their possible values. The hyparameters are partitioned into those related to the ANN architecture and those related to the ANN training.

	Hyper-parameter	Possible values
ANN architecture	Weights/biases	$\mathbb{R}$
	Activation function	tanh, σ, S
	Hidden layers	$\mathbb{Z}_+$
	Features	$\mathbb{Z}_+$
ANN training	Gradient-based optimizer parameters	Optimizer-dependent
	Learning rate	$\mathbb{R}_+$
	Training epochs	$\mathbb{Z}_+$

Hyper-parameter Optimization. Hyper-parameter optimization is handled by the Keras-tuner library. The three tuners available in the library are random search, bayesian optimization, and hyperband. For an explanation of the random search algorithm see Rastrigin [26], for bayesian optimization see Pelikan et al. [17], and for hyperband see Li et al. [15]. The parameters optimized by the hyper-parameter optimization are shown in Table 1.

Meta-parameter Optimization. Pattern search is one of many derivative-free optimization algorithms that are acceptable. Pattern search has all the traits required. Pattern search is used because it is an algorithm that is relatively easy to implement.

Further optimization could be conducted by comparing additional search algorithms. Choosing the best meta-parameter optimization is a "trial and error" search. Finding the optimal meta-parameter optimizer is too resource expensive at this stage.

Algorithm 1 details the pattern search algorithm where $X^{(\text{new})}$ is the new base point, X' is the new temporary base point, X is the initial base point, δ is the pattern step size, and α is an acceleration factor. The meta-parameters and their potential values are given in Table 2.

Algorithm 1. Pattern search algorithm [3, p. 51]

---

procedure PATTERNSEARCH(*input,variables,here*)
    Define parameters for the algorithm.
    Generate a random base point X.
    while The difference between the previous base point best fitness and the current base point best fitness is greater than the minimum difference. **do**
        Generate exploratory points in a pattern, the mesh, around the base point X.
        $X^{(\text{new})}$ = the best exploratory point
        if The fitness of the best exploratory point $X^{(\text{new})}$ is better than the fitness of the base point X **then**
            $X^{(\text{new})} \leftarrow$ best exploratory point
            $\mu \leftarrow \mu_0$ ▷ reset mesh size
            while $X^{(\text{new})}$ is better than X **do**
                $X' \leftarrow X$ ▷ set exploratory point as new base point
                $X \leftarrow X^{(\text{new})}$
                $X^{(\text{new})} \leftarrow X' + \alpha \cdot (X - X')$ ▷ pattern move
                Generate exploratory points in a pattern around the new base point.
                    $X^{(\text{new})} \leftarrow$ the best new generated point
            end while
        else $\mu^{(\text{new})} \leftarrow \mu - \delta$ ▷ decrease the mesh size
        end if
    end while
end procedure

Table 2. A list of meta-parameters optimized through pattern search and their possible values. The meta-parameters are partitioned into those related to the atom embeddings and those related to the ANN.

	Meta-parameter	Possible values
Embeddings	Projection/output dimensions	$\mathbb{Z}_+$
	Word em. model/input dimensions	$\mathbb{Z}_+$
	Keyword weighting	$\mathbb{R}_+$
	Atom embedding method	BOWΣ, BOWμ, PVDM, ∇
ANN	Gradient-based optimizer	SGD, Adam, AdaGrad, AdaDelta, AdaMax, RMSprop
	ANN architecture	FFNN, RNN
	Tuner optimizer	Random search, hyperband, Bayesian
	Tuner parameters	Optimizer-dependent

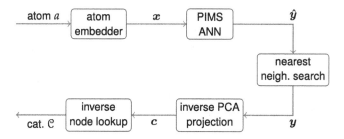

Fig. 4. An atom classifier derived from the atom embedder, PIMS ANN, the inverse PCA projection, and an inverse node lookup. The ANN has been trained on the user's PIMS structure, thereby making its output a low-dimensional estimate of the atom's "location" in the user's PIMS. Converting this estimate into "node space" requires a nearest-neighbor search, which can occur as shown, before inverse projection, or after [20].

2.6 PIMS ANN as a Classifier, A Bonus Application

As has been noted, the new metastimuli architecture circumvents the need to explicitly classify each atom. However, and this classification is in a sense implicit in the output of the PIMS ANN $\hat{y}$. All that is needed to yield an explicit classification of each atom is a relatively simple procedure depicted in Fig. 4: a (one) nearest-neighbor search, an inverse principle component analysis (PCA) projection, and an inverse node lookup. This is superfluous for metastimuli, but can be deployed as an auto-classifier for other applications with similar PIMS structures.

3 Results

Several new methods of metastimuli generation are presented, including an improvement to the overall metastimuli architecture. Variations on each method are compared, resulting in application-specific recommendations. The software tools we develop and present are made available as public repositories (those already available are [23,35,36]).

3.1 Learning by Epoch

During optimization, each generated ANN model with its meta-parameter and hyper-parameter set is trained for 10 epochs. This is not enough training to produce a usable model but is sufficient as a comparison. Better meta- and hyper-parameter sets produce better models that demonstrate lower fitness. The short training is necessary to conserve resources as a single optimization may require hundreds of models to be trained.

Therefore, at the end of optimization, the model with the optimal meta- and hyper-parameters must be trained significantly longer to complete the optimization process with a fully optimized ANN.

In deep learning, which we use here, longer training will continue to improve the loss of the ANN for the dataset upon which it trains.

The optimal ANN with meta- and hyper-parameter is trained for 200 epochs [as shown in Fig. 5]. After each training epoch, the ANN evaluates the testing dataset, which is labeled data withheld during the training process. Evaluating the testing set after each training epoch demonstrates the ANN is learning from similar data and not merely memorizing the dataset it trains on, which is called overfitting.

Upon completion of the test dataset evaluation, the model was tested on the null dataset. For a full discussion on the use of the null dataset, see Subsect. 2.3.

3.2   Meta- and Hyper-parameter Optimization

Figure 6 shows the pattern search fitness for each iteration. The first chosen value is the initial, randomly generated base point or set of meta-parameters. The second chosen value is the set of meta-parameters that results in a ANN with the lowest fitness compared with the initial set of meta-parameters and the parent exploratory set of meta-parameter sets. This chosen value is the new base point $X^{(new)}$. A pattern move creates a new temporary base point with a new temporary exploratory set. This sequence is repeated for the third chosen meta-parameter set.

Iterations after the third chosen meta-parameter did not result in a ANN with lower fitness. The pattern search algorithm continued creating exploratory sets with changing mesh sizes probing the design space until the search limit was reached. The maximum of number of exploratory sets without a change in base point is set at three for this run. The maximum number of exploratory sets is set at three to reduce computation expenses as continuing the pattern search algorithm would be result in a large increase in computation time with nominal reduction in fitness.

4   Discussion

The results depend on a significant number of meta- and hyper-parameters, optimized according to the methods described above. Beyond the results themselves, it is challenging to make general statements that are not potentially misleading; for instance, that technique X is better than technique Y. However, with these qualifications and despite the risk of black swans,[2] we present comparisons among techniques despite the limited scope of evidence.

4.1   Optimal Meta-Parameters and Hyper-parameters

The optimal hyper-parameters of Table 3 and Table 4 and optimal meta-parameters of Table 5 represent the "best" of each parameter found in this study. Focusing on the meta-parameters of Table 5, the optimal number of projection/output dimensions, which is the dimension of the metastimuli, is four, a

---

[2] See Hume and the "problem of induction.".

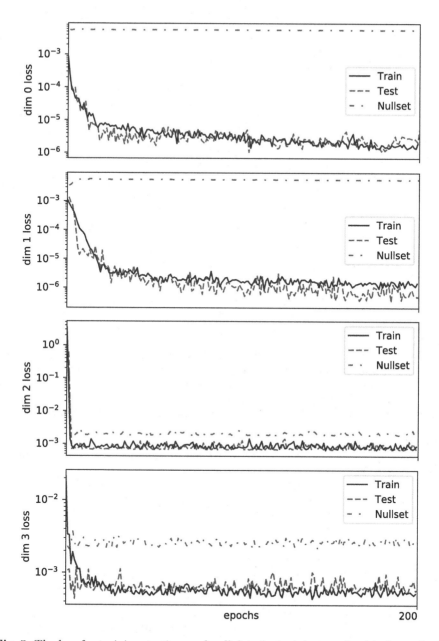

Fig. 5. The loss for training, testing, and null data by training epoch with the optimal meta- and hyper-parameters. As we expect, the null loss, which is the mean loss of five models, performs poorly compared to the training and testing loss. The training loss is used for ANN backpropagation. The testing loss shows how the model performs at that epoch. It is important to note that the models were not updated based on testing or null loss, only based on training loss.

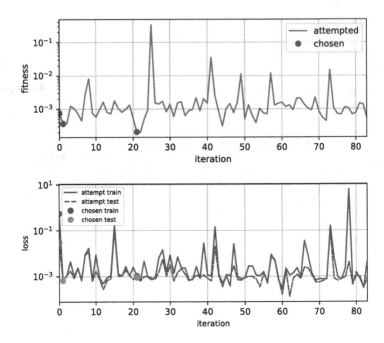

Fig. 6. Meta-parameter and hyper-parameter search results in the form of the (top) pattern search fitness and (bottom) final loss (averaged over dimensions) for each pattern search iteration. The zero iteration chosen meta-parameter set is the initial "base point" or randomly generated set of meta-parameters. Subsequent chosen sets are exploratory points with the better fitness than the base point and their set. The ANN is trained for ten epochs with a given set of meta-parameters and hyper-parameters.

Table 3. Optimal hyper-parameters learning rate, optimizer parameters, and number of hidden layers. The first value of the activation function and features is the input layer.

Dimension	Hyper-parameter	Optimal values
0	Learning rate	3.76×10^{-4}
	Optimizer parameters	$\beta_1 = 0.900, \beta_2 = 0.996$
	Hidden layers	8
1	Learning rate	4.45×10^{-4}
	Optimizer parameters	$\beta_1 = 0.900, \beta_2 = 0.936$
	Hidden layers	3
2	Learning rate	5.06×10^{-3}
	Optimizer parameters	$\beta_1 = 0.950, \beta_2 = 0.936$
	Hidden layers	2
3	Learning rate	9.25×10^{-3}
	Optimizer parameters	$\beta_1 = 0.900, \beta_2 = 0.992$
	Hidden layers	5

Table 4. Optimal hyper-parameters activation function and number of features for each ANN layer and projection/output dimension. Layer 0 is the input layer.

Dim	Hyper-parameter	ANN layer								
		0	1	2	3	4	5	6	7	8
0	Activation fun	tanh	σ	tanh	tanh	tanh	tanh	tanh	tanh	tanh
	Features	760	88	8	8	8	8	8	8	8
1	Activation fun	tanh	σ	tanh	tanh					
	Features	328	1368	8						
2	Activation fun	tanh	S	tanh						
	Features	784	1216	8						
3	Activation fun	σ	tanh	tanh	tanh	tanh	tanh			
	Features	696	1168	8	8	8	8			

Table 5. The optimal meta-parameters from the meta-parameter optimization.

	Meta-parameter	Optimal values
Embeddings	Projection/output dimensions	4
	Word em. model/input dimensions	20
	Keyword weighting	5
	Atom embedding method	PVDM
ANN	Gradient-based optimizer	Adam
	ANN architecture	FFNN
	Tuner optimizer	Random search

manageable number in terms of current haptic devices. The optimal number of word embedding or model input dimension was 20. Keyword weighting optimized at five, which means scaling keyword embeddings derived directly from PIMS category names was effective (a weight of unity would imply no improvement); however, it is not so high as to imply that semantic content was irrelevant. The distributed memory paragraph vector (PVDM) was the optimal atom embedding method, implying it was superior to the bag-of-words and ∇ methods, which is not particularly surprising given that it is a more advanced technique.

Regarding the gradient-based hyper-parameter optimizer technique, the Adam optimizer proved superior to SGD, AdaGrad, AdaDelta, AdaMax, and RMSprop. The Adam optimizer is a stochastic gradient descent method developed by Kingma and Ba [11]. Surprisingly, the feed-forward neural network performed better than the recurrent neural network. It should be noted, however, that the meta-parameter optimizer switched back-and-forth several times between the two architectures; we suspect further study may show the RNN to perform better. The optimal hyper-parameter tuner optimizer was random search, outperforming the hyperband and Bayesian optimizers.

4.2 Directions of the Work

The results presented here are promising: the ANNs can learn on relatively limited datasets and perform reasonably well at associating a meaningful (in terms of a user's PIMS) low-dimension real vector to atoms not previously seen. However, much work remains before the hypothesis of the "metastimulus bond effect" [22] on human learning can be studied directly. Before a study can be conducted, two significant results must be achieved:

1. a haptic interface must be developed to apply the real vectors resulting from the work presented above (i.e. to apply metastimuli) and
2. users (study participants) must be provided a software environment for creating their own PIMSs that can be processed by the PIMS filter software.

Both directions are currently being pursued by the authors.

Acknowledgements. This work used the Extreme Science and Engineering Discovery Environment (XSEDE), which is supported by National Science Foundation grant number ACI-1548562, through the allocation for Shawn Duan (user: Dane Webb) [33,39]. Specifically, it used the Bridges system (bridges-gpu.psc.xsede.org), which is supported by NSF award number ACI-1445606, at the Pittsburgh Supercomputing Center (PSC) [16]. We thank TJ Olesky of PSC for their assistance with porting code over to Bridges.

A   Software repositories

The software written to generate the results presented in this work is open-source and can be found in the permanent software repository of [38]. The ongoing development of the software is hosted at the GitHub repository [37]. Several sub-repositories are included: [23,35,36].

References

1. Arora, S., Liang, Y., Ma, T.: A simple but tough-to-beat baseline for sentence embeddings (2016)
2. Bird, S., Klein, E., Loper, E.: Natural Language Processing with Python: Analyzing Text with the Natural Language Toolkit. O'Reilly, Beijing (2009). http://my.safaribooksonline.com/9780596516499. http://www.nltk.org/book
3. Bozorg-Haddad, O., Solgi, M., Loï, H.A., et al.: Meta-heuristic and Evolutionary Algorithms for Engineering Optimization. Wiley, Hoboken (2017)
4. Cer, D., et al.: Universal sentence encoder. arXiv preprint arXiv:1803.11175 (2018)
5. Charniak, E.: An Introduction to Deep Learning. Addison-Wesley Data & Analytics, Addison Wesley Professional (2018). https://mitpress.mit.edu/books/introduction-deep-learning
6. Cohan, A., et al.: A discourse-aware attention model for abstractive summarization of long documents. In: Proceedings of the 2018 Conference of the North American Chapter of the Association for Computational Linguistics: Human Language Technologies, Volume 2 (Short Papers) (2018). https://doi.org/10.18653/v1/n18-2097

7. Fredembach, B., de Boisferon, A.H., Gentaz, E.: Learning of arbitrary association between visual and auditory novel stimuli in adults: the "bond effect" of haptic exploration. PloS One **4**(3), e4844 (2009)

8. Jung, J., et al.: Speech communication through the skin: design of learning protocols and initial findings. In: Marcus, A., Wang, W. (eds.) DUXU 2018. LNCS, vol. 10919, pp. 447–460. Springer, Cham (2018). https://doi.org/10.1007/978-3-319-91803-7_34

9. Kant, I., Guyer, P., Wood, A.: Critique of Pure Reason. The Cambridge Edition of the Works of Immanuel Kant. Cambridge University Press, Cambridge (1999)

10. Karim, M.R.: Deep-learning-with-tensorflow, April 2017. https://github.com/PacktPublishing/Deep-Learning-with-TensorFlow/graphs/contributors

11. Kingma, D.P., Ba, J.: Adam: a method for stochastic optimization (2017)

12. Kowsari, K., Heidarysafa, M., Brown, D.E., Meimandi, K.J., Barnes, L.E.: RMDL: random multimodel deep learning for classification. CoRR abs/1805.01890 (2018). http://arxiv.org/abs/1805.01890

13. Le, Q., Mikolov, T.: Distributed representations of sentences and documents. In: International Conference on Machine Learning, pp. 1188–1196 (2014)

14. Lehoucq, R., Maschhoff, K., Sorensen, D., Yang, C.: ARPACK Software. https://www.caam.rice.edu/software/ARPACK/

15. Li, L., Jamieson, K., DeSalvo, G., Rostamizadeh, A., Talwalkar, A.: Hyperband: a novel bandit-based approach to hyperparameter optimization. J. Mach. Learn. Res. **18**(1), 6765–6816 (2017)

16. Nystrom, N.A., Levine, M.J., Roskies, R.Z., Scott, J.R.: Bridges: a uniquely flexible HPC resource for new communities and data analytics. In: Proceedings of the 2015 XSEDE Conference: Scientific Advancements Enabled by Enhanced Cyberinfrastructure. XSEDE 2015. Association for Computing Machinery, New York (2015). https://doi.org/10.1145/2792745.2792775

17. Pelikan, M., Goldberg, D.E., Cantú-Paz, E., et al.: BOA: the Bayesian optimization algorithm. In: Proceedings of the Genetic and Evolutionary Computation Conference GECCO-99, vol. 1, pp. 525–532. Citeseer (1999)

18. Picone, R.: Null data for machine learning, December 2020. https://doi.org/10.6084/m9.figshare.13473834.v1

19. Picone, R.: Artificial neural network training with personal information management system integration, February 2021. https://doi.org/10.6084/m9.figshare.13886231.v1

20. Picone, R.: An atom classifier architecture for an artificial neural network trained on a personal information management system, February 2021. https://doi.org/10.6084/m9.figshare.13886450.v1

21. Picone, R.: Metastimuli system architecture, February 2021. https://doi.org/10.6084/m9.figshare.13884095.v1

22. Picone, R.A.R., Webb, D., Powell, B.: Metastimuli: an introduction to PIMS filtering. In: Schmorrow, D.D., Fidopiastis, C.M. (eds.) HCII 2020. LNCS (LNAI), vol. 12197, pp. 118–128. Springer, Cham (2020). https://doi.org/10.1007/978-3-030-50439-7_8

23. Picone, R.A.: Ricopicone/PIMS-filter: PIMS filter, January 2020. https://doi.org/10.5281/zenodo.3633355

24. Picone, R.A.R., Lentz, J., Powell, B.: The fuzzification of an information architecture for information integration. In: Yamamoto, S. (ed.) HIMI 2017. LNCS, vol. 10273, pp. 145–157. Springer, Cham (2017). https://doi.org/10.1007/978-3-319-58521-5_11

25. Picone, R.A.R., Powell, B.: A new information architecture: a synthesis of structure, flow, and dialectic. In: Yamamoto, S. (ed.) HIMI 2015. LNCS, vol. 9172, pp. 320–331. Springer, Cham (2015). https://doi.org/10.1007/978-3-319-20612-7_31

26. Rastrigin, L.: The convergence of the random search method in the extremal control of a many parameter system. Autom. Remote Control **24**, 1337–1342 (1963)

27. Saerens, M., Fouss, F., Yen, L., Dupont, P.: The principal components analysis of a graph, and its relationships to spectral clustering. In: Boulicaut, J.-F., Esposito, F., Giannotti, F., Pedreschi, D. (eds.) ECML 2004. LNCS (LNAI), vol. 3201, pp. 371–383. Springer, Heidelberg (2004). https://doi.org/10.1007/978-3-540-30115-8_35

28. de Saussure, F.: Course in General Linguistics. Columbia University Press, New York City (1916)

29. SciPy: Sparse eigenvalue problems with ARPACK. https://docs.scipy.org/doc/scipy/reference/tutorial/arpack.html

30. Shahid, N., Perraudin, N., Kalofolias, V., Puy, G., Vandergheynst, P.: Fast robust PCA on graphs. IEEE J. Sel. Top. Sig. Process. **10**(4), 740–756 (2016). https://doi.org/10.1109/JSTSP.2016.2555239

31. Sporleder, C., Lapata, M.: Automatic paragraph identification: a study across languages and domains. In: Proceedings of the 2004 Conference on Empirical Methods in Natural Language Processing, pp. 72–79 (2004)

32. Stein, B.E., Meredith, M.A., Wallace, M.T.: Development and neural basis of multisensory integration. In: The Development of Intersensory Perception: Comparative Perspectives, pp. 81–105 (1994)

33. Towns, J., et al.: XSEDE: accelerating scientific discovery. Comput. Sci. Eng. **16**(5), 62–74 (2014). https://doi.org/10.1109/MCSE.2014.80. https://doi.ieeecomputersociety.org/10.1109/MCSE.2014.80

34. Virtanen, P., et al.: SciPy 1.0-Fundamental Algorithms for Scientific Computing in Python. arXiv e-prints arXiv:1907.10121 (Jul 2019)

35. Webb, D.: danewebb/tag-classification: Initial release of tag-classification (2020). https://doi.org/10.5281/zenodo.3633402

36. Webb, D., Picone, R.A.: danewebb/tex-tagging: Initial release of tex-tagging (2020). https://doi.org/10.5281/zenodo.3633400

37. Webb, D., Picone, R.A., Obierefu, F.: Metastimuli-Project. https://github.com/dialectic/Metastimuli-Project (2021)

38. Webb, D., Picone, R.A., Obierefu, F.: Metastimulighter, February 2021. https://doi.org/10.5281/zenodo.4539755

39. Wilkins-Diehr, N., et al.: An overview of the XSEDE extended collaborative support program. In: Gitler, I., Klapp, J. (eds.) ISUM 2015. CCIS, vol. 595, pp. 3–13. Springer, Cham (2016). https://doi.org/10.1007/978-3-319-32243-8_1

40. Wittgenstein, L., Anscombe, G.: Philosophical Investigations: The German Text, with a Revised English Translation. Blackwell, Oxford (2001)

41. Zaccone, G., Karim, M.: Deep Learning with TensorFlow: Explore Neural Networks and Build Intelligent Systems with Python, 2nd edn. Packt Publishing, Birmingham (2018)

Holarchic HCI and Augmented Psychology ("AugPsy")

Suraj Sood[✉]

The Sirius Project, Carrollton, USA

Abstract. Consciousness enables experience, and each can be placed on a spectrum [1, 14]. Experience is more robust and multidirectional, though the possibility exists for it to be bidirectional (particularly for the geometrician working along a line, but also generally when considering between two given options). Consciousness is synonymous informally with awareness. When one is conscious, they are aware, and vice versa. Awareness can be quantified in terms of being "greater" or "lesser". For example, one may be more aware of certain aspects of experience than others given selective attention.

Experience is the basic unit of analysis for phenomenology. While experience may be operationalized as qualia to address "what things are like" [20], the former may also be treated as a formal primitive. Phenomena are events as they appear to or present themselves for conscious perceivers. In ordinary use, experiences are assumed to be significant events or happenings.

Phenomenal experience is qualitative. It is characterized as such by description through adjectives (e.g., "good" or "bad"). Experiences can be categorized into types, e.g. into the learning kind (as in the "learning experience"). If an experience is rich, then it has richness that may be qualified—described further in terms of what makes it so—or quantified. Growth may result from the victorious experience. This is so in battle-based role playing games (RPGs), where successfully defeating one's opponent earns experience points that contribute to the possible level-up of one or more of the player's team members (as in *Pokémon* and *Fire Emblem*, two of the most popular Japanese action-adventure RPG series).

It is posited that the self, after being immersed in something greater than it, has potential to emerge greater than it was prior [2, 3]. Positive psychology recognizes such an immersed state as being one of flow or engagement. Subjective immersion [6] can be reported on to certain extents of meaningfulness and accuracy. Immersion can be qualified, e.g. via description of an activity's meaning to the human actor, or perhaps quantified. Perhaps the optimal flow experience is only quantifiable as being infinitely enjoyable, enriching, engaging, and/or meaningful, among other possible measures.

Augmented psychology was argued for in [11] with the proposal of augmented mind, including augmented cognition, affect, and conation. AugPsy may also include augmented body [65], consisting of the device-attaching human and their technologically extended self [66]. The AugPsy program propounded in this chapter is to be distinguished from Augmented Psychology as the psychological intervention using met-aphorical experiences in virtual reality (VR), conceived on the basis of hypothesized "last frontiers" of neuroscientific research [70].

© Springer Nature Switzerland AG 2021

D. D. Schmorrow and C. M. Fidopiastis (Eds.): HCII 2021, LNAI 12776, pp. 305–330, 2021.

https://doi.org/10.1007/978-3-030-78114-9_22

Keywords: Consciousness · Experience · Qualia · Immersion ·
Postphenomenology

1 Introduction

Consciousness enables experience. Consciousness and experience can each be understood as existing along a spectrum [1, 14]. (Affect can be as well, but the affective spectrum is devoted more exclusively to disorders [54].) Experience is more whole and multidirectional than consciousness, though the possibility exists for the former to be bidirectional (particularly for the geometrician working along a line, but also in general when deliberating between any two given options).

Consciousness is synonymous with awareness. When one is conscious, they are aware, and vice versa. Awareness can be quantified in terms of being "greater" or "lesser". For example, one may be more aware of certain aspects of experience than others, given selective attention. Exclusion of extraneous data, and the suppression or repression of cognition, affect, or conation, can each be psychological augmentative mechanisms if and only if they afford better task performance.

Experience is the basic unit of analysis for phenomenology. The central insight of phenomenology is that "pure experience is…a unity which is neither subject nor object but potentially both" ([43], p. 202). While experience may be operationalized as qualia to address "what things are like" [20], the former may also be treated as a formal primitive. Phenomena are events as they appear to or present themselves for conscious perceivers. In ordinary use, experiences are assumed to be significant events or happenings.

Phenomenal experience is qualitative. It is to be characterized as such by description through adjectives (e.g., "good" or "bad"). Experiences can be categorized into types, e.g. as of the learning kind (one's life may be full of "learning experiences"). If an experience is rich, then it has richness that may be qualified—described further in terms of what makes it so—or else quantified in terms of ≥ 0 experiences.

Growth may result from victorious experience. This is so in battle-based role-playing games (RPGs), where successfully defeating one's opponent earns experience points that contribute to the possible level-up of one or more of the player's team members. This much is operative in Pokémon and Fire Emblem, two of the most popular Japanese action-adventure RPG series.[1]

It is posited that the self, after being immersed in something greater than itself, emerges from immersion greater than before [2, 3]. Positive psychology recognizes such

---

[1] Though the popular *Yu-Gi-Oh!* trading card game (TCG) does not have a corresponding game element of experience, it is relevant to HCI in ways distinct from the two other franchises mentioned. Specifically, *Yu-Gi-Oh!* emphasizes technology heavily in its anime: this is exemplified in the character Seto Kaiba and his invention of "duel technology" in the form of the "duel disk". Using the duel disk allows players to play the card game while summoning realistic holograms of magic, "trap cards", and fantasy monsters that do battle. *Yu-Gi-Oh!* is meta-technological in that, while interacting with one's computer (to watch the anime or play the franchise's video games), one also confronts technological possibilities not presently existent in the actual world.

an immersed state as being one of flow or engagement ("being one with the music[2]" when involved in a certain kind of activity). Subjective immersion [6] can be reported on to certain extents of meaningfulness and accuracy. Immersion can be qualified, e.g. via description of an activity's meaning to a given human actor, or else quantified by answering how immersive said activity was or how many immersive experiences one or more subjects have had. Perhaps the optimal flow experience is just quantifiable as being infinitely enjoyable, enriching, engaging, and/or meaningful, among other possible measures. Related to flow as optimal experience is defining what constitutes optimal human-computer interaction (HCI). Examples of suboptimal HCI are illicit system hacking (e.g., of video game consoles like the New Nintendo 2DS), while optimal HCI may include practices like white hat (defensive) hacking in cybersecurity.

In this chapter, the above understanding of experience and consciousness will be related to formal-mathematical psychology. Related work leads to reported results of a semantic psychological study originating from experiments conducted in a virtual community of practice (VCoP) [55]. These experiments included neologism, conceptual innovation, and construct proposal, among other related activities (e.g., that of naming new fields and super-fields). Based on the semantic approach undertaken, three novel psychological constructs are generated. These are "memsight" and "foremory"—both denoting a hybrid memory-foresight construct—as well as "momeihor", a compromise term between the former two. Other constructs that follow from state-dependent memory are next generated, including trait-dependent, state-independent, trait-independent, state-interdependent, and trait-interdependent memories. "Associative identity superorder" and "innate helpfulness" follow from dissociative identity disorder (DID) and learned helplessness, respectively. (Identity itself is conceptualized holistically as a function of disposition, cognitive style, affect, judgment, and value [60].)

Following introduction to the above terms, it is argued that theoretical Type C-Z personality types follow from the Type A and Type B personality types. The Type C personality is regarded as either more passive than both Type A and B ones, or else as assertive (i.e., in between the aggressive Type A and passive Type B). Lastly, a program for generating psychological laws dubbed "psycholawgy" is proposed, along with candidate laws that could begin to populate this hitherto unfulfilled area of research. Each of the efforts undertaken in this chapter are important for human-computer interaction and augmented cognition in that—to understand the ideal mode of being-in-virtuality (including being-with-others, i.e. the Heideggerian Mitsein)—evaluations of both old and new constructs might be prerequisite for the discussion necessary. The present work also has broader potential value for the fields of psychology and philosophy.

2 Related Work

Person was formalized as a function of self and other; they were further granted to be romantic, existential, humanistic, chemical, environmental, hedonic and eudaimonic (happiness-seeking), conservative, and liberal [11]. These are in addition to persons being physical, chemical, biological, psychological, social, cultural, and spiritual (as explicated

---

[2] Immersion in musical listening—along with the accompanying change in one's affective state to reflect the music's intended mood—can be viewed as an instantaneous flow state.

in Sood's [5] theory of reality). The holarchic, subjective-objective, holonic ontology of persons—a "psycho-ontology" [45] using a novel mathematics to represent reality and mind formally—was enlarged. It is now granted that reality can be unconscious (i.e., dreamless deep sleep)[3], subconscious (in hypnogogic and hypnopompic liminal states), conscious while in the default mode network (DMN), or superconscious when a peak-experience or self-transcendence [35] have occurred.

It remains an open question whether psychologists have fully accounted for both people and their situations. What determines their interaction? People and situations have power relative to one another. A person might overcome a challenging situation or be overcome by it. In the optimal case, people and situations have equal power relative to one another regardless of what determines the interaction. It may be hypothesized that what determines such an equal interaction is itself ideal.

Sood's multidimensional notion of person was expanded before being formalized in terms of more basic, psychological primitives. Such primitives have been introduced in previous works to address what has been called "the units of analysis problem in psychology" ([21], p. 177). However, Sood did not discuss the follow-up problem of quantifying psychology's basic units. (This problem is addressed in Sect. 4.1 of the present chapter.)

Sood's personology includes the following 27 properties of the human person[4]:

1. *Physical* – People's bodies are composed of matter. Further, people interact with other physical objects.
2. *Biological* – People breathe, eat, and drink; and a great many of them have sex and reproduce.
3. *Temporal* – People are born, they live, and they die; they experience time.
4. *Cultural* – People are embedded in cultures characterized by unique but shared ways of being.
5. *Social* – People participate in societies consisting of concrete relations between themselves and others.
6. *Economic* – People are agents who trade goods and services with one another in marketplaces.
7. *Technological* – People invent and utilize tools to perform tasks they were previously unable or less able to accomplish.
8. *Artistic* – People express themselves through the creation of original works such as paintings and songs.
9. *Intellectual* – People aim to comprehend reality and achieve accurate understandings of it.
10. *Moral* – People have unique and shared ideas of wrong versus right action.
11. *Spiritual* – People seek enlightenment, wisdom, and contact with the divine or supernatural via practices such as meditation and prayer.

---

[3] "Unconscious reality" was encountered in the name and lyrics of a song by the former pop-rock band Artist Vs. Poet. It is forwarded that psychological insight can be reached, and cognition thus augmented, via analysis of lyrics by such artists (including hard-rock band A Day to Remember, among many others).

[4] The human person has typically been discussed in theological, ethical, and philosophical contexts [36, 37].

12. *Religious* – People worship what they deem as sacred (e.g., God or Gods; Goddess or Goddesses) through rituals and organized communion.

13. *Political* – People negotiate and have interests that are in line or at odds with those of others.

14. *Athletic* – Whether for fitness or organized play, people exercise their bodies and minds.

15. *Professional* – People work toward goals, including earning money and achieving satisfaction.

16. *Recreational* – People enjoy leisurely activities such as taking walks and attending parties.

17. *Linguistic* – People communicate via representational symbol systems characterized by semantics, syntax, and pragmatics.

18. *Psychological* – People have minds and engage in behaviors. More specifically, they think, feel, have personalities, interact with situations, are motivated, sense, perceive, experience, learn, and pay attention.

19. *Romantic* – People become emotionally involved with one another. Most get married.

20. *Existential* – People are responsible and free: they have psychological wills.[5]

21. *Humanistic* – People are creative, spontaneous, and active beings who contribute to the furthering of humanity.

22. *Chemical* – People are composed in part of physical reactions taking place throughout their bodies.

23. *Environmental* – People engage in a variety of ways with their surroundings.

24. *Hedonic* – People seek happiness in the form of pleasure.

25. *Eudaimonic* – People seek happiness in the form of fulfillment.[6]

26. *Conservative* – People live in accordance with rules and principles designed with security in mind.

27. *Liberal* – People live freely to maximize (e.g.) diversity, inclusion, and peace.

19 was added since it is subsumable under neither 5 (social) nor 9 (intellectual). (Contra-cognitivist models that view affect as merely a class of cognition: see [13] for a treatment of this perspective). Various existential theories of psychological will have been proposed in the past two centuries, ranging from Friedrich Nietzsche's "will to power" to Viktor Frankl's "will to meaning". Will is used in the present context to refer simply to volition, i.e. purposive striving evidenced when one or more individuals decides on and commits to certain action.

---

[5] This chapter's notion of existential humanness is intended to be fully compatible with Yalom's existential givens, including freedom, death, isolation, and meaning [44].

[6] An interesting question for affective HCI and positive computing, as well as for positive psychology, is whether the process of attaining eudaimonic fulfillment feels similarly to flow. Since cognition theoretically disappears during flow (as Seligman once claimed), does the same happen when one is maximally engaged in a flow activity that does not necessarily involve thought? If so, eudaimonia may be equated to Aristotelian flow. In any case, the question of where pleasure ends and fulfillment begins is a more general and worthy quantitative question to answer. Additionally, when non-cognitive, flow cannot be a form of augmented cognition (by definition), but may still be one of augmented psychology.

Learning has been covered by Bandura & Huston [24] and attention by philosophical, perceptual, and cognitive psychologists (e.g., William James). The formation of learned habits is essential for the development of procedural knowledge and memory. One interesting consideration regarding learning and attention is that "meta" or naturally-augmented versions of both learning and attention (as well as cognition) are at least conceivable, if not existent. Meta-learning occurs when one reflects on or operates on his or her procedural knowledge; meta-attention or meta-awareness occurs when we cognize over the nature of our awareness. Meta-awareness is the domain of phenomenology.

Marriage is an established social and religious (12) convention. Moreover, romantic being in the present sense is mostly meant as being affective (in the same sense as in 18: people "feel"). It could be expressed artistically (8) but is not reducible to such. 19 could thereby be viewed as a product of 5, 8, 9, 12, and 18, though it need not be necessarily. 26 and 27 were meant not merely in their political senses, but more broadly to encompass human being and doing.

People were also granted to be inherently humanistic and environmental. For the theoretical psychologist, the latter is to be distinguished from persons' being situational as in 18. Varela et al. [47] propounded the original enactive framework unifying cognitive science with phenomenology, asserting that "the organism both initiates and is shaped by the environment" (p. 174). Sood [4] substituted "organism" and "environment" in this statement with "person" and "situation" respectively, asserting that doing so rendered his treatment more topically psychological. Lewin [22] formalized human behavior as

$$Be = F[P, E] \tag{1}$$

Where Be equaled "behavior", P equals "person", and E equals "environment". Lewin's statement reads "Behavior = Function of person and environment" (p. 878). Sood's [5] formalization of human behavior was assigned the variable B, which equaled $F[Sm, Rp]$

$$B = F[Sm, Rp] \tag{2}$$

Where Sm equals "stimulus" and Rp equals "response". Sood revised Lewin's behavioral formula to align more with traditional behavioristic psychology (viz., Skinner's [29]) and truncated the latter's Be variable to simply B.

Sm could be regarded as analogous, if not identical, with E in that for behaviorists like Skinner, stimuli were objects in the subject's surrounding (external) environment. For Rauthmann et al. [23], situations are composed partially of environmental *cues* that are physical, objectively quantifiable stimuli. While this framing suggests that the environment should be conceived as being part of situationality, for the present discussion, the interchangeability of E, Sm, and situationality (formalized later in this chapter) is noteworthy.

2.1 Person-Computer Interaction (PCI)

Psychological persons may be said to be either selves or others. Psychological notions of *self* and *other* pervade the existential psychological literature [16, 33]. Sood [1] formalized person-situation interaction as a complex, interdependent function of mental and behavioral structures (i.e., states and traits) and processes. He did so as follows

$$[P, S] = F[St_{(T,Se)}, Pc]_{(M,B)} \qquad (3)$$

Where P equals "person", S equals "situation", St equals "structure", T equals "trait", Se equals "state", Pc equals "process", M equals "mind"[7], and B equals "behavior" [20]. (Traits and states are treated as distinct types of psychological structures.) $[P, S]$ is a whole composed entirely of parts St_{MSe}, St_{BSe}, St_{MT}, St_{BT}, Pc_M, and Pc_B, which respectively denote "mental states", "behavioral states", "mental traits", "behavioral traits", "mental processes", and "behavioral processes". Informally, (3) reads: *person-situation interaction is a function of mental and behavioral structures and processes.* Such mental and behavioral structures may be either traits, states, or hybrid *trates* [11]. The use of trate over both state and trait would eliminate the need to use latter in formalisms such as (3).

The more direct formalization of P[8] was undertaken

$$P = F[Sl, Ot] \qquad (4)$$

Where Sl equals "self" and Ot equals "other". Self has received a recent psychological treatment by Klein [31], where William James' classical notions of "self-as-known" and "self-as-knower" received updates to a more holarchic notion. Klein identifies two distinct kinds of selves from cognitive neuroscience and clinical case work involving memory and knowledge, in particular. Klein's epistemological self is "the self of neural instantiation: the neuro-cognitive categories of self-knowledge" (p. 20); his ontological self is "the self of first-person subjectivity...that consciously apprehends the content of the epistemological self" (p. 46). Klein's dualistic view of self may be characterized as holarchic—i.e., subjective-objective—to the extent that neuro-cognition is ontologically objective whereas first-person subjectivity is ontologically subjective. Dennett [32] also offered a novel theory of self, defining it as a center of narrative gravity, a "purely abstract object...[and] fiction". This treats self entirely as an ontologically subjective phenomenon.

Other is a concept that, while theoretically opposed from the notion of self, has received marginal attention from psychologists. The possibilities of the psychological study of other open numerous such constructs. Hyphenated concepts and constructs for the same study of self include: *self-relationship, self-possessed, self-hatred,* self-disorder, self-compassion, self-confidence, self-control, self-distancing, self-doubt, self-efficacy,

---

[7] Overmier and Lawry defined M instead as "mediator" in the incentive motivation formula.

[8] A useful contribution to continental philosophy relevant to the present discussion of person would be the introduction of the concept "person-in-themself" (or "person-in-himself" and "person-in-herself"). This may exist as a counterpart to Immanuel Kant's "thing-in-itself", an object which appears to us but that we only can assume exists independent of our relation (e.g., observatory) to it. While person may be subsumed as a kind of noun along with *thing*, the former refers to an ontologically subjective rather than objective noun. Of course, based on the sub-discussion of self and other here, additional concepts may be introduced: "thing-in-itother" and "person-in-itother"; acceptance of the term "itother" (following from *itself*) would need to precede this.

self-expansion, self-harm, self-reflection, self-suppression, self-determination, self-care, self-loathing, self-comparison, self-concept, self-esteem, self-handicapping, self-image, self-perception, self-regulation, self-reference, self-referential, self-actualization, self-transcendence, self-knowledge, self-ignorance, self-interest, self-report, self-replication, self-directed, self-talk, self-reliance, self-realization, self-defeating, self-concept, self-identify, self-as-known, self-as-knower, self-sabotage, self-aggrandizement, self-effacement, self-evident, self-love, self-consciousness, self-promotion, self-assessment, self-motivated, self-deception, and self-pity.

Based on the above, concepts and constructs for the study of other include: *other-relationship, other-possessed, other-hatred, other-disorder,* other-compassion, other-confidence, other-control, other-distancing, other-doubt, other-efficacy, other-expansion, other-harm, other-reflection, other-suppression, other-determination, other-care, other-loathing, other-comparison, other-concept, other-esteem, other-handicapping, other-image, other-perception, other-regulation, other-reference [73], *other-referential,* other-actualization, other-transcendence, other-knowledge, other-ignorance, other-interest [34], other-report, other-replication, other-directed, other-talk, other-reliance, other-realization, other-defeating, other-concept, other-identify, other-as-known, other-as-knower, other-sabotage, other-aggrandizement, other-effacement, other-evident, other-love, other-consciousness, other-promotion, *other-assessment, other-motivated, other-*deception, and *other-pity.* Further self and other concepts and constructs likely remain to be theorized on and scientized. The set of elements just delineated can be expanded based on interchanging suffixes, e.g. changing self-motivat-*ed* to self-motivat-*ional.*[9]

In the context of augmented cognition, the central role of the self who thinks (i.e., from Descartes' original *cogito*) is easily imagined and difficult, if not impossible, to successfully refute. Resolving the philosophical problem of other minds [30], which consists in answering whether we may come to know that other people's minds exist, would be tantamount to knowing how we could know of other people's cognitions (and affects and motivations in Sood's Platonic-Freudian model of mind). Such knowledge would be requisite for its instrumentalization; and, if technology consists in the instrumentalization of knowledge—not merely of information, which is truth value-neutral—then knowledge of other minds is requisite for any technology that would augment user cognition. The problem of other minds thus also represents a problem for the philosophy of HCI.

The problem of other minds may be attempted to be solved in one or more of the following broad ways:

1. *Technological*: Deeply immersive social networking. Ubiquitous communication and interaction between agents via, e.g., heavily networked virtual reality (VR) simulation.
2. *Spiritual:* Collective immersion in flow, peak, religious, or meditative experiences. Transpersonal overcoming of the manifest, illusory self-other distinction; feeling

---

[9] Concepts following from (3)–(4) include: *personal situation; situational person; personal self; personal other; situational self* (i.e., who one is in a given context or setting); and *situational other.*

one with the world or universe as either a state (e.g., the peak experience [35]) or trait.

3. *Biopsychosocial:* Empathy, abductive inference, and conviction or faith in the existence of other minds.

The technological possibility is relevant for human-computer interaction, and more specifically for the projects of augmented cognition and psychology. (Relatedly, the project of augmented cognition may be defined as that of aligning thought with reality.) The biopsychosocial possibility above refers to the theory of mind phenomenon, where social agents hold intuitive beliefs in the existence of other minds.

Knowledge is understood here as a form of cognition represented in one's mind or being enacted procedurally via the skilled use of one's body.[10] In either case, knowledge is encoded in an embodied, neurocognitive substrate. Representing knowledge via formal syntax and operations is the domain of mathematical logic, which also extends into computation primarily in the form of discrete logical operations determined by the programmer.[11]

2.2 The Platonic-Freudian Model of Mind

Sood [5] formalized *M mind* as a portion of ψ, *psychology* (denoting the field of psychology, including its two most eminent and high-level, modern topics of study). He did so as follows

$$\psi = F[M, B] \tag{5}$$

Where *B* equals *behavior*. Sood's formalism was disciplinary in nature; person-situation interaction (with (M, B) operating as a subscript to $[St_{(T,Se)}, Pc]$) could just as easily have been set equal to ψ. In any case, *M* was next formalized as follows

$$M = F[(A, C, Mv)_{(U-,Sb-)Cs}] \tag{6}$$

Where *A* equals "affect", *C* equals "cognition", *Mv* equals "motivation", $U-$ equals "un-", $Sb-$ equals "sub-", and *Cs* equals "consciousness". According to the right portion of (6)'s subscript, each of these elementary mental phenomena may be either unconscious, subconscious, or conscious. (8) yields the following nine constructs: "unconscious affect", "subconscious affect", and "conscious affect"; "unconscious cognition", "subconscious cognition", and "conscious cognition"; and "unconscious motivation", "subconscious motivation", and "conscious motivation". Any of these constructs could informally be considered subminds in a manner analogous to how each of

---

[10] Procedural memory consists in the storage of and retrieval from embodied knowledge. An interesting consideration is its connection with expert intuition, which does not yet seem to have been rendered explicit. Procedural memory and expert intuition draw from one's stored set of embodied "know-how" and "know-that", respectively.

[11] Related to the formal representation of knowledge is the question of how to quantify knowledge. One may answer this by counting all propositional statements that an agent knows to be true.

the five-factor model's traits (Openness, Conscientiousness, Extraversion, Agreeableness, and Neuroticism) could be regarded as subpersonalities of a given person's overall personality.

Formula (6) drew from Freud's topographical model of mind [18] on one hand—where mental content passes between the unconscious and conscious sub-minds via the intermediary subconscious—and Revelle's recent attempt to synthesize Plato's tripartite model of mind (consisting of precursors for affect, cognition, and motivation) into a formal personality framework [19]. (6) is presumed to be compatible with Mischel & Shoda's [42] "cognitive-affective system theory" of personality (p. 246).

The fusion of (2), (3), and (6) was undertaken

$$[P, S] = F[St_{(T,Se)}, Pc]_{[(A,C,Mv,B)_{(U-,Sb-)Cs}]} \tag{7}$$

(7) reads: *Person-situation interaction is a function of unconscious, subconscious, and conscious affective, cognitive, motivational, and behavioral traits, states, and processes.* B here was not part of Sood's original Platonic-Freudian model of mind, nor does (7) need to imply that it now is. It has been added to (7) (and subsequent invocations of $F[St_{(T,Se)}, Pc]_{...}$) given its historical closeness with Mv (see the *conation* concept as in Plato's work [25]), and to accommodate Maslow's view of behavior almost always requiring motivation in order to occur. The tripart primitives listed in Table 1 follow from the compound psychological primitives named between (6) and (7).

The mathematical-theoretic approach to psychology undertaken [1, 2] requires an expansion of Freudian topography. Specifically, if unconsciousness is zero (0) awareness; subconsciousness is half (0.5) awareness; and consciousness is full (1) awareness, then mathematically, one could speak equally of negative subconsciousness and consciousness: -0.5 and -1 awareness, respectively.[12] Numerous typologies of consciousness exist. Subconsciousness and unconsciousness may be considered grades of consciousness, but as with experience, one may speak of kinds of consciousness, such as technological and literary consciousnesseses.[13]

Sood [1, 2] formalized the sub-primitives of Table 1's triads into his person-situation and mind formulae but neglected to explicate them rigorously. Affect is a "a non-conscious experience of intensity...a moment of unformed and unstructured potential" [39]. It "cannot be fully realized in language" and "is always prior to and/or outside of consciousness". It is "the body's way of preparing itself for action in a given circumstance by adding a quantitative dimension of intensity to the quality of an experience".

Starting with Kahneman and Tversky [26], cognition in modern psychology has frequently been defined as consisting of Systems 1 and 2. In this "dual-process" theoretic model, System 1 consists of thought that is fast, instinctive, affective, and unconscious. (Intuition is an unconscious process, but its outputs—occurring as insight, e.g. realized by a subject in an "aha!" moment—are conscious.) System 2, on the other hand, consists

---

[12] The unconscious sub-mind can be formally defined as the set of all holons that exist outside of awareness.

[13] [50] describes eight kinds of consciousness, including organism, control, intentional, state/event, reportable, introspective, subjective, and self-consciousnesses. Introspective consciousness is speculated to be a "special case" of intentional consciousness and is proposed to explain state/event consciousness (p. 4).

Table 1. Tripart primitives of Sood's Platonic-Freudian model of mind[14]

Structures and Processes	Freudian topography		
Platonic triad (including *Mv* instead of *B*)	*CsASe*: Conscious affective state (e.g., palpable moods; feelings "of the moment")	*CsMvSe*: Conscious motivational state (e.g., realizing to reach a goal state or overcome a given situation)	*CsCT*: Conscious cognitive trait (e.g.: *woke*[a] *Openness*)
	CsAT: Conscious affective trait (e.g., woke *Neuroticism*)	*CsMvT*: Conscious motivational trait (e.g., woke *Conscientiousness*)	*CsCSe*: Conscious cognitive state (e.g.: being pensive; being momentarily lost or absorbed in thought, i.e. introspective, reflective, ruminative, imaginative, cogitative; daydreaming)
	SbCsCSe: Subconscious cognitive state (e.g., REM-dreaming)	*SbCsASe*: Subconscious affective state (half-awareness of mood, fleeting feelings or emotionality)	*SbCsMvSe*: Subconscious motivational state
	SbCsCT: Subconscious cognitive trait (e.g., Jungian/Myersian "iNtuitive" type)	*SbCsAT*: Subconscious affective trait (half-awareness of *Neuroticism* or *Extraversion – Enthusiasm*)	*SbCsMvT*: Subconscious motivational trait
	UCsMvSe: Unconscious motivational state	*UCsASe*: Unconscious affective state (e.g., subject undergoing intuitive processing)	*UCsCSe*: Unconscious cognitive state (e.g., subject undergoing intuitive processing)
	UCsMvT: Unconscious motivational trait (e.g., *Conscientiousness – Industriousness*)	*UCsAT*: Unconscious affective trait	*UCsCT*: Unconscious cognitive trait (e.g., *Openness – Intellect* or *Imagination*)

(continued)

[14] References to constructs of the five-factor model of personality (a.k.a. the "Big Five") are derived from [38].

Table 1. (*continued*)

Structures and Processes	Freudian topography		
	CsAPc: Conscious affective process (e.g., processing of emotions during appropriate psychotherapeutic intervention)	*CsMvPc*: Conscious motivational process (setting one's mind to accomplish a goal or complete a task)	*CsCP*: Conscious cognitive process (woke thought)
	SbCsCPc: Subconscious cognitive process	*SbCsAPc*: Subconscious affective process	*SbCsMvPc*: Subconscious motivational process
	UCsMvPc: Unconscious motivational process	*UCsAPc*: Unconscious affective process (e.g., System 1 intuition)	*UCsCPc*: Unconscious cognitive process (e.g., System 1 intuition)

[a]Woke was defined formally in [11] as meaning "subjectively self-aware". This could be expanded into "a trate of being subjectively self- or other-aware: often, but not necessarily, as such awareness is of perceived social injustice".

of slower, more deliberative, logical, and conscious cognition. A triple-process theory of love, in which such a dual-process one consists of System 1 romantic love and System 2 care, would be a novel and valuable contribution to the cognitive psychology of love.[15] Such a theory would build upon theories positing that romantic love consists of joy, interest, and sexual arousal [57], while love itself consists of passion, commitment, and intimacy [58].[16]

Motivation has been defined differently by theorists. The basic question for the science of motivation is why beings (viz.: humans, animals, and/or robots; possibly aliens) do what they do. Anthropological theories of motivation abound. In psychology, prominent such theories are ones of drive-reduction, evolutionary, and optimal arousal. A parsimonious, complete theory of motivation would minimally need to answer the questions of why such beings want to, should, need to, and do carry out their behaviors.

Maslow developed the hierarchy of needs. His theory posits that humans successively fulfill needs of varying classes [27]. He believed that motivations could be meaningfully separated into groups based on two criteria: 1) which of them must be acted upon

---

[15] Further, speaking of the "head" and "heart" in metaphorical terms could lead to the quantification of just how "ahead" (i.e., mature) cognition or affect might be in relation to the other (assuming the metaphor holds literally).

[16] A Platonic theory of love can also be added. In such a model, love can be conceptualized as being affective (consisting of emotions like joy), cognitive (containing fond thoughts of the object of love), or conative (demanding action on the part of the lover to better the state of the loved object).

first in order for a person to survive, and 2) which are necessary to act upon to reach self-actualization. Maslow and Horney considered self-actualization respectively as a syndrome and trait of neurotic personalities, reflecting the state of psychological theory during the early/mid-20th century as psychoanalytic and clinical more so than positive: i.e., being more interested in human growth and potential, flourishing, and well-being.

In decreasing order of their relative degrees of necessary fulfillment, Maslow's motivations were physiological, safety, love, esteem—"D-needs", i.e. deficiency needs or survival needs—and self-actualization needs, i.e. "B-needs" or being needs (perhaps more accurately re-termed "B-wants"). Still, the question of how motivations such as these interact—both with one another and with other factors (cognitive, affective, behavioral)—has not yet been answered. For Maslow, motivation was almost always necessary for behavior; additionally, he believed that more than one motivation typically figures into a single behavior ([27], p. 370). The Maslowian science of motivation must work first from behavior to motivation, and possibly afterward, from motivation to other, equally-fundamental psychological phenomena (viz., affect and cognition).

Maslow [27] stated that "any conscious desires (partial goals) are more or less important as they are more or less close to the basic needs [of Maslow's hierarchy]" (p. 384). Since Maslow recognized some fundamental connection between desires and goals, it follows from an earlier statement he made—that "conscious, specific, local-cultural desires are not as fundamental in motivation theory as the more basic, unconscious goals" (p. 370)—then unconscious wants will always be closer to basic human needs than will conscious ones.

The theory that unconsciousness is more influential motivationally than consciousness goes back to at least Freud; this theory may be more amenable to a truly scientific analysis today. There remain the scientific questions associated with motivation's operationalization. Two such questions may be posed. First: How do we identify distinct motivations as such—both in terms of their relatively more autonomous properties, and their interactions in a person or persons' overall motivational system(s)? It may be easiest to start with the more basic but core concept of motive. Different motives for behavior exist: people do things to reduce drives, adapt, or achieve optimal arousal. These may be taken to be the human's most fundamental motivations after the fulfillment of D-needs. Motive illustrates the utility of hermeneutic methods applied in psychology, viz. within phenomenology. Conscious motives can be interpreted on at least three levels: first-, second-, and third-person [47–49].

First-, second- and third-person approaches in cognitive science have been applied only to consciousness. It remains to be elucidated theoretically whether a "zeroth-person" approach could be suited to the study of unconsciousness. A zeroth-person approach would precede the possibility of the first-person one, thus being appropriate for the study of preconscious trates. The zeroth-person would be the Homo sapiens' most recent ancestor who lacked consciousness enabled by a central nervous system (CNS). Similarly, one could also speak of a "half-person" approach to the study of subconsciousness, possibly referring to half the normal degree of human consciousness. Typing in this manner also allows for the possibility of consciousness containing an indeterminate number of possible degrees, i.e., a trigonometry of visual consciousness.

The first-person perspective interrogates or defines motives to oneself: i.e., I did X because X or Y. (One may be motivated by means or ends.) The first-person analysis of motive is thus personal and (at least ontologically) subjective. The second-person level involves how others frame our motives: "He or she did X because X or Y". This perspective is interpersonal and (at least ontologically) intersubjective. (Ontological intersubjectivity follows from Searle's treatment [52] considered alongside Wilber's metaphysical ontology [53].) Finally, third-person perspectives are more likely to appeal to physical, chemical, or biological (ontologically objective) motives. In this case, drive-reduction and optimal arousal theories may be favored more readily. Such a perspectival analysis complicates the fact already acknowledged that motivation may be unconscious, subconscious, conscious, negative-subconscious, or negative-conscious. For example, one agent may be unconsciously motivated at the first-person level, while another agent might be conscious of the former's motivation at the second- or third-person level(s).

A second question for motivational science is: How do motivations interact with other psychological phenomena like cognitions and affects? Motivation may be felt in response to a desire. For example, if one desires a long-term mate, one could become motivated to seek out and become involved with a promising candidate. One may then plan how to go about getting to know said candidate sufficiently to evaluate long-term mating potential. Considered in this way, the search for a long-term romantic partner includes affective, motivational, and cognitive factors and processes that follow from one another (possibly, in this order).[17]

Kelly [18] considered laziness, appetite, and affection as motivational concepts. Kelly understood motivations as being parts of greater systems of construction evidenced by individuals (e.g., through dialogue). Considered this way, motives can be thought to play out within proximity to beliefs. However, "appetite" is closer to one of Maslow's basic needs and is also something of a raw instinctual property characterizing a living being's consumptive capacity with respect to a suitable object Y (e.g., food). Kelly also provided a more historical framing of motivation in terms of the synonymous triads of "cognition, conation, and affection", "intellect, will, and emotion", and (in more modern terms) "thought, action, and feeling" (pp. 68–9).[18] Motivation, then—to the extent that it is will manifest in one's action—may be determined as such in reverse fashion from behaviors. However, Maslow [19] asserted that "Motivation theory is not synonymous with behavior theory… While behavior is almost always motivated, it is almost always biologically, culturally, and situationally determined as well" (p. 371).

Maslow's hierarchical view of motivation has been contrasted with Kelly's more dynamic one [11]. For Kelly, a more socially-enactive, cognitive path would render

---

[17] Related to the topic of long-term romantic partnership is the more general role of affect in interpersonal relations. One relevant question is: Can we behave to determine—rather than merely influence—a given being's affective trate? If so, the door is opened to affective governance in everyday contexts. Such social engineering in the form of institutionalism would seek to negate the neoliberal view of the autonomous subject, where individuals are solely self-responsible [56].

[18] In [63], it is noted that affection, cognition, and conation correspond respectively with pathos, logos, and ethos. It may be considered whether the respective groupings, when included equally by a given mind or persuasion and transcended, yield a super-mind or super-persuasion.

motivation a clearer construct for psychological scientists (including personality psychologists) to operationalize. Regarding the possibility of unmotivated behavior, Maslow stated that "expressive behavior is either unmotivated or...less motivated than coping behavior" ([28], p. 138). Expressive behavior is unconscious (UCsB) while coping behavior is conscious (CsB).

2.3 The *S* Equation

The psychological situation concept has been lamented by Rauthmann et al. [23] as being used often "haphazardly, ambiguously, [and] inconsistently" in the literature (p. 363). To ameliorate this, these authors proposed "three different basic kinds of situational information: cues (composition information), characteristics (psychological meaning information) and classes (category information)" (p. 363). Cues represent "physically present, scalable and (relatively) objectively quantifiable stimuli" (p. 364). Characteristics capture the *"psychologically important meanings* of perceived cues, thus summarizing a situation's psychological 'power'" (p. 364). Finally, classes represent "abstract groups, or types, of situations" (p. 364).

The formalization of Rauthmann et al.'s situation framework was undertaken in [11]

$$S = F[Cu, Ch, Ce] \tag{8}$$

Where *S* equals "situation", *Ce* equals "class", *Ch* equals "characteristic", and *Cu* equals "cue". Given (3), (4), and (8) and the transitive property, (9) resulted

$$[P, S] = [F[Sl, Ot], F[Cu, Ch, Ce]] \tag{9}$$

By (9), person-situation interaction was extended as a function of the interaction between selves and others with cues, characteristics, and classes.

The following equation fused (2)–(8), above

$$[F[Sl, Ot], F[Cu, Ch, Ce]] = F[St_{(T,Se)}, Pc]_{[(A,C,Mv,B)_{(U-,Sb-)Cs}]} \tag{10}$$

(10) read: *Person-situation interaction as a function of self and other–cue, characteristic, and class interaction is a function of unconscious, subconscious, and conscious affective, cognitive, motivational, and behavioral traits, states, and processes.* It is a meta-psychological statement incorporating the major psychological constructs considered here and in previous work. The system of functions formulated in Eqs. 1–10 is recursive in being self-referential: each function is definable in terms of itself.[19]

As an example of recursion in HCI, Eqs. 1–10 also point to the inherent reflexivity of HCI work (e.g., programming) and research (e.g., browsing). HCI is inherently reflexive to the extent that the humans involved work on or with computers, thus instantiating human-computer interaction while operating in to said field. HCI in general may be said to be recursive if and only if (iff) its work refers explicitly to the reflexive loop just mentioned.

---

[19] In the spirit of (4) and its description in this chapter, it is encouraged that future studies consider an "other-referential" counterpart to the concept of recursion. In an other-referential formal system, functions or other mathematical objects would be definable as other terms occurring within a given universe of discourse. In terms of mathematical equations, such reverse-recursion ("cursion") could simply refer to one value on a side of an equation equaling values on the other.

3 Semantic Averaging and Enumeration: Novel Concepts and Constructs

The motivation for proposing novel concepts and constructs is important for any psychological science to clarify. Kukla [51] describes the process of conceptual innovation in psychology. At times, it may prove necessary for the augmented cognition researcher to assess the value of existing concepts and constructs in terms of their utility or semantics (as well as their historical relevance). Certain constructs may have fit better in a previous iteration of science with respect to their "discursive roles", i.e., how they were taken up in dialogue.

An example of a psychological concept that arguably never evolved into a construct is Plato's notion of conation. Whereas by it, Plato referred to something exactly between the modern-day understandings of motivation and behavior, there is no well-established science of conation itself. Given the respective states of our psychological sciences of motivation and behavior, as well as the potential value of understanding these two phenomena together, a science of conation's value would unite two fundamental psychological phenomena through a common construct.

The above may apply in the case of constructs like foresight [15] and memory, both of which are studied in modern psychology. Following from the enumeration of several novel terms for the psychologies of self and other [11], otherish is proposed as a counterpart to selfish (for philosophical psychology, in particular [16]). Whereas being selfish can be defined as being excessively self-interested, to be otherish would be to act excessively other-interested. This may be applied to understanding scenarios like the prisoner's dilemma [17] in which agents should act to balance self- and other-interest. Superconcepts containing two or more subconcepts [61] are also considered.

3.1 Semantic Averaging: "Foremory" and "Memsight"

Based on a shared neuropsychological basis [15], one may wish to understand memory and foresight in terms of a common unit. In such a case, one may apply a "semantic averaging" method to both constructs in the interest of generating one or two novel constructs. A pseudo-mathematical approach may be as follows

$$\left[\frac{Foresight + Memory}{2} \right] = \{Foremory, Memsight\} \tag{11a}$$

Like the research summarized in Sect. 2, foresight and memory may be assigned variables[20]. Foresight can be denoted by Fs and Memory by Mo

$$\left[\frac{Fs + Mo}{2} \right] = \{Foremory, Memsight\} \tag{11b}$$

---

[20] The neologism of psychological portmanteaus like foremory and memsight can be traced historically to [59] with the coinage of "idiothetic". As a portmanteau of *idiographic* and *nomothetic*, the idiothetic approach to personality seeks a middle ground between qualitative case study and quantitative population analysis.

If there is sufficient utility in using either foremory or memsight to denote the hybrid memory-foresight phenomenon, researchers may choose either. It is recommended that only one be committed to ensure that studies of it proceed using a shared term. Foremory or memsight can be used, or else semantic averaging can be applied to these two terms as in the following subsection.

3.2 Foremory and Memsight: "Momeiohr"

Memsight and foremory theoretically both refer to the hybrid memory-foresight or foresight-memory construct. Which is used may depend on the subjective position of a researcher as being interested in either of memory or foresight more than the other. If memory is preferred, memsight may be decided on; and if foresight is preferred, foremory may be chosen.

If memory and foresight are valued equally in a study of their joint construct, one may apply sematic averaging to memsight and foremory as follows

$$\left[\frac{Memsight + foremory}{2} \right] = Momeiohr \tag{12}$$

Momeiohr (pronounced *moe-may-oar*) was generated by selecting the first letter of memsight, the second one of foremory, the third one of memsight, the fourth of foremory, and so on until the final letter being borrowed from foremory. Privilege was given to the first letter of momeiohr being *m* given its status as the first letter of memory, which preceded foresight as used here in psychological theorizing.

3.3 Trate-(In(ter))Dependent Momeiohr

From state-dependent memory (the phenomenon of greater recall occurring in situations similar to when information was absorbed) as well as Stephen Covey's lifespan developmental philosophy of increasing interdependence from previous independence and dependence [13], several novel concepts can be derived. These include:

- Trait-independent memory (T-IdM)
- State-independent memory (S-IdM)
- Trait-dependent memory (T-DM)
- State-dependent memory (S-DM)
- Trait-interdependent memory (T-ItdM)
- State-interdependent memory (S-ItDM)
- Trait-independent foresight (T-IdF)
- State-independent foresight (S-IdF)
- Trait-dependent foresight (T-DF)
- State-dependent foresight (S-DF)
- Trait-interdependent foresight (T-ItdM)
- State-interdependent foresight (S-ItdF)

Lifespan considerations are relevant here. For example: for 1st-world citizens, does the average person start dependent (ideally, ages 0–33), then become more independent (33–66), and finally interdependent (66–100)?

3.4 "Associative Identity Superorder" and "Innate Helpfulness"

Superconcepts consist of two or more subconcepts. A novel example would be the superconcept of an "inner child-adult self", which may be operationalized as a loop (thus rendering it a construct). This superconcept combines the subconcepts of inner child and adult self, which have been discussed in relation to one another in the context of abandonment grief [62].

"Associative identity superorder" can be derived from dissociative identity disorder (DID). *Associative identity superorder* (AIS) can be defined as having the parts of one's identity reinforce one another in a way that boosts one's well-being. "Innate helpfulness" can be derived from learned helplessness [71]. If learned helplessness is the acquired reaction to a hopelessly harmful situation, *innate helpfulness* could be the unlearned response to hopefully beneficial persons.

Festinger's cognitive dissonance, rather than referring to a logically inconsistent set of 2+ cognitive propositions, is technically cognitive-behavioral dissonance [7]. According to [7]: "[Dissonance], that is, the existence of non fitting relations among cognitions, is a motivating factor in its own right. By the term *cognition*...[Festinger meant] any knowledge, opinion, or belief about the environment, about oneself, or about one's behavior. Cognitive dissonance can be seen as an antecedent condition which leads to activity oriented toward dissonance reduction just as hunger leads to activity oriented toward hunger reduction" (p. 3). Behavioral, motivational, and affective dissonances follow from cognitive dissonance. *Behavioral dissonance* consists of conflicting behaviors: e.g., "hot-and-cold" relationship[21] styles. *Motivational dissonance* consists of ambivalence in the form of "I want to/should/must" vs. "I do not want to/should not/must not", e.g. when faced with a possible task. *Affective dissonance* can take the most basic form of "I like it" vs. "I dislike it", pertaining to ambivalence regarding one's feelings (possibly toward one's intimates [68]).

Naturally, positive variants of the above concepts can also be proposed. *Affective consonance*, i.e. agreement between affects, consists in either total liking or total disliking. *Behavioral consonance* can be defined simply as being in flow, totally immersed in an activity [6]. *Motivational consonance* may consist of total (un)wanting. Finally, *cognitive consonance* consists of logical consistency within one's mind.

3.5 Type {A, B, ... Z} Personalities and Ideal Persons

Type A and B personality types exist in both the literature [39] and common parlance. Type A individuals are defined as overtly aggressive; Type B individuals are behaviorally passive. The Type A-B hybrid personality may be considered optimal, ideal, and balanced. Neurotic Type C and D personalities have also been posed [69]. Theoretically, one could speak of personality types E-Z, though all such types would need to be defined in terms of their proneness to cardiac disease as the original Type A and B were.

---

[21] Also of relevance to relationships vis-à-vis augmented cognition is the former's increasing technological mediation. Such mediation takes the forms of text, voice, and video chats, messaging, and meetings. A typology may be sketched out where long-distance relationships are assumed to be the most technologically mediated, necessarily relying on the aforementioned communication channels.

One may speak of ideal psychological persons in terms of ruling style, communication style, and personality. The ideal ruler from a psychological view is authoritative in the first place. Any given ideal person, particularly from the vantage point of American psychology, is assertive rather than passive or aggressive. The ideal personality from the perspective of the five factor model may be interpreted as being Open, Conscientious, Extraverted, Agreeable, and Emotionally Stable, possibly scoring in the middle of these scales.

4 Psychological Laws ("Psycho-*Law*-Gy")

A successful science generates laws governing the phenomena of interest. To date, psychology has not successfully done such. An example of a psychological law is as follows: Personality types, as in the popular Myers-Briggs Type Indicator (MBTI), are characterized by the more frequent presence of certain personality traits. Such statements can prevent conflations of personality constructs from differing models (e.g., MBTI vs. five factor model or "Big Five").

Below is an attempt to established psychological axioms inspired by the formal mathematical approach summarized in Sect. 2. Such an attempt is intended to build upon the kind of psychological law (what can henceforth be referred to as "psycholawgy") attempted in the preceding paragraph.

1. *Persons interact with situations.* This is taken for granted in the study of person-situation interaction.
2. *Person-situation interaction consists of mental and behavioral structures ("trates", i.e. state-trait hybrids or fusions) and processes.*
3. *Mental trates are affective, cognitive, and conative.* Conation can refer to behavioral motivation or motivated behavior. It is a preexisting hybrid concept uniting modern psychology's constructs of behavior and motivation. Motivated behavior is not *expressive.* Expressive behavior is not engaged in to cope with reality. Rather, it is done for its own sake: expressive behavior is self-justified.
4. *Behavior is affectively and cognitively motivated.* This is reflected in the formalism $B = F[Mv_{A,C}]$, i.e., behavior is a function of cogfective (affective-cognitive) motivation.

The principal questions for conative (motivational-behavioral) philosophy to ask, and for conative science to answer, are: 1) Why do beings do what they do? And 2) How do they do such? 1 must be answered in terms of psychological beings' guiding motives. 2 would be answered in terms of behavioral mechanisms, i.e., stimulus-response (Sm-Rp) interaction and reinforcement-punishment dynamics. Behavioral reinforcement strengthens the frequency or intensity of a given set of action(s), while such punishment weakens either or both.

The "triple-process theory" follows from [8], which expanded the dual-process theory of cognition [9, 10] consisting of the intuitive System 1 and analytical System 2. Per [11]'s neologized construct cogfect (see 4 in this section), and the fact intuition is treated as both cognitive and affective (hence its being "cogfective"), triple-process theory is transitorily cogfective. There is good reason to reject cognitive psychology's claim to affect, particularly if Hume's [12] adage that "reason is…the slave of the passions" holds interpersonally (or epistemic- intersubjectively—i.e., irrationally and ineffably). However, System 3 decision-making combining intuitive affect[22] and analytical cognition is also conative in its motivational underpinning and behavioral output. Such decision-making involves determining a desired, existential (mid- to long-term) goal state.[23]

4.1 Quantification of Psychological Units

The formulation of psychological laws can benefit from the quantification of psychological variables or constants. In the case of Eq. (6), cognition C, affect A, and motivation Mv were included as sub-domains of mind M. Along with behavior B, the quantification of these four factors is straightforward. Once they are identified as such, one may count cognitions, affects, motivations, behaviors, and minds. Cognition is reducible to thought: thus, once one has counted discrete thoughts, the quantification of cognition can be undertaken. Thoughts may be considered as either "complete" or "incomplete". Complete thoughts, i.e. complete cognitions, consist of verbal thoughts taking the form of complete grammatical sentences. A complete cognition in the English language may be: *I am hungry for a burrito*. In contrast, an incomplete cognition in English may be: *want burrito*. Incomplete cognitions may in fact be viewed as more affective: they may express a desire of the subject, possibly of a stronger nature given their incompleteness. If this view is adopted, affects can be quantified as incomplete cognitions, though the question of whether compete versus incomplete affects exist may arise.

Behaviors are easy to quantify so long as it is agreed what constitutes a discrete one. A discrete behavior may be as general as "standing". One may count the instances of standing that occur across a given set of subjects within a time range and count these as one kind of behavior. Behavior may be quantified in terms of its types, or more generally based on the number of times a subject is observed to respond to a stimulus. Here as before, responses Rp and stimuli Sm may be quantified by themselves, but as the parameters governing behavior. Defined in these terms, a behavior is governed by a distinctly-bonded pair between stimulus and response.

5   Discussion

One obvious limitation of the semantic averaging method proposed is that it is not always necessary. If at least one term exists denoting a novel phenomenon for a given (culturally-situated) observer, then of course it should simply be used. The process of searching for existing terms should first extend to other languages. If and only if a term exists neither in one's own nor other languages should semantic averaging be undertaken. This satisfies Occam's razor, where explanatory simplicity trumps superfluous complexity in

---

[22] See [41] for a discussion of intuitive cognition.

[23] Related to dual-process cogfective decision-making is the growing belief that System 1 affect is best understood in terms of "embodied, embedded" mental science [44]. Augmented psychology must test whether decision-making is augmented overall by the respective enactments of distinct types of embodiment (i.e., human vs. computer).

scientific theorizing. It is more conscientious to mix two distinct ethnic languages before attempting to invent an entirely new term.[24]

Semantic averaging is also not the only method used to generate concepts. This is observed in the following generation and definition: *conat* (n.) – a volitional network; see cognit [64], which implies the redefinition of affect as a cardiac network. Conat follows from the existence of cognit and its derivation from cognition: conat has been similarly derived from conation.

Another consideration is defining which phenomena hybrid constructs might refer to. In the case of momeiohr, what—if anything—is it for both the past and future to exist simultaneously in a given mind? Two possibilities exist here. One is that any of cognition, affect, motivation, and behavior have intentionality in Brentano's sense (i.e., "aboutness" or pertinence). Said intentionality might be shared between two or more of these four facets of mind. Cognition's intentionality might pertain to the future, while affect's might pertain to the past: this could represent an example of cognitive-affective dissonance [46] and (in at least one sense) momeiohr. Another potential sense of momeiohr is thinking or feeling about, being motivated by, or acting in relation to the present, which exists temporally between the past (which memory focuses on) and future (the domain of foresight). In evaluating what a hybrid phenomenon like momeiohr is like, intentionality among the four factors of mind discussed can be considered in terms of dissonance or consonance between one another.

Related to the preceding sub-discussion is parsimony. Irrespective of novel concept generation, any of affect, cognition, motivation, or behavior can have shared or distinct intentionality within operation of the original, unitary construct (memory in momeiohr's case) or concept (foresight). One may think X about the future but feel Y about it. Both thinking and feeling X about the past or future, if possible, could be spoken of as an example of cogfect, a phenomenon whose existence has been postulated in past work [11].

It is reasonable to doubt the necessity of momeiohr. While a theorist might find either memsight or foremory adequate, momeiohr defined as psychological intentionality of the present might seem overly similar to mindfulness. Mindfulness is an established construct in psychology [67] that is often defined as awareness of the present. Mindfulness is distinct from momeiohr in that the latter necessarily regards the present (being derived explicitly from the temporal constructs memory and foresight). Mindfulness is not necessarily of the present: one can also be mindful of the past or the future (and perhaps of both, though this is kept open).[25]

Phenomena like cogfect and momeiohr must be treated as speculative at this stage of psychological science. Evaluation of whether these concepts have internal or external validity is a project that might be best initiated in an introspective, intersubjective,

---

[24] In the case of blending memory and foresight, my study was confined to Western (Euro-American) psychology. No competing constructs to memory nor such concepts to foresight were found, though my study did not consider whether a term for momeiohr exists in any non-English language.

[25] Related is the common notion of intention as one's aim to carry out a task for X purpose. Intentions of this kind are usually framed as conscious, but they can be unconscious or subconscious (and possibly superconscious) as well.

and phenomenological manner. If two people believe strongly enough that they have experienced cogfect or momeiohr, then the more concrete defining of these phenomena could commence. Going even further, if two psycho-philosophers could communicate sincerely and truthfully that they have both, at any given point(s) of time t, experienced conation as motivated behavior or behavioral motivation (the former should be easy to agree on at this folk level), then they can move on to the more challenging notions of cogfect[26] and momeiohr. In any case, it is advised that theorists interested in concept generation reflect critically before proposing novel concepts, for they can be erroneously termed or defined. An example of such a concept is confirmation neutrality [11], which was defined as seeking evidence to support only one's true beliefs. Defined this way, confirmation neutrality is really just a positive form of confirmation bias: it must be clarified as such, or the definition offered for the former concept should be revised as seeking evidence to support none of one's beliefs.

Proposed psychological laws 1–4 have not been derived empirically. Scientific laws must apply to general cases of phenomena. The four laws proposed in Sect. 4 have been intended as *a priori* axioms more appropriately considered as formal laws. Nonetheless, psycholawgy can (and, at this stage, should) be regarded as formal science at the nexus between analytic philosophy and theoretical psychology.

6 Conclusion

"Indivectivism" is an additional concept that is derivable from collectivism and individualism, two mainstay concepts in cultural psychology. Cognition can be augmented through a hybrid holistic-analytic (East-West) cognitive style situated within indivectivism. Inspiration for this concept arose from consideration of the characteristics of self-actualization as proposed by Maslow, particularly *resolution of certain dichotomies* and *transcendence of one's culture*. Terms introduced throughout this chapter have potential to not only contribute to augmented cognition, but may assist in the augmentations of consciousness, experience, culture [72], subjectivity, mind, and body as well.

Related to Sect. 4's proposal of a psycholawgy is a possible law that draws inspiration from physics' conservation of energy. Such a psychological law would be the "conservation of affect", stating that *affect can be neither created nor destroyed*. An example of this law in action is the fact that feelings often change: whether they can disappear forever or not would be an important hypothesis to test in assessing the speculated law. Much as matter is also conserved as well as energy, if the conservation of affect is found to hold, perhaps it could also apply for cognition or conation.

Continuing with physics: are entropy and gravity opponent forces? Gravitation binds low-mass objects to high-mass ones. Entropy is the scattering of matter and its conversion from such to energy. Gravity consists of gravitons; dark matter is speculated to make up entropy. If eventually discovered empirically, dark matter particles should be referred

---

[26] In [11], intuition was defined as a term that is referred to in its psychological literature as affect and cognition in different places. It seems both more faithful and parsimonious to treat intuition less as cogfective (which was a compromise attempted in [11] given the divergence of how to conceive of intuition), and more as simply affective. If this is done, no concrete phenomenon will have yet been identified as being definitionally cogfective.

to as "entropons". This speculative discussion venturing into theoretical physics and cosmology follows from the proposal of *wholicle* as a novel concept for holarchic theory (which, via holarchic-informatic psychology, is related to human-computer interaction).

References

1. Wilber, K.: The Spectrum of Consciousness
2. Csikszentmihalyi, M.: Flow: The Psychology of Optimal Experience. HarperCollins ebooks
3. Seligman, M.: Authentic Happiness: Using the New Positive Psychology to Realize Your Potential for Lasting Fulfillment [Kindle DX Version]. Simon & Schuster, New York (2002)
4. Sood, S.: The psychoinformatic complexity of humanness and person-situation interaction. In: Arai, K., Bhatia, R. (eds.) FICC 2019. LNNS, vol. 69, pp. 496–504. Springer, Cham (2020). https://doi.org/10.1007/978-3-030-12388-8_35
5. Sood, S., Lee, C., Hovhannisyan, G., Lee, S., Rozier, G., Hadgis, A., Sproul, K., Higgins, T., Henson, A., Shrider, M., Hancock, M.: Holarchic psychoinformatics: a mathematical ontology for general and psychological realities. In: Schmorrow, D.D., Fidopiastis, C.M. (eds.) HCII 2019. LNCS (LNAI), vol. 11580, pp. 345–355. Springer, Cham (2019). https://doi.org/10.1007/978-3-030-22419-6_24
6. Hovhannisyan, G., Henson, A., Sood, S.: Enacting virtual reality: the philosophy and cognitive science of optimal virtual experience. In: Schmorrow, D.D., Fidopiastis, C.M. (eds.) HCII 2019. LNCS (LNAI), vol. 11580, pp. 225–255. Springer, Cham (2019). https://doi.org/10.1007/978-3-030-22419-6_17
7. Festinger, L.: A Theory of Cognitive Dissonance. Stanford University Press, Stanford (1957)
8. Dijksterhuis, A., Strick, M.: A case for thinking without consciousness. Per. Psychol. Sci. 11(1), 117–132 (2015). https://www.researchgate.net/publication/292188707_A_Case_for_Thinking_Without_Consciousness. Accessed 19 Feb 2020
9. Gore, J., Sadler-Smith, E.: Unpacking intuition: a process and outcome framework. Rev. Gen. Psychol. 15(4), 304–316 (2011)
10. Kahneman, D.: Thinking, Fast and Slow [Kindle DX version]. Farrar, Straus and Giroux (2011)
11. Sood, S.: The platonic-Freudian model of mind: defining "Self" and "Other" as psychoinformatic primitives. In: Schmorrow, D.D., Fidopiastis, C.M. (eds.) HCII 2020. LNCS (LNAI), vol. 12196, pp. 76–93. Springer, Cham (2020). https://doi.org/10.1007/978-3-030-50353-6_6
12. Hume, D.: A Treatise of Human Nature. https://www.pitt.edu/~mthompso/readings/hume.infuencing.pdf. Accessed 1 July 2020
13. Covey, S.: Moving from independence to interdependence. https://goskybound.com/independence-to-interdependence/. Accessed 1 July 2020
14. Gerlenter, D.: The Tides of Mind: Uncovering the Spectrum of Consciousness. Liveright, New York (2016)
15. Suddendorf, T.: Episodic memory versus episodic foresight: similarities and differences. WIREs Cogn. Sci. 1, 99–107 (2010)
16. Zahavi, D.: Self and Other: Exploring Subjectivity, Empathy, and Shame. Oxford University Press, Oxford (2014)
17. Neumann, S., Sood, S., Hollander, M., Wan, F., Ahmed, A., Hancock, M.: Using bots in strategizing group compositions to improve decision-making processes. In: Schmorrow, D., Fidopiastis, C. (eds.) Augmented Cognition 2018. LNCS, vol. 10916, pp. 305–325. Springer, Cham (2018)
18. Kelly, G.: Clinical Psychology and Personality: The Selected Papers of George Kelly. Wiley, New York (1969)

19. Revelle, W.: Integrating personality, cognition, and emotion: Putting the dots together? (2011). https://www.personality-project.org/revelle/publications/BPSP-revelle.pdf. Accessed 9 Jan 2019

20. Nagel, T.: What is it like to be a bat? Philos. Rev. **83**(4), 435–450 (1974)

21. Horley, J.: The units of analysis problem in psychology: an examination and proposed reconciliation. In: Baker, W.J., Mos, L.P., Rappard, H.V., Stam, H.J. (eds.) Recent Trends in Theoretical Psychology. Recent Research in Psychology, pp. 177–187. Springer, New York (1989). https://doi.org/10.1007/978-1-4612-3902-4_18

22. Lewin, K.: Field theory and experiment in social psychology: concept and methods. Am. J. Soc. **44**, 868–896 (1939)

23. Rauthmann, J., Sherman, R., Funder, D.: Principles of situation research: towards a better understanding of psychological situations. Eur. J. Pers. **29**, 363–381 (2015)

24. Bandura, A., Huston, A.C.: Identification as a process of incidental learning. J. Abnorm. Soc. Psych. **63**(2), 311–318 (1961)

25. Plato: The Republic, 2nd edn. Penguin Books, London (2007). (Original Work Published in ~375 B.C.)

26. Kahneman, D.: Thinking, Fast and Slow. Farrar, Straus and Giroux [Kindle DX version] (2011)

27. Maslow, A.H.: A theory of human motivation. Psychol. Rev. **50**, 370–396 (1943)

28. Maslow, A.H.: Toward a Psychology of Being, 1st edn. Wilder Publications, Blacksburg (2011). (Original Work Published in 1962)

29. Skinner, B.F.: Generic nature of the concepts of stimulus and response. J. Gen. Psychol. **12**, 1240–1265 (1935)

30. Solipsism and the Problem of Other Minds. https://www.iep.utm.edu/solipsis/. Accessed 12 Nov 2019

31. Klein, S.: The self and science: is it time for a new approach to the study of human experience? Curr. Dir. Psychol. Sci. **21**(4), 253–257 (2012)

32. Dennett, D.C.: The self as a center of narrative gravity. In: Kessel, F., Cole, P., Johnson, D. (eds.) Self and Consciousness: Multiple Perspectives. Erlbaum, Hillsdale (1992)

33. Buber, M.: I and Thou (1958)

34. Gerbasi, M.E., Prentice, D.A.: The self- and other-interest inventory. J. Pers. Soc. Psychol. **105**(3), 495–514 (2013)

35. Maslow, A.H.: Religions, Values, and Peak-Experiences. Penguin Compass, New York (1976)

36. Velkley, R.: Freedom and the Human Person. Catholic University of America Press, Washington, D.C (2007)

37. Spalding, T., Stedman, J., Gagné, C. L., Kostelecky, M.: The Human Person: What Aristotle and Thomas Aquinas Offer Modern Psychology. Springer, Cham (2019). https://doi.org/10.1007/978-3-030-33912-8

38. DeYoung, C.G., Weisberg, Y.J., Quilty, L.C., Peterson, J.B.: Unifying the aspects of the Big Five, the interpersonal circumplex, and trait affiliation. J. Pers. **81**(5), 465–475 (2013)

39. Brand, R.J., Rosenman, R.H., Sholtz, R.I., Friedman, M.: Multivariate prediction of coronary heart disease in the Western collaborative group study compared to the findings of the Framingham study. https://pubmed.ncbi.nlm.nih.gov/1245042/. Accessed 6 July 2020

40. Shouse, E.: Feeling, emotion, affect. M/C J. **8**(6) (2005). http://journal.media-culture.org.au/0512/03-shouse.php. Accessed 18 Nov 2019

41. Patterson, R.E., Eggleston, R.G.: Intuitive cognition. J. Cogn. Eng. Decis. Mak. **11**(1), 5–22 (2017). https://www.deepdyve.com/lp/sage/intuitive-cognition-fdpCmqLtLc?key=sage

42. Mischel, W., Shoda, Y.: A cognitive-affective system theory of personality: reconceptualizing situations, dispositions, dynamics, and invariance in personality structure. Psychol. Rev. **102**(2), 246–268 (1995)

43. Arisaka, Y.: 'Self and other' in Japanese philosophy. In: Thompson, E. (ed.) Between Ourselves: Second-Person Issues in the Study of Consciousness. Imprint Academic, Thorverton (2001)

44. de Bellini-Leite, S.C.: The embodied embedded character of System 1 processing. https://www.ncbi.nlm.nih.gov/pmc/articles/PMC3653224/. Accessed 20 Aug 2020

45. Hazony, Y.: Domain-general operations in the mind's 'central processing system'? A test case for psycho-ontology. https://www.psychoontology.org/docs/yoram-hazony.pdf. Accessed 22 Aug 2020

46. Marshall, S.: Cognitive-affective dissonance in the classroom. https://www.tandfonline.com/doi/abs/10.1080/00922013.1980.11000222. Accessed 22 Aug 2020

47. Varela, F., Thompson, E., Rosch, E.: The Embodied Mind: Cognitive Science and Human Experience. The MIT Press, Cambridge (1991)

48. Thompson, E.: Between Ourselves: Second-Person Issues in the Study of Consciousness. Imprint Academic, Thorverton (2001)

49. Varela, F., Shear, J.: The View from Within: First-Person Approaches to the Study of Consciousness. Imprint Academic, Thorverton (1999)

50. Lycan, W.G.: Consciousness and Experience. The MIT Press, Cambridge (1996)

51. Kukla, A.: Methods of Theoretical Psychology. The MIT Press, Cambridge (2001)

52. Searle, J.: The Mystery of Consciousness. New York Review Books, New York (1997)

53. Wilber, K.: Sex, Ecology, Spirituality: The Spirit of Evolution. Shambhala Publications, Boston (2000)

54. https://en.wikipedia.org/wiki/Affective_spectrum#:~:text=The%20affective%20spectrum%20is%20a,than%20would%20normally%20be%20expected. Accessed 11 Sept 2020

55. https://en.wikipedia.org/wiki/Virtual_community_of_practice. Accessed 12 Sept 2020

56. Wrenn, M.V., Waller, W.: Care and the neoliberal individual. https://www.tandfonline.com/doi/abs/10.1080/00213624.2017.1321438?journalCode=mjei20. Accessed 13 Sept 2020

57. Cornelius, R.R.: The Science of Emotion: Research and Tradition in the Psychology of Emotions. Prentice Hall, Hoboken (1996)

58. Sternberg, R.J.: A triangular theory of love. Psychol. Rev. **93**(2), 119–135 (1986)

59. Lamiel, J.T.: Toward an idiothetic psychology of personality. Am. Psychol. **36**(3), 276–289 (1981)

60. Osbeck, L.M., Nersessian, N.J.: Epistemic identities in interdisciplinary science. Perspect. Sci. **25**(2), 226–260 (2017)

61. Huang, J., Huhns, M.N.: Superconcept formation system—An ontology matching algorithm for service discovery. https://cse.sc.edu/~huhns/confpapers/sd06-huang-v2.pdf. Accessed 7 Oct 2020

62. https://www.abandonment.net/. Accessed 7 Oct 2020

63. Scalambrino, F.: Philosophical Principles of the History and Systems of Psychology: Essential Distinctions. Springer, New York (2018). https://doi.org/10.1007/978-3-319-74733-0

64. https://www.yourdictionary.com/cognit. Accessed 8 Oct 2020

65. https://arxiv.org/ftp/arxiv/papers/1604/1604.06158.pdf. Accessed 14 Oct 2020

66. Abel, C.: The Extended Self: Architecture, Memes, and Minds. Manchester University Press, Manchester (2015)

67. Langer, E.J.: Mindfulness, 25th Anniversary edn. Da Capo Press, Boston (2014). (Original Work Published in 1989)

68. Fromm, E.: The Art of Being. Open Road, New York (2013)

69. https://www.healthyway.com/content/type-c-and-d-two-unique-often-overlooked-personality-types/. Accessed 14 Oct 2020

70. https://become-hub.com/en/#:~:text=Augmented%20Psychology%20is%20an%20innovative,last%20frontiers%20of%20neuroscientific%20research. Accessed 9 Nov 2020

71. Seligman, M.: Learned helplessness. https://www.annualreviews.org/doi/pdf/10.1146/ann urev.me.23.020172.002203. Accessed 9 Nov 2020

72. https://newprairiepress.org/oz/vol33/iss1/7/. Accessed 9 Nov 2020

73. Maki, R.H., McCaul, K.D.: The effects of self-reference versus other reference on the recall of traits and nouns. Bull. Psychon. Soc. **23**(3), 169–172 (1985). https://doi.org/10.3758/BF0 3329817

Augmented Cognition in Complex Environments

Human Characteristics and Genomic Factors as Behavioural Aspects for Cybersecurity

Laima Ambrozaitytė[1]([✉])[iD], Agnė Brilingaitė[2][iD], Linas Bukauskas[2][iD], Ingrida Domarkienė[1][iD], and Tautvydas Rančelis[1][iD]

[1] Department of Human and Medical Genetics, Institute of Biomedical Sciences, Faculty of Medicine, Vilnius University, Vilnius, Lithuania
{laima.ambrozaityte,ingrida.domarkiene,tautvydas.rancelis}@mf.vu.lt
[2] Cybersecurity Laboratory, Institute of Computer Science, Vilnius University, Vilnius, Lithuania
{agne.brilingaite,linas.bukauskas}@mif.vu.lt

Abstract. Modern behavioural genetic studies of personality investigate the genetic and environmental contribution to the development of personality and the genetic and environmental covariance with a range of characteristics, as well as stress, impulsiveness, and addiction. Cyber kill chains are used to define stages of the incident and to position an event. The risky behaviour, possible human addictions, and weaknesses are used in the evaluation, selecting the best human-to-human or human-machine-human interactions strategy. An unintentional human error can cause cybersecurity breaches, because stress, long working hours, and set of wide-range responsibilities lower caution and increase the impact of individual characteristics on the decision rationality. This work aims to hypothesise a possible holistic architecture for specific human behaviour factors involved in cybersecurity risks. A good cybersecurity habit could prevent incidents and protect against attacks. Habits are mostly initiated automatically. Therefore, they can dominate personal behavioural patterns under specific circumstances. Genetic heritability of impulsiveness is considered as moderate from 33% to 50%. Genomic data study of particular individuals can help identify one's behaviour patterns and show the risks in cybersecurity for that individual. An individual risk profile could be generated by combining known genome variants linked to a trait of particular behaviour analysing molecular pathways of Dopamin, Serotonin, Catecholaminergic, GABAergic, neurons migration, Opioid, cannabinoid system and other addiction genes. Construction of a model strategy when including genomic information results for the specification of human behavioural characteristics might benefit towards higher risk assessment in cybersecurity processes.

Keywords: Behaviour genomics · Impulsiveness · Risky behaviour · Decision-making · Impulse control · Genome variation · Cybersecurity · Cyber kill-chain

ⓒ Springer Nature Switzerland AG 2021
D. D. Schmorrow and C. M. Fidopiastis (Eds.): HCII 2021, LNAI 12776, pp. 333–350, 2021.
https://doi.org/10.1007/978-3-030-78114-9_23

1   Introduction

Advancements in various technologies have been reshaping workplaces, economic processes, and individual lives. The blurred boundaries between physical and digital worlds press to update skills and ensure efficiency when keeping humans and machines together. In everyday life, humans face digital as well as all other environments that feature uncertain and volatile and ever changing situations. Efficient adaptive behaviour must consider uncertainty and volatility [27]. Timely decisions and actions, also, careful attention could ensure stability in business and public sectors.

Modern behavioural genetic studies of personality investigate the genetic and environmental contribution to the development of personality in addition to the genetic and environmental covariance with a range of characteristics, as well stress, impulsiveness, and addiction. Many different personality traits and dimensions show moderate to large phenotypic covariance [73]. In the era of direct-to-consumer genetic testing (DTC-GT) and fast pace of genetic data generation and accumulation, it is still unclear to what extent this sensitive data can be used. While DTC-GT continues to provide people with controversial interpretation [57] of the data of unknown quality [57, 71], researchers hesitate to broaden the research. There is a need to investigate the usage of genetic factors as much as possible to know where it could add value and then make inferences and proposals.

In the context of behavioural patterns, genetics could be used as an additional aid to evaluate personal risk at the workplace and follow with personalised training. Incorporating genetic component to the person evaluation sheet, employee and employer can benefit in many ways, starting with better self-awareness to the capacity of individual abilities—norm of reaction.

Cybersecurity behaviour is an application area where a genetic component could find its purpose. An unintentional human error can cause security breaches, because stress, long working hours, and set of wide-range responsibilities lower caution and increase the impact of individual characteristics on the decision rationality. Also, adversaries can find victims among organisation insiders based on the exposed digital profile for a modern social engineering attack. Besides, sometimes in cybercrime situations it could be difficult to run a test for psychological portrayal to predict actions of the particular person. If available, genetic data could be profiled according to the traits of interest and partially do the job.

This work aims to hypothesise a possible holistic architecture to distinguish and assess specific human behaviour factors involved in cybersecurity risks. The research goal is to explore to what extent those risks could be predicted and controlled. The paper seeks to explain the link between natural human and digital-self. Specific genetic markers of the given behaviour complemented with digital information could add some value when evaluating personal risks in cybersecurity behaviour. Cyber kill-chain stages involve specific human behaviours critical for the outcome. For better cybersecurity risk prognosis, the study suggests to overthink the underlying factors. Inclusion of genetic factors would give an additional dimension in personal risk assessment. Genome is a primary source of biological signal, and variation makes it responsive to the environmental signals at different levels. Behaviour genomics should start at critical phases and operations in cyberspace/cybersecurity. Decision-making and impulse control seem to be the important consequential elements. Human decision and reaction to the impulse is a result of intricate biological networks within the organism functioning reciprocally to the environment (in a broad sense).

The paper is structured as follows. Section 2 makes the background of the research including association of cybersecurity aspect and human risk factors. Then, Sect. 3 deconstructs impulsivity from the perspective of human genome. The paper concludes with discussion in Sect. 4 that also covers future work directions.

2 Methods

2.1 Background

The European Union Agency for Network and Information Security (ENISA) emphasises that the industry should shift from technology and process-centric to a human-centric view [22]. Cybersecurity training is needed to build skills, but cybersecurity behaviour also depends on the surrounding and ability to cope with threats under certain circumstances. Ertan et al. [24] identify four behavioural sets that influence how people follow cybersecurity compliance rules. However, they also define the future research direction to consider the types of employees and organisational culture to improve security. Hadlington [35] highlighted that Internet addiction and personal feature impulsivity were significant factors to predict risky cybersecurity behaviour.

Cyber kill-chains are used to define stages of the attack from the preparation to the execution. Introduced by Lockheed Martin [39, 40], cyber kill-chain structures the incident in the most general way. More specific chains can be set up to represent an internal organisation kill-chain and person-oriented and target manipulation kill-chains. Table 1 presents the general cyber kill-chain with properties related to target manipulation and human trait-specific. It also depicts the counter kill-chain. The cyber kill-chain begins with the target's reconnaissance by looking for private data leaks and third party co-alignment on social networks. The weaponization stage is related to developing the possible attack scenario based on the data gathered during the reconnaissance. The risky behaviour, possible human addictions, and other weaknesses are used to select the best strategy for human-to-human or human-machine-human interactions. Dark traits and observable weaknesses of the person might be integrated into the cyber operation scenario. The delivery and exploitation phases have seamless borders with the possible scenario applied and executed/played against a victim. Such the phase takes place using direct relayed communication. The installation phase very much depends on the process of exploitation. It can involve repetitive actions to strengthen the attack effect or impact on the victim, reassuring with

Table 1. Cyber kill chain

Cyber Kill-chain	Properties	Counter Kill-chain
Reconnaissance	– Data leaks – Third party alignment – Social behaviour	Detect
Weaponization	– Risky behaviour – Addiction – Weaknesses – Dark traits	Deny
Delivery & Exploitation	– Impulsivity – Attention to detail	Disrupt and Degrade
Installation	– Persistent actions – Blackmail – Extortion	Deceive
Command & Control and Exfiltration	– Persistent manipulation – Blackmail – Hidden goals – Extortion	Contain

persistent actions of blackmail or extortion schemes. The command & control and exfiltration phases are the final phases. The possible target is governed and controlled to deliver the objective data. In many cases, the person is not the target, but valuable data, responsibilities, functions, and related entities are.

All the cyber kill-chain phases are related to the impulsive decision of the victim. Actions triggered consciously or unconsciously to behave on social networks and making a decision by the lack of deliberation or long term foresight lead to an inability to counter the cyber kill-chain challenges. For example, early training to detect future threats and emphasise future actions can minimise data leaks and reduce impulsive decisions that would directly disrupt reconnaissance, deny possible extraction of traits and weaknesses during weaponisation. Training to cope with impulsiveness could disrupt the victim's exploitation and degrade the impact of the incident.

Genetic factors underlying certain phenotype can be identified only when the trait is carefully defined, and criteria are clear. Behavioural patterns that might affect decision-making, impulse control or consciousness comprise a complex of impulsive behaviours (impulsiveness) which coalesce into the group of externalising behaviours. In Fig. 1, externalising problems include a bouquet of behavioural characteristics classified as psychiatric disorders, personality characteristics, or non-clinical behaviour. Impulsive behaviours usually are subdivided into three

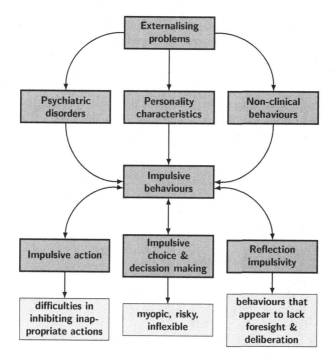

Fig. 1. Deconstructing impulsiveness

domains: impulsive action, reflection impulsivity, and impulsive choice/decision-making. An impulsive action describes difficulties in inhibiting inappropriate actions, reflection impulsivity—behaviours that appear to lack foresight and/or deliberation, and impulsive choice/decision-making—choices that favour immediate rewards over long-term rewards, involve the acceptance of undue risk or uncertainty, or are inflexible to environmental changes [2,32]. In other words, impulsive behaviour as a construct represents different behaviours that are deficiently realised, early expressed, unduly risky, and inadequate [25,61,80] such as alcohol or substance misuse, antisocial behaviours, aggression, and risk taking [48,64,82].

Genotype (e.g., genetic variants) and phenotype (e.g., certain behaviour) relation deconstruction requires understanding of the structure and functioning of the organism at all levels, starting from a single cell genome. Phenotypic diversity and capability to adapt mainly lies within the gift of variability. Genomic variation translated to the stuctural, functional, and/or regulatory variation alltogether interacting with changing environment is the matter that should be addressed first. Three neurobiological systems including the control/regulatory, reward, and threat systems, mediated by the medial and ventral prefrontal cortices, the ventral striatum and midbrain dopaminergic system, and the amygdala, respectively, provide an overlapping pathway linking brain circuitries and neurotransmitter systems associated with addiction risk and impulsivity [46]. In

Fig. 2, starting from a single gene regulation in the genome, an expression of a protein begins. Proteins are structural and functional units of the cell. They are involved in different signalling pathways, which organises into interacting networks. Everything forms an integrative reactive system reciprocally linked with environment under the all-changing ever-present variation. Four different neuromodulator circuits were shown to be responsible for a specific decision-making phenotype. Disruptions in different neuromodulator systems at all levels may give rise to different types of impulsive decision-making [32].

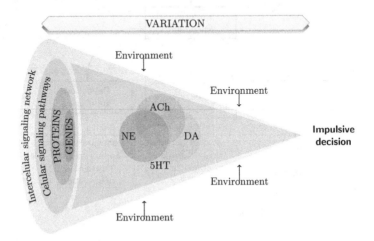

Fig. 2. The biology of impulsive decision making (DA—dopamine, ACh—acetylcholine, 5HT—serotonin, NE—norepinephrine)

2.2   Cybersecurity in a Work Role

Typically, individuals with high level work locus of control and tight relationship (strong work identity) to the workplace environment have stronger information security awareness [36].

Organisations focus on extrinsic factors, e.g. general security awareness, to ensure and stimulate security compliance behaviour via training and awareness campaigns. Yet, the dominant decision style is an intrinsic variable, thus, decision-makers can apply specific management practices [20].

But one of the factors behind human cybersecurity behaviour is time pressure. Task, user, and workplace characteristics make moderating factors how time pressure makes an impact on the behaviour, and personality traits may be considered in the design of job roles [16]. Cyber users are not super humans, they have personal traits, and more training is not always the path to follow. Modelling and simulations with personalised aspects could be proper directions to increase cybersecurity in organisations [50].

2.3 Impulsiveness Assessment Methods

Animal models are inevitable in behavioural studies. No model is ideal but still can bring useful insights. To study impulsive behaviour non-human animals are used, e.g. to study addiction a plethora of methods are used to model rodents [49]. Major understanding of neural circuits of impulsivity is rodent experiments-driven. Many studies used rat models and later were accompanied by mice models when genetically engineered animals were available [13]. There are laboratory techniques established to evaluate animal model impulsive behaviour. And vice versa, there are human impulsive behaviour assessment methods that are adapted for animal model research.

Models are divided into two main categories regarding impulsive behaviours—impulsive choice and action. In other words, impulsive behaviour is assessed either as the capability to suppress the behaviour/reaction in advance, or stop and get rid of behaviour that is already in progress [58]. For instance, this could be the tasks of Delay Discounting [53], Go/No-Go [30], Stop Signal [51], or Continuous Performance [63]. Mentioned tasks evaluate different, albeit in part possibly coinciding, behaviours that may be underlied by different neurobiological processes [58]. Understanding of that is essential starting point for further research and application. As every model has its weakness, research must look for additional methods, evaluation/analysis components or so to cover the existing gaps (to make prognosis/prediction more accurate). Genetic factor inclusion may complement behaviour evaluation model by providing state-of-the-art gene-driven human behaviour reaction norm.

2.4 Impulsiveness Genetic Analysis Methods

Complex trait (including human behaviour) genetics starts with the twin and family studies seeking to evaluate the extent of variation explained by genetic factors. In narrow sense it is determined by heritability (h^2) coefficient. Under several assumptions it is a genotypic variance versus phenotypic (trait) variance: $h^2 = \frac{Var(A)}{Var(P)}$. During past decades, studies analysing genetic factors of various traits grew significantly. Early genetic studies focused on candidate gene analysis. This approach is hypothesis driven and requires *a priori* knowledge on the putative biological pathway that is to be tested for genetic factors. Research mainly focused on genes or genetic variants in the serotonergic or dopaminergic region. However, this methodology did not escape flaws such as false positive results, underpowered studies, publication bias, hypothesis formulation errors [9,21]. That is why hypothesis free methods came to thrive. Together with technological breakthrough understanding how to properly handle genome-wide association analysis started since the 2007 precedent made by first results of The Welcome Trust Case Control Consortium [79]. Genome-wide association study (GWAS) design fits the current theory of complex trait genetics, whereby phenotypes are explained as a result of many genome variants of small effect acting together and interacting with each other as well as environment [77]. GWAS compares frequencies of genetic variants (alleles of SNPs) within the case (of given trait) and control groups. Powerful studies, achieving high p-values by testing thousands of genomic variants in a large cohorts, brings out genomic loci significantly associated with the trait under research and then can further be finely mapped. Environmental conditions can alter the importance of genetic influences on the phenotype and this brings in additional types of analysis investigating gene-environment interactions (GxE) [19]. For externalizing phenotypes including impulsiveness, methods could be divided into two different models: the social control/opportunity and the social distinction [8,66]. Overwhelming GWAS findings showed high genetic overlap between externalizing behaviour traits [2]. In other words, genetic component for several different behavioural patterns turns out to be the same [47,65,78]. It was demonstrated by calculating correlations using bivariate LD score regression [11].

Science moves forward seeking for methods that would be able to condense existing results and lift research up from the univariate analysis to multivariate. The example of such efforts could be Genomic Structural Equation Modeling [33]. A set of phenotypes from GWAS summary statistics are used to find joint genetic architecture through genetic correlations. This method also raises the power of predictive scores. There are many methods for prediction calculations, but one of the most used linear models is Polygenic Risk Score (PRS) [41]. It can be calculated summing up trait-associated alleles across many genetic loci usually weighted by effect sizes extracted from GWASs summary data. PRS can prove itself to be valuable tool for a given phenotype prognosis.

3   Results

The review of publications shows that impulsiveness is highly related with other negative behaviour such as suicides, aggression, addiction and psychiatric disorders. Impulsive behaviour could help to predict suicidal behaviour, psychopathy, drug, alcohol, internet addiction problems [76]. Such human factor as impulsive behaviour is highly related with cybersecurity problems. Impulsive behaviour can lead to information, data security breaches, ransomware attacks, increase chance to fall victim to cybercrime and negatively affect decision making. Genetic heritability of impulsiveness is considered as moderate and in various twin studies accounts from 33% to 50% [7,43,44]. Genomic data study of particular individual can help to identify ones behaviour patterns and show the risks in cybersecurity for that individual.

As previously described impulsivity is highly related with neuromodulator systems. Genes that encode proteins that are directly involved with each neurotransmitter could have high impact for impulsive behaviour as well. Dopamine is neurotransmitter that has a vital role in reward and movement regulation and is related with human behavioural characteristics such as sleep, mood, motivation, learning, impulsivity as well highly related to drugs addiction [42]. As dopamine is known to be related to impulsivity, high number of research studies are performed with genes associated with this neurotransmitter and impulsivity, as well genome-wide association studies (GWAS) that allowed to determine the relationship of genes to dopamine. A high number of research studies been done on *SLC6A3* (Solute Carrier Family 6 Member) gene that encodes a dopamine transporter and mediates the re-uptake of dopamine from the synapse. Kim and his colleagues showed that this gene is related with attention deficit hyperactivity disorder (ADHD) as well to impulsivity behaviour directly. Robertson et al. published study showed that this gene is related with Parkinson's disease and with impulsivity [62]. Cummins el at. work showed that polymorphisms (rs37020; rs460000) in this dopamine transporter gene allow to predict individual differences in stop-signal reaction time (SSRT) and have impact on impulsivity and ADHD disorder [18]. Studies that have been focused not on impulsivity showed that this gene is related with alcohol, cocaine, and internet addictions. Other genes that are related with dopamine and impulsivity are *DRD2* (Dopamine Receptor D2) gene, which encodes dopamine receptor and *ANKK1* (Ankyrin Repeat And Kinase Domain Containing 1) gene, which is highly linked to *DRD2* gene and controls the synthesis of dopamine in the brain. The rs4938012 variant in the *ANKK1* gene by Koeneke et al.was emphasised as one of the strongest associated variant to alcohol consumption variation and antisocial personality [45].

Another important neurotransmitter related with impulsivity is serotonin. Serotonin is neurotransmitter that carries signals between neurons and is related to modulation of mood, impulsivity, learning, memory. *SLC6A4* is main serotonin transporter gene and transports serotonin from synaptic spaces into presynaptic neurons. There is high number of publications of this gene and human behaviour. In one of them genome variant rs25531 showed as causing significantly higher hyperactivity and impulsivity [28]. Associated with impulsivity are serotonin genes *TPH1*, *TPH2* (Tryptophan Hydroxylase) that encode proteins related to the biosynthesis of serotonin. Landt et al. study shows that rs1473473 genome variant in *TPH2* gene is associated with impulsivity and impulsive eating habit [67]. Gene family *HTR1A*, *HTR1B*, *HTR2A*, *HTR2B*, which encodes serotonin receptors is associated with impulsivity as well. There is high number of variants related with impulsive behaviour in these genes (see Table 2), from which very important is rs17110563 genome variant causing stop mutation in *HTR2B* gene that leads to severe impulsivity [6].

Common gene related to impulsive behaviour is *COMT* (Catechol O Methyltransferase). It is important catecholaminergic system gene, which is related with major degradation pathways of the catecholamine transmitters. Good example of variant in this gene related to impulsivity is rs4680 which is mentioned in several publications [60].

Genes from GABAergic system, which are mostly related with eating habits, obesity are well descried in the Bauer et al. study, which showed that variant rs279858 in *GABRA2* gene, which encodes a gamma-aminobutyric acid (GABA) receptor, is significantly associated with impulsivity and body mass index [4].

There are a high variety of genes both related with some kind of addiction and with impulsivity, for example *MAOA*, *OPRM1*, *OPRK1*, *CHRNA4* genes (see Table 3). In this category for problems relating to cybersecurity risks it is worth

Table 2. Genes related to impulsivity

Gene	Full gene name	Genome variants	Ref.
Dopamine System			
SLC6A3 (DAT1)	Solute Carrier Family 6 Member	rs37020, rs460000	[10]
Encodes a dopamine transporter, mediates the re-uptake of dopamine from the synapse			
DRD2	Dopamine Receptor D2	rs1799978, rs4245149	[18]
Encodes the D2 subtype of the dopamine receptor			
ANKK1	Ankyrin Repeat And Kinase Domain Containing 1	rs4938012	[14]
Gene is closely linked to *DRD2* gene, controls the synthesis of dopamine			
Serotonin System			
SLC6A4	Solute Carrier Family 6 Member 4	rs25531	[69]
Serotonin transporter gene, transports serotonin from synaptic spaces into presynaptic neurons			
TPH2	Tryptophan Hydroxylase	rs1473473	[67]
Encodes protein that is important in biosynthesis of serotonin			
MAOA	Monoamine Oxidase A	rs1465108	[15]
Encodes mitochondrial enzymes which catalyze dopamine, norepinephrine, and serotonin			
HTR1A	5-Hydroxytryptamine Receptor 1A	rs6295	[5]
Encodes a G protein-coupled receptor for serotonin			
HTR1B	5-Hydroxytryptamine Receptor 1B	rs6296, rs6297, rs13212041	[17, 75]
Encodes a G protein-coupled receptor for serotonin			
HTR2A	5-Hydroxytryptamine Receptor 2A	rs6311, rs6313	[29]
Encodes one of the receptors for serotonin			
HTR2B	5-Hydroxytryptamine Receptor 2B	rs17110563	[6]
Encodes one of the receptors for serotonin			
TPH1	Tryptophan Hydroxylase 1	rs1799913	[3]
Encodes a protein catalyzes the first and rate limiting step in the biosynthesis of serotonin			
Catecholaminergic system			
COMT	Catechol-O-Methyltransferase	rs4680	[68]
Encodes Catechol-O-methyltransferase, which is one of the major degradative pathways of the catecholamine transmitters			
GABAergic system			
GABRA2	Gamma-Aminobutyric Acid Type A Receptor Subunit Alpha2	rs279858	[4]
Encodes a gamma-aminobutyric acid (GABA) receptor, which is the major inhibitory neurotransmitter			
Neurons migration			
RELN	Reelin	rs362794	[26]
Related to signaling pathway which underlies neurotransmission, memory formation and synaptic plasticity			

to mention the *CHRNA4* gene, which has a role in fast signal transmission at the synapses. Not only it relates with impulsive behaviour, but also with addiction to internet usage, for example genome variant rs1044396 [55].

Table 3. Other impulsivity related genes and addiction genes

Gene	Full gene name	Genome variants	Ref.
Other impulsivity ralated genes			
VDR	Vitamin D Receptor	rs2228570	[81]
Encodes vitamin D3 receptor, functions as a receptor for the secondary bile acid, lithocholic acid			
NRXN3	Neurexin 3	rs11624704	[70]
Encodes a member of a family of proteins that function in the nervous system as receptors			
Opioid, cannabinoid system/other addiction genes			
OPRM1	Opioid Receptor Mu 1	rs1799971	[31]
Encodes the mu opioid receptor in humans, which have important role in dependence to other drugs of abuse, such as nicotine, cocaine, and alcohol			
OPRK1	Opioid Receptor Kappa 1	rs1051660, rs6090041, rs6090043	[12]
Encodes an opioid receptor, a receptor for various synthetic opioids			
CHRNA4	Cholinergic Receptor Nicotinic Alpha 4 Subunit	rs1044396	[55]
Encodes a nicotinic acetylcholine receptor, which belongs to a superfamily of ligand-gated ion channels that play a role in fast signal transmission at synapses			

An individual impulsivity risk profile could be created combining mentioned known genome variants using a special biostatistical approach such as polygenic score. For complex inheritance genomic factor will not provide full profile of individual behaviour, however, combining with data from digital self analysis, it could create a strong model of particular individual behaviour.

4 Discussion

According to the recent evolutionary-inspired theories (i.e., differential suscepti-bility, biological sensitivity to context), humans, like many other species, differ substantially in their sensitivity to contextual factors, with some more suscepti-ble to environmental influences than others. These prominent theories converge on the proposition that genetic factors play a significant role in individual dif-ferences in Environmental Sensitivity [1].

Cognition as a quality of human or personality is a complex feature. Seeking to augment cognition, first we must deconstruct what are the main components that might be targeted by some existing and evolving techniques. The theory underlying cognitive genomics includes interdisciplinary integrated knowledge from genetics, evolutionary and molecular biology, cognitive and behavioural psychology, neurophysiology, and neuroanatomy. Approximately 70% of all human genes are expressed in the brain [37] and heritability was found of 40–70% for various aspects of cognition, temperament, and personality [54]. The behavioural and neurobiological relationships between impulsivity and addictive behaviours have been well established [59].

Impulsivity is defined as a bottom-up control mechanism regulated by auto-matic or reward-driven responses with diminished cognitive control to demands that may not be appropriate [52]. Impulsivity holds four constructs—deficit of premeditation and perseverance, sensation seeking, and urgency [80], contributes to addiction risk [23] and vice versa [59]. Human behaviour such as impulsivity or certain addictions increase the possible breach in cybersecurity, for example Ransomware attacks. Genomic data study of a particular individual can help to identify his biology driven behaviour patterns and show the potential risks in cybersecurity for that individual. Almost every human behavioural trait is a result of many genomic variants in action altogether with the environmental factors. Genetics as such will not provide a full profile of individual behaviour, but combining with data from digital analysis can create a strong model of particular individual behaviour.

4.1   Behavioural Patterns and the Environment

A good cybersecurity habit could prevent incidents and protect against attacks. Habits are initiated automatically, therefore, they can dominate personal behavioural patterns under specific circumstances. Cybersecurity behavioural habits can be created by promoting self-efficacy, response efficacy, and behavioural comprehensiveness [38]. Adaptive decision-making in changeable environments requires drawing probabilistic inferences about stimulus–action–outcome contingencies based on previous experience and external sources of information, which may be inaccurate and uncertain themselves [74]. As the fight against susceptibility to cybercrime and the prevention of digital attacks within businesses moves an emphasis away from technology towards human factors, research of this nature becomes more and more important [35]. Different research studies highlights how aspects of personality and technical skills impact on the potential to engage in effective information security behaviours.

4.2   Ethical Issues

Genome information and person behavioural profile are considered as personal and sensitive data. Therefore, data storage requires to follow (inter-)national policies regarding the management of private and sensitive data. For example, within the European Union, main rules and restrictions are defined by General Data Protection Regulation [72]. Thus, access to the genome and behavioural profile data should be strictly controlled and used only upon informed consent of a person.

Usage of genome data to profile business personnel and to distinguish employees based only on predicted undesirable behaviour could be discriminatory. Therefore, demonstrated behaviour under specific circumstances should make a high impact on some evaluation procedures. Also, the inclusion of genetic factors into risk assessment should be considered only in specific positions related to confidential data, critical infrastructure, or business that if compromised, makes instabilities at (inter-)national level. Also, an employee could need to make self-evaluation to learn personal traits before deciding on a position.

4.3   Future Research Directions

Impulsivity is increasingly recognized as a phenotypically heterogeneous construct [56] and study demonstrates Gustavson et al. [34] researches that large-scale genome association results can be used to evaluate theoretical models of impulsivity and psychology more broadly. In the present work we have analysed the methods for the analysis of human behavioural characteristics for the cybersecurity. The risky behaviour, possible human addictions and weaknesses are used in evaluation selecting the best strategy for human-to-human or human-machine-human interactions. In many cases the person is not the target, but valuable data, responsibilities, functions, and related entities. And genomic information about human behaviour cannot be interpreted without additional contexts.

As every investigation model has its weaknesses, research should look for additional or deeper systematic methods, evaluation components or so to cover the existing gaps (to make prognosis/prediction more accurate). Genetic factor inclusion may complement behaviour evaluation model by providing state-of-the-art gene-driven human behaviour reaction norm. Thus, the aim for ongoing research is to construct and suggest a model strategy when including results of genomic information for the improvement of human (self)training in cybersecurity, addressing the actionable target risks.

Acknowledgements. This work was partially supported by project *Advancing Human Performance in Cybersecurity*, ADVANCES. The ADVANCES is funded by Iceland, Liechtenstein and Norway through the EEA Grants.

References

1. Assary, E., Zavos, H.M., Krapohl, E., Keers, R., Pluess, M.: Genetic architecture of environmental sensitivity reflects multiple heritable components: a twin study with adolescents. Mol. Psychiatry **2020**, 1–9 (2020). https://doi.org/10.1038/s41380-020-0783-8
2. Barr, P.B., Dick, D.M.: The genetics of externalizing problems. In: de Wit, H., Jentsch, J.D. (eds.) Recent Advances in Research on Impulsivity and Impulsive Behaviors. CTBN, vol. 47, pp. 93–112. Springer, Cham (2019). https://doi.org/10.1007/7854_2019_120
3. Barrot, C., et al.: Relationships between the molecular basis of impulsivity and suicidal behavior. Forensic Sci. Int.: Genet. Suppl. Ser. **5**, e530–e531 (2015)
4. Bauer, L.O., Yang, B.Z., Houston, R.J., Kranzler, H.R., Gelernter, J.: GABRA2 genotype, impulsivity, and body mass. Am. J. Addict. **21**(5), 404–410 (2012)
5. Benko, A., et al.: Significant association between the C(- 1019) G functional polymorphism of the HTR1A gene and impulsivity. Am. J. Med. Genet. Part B: Neuropsychiatric Genet. **153**(2), 592–599 (2010)
6. Bevilacqua, L., et al.: A population-specific HTR2B stop codon predisposes to severe impulsivity. Nature **468**(7327), 1061–1066 (2010)
7. Bevilacqua, L., Goldman, D.: Genetics of impulsive behaviour. Philos. Trans. Roy. Soc. B: Biol. Sci. **368**(1615), 20120380 (2013)

8. Boardman, J.D., Daw, J., Freese, J.: Defining the environment in gene-environment research: lessons from social epidemiology. Am. J. Public Health **103**(S1), S64–S72 (2013)

9. Border, R., et al.: No support for historical candidate gene or candidate gene-by-interaction hypotheses for major depression across multiple large samples. Am. J. Psychiatry **176**(5), 376–387 (2019)

10. Brewer III, A.J., et al.: Genetic variation of the dopamine transporter (DAT1) influences the acute subjective responses to cocaine in volunteers with cocaine use disorders. Pharmacogenet. Genomics **25**(6), 296 (2015)

11. Bulik-Sullivan, B.K., et al.: LD score regression distinguishes confounding from polygenicity in genome-wide association studies. Nat. Genet. **47**(3), 291–295 (2015)

12. Burns, J.A., et al.: Molecular imaging of opioid and dopamine systems: insights into the pharmacogenetics of opioid use disorders. Front. Psychiatry **10**, 626 (2019)

13. Capecchi, M.R.: Gene targeting in mice: functional analysis of the mammalian genome for the twenty-first century. Nat. Rev. Genet. **6**(6), 507–512 (2005)

14. Chan, T., et al.: Impulsivity and genetic variants in DRD2 and ANKK1 moderate longitudinal associations between sleep problems and overweight from ages 5 to 11. Int. J. Obesity **38**(3), 404–410 (2014)

15. Chester, D.S., et al.: Monoamine oxidase a (MAOA) genotype predicts greater aggression through impulsive reactivity to negative affect. Behav. Brain Res. **283**, 97–101 (2015)

16. Chowdhury, N.H., Adam, M.T., Teubner, T.: Time pressure in human cyberse-curity behavior: theoretical framework and countermeasures. Comput. Secur. **97** (2020). https://doi.org/10.1016/j.cose.2020.101931

17. Conner, T.S., Jensen, K.P., Tennen, H., Furneaux, H.M., Kranzler, H.R., Covault, J.: Functional polymorphisms in the serotonin 1B receptor gene (HTR1B) predict self-reported anger and hostility among young men. Am. J. Med. Genet. Part B: Neuropsychiatric Genet. **153**(1), 67–78 (2010)

18. Cummins, T., et al.: Dopamine transporter genotype predicts behavioural and neural measures of response inhibition. Mol. Psychiatry **17**(11), 1086–1092 (2012)

19. Dick, D.M.: Gene-environment interaction in psychological traits and disorders. Ann. Rev. Clin. Psychol. **7**, 383–409 (2011)

20. Donalds, C., Osei-Bryson, K.M.: Cybersecurity compliance behavior: exploring the influences of individual decision style and other antecedents. Int. J. Inf. Manag. **51** (2020). https://doi.org/10.1016/j.ijinfomgt.2019.102056

21. Duncan, L.E., Keller, M.C.: A critical review of the first 10 years of candidate gene-by-environment interaction research in psychiatry. Am. J. Psychiatry **168**(10), 1041–1049 (2011)

22. ENISA: Cybersecurity culture guidelines: behavioural aspects of cybersecurity. European Union Agency for Network and Information Security (2018). https://doi.org/10.2824/324042

23. Ersche, K.D., Turton, A.J., Pradhan, S., Bullmore, E.T., Robbins, T.W.: Drug addiction endophenotypes: impulsive versus sensation-seeking personality traits. Biol. Psychiatry **68**(8), 770–773 (2010)

24. Ertan, A., Crossland, G., Heath, C., Denny, D., Jensen, R.B.: Cyber security behaviour in organisations. CoRR abs/2004.11768 (2020). https://arxiv.org/abs/2004.11768

25. Evenden, J.L.: Varieties of impulsivity. Psychopharmacology **146**(4), 348–361 (1999). https://doi.org/10.1007/PL00005481

26. Fatemi, S.H.: Reelin glycoprotein: structure, biology and roles in health and disease. Mol. Psychiatry **10**(3), 251–257 (2005)

27. Findling, C., Chopin, N., Koechlin, E.: Imprecise neural computations as a source of adaptive behaviour in volatile environments. Nat. Hum. Behav. **5**, 99–112 (2021). https://doi.org/10.1038/s41562-020-00971-z

28. Gadow, K.D., et al.: Allele-specific associations of 5-HTTLPR/rs25531 with ADHD and autism spectrum disorder. Progr. Neuro-Psychopharmacol. Biol. Psychiatry **40**, 292–297 (2013)

29. Genis-Mendoza, A.D., et al.: Genetic association analysis of 5-HTR2A gene variants in eating disorders in a Mexican population. Brain Behav. **9**(7) (2019)

30. Gordon, B., Caramazza, A.: Lexical decision for open-and closed-class words: failure to replicate differential frequency sensitivity. Brain Lang. **15**(1), 143–160 (1982)

31. Gray, J.C., et al.: Genetic analysis of impulsive personality traits: examination of a priori candidates and genome-wide variation. Psychiatry Res. **259**, 398–404 (2018)

32. Groman, S.M.: The neurobiology of impulsive decision-making and reinforcement learning in nonhuman animals. In: de Wit, H., Jentsch, J.D. (eds.) Recent Advances in Research on Impulsivity and Impulsive Behaviors. CTBN, vol. 47, pp. 23–52. Springer, Cham (2020). https://doi.org/10.1007/7854_2020_127

33. Grotzinger, A.D., et al.: Genomic structural equation modelling provides insights into the multivariate genetic architecture of complex traits. Nat. Hum. Behav. **3**(5), 513–525 (2019)

34. Gustavson, D.E., et al.: The latent genetic structure of impulsivity and its relation to internalizing psychopathology. Psychol. Sci. **31**(8), 1025–1035 (2020)

35. Hadlington, L.: Human factors in cybersecurity; examining the link between internet addiction, impulsivity, attitudes towards cybersecurity, and risky cybersecurity behaviours. Heliyon **3**(7) (2017). https://doi.org/10.1016/j.heliyon.2017.e00346

36. Hadlington, L., Popovac, M., Janicke, H., Yevseyeva, I., Jones, K.: Exploring the role of work identity and work locus of control in information security awareness. Comput. Secur. **81**, 41–48 (2019). https://doi.org/10.1016/j.cose.2018.10.006

37. Hariri, A.R., Weinberger, D.R.: Imaging genomics. Br. Med. Bull. **65**(1), 259–270 (2003). https://doi.org/10.1093/bmb/65.1.259

38. Hong, Y., Furnell, S.: Understanding cybersecurity behavioral habits: insights from situational support. J. Inf. Secur. Appl. **57** (2021). https://doi.org/10.1016/j.jisa.2020.102710

39. Hutchins, E., Cloppert, M., Amin, R.: Intelligence-driven computer network defense informed by analysis of adversary campaigns and intrusion kill chains. Lead. Issues Inf. Warfare Secur. Res. **1**(1), 80 (2011)

40. Hutchins, E.M., Cloppert, M.J., Amin, R.M.: Intelligence-Driven Computer Network Defense Informed by Analysis of Adversary Campaigns and Intrusion Kill Chains (2011). https://www.lockheedmartin.com/content/dam/lockheedmartin/rms/documents/cyber/LM-White-Paper-Intel-Driven-Defense.pdf. Lockheed Martin Corporation. White paper

41. International Schizophrenia Consortium, et al.: Common polygenic variation contributes to risk of schizophrenia and bipolar disorder. Nature **460**, 748–752 (2009). https://doi.org/10.1038/nature08185

42. Juárez Olguín, H., Calderon Guzman, D., Hernandez Garcia, E., Barragan Mejia, G.: The role of dopamine and its dysfunction as a consequence of oxidative stress. Oxidative Med. Cell. Longevity **2016**, 1–13 (2016)

43. Keller, M.C., Coventry, W.L., Heath, A.C., Martin, N.G.: Widespread evidence for non-additive genetic variation in Cloninger's and Eysenck's personality dimensions using a twin plus sibling design. Behav. Genet. **35**(6), 707–721 (2005). https://doi.org/10.1007/s10519-005-6041-7

44. Khemiri, L., Kuja-Halkola, R., Larsson, H., Jayaram-Lindström, N.: Genetic overlap between impulsivity and alcohol dependence: a large-scale national twin study. Psychol. Med. **46**(5), 1091 (2016)
45. Koeneke, A., Ponce, G., Troya-Balseca, J., Palomo, T., Hoenicka, J.: Ankyrin repeat and kinase domain containing 1 gene, and addiction vulnerability. Int. J. Mol. Sci. **21**(7), 2516 (2020)
46. Kozak, K., Lucatch, A.M., Lowe, D.J., Balodis, I.M., MacKillop, J., George, T.P.: The neurobiology of impulsivity and substance use disorders: implications for treatment. Ann. New York Acad. Sci. **1451**(1), 71 (2019)
47. Kranzler, H.R., et al.: Genome-wide association study of alcohol consumption and use disorder in 274,424 individuals from multiple populations. Nat. Commun. **10**(1), 1–11 (2019)
48. Krueger, R.F., Hicks, B.M., Patrick, C.J., Carlson, S.R., Iacono, W.G., McGue, M.: Etiologic connections among substance dependence, antisocial behavior, and personality: modeling the externalizing spectrum. J. Abnormal Psychol. **111**(3) (2009)
49. Kuhn, B.N., Kalivas, P.W., Bobadilla, A.C.: Understanding addiction using animal models. Front. Behav. Neurosci. **13**, 262 (2019)
50. Lahcen, R.A.M., Caulkins, B.D., Mohapatra, R., Kumar, M.: Review and insight on the behavioral aspects of cybersecurity. Cybersecurity **3**(1), 10 (2020). https://doi.org/10.1186/s42400-020-00050-w
51. Logan, G.D., Cowan, W.B.: On the ability to inhibit thought and action: a theory of an act of control. Psychol. Rev. **91**(3), 295 (1984)
52. Martel, M.M., Levinson, C.A., Lee, C.A., Smith, T.E.: Impulsivity symptoms as core to the developmental externalizing spectrum. J. Abnormal Child Psychol. **45**(1), 83–90 (2017)
53. Mazur, J.E.: An adjusting procedure for studying delayed reinforcement. In: Commons, M.L., Mazur, J.E. Nevin, J.A. (eds.) pp. 55–73 (1987)
54. McGuffin, P., Riley, B., Plomin, R.: Toward behavioral genomics. Science **291**(5507), 1232–1249 (2001)
55. Montag, C., Kirsch, P., Sauer, C., Markett, S., Reuter, M.: The role of the CHRNA4 gene in internet addiction: a case-control study. J. Addict. Med. **6**(3), 191–195 (2012)
56. Niv, S., Tuvblad, C., Raine, A., Wang, P., Baker, L.A.: Heritability and longitudinal stability of impulsivity in adolescence. Behav. Genet. **42**(3), 378–392 (2012). https://doi.org/10.1007/s10519-011-9518-6
57. Oh, B.: Direct-to-consumer genetic testing: advantages and pitfalls. Genomics Inform. **17**(3), e33 (2019)
58. Pattij, T., Vanderschuren, L.J.M.J.: The neuropharmacology of impulsive behaviour, an update. In: de Wit, H., Jentsch, J.D. (eds.) Recent Advances in Research on Impulsivity and Impulsive Behaviors. CTBN, vol. 47, pp. 3–22. Springer, Cham (2020). https://doi.org/10.1007/7854_2020_143
59. Perry, J.L., Carroll, M.E.: The role of impulsive behavior in drug abuse. Psychopharmacology **200**(1), 1–26 (2008). https://doi.org/10.1007/s00213-008-1173-0
60. Pietrzak, R.H., Sprague, A., Snyder, P.J.: Trait impulsiveness and executive function in healthy young adults. J. Res. Pers. **42**(5), 1347–1351 (2008)
61. Reynolds, B., Ortengren, A., Richards, J.B., De Wit, H.: Dimensions of impulsive behavior: personality and behavioral measures. Pers. Individ. Differ. **40**(2), 305–315 (2006)

62. Robertson, B.D., et al.: SLC6A3 polymorphism predisposes to dopamine overdose in Parkinson's disease. Front. Neurol. **9**, 693 (2018)
63. Rosvold, H.E., Mirsky, A.F., Sarason, I., Bransome Jr., E.D., Beck, L.H.: A continuous performance test of brain damage. J. Consult. Psychol. **20**(5), 343–350 (1956)
64. Salvatore, J.E., Dick, D.M.: Genetic influences on conduct disorder. Neurosci. Biobehav. Rev. **91**, 91–101 (2018)
65. Sanchez-Roige, S., et al.: Genome-wide association studies of impulsive personality traits (BIS-11 and UPPS-P) and drug experimentation in up to 22,861 adult research participants identify loci in the CACNA1I and CADM2 genes. J. Neurosci. **39**(13), 2562–2572 (2019)
66. Shanahan, M.J., Hofer, S.M.: Social context in gene-environment interactions: Retrospect and prospect. J. Gerontol. Ser. B: Psychol. Sci. Soc. Sci. **60**(Special_Issue_1), 65–76 (2005)
67. Slof-Op't Landt, M.C., et al.: Genetic variation at the TPH2 gene influences impulsivity in addition to eating disorders. Behav. Genet. **43**(1), 24–33 (2013). https://doi.org/10.1007/s10519-012-9569-3
68. Soeiro-De-Souza, M.G., Stanford, M.S., Bio, D.S., Machado-Vieira, R., Moreno, R.A.: Association of the COMT Met158 allele with trait impulsivity in healthy young adults. Mol. Med. Rep. **7**(4), 1067–1072 (2013)
69. Sonuga-Barke, E.J., et al.: A functional variant of the serotonin transporter gene (SLC6A4) moderates impulsive choice in attention-deficit/hyperactivity disorder boys and siblings. Biol. Psychiatry **70**(3), 230–236 (2011)
70. Stoltenberg, S.F., Lehmann, M.K., Christ, C.C., Hersrud, S.L., Davies, G.E.: Associations among types of impulsivity, substance use problems and neurexin-3 polymorphisms. Drug Alcohol Depend. **119**(3), e31–e38 (2011)
71. Tandy-Connor, S., et al.: False-positive results released by direct-to-consumer genetic tests highlight the importance of clinical confirmation testing for appropriate patient care. Genet. Med. **20**(12), 1515–1521 (2018)
72. The European Parliament and the Council of the European Union: Regulation (EU) 2016/679 of the European Parliament and of the Council of 27 April 2016 on the protection of natural persons with regard to the processing of personal data and on the free movement of such data, and repealing Directive 95/46/EC (General Data Protection Regulation). Official Journal of the European Union (2016)
73. Torgersen, S.: Behavioral genetics of personality. Cur. Psychiatry Rep. **7**, 51–56 (2005). https://doi.org/10.1007/s11920-005-0025-4
74. Ullsperger, M.: Imprecise learning and uncertainty. Nat. Hum. Behav. 1–2 (2020)
75. Varga, G., et al.: Additive effects of serotonergic and dopaminergic polymorphisms on trait impulsivity. Am. J. Med. Genet. Part B: Neuropsychiatric Genet. **159**(3), 281–288 (2012)
76. Verdejo-García, A., Lawrence, A.J., Clark, L.: Impulsivity as a vulnerability marker for substance-use disorders: review of findings from high-risk research, problem gamblers and genetic association studies. Neurosci. Biobehav. Rev. **32**(4), 777–810 (2008)
77. Visscher, P.M., et al.: 10 years of GWAS discovery: biology, function, and translation. Am. J. Hum. Genet. **101**(1), 5–22 (2017)
78. Walters, R.K., et al.: Transancestral GWAS of alcohol dependence reveals common genetic underpinnings with psychiatric disorders. Nat. Neurosci. **21**(12), 1656–1669 (2018)

79. Wellcome Trust Case Control Consortium and others: Genome-wide association study of 14,000 cases of seven common diseases and 3,000 shared controls. Nature **447**(7145), 661 (2007)
80. Whiteside, S.P., Lynam, D.R.: The five factor model and impulsivity: using a structural model of personality to understand impulsivity. Pers. Individ. Differ. **30**(4), 669–689 (2001)
81. Wrzosek, M., et al.: Association between Fok I vitamin D receptor gene (VDR) polymorphism and impulsivity in alcohol-dependent patients. Mol. Biol. Rep. **41**(11), 7223–7228 (2014)
82. Young, S.E., Stallings, M.C., Corley, R.P., Krauter, K.S., Hewitt, J.K.: Genetic and environmental influences on behavioral disinhibition. Am. J. Med. Genet. **96**(5), 684–695 (2000)

A Supervisor Agent-Based on the Markovian Decision Process Framework to Optimize the Behavior of a Highly Automated System

A. Castellano[1], M. Karimshoushtari[2], C. Novara[2(✉)], and F. Tango[3]

[1] RE:Lab, 42122 Reggio Emilia, Italy
andrea.castellano@re-lab.it
[2] Politecnico di Torino, 10129 Turin, Italy
{milad.karimshoushtari,carlo.novara}@polito.it
[3] Centro Ricerche Fiat, 10043 Orbassano, Italy
fabio.tango@crf.it

Abstract. In this paper, we explore how MDP can be used as the framework to design and develop an Intelligent Decision Support System/Recommender System, in order to extend human perception and overcome human senses limitations (because covered by the ADS), by augmenting human cognition, emphasizing human judgement and intuition, as well as supporting him/her to take the proper decision in the right terms and time.

Moreover, we develop Human-Machine Interaction (HMI) strategies able to make "transparent" the decision-making/recommendation process. This is strongly needed, since the adoption of partial automated systems is not only connected to the effectiveness of the decision and control processes, but also relies on how these processes are communicated and "explained" to the human driver, in order to achieve his/her trust.

Keywords: Intelligent decision support system · Recommender system · Autonomous driving · Markovian decision process

1 Introduction

Autonomous Vehicles (AVs) arise as a technological solution to mitigate the shortcomings of manual driving: reduction of human-caused accidents and the realization of a more efficient driving task in terms of energy consumption, traffic flow and driver's workload. Under this perspective, AVs are expected to fundamentally change road transport and improve life quality. In fact, the automation of vehicles has been identified as one major enabler to master the Grand Societal Challenges "Individual Mobility" and "Energy Efficiency" and highly automated driving functions (ADF) are one major step to be taken.

However, this technology is not mature enough yet for massive implementation and, in addition, it can bring to specific side-effects. In particular, the automation of the dynamic driving task removes humans from the control loop, leaving to the driver the

© Springer Nature Switzerland AG 2021
D. D. Schmorrow and C. M. Fidopiastis (Eds.): HCII 2021, LNAI 12776, pp. 351–368, 2021.
https://doi.org/10.1007/978-3-030-78114-9_24

monitoring loop. If we consider the Skills, Rules, Knowledge framework of Rasmussen in manual operation of a vehicle [1], we can say that moving from the skill-based behavior to the rule-based behavior up to the knowledge-based behavior makes the workload and the probability of errors more likely to increase (Fig. 1).

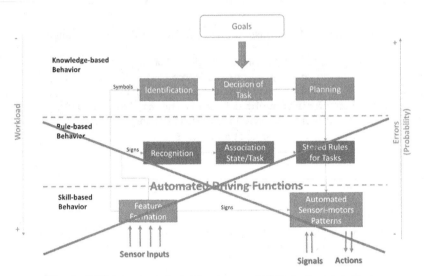

Fig. 1. SRK framework, including the use of ADFs in the driving task.

This is exactly the risk of Automated Driving Systems (ADSs), where the first two lower levels are performed by the system, leaving the upper level (namely, knowledge-based behavior) to humans, indeed characterized by high workload and high probability of error. Under this perspective, there is also the risk that humans lose some skills, thus fundamental changes can occur to what humans are expected to learn.

Especially as machines acquire capabilities to learn deeply and actively from data [2], adaptation and personalization to human needs shall be considered. In this context, intelligent agents should be able to think and behave in ways that support humans, by providing personalized, adaptive, responsive and proactive services in a variety of settings and scenarios.

The European ECSEL research project PRYSTINE realizes Fail-operational Urban Surround perceptION (FUSION)[1] based on robust Radar and LiDAR sensor fusion and control functions, in order to enable safe automated driving in urban and rural environments. With reference to the latest innovations of the PRYSTINE project, in this paper, we explore how an Intelligent Decision Support System (IDSS) can be designed and developed, in order to extend human perception and overcome human senses limitations (because covered by the ADS), by augmenting human cognition, emphasizing human judgement and intuition, as well as supporting him/her to take the proper decision in the right terms and time. A critical aspect needed to design adaptive systems is the decision-making task, which has to weight several possibly conflicting data sources in

---

[1] For more information, see the website: https://prystine.eu/.

order to decide a safe driving plan. The theory of Markov Decision Processes (MDPs) [3] provides the standard semantic foundation for a wide range of problems involving decision-making tasks. Indeed, MDP formalism allows a modeler to specify a stochastic decision process by means of a set of states S, in which a decision maker has to choose an action from a set of available actions Act. Then, the process randomly evolves according to a specified transition probability associated with the selected action, and it returns to the decision maker a reward depending on the chosen action and by the source and destination states.

Under this perspective, the supervisor agent based on MDP is a kind of recommendation system (RS), which aims at predicting if an item would be useful to a user based on given information (following the definition of [7] and [8]). In this sense, it can solve the information overload problem, by suggesting the proper action and personalizing the user experience, delivering accurate, personalized recommendations to users (i.e., drivers in our case), according to some criteria, such as safety and preferences. In fact, it can be challenging for a user to filter through all the available information and take away essential aspects information overload or, for a system, to decide about the optimal action to take, satisfying different and, sometime, contradictory criteria [9].

Moreover, we develop Human-Machine Interaction (HMI) strategies able to make "transparent" the aforementioned decision-making process. This is strongly needed, since the adoption of partial automated systems is not only connected to the effectiveness of the decision and control processes, but also relies on how these processes are communicated, and "explained" to the human driver, in order to achieve his/her trust. This is a crucial topic, since it is common opinion that the HMI has a crucial role in the adoption of partially and highly automated vehicles [10]. The main challenge related to this topic relies on the responsibility of the HMI as "enabler of the cooperation", i.e. on being the tool that allows the vehicle to explain its intentions and, at the same time, allows the driver to provide inputs and act as decision-maker in the driving process. Recent studies have shown the relevance of providing the correct type and amount of information and the impact of these design choices on the improvements of the decision-making capabilities [11]. At the same time, different experimental studies have demonstrated the relevance of the approach focus on increasing the transparency of the automation [12].

The HMI proposed in this paper will be a multimodal state-adaptive system, able to tailor the interaction modality according to the outcome of the intelligent decision maker and the cognitive (as well as behavioral) state of the driver. The proposed system will focus on the design and implementation of the perception-decision-action (plus interaction) cycle in common traffic situations that, even if representing most of the driving task, are currently less explored in industry and research.

2   The Supervisor Agent as an Intelligent Decision Support System

Consider now an ADS, which applies appropriate controls to the vehicle (both lateral and longitudinal) so that collisions may be avoided. When a collision is imminent, there is no doubt about what to do: the system has to react to an immediate danger (following the "sensori-motor" level of Piaget [4] or the "Control level" in the hierarchical structure of Janssen and Michon [5]) by braking as hard as possible to bring the host-vehicle in a safety zone. This is exactly what nowadays ADAS applications do.

When there is a normal (i.e., safe) driving situation, it is less clear what the optimal actions are. For example, when approaching a slower car, should the host-vehicle follow the one ahead, or change lane for an overtaking maneuver? From one side, a car-following decision can be the "safest" solution, but on the other side it can make the trip longer and can waste time. Therefore, a decision system that supports the human driver and takes the optimal actions can really help. In particular, deciding the optimal action to perform, or what corrective controls to exercise in order to avoid a possible collision, is essentially a problem of "credit assignment": supposing an outcome is a consequence of a sequence of decisions. In other words, the credit assignment problem calls for a system to associate decisions to their long-term outcomes. One of the most important theories for formulating and solving credit assignment in sequential decision-making problems is the aforementioned MDP theory [6]. In modelling a problem as an MDP, we contemplate a decision-maker who is required to take decisions over a sequence of discrete time periods.

2.1 Use-Cases and Scenarios of Interest

In the PRYSTINE project, all the SW and HW components are implemented and integrated in some demonstrators. In particular, the IDSS described in this paper is included in one project application for the passenger car, employing PRYSTINE's fail-operational autonomous driving functions (ADFs) and the related sensor data fusion (SDF) from a wide range of sensors (Radar, LiDAR, camera, V2X communication and feedback devices).

Fig. 2. Maserati prototype vehicle used by the PRYSTINE Project. The car is equipped with a range of cameras, radars, communication sensors and feedback devices, serving as a testbed for both level 2 and level 3 ADFs.

Current ADSs rely on SDF to identify the driving scenario in the vehicle proximity (i.e., in the field of view/range of sensors), possibly extended by information through V2X communication. Data from heterogeneous sources/sensors are fused to provide an overview of traffic in the surroundings of the vehicle. This information can be used to let the ADS anticipating the evolution of traffic, providing a more comfortable and efficient driving performance, especially in urban scenarios.

In the project, three use-cases (UCs) are developed: the *"Traffic Light Time-To-Green"*, *"Trajectory Recognition and VRU"* and the *"Emergency Lateral Lane Stop"*. For the application of our IDSS, based on MDP framework, we started from the third one, which is sketched in the following figure:

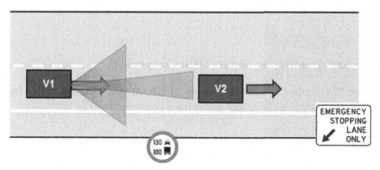

Fig. 3. Sketch of the UC3, named emergency lateral lane stop, specific for different types of scenarios.

In this scenario, the AV is travelling at a given speed, when it approaches a slower vehicle. In this case, the decision-maker has to define the next optimal action: is it better to follow the car ahead, or to overtake it? It is worth to noting here that the developed IDSS can either inform the driver about the best maneuver to do or intervene on the vehicle actuators to perform the same maneuver. Of course, the final decision depends on some factors, such as the safety of the action (e.g., if another vehicle is already overtaking the AV from the left adjacent lane, the overtaking is not considered or at least delayed), the optimization of the travelling time (i.e., maybe the car-following decision can minimize fuel consumption but make the travel too much longer) and even from the cognitive status of the driver (e.g., s/he is distracted or attentive).

The inputs of the system are related to the perception of the external environment, constituted by the Radar (front/blind spot), front camera, ultrasonic sensors and LiDAR. In addition, the system considers the use of a Driver Monitoring System (DMS), which detects the driver status to understand if s/he is still capable to control the vehicle, or alternatively, if s/he is able to get back into the control-loop in case of a "take over request" (TOR) from the system. If a critical case is detected, a safe-stop maneuver is necessary (e.g., the driver is impaired for drowsiness). In details, the DMS includes biometric devices and dynamic vehicle algorithm, to detect drowsiness, cognitive load and visual distraction.

The output is represented by the longitudinal/lateral controls of the vehicle, to avoid potential collision, to act an overtaking and, if necessary, to perform a safe stop maneuver (emergency lights activation and stop in the emergency lane, if possible).

As it is now, in the current ADAS/ADS applications (even at prototypical level), the choice between an overtaking and a car-following action can be conflictual and not smooth (if the "adaptive cruise control" and the "support to overtaking" functions do not communicate each other); moreover, if the driver is not responding (as aforementioned, due to drowsiness, for example) to a TOR after some time (because the system reached the limits of its Operational Design Domain, or ODD in short), the AV "simply" stops in the current driving lane. Thanks to the super-visor agent, which "knows" the situation, the most appropriated action is taken: with reference to the previous example, the system can decide to minimize the travelling time and, given that such a decision is safe and the driver is attentive, an overtaking maneuver is initiated. On the other way, if the driver is impaired, after checking that the emergency lane is present, a safe lane change is performed.

2.2 The System Architecture and Its Main Components

Following the "*Perception Cognition Action*" (PCA) framework, the following figure shows the overall system architecture and related components (Fig. 4):

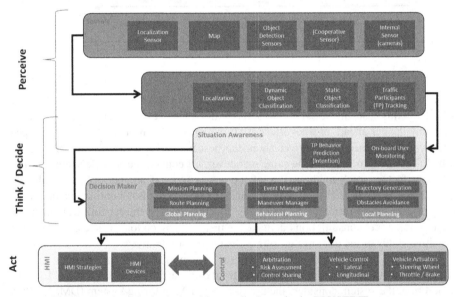

Fig. 4. Sketch of the logical architectural scheme in the PRYSTINE system.

The first layer, **Perceive**, includes both the sensing and the perception parts, where the raw information coming from the sensors are elaborated and processed, in order to derive a detailed picture of the external scene. Of course, in case a driving simulator is used, this is done automatically in the simulation.

Then, such an information is assessed in the second layer, **Think/Decide**, which includes a module (named *situation awareness*) for the prediction of the dynamic evolution of the external scene and the monitoring of the internal scene (namely, the status of the driver, what s/he is doing, and so on). The Decision-maker module that we have developed, is part of this layer; considering the three parts in which it is divided, we focused on the **behavioral planning**: our system can manage the events and the related maneuver, identifying the optimal actions to do.

This output, third layer (**Act**), can be provided directly to the user (in case of a Recommender system in ADAS applications) or to the vehicle actuators (in case of AD applications). In both situation a dedicated HMI is necessary: to support the driver and help to select the best solution in the first option; to inform the driver about what the systems is doing and what is expected from him/her in the second option.

3 Implementation of the IDSS

In this section, we first recall the general definition of MDP. Then, we propose an MDP for the considered use case (overtaking maneuver). The subsequent parts of the section are dedicated to present the proposed HMI concept and implementation.

3.1 MDP Definition

A MDP is a control or decision-making process, finalized at obtaining a desired behavior of a system of interest. The system of interest is often called the process to control or also the plant.

Mathematically, a MDP is defined as a 4-tuple (S,A,P,R), where:

S is the set of all plant states of interest. S is called the state space.

A is the set of actions that can be performed at a given time instant.

P is the state probability transition. In particular, given two states $S1,S2 \in S$ and an action $a \in A$, $P(a,S1,S2)$ is the probability that the action a yields a transition from state $S1$ to state $S2$.

R is the immediate reward. It is possible to assign a reward to promote desire state transitions (positive reward) and penalize other transitions (negative reward).

3.2 The Super-Visor Agent Implementation

As discussed in Sect. 2.1, three UCs are developed in the PRYSTINE project. For the application of our IDSS-MDP framework, we consider the third one, sketched in Fig. 2. In this scenario, the AV is traveling at a given speed, when it approaches a slower vehicle in the same lane, and the decision-maker has to define the next action. In the following, we formally introduce all the quantities that define the proposed MDP, that is the core of our IDSS.

Road scenario
Road, 3 lanes, from right to left:

- Lane 0: emergency lane.
- Lane 1: normal traveling lane.
- Lane 2: overtake lane.

Vehicles:

- AV: autonomous vehicle, initially in lane 1.

- PV: vehicle preceding AV, always in lane 1.
- OVs: other vehicles but AV and PV, possibly traveling in lane 1 and/or lane 2.

Main variables:

- v_x: longitudinal speed of AV.
- v_m: maximum longitudinal speed allowed on lanes 1 and 2.
- $v_r \leq v_m$: AV desired speed.
- $v_p < v_r \leq v_m$: longitudinal speed of PV.

MDP states

We consider a road scenario in a suitable neighborhood of AV.

AV states:

- $L0$: AV stopped in lane 0, $v_x = 0$.
- $L1$: AV lane 1 keeping, $v_x = v_p$ (before overtaking), $v_x = v_r$ (after overtaking).
- $L2$: AV lane 2 keeping, $v_x = v_m$.

Lane 1 states:

- $F1$: no PV, no OVs in lane 1.
- $P1$: PV in lane 1, no OVs in lane 1.
- $O1$: PV and OVs ahead of PV in lane 1.

Lane 2 states:

- $F2$: no OVs in lane 2.
- $O2$: OVs in lane 2.

Driver States:

- DA: healthy driver.
- DD: impaired driver.

The full scenario state is $S = (S_E, S_{L1}, S_{L2}, S_D) \in \mathcal{S}$, where $S_E \in \{L0, L1, L2\}$, $S_{L1} \in \{F1, P1, O1\}$, $S_{L2} \in \{F2, O2\}$, $S_D \in \{DA, DD\}$. The state space $\mathcal{S}$ is defined as $\mathcal{S} \doteq \{L0, L1, L2\} \times \{F1, P1, O1\} \times \{F2, O2\} \times \{DA, DD\}$. The total number of possible states is $\text{card}(\mathcal{S}) = 3 \times 3 \times 2 \times 2 = 36$. For the sake of simplicity, we define a smaller number of aggregate states, allowing us to capture the relevant situations that may occur. In the following, the logic symbols $\forall$ (for all, for any), $\vee$ (or), $\wedge$ (and) will be used.

Aggregate States:

- $S0 \doteq (L0, \forall, \forall, \forall)$: AV stopped in lane 0, end state (12 non-aggregate states).

- $S11 \doteq \{(L1, F1, \forall, \forall), (L1, P1, F2, DD), (L1, P1, O2, \forall), (L1, O1, \forall, \forall)\}$: AV traveling in lane 1, overtaking not possible/not useful (11 non-aggregate states).
- $S12 \doteq (L1, P1, F2, DA)$: AV traveling in lane 1, overtaking possible (1 non-aggregate state).
- $S21 \doteq \{(L2, P1, \forall, \forall), (L2, O1, \forall, \forall)\}$: AV traveling in lane 2, re-entry in lane 1 not possible (8 non-aggregate states).
- $S22 \doteq (L2, F1, \forall, \forall)$: AV traveling in lane 2, re-entry in lane 1 possible (4 non-aggregate states).

The corresponding state space is $S_A \doteq \{S0, S11, S12, S21, S22\}$.

MDP Actions

We distinguish between two kinds of actions: inputs, i.e., actions decided by the MDP system (or by the driver), and events, i.e., actions coming from the external world, independent of the MDP.

Inputs:

- *llc*: left lane change.
- *rlc*: right lane change.

Events:

- *vea*: one or more OVs arrive in lane 1 ahead of PV and/or in lane 2, impeding to change lane.
- *vem*: all OVs in lane 1 and/or in lane 2 which impede to change lane get sufficiently far from AV.
- *dba*: driver becomes healthy.
- *dbd*: driver becomes impaired.

Aggregate Events:

- $ovn = vea \vee dbd$: overtaking becomes impossible.
- $ovy = (vem \wedge (dba \vee DA)) \vee (P1 \wedge F2 \wedge dba)$: overtaking becomes possible.
- $rey = vem$: re-entry becomes possible.

The set of input is $U \doteq \{llc, rlc\}$, the set of aggregate events is $E \doteq \{ovn, ovy, rey\}$ and the overall set of actions is $A \doteq U \cup E$.

MDP Probability Functions

The state transition probability functions for the two input actions *llc* and *rlc* are as follows:

$$P(llc, S_a, S_b) = \begin{cases} p_o, & S_a = S12, \ S_b = S21 \\ 1 - p_o, & S_a = S12, \ S_b = S12 \\ 0, & \text{otherwise} \end{cases}$$

$$P(rlc, S_a, S_b) = \begin{cases} 0.5, & S_a = S22, \; S_b = S11 \\ 0.5, & S_a = S22, \; S_b = S12 \\ 0, & \text{otherwise.} \end{cases}$$

MDP Graph

The MDP graph is shown in the figure below. It can be noted that, for each state, at most one action is defined. The MDP thus corresponds to a Markov Chain and no rewards need to be defined. In more complicated scenarios, rewards can be used to provide the MDP with more flexibility and capability to deal with different situations (Fig. 5).

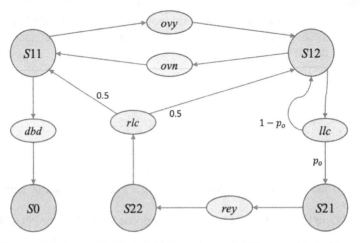

Fig. 5. MDP graph. Where not indicated, the transition probability associated with an edge is 1.

3.3   The Human-Machine Interface (HMI) Implementation

In the context mentioned in Chapter 1, the main goal of a Human-Machine Interaction system is to maximize the effectiveness of the cooperation between the human and the automated agent. In order to do that, this system shall be able to be easily understood by the driver, to increase his/her awareness about the situation, and (most important) to be trusted.

The HMI described in this paper is designed to exploit the potential of the Supervisor Agent, i.e., to easily represent its mental model in order to:

- Provide effective information/explanation when decisions are taken by the system.
- Encourage the cooperation when decisions and actions are shared between the human and the automated agents.
- Avoid unnecessary information when decisions and actions are delegated to the human driver, in order to avoid an overload in terms of cognitive and physical resources.

The HMI is deployed in a multimodal full-digital instrument cluster. It includes all relevant information related to the driving task (e.g., current speed, gear, automation mode etc.) as well as evidence about the driver's state (e.g. if he/she is distracted) and the action required to achieve an optimal driving (i.e. the suggested behavior). The HMI has been designed following the theories related to the negotiation-based interaction approach [13]. This means that the main goal of the HMI is to "explain rather than warn", in order to cooperate with the driver in achieving a pleasant, comfortable and safe drive.

According to the decision made by the supervisor agent, the HMI will inform the driver about what the vehicle expects from him/her, and provides messages related to the reasons that lead to the request of interaction. This is provided through:

- **Graphical explanations** provided through interactive 3D representation at the center of the HMI, where the road environment as well as the surrounding road actors are reconstructed (e.g., from digital maps plus vehicle's sensors) and displayed through a stylized representation
- **Messages** provided through audio signals and text.

The following figure, for example, shows a situation where the driver and the automation are sharing the vehicle control, and the car informs the driver that they are approaching a vehicle, that will be followed (Fig. 6).

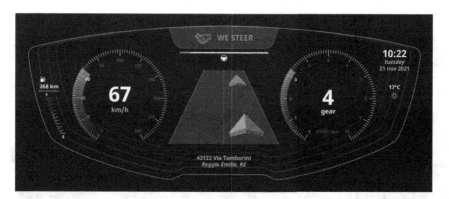

Fig. 6. Sketch of HMI for a control sharing between human driver and automated system.

The following figure shows a situation where the automation is engaged and, due to a combination of sensory limitation – i.e., lack of visibility - and the implementation of a cautious behavior, it actually informs that driver that the "car following" (CF) will results, unless the driver would intentionally override the system to perform a manual overtake. In this case, the 3D representation is highly focused on explaining the reasons behind the behavior (i.e., the visibility constraint) rather than the actual action requested to the driver, that is relegated to a small message on the upper right part of the screen. This design choice relies on the implicit interactions [14], since it is aimed at fostering a behavior rather than explicitly force a reaction (Fig. 7).

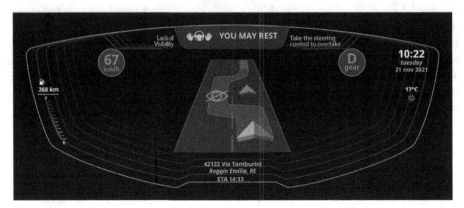

Fig. 7. Sketch of HMI informing driver about the action selected by the system (CF maneuver in this case).

Finally, the figure below shows the case where an automatic emergency maneuver is actuated by the vehicle; in this case, the explanation is provided before the actual stop of the vehicle, to allow the human driver to take back the control before the stop of the car. The cooperation here is provided showing the upcoming decision/behavior of the automation, i.e., to stop in the emergency lane (Fig. 8).

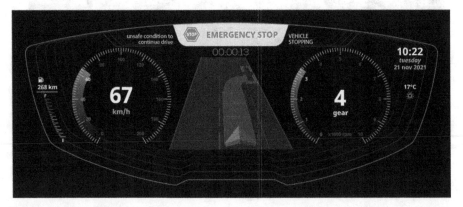

Fig. 8. Sketch of the HMI that informs the driver about the reason of the actuation for an emergency maneuver.

4 Data Analysis and Results

In the considered scenario, the autonomous vehicle (AV) is travelling at a speed of 70 km/h, when it approaches a preceding vehicle (PV), travelling at the lower speed of 45 km/h in the same lane, see Fig. 3 (AV = V1, PV = V2). The decision-maker has to choose in real-time the action to perform. Note that the IDSS can either inform the driver about the best maneuver to do or intervene on the vehicle actuators to perform the same maneuver. In the present case study, we have adopted the second approach, where the IDSS takes the action, based on what decided by the MDP. One important constraint that we impose is that the IDSS-MDP module cannot work completely alone: it needs in any case the driver to be healthy and aware. The following sub-scenarios have been considered:

Sub-scenario 1. The driver is healthy and aware. The MDP decides to either overtake or follow the preceding vehicle. Other two vehicles are traveling at a speed of 45 km/h in the opposite direction on the lane to be used for overtaking.

Sub-scenario 2. At a certain time, the driver becomes impaired. According to the imposed constraint, the IDSS-MDP module cannot work in a completely autonomous mode. Hence, after checking that the emergency lane is present, the MDP imposes a safe right lane change and a stop in the emergency lane.

For both sub-scenarios, two simulations were carried out: one corresponding to a MDP sporty strategy ($p_o = 1$), the other one corresponding to a MDP cautious strategy ($p_o = 0.1$). According to the probability functions defined, the sporty strategy performs an overtaking every time that is possible, while the cautious strategy performs an overtaking when it is possible but only with probability p_o.

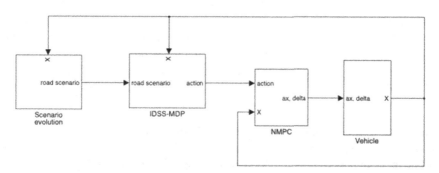

Fig. 9. Autonomous driving simulator block diagram.

The simulations were carried out by means of an autonomous driving simulator developed in MATLAB/SIMULINK. The simulator block diagram is shown in Fig. 9 and is characterized by the following blocks:

Scenario Evolution: This block generates the road scenario, (roads, vehicles, obstacles) and computes its evolution over time. Mathematically speaking, it provides the IDSS-MDP module with the coordinates of all elements that appear in the scenario.

Vehicle: Block describing the vehicle lateral and longitudinal dynamics. The block is essentially the "Vehicle Body 3DOF Dual Track" model, taken from the MAT-LAB Vehicle Dynamics Toolbox. The following parameter values were used: $l_f = 1.2\,\text{m}$, $l_r = 1.6\,\text{m}$ (lengths of front and rear longitudinal semi-axes), $m = 1575\,\text{kg}$ (mass), $J = 4000\,\text{kg m}^2$ (moment of inertia), $c_f = 27e3\,\text{N/rad}$, $c_r = 20e3\,\text{N/rad}$ (front and rear cornering stiffness coefficients). X is the vehicle state vector, containing the relevant kinematic and dynamic variables (linear and angular positions, linear and angular velocities), a_x is the requested longitudinal acceleration and δ is the commanded steering angle.

NMPC: Low-level controller, performing trajectory planning, and lateral and longitudinal AV dynamics control. The controller is based on a Nonlinear Model Predictive Control (NMPC) approach, see, e.g., [15, 16]. NMPC is a general and flexible approach to nonlinear system control. It allows us to deal with input and trajectory constraints, and to manage systematically the trade-off between performance and command effort. The approach is based on two main operations (accomplished at each time step): (i) a prediction over a given time horizon is performed, using some vehicle model; (ii) the command input is chosen as the one yielding the "best" prediction (i.e., the prediction closest to the desired behavior) by means of some on-line optimization algorithm. The NMPC controller works with a sampling time $T_s = 0.05$ s.

IDSS-MDP: Intelligent Decision Support System, based on the MDP designed in Sect. 3.2. This block collects the information coming from the road scenario and the AV and indicates to the NMPC block the best action to perform at each time step, with a sampling time $T_d = 0.5$s. Note that the AV consists of the three blocks Vehicle, NMPC and IDSS-MDP.

The simulation results can be summarized as follows (see also Fig. 10 to Fig. 12).

Simulation 1 (Sub-Scenario 1 and Sporty MDP Strategy). AV (traveling with speed 70 km/h) approaches PV (traveling with speed 45 km/h). Since another vehicle (OV1) is traveling in the opposite direction, AV reduces its speed, in order to follow PV. As soon as OV1 has gone, AV overtakes PV. After the overtake, a fourth vehicle (OV2) comes from the opposite direction, but this does not affect the behavior of AV.

Simulation 2 (Sub-Scenario 1 and Cautious MDP Strategy). AV (traveling with speed 70 km/h) approaches PV (traveling with speed 45 km/h). Since another vehicle (OV1) is traveling in the opposite direction, AV reduces its speed in order to follow PV. Here, the cautious strategy prefers to wait to overtake. In the meanwhile, OV2 comes from the opposite direction. AV waits also OV2 to move away and then it overtakes PV.

Simulation 3 (Sub-Scenario 2 and Sporty MDP Strategy). When the driver becomes impaired, AV performs a right lane change and then stops in the emergency lane.

Simulation 4 (Sub-Scenario 2 and Cautious MDP Strategy). Results similar to those of Simulation 3 (Fig. 11).

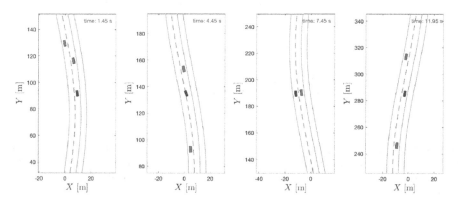

Fig. 10. Simulation 1. AV and PV travel upward. The other vehicles travel downward.

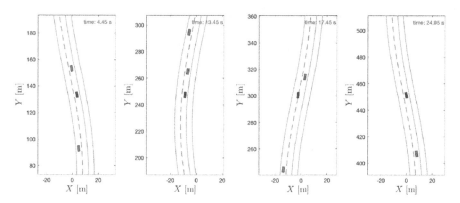

Fig. 11. Simulation 2. AV and PV travel upward. The other vehicles travel downward.

To evaluate the performance of the IDSS-DMP strategies in the two sub-scenarios, the following KPIs have been used:

- KPI1 [s]: Time taken to cover a given distance (450 m).
- KPI2 [s]: Time taken to stop in the emergency lane.
- KPI3 [m/s^2]: Root Mean Square (RMS) value of the lateral acceleration.
- KPI4 [m/s^2]: RMS value of the longitudinal acceleration. This KPI is clearly related to the fuel consumption.

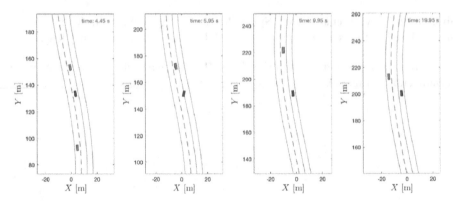

Fig. 12. Simulation 3. AV and PV travel upward. The other vehicles travel downward.

The KPI values obtained in the various simulations are reported in Table 1. As expected, the MDP sporty strategy allows quicker maneuvers but implies larger lateral and longitudinal accelerations (and thus a higher fuel consumption) with respect to the cautious strategy. In any case, according to the MDP designed in Sect. 3.2, both strategies are allowed to overtake only if this maneuver is safe and both of them are able to command an emergency stop in short times.

Table 1. KPI values obtained in the simulations.

Simulation	KPI1	KPI2	KPI3	KPI4
1	20.15	–	1.37	1.69
2	24.6	–	1.23	1.54
3	–	18.8	1.52	2.35
4	–	19.3	1.52	2.35

5 Conclusions

The system we illustrated in this paper, based on MDP framework, can be regarded as a decision-maker (when applied to ADFs) and even as a recommender tool (when applied to ADAS). These types of systems are widely used in many fields, to provide recommendations and suggestions based on some criteria, such as user's preferences and styles (see the "sporty strategies" and the "caution strategies" in our simulations), safety (e.g., no other vehicles are already overtaking the AV in the adjacent lane) and comfort (avoiding too strong lateral/longitudinal accelerations). With the ever-growing volume of information online, these systems can be a useful tool to overcome information overload, or to suggest a proper action to automation, with the related explanation to the user about what is happening and why. In literature, there are many types of recommendation/decision-making systems with different methodologies and concepts.

Various applications include e-commerce, healthcare, transportation, agriculture, and media. This paper provided our proposed solutions for an intelligent system supporting the decision (IDSS) in the context of AD. We defined it as "intelligent", because it is able to adapt to the different states of the user (e.g., aggressive/cautious, distracted/attentive, and so on) and to the external conditions (e.g., the lane for overtaking is free), as well as because it provides the best actions, in the sense that it satisfies optimal criteria in terms of travelled time, safety and comfort.

This work is preparatory for the final phase of the PRYSTINE project, in which the MDP-based IDSS will be integrated and implemented in the project demonstrator, the prototype Maserati vehicle (presented in Fig. 2). In particular, we will apply our solution to the use-case 3, for the emergency lane-change maneuver (described in Fig. 3).

Declarations

Funding. This work was supported by the Electronic Components and Systems for European Leadership Joint Undertaking (ECSEL), which funded the PRYSTINE project under Grant 783190.

Conflict of Interest. Authors declares that there are no conflicts of interests.

References

1. Rasmussen, J.: Human errors. A taxonomy for describing human malfunction in industrial installations. J. Occup. Accid. **4**(2–4), 311–333 (1982)
2. Siau, K., Wang, W.: Building trust in artificial intelligence, machine learning, and robotics. Cutter Bus. Technol. J. **31**(2), 47–53 (2018)
3. Puterman, M.L.: Markov Decision Processes. Discrete Stochastic Dynamic Programming. Wiley, Chichester (2005)
4. Jean Piaget's Theory and Stages of Cognitive Development, by Saul McLeod, Simply Psychology. Accessed 2018
5. Michon, J.A.: A critical view of driver behavior models: what do we know, what should we do? In: Evans, L., Schwing, R.C. (eds.) Human Behavior and Traffic Safety, pp. 485–524. Springer US, Boston, MA (1986). https://doi.org/10.1007/978-1-4613-2173-6_19
6. Tango, F., Aras, R., Pietquin, O.: Learning Optimal Control Strategies from Interactions with a PADAS. In: Cacciabue, P.C., Hjälmdahl, Magnus, Luedtke, Andreas, Riccioli, Costanza (eds.) Human Modelling in Assisted Transportation, pp. 119–127. Springer Milan, Milano (2011). https://doi.org/10.1007/978-88-470-1821-1_12
7. Ricci, F., Rokach, L., Shapira, B.: Introduction to recommender systems handbook. In: Ricci, F., Rokach, L., Shapira, B., Kantor, P.B. (eds.) Recommender Systems Handbook, pp. 1–35. Springer, Boston, MA (2011). https://doi.org/10.1007/978-0-387-85820-3_1
8. Fayyaz, Z., Ebrahimian, M., Nawara, D., Ibrahim, A., Kashef, R.: Recommendation systems: algorithms, challenges, metrics, and business opportunities. Appl. Sci. **10**(21), 7748 (2020). https://doi.org/10.3390/app10217748
9. Beel, J., Langer, S., Genzmehr, M., Gipp, B., Breitinger, C., Nürnberger, A.: Research paper recommender system evaluation: a quantitative literature survey. In: Proceedings of the International Workshop on Reproducibility and Replication in Recommender Systems Evaluation, Hong Kong, China, 12 October (2013), pp. 15–22 (2013)
10. Carsten, O., Martens, M.H.: How can humans understand their automated cars? HMI principles, problems and solutions. Cogn. Technol. Work **21**(1), 3–20 (2018). https://doi.org/10.1007/s10111-018-0484-0

11. Sharma, A., et al.: Is an informed driver a better decision maker? a grouped random parameter with heterogeneity-in-means approach to investigate the impact of the connected environment on driving behavior in safety-critical situations. Anal. Meth. Accid. Res. **27**, 100127 (2020)
12. Castellano, A., et al.: Is your request just this? New automation paradigm to reduce the requests of transition without increasing the effort of the driver. In: 25th ITS World Congress. Copenhagen, Denmark, vol. 17 (2018)
13. Gowda, N., Ju, W., Kohler, K.: Dashboard design for an autonomous car. In: Adjunct Proceedings of the 6th International Conference on Automotive user Interfaces and Interactive Vehicular Applications (2014)
14. Ju, W.: The design of implicit interactions. Synth. Lect. Hum.-Centered Inf. **8**(2), 1–93 (2015)
15. Findeisen, R., Allgower, F., Biegel, L.: Assessment and future directions of nonlinear model predictive control. In: Lecture Notes in Control and Information Sciences. Springer (2007). https://doi.org/10.1007/978-3-540-72699-9
16. Grune, L., Pannek, J.: Nonlinear model predictive control - theory and algorithms. In: Communications and control engineering. Springer (2011) https://doi.org/10.1007/s12555-011-0300-6

The Cognitive Study of Immersive Experience in Science and Art Exhibition

Ching-Wen Chang(✉)

Graduate School of Creative Industry Design, National Taiwan University of Art,
New Taipei City, Taiwan
lizchang@cycu.org.tw

Abstract. In terms of the history of design development, human engineering emerged after World War II in the 1950s, and continued to the rise of personal computers in the 1980s. Human-oriented interface design and human-oriented interactive interfaces are more important. In the 21st century, the age of sensibility is approaching. The so-called pleasure or experience, when it comes to cultural creativity, its interaction with "people" becomes more important.

Since the 1980s, science and technology art exhibitions have begun to focus on audience participation. Facing the challenges of the new century, why do you need to apply interactive technology in the art exhibition scene? What are the factors that affect the audience's experience of the immersive space? How to integrate resources to provide service innovation? It is a topic of contemporary art exhibition.

This research is based on literature discussion and case studies. It first sorts out the application of technology in Taiwan's art exhibitions in the past three years, and then focuses on the case of all-tech immersive performances. Through observation of the audience experience and focus group interviews at the exhibition site, we can understand the audience's perception of immersive immersion. The cognitive model of space is used as a reference for the modification of exhibition design.

In the future cultural performance stage, it is necessary to combine interactive technology with cultural connotation through the audience's experience, with educational concepts and interpretation creation as the purpose, and practical application in the new creative planning project of the exhibition space to complete cultural added value. And further develop service innovations to achieve the goals of "Co-produce", "Co-design" and "Co-deliver" for exhibitors and participants.

Keywords: Immersive experience · Hermeneutic theory · Metacognition · Service innovation

1 Introduction

In terms of the history of design development, human engineering emerged after World War II in the 1950s, and continued to the rise of personal computers in the 1980s. Human-oriented interface design and human-oriented interactive interfaces are more important. In the 21st century, the age of sensibility is approaching. The so-called pleasure or

© Springer Nature Switzerland AG 2021
D. D. Schmorrow and C. M. Fidopiastis (Eds.): HCII 2021, LNAI 12776, pp. 369–387, 2021.
https://doi.org/10.1007/978-3-030-78114-9_25

experience, when it comes to cultural creativity, its interaction with "people" becomes more important [1].

With the development and popularization of emerging technologies, the way people see and experience the world is gradually changing. Human are no longer satisfied with the traditional ways of sharing, communicating and transmitting information, but need to use more diverse media to enhance the sense of entertainment. Enjoy and attract more people to participate, and at the same time effectively transfer knowledge, cultural meaning and value. Among museums, cultural relics, and historical exhibition sites, guided explanations, displays, are impacted and challenged by new technologies, but also benefited from new technologies and have high potential to create a new way of pavilion interpretation. In fact, many museums and cultural fields have invested in the development and introduction of emerging technologies, such as immersive technologies (AR, VR), which allows the guided experience to escape the past one-way interpretation mode, and then the possibility of more immersive, more diverse, more interesting interaction and exhibit display [2].

As early as 2012, the Science Museum in London, UK, using AR technology in the museum, invited the well-known BBC host James May to use AR technology to create a virtual tour guide, just open the application in the mobile phone, tablet, and use the camera of the mobile phone after aligning the identification map of the mark, an image of the host will appear on the screen to explain, adding to the interactive nature of the museum tour [3]. In Taiwan, most of the common technology applications at the art exhibition site are digital navigation apps, and there are also use "five senses" (visual, tactile, auditory, technological, and historical) as the interactive main axis, combined with AR technology and AR Glasses and LBS real-time positioning services to create a Mobile Museum with educational functions are indeed the most innovative and eye-catching application examples of AR technology.

This research focuses on the immersive experience of science and technology art exhibitions. Through literature discussion and case studies, to understand domestic art exhibition activities, which technologies are used in the content of the exhibition? Why do exhibition spaces such as museums need digital content? Secondly, through trend research and expert interviews, what are the factors that affect the audience's immersive experience? Finally, use the service innovation design framework in the practical cases of domestic landmark museums, and during the trial operation stage, use Focus Group Interviews (FGI) to explore the effectiveness of the audience experiencing the immersive and fully interactive exhibition space. To serve as a reference for future space design and management amendments.

2 Literature Review

British industrial designer, the founder of IDEO design company in Silicon Valley, Bill Moggridge proposed to get industrial design from the perspective of "user-centered" and "interactive design", and creating the first notebook computer in history. In recent years, digital technology has been applied to the innovation and interactive design of different products and services. The overall picture of digital technology productization is a characteristic of design science and education, and design is regarded as a knowledge with both intellectual and perceptual. In the era of knowledge economy, the key to industrial growth lies in how to integrate knowledge and create value. The key to the success or failure of the innovation of the digital product content (including E-services) industry is how to use the practical value function of technological innovation through interactive design to create a product that conforms to product innovation strategies, market positioning, and is usable to target groups, easy to use, and can experience moving products during use [4]. An immersive experience is not only interactive entertainment but also sensory feast. More emphasis is placed on the connection of senses, ontology, interest, spatial cognition, narration, and emotion [5].

2.1 Science and Art Exhibition

Disney and Pixar Animation Director John Lasseter said that "Art challenges technology, technology inspires art". Walter Benjamin also mentioned in *"The work of Art in the Age of Mechanical Reproduction"* that "Artwork can be copied mechanically: this fact has changed everyone's perception of art." [6]. Technology and art are not two areas with clear boundaries. Intervene, challenge and merge with each other, and even copy each other. The form and connotation of artistic creation changed with the development of human society; perspective and anatomy were used in the 15th century Renaissance, and the 18th century used photographic technology for experimental creation. In the 1960s and 1970s, the camera, video recorder and television generally, artists are allowed to create audio-visual products. After the 1970s, computer software and hardware equipment, the internet, virtual reality, etc., were researched and developed with increasingly mature technology and media, making the development of technology and art more vigorous.

Since the development of science and art, the reason why interactive design that emphasizes returning to the human level for thinking has been valued in recent years is that it transcends technology and takes human needs and experience as considerations to create a perfect relationship between technology and human link. The focus is not on pursuing the newest technology, nor on how to create beautiful compositions, but on a creative process that uses wisdom to make technology truly "serve people." The "service" referred to here is not a waiter or simply the service industry. Commercially, the difference between products and services is that "the product itself is used to solve the functional needs of users, but other needs derived from the purchase of the product will be solved by the service." When this concept is applied to a technological art exhibition, it means that "the technological art itself may attract the participation of the audience, but the emotional cognition and in-depth experience derived from participation will be solved by the service." This concept is the same as the design thinking concept proposed by Tim Brown, that is, "Continuously evaluate and modify each design link, and at the three levels of Desirability, Feasibility, and Viability to strike a balance." [7].

In terms of technical characteristics, both "Technology Art" and "Media Art" have "dynamic", "media", "connectivity", "interactivity" and "timeliness", or the above permutations or combinations of characteristics [8]. The main characteristics presented by interactive art are: Interactivity, Immersion, Imagination and Creativity, Hypermedia. Users can get cross-domain and cross-disciplinary perception from sound, light, interactive programs, and even smell [9]. Virtual reality works of art use sound guidance and unique interactive equipment between the artist's design and audience immersion to create and explore elements such as space, time and perception, and in the fields of architecture, cognitive neurology, installation, sound composition, and visual art cooperating. Virtual reality technology highlights three notable features: "immersion" that emphasizes spatiality, "interaction" that emphasizes technological innovation, and "imagination" in perceiving time experience [10].

Museum researcher and scholar Wang Songshan sorted out and reviewed the research literature of Taiwan museums, and pointed out that the progress of science and technology has changed the aspects of research, collection and preservation, exhibition and education, and social and cultural services in museum practice. The three aspects of Museum Substances existence, Museum Qualities and Museum Relations all have different degrees of influence. The advancement of science and technology has created new display possibilities; the expansion of information systems has changed the interpretation and communication of museums, such as attempts to achieve aesthetic goals through scientific means. Not only that, the design field of the museum is also trying to develop a more extensive and scientific design calculation model. In addition, as museums move from "education-oriented" to "learning-oriented", the importance and complexity of learning tools have increased. The software design that advocates the integration of "human, machine, and environment" interaction can allow the hardware functions of the exhibition hall to be fully utilized. New technology enables the museum to extend virtual display and sensory experience in addition to the traditional physical display. Wang Songshan also believes that future research on the application of new technologies in museums and other exhibition spaces should at least respond to the following trends:

1. Not only pursue in-depth research foundation, but also no ignore the innovation of visual effects;
2. Attach importance to the effects of leisure and entertainment, emphasize regional characteristics and encourage people to participate;
3. Deepening and popularizing the subject research;
4. Caring for social issues as a forum reflecting diverse opinions;
5. Technology instigates actions and changes in community organizations [11].

Technological art blurs the boundary between art and media, allowing viewers to have a close dialogue with the works, bringing novel spatial experiences and psychological fluctuations. The newness of new media technology does not lie in the new technology, but the new concept. The new technology of every era has promoted the advancement, innovation and reflection of contemporary art. Art critic John Berger wrote in "*Another Image Narrative*": The camera was invented in 1839, so Positivism, Sociology, and Photography can be said to be born and grown together. All three believe that scientists can record, observe, and measure truth, precision and accuracy will replace metaphysics, and scientific truth will replace individual subjectivity. In the same way, the most widely used AR/VR/MR technology in the modern era of technology and art may also drive the entire era of advanced understanding of human interaction, immersive experience, theater interpretation, and service experience. Become the era of desirable, feasible and sustainable participation in art. (see Table 1).

Table 1. Keywords and commonality of art/design of technology application.

Scholars	Theory	Keywords	Commonality
Wang Songshan (2006)	Museum display	Audience, technology, field, narration	Feasible/interactive Desirable/immersive Renewable/theatre Education/learning Entertainment/pleasure Experience/enrichment
Yuan Guangming (2006)	Technology and art	Power, media, time, connection, interaction	
Bill Moggridge (2008)	Industrial design	Useful, easy to use, attractive	
Tim Brown (2010)	Design thinking	Demand, feasibility, survival	
Ye Jinrui (2010)	Interactive design	Effective, simple, enjoyable	
Lin Peichun (2012)	New media art	Interaction, integration, imagination, hypermedia	
Roberto Diodato (2012)	Virtual reality	Space immersion, technological interaction, perception imagination	
Feng Mingzhu (2015)	Museum challenge	Digital technology, cultural equality, localization	

2.2 Immersive Experience

According to Csikszentmihalyi's original definition, immersion is "the user enters a common experience mode, in which the user seems to be attracted, and the consciousness is concentrated in a very narrow range, so some irrelevant perceptions and thoughts are filtered out. He also loses consciousness, only responds to specific goals and clear feedback, and produces a sense of control through the manipulation of the environment." [12]. Thinks that people will do what they want to do based on their internal drive, not external ones. The priority of factors depends on individual needs, and immersion (flow) experience is the prototype of the true motivation for this state of consciousness.

In the theory of immersion, skill and challenge are two important factors. The two must balance each other and drive the self to a higher and more complex level; what is produced by immersion is a kind of self-harmony. Enjoying "merging of activity and awareness" in the activity, because the participants are fully engaged in the activity, and may have completed tasks that are usually impossible, but the participants are completely unaware of the activity the challenges brought by them have long been beyond what they can handle in the past. This feeling will make more surely of themselves and encourage individuals to work harder to learn new skills. When the individual's self-evaluation continues to improve, the experience of "it has its own purpose", that is, the individual will continue to work hard to continue to get this feeling [13].

Immersion theory has been used in Computer and Internet research in recent years, and it has confirmed that there is indeed immersion in Internet usage. Research by foreign scholars Lombard, Reich and Grabe pointed out that the process of individual participation in game context interaction will begin to have a sense of control over the manipulation of the environment, respond to specific goals, and filter out the impact of irrelevant perceptions, and enter the immersive state at this time [14]. The research of Johnson and Wiles has an in-depth analysis of the impact of game interface design on users, pointing out that players will have a positive emotional experience during the game due to the full control and sense of play, which makes the players focus and filter the feeling of irrelevance is to enter the state of selflessness, so it is believed that through the game, the user can enter a state of immersion [15]. The research of Hsu and Lu pointed out that in the environment of online games, immersion is defined as a kind of fun experience, including the fun, control, concentration and inner interest gained during the game [16]. Sweetser and Wyeth extended their research on immersion theory in games, and proposed a complete theoretical model for "user experience" and "enjoyment," called "Game Flow". Believe that enjoyment is an important factor and characteristic of users' willingness to play games. It contains eight aspects, including games, concentration, challenges and skills, control, clear goals, feedback, indulge and social activities, etc., bringing the theory of immersion into the discussion of the game [17].

Most of the theoretical aspects can echo the characteristics of the immersion theory proposed by the scholar Csikszentmihalyi. On the whole, participants will focus on challenging tasks, and use their skills to break through and successfully complete tasks. In the process of participating wholeheartedly, because was immersed in it, so ignored existence and distorted the sense of time. When people are engaged in certain things, it is particularly easy to enter a state of full devotion and selflessness, and even not aware of the passage of time, after this event is over, they will feel very satisfied and happy, to achieve this state is "Experience of Flow". The scope of the discussion is very wide, there are not only a lot of follow-up studies in academics, but also widely used in leisure, sports, entertainment and education in life. Csikszentmihalyi further concluded that immersion experience has nine characteristics, namely:

1. Clear goals
2. Challenge-skills balance
3. Unambiguous feedback
4. Focused attention (focus)
5. Merging of action and awareness
6. Sense of control
7. Loss of self-consciousness
8. Distortion of time
9. Intrinsic motivation cycle [18].

If distinguished by "Immersion Object", it can be divided into the following six different types of immersion dimensions: sensory, ontology, sense of interest, spatial cognition, narration, and emotion. These six kinds of immersion are not mutually exclusive concepts, they are often mixed in real time, or exist in a work of art at the same time [19]. In addition to these six types, this study believes that it is necessary to add the type of "Time Immersion", for example, when watching certain virtual reality works, the viewer's body does not actually move, but spatial cognition is closely related to the concept of time (see Table 2).

Table 2. International scholars discuss the definition of immersion, drawn by this research.

Scholar	Definition
Csikszentmihalyi (1998)	Concentrated on the task of challenge, selflessness, unawareness of the passage of time, satisfaction and joy after the task was completed
Chen et al. (1999) Novak et al. (2000)	Novak et al. (2000) are completely involved in the activity situation, concentrate and filter out all irrelevant perceptions, that is, enter the immersion state
Johnson, Wiles (2003)	Immersion is a state of concentration and pleasure
Hsu and Liu (2004)	Immersion is a kind of fun experience, including the fun and sense of control obtained in game activities, and the concentration and inner fun in the process
Wen and Yang (2005)	Immersion is a state of concentration and contemplation. When people enter this state, they will feel an uplifting force in their body and mind
Sweetser and Wyeth (2005)	Extended the study of immersion theory in games, and proposed a complete theoretical model for "user experience" and "enjoyment", and called it "game immersion"
M. V. Sanchez-Vives and M. Slater (2005)	Aware of both "location" and "event" and at the same time that there is no such location or event. The confusion about the difference between real and virtual places and events
J. Löwgren (2007)	The system needs to be able to induce a sufficient sense of "perceived reality". The important element of this "perceived reality" is the system's technical ability to provide "non-mediated perceptual illusion."
C. C. Bracken, G. Pettey, T. Guha, B. E. Rubenking (2010)	This state of existence is in a psychological state or subjective perception, where even if the experience is produced by technology, part or all of the personal perception cannot recognize the effect of technology in the virtual experience

(continued)

Table 2. (*continued*)

Scholar	Definition
Gordon Calleja (2011)	Immersion dimensions: senses, ontology, sense of interest, spatial cognition, narration, emotion
Ostrom, Parasuraman, Bowen, Patricio, Voss (2015)	Using reality and virtual technology can enable consumers to play a more dynamic and autonomous role in their experience
S. Turner, C. W. Huang, L. Burrows, P. Turner (2016)	Positively related to the richness of the feeling of technological intervention, which promotes isolation or decoupling from the real world
Lemon & Verhoef (2016)	Significantly affect customer experience, defined as "the customer's cognition, emotion, behavior, sensory and social response to the company's products throughout the purchase process
Nikolai Tenev (2019)	Types of immersive experience: 360-degree panoramic view, digital avatar, virtual reality, augmented reality, mixed reality, and extended reality
Chenyan Zhang (2020)	Realize the purpose of XR entertainment, create a complete sensory simulation close to reality, and study mentality phenomena or problems

2.3 Hermeneutic Theory

This research focuses on the cognition of immersive experience. Therefore, hermeneutics is adopted as the philosophical position of metacognition. Cognition and metacognition are the two main factors of thinking. Cognition includes elements such as recall, coding, information processing, creative thinking, critical thinking, decision-making, problem solving, and conceptualization; Metacognitive thinking operations include planning, monitoring, and evaluation. Metacognition includes two fields: Metacognitive Knowledge and Metacognitive Experience; Metacognitive Knowledge refers to a person possessing knowledge related to cognitive matter; Metacognitive Experience is the individual the conscious experience of cognition and affection, Metacognition is to plan, monitor, test, modify, and evaluate personal learning habits [20].

Because Hermeneutics is a science and method related to "understanding", and art performances involve various phenomena, the "part and whole", "contextual context", "historical consciousness", "experience" and "dialogue" emphasized by Hermeneutics concepts can provide a path to in-depth understanding of art, as well as aspects such as customer perception verification and subjective reflection. Although Hhermeneutics is one of the common theoretical viewpoints in research methods, it is widely used in the research of humanities and sociology. There are few related discourses on technology or art research methods, or only the research applies hermeneutics methods to art research. Multiple interpretations, such as: Paul Ricoeur's Hermeneutics is a method of analyzing the meaning of time implicit in images, movies, animations or photographic images. That is, the cycle of narrative and time, Paul Ricoeur believes that the text shows the "Historical feature of human experience is that it is at a distance, or through communication from a distance." [21].

However, if the science and technology art exhibition is regarded as a readable or writable text, a theater, a cultural product, or a service system, it is necessary to actively explore the original intention of the author and the work and the possible extension of the meaning. According to Ricoeur's view, an interpretive text is a dialectical process between "understanding" and "interpretation", and both are the constituent elements of Hermeneutics. The important thing is not what is hidden behind the text, but the meaning it reveals. Understanding is not just about the author's intention in the text, but the meaning it projects to the reader. Such a text is "an invitation, an accessible space, and an opportunity to create a new reality" [22]. Gadamer said: "The interpretation and understanding of the text is the fusion of two horizons." These two horizons are the horizons of readers and the horizons that people want to try to understand in the past. Through mutual experience, cognition and mutual influence, the mutual commonality or the same rationality in cognition is formed, which is also the basis of human interaction and communication. And the life world is not a self-centered solipsistic world, but a world shared, understood and experienced with others. Gadamer regards understanding as a process of dialogue. Therefore, there must be an act of communication between subject and object to form a Relevance, a new experience, proceed like a "game" [23].

3   Research Methods

This research is based on literature discussion and case studies. As the subject of discussion is the immersive experience of science and technology art exhibitions and the subject of the case is the Museum, therefore, we will first carry out the application of technology in domestic art exhibitions in recent years, sort out the immersive experience, and at the same time make an extended collection of the literature on the interpretation theory and service design that affects the audience's experience.

For practical cases of all-tech immersive exhibition space design, we started with the "Interpretive case study" at the pre-research stage, emphasizing that the number of cases is refined, and re-understanding the problem is the focus. The angle determines the resolution, reasoning must be integrated into dialectics, and see what has not been seen before [24]. Then, through in-depth interviews with museum researchers, educational expert advisors, and exhibition design leaders, we will study the cognitive attributes, emotional depth, and design value of various types of technology applications in the minds of audiences, designers, and business owners. Through exploring the context and research collecting data, integrating new and old resources, summarizing experience services and new creation attributes, as the prototype of service innovation for exhibition space design based on design thinking and service design process planning.

The evaluation criteria refer to the literature review of Tim Hilken and others, and evaluate the design, service, and experience from the aspects of AR variables, experience reality, experience evaluation, decision-making, behavioral intention, and brand recognition [25]. Before launching, conduct in-depth interviews with experts and stakeholders; after launching, in addition to on-site observation, also focus group interviews (FGI, cognition, technical operation, drama guide), and audience surveys (experience, service process, cultural acupuncture).

3.1 Trend Research: Immersive Experience Application of Taiwan Science and Art Exhibition

Over the past few decades, neuroscience has discovered a wealth of new information about our senses and how they act as our gateway to the world. Dr. Rob DeSalle, curator of the Invertebrates at the American Museum of Natural History, explained how we see, hear, smell, touch, taste, maintain balance, feel pain, and rely on other unfamiliar senses. He also explained how these senses are aesthetically, Art and music shape our perception of the world. Immersive experience is "the perception of physical existence in the non-physical world" [26]. "Our ability to perceive the world may have begun before the human species began to think. Exploring how and why we perceive the environment around us is the topic of our museum's exploration. Therefore, the "Our Senses" exhibition will provide visitors with an immersive experience." The curator Rob Desalle also mentioned that he hopes visitors can learn without knowing it.

In Taiwan, an immersive environment is a new trend in the field of technology and art exhibitions. The five senses are fully open, allowing participants to experience (meta) the experience (cognition) of others. As the connotation of science and technology continues to evolve, the traditional digital content industry is facing dynamic adjustments. From the original three core industries: Digital games, Computer animation, and Digital learning, it has expanded to a digital content industry that combines Emerging technologies (somatosensory) and Fusion.

With the development and popularization of emerging technologies, the way people see and experience the world is gradually changing. Museums, art galleries, historical sites and other arts and cultural institutions have long played the role of conveying culture, inheriting value, and giving play to the "4E" (Education, Ecstatic, Entertain, Enrich) society Function, it is undeniable that "Entertain" is one of the most critical functions. Therefore, the experience provided by art institutions to users is extremely important. In the era of digitization of everything, the physical art field has the spatial characteristic of "experience first".

This means that it is not difficult to select the pieces of works to be exhibited, but facing "how to transform the work" and "how to interpret" is a big challenge. For example, if you think about the characteristics of immersive experience such as VR/AR, you can think further, and have a step-by-step, layered experience, so that the experiencer can deeply understand perception. Therefore, when using virtual technology in art, it must be the three principles of display of "virtual reality", "enhanced reality" and "surpassing reality" proceed to research and create. In terms of space design, it is also necessary to take into account the "virtual and real integrated dual-situation field", "the cultural relic-based virtual theater", and "design in line with the characteristics of the VR experience" (all-directional scene construction, good movement guidance) [27] (see Table 3).

Table 3. Multimedia and immersive art exhibition and related technologies in Taiwan.

Exhibition name	Year/location	Technology application
Underwater archaeology immersive theater-ocean magic cube	2018/New Taipei city shihsanhang museum of archaeology	All-age immersive theater. 36 pieces of 55-inch borderless spliced TV wall, 720-degree three-dimensional surrounding space
Taipei machinery factory exhibition	2018/Ministry of culture	All-age immersive theater. AR multimedia tour of the whole area
Penghu navy story exhibition	2019/Cultural assets bureau, ministry of culture	All-age immersive theater. 360-degree panoramic video, somatosensory interaction, interactive light table, animation, dynamic image. Gold Medal at the 52nd Houston International Film Festival in 2019
Steam dreamworks	2019/National taiwan museum	All-age immersive theater. VR real 3D interaction, large-scale train entity light sculpture, interactive huge projection in the whole area, light sculpture theater
Reflections along the river NPM x WEIWUYING: new media art exhibition	2019/Kaohsiung weiwuying national art and culture center	AI guided tour, huge scrolls of ancient paintings and animations, virtual reality VR, high-quality promotional videos
Science and technology archaeology	2020/New Taipei City Shihsanhang Museum of Archaeology	3D printing, 2D image 3D stereo, AR guide, situational participation (archaeological detective)
Asia wineware exhibition	2020/Cultural assets bureau, ministry of culture 、shihsanhang museum of archaeology	All-age immersive theater. Multi-human interaction

(continued)

Table 3. (*continued*)

Exhibition name	Year/location	Technology application
Children's gallery 2.0	2020/National palace museum	All-age immersive theater. High-tech electronically controlled glass, interactive drawing and sculpture, multi-sensory theater, AI study table, digital deep learning, high-tech radar interactive wall
Bestiarum vocabulum: NPM x hsinchu 241 new media art exhibition	2020/Hsinchu 241 art space	All-age immersive theater. VR real 3D interactive, huge projection, 7-m high projection projection
Listen! the river is talking—children's experience hall	2020/Tamsui heritage museum	All-age immersive theater. 3D floor stickers, AR guide, highly interactive and comprehensive projection, huge light sculpture mountain, somatosensory interactive fishing, historical scene AR battle game
Century Journey-Taipei City centennial exhibition	2020/Taipei municipal archives academia	GIS synthesis, high-tech radar interactive wall, AR US military airstrike interactive, antique typewriter interactive table
The one-hundred-year commemoration of historic events	2021/Beitou hot spring fraternity permanent exhibition	AR interactive full-length mirror, light sculpture projection, old-fashioned counter AR check in interactive

3.2   Interpretive Case Study: NPM Children's Gallery 2.0

Wu Micha, the current director of the National Palace Museum (NPM): "Among the international museums, the National Palace Museum is the first to incorporate new media art into the national treasure collection. Many works win prizes at international film festivals every year. This is due to Taiwan's advanced digital technology. If there is no Taiwan's high technology, the National Palace Museum's cultural relics are just the National Palace Museum's cultural relics. Because of technology, the National Palace Museum has undergone tremendous changes. This is not just an addition, but a multiplicative effect." Expectations for innovation; to break away from the stereotypes of traditional museums, to make strides towards cutting-edge technology combining art and technology, and to become the domestic leader in applying technological immersion experience to children's art spaces. At the beginning of the preparation for the Children's Gallery 2.0 permanent exhibition space, Xu Xiaode, Director of the Education Exhibition Office, also specifically requested, "The exhibition space should be designed in the spirit of research, and should not be interactive for interaction, but must have educational connotations."

In Taiwan, the National Palace Museum (NPM) is like the epitome of social and economic development. Since 2006, on the basis of digital collections, the Palace Museum has begun to cooperate with colleges and universities and the industry to combine technology and art to move towards new media art creation. The main types are Ancient painting animation, 3D animation film, special exhibition of new media art. The exhibition venues are not limited to the NPM, including airports, cultural and creative parks, campuses, friend halls, local arts and cultural institutions, and other areas outside the hospital, and even go overseas, or synchronize with foreign museums, and online joint virtual exhibitions. It has almost transformed an ancient traditional museum into a museum without walls, and then moved towards a mobile museum and a cloud museum. In response to the advent of the digital technology era, no matter in the collection, education, service and new media applications, there are rapid and huge contingency measures. As a result, the original operation and operation methods of the NPM have almost changed, and the established image of the NPM has been reversed for more than 30 years. Since then, in the face of social changes, it has also adjusted its operating policies and development direction to meet six major challenges:

1. Challenges in the era of digital technology;
2. Caring for the challenges of Taiwan's native culture;
3. Challenges from the aspirations of "Balance between North and South. Cultural Wealth";
4. The challenge of rising social welfare awareness;
5. Challenges from the rise of cultural and creative industries;
6. The increasingly prosperous business has caused a serious shortage of museum space [28].

Therefore, Cimi Design which the design executive unit, adheres to the three cores of ART (Antique, Reality, Tech) cultural relics, reality, and technology, as the main axis of the space design and planning, and runs through the entire audience. The character "Xiao Cui" is an animation transformed from the National Treasure of the NPM, serves as a virtual tour guide for the audience to enter the expedition. In the process of exploration, the audience can experience the wisdom and taste of ancient people's life. The use of multimedia makes ancient cultural relics come to life, full of imagination space, increase the perception of memory, and create a new narrative power, no longer just passive receivers. Rather, it has the opportunity to become a part of history and even the leader of interpretation.

3.3   Evaluation Criteria: Evaluation Criteria for Immersive Experience

Immersive experience is a new way that accompanies the experience economy. The purpose is to create a comprehensive experience for participants that is, by shaping the senses and thinking, emotional experience, attracting the attention of consumers, and causing emotional resonance or thinking identification, for Products and services find new value and living space. At present, the major exhibition venues focus on the introduction and design of 360-degree holographic images, AR augmented reality, VR virtual reality, MR mixed reality, and digital twin, which are full of fun and Interactivity. There are three E indicators for evaluating the effectiveness of interactive design: Effectiveness of the functional side (Effective), Easy operation of the operation side (Easy), and Enjoyable side of the pleasure (Enjoyable) [29].

Immersion is one of the characteristics that must exist after the user interacts with the virtual environment. Why is immersive experience important when designing and experimenting with virtual environments? Chenyan Zhang believes that the following three aspects are the most relevant: Realizing the purpose of XR Entertainment, Create a complete sensory simulation close to reality, Research on mentality phenomena or problems [30].

In the process of literature discussion, most researchers will first find the "process" (mode) of using technology to communicate from the aspects of function, operation, and pleasure perception, and summarize the "dimensions" (factors) from the literature as evaluation criteria, and then select "tools" (methods) to analyze the effectiveness of "experience" (metacognition). For example: Scholar Chenyan Zhang measures immersive experience in five dimensions: validity, reliability, sensitivity, non-invasiveness, and novelty, using psychometric questionnaires, continuous active observation, primary and secondary task performance, neuropsychology, etc. the quality of.

There are also context-aware theories as the framework, through literature review, trying to summarize the research framework of AR's omni-channel experience, helping to explain how people naturally participate in information processing and the formation of preferences and decision-making. More and more researchers use situational cognition to explain customer experience and behavior. Contextual awareness means that when customers experience the integration of information about products and services (Embedded) when they experience immediate decision-making, allow physical interaction with the product or service (Embodiment) and provide opportunities, their experience seems to be closest to reality, and willing to share (Extend). When the customer experience reaches the cognitive level of "Embedding", "Embodiment", and "Expansion", it can best enhance the reality basis of the experience, contrary to other emerging technologies that immerse customers in a fully integrated environment (such as virtual reality). AR complements reality rather than replaces reality. Therefore, the specific concepts and metrics unique to AR are summarized [25].

This research will verify the concept and service of the prototype design in the future, it is planned to adopt the literature review of Tim Hilken et al. as a criterion reference for evaluation, from AR variables, experience reality, experience evaluation, decision-making, behavioral intention, brand recognition and other aspects are evaluated.

Before the exhibition, first conduct a focus interview group, co-hosted by the education consultant and design director, invite the target audience of the children's art space:

two classes in elementary schools (60 people) and one class in junior high schools (30 people) for in-depth interviews and interactive discussions. Bring the science and technology model applied to the exhibition hall to the class for the participants to try it out. During Trial operation stage, the design team arranges a parent-child group (five groups, about 20 people) to participate in the experience of all interactive exhibits in the entire exhibition area, and at the same time shoot the promotional video. And after the exhibition, museum management staff will first conduct guided training and assessment, and arrange holiday drama guided activities, inviting parent-child groups to participate (each time 30 min, 20 groups of families, a total of 10 games, online reservation is required), and service providers after the event (Volunteers, guides) and audience surveys.

4   Results and Discussion

4.1   IEDSP: Immersive Experience Design Service Prototype for NPM Children's Gallery 2.0 Full-Tech Immersion Space Exhibition

Under the request of the owner to inject the spirit of academic research into the exhibition venue design, this research uses the service experience engineering method to construct an Immersive Experience Design Service Prototype (**IEDSP**) (see Fig. 1). The newly launched National Palace Museum Children's Gallery 2.0 in July 2020, the design executive unit Cimi Design adheres to the three cores of **ART** (Antique, Reality, Tech) cultural relics, reality, and technology, as the design main axis of the all-tech immersive space. The entire exhibition area is like a large-scale picture book, like a vehicle that can fly over the long river of history.

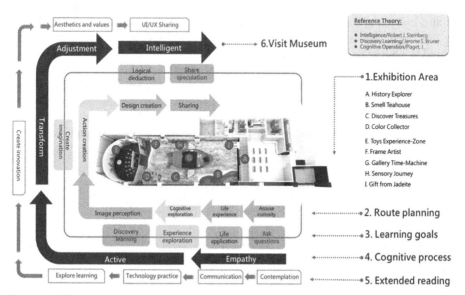

Fig. 1. IEDSP: immersive experience design service prototype of national palace museum children' gallery 2.0 full-tech immersion space exhibition, drawn by this research.

The characters run through the audience. The animated character "Xiao Cui" transformed from the NPM national treasure jade cabbage is used as a virtual tour guide for the audience to enter the expedition. All are invited visitors explore the beauty of cultural relics together through the stages of curiosity, experience, cognition, memory, creation, and sharing. The imaginative story situation not only allows the audience to enter the immersive fantasy theater, but also provides museum guides with more innovative options for theatrical tour. In the process of exploration, the audience can experience the wisdom and taste of ancient people's life. The use of multimedia makes ancient cultural relics come alive, full of imagination space and increased memory perception, thereby creating a new narrative power, no longer just passive receivers, but It has the opportunity to become a part of history and even the leader of interpretation.

Even if a wealth of technological components used, the inheritance or establishment of cultural context cannot be ignored. The design of the NPM Children's Gallery 2.0 exhibition space is still centered on the museum's "*Illustrated Album of Sea Oddities*", "*Along River During the Qingming Festival*" and selected cultural relics in the collection. It is used by museum researchers, educators, and new media artists. Under the cooperation, plan the route from the perspective of sharing and close to the people, complete the learning process under the goal of sharing, at the same time expand the reading with potential development as the topic, and design teaching aids with the level of cognitive computing, and finally enter the museum as the purpose of operating with the returning audience, the cultural mission is always on top.

4.2 IECPM: Immersive Experience Cognitive Process Model

Through literature discussion and case studies, this research not only establishes the prototype of full technology Immersive Experience Design Service Prototype (**IEDSP**), but also constructs the Immersive Experience Cognitive Process Model (**IECPM**, see Fig. 2). The aim is to explore the immersive experience of technology art exhibitions. It should be based on interaction, immersion, education, and games, and then advanced through interpretive theories, to help participants "experience" the multi-valued field of art and gain full self-presence. It may even become one of the reference elements of the service innovation model. The **IECPM** tool can assist in observing how participants can make themselves a part of the work from the Intervention → Incarnation → Extended experience process. After converting experience, the extended metacognition can be expressed, which is the use of experience and experience, classify and structure the experience mode of knowledge content.

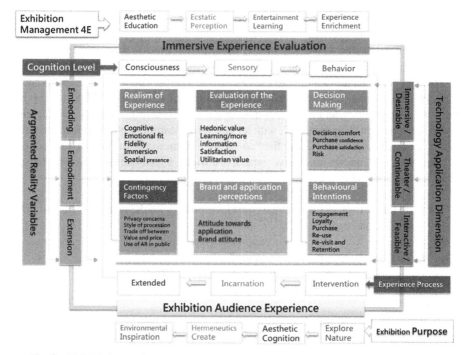

Fig. 2. IECPM: immersive experience cognitive process model, drawn by this research.

5   Conclusion

With the rapid development of technology, all walks of life are using technology, intelligence and mobility to drive product sales and service innovation. In addition to the rapid delivery of products or services, flow and experience are more valued. During this research period, I proposed "**IEDSP + IECPM**", which can be practically used in the design of service innovation processes for cultural and artistic exhibitions. At the same time, in the verification stage, try to echo Carlos Flavián, Sergio Ibáñez-Sánchez, Carlos Orús mentioned in their research that the future experience in the field of science and technology can be considered:

I.   Do customers perceive the meaning of technology in the same way?
II.   How do users' cognition, emotion, behavior, sensory and social reactions work when experiencing technological art? Which are the main variables?
III. What is the role of technology in driving customer behavior? Is the embodied technology more immersive and multi-perceptive than external technologies? [31]

Although the introduction of technology has changed the existing visit experience of art exhibitions, people seem to be able to appreciate the exhibits up close without going to the scene, and even get supplementary information or interaction in real time than visiting the physical exhibition. However, how to balance the virtual and the interaction in the application in fact, it is the key point to choose. When the wave of construction surges, if you don't want to make the immersive experience short-lived, you must continue to pay attention: Is the exhibits the main core? Do you plan a good experience space? Is there a complete maintenance service? Is there a relief plan for traffic management? Does it connect with education promotion and take root down?

Through the guidance of immersive interactive design, performance participants have more opportunities to go from the traditional passive and stereotyped "Making" (operation), to open thinking and exploring trial and error "Tinkering" (repair), to problem solving and creation "Engineering", with an innovative learning rhythm to face the new century art exhibition space. Under the "co-creation framework" of interactive creation [32], this research endows immersive experience with the connotation of interpretation in the science and technology art exhibition space, trying to construct:

1. Integrate the "Co-produce" inclusive product model with the resources of "cultural relics, reality, and technology";
2. Emphasize the "Co-design" co-creation design model at the core of the experience of "history, interpretation, and education";
3. Link the co-learning creative spirit of "Co-deliver" through "interaction, immersion, theater" drama guides and educational activities.

To welcome the traditional innovation of the era of "community", the technology and art exhibition space is regarded as the adaptable option of "cultural life".

References

1. Lin, R.: Exploring the Prospect of Design Education in Taiwan from the Bauhaus Style. Department of Applied Fine Arts of Fu Jen Catholic University (Editor-in-Chief). In: Proceedings of the International Symposium in Commemoration of the 90th Anniversary of Bauhaus, pp. 59–76. Fu Jen Catholic University Press, New Taipei City (2009)
2. Zhong, Y.: Experience economy: museum immersion technology development and application. Evaluation and analysis of the MIC industry by the Information Technology Council. https://www2.itis.org.tw/netreport/NetReport_Detail.aspx?rpno=961231832. 30 July 2019
3. Moggridge, B.: Key design report: changing the interaction design principles of the past and the future. Published by Machaus, Taipei (2008). Translated by Xu Yuling. The original publication year: 2007
4. Yumeng Digital Technology Company, AR Augmented Reality Enriches Navigation Experience, Becoming a Museum's New Revolution, Artplant. https://www.arplanet.com.tw/trends/artrends/arinmuseums/. 27 March 2020
5. Xiangyun, H.: Is immersive art Buzzword, or is it an indispensable "innovative concept"? The experimental field of contemporary culture of Air Force, CLABO experimental wave. https://mag.clab.org.tw/category/feature/immersion/. 31 March 2020
6. Benjamin, W.: Art Works in the Age of Mechanical Copy: A Collection of Ban Yaming. Business Weekly Publications, Inc., Taipei (2019). Translated by Zhuang Zhongli. The original publication year: 2013
7. Brown, T.: Change by Design: How Design Thinking Transforms Organizations and Inspires Innovation. Harper Collins, Scotland (2009)
8. Yuan, G.: Overview of the Development of Media Art. Taiwanese digital art. https://www.digiarts.org.tw/DigiArts/DataBasePage/4_88361759652866/Chi. September 2016

9. Lin, P.: (Editor-in-Chief): Taiwan Digital Art e Archives. Artist Publishing Co., Taipei. (2012)
10. Diodato, R.: Aesthetics of the Virtual. NY: State University of New York Press, New York, p. 36. (2012)
11. Wang, S.: Technology, society and museums. Museology Quarterly, 20(1) (2006)
12. Csikszentmihalyi, M.: Beyond boredom and anxiety. Jossey-Bass, California, p. 75 (1975).
13. Csikszentmihalyi, M., LeFevre, J.: Optimal experience in work and Leisure. J. Pers. Soc. Psychol. **56**(5), 815–822 (1989)
14. Lombard, M., Reich, R., Grabe, M.E., Bracken, C., Ditton, T.: Presence and television: the role of screen size. Hum. Commun. Res. **26**(1), 75–98 (2000)
15. Johnson, D., Wiles, J.: Effective affective user interface design in games. J. Ergon. **46**, 1332–1345 (2003)
16. Hsu, C.L., Lu, H.P.: Why do people play on-line games? An extended TAM with social influences and flow experience. J. Inf. Manage. **41**, 853–868 (2004)
17. Sweetser, P., Wyeth, P.: Game flow: a model for evaluating player enjoyment in Games. ACM Comput. Entertainment **3**(3), 3 (2005)
18. Csikszentmihalyi, M.: Flow: The psychology of optimal experience. Harper & Row, New York (1990)
19. Calleja, G.: In-Game from Immersion to Incorporation. MIT Press, Cambridge (2011)
20. Flavell, J.H.: Cognitive Development, 2nd edn. Prentice-Hall, New Jersey, Englewood Cliffs (1985)
21. Ricoeur, P.: Time and Narrative, vol. I. The University of Chicago Press, Chicago (1990)
22. Hilligoss, S.: Robert Coles. Twayne Publishers, New York (1997)
23. Gadamer, H.: Truth and Method (2nd ed.). The Continuum Publishing Company, New York, p. 269. (1989)
24. Dyer, W.G., Wilkins, A.L.: Better stories, not better constructs, to generate better theory a rejoinder to eisenhardt. Acad. Manag. Rev. **16**(3), 613–619 (1991)
25. Hilken, T., Heller, J., Chylinski, M.: Debbie Isobel Keeling, Dominik Mahr, Ko de Ruyter: Making omnichannel an augmented reality: the current and future state of the art. J. Res. Interact. Mark. **12**(4), 509–523 (2018)
26. DeSalle, R.: Our Senses: An Immersive Experience, p. 7. Yale University Press, London (2018)
27. Pu, L.: The past and present of technology and humanities: NPM Tide: Taiwan Chinese Creative Park Tour Calligraphy and Painting Art 4G New Media Art Exhibition, NPM Cultural Relics Monthly, 402, pp. 117–128 (2016)
28. Feng, M.: Challenges and Responses: On the Changes of the National Palace Museum in the Past 30 Years, NPM Academic Quarterly, 33(1) (2015)
29. Jinrui, Y.: Introduction to Interactive Design. Artist Publishing Co., Taipei (2010)
30. Zhang, C.: The Why, What, and How of Immersive Experience. IEEE Access, 8 (2020)
31. Flavián, C., Ibáñez-Sánchez, S., Orús, C.: The impact of virtual, augmented and mixed reality technologies on the customer experience. J. Bus. Res. **100**, 547–560 (2018)
32. Ramaswamy, V., Ozcan, K.: What is co-creation? an interactional creation framework and its implications for value creation. J. Bus. Res. **84**, 196–205 (2018)

Evaluation of a Virtual Reality Simulation Tool for Studying Bias in Police-Civilian Interactions

Long Doan$^{(\boxtimes)}$ ⓘ, Rashawn Ray ⓘ, Connor Powelson ⓘ, Genesis Fuentes, Rebecca Shankman, Shaun Genter, and Jasmón Bailey

University of Maryland, College Park, MD 20742, USA
longdoan@umd.edu

Abstract. Racial inequities in police use of force has led scholars and policy makers to pursue ways to explain and reduce this gap. Many point to implicit bias in policing as a key driver in this disparity. However, there is limited evidence linking implicit cognitions and differences in behaviors. We argue that difficulties associated with recreating life-like situations with adequate experimental control in research settings designed to measure discriminatory behaviors obscure the relationship between implicit bias and behavior in policing. To address this, we rely on virtual reality to create experimental settings that better mimic officers' experiences in the field. We evaluate the effectiveness of such a VR system in recognizing officers' speech and correctly categorizing them. We find modest accuracy in both speech recognition and affective coding. However, the system has a significant and positive association with human generated codes for all but the most egregious cases of incorrect speech recognition. In quantifying and assessing the system's effectiveness, we demonstrate VR's potential in studying bias in policing.

Keywords: Virtual reality · Policing · Bias · Human computer interaction

1 Introduction

Research shows disparities in police use of force. Research and policy makers have pursued ways to explain and reduce this gap, with many pointing to implicit bias as a key driver in this disparity. The implicit association test is the most prominent method for measuring implicit social cognitions–unconscious mental associations that can influence perceptions, actions, and decisions [1], and has been lauded as a Galilean discovery in social psychology [2]. Nevertheless, considerable debate surrounds the validity and reliability of the measure [3], and its predictive validity [4]. Indeed, the debates surrounding the measurement and predictive power of implicit cognitions, and in particular implicit biases, has animated much academic research and even public interest [5].

We argue that, as observed in past work [6], a major part of the issues in studying the behavioral manifestations of implicit bias is the difficulty in recreating environments under which discriminatory behaviors are likely and measurable in the lab while maintaining good experimental control. Our approach to minimize this methodological

© Springer Nature Switzerland AG 2021
D. D. Schmorrow and C. M. Fidopiastis (Eds.): HCII 2021, LNAI 12776, pp. 388–399, 2021.
https://doi.org/10.1007/978-3-030-78114-9_26

problem is to rely on advances in virtual reality (VR) technology to create life-like scenarios that has the potential to better mimic real-world settings where implicit bias may be expected to have the strongest and most reliable effects. But, in order to accomplish this goal, VR simulations need to both be able to adapt in real time to officers' input and remain experimentally controlled. This study presents an assessment of whether such a VR system can be used to study bias in police-civilian interactions.

In this study, 79 officers run through three VR simulations involving three different scenarios commonly encountered in the field: (1) a domestic, (2) suspicious person, and (3) convenience store call. In all three simulations, officers are tasked with investigating the scene and resolving the call. Each scene involves an interaction with one person of interest. The person of interest uses speech recognition to parse and categorize the officer's commands and requests. Based on how the VR simulation categorizes these requests, the person of interest responds using one of several hundred preprogrammed responses developed in consultation with subject matter experts. In this way, the VR simulations are realistic and adaptive to each officer, while maintaining strict experimental control. Officers run through the three scenarios in random order to reduce order effects. In each scenario, we experimentally manipulate the race and gender of the person of interest. Each person of interest can be black or white and female or male.

2 Background

Bias in policing can potentially be dangerous, and even deadly, for citizens as well as police officers [7]. Existing literature in sociology [8–11], psychology [12–16], public health [17, 18], and criminology [19] provide evidence of racial bias in policing. Department of Justice reports conducted in Baltimore, Newark, and St. Louis show similar patterns. Research documents that police officers are more likely to use force against Blacks and Latinos relative to Whites [20]. In their analysis of police killings over time, Krieger and colleagues found that Blacks are 3.5 times more likely to be victims of police killings than Whites [17]. Gilbert and Ray argue that existing laws provide liberties to the police to use excessive force [18]. Although some may assert that Blacks' higher tendency to commit crime is the reason for their higher likelihood of being killed by police, data from the Federal Bureau of Investigation do not support this claim. First, violent crime has significantly decreased since the 1990s despite an increase in justifiable homicides. Second, data show that Blacks, compared to Whites, are less likely to be fighting the police or have a gun at the time they are killed by police [18].

Perceived negative attributes may anticipate criminal behavior and lead to members of certain groups being perceived as more suspicious and dangerous than others. Besides explicit bias, research draws attention to racial profiling and implicit bias as factors for racial differences in police treatment [9, 13]. Entman and Rojecki found that Black suspects and criminals are more likely to be featured in news reports than White suspects and criminals [21]. With limited interpersonal interactions across racial divides, these images may lead to stereotypical thinking that all Black men are dangerous and threatening. Respondents in their study estimated that Blacks commit 40% more violent crime than they actually do [21]. A 2011 study using stop and frisk data from New York City found that Blacks and Latinos were more likely than Whites to be stopped and have force used against them. The study also found that the police were less likely to find weapons or contraband on Blacks and Latinos relative to Whites [22]. The explanation for this finding is that, on one hand, police officers use other factors among Whites that might suggest criminality. On the other hand, they primarily use skin tone to attribute criminality onto Blacks and Latinos. As a result, police officer's implicit biases of the personal attributes of pedestrians and drivers inform their investigatory selections.

A major part of the issues in studying the behavioral manifestations of implicit bias is the difficulty in recreating environments under which discriminatory behaviors are likely and measurable in the lab while maintaining good experimental control [6]. Our approach to minimize this methodological problem is to rely on advances in VR technology to create life-like scenarios that have the potential to better mimic real-world settings where implicit bias may be expected to have the strongest and most reliable effects.

Recent research in cognitive psychology [23] suggests that the mind is inherently embodied. The way we create and recall mental constructs is influenced by the way we perceive the world and move about it [24, 25]. Therefore, an important component of the virtual environments is the subjective experience of being virtually present, even when one is physically elsewhere. This growing body of work suggests that immersion and embodiment can have a profound impact on attitudes and behaviors. Although recent studies have examined bias in policing, and especially racial bias in policing [26, 27], the use of VR rather than video vignettes or body camera footage represents a methodological innovation that can yield higher quality and more internally valid data. Further, we argue that VR scenarios present a best-case test for the relationship between implicit bias and behaviors. If findings support expectations, these methodological innovations can be applied to the study of implicit bias and behavioral manifestations more broadly.

3   Experimental Design

We recruited 79 police officers from police departments in the Mid-Atlantic, Southern, and Mid-Western regions of the United States. Officers ran through three VR simulations involving three different scenarios commonly encountered in the field: (1) a domestic, (2) suspicious person, and (3) convenience store call. The VR simulations were designed based on pilot work we had completed with local police departments. In our preliminary work, the most common criticism officers had with existing training tools was that they did not adapt in real time to what the officers were doing in the simulations. Our simulations accounted for this criticism by having the persons of interest in each scenario adaptively respond to officers. Using speech recognition and a coarse dictionary of respectful or disrespectful language based on LIWC dictionaries [28], the VR simulation picked the best response to give to officers in the moment. This automatically generated (AG) deference score was calculated by matching words to a dictionary of respectful and disrespectful words, summing over the words in an utterance, and normalizing the sum. The AG deference score thus ranged from -1 representing a completely disrespectful utterance to $+1$ representing a completely respectful utterance.

Using this approach allowed us to maintain the internal validity associated with having tightly controlled sets of responses that are consistent across officers. At the same time, this approach increased the external validity of the simulations by having simulations that are responsive to officers as persons of interest would in real life. Officers ran through the three scenarios in random order to reduce order effects. In each scenario, we experimentally manipulated the race and gender of the person of interest. The focus of the larger experiment was on this race by gender comparison across three outcomes of interest: (1) explicit bias, (2) implicit bias, and (3) differential treatment of persons of interest. However, results presented in this paper are focused on an evaluation of the VR system's ability to adequately recognize and measure differential treatment in real time. Explicit and implicit bias was measured using the symbolic racism scale and the implicit association test [30, 31], respectively. Differential treatment was measured using an index of respectful language use at the utterance level. Across the 79 officers, a total of 8,178 utterances were spoken.

Table 1. Sample characteristics

Characteristics	Distribution	Category
Age category	39%	18–34 years
	29%	35–44 years
	31%	45+ years
Gender	84%	Men
	16%	Women
Race	54%	White
	38%	Black
	8%	Another race
Region	15%	Mid-Atlantic
	62%	South
	23%	Midwest
Experience	32%	0–5 years
	14%	5–10 years
	22%	10–15 years
	32%	15+ years

Table 1 includes a breakdown of officer characteristics in the sample. To maintain confidentiality of participants, we collected characteristics in broad categories and collapse categories with fewer than 5% of the sample. As reported in Table 1, the sample was roughly stratified by age, with about a third of the sample between the ages of 18–34, a third between 35–44, and a third 45 or over. Reflecting the demographics of police officers in general, the sample was predominantly men [29]. Over half of the sample identifies as White, about 40% identify as Black, and a smaller subset identified as another race. Participants came from several departments in the Mid-Atlantic (15%),

South (62%), and Midwest (23%) regions of the United States. Finally, there was substantial variation in officer experience on the job with about a third of the sample having fewer than 5 years of experience, a third between 5–15 years, and a third with 15 or more years of experience.

Session notes from experimental sessions indicated that the VR simulations generally performed well, with officers lauding the program's ability to respond to their input in realistic manners. However, there was also negative feedback indicating that some responses were *non sequiturs*. Although the use of automated text coding is growing in the social sciences [32], the combination of speech recognition with automated coding is relatively untested [33]. As such, our goal in this paper is to quantify the VR system's effectiveness and assess the transcription and coding done in real time. To do so, we manually transcribed and coded a random subset of responses to compare the automated scores feeding the system to human generated codes.

4   Assessment Methodology

We assess the efficacy of the VR program's ability to mimic police-civilian interactions along two main metrics: (1) the transcription accuracy of officers' verbal interactions with VR characters and (2) the correlation between automatic and manual coding of deference based on these transcriptions. We randomly sampled 10% of recorded experimental sessions and manually transcribed and content-coded them to compare to automated transcription and coding. Once transcribed and de-identified if officers accidentally volunteered identifying information, we use the manual transcriptions as the ground truth to compare to the automated transcriptions. Transcription accuracy is measured using the word error rate [34], a commonly used metric of performance for speech recognition systems. The word error rate (WER) is computed for each utterance spoken by an officer as:

$$WER = \frac{S + D + I}{N} \tag{1}$$

where S is the number of substitutions, D is the number of deletions, I is the number of insertions, and N is the total number of words in an utterance. We use the Python package jiwer to loop through each utterance and calculate a WER [35].

To assess the performance of the automatically generated deference scores used in the VR simulations, we compare them to human coded deference scores. We sampled 1,000 respondents from Prolific Academic to code for deference. Prolific Academic is a crowdsourcing platform used by scholars, among others, to recruit participants for online studies [36]. Prolific has been found to produce high quality data using traditional metrics such as satisficing and attention checks, participant naivety, and the sample's ability to reproduce well-documented effects in prior studies [36]. Each respondent is randomly assigned 20 to 25 quotes from experimental sessions to code. Collective, respondents produced 20,232 codes for the 861 sampled quotes spoken by officers during the experiment.

For each quote, we followed Voigt and colleagues' work by asking respondents to indicate how respectful, formal, polite, friendly and impartial the officer is being toward the VR characters [27]. All items are asked on a scale of 1 to 10 with bipolar labels on the scales representing disrespect, informality, impoliteness, unfriendliness, and partiality on the low end of the scale and respect, formality, politeness, friendliness, and impartiality on the high end of the scale. These five items had high construct validity (Cronbach's $\alpha = .89$), so we created a mean scale representing manually coded (MC) deference. We examine the correlation between automatic and manual coding of deference in the aggregate as well as by WER to parse out whether any lack of correlation is due to a failure in the deference score generation or due to a failure in the speech recognition.

5 Results and Discussion

Table 2 includes descriptive statistics for the key assessment variables in this study. AG deference has a mean of .01, a range of −.72 to +1, and a standard deviation of .15. This means that on average, officers are fairly neutral toward the person of interest in the VR simulations. They tended to be more respectful than disrespectful, with no officer speaking entirely in a disrespectful tone. Corresponding to this, MC deference is slightly above the midpoint of the 1–10 scale with a mean of 5.98 and standard deviation of 1.96. Component scores indicate high correspondence between the 5 measures that make up the MC deference scale. Finally, the word error rate has a mean of .44 across the utterances, suggesting that on average 44% of words in an utterance is incorrectly recognized by the speech recognition system.

Table 3 includes correlations between AG and MC deference scores. All correlations are statistically significant ($p < .05$), but they range in their magnitude. On the aggregate, the correlation between AG and MC deference is .06, suggesting that there is minimal but positive correspondence between the two deference scores. Higher AG deference scores tend to be positively related to higher MC deference scores and vice-versa. Note that out of the 20,232 codes humans coded, only 18,518 have corresponding AG deference scores. This is due to the speech recognition not being able to transcribe 72 utterances that human transcribers were able to identify. To assess whether the low correlation is due to a lack of correspondence itself or due to error in the automated transcriptions, we next break down the correlation by WER. To simplify results, we binned WER into quartiles. The 1st quartile includes utterances with WERs between 0 and .143, the 2nd quartile includes utterances with WERs between .143 and .375, the 3rd quartile includes utterances with WERs between .375 and .75, and 4th quartile includes utterances with WERs between .75 and 1.

As shown in the table, correlations remain constant, ranging from .06 to .08 for the first 3 quartiles. However, AG deference has a significantly negative but small correlation with MC deference for utterances in the 4th quartile of WER. This suggests that for utterances where 75 to 100% of the words are incorrectly recognized, the VR system erroneously codes the deference in the opposite direction as human coders.

Because AG deference is generated based on a pre-existing dictionary of respectful and disrespectful words, words that are not in the dictionary are assigned a value of 0. Another potential source of low correlations is due to this overinflation of zeros in the AG deference scores. In the next set of analyses, we exclude zero AG deference scores to see if this is a contributing factor in the low correlation between AG and MC deference.

Table 2. Descriptive statistics for key assessment variables

Variable	Mean (Min–Max)	SD
Automatically generated deference	.01 (−.72–1.00)	.15
Manually coded deference scale ($\alpha = .89$)	5.98 (1–10)	1.96
Respect	6.42 (1–10)	2.27
Formal	5.36 (1–10)	2.68
Polite	6.20 (1–10)	2.29
Friendly	6.04 (1–10)	2.23
Impartial	5.86 (1–10)	2.22
Word error rate	.44 (0–1)	.35

Table 3. Correlations between automatically generated and manually coded deference scores

Specification	Correlation	Observations
Overall	.06	18,518
By WER quartiles		
1st quartile	.06	4,737
2nd quartile	.08	5,015
3rd quartile	.07	5,198
4th quartile	− .02	3,568
Excluding zeros	.13	2,798
Non-zeros by WER quartiles		
1st quartile	.13	892
2nd quartile	.16	857
3rd quartile	.21	652
4th quartile	− .05	397

Excluding zeros from the analyses doubles the overall correlation between AG and MC deference, suggesting that a major factor in low correlations is a limited dictionary used in generating deference scores.

Breaking the correlations by WER quartiles shows a similar pattern to before where correlations remain constant across WER quartiles until the 4th quartile, where the correlation between AG and MC deference once again becomes negative. Interestingly, correlations are higher in the middle of the WER distribution than at either ends. To determine if this is an artifact of binning or a true finding, we graph the relationship between AG and MC deference across the continuous range of the variable in Fig. 1.

Figure 1 shows the marginal effect of AG deference on MC deference from a regression predicting MC deference using AG deference and WER and its quadratic form. The solid line is the marginal effect across the WER range, and the shaded area is the 95% confidence interval of that effect. Consistent with the binned results, AG has a stronger effect as WER increases to about the mean WER rate where it starts to have weaker effects. The confidence interval of the marginal effect does not cross 0, indicating no significant effect, until a WER of about .8. This means that AG deference is generally predictive of MC deference *except* for cases of extreme error in the speech recognition system.

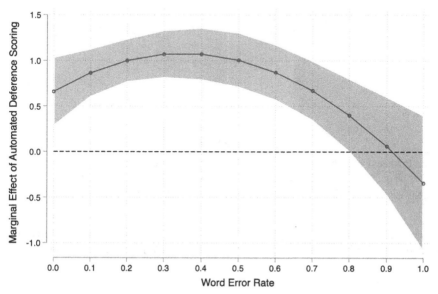

Fig. 1. Marginal effect of automatically generated deference scores on manually coded deference scores over the range of the word error rate. Shaded area is the 95% confidence interval of the marginal effect. (Color figure online)

Contrary to our intuition, error-free speech recognition does not lead to stronger relationships between AG and MC deference. This led us to further explore the features of the two ends of the WER continuum. Is there a reason why AG deference is most predictive of MC deference in the middle of the WER continuum instead of either end of the continuum? As a data quality check, we ask human coders to flag utterances that they were unable to code either because it is too short or requires more context to make sense of the underlying meaning and respectfulness of the language. We suspected that the two extremes of the WER distribution are more likely to be one- or two-word utterances, which will be more likely to be 100% correct or incorrect than longer utterances. To explore this possibility, we ran a binary logistic regression of an utterance being flagged as uncodable on the WER.

Figure 2 includes the predicted probability of an utterance being flagged as uncodable across the WER distribution. The solid line is the predicted probability, and the shaded area is the 95% confidence interval for the predicted probability. As shown in the figure, there is a strong curvilinear relationship between WER and an utterance being flagged

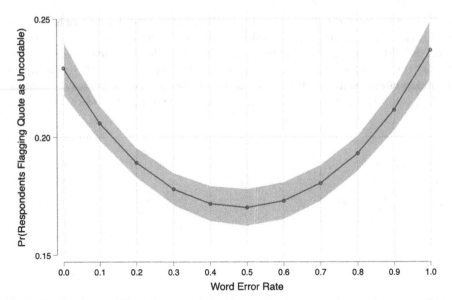

Fig. 2. Predicted probability of a quote being flagged by the respondent as being uncodable because the quote is too short or requires more context to be understood. Shaded area is the 95% confidence interval for the predicted probability. (Color figure online)

by human coders as uncodable. Utterances with a WER of 0 or 1 are significantly more likely to be flagged as uncodable than utterances with a WER toward the middle of the distribution.

Collectively, the findings paint a clear picture regarding the VR system's performance. There is a modest but positive relationship between AG and MC deference that is largely constant across the range of WER except for the highest WERs. Above a WER of .8, there is a negative relationship between AG and MC deference. Very short utterances are more likely to both be flagged as uncodable and to have a WER on either end of the WER continuum, suggesting that the VR system works best with moderately long phrases. More important than the WER, the relationship between AG and MC deference is much stronger for non-zero deference scores, suggesting that a more robust dictionary of words will improve the VR system's ability to generate accurate scores in real time.

6   Conclusion

In this paper, we sought to evaluate the effectiveness of a realistic and adaptive VR system as a tool for studying bias in policing. We collected data from 79 police officers who ran through the VR simulations and generated 8,178 utterances of speech that can be used to study differential treatment in policing as has been done with observational data in prior work [27]. To assess the effectiveness of the VR system, we had manually transcribed a random subset of experimental sessions and had human coders rate the utterances in terms of respect, formality, politeness, friendliness, and impartiality. This paper reports results from a comparison of the performance of the automatically generated deference scores with the human coded scores.

Overall, we found that a system that transcribes, categorizes, and codes human input in real time is feasible, generates codes that generally matched human intuitions about deference and respect, and can be successfully deployed in the field. Two major caveats temper this conclusion. First, the AG deference scores only perform substantially better than chance (i.e., have a correlation substantively larger than 0) in cases where the dictionary of respectful and disrespectful words exists. Second, transcriptions with over 80% incorrectly recognized words lead to a distorted picture in terms of deference and the AG and MC deference scores are negatively related in this space. As speech recognition systems continue to improve, we should be able to easily correct the latter point in future iterations of the VR system. The corpus of respectful and disrespectful words will be a harder problem to solve and developing a larger and more context-sensitive dictionary will be worthwhile endeavor for future research.

Acknowledgements. We thank David Johnson and Robert Koulish for contributions to the early design of the project. We also thank Clayton Buck, Racheli Cohen, Ellie Pokress, Nick Provenzano, Michael Ros, Wanda Segura Acevedo, and Olivia Sharon for excellent research assistance. This research was approved by the University of Maryland Institutional Review Board protocol no. 1363074.

References

1. Nosek, B.A., Greenwald, A.G., Banaji, M.R.: The implicit association test at age 7: a methodological and conceptual review. In: Bargh, J.A. (ed.) Automatic Processes in Social Thinking and Behavior, pp. 265–292. Psychology Press (2007)
2. Kester, J.D.: A revolution in social psychology. APS Observer 14 (2001). http://www.psychologicalscience.org/observer/0701/family.html
3. Egloff, B., Schmukle, S.C.: Predictive validity of an implicit association test for assessing anxiety. J. Pers. Soc. Psychol. **83**(6), 1441–1455 (2002)
4. Greenwald, A.G., Banaji, M.R., Nosek, B.A.: Statistically small effects of the Implicit Association Test can have societally large effects. J. Pers. Soc. Psychol. **108**, 553–561 (2015)
5. Singal, J.: Psychology's favorite tool for measuring racism isn't up to the job. The Cut (2017). https://www.thecut.com/2017/01/psychologys-racism-measuring-tool-isnt-up-to-the-job.html
6. List, J.A.: Field experiments: a bridge between lab and naturally occurring data. B.E. J. Econ. Anal. Policy **5**, 1–47 (2007)
7. President's Task Force on 21st Century Policing: Final Report of the President's Task Force on 21st Century Policing. Office of Community Oriented Policing Services, Washington, DC (2015)
8. Feagin, J.R.: Racist America: Roots, Current Realities, and Future Reparations, 2nd edn. Taylor & Francis Group, New York (2010)
9. Davenport, C., Soule, S.A., Armstrong, D.A.: Protesting while black? The differential policing of American activism, 1960 to 1990. Am. Sociol. Rev. **76**(1), 152–178 (2011)
10. Ray, R.: "If only he didn't wear the hoodie…" selective perception and stereotype maintenance. In: McClure, S., Harris, C. (eds.) Getting Real about Race: Hoodies, Mascots, Model Minorities, and Other Conversations, pp. 81–93. Sage, Los Angeles (2015)

11. Ray, R., Marsh, K., Powelson, C.: Can cameras stop the killings? Racial differences in perceptions of the effectiveness of body-worn cameras in police encounters. Sociol. Forum **32**, 1032–1050 (2017)

12. Oliver, M.B.: African American men as "criminal and dangerous": implications of media portrayals of crime on the "criminalization" of African American men. J. Afr. Am. Stud. **7**(2), 3–18 (2003)

13. Eberhardt, J.L., Goff, P.A., Purdie, V.J., Davies, P.G.: Seeing black: race, crime, and visual processing. J. Pers. Soc. Psychol. **87**(6), 876–893 (2004)

14. Correll, J., Urland, G.R., Ito, T.A.: Event-related potentials and the decision to shoot: the role of threat perception and cognitive control. J. Exp. Soc. Psychol. **42**, 120–128 (2006)

15. Trawalter, S., Todd, A.R., Baird, A.A., Richeson, J.A.: Attending to threat: race-based patterns of selective attention. J. Exp. Soc. Psychol. **44**, 1322–1327 (2008)

16. McConnaughy, C.M., White, I.K.: Racial politics complicated: the work of gendered race cues in American politics. In: New Research on Gender in Political Psychology Conference (2011)

17. Krieger, N., Kiang, M.V., Chen, J.T., Waterman, P.D.: Trends in US deaths due to legal intervention among black and white men, age 15–34 years, by county income level: 1960–2010. Harvard Public Heal Rev. **3**, 1–5 (2015)

18. Gilbert, K., Ray, R.: Why police kill black males with impunity: applying critical race and public health theory to address determinants of policing behaviors and the justifiable homicides of black men. J. Urban Health **93**(1), 122–140 (2016)

19. Brown, K.R.: The Color of Crime: Racial Hoaxes, White Fear, Black Protectionism, Police Harassment, and Other Macroaggressions, 2nd edn. New York University Press, New York (2008)

20. Gabrielson, R., Jones, R.G., Sagara, E.: Deadly force in black and white: a ProPublica analysis of killings by police shows outsize risk for young black males. ProPublica: Journalism in the Public Interest (2015)

21. Entman, R.M., Rojecki, A.: The Black Image in the White Mind: Media and Race in America. University of Chicago Press, Chicago (2000)

22. Krupanski, M., Park, A.R., Melodia, L.: Racial disparity in NYPD stops-and-frisks: the center for constitutional rights preliminary report on UF-250 data obtained for 2005 through June 2008 (2009). http://ccrjustice.org/sites/default/files/assets/Report-CCR-NYPD-Stop-andFrisk_3.pdf

23. Repetto, C., Serino, S., Macedonia, M., Riva, G.: Virtual reality as an embodied tool to enhance episodic memory in elderly. Front. Psychol. **7**, 1839 (2016)

24. Barsalou, L.W.: Grounded cognition. Annu. Rev. Psychol. **59**, 617–645 (2008)

25. Shapiro, L.: Embodied Cognition. Routledge (2010). ISBN 978-0415773423

26. James, L.: The stability of implicit racial bias in police officers. Police Q. **21**, 30–52 (2017). https://doi.org/10.1177/1098611117732974

27. Voigt, R., et al.: Language from police body camera footage shows racial disparities in officer respect. Proc. Natl. Acad. Sci. **114**, 6521–6526 (2017)

28. Pennebaker, J.W., Booth, R.J., Boyd, R.L., Francis, M.E.: Linguistic inquiry and word count: LIWC 2015. Pennebaker Conglomerates, Austin (2015). www.LIWC.net

29. Sklansky, D.A.: Not your father's police department: making sense of the new demographics of law enforcement. J. Crim. Law Criminol. **96**, 1209–1244 (2005)

30. Henry, P.J., Sears, D.O.: The symbolic racism 2000 scale. Polit. Psychol. **23**(2), 253–283 (2002)

31. Greenwald, A.G., Andrew Poehlman, T., Uhlmann, E.L., Banaji, M.R.: Understanding and using the Implicit Association Test: III. Meta-analysis of predictive validity. J. Pers. Soc. Psychol. **97**, 17–41 (2009)

32. Nelson, L.K., Burk, D., Knudsen, M., McCall, L.: The future of coding: a comparison of hand-coding and three types of computer-assisted text analysis methods. Sociol. Methods Res. **50**(1), 202–237 (2021)
33. Arumugam, D., Karamcheti, S., Gopalan, N., Wong, L.L., Tellex, S.: Accurately and efficiently interpreting human-robot instructions of varying granularities. arXiv preprint arXiv: 1704.06616 (2017)
34. Morris, A.C., Maier, V., Green, P.: From WER and RIL to MER and WIL: improved evaluation measures for connected speech recognition. In: Eighth International Conference on Spoken Language Processing (2004)
35. Vaessen, N.: JiWER: similarity measures for automatic speech recognition evaluation (2021). https://pypi.org/project/jiwer/
36. Peer, E., Brandimarte, L., Samat, S., Acquisti, A.: Beyond the Turk: alternative platforms for crowdsourcing behavioral research. J. Exp. Soc. Psychol. **70**, 153–163 (2017)

Utilizing Current Technologies to Foster Augmented On-line Learning

T. Liam Herman, Michael-Brian C. Ogawa(✉), and Martha E. Crosby

University of Hawai'i at Mānoa, Honolulu, HI 96822, USA
{hermantw,ogawam,crosby}@hawaii.edu

Abstract. Science involving the human brain, psychology, and cognition has progressed sufficiently that the technology exists to develop a mutually beneficial exchange of information between a human and an AI. Dubbed "AI Symbiosis," this process enables positive feedback between humans and adaptive computer algorithms in which both human and AI would "learn" how to perform tasks more efficiently than either could alone. Several new technologies and inventions allow a vast array of augmented input and/or output between humans and AI, including mental activity wirelessly operating computers, manipulation of targeted neurons with or without implants, non-invasive, surface-level implants the size of a coin transmitting real-time neural activity of senses, real-time video feed of human mental images, and estimation of thoughts and emotions. A research project is planned to study students' divided attention when they are learning content in on-line environments. The research will target eye-tracking, click timing, and task performance data to determine the levels of impact divided attention has on student learning. We believe that this line of research will also inform best practices in on-line instructional settings.

Keywords: Augmented cognition educational applications · Artificial intelligence · Consumer-grade sensors

1   Introduction

Understanding of the human brain has grown exponentially over the last millennia. Long gone are the days of ancient Egyptians who during mummification discarded the brain as if mucus, rather than preserving it as they did with organs considered more important such as the intestines [5]. Only within the last century have psychology and cognitive science emerged, which have already become involved in some of the most competitive research in modern times. Leaps and bounds in progress have been made in developing scientific methods to treat, manipulate, and emulate human behavior. Academia at large has recognized the brain's complexity and plethora of functions to include perception interpretation, the regulation of body functions, and information processing capabilities. Since the invention of electronic computers, the human brain has increasingly been considered as an organic carbon-based computer as opposed to today's silicon-based electronic systems. This comparison has inspired a remarkable amount

© Springer Nature Switzerland AG 2021
D. D. Schmorrow and C. M. Fidopiastis (Eds.): HCII 2021, LNAI 12776, pp. 400–406, 2021.
https://doi.org/10.1007/978-3-030-78114-9_27

of research seeking to develop a passible digital equivalent of human consciousness. Despite being unknown decades from either developing true artificial intelligence (AI) or potentially uploading a human brain's contents to an electronic equivalent, a new stage of human evolution has already been reached dubbed "AI Symbiosis" [6] signifying the development of mutually beneficial relationships between humans and AI.

Such capabilities once only dreamed of are now upon us after numerous recent advancements in a variety of academic fields such as psychology, cognitive science, and nanobiotechnology. Altogether, these discoveries and inventions have realized computer-assisted augmentations which can provide a feedback loop between AI and human intelligence (HI). Now that computers capable of hosting AI have reached such miniscule sizes, humans can be outfitted with inobtrusive augments complete with an onboard AI and input/output functionality, also known as intelligent agents (IA). These IA enable a give and take of assistance to its wearer in near-real time, as well data monitoring and interpretive processes allowing them to undergo mutual adaptations and advancements towards higher efficiency and expanded capabilities—not only toward the task at hand, but towards each other as well. Initially the augmented subjects will perform simple tasks while the AI would use the gathered data to develop an algorithm attempting to mimic the actions of the subject, complete the specified tasks, and develop a model sufficient to recognize variations of initial conditions such that it can adapt to modified parameters without human intervention (i.e. manually altering the code). Overall, a primary goal of AI Symbiosis is to develop and provide augments for human use to provide them with enhanced abilities beyond that which a human, AI, or robot could do on their own. In time HI/AI interfaces will inevitably become commonplace, incorporating a vast array of technologies and functions such that our civilization will undergo a fundamental shift more impactful than any other in the history of mankind.

2 Research Foundation

2.1 Background

Research into AI incorporates a diverse community of scientists and philosophers who analyze the human brain with the intent to develop understanding of our own species' cognition, which is then utilized to further AI capabilities by reverse engineering our own cognitive processes. A common theory among these researchers is that a human brain can be emulated using electronics. There are several factors which support this perspective. Computers are inherently modular, not unlike the brain, with different sections specialized for certain tasks [3]. Both AI and HI use electrical signals to perform operations within milliseconds. In another significant similarity, humans have distinctly separate short-term memory and long-term memory functions [3] similar to computers—random-access memory (RAM) and non-volatile memory (e.g. HDDs and SSDs). Although the central processing unit (CPU) of a computer is a single component, unlike the neural network of the brain, both can process data at a rate too fast for humans to consciously keep up with. These comparisons inspire possibilities for IAs to supplement humans with expanded abilities. For example: many inputs and stimuli go unnoticed to humans (as we can only focus on so much at the same time) yet incorporating IAs could store such data for later examination *and* represent information in a far more resilient and trustworthy form than human memories alone, which have a wide range of reliability. As such, there is a foundation of similarities upon which scientists can bridge the gap between HI and AI.

2.2 Potential Applications of Augmented Intelligence

Beyond simply allowing humans and AI to interact and adapt to each other, our bodies can be controlled by either humans or AI. Electrical manipulation of neurons using hardwired implants were discovered decades ago, and advancements in its usage are ongoing [3]. Another form of cerebral manipulation called optogenetics involves modifying the DNA of neurons causing them to activate when a specific wavelength of light is applied. This process enables stimulating specific neurons in the brain with only a colored flashlight, which has the advantage over electrical manipulation that it does not require a hardwired cerebral interface [3]. These methods could be supplemented by an AI-influenced exoskeleton with input from the brain, remote guidance systems, electronic monitoring equipment, and even an AI program capable of autonomous movement such as a robot developed by Google researchers [4]. Such a rig could react to stimuli 50x faster than a human could (5 ms vs 250 ms), allowing an appropriate response to be taken about a quarter second sooner than a single focused individual or even more if no human consciousness was initially aware of the event. Astronauts, construction workers, spelunkers, soldiers, and mountain climbers could all benefit from this technology, both in efficacy and hazard mitigation.

Additional opportunities exist allowing interaction and learning between brain and AI with the digitization of sensory inputs. Gertrude, Elon Musk's cyborg pig, has an implant that transmits sensory input from its snout and displays a visual representation of what she smells on a display monitor allowing real-time analysis [9]. This reveals the potential to examine and understand brain activity in the context of its input, as well as combine the extraordinary senses of certain animals with human analysis to improve sensory detection and tracking methods. For example, an implant used on a police dog could display all detected scents on a monitor, quickly identify odors of specific illicit substances, and verify the K9 unit has not lost the scent trail. Sensory impressions can also be interpreted from human brains without a need for implants- visual and conceptual images held by humans can be recorded from scans of their cerebral activity. Researchers have been able to create videos representative of mental pictures held by volunteers via the utilization of an MRI to monitor their medial prefrontal cortex. By comparing the signals to the frames of the movie observed at the corresponding moment, researchers were able to derive an algorithm to convert brain signals to video. This experiment was successful to the extent that they could correctly identify which individual of a group the volunteer was thinking about by analyzing the brain scans [2]. Another example of HI-AI interactivity is the development of technology allowing a person to mentally operate computers. Implants of various types have achieved this outcome, most notably the development of a microscopic device at the end of an ultrathin wire which can be inserted for navigation to the brain's motor cortex, where it wirelessly transmits the subject's intentions to move as input to a computer. Several volunteers paralyzed with Lou Gehrig's disease (amyotrophic lateral sclerosis) were able to send texts and browse the internet freely without using a muscle in their body [7]. This afforded them with new levels of enjoyment and interactivity.

2.3 AI Symbiosis

Although several computer-enhanced abilities for humans have been discussed, we have not yet examined furthering development of AI itself. Symbiosis is built upon mutual benefits, so it is important consider the benefits to AI from the perspective of current technologies. Consider the recent findings of Neuralink, a business venture with the goal of developing brain-machine interface (BMI) technology achieved in the mid-2000s to make them accessible to consumers. Non-invasive implants the size of a coin have been fitted to animals (such as Gertrude) that can gather signals related to movement, smell, vision, and hearing without probing beyond the brain's surface. An AI gathering these types of data paired with separate sensory inputs such as cameras and microphones would be able to comprehend such signals given sufficient analysis. The next logical step would be to use this information to emulate those modules, which would be a significant contribution towards an electronic simulation of a human's cerebral activity. Elon Musk said that the *ultimate goal* would be to perfect AI symbiosis [9], with the AI and human learning from each other in such a way that would be far more efficient and powerful than all prior applications.

Even if AI can learn and adapt from the plethora of data accessible via human interaction, how can we know for sure when an AI can sufficiently act like a human? The Chinese Room experiment [9] illustrates asynchronous communication providing enough ambiguity that it is difficult to be certain of whether the other entity is sentient. Taking that into account, the Turing test has been modified to include visual signals and other methods of gauging interpretations and responses, which begin to test for intentionality. Interpreting symbols according to a constant set of rules is one thing but understanding complex objects, or concepts beyond a list of characteristics, is another entirely. The concept of intentionality involves the subject understanding an object beyond its symbolization and characteristics and is a popular topic among those debating the possibility of AI reaching consciousness [9]. Theoretically, giving computers an array of sensory inputs, social behaviors, and physical interaction programming could lead to intentionality the way humans may have developed it by using perception, prior knowledge, and the ability to think critically. In the future, AI avatars may be able to engage in physical interactions such as exercise, work, and even human conversations on our behalf - in our own bodies, as we cognitively experience virtual reality. It currently appears to be imaginary, but as AI Symbiosis evolves and nanobiotechnology becomes more capable and specialized the potential will seem more tangible with each passing year.

It seems undeniable that AI development is inextricably linked with HI as advances in one field of study advances the other as well, like the mutual learning inherent to AI symbiosis. There are a multitude of ways that computers can control or assist humans and vice versa, and beyond certain constrictions such as quantum processing and digitization of cognition there is much potential for progress. Evidence exists that the minimum requirements of obtaining AI Symbiosis are exceeded on a fundamental level as demonstrated by Musk's Neuralink experiments [9]. Both HI and AI can sense, process, interpret, transmit, and receive data - thus enabling the mutual learning process. The future of human enhancement is approaching; quantum processing and mind digitization could catalyze development with AI Symbiosis as a foundational component. The technological capabilities of AI, IAs, and BMIs that exist today illustrate the beginnings of this approach. Humans can fully operate personal computers remotely using an implant and their mind, which among other possibilities can give quadriplegics an opportunity to be active in different ways in modern society. Noninvasive brain scans can display a visual representation of a subject's mental images, an invaluable tool with disabled patients. Implants can gather sensory input from an animal and transmit it to a computer for storage and further analysis. AI interfaces can shave tenths of seconds off the average human reaction time, similar to the near-instantaneous responses displayed by Tesla cars utilizing video cameras in conjunction with predictive algorithms to avoid accidents [1]. With the many advancements of science in recent years, the potential to utilize these technological breakthroughs continuously increases.

3 Proposed Research

3.1 Divided Attention

Divided attention is a common phenomenon associated with multitasking, where a person performs multiple tasks in rapid succession [9]. Performing tasks in this manner creates the illusion of multitasking and results in reduced task performance or an increased time on task when getting accustomed to the new assignment. Van der Stigchel described in detail the impact of divided attention on work and learning environments. In many working environments, employers often ask that subordinates immediately respond to their email, text messages, and phone calls. This tends to result in superficial levels of depth in productivity, where major breakthroughs and critical thinking tasks may be delayed or not completed at all. Therefore, the attempted parallel process dynamic prevalent in offices and schools alike known as multitasking actually causes lower levels of productivity than if each of the tasks were performed individually in series.

In education, the deepest levels of learning and profoundest insights typically take place with high levels of focus on content [9]. Students can still learn while multitasking but later will not be able to use the information as effectively as those who focused solely on the material. For many multitasking during the learning process may result in short-lived benefits but will inevitably result in long-term disadvantages. Not only will these multitaskers have greater difficulty recalling pertinent information, but their aptitude for critical thinking skills with the subject-matter will be significantly diminished.

Divided attention and multitasking in students is a growing concern in learning environments due to the myriad distractions that exist. These adverse behaviors can be mitigated to an extent in the physical classroom environment, where students are less likely to pay attention to non-educational tasks such as checking social media, watching videos, or playing games. However, due to the COVID-19 pandemic leading to the growth of on-line learning and learning from home, these counterproductive habits have risen to the forefront of obstacles to modern-day education. Researchers teaching synchronous classes online have experienced an increase in their students multitasking, to an extent which would be impossible in a physical classroom. Many teachers have discussed their concerns with students watching television, playing games, and browsing social networking feeds while attending class. In some cases, the researchers and teachers observed students manipulating their game controllers, using a television remote, and scrolling on their phones during class sessions. Students mute themselves to hide evidence of their divided attention while their video continues to stream, and it is impossible to tell how many students are multitasking who are scrupulous enough to hide their distracting devices.

While ongoing pandemic precautions have resulted in many schools pivoting to online education indefinitely, we believe that online educational opportunities will continue to experience widespread use even after the pandemic is over and schools again open their doors. Therefore, it is vital to educational professionals to study divided attention such that augmented cognition could be developed to create applications for AI Symbiosis resulting in students reaching higher levels of comprehension and retention in a variety of learning environments.

3.2 Methodology

The researchers plan to conduct a study targeting divided attention when learning content in on-line environments. The research will target eye-tracking, click timing, and task performance data to determine the levels of impact divided attention has on student learning. We believe that this line of research will also inform best practices in on-line instructional settings.

The researchers partner with a large-enrollment course in computer science that typically enrolls between 200 and 300 students per semester. The course focused on computer science principles, application usage, and technology and its impact in society. Due to the general content of the course, the students come from a variety of backgrounds including over 30 different majors. The class includes a 75-min synchronous lecture each week and two 75-min synchronous lab sessions per week. The lectures are conducted via Zoom and include multiple interactive elements including *polls,* where students can respond to multiple choice questions posed by the instructor. Students are also asked to respond to questions in the chat for open-ended type questions. After the lecture, a multiple-choice quiz is posted to the course management system for students to complete within a few days. These elements make the lecture portion of the course a strong area to study augmented cognition using consumer-level devices. The proposed methods are pending institutional review board approval.

Since most students use a laptop with a built-in web camera, we plan to collect eye-tracking data during the synchronous lecture sessions. The eye-tracking data and timing will be aligned with slide and audio content to acquire evidence of the students' focus on content throughout the session. Since the poll questions used in the lectures focus on recalling or applying information learned, we will collect the data submitted to the polls and timing related data. This data will indicate the amount of time taken to respond to each question and the correct or incorrect nature of the response. Lastly, we will collect the students' end of lecture quiz in the course management system to determine if they could apply knowledge after learning the material.

These data align with the divided attention framework, where the researchers plan to use a repeated measures design for each student to determine if how their focus shifts during a lecture and if it impacts their poll response correctness and timing. Based on Van der Stigchel's work [8], we also plan to use the post lecture CMS quiz as a dependent variable to determine the amount of impact divided attention has on longer term performance in learning (Fig. 1).

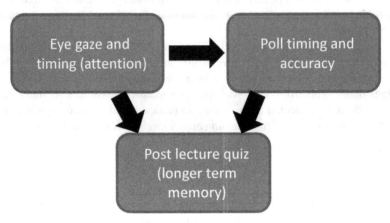

Fig. 1. Research design

We believe that the findings of the proposed study will serve as a foundational component of AI symbiosis research. It will provide insights into the impact of divided attention on learning. These insights could be used in the feedback loop for AI symbiosis research.

References

1. Autopilot (n.d.). https://www.tesla.com/autopilotAI?redirect=no. Accessed 11 Feb 2021
2. Choi, C.: Brain researchers can detect who we are thinking about (2013). https://www.scient ificamerican.com/article/brain-researchers-can-detect-who-we-are-thinking-about/. Accessed 5 Dec 2020
3. Friedenberg, J., Silverman, G.: Cognitive Science: An Introduction to the Study of Mind. SAGE Publications, Thousand Oaks (2016)
4. Hao, K.: This robot taught itself to walk entirely on its own (2020). https://www.technolog yreview.com/2020/03/02/905593/ai-robot-learns-to-walk-autonomously-reinforcement-lea rning/. Accessed 16 Dec 2020
5. Harris, T.: How mummies work (2020). https://science.howstuffworks.com/mummy2.htm. Accessed 16 Dec 2020
6. Nair, A.: The 'symbiosis' between human brain and AI - Elon Musk (2018). https://analyticsind iamag.com/elon-musk-wants-to-create-symbiosis-between-human-brain-and-ai/. Accessed 16 Dec 2020
7. Rogers, A.: A new way to plug a human brain into a computer: via veins (2020). https://www. wired.com/story/a-new-way-to-plug-a-human-brain-into-a-computer-via-veins/. Accessed 5 Dec 2020
8. Van der Stigchel, S.: Dangers of divided attention. Am. Sci. **109**(1), 46–53 (2021)
9. Wetsman, N.: Elon Musk trots out pigs in demo of Neuralink brain implants (2020). https://www.theverge.com/2020/8/28/21406143/elon-musk-neuralink-ai-pigs-demo-brain-computer-interface. Accessed 16 Dec 2020

Configurable Parallel Induction Machines

Karina Ionkina[1], Monte Hancock[1,2], and Raman Kannan[2(✉)]

[1] Hunter College, 695 Park Avenue, New York, NY 10065, USA
[2] Tandon School of Engineering, NYU, Brooklyn, NY 11201, USA
rk1750@nyu.edu

Abstract. Machine Learning practice in general offers significant opportunities for parallel computing and practicing sound software engineering. More often than not, practitioners routinely write dataset specific scripts and learners focus on model building and refining. Focusing on particular models is not consistent with NFL, a fundamental theorem in Machine Learning. Not minding time-honored software engineering principles is inefficient. In this paper, we present our implementation of MISD machine, consistent with No Free Lunch Theorem, problems we encountered and our approach to solve those problems.

Keywords: No Free Lunch Theorem · Flynn's Taxonomy · Parallel computing

1 Parallelism

1.1 No Free Lunch Theorem

No Free Lunch [1, 2] is a consequential theorem for Machine Learning practitioners. NFL posits that there is no "super algorithm" that outperforms all other algorithms for all datasets. We may consider Machine Learning to be an emergent discipline but induction is an age old field of enquiry in philosophy, going all the way back to Hume [3].

2 Supervised Learning

In [4] Wolpert elaborates the general purpose No free lunch theorem and its relevance and application to supervised learning algorithms [5] in machine learning. The process of classification exercise in machine learning involves two phases:

- Learning (or induction) during which supervised learning algorithms are trained on known examples
- And a scoring (or generalization) phase where the trained algorithm is presented "never seen before" data to be classified.

The NFL theorem tells us that there are no super-algorithms that can out-perform all other algorithms on all the data. The implication is that, during the learning phase, practitioners have an obligation to evaluate, compare more than one algorithm, and select most performant algorithm, for generalization phase.

© Springer Nature Switzerland AG 2021
D. D. Schmorrow and C. M. Fidopiastis (Eds.): HCII 2021, LNAI 12776, pp. 407–417, 2021.
https://doi.org/10.1007/978-3-030-78114-9_28

3   NFL and Machine Learning

To be compliant with NFL, then we have to train multiple models against a given dataset. The multiple models can be trained in parallel and there is no need to synchronize them. This represents a classic case of Multiple Instruction Single Data (MISD) in the Flynn's Taxonomy [6].

In practice, to be NFL compliant, practitioners must evaluate several algorithms to determine the best performing algorithm for each dataset. This presents an enormous opportunity to exploit parallel computing. NFL dictates that one run multiple algorithms against any dataset before selecting an algorithm for further analysis.

4   Machine Learning and Parallel Computing

Machine Learning lends itself for parallel computing in numerous ways including:

1. Cross Validation [7, 8] (SIMD)
2. Bagging [9] (SIMD) and RandomForest [10]
3. Stacking [11] (MISD).

In Cross Validation, given dataset is split into N disjoint subsets, called a Fold. Then, we iterate over all the N-Fold, keeping 1-Fold as the test/validation fold, and the other (N − 1) folds are used to train the model. Note that all the iterations can be run in parallel. Here, in each iteration, the test data and the training data are different, thus multiple data (MD). In each iteration while the training dataset is different, the algorithm remains the same, single instruction (SI), resulting in a SIMD machine. Bagging is very similar where bootstrapped [12] samples (with replacement) is used to train the same algorithm, also resulting in SIMD machine. Stacking, on the other hand implements MISD, as one trains many different models (MI) on the same data set (SD). In stacking instances are assigned a class label using majority vote or other such aggregation strategy.

There are numerous opportunities for parallelization and yet it is not common practice except when Spark [13] is used. Custom scripts are written as a general purpose parallel utility; such is not available. In this effort one of our main goals is to make available a parallel execution environment.

5   Software Engineering

Reusability is a major objective for Software Engineering [14]. In practice, custom scripts are written, for each and every distinct dataset. Essentially there is no reuse. In order to analyze a dataset, the learner must know the variables (feature vector) in consideration, class variable the classifier has to learn to associate given a feature vector, a formula specifying the model. Dataset specific processing is required for the following reasons:

1. Some classifiers are not capable of handling more than two classes. Based on the number of classes the framework must handle classifier differently.
2. Class imbalance, when present, has to be handled appropriately

3. Some classifiers require encoding as they cannot handle categorical domain
4. In the presence of highly correlated variables or when there are a large number of covariates, dimensionality reduction may be required
5. Features have to be either normalized or standardized, when warranted, in a multivariate setting
6. Missing values have to be handled
7. Variable Importance – not all features are equally important and has to be managed
8. Data structure conversion.

When datasets are pre-processed to manage conditions 2–5, the encoding scheme and standardization schemes have to be maintained to transform data from original space to transformed space and vice versa at the time of scoring.

5.1   Handling Binary vs Multi-class Datasets

Both SVM and Logistic Regression determine a linear separator and are not designed to discriminate more than two classes without special processing (repetitive one-vs-all processing). To maintain strict adherence to Ockhams Razor [15], we avoid such special processing, by default. The execution mechanism determines the algorithms to be trained, avoiding both SVM and Logistic Regression in the case of multi-class datasets, unless the meta-data definition is configured to run one-vs-all strategy to handle multi-class strategy.

5.2   Handling Class Imbalance [16]

Neither under-sampling the majority class nor over-sampling minority class is necessarily optimal as the underlying distribution is being modified. Users can specify the strategy to be used, in the meta-data definition.

5.3   Encoding Scheme

Categorical variables are generally encoded using one of two popular encoding schemes, ordinal and one-hot scheme [17]. One-hot encoding scheme is considered stronger and the encoding scheme can be specified in the meta-data definition. When used the encoding schemes are persisted to process never seen before data consistently during scoring process.

5.4   Dimensionality Reduction [18]

More often than not, datasets are multi-variate and dimensionality reduction is a consequential data preparation step. Dimensionality Reduction preferences can also be specified in the metadata definition. As in the case of encoding scheme, the load factors are persisted so that values can be converted back to the original coordinate space.

5.5 Scaling [19]

Scaling is done automatically when needed and the factors are persisted as in other cases so that values can be scaled as needed.

5.6 Variable Importance [20]

Variable Importance factors and VIF factors are computed and included in the output reports. Retention criteria can be specified in the meta-data specification. These options are persisted and applied at the time of scoring.

5.7 Outliers [21]

In Machine Learning and in all of data analytics, the goal almost always is to find observations that do not conform to the norm. And, yet, those observations, that differ significantly from other observations, can unduly influence the rules we seek to extract to generalize. Practitioners have to make a decision, should the outliers be removed or included? And, determine under what conditions an observation may be removed. These may be specified in the metadata with outlier_ceiling (any value above this will be identified as outlier), outlier_floor (any value below this will be identified as outlier), and outlier action to remove (when set to remove the observation will be removed).

5.8 Missing Values [22]

Poor Quality derails any machine learning exercise, regardless of the process discipline. Missing Values are the norm and may be present in various form, such as, NA, no value, blank, empty string. If a value is found missing, one can either remove the observation with the missing value or impute the missing value using mean, median or other advanced techniques. Practitioners have to specify missing_value_action. The permitted values are (remove_observation, or impute_by_mean or impute_by_median or impute_by_mode or impute_by_classifier). When set to remove_observation, the observation will be removed and when set to impute_by_mean or by impute_by_median or by impute_mode, the framework assigns the specified central tendency measure. When it is set to impute_by_classifier, framework uses one of the appropriate supervised learner to assign a value.

5.9 Data Preparation

Practitioners spend an inordinate amount of time preparing data prior to training. Simplifying, cleaning and reducing the data are important subtasks and the framework can be programmed to perform all the necessary preparatory steps via the metadata description, as outlined above. In summary data can be prepared without writing custom or dataset specific software and much of the metadata specification can be reused, compressing classification cycle times.

5.10   Data Structure Conversion

Datasets are 2-dimensional and often have to be converted into matrices suitable for leveraging linear algebra procedures. Many other states are managed and all such data structures are internal to the execution process and does not affect scoring.

6   Meta-data = Koenig's Principle

As alluded to in the previous section, all data preparation tasks are specified in the meta-data specification and it is handled independent of datasets. Dataset specific processing is unnecessary, as Andrew Koenig declared "we can solve any problem by introducing an extra level of indirection" [23]. We apply Koenig's principle to split the data into two parts, actual and a description of the dataset. We capture essential discriminating characteristics of the dataset into meta-data as shown below. The data loader reads any dataset using the meta-data, as shown below. This is for the heart dataset from UCI [24].

As mentioned before promoting robust reuse is another goal. In summary, achieving compliance with NFL and Ockham's Razor, while promoting parallelism and software reuse are the objectives for this initiative. Reusability forces us to be dataset independent and learner independent.

We show below the metadata specification schema used in our framework.

```
rkannan@F4Linux2:~/ML/metadata$ cat heart.metadata.csv.pr
dataset=heart
dataset.file="/home/rkannan/ML/Heart/heart.csv"
dataseturl="https://www.kaggle.com/ronitf/heart-disease-uci"
header.present=T
separator=,
trainsplit=0.70
keep_split_statistics=T
seed=43
nObs=303
nCols=14
predictorCount=13
labelColPos=14
allCols="age","sex","cp","trestbps","chol","fbs","restecg","thalach","exang","oldpeak","slope","ca","thal","target"
predictorCols="age","sex","cp","trestbps","chol","fbs","restecg","thalach","exang","oldpeak","slope","ca","thal"
labelCol="target"
scale=F
encode=F
removeCols=
removeLowPValueColumns=F
remove_minority_class=F
multi_class_strategy=bayesian    #|one-vs-all
learnerlist="vglm","lda","nb","rF","SVM","dTree","knn","glm","gbm","xgb","bag","stack"
stack_by=vote                    #|nn
keep_learner_statistics=separate        #|tabulate
runcv5=T
runcv10=T
runjackknife=T
compute_VIF=T
compute_variableImportance=T
runForwardSelection=T
runBackwardSelection=T
generate_pairwise_correlations=F
generate_entropy=F
generate_information_gain=F
collect_compute_performance=T
keep_label_matrix=T
# data cleansing hints
# how to handle missing value complete (runs complete.cases) in the future we will
# NA will be removed
missing.policy=complete
# have more options including zoo what to do when a value is black not NA not null just blank character
blank.policy=complete
```

6.1 Traditional Machine Learning Exercise

Following architecture captures the traditional ML Task exercise. In this model, software engineers write custom software to read the dataset (the scripts are dataset aware number of attributes, target variable and the formula). Prepare the dataset for a specific learner, train the model, gather metrics and results.

Custom scripts are dataset aware, specific to a particular classifier, generate performance metric for that classifier.

6.2 Framework

The objective for our framework is to be independent of dataset and learner. To achieve dataset independence a config object is created as shown above and pre-processed data is passed on to the execution layer where a parallel task tree is activated – multiple learners are trained and induced using the prepared dataset – in a MISD configuration. Each learner is an instruction and all of them learn from a single dataset (SD), hence MISD.

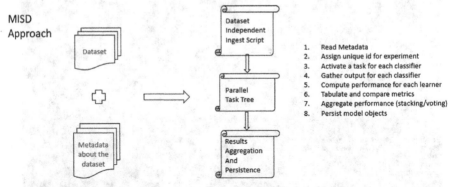

A detailed view of this framework is shown below. Metrics for each learner is gathered and persisted along with model objects and data preparation objects against a unique execution id. During the generalization phase, these objects are retrieved and the never seen before data is scored.

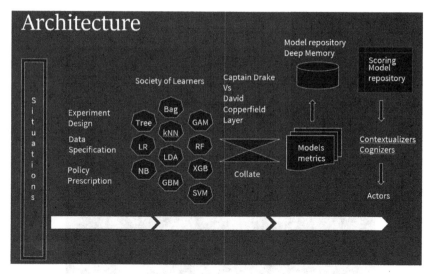

The framework has been implemented in R programming language [25].

7   Task Execution

Using parallel package [26] a list of tasks are executed in parallel as shown below

```
require(parallel)
#tasks<-list(vglm=run_vgam,lda=run_lda)

out<-mclapply(tasks,function(f)f(),mc.cores = length(tasks) )
```

7.1   Multiclass vs Binary Class

SVM and LogisticRegression are binary classifiers as they seek to find a linear separation boundary, and cannot be used, as is, when there are more than two classes in the dataset. In contrast, Bayesian classifiers, such as, NaiveBayes, LDA and logic based classifier Trees and distance based classifier kNN, can handle multi-class classifiers.

7.2   Ensemble Methods

We also run multiple ensemble classifiers (randomForest, bagging and boosted machines). These classifiers are discussed in detail [28]

7.3 Classifier Performance Metrics

```
rkannan@F4Linux2:~/ML/p-run-output/09162020$ more OUT_gbm3_cmx.txt
Confusion Matrix and Statistics


          unacc acc vgood good
   unacc    352 106     0   23
   acc        0  15     1    0
   vgood      0   0    21    0
   good       0   0     0    0

Overall Statistics

               Accuracy : 0.749
                 95% CI : (0.7094, 0.7858)
    No Information Rate : 0.6795
    P-Value [Acc > NIR] : 0.0003259

                  Kappa : 0.303

 Mcnemar's Test P-Value : NA

Statistics by Class:

                     Class: unacc Class: acc Class: vgood Class: good
Sensitivity                1.0000    0.12397      0.95455      0.0000
Specificity                0.2229    0.99748      1.00000      1.0000
Pos Pred Value             0.7318    0.93750      1.00000         NaN
Neg Pred Value             1.0000    0.78884      0.99799      0.9556
Prevalence                 0.6795    0.23359      0.04247      0.0444
Detection Rate             0.6795    0.02896      0.04054      0.0000
Detection Prevalence       0.9286    0.03089      0.04054      0.0000
Balanced Accuracy          0.6114    0.56072      0.97727      0.5000
```

Most widely used metrics, computed using Caret [29] package, are persisted.

7.4 Comparative Analysis

```
rkannan@F4Linux2:~/ML/R11022020/icu$ more icu_perfmx.csv
"name","sensiivity","specificity","pos_pred_val","neg_pred_val","precision","recall","f1","prevalence","balAccuracy"
"C50",1,0.3077,0.8393,1,0.8393,1,0.9126,0.7833,0.7833
"nb",1,0.3077,0.8393,1,0.8393,1,0.9126,0.7833,0.7833
"vglm",1,0.3077,0.8393,1,0.8393,1,0.9126,0.7833,0.7833
"glm",1,0.3077,0.8393,1,0.8393,1,0.9126,0.7833,0.7833
"rda",1,0,0.7833,NA,0.7833,1,0.8785,0.7833,0.7833
"lda",1,0.3077,0.8393,1,0.8393,1,0.9126,0.7833,0.7833
"esvm",1,0.3077,0.8393,1,0.8393,1,0.9126,0.7833,0.7833
"rpart",1,0.3077,0.8393,1,0.8393,1,0.9126,0.7833,0.7833
"bag",0.8936,0.3846,0.84,0.5,0.84,0.8936,0.866,0.7833,0.7
"RF",1,0.3077,0.8393,1,0.8393,1,0.9126,0.7833,0.7833
"gbm",0.9574,0.3077,0.8333,0.6667,0.8333,0.9574,0.8911,0.7833,0.75
"gbm3",0.9574,0.3077,0.8333,0.6667,0.8333,0.9574,0.8911,0.7833,0.75
"gbm5",0.9574,0.3077,0.8333,0.6667,0.8333,0.9574,0.8911,0.7833,0.75
"xgb2",1,0.3077,0.8393,1,0.8393,1,0.9126,0.7833,0.7833
"xgb4",1,0.3077,0.8393,1,0.8393,1,0.9126,0.7833,0.7833
"xgb5",0.9149,0.3077,0.8269,0.5,0.8269,0.9149,0.8687,0.7833,0.7167
```

Metrics generated by individual learners are then aggregated as shown below.

7.5 Stacking

The results from the base models are then combined using stacking wherein we use majority vote to assign class label, as shown below.

	actual	c50	nb	vglm	glm	rda	lda	esvm	rpart	bag	rf	gbm5	xgb5	stackv
1	0	0	0	0	0	0	0	0	0	0	0	0	0	0
2	0	0	0	0	0	0	0	0	0	0	0	0	0	0
3	0	0	0	0	0	0	0	0	0	0	0	0	0	0
4	0	0	0	0	0	0	0	0	0	0	0	0	0	0
5	0	0	0	0	0	0	0	0	0	0	0	0	0	0
6	0	0	0	0	0	0	0	0	0	0	0	0	0	0
7	0	0	0	0	0	0	0	0	0	1	0	0	0	0
8	0	0	0	0	0	0	0	0	0	0	0	0	0	0
9	0	0	0	0	0	0	0	0	0	0	0	0	0	0
10	0	0	0	0	0	0	0	0	0	0	0	0	0	0
11	0	0	0	0	0	0	0	0	0	0	0	0	0	0
12	0	0	0	0	0	0	0	0	0	0	0	0	0	0
13	0	0	0	0	0	0	0	0	0	1	0	1	0	0
14	0	0	0	0	0	0	0	0	0	0	0	0	0	0
15	0	0	0	0	0	0	0	0	0	0	0	0	0	0
16	0	0	0	0	0	0	0	0	0	0	0	0	0	0
17	0	0	0	0	0	0	0	0	0	0	0	0	0	0
18	0	0	0	0	0	0	0	0	0	0	0	0	0	0
19	0	0	0	0	0	0	0	0	0	0	0	0	0	0
20	0	0	0	0	0	0	0	0	0	0	0	0	0	0
21	0	0	0	0	0	0	0	0	0	0	0	0	0	0
22	0	0	0	0	0	0	0	0	0	1	0	0	0	0
23	0	0	0	0	0	0	0	0	0	0	0	0	0	0
24	0	0	0	0	0	0	0	0	0	0	0	0	0	0
25	0	0	0	0	0	0	0	0	0	0	0	0	0	0
26	0	0	0	0	0	0	0	0	0	0	0	0	0	0
27	0	0	0	0	0	0	0	0	0	0	0	0	1	0
28	0	0	0	0	0	0	0	0	0	0	0	0	0	0
29	0	0	0	0	0	0	0	0	0	0	0	0	0	0
30	0	0	0	0	0	0	0	0	0	0	0	0	0	0
31	0	0	0	0	0	0	0	0	0	0	0	0	0	0
32	0	0	0	0	0	0	0	0	0	0	0	0	0	0
33	0	0	0	0	0	0	0	0	0	1	0	1	1	0
34	0	0	0	0	0	0	0	0	0	0	0	0	0	0
35	0	0	0	0	0	0	0	0	0	0	0	0	0	0

Here each row represents an observation and columns represent the labels assigned by individual base learners. At the time of stacking, a stacked class label is assigned based on simple majority voting as shown above. Stacking does improve to near perfect accuracy, improving accuracy over all the learners stacked.

8   Model Management

Each experiment and the induced learners are persisted such that never seen before observations can be scored, as needed. The observation can then be scored as per the stacking policy.

9   Learner Management

Currently, the framework supports 17 different classification models. We are evaluating ideas and approaches to allow users to register custom classifiers and leverage proprietary learners.

10 Summary

Machine Learning and applications of Machine Learning is quite common and has become a mature and viable technology. In our observation the practice of M/L has evolved in isolation, resulting in inefficient practice. Both

1. Software Reuse is absent as custom data preparation and classification solutions are crafted; and
2. More often than not these tasks run without any parallelization.

And, most importantly with single learner analysis, without incorporating NFL.

We have presented a reusable framework that allows users to specify complex machine learning tasks, in the form of metadata file, encapsulating dataset specific characteristics, model run-time characteristics and data preparation preferences. Most classification task can be completed without ever writing an additional like of code. The caret [29] package, in contrast, provides a unified interface. The caret package allows you to learn once and run any classifier with that expertise. Our goal was to eliminate any coding to run a classifier or many classifiers.

Practitioners can effortlessly train multiple classifiers of their choosing in parallel and optionally stack the results.

Acknowledgements. IBM Power Systems Academic Initiative IBM PSAI for their generous support for all my courses.

References

1. Wolpert, D.: The lack of a priori distinctions between learning algorithms. Neural Comput. **8**(7), 1341–1390 (1996). https://doi.org/10.1162/neco.1996.8.7.1341
2. http://no-free-lunch.org/
3. https://www.kdnuggets.com/2019/09/no-free-lunch-data-science.html
4. Wolpert, D.H.: The supervised learning no-free-lunch theorems. In: Roy, R., Köppen, M., Ovaska, S., Furuhashi, T., Hoffmann, F. (eds.) Soft Computing and Industry, pp. 25–42. Springer, London (2002). https://doi.org/10.1007/978-1-4471-0123-9_3
5. Kotsiantis, S.B.: Supervised machine learning: a review of classification techniques. https://datajobs.com/data-science-repo/SupervisedLearning-%5bSB-Kotsiantis%5d.pdf
6. https://hpc.llnl.gov/tutorials/introduction-parallel-computing/flynns-classical-taxonomy
7. Mosier, M.W.: I. Problems and design of cross-validation. Educ. Psychol. Measur. **11**, 5–11 (1951)
8. Gerber, F., Nychka, D.W.: Parallel cross validation: a scalable fitting method for Gaussian process models. Comput. Stat. Data Anal. **155**, 107113 (2021). https://doi.org/10.1016/j.csda.2020.107113
9. Breiman, L.: Bagging predictors. Mach. Learn. **26**, 123–140 (1996)
10. Breiman, L.: Random forests. Mach. Learn. **45**, 5–32 (2001)
11. Wolpert, D.H.: Stacked generalization. Neural Netw. **5**, 241–259 (1992)
12. Efron, B.: Bootstrap methods: another look at the jackknife. Ann. Stat. **7**(1), 1–26 (1979). https://doi.org/10.1214/aos/1176344552

13. Zaharia, M.: Apache Spark: a unified engine for big data processing. Commun. ACM **59**, 56–65 (2016). https://cacm.acm.org/magazines/2016/11/209116-apache-spark/abstract
14. Sommerville, Software Engineering, 10 edn, chap. 15
15. http://www.cs.iastate.edu/~honavar/occam.pdf
16. He, H., Ma, Y. (eds.): Imbalanced learning: Foundations, Algorithms, and Applications. Wiley, New York (2013)
17. https://docs.h2o.ai/h2o/latest-stable/h2o-docs/data-science/algo-params/categorical_enc oding.html
18. https://en.wikipedia.org/wiki/Dimensionality_reduction
19. https://www.analyticsvidhya.com/blog/2020/04/feature-scaling-machine-learning-normal ization-standardization/
20. https://www.r-bloggers.com/2020/07/comparing-variable-importance-functions-for-mod eling/
21. https://www.itl.nist.gov/div898/handbook/prc/section1/prc16.htm
22. https://stats.idre.ucla.edu/spss/modules/missing-data/
23. https://en.wikipedia.org/wiki/Fundamental_theorem_of_software_engineering
24. https://archive.ics.uci.edu/ml/datasets/Heart+Disease
25. R Core Team: R: a language and environment for statistical computing. R Foundation for Statistical Computing, Vienna, Austria (2018). https://www.R-project.org/
26. https://nceas.github.io/oss-lessons/parallel-computing-in-r/parallel-computing-in-r.html
27. Aly, M.: Survey on multiclass classification methods. Neural Netw. **19**, 1–9 (2005)
28. Witten, I.H., Frank, E., Hall, M.A., Pal, C.J.: Data Mining, pp. 479–501 (2017)
29. Kuhn, M.: Building predictive models in R using the caret package. www.jstatsoft.org/article/view/v028i05/v28i05.pdf

Digital Human in Cybersecurity Risk Assessment

Aistė Jurevičienė⬡, Agnė Brilingaitė⬡, and Linas Bukauskas(✉)⬡

Cybersecurity Laboratory, Institute of Computer Science, Vilnius University,
Vilnius, Lithuania
aiste@jurevic.com, {agne.brilingaite,linas.bukauskas}@mif.vu.lt

Abstract. Cybersecurity focuses on technological solutions, skills, and setup. Nevertheless, advanced cyber attacks include aspects of social engineering and exploit the weaknesses of an individual. Advanced persistent threat actors are invisible. Therefore, after harvesting large amounts of publicly available data, they have overabundant time to stage a possible attack and choose a victim as the weakest link. On social media, people tend to disclose personal information in implicit and explicit ways. User profiles and *What is on your mind* messages on the social network can contain sensitive and private data, e.g. location, address, and birth date. However, user comments, *Likes*, and shared photos can determine the user's personality during a personality trait analysis. Habits, interests, locations, and exposed loved ones are vulnerabilities that can be exploited during the cyber attack. Comprehensive image analysis, application of state of the art recognition techniques could be used to analyse shared photos of the individual, assume specific weaknesses, and predict behaviour-related features.

The work aims to build a formal ontology-based model for cybersecurity risk assessment that considers digital human characteristics. A multi-layered architecture solution was build as a proof of concept to maintain a set of artificial intelligence algorithms and specially developed questionnaires for data gathering and processing. The prototype enabled us to organise a small scale experiment to validate trait analysis methods. Also, it opened further research directions.

Keywords: Digital human · Cybersecurity · Personal risk assessment · Ontology-based model · Artificial intelligence

1 Introduction

A cyber attack by CISCO is defined as "... *a malicious and deliberate attempt by an individual or organisation to breach the information system of another individual or organisation. Usually, the attacker seeks some type of benefit from disrupting the victim's network*" [18]. Unfortunately, the number of victims of cyber attacks and the damage to society is increasing. A number of security breaches are rising. Compared to 2013 and 2018 [15], the number of security

D. D. Schmorrow and C. M. Fidopiastis (Eds.): HCII 2021, LNAI 12776, pp. 418–432, 2021.
https://doi.org/10.1007/978-3-030-78114-9_29

breaches increased by 67%, and the average cost of cybercrime increased by 72%. The average cost of cybercrime in 2018 was US$13.0 Million for each company. During attacks, business is disrupted, valuable information and revenue are lost, equipment is damaged. Most losses are due to malware, Web-based attacks, and denial-of-service.

Risk assessment models are used to observe, improve, and prevent possible cyber incidents. They ensure information and system security. Traditional risk assessment techniques are focused on saving the digital assets. In many cases, consideration of human properties would lead to undetermined, extensive, and open interpretation evaluation. Implementation of a risk assessment with human characteristic in mind becomes very complicated. Moreover, many additional and specific factors may impact results. Advanced persistent threat actors already take advantage of human properties as possible factors for the target acquisition. Therefore, a cybersecurity risk assessment should include the same or even more factors to counter attackers in advance.

Smart devices such as mobile phones and smartwatches can track the person's whereabouts and individual health condition. Machine learning algorithms can recognise and predict not just apparent things as ethnicity, age, gender, but also certain diseases or social habits. Furthermore, the analysis of social network comments with machine learning can predict whether a person has an eating disorder, depression, or post-traumatic stress disorder. Often, the presence of one trait determines the manifestation of another. For example, neuroticism at the genetic level [17] correlates with depression, schizophrenia, ever-smoker. And schizophrenia, like bipolar syndrome, affects facial proportions [10]. Thus, based on the data obtained from digital human data such as facial symmetry or frequent smoking observations, the algorithm can derive a broader spectrum of human features, and the malicious actors could use them for social engineering style attacks.

Some human traits are known to have direct links with cyber hygiene and susceptibility to social engineering attacks. For example, neurotic people are distrustful, cautious [30], and this results in low-level risk. The individuals with avoidant decision-making [7] style are characterised by poor cyber hygiene. A direct link between other traits and cyber risk may be found in trait correlation studies. However, an attacker can exploit characteristics that may not be directly related to security. For example, people in certain regions have an inherited trait of aldehyde dehydrogenase deficiency. This feature can potentially create a favourable scenario for an attacker to exploit a human under certain circumstances.

This paper presents a theoretical ontology-based model that is the basis for human trait semantic network in cybersecurity. A semantic network is like a digital human skeleton with fragmented human characteristics. For a given human property, digital recognition is or can be developed using various algorithms. Artificial intelligence algorithms are used to identify traits from a given digital source based on a semantic network depending on the group of specified properties. Different combinations of traits result in specific human behaviour in critical situations and under stress, such as cyber attacks. Therefore, a personalised risk assessment is essential for security training, development of individualised carrier paths or building defensive mechanisms to disrupt cyber kill-chains in progress. The prototype multi-layer architecture solution was built as a proof of the concept to combine a set of algorithms and questionnaire-based sub-system to validate our hypotheses.

The paper is structured as follows. Section 2 covers related work about humans in the context of risk assessment and provides the background for the research. Section 3 presents an ontology-based model. Sections 4 covers a methodology on how risk assessment model was implemented. Section 5 presents results of the experiments. The paper ends up with conclusions and future work in Sect. 6.

2   Background

The human is the weak point in cyber attacks. Firstly, personal computers are more vulnerable and in a worse condition than business computers that are in professional care. Therefore, 95% of attacks are directed to personal computers [3]. Secondly, people share a lot of personal information on the internet. Thus, adversaries can use personal traits to develop an attack strategy by social engineering. For example, women and older people have worse cybersecurity habits than others [7]. Usually, open people have relaxed social networking settings, and agreeable, conscientious or extroverted people are susceptible to social engineering attacks [30].

People with different traits behave differently in the same situations to achieve the desired result or avoid the problems. For example, for extroverted gymnasts, setting a particular goal helps to maintain concentration, and for those characterised by neuroticism, emotional control helps them cope with difficulties [22]. Furthermore, people with a sense of conscientious turn better in strategic situations when they focus on problems. Also, people who have a combination of characteristics: high extrovertability, openness, and low neuroticism cope with difficulties in a concentrated way. Therefore, knowledge of personal weaknesses, characteristics, and actions when solving complex problems opens possibilities reaching objectives.

Cyber hygiene, social network settings, addictions, and behaviour in stressful situations are directly related to cyber risks. Still, at the same time, they depend on the appearance of specific characteristics. Researchers have been analysing traits such as age, gender, Big Five traits, decision-making styles, risk-taking preferences, interest areas [5–7,16,27]. Therefore, attackers can take advantage of many other characteristics when provoking a victim. Anthropometric data such as gender, age, body complexity, ethnicity, facial features are relatively well studied, and their recognition with machine learning is widely used. More personal data, e.g. psychological condition such as depression, PTSD, eating disorders, stress, or propensity to commit suicide, can be recognised from social media and speech artefacts using machine learning algorithms. However, the psychological condition is not easy to recognise in an automated way because of language differences, new terms within social networks, misspelt words, and extra characters. Although it may be argued that the human psychological state is an individual matter, certain disorders occur in specific segments of the population. For example, the United States face armed attacks at school, colleges [24], and mass shootings in public areas. As a result, many witnesses are exposed to stress and depression that makes them negligent to the cyber domain.

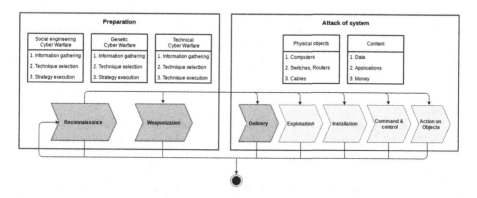

Fig. 1. Cyclic social engineering kill-chain

The general cyber kill-chain [11] characterises a sequence of actions of the attacker. It is observed that the attacks are reoccurring and repeated to achieve the desired goal. Certain stages can be skipped, interrupted, terminated, or fed back to make a loop (see Fig. 1). *Reconnaissance* and *Weaponization* stages are performed to gather data, choose a technique and build a strategy for the attack execution without interaction with a victim. In contrast, *Delivery* and later stages represent the attack on the system with possible human victim involved. Threat intelligence information systems, defence tools and cybersecurity methods are improved from the technology side. Often, defenders notice and stop a computer attack in time. However, it is difficult to control the situation when it comes to social engineering or human interaction domain as a human vulnerability is exploited [28]. For example, an interrupted attack can be resumed by collecting and applying information about the person responsible for the system protection. Human vulnerabilities are exploited at any time during an attack.

The cyber domain uses ontologies to structure knowledge. Ontologies in the areas of vulnerability, operations, social networks, privacy, and organization security management are defined [29]. Cyberoperations are defined as actions in cyberspace to achieve a goal. In the ontology definition, the cyber operation is the action a cyber operator makes during an attack [20]. There are three operation domains, one of which is Knowledge Accumulation [29]. This domain is related to the accumulation and structuring of existing knowledge. It covers the human traits and the associated cyber vulnerabilities that the cyber operator can manipulate during the cyber attack.

Different algorithms are used for data analysis, depending on the area under study. For example, identifying traits from the human face takes place in several stages, the first of which is the detection of the face [26]. For face detection, several methods are used: knowledge-based, feature invariant, template matching, appearance-based, and agent-based. The most popular face detection algorithms are Histogram of Oriented Gradient (HOG), Haar Feature-Based Cascade Classifier, and convolutional neural networks (CNN). Haar Cascade and HOG run in real-time on CPU, but HOG does not detect small faces, and the formatted bounding box does not cover the entire face [8]. Nevertheless, HOG is better for the detection of non-frontal or faces with small occlusion. Compared to the two other, CNN is the best in non-frontal faces detection, and easily get hold of with occlusions. HOG does not detect looking down or up faces of people. And for identification of other traits, various neural networks are used, e.g. deep neural networks (DNN)—sexual orientation [31], CNN—gender and age [9,14,23] identification.

The risk assessment is based on the high impact of vulnerability probability [1]. The risk assessment is essential to ensure information security, as it identifies weaknesses and threats to identify and assign preventive measures. Risk assessment consists of two parts—analysis and evaluation. There are various systems to assess the cyber risks posed mostly by technological vulnerabilities. These risk assessment systems are based on models that calculate the risk by the sum of multiplications of vulnerability probabilities and consequences [32]. However, in assessment, an additional component may be used—the impact of vulnerability [4].

3   An Ontology-Based Model

Ontology-based semantic networks from top to bottom must perform accurate searches on the questions asked [19]. The data source used should be accessible when rising from the bottom to up. An ontology should have several levels, such as top, middle, and domain; when going from the top, the level of abstraction should decrease. Any semantic network is a global network of ontologies.

An ontology is a collection of triplets. Any triplet t belongs to the set $\mathcal{T}$. Triplets can also have [21]: URI/IRI links—**U**, literals in text or numbers—**L**, or empty blank nodes—**B**.

Definition 1 (Triplet set). *Let us have a set of triplets $\mathcal{T}$, where each triplet t is in at least one ontology $t \in \mathcal{O}$:*

$$\mathcal{T} ::= \{t(s, p, o) | s \in \mathbf{U} \cup \mathbf{B} \wedge p \in \mathbf{U} \wedge o \in \mathbf{U} \cup \mathbf{B} \cup \mathbf{L}\}.$$

Here, variables s, p, and o represent a subject, a predicate, and an object, respectively.

Predicate examples can be `isA`, `has`, `describe`, `implements`, `depend`, `trigger`, `partOf`, `influence`, `threatProbability`, `risk`, and `property`. Table 1 presents examples of triplets. The left side of the table shows the predicate name that can be used in the semantic network, and the right side provides a full triplet example with a particular predicate usage. For example, the identification of subject *Age* can be implemented using algorithm *CNN* (object *Algo/CNN/1*).

Table 1. Triplet examples

Predicate	Usage example
has	Head —has→ Face
describe	Circadian phenotype —describe→ Lifestyle
implements	Age —implements→ Algo/CNN/1
depend	Eye color —depend→ Genetic
trigger	Environment —trigger→ Psychological condition
partOf	Eyes —part of→ Face
threatProbability	Openness —threatProbability→ 1.5
risk	Human —risk→ 4.5

Any triplet set $\mathcal{T}$ can be transformed into non-homogeneous graph $\mathcal{G} = (\mathcal{V}, \mathcal{E})$. Here, sets $\mathcal{V}$ and $\mathcal{E}$ denote vertices and edges, respectively, $|\mathcal{V}| > 0$ and $|\mathcal{E}| > 0$. Set $\mathcal{V}$ includes all objects and subjects from the triplet set $\mathcal{T}$, and set $\mathcal{E}$ includes dependencies among subjects and objects via predicates. Edges are represented as 3-tuples $e(s, o, p)$ for each dependensy between subject s and object o via predicate p. Graph $\mathcal{G}$ is an ontology schema.

Definition 2 (Ontology schema). *Ontology schema $\mathcal{G}$ is a resource-defined graph constructed from the triplet set $\mathcal{T}$:*

$$\mathcal{G} ::= \forall t_i(s_i, p_i, o_i), t_j(s_j, p_j, o_j) \exists t_k(s_k, p_k, o_k) | t_i \neq t_j \wedge t_k \neq t_i \wedge t_k \neq t_j,$$
$$t_k(s_k, p_k, o_k) = ((s_j, *, o_i) \vee (s_i, *, o_j) \vee ((o_i, *, s_j) \wedge o_i \notin \mathbf{L}) \vee$$
$$((o_j, *, s_i) \wedge o_j \notin \mathbf{L}) \wedge t_i, t_j, t_k \in \mathcal{T} \wedge$$
$$\nexists t(o, p, s) \in \mathcal{T} : o \notin \mathcal{V} \vee s \notin \mathcal{V} \vee e(o, s, p) \notin \mathcal{E}.$$

As an example in Table 1, *Age* and *Face* vertices are used in different triplets, but they can be associated via predicate describe, *Face* describe *Age*.

Definition 3 (A property path). *Property path $\mathcal{P}$ is a path with in the graph $\mathcal{G} = (\mathcal{V}, \mathcal{E})$ among two vertices v_i and v_k. The path is denoted as a sequence $v_1 \xrightarrow{p_1} v_2 \xrightarrow{p_2} \ldots \xrightarrow{p_{k-1}} v_k$. All paths belong to the set of property paths $\mathcal{PP}$.*

For example, the path can be found between node *Body part* and algorithm *Algo/DNN/5* to identify movement patterns from the video feed.

Definition 4 (Likelihood of a threat). *Likelihood of the threat is the function $l : \mathcal{PP} \rightarrow \mathbb{R} \cup \perp$ producing a value if the path ends with an edge with predicate value* threatProbability. *Otherwise, an undefined value $\perp$ is returned. The function is defined as:*

$$l(\mathcal{P}) ::= \begin{cases} v_j, & \Longleftrightarrow \exists v_i, v_j : (v_i, \texttt{threatProbability}, v_j) \in \mathcal{P}, \\ \perp, & otherwise. \end{cases}$$

In some cases, only the existence of traits is already a threat in itself. In other cases, external factors are required to trigger the threat, described along the path.

Definition 5 (Impact of a vulnerability). *An impact of vulnerability is the function $g : \mathcal{PP} \rightarrow \mathbb{R} \cup \perp$ producing a value if the path ends with an edge with predicate value* impact. *Otherwise, an undefined value $\perp$ is returned. The function is defined as:*

$$g(\mathcal{P}) ::= \begin{cases} v_j, & \Longleftrightarrow \exists v_i, v_j : (v_i, \texttt{\textit{impact}}, v_j) \in \mathcal{P}, \\ \perp, & otherwise. \end{cases}$$

Definition 6 (Risk on a property path). *The risk on the property path is a function that given a property path $\mathcal{P}$ calculates the risk using its vertices, $\mathcal{R} : \mathcal{PP} \rightarrow \mathbb{R}$. The risk $\mathcal{R}$ is defined as follows:*

$$\mathcal{R}(\mathcal{P}) ::= \sum_{\forall v_i \in \mathcal{P}} l_i(\mathcal{P}'') g_i(\mathcal{P}') c_i, \exists \mathcal{P}' = v_i \xrightarrow{impact} *, \exists \mathcal{P}'' = v_i \xrightarrow{threatProbability} *,$$

where c_i is a consequence multiplier for a probable impact if the vulnerability is found. Consequence multiplier acts as importance factor to highlight the property path.

The risk calculation on the path enables the collection of all possible components that impact the individualised risk assessment process. The richness of property paths represents different attack vectors. Therefore, the model implementation with automated algorithms and dynamic data feeds enables digital human risk assessment.

4   Methodology

This paper's research goal was to explore ontology-based risk assessment, including digital human properties and existing technological solutions. Data was gathered using the prototype system. The prototype system supported the collection of questionnaires, and multi-modal data feeds.

Figure 2 depicts the general architecture and components of the prototype system that collects and processes data. Multi-modal input from video and photo were captured to analyse external human properties using several classification algorithms. The aggregation component enabled the evaluation output. Social behaviour component was responsible for questionnaire data management.

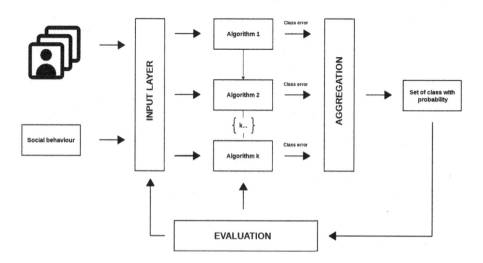

Fig. 2. General architecture of the prototype system

Image data gathering was the initial stage to collect data about the person without direct human interaction. Implemented and integrated algorithms were able to determine age, gender, ethnicity, parts of the body and face, eye colour, and family relationships among participants. The correct face detection has a significant impact on trait recognition. The snapshot by a computer camera solves the photo quality problem for different algorithms. The most traits are recognised using multiple neural networks, considerable computational resources are required—the prototype used neural network layouts with different training data to construct classifiers. Separate training was required for each particular component of the ontology, e.g. age, gender, and body parts. Thus, within the semantic network, an algorithm, e.g. DNN, is reached via the property path $\mathcal{P}$ through the traits identified using image data. For example, if a head is recognised on the image and the face is detected, an attempt can be made to recognise the eyes' location, eye geometry, and eye colour using a specific algorithm. The MTCNN algorithm is used for eye colour recognition in the prototypical system.

The questionnaire supported specific information about a person traits related to cybersecurity risk. A person visited the page to take a photo snapshot using a computer camera and answered questions to identify Big Five characteristics, decision-making style, and risk-taking preferences. The questionnaire was based on trait identification standards. The Big Five traits are identified using a 50-item International Pool of Personality Item Pool [12] that was compiled in collaboration with researchers seeking to have advanced personality measures. For each of the five traits, agreeableness, conscientious, extroversion, neuroticism, and openness, ten questions are used. They have negative and positive wordings to ensure consistency and cross-validation of participant answers. Five decision-making styles are—avoidant, dependent, intuitive, rational, and spontaneous. The General Decision-Making Style Questionnaire (GDMS) [25] applied to determine the decision-making style. A subset of non-overlapping questions was used in our work. Instead of unused questions, five situations were formulated with five behavioural invariants to reflect each human decision-making style. Also, there were five distinguished risk-taking preferences—ethical, financial, health/safety, recreational, and social. The risk-taking tendency was assessed using a Domain-Specific Risk-Taking (DOSPERT) Scale consisting of 30 hearings [2]. Results were obtained evaluating answers to questions and identifying features from the photos. The total risk score was calculated according to the model following the ontology paths. If the family picture was uploaded (or snapshot was made with the camera) each identified individual with a kinship increased the risk accordingly. In the prototype, a neural network architecture for kinship recognition was a Siamese neural network where two input vectors were used with the same weights.

5   Experiments

The study to evaluate the prototype, assess the model and compute individual risk in cybersecurity involved 23 families of volunteers. They included two to nine family members and two individuals. Altogether 87 people returned the questionnaires. Some families were made up of just husbands and wives, but they were not counted as kinships. More women (63.6%) than men (36.4%) participated in the study. Age groups from 18 years are studied; most individuals (43.2%) aged 25–34, aged 35–44 made 4.5%, and the rest were over 65 (5.7%). Only 9 of the respondents were students. Most of the rest had a higher education degree. Study participants have education in different fields—social sciences, engineering, life sciences. And, seven students were graduating in computer science. However, 74.7% of participants marked computer literacy as advanced or experienced. In the question *how much time you spend at the computer*, the answer 5–6 h were marked by 12.6% of respondent. Thus, the study population was quite diverse. The subjects were local residents (Lithuanian). Most of the research subjects did not belong to the university community and were family members of participating students.

Based on the response analysis, participants were quite extroverted and open (see Fig. 3(b)) and several participants with apparent neurotic characteristic.

However, the participants were also quite agreeable and conscientious because volunteering to participate in the survey is often agreed upon by pleasant enough, helpful people. The neurotic and open people had a higher cyber risk than people with other characteristics based on the privacy settings in social networks. But, respondents with other factors also had a high-risk value. For example, agreeableness makes them susceptible to manipulations with dark patterns. The survey did not show many people with apparent risk-taking preferences (see Fig. 3(a)). In this research, most people had recreational and social risk-taking choices. Regarding situational decision-making questions, questionnaire results showed that people made decisions depending on the situation, possibly determined by human values (see Fig. 4(a)). Most respondents had a rational decision-making style.

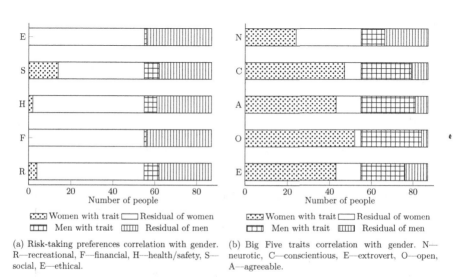

(a) Risk-taking preferences correlation with gender. R—recreational, F—financial, H—health/safety, S—social, E—ethical.

(b) Big Five traits correlation with gender. N—neurotic, C—conscientious, E—extrovert, O—open, A—agreeable.

Fig. 3. Big five traits and risk-taking preferences correlation with gender and age

Although several algorithms were used to determine age, only 46% of people are assigned to the appropriate age group automatically (see Fig. 4(b)). The age was most correctly identified for younger participants. Within 25–34 age group, the age was identified correctly for approximately 78% participants. Algorithms assigned participants to the younger groups quite often due to several reasons. First of all, the groups are relative. The age on the threshold is difficult to distinguish, and the error is treated as sufficient. Secondly, algorithms are trained to assign people to a younger group, as it is more acceptable than the opposite. When a person is recognised as younger, he or she is less likely to take an offence. For example, the study involved people over 65, and all of them were assigned to the age group between 55–64. Thirdly, such a situation could arise due to personal appearance, the living environment, health-associated habits, and national characteristics. Most of the images belonged to women in a stocky position. Therefore, they often looked younger. Also, cosmetics could hide the signs of old age. Also, photo quality and lighting could make an impact on the results.

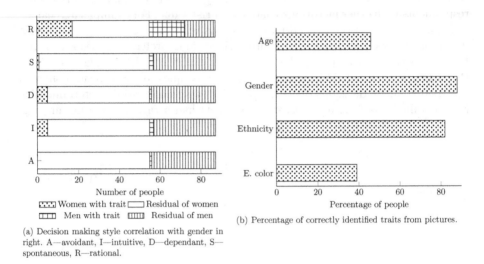

(a) Decision making style correlation with gender in right. A—avoidant, I—intuitive, D—dependant, S—spontaneous, R—rational.

(b) Percentage of correctly identified traits from pictures.

Fig. 4. Traits recognized from answers and photos

The human gender was best identified in the study, and even in 88% of cases, the algorithms identified it correctly. All men were identified as men, with only a few women assigned to the male category, except for one woman. The assigned woman had short hair and without makeup. Ethnicity was correctly identified in about 82% of cases. The majority of misidentified people were assigned to Latino-Hispanic and Asian groups. Most smiling people were identified as Asian due to their face mimicry. Moreover, tanned and rounder-faced people were attributed to Latino-Hispanic group.

Trends in the correlation between traits were observed, but they cannot be described as rules. Parallel coordinates diagram was designed to represent a multidimensional diagram in a 1D plot. This method of data representation was applied to elucidate the possible correlations of certain features. Initially, an attempt was made to look at the general trends that could be identified from traits depicted in the questionnaire. For better data comparison, numerical data was scaled. As most of the respondents were identified as extroverted, to find trends, the median of extrovertability score was calculated. As a mode of classification, respondents were divided into more extroverted and less extroverted. Figure 5 depicts traits that show correlation with cyber hygiene habits.

Extroverted people were more likely to score high openness and agreeability scores; they were less neurotic. Extrovert more often did not avoid making decisions, and they did not need other opinions. They also loved more extreme entertainment and were not afraid to take risks in that area of entertainment.

More introverted people were more likely to report worse updating and applying security awareness practices but better device protection. Extroverted ones showed good enough cyber hygiene. However, together with low neuroticism, high agreeableness and openness, high extrovertability scored higher social engineering risk. Neurotics, due to their suspicion and distrust, were less susceptible to social engineering attacks. However, all other Big Five traits under the "Social Engineering Personality Framework" (SEPF) [30] increased the risk due to the potential number of principles. Therefore, an attacker can access a person with the above characteristics based on all six principles: liking, authority, reciprocity, social proof, scarcity, commitment, and consistency.

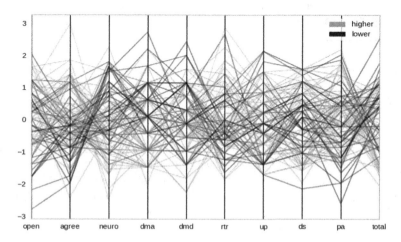

Fig. 5. Extroversion correlation with other traits. The vertical axis contains scaled score points. Abbreviations: open—openess, agree—agreeableness, neuro—neuroticism, dma—avoidant and dmd—dependant decision making styles, rtr—recreational risk-taking preference, up—updating, ds—device securement, pa—protective awareness, total—risk score

Our research confirmed existing results [13] that women are more neurotic and agreeable compared to men, and they also had a higher interest in Domestic-Manual, Social-Educational, and Hedonistic-Enterprising. On the other hand, men were more technical, Logic-Minded, and more interested in research and science. Young people also have more Technical-Logical thinking. They are also more hedonistic, more open, and more neurotic than older people. Furthermore, the older ones are more agreeable, conscientious; they have a domestic, Cultural-Intellectual, Social-Educational interest. Based on the associations of such external traits with Big Five traits, one could make initial risk assessment from the images based on these character traits. Thus, having both images and personality traits identified from the survey questions, one could conclude that pictures would suffice for a generalised identification of at least the Big Five characteristics.

6   Conclusions and Future Work

This work focused on the development of the ontology-based methods for cybersecurity risk assessment that considers digitally acquired human characteristics. Machine learning methods were used to recognise facial features from image snapshots, and questionnaires supported verification of the automatically calculated results. We proposed the general multi-layer architecture solution that can encapsulate classical machine learning algorithms. The artificial intelligence algorithms were implemented to integrate image/video feed analysis and questionnaire subsystems into the architecture. Statistical data processing and data mining algorithms were applied to analyse traits and digital human properties. Implemented architecture, tested algorithms, and experimental results confirmed hypotheses from other researchers and enabled an integrated cybersecurity risk assessment approach.

The assessment of digital human traits in the cybersecurity area is rapidly developing research direction. Considering the evolution of artificial intelligence algorithms and vast numbers of publicly shared personal data, the problem at hand is still to be recognised as important. The future research directions could include detailed analysis of algorithms to be applied for automated and semiautomated extraction and aggregation of digital human characteristics. These directions would open new possibilities for better identification and qualitative evaluation of artificial intelligence classification algorithms applied in human trait analysis and compare them to classical implementations. The other research direction is to narrow down trait analysis towards cybersecurity specialist identifying important characteristics or choosing different questioning strategies. As a continuation of the project, an investigation of possible attack prevention scenarios should be considered. The emphasis on competencies that cover up disadvantageous traits could further enhance the work and help improve cybersecurity situation. Finally, the ontology-based model could be extended and implemented with a set of predicates for specific scenarios to tune the risk assessment calculation.

Acknowledgements. This work was partially supported by project *Advancing Human Performance in Cybersecurity*, ADVANCES. The ADVANCES is funded by Iceland, Liechtenstein and Norway through the EEA Grants.

References

1. Akinrolabu, O., Nurse, J.R., Martin, A., New, S.: Cyber risk assessment in cloud provider environments: current models and future needs. Comput. Secur. **87**, 101600 (2019). https://doi.org/10.1016/j.cose.2019.101600
2. Blais, A.R., Weber, E.: A domain-specific risk-taking (DOSPERT) scale for adult populations. Judg. Decis. Making **1**, 33–47 (2006). https://doi.org/10.1037/t13084-000
3. Cain, A.A., Edwards, M.E., Still, J.D.: An exploratory study of cyber hygiene behaviors and knowledge. J. Inf. Secur. Appl. **42**, 36–45 (2018). https://doi.org/10.1016/j.jisa.2018.08.002

4. Cox, L.: Some limitations of "risk = threat × vulnerability × consequence" for risk analysis of terrorist attacks. Risk Anal.: Off. Publ. Soc. Risk Anal. **28**, 1749–61 (2008). https://doi.org/10.1111/j.1539-6924.2008.01142.x

5. Egelman, S., Peer, E.: Scaling the security wall: developing a security behavior intentions scale (SeBIS). In: Proceedings of the 33rd Annual ACM Conference on Human Factors in Computing Systems, CHI 2015, pp. 2873–2882. Association for Computing Machinery, New York (2015). https://doi.org/10.1145/2702123.2702249

6. Gavett, B., Zhao, R., John, S., Bussell, C., Roberts, J., Yue, C.: Phishing suspiciousness in older and younger adults: the role of executive functioning. PLoS One **12**, e0171620 (2017). https://doi.org/10.1371/journal.pone.0171620

7. Gratian, M., Bandi, S., Cukier, M., Dykstra, J., Ginther, A.: Correlating human traits and cybersecurity behavior intentions. Comput. Secur. **73**, 345–358 (2017). https://doi.org/10.1016/j.cose.2017.11.015

8. Gupta, V.: Face detection - OpenCV, Dlib and deep learning (C++/Python) (2018). https://www.learnopencv.com/face-detection-opencv-dlib-and-deep-learning-c-python/. Accessed 16 June 2020

9. Hacibeyoglu, M., Ibrahim, M.H.: Human gender prediction on facial mobil images using convolutional neural networks. Int. J. Intell. Syst. Appl. Eng. **6**(3), 203–208 (2018). https://doi.org/10.18201/ijisae.2018644778

10. Hennessy, R., Baldwin, P., Browne, D., Kinsella, A., Waddington, J.: Frontonasal dysmorphology in bipolar disorder by 3D laser surface imaging and geometric morphometrics: comparisons with schizophrenia. Schizophrenia Res. **122**, 63–71 (2010). https://doi.org/10.1016/j.schres.2010.05.001

11. Hoffmann, R.: Stochastic model of the simple cyber kill chain: cyber attack process as a regenerative process. In: Saeed, K., Dvorský, J. (eds.) CISIM 2020. LNCS, vol. 12133, pp. 355–365. Springer, Cham (2020). https://doi.org/10.1007/978-3-030-47679-3_30

12. International Personality Item Pool: Administering IPIP measures, with a 50-item sample questionnaire (2019). https://ipip.ori.org/New_IPIP-50-item-scale.htm. Accessed 25 Oct 2020

13. Kandler, C., Bleidorn, W., Riemann, R., Angleitner, A., Spinath, F.: The genetic links between the big five personality traits and general interest domains. Pers. Soc. Psychol. Bull. **37**, 1633–1643 (2011). https://doi.org/10.1177/0146167211414275

14. Levi, G., Hassncer, T.: Age and gender classification using convolutional neural networks. In: IEEE Conference on Computer Vision and Pattern Recognition Workshops (CVPRW), pp. 34–42 (2015). https://doi.org/10.1109/CVPRW.2015.7301352

15. LLC, P.I.: Ninth annual cost of cybercrime study unlocking the value of improved cybersecurity protection (2019). https://www.accenture.com/_acnmedia/pdf-96/accene-2019-cost-of-cybercrime-study-final.pdf. Accessed 25 Jan 2020

16. McCormac, A., Zwaans, T., Parsons, K., Calic, D., Butavicius, M., Pattinson, M.: Individual differences and information security awareness. Comput. Hum. Behav. **69**, 151–156 (2016). https://doi.org/10.1016/j.chb.2016.11.065

17. Nagel, M., et al.: Meta-analysis of genome-wide association studies for neuroticism in 449,484 individuals identifies novel genetic loci and pathways. Nat. Genet. **50**, 920–927 (2018). https://doi.org/10.1038/s41588-018-0151-7

18. Navabifar, F., Emadi, M., Yusof, R., Khalid, M.: What are the most common cyber attacks? https://www.cisco.com/c/en/us/products/security/common-cyberattacks.html. Accessed 16 June 2020

19. Obrst, L., Chase, P., Markeloff, R.: Developing an ontology of the cyber security domain. In: da Costa, P.C.G., Laskey, K.B. (eds.) Proceedings of the Seventh International Conference on Semantic Technologies for Intelligence, Defense, and Security, Fairfax, VA, USA, 23–26 October 2012. CEUR Workshop Proceedings, vol. 966, pp. 49–56. CEUR-WS.org (2012)

20. Oltramari, A., Cranor, L., Walls, R., McDaniel, P.: Building an ontology of cyber security. In: CEUR Workshop Proceedings, vol. 1304, pp. 54–61 (2014)

21. Pérez, J., Arenas, M., Gutierrez, C.: Semantics and complexity of SPARQL. In: Cruz, I., et al. (eds.) ISWC 2006. LNCS, vol. 4273, pp. 30–43. Springer, Heidelberg (2006). https://doi.org/10.1007/11926078_3

22. Roberts, R., Woodman, T.: Personality and performance: moving beyond the big 5. Curr. Opin. Psychol. **16**, 104–108 (2017). https://doi.org/10.1016/j.copsyc.2017.03.033

23. Rodrìguez, P., Cucurull, G., Gonfaus, J.M., Roca, F.X., Gonzàlez, J.: Age and gender recognition in the wild with deep attention. Pattern Recogn. **72**, 563–571 (2017). https://doi.org/10.1016/j.patcog.2017.06.028

24. Saha, K., Choudhury, M.: Modeling stress with social media around incidents of gun violence on college campuses. In: Proceedings of the ACM on Human-Computer Interaction, vol. 1, pp. 92:1–92:27 (2017). https://doi.org/10.1145/3134727

25. Scott, S., Bruce, R.: Decision-making style: the development and assessment of a new measure. Educ. Psychol. Meas.- EDUC PSYCHOL MEAS **55**, 818–831 (1995). https://doi.org/10.1177/0013164495055005017

26. Shaily Pandey, S.S.: Review: face detection and recognition techniques. Int. J. Comput. Sci. Inf. Technol. **5**(3), 4111–4117 (2014)

27. Sheng, S., Holbrook, M., Kumaraguru, P., Cranor, L.F., Downs, J.: Who falls for phish? A demographic analysis of phishing susceptibility and effectiveness of interventions. In: Proceedings of the SIGCHI Conference on Human Factors in Computing Systems, CHI 2010, pp. 373–382. Association for Computing Machinery, New York (2010). https://doi.org/10.1145/1753326.1753383

28. Shin, K., Kim, K.M., Lee, J.: A study on the concept of social engineering cyber kill chain for social engineering based cyber operations. J. Korea Inst. Inf. Secur. Cryptol. **28**(5), 1247–1258 (2018). https://doi.org/10.13089/JKIISC.2018.28.5.1247

29. Takahashi, T., Kadobayashi, Y.: Reference ontology for cybersecurity operational information. Comput. J. 2297–2312 (10 2014). https://doi.org/10.1093/comjnl/bxu101

30. Uebelacker, S., Quiel, S.: The social engineering personality framework. In: 2014 Workshop on Socio-Technical Aspects in Security and Trust, pp. 24–30 (2014). https://doi.org/10.1109/STAST.2014.12

31. Wang, Y., Kosinski, M.: Deep neural networks are more accurate than humans at detecting sexual orientation from facial images. J. Pers. Soc. Psychol. **114**, 246–257 (2018). https://doi.org/10.1037/pspa0000098

32. Wawrzyniak, D.: Information security risk assessment model for risk management. In: Fischer-Hübner, S., Furnell, S., Lambrinoudakis, C. (eds.) TrustBus 2006. LNCS, vol. 4083, pp. 21–30. Springer, Heidelberg (2006). https://doi.org/10.1007/11824633_3

Initial Reflections on the Use of Augmented Cognition in Derailing the Kill Chain

Geir M. Køien[(✉)] [ID]

University of South-Eastern Norway (USN), Campus Vestfold, Horten, Norway
geir.koien@usn.no

Abstract. Digital systems are now our new critical infrastructures. In contrast to traditional infrastructures, a digital system can be attacked remotely by software weapons. The so-called Advanced Persistent Threat (APT) actors are nation-state actors or advanced organized crime groups (ransomware and industrial espionage), and they pose a threat to corporations, critical infrastructures and even nation states. The "Kill Chain" represents a model of the attack pattern of an APT group. Augmented cognition (AC) is poised to become an important part of the tool chest of the defenders. In this paper we outline some areas where AC could make a difference.

Keywords: Cybersecurity · Augmented cognition · Advanced persistent threat · Kill chain · Biases · Misconceptions

1 Introduction

1.1 Context

This paper is concerned with cybersecurity and Augmented Cognition (AC). Specifically, it is concerned with mitigation and protection against a class of adversaries known as Advanced Persistent Threat (APT) actors. These threat actors are often nation-state actors, they are sophisticated, they have considerable resources and they are willing to conduct prolonged campaigns to carry out intrusion into digital infrastructures/systems. The "Kill Chain" is a model of how APT actors engage, and it is defined by a set of distinct steps and events.

To defend against an APT actor is not easy. The system defenders, known as the Blue Team (BT), have a difficult task, and will have to persist being vigilant during prolonged periods of (seeming) inactivity. Every technological measure that may help and facilitate is obviously welcomed. In addition to automation tools of many kinds, it is hoped AC methods will help emphasising small, but significant, events and that it will help the BT stay focused. Additionally, we hope that AC can help to alleviate problems associated with attention deficits and help with correcting "false beliefs" that the BT may come to hold. There are a number of biases that humans may fall for, and with the APT playing tricks of deception, it is essential that the BT stay factual and focused.

D. D. Schmorrow and C. M. Fidopiastis (Eds.): HCII 2021, LNAI 12776, pp. 433–451, 2021.
https://doi.org/10.1007/978-3-030-78114-9_30

1.2 Augmented Cognition in General

In [41], the authors give a broad outline of the AC field. In general, AC is seen as tool-aided enhanced cognition. The AC system should be able to detect or deduce the human cognitive state. It should also provide means for extended sensory inputs and an ability for augmented interaction with whatever external system there is. There are different aspects to AC, ranging from modest non-invasive user-interface/visualization tools to advanced invasive brain-computer interfaces. One may also differentiate AC on whether the humans have to adapt to the tools (technology-driven approach) versus the tools being made to adapt to humans (usage driven approach).

Modern AC tools involves augmented senses and augmented actions, e.g. use of speech recognition, accepts gestures, eye gaze, etc. One may also include sensors to pick up heart rate, sweating, and similar to pick up signs of stress and agitation. This may be useful when the system needs to let the human user recover before proceeding. For an AC system that needs to work with human operators during emergency situations, it may be extremely useful for the system to avoid overloading the operators at critical times.

An AC system can be set up to provide the user with information through various modalities in real-time, including visual, auditory and haptic presentations. For our purpose, these modalities should be tailored towards the needs for the BT members, and should allow for individual adaptations. What is actually going to be useful here is outside the scope of the present paper, but suffice to say that development of these modalities is of the essence for effective use of AC. We also have technologies that let humans explore computational models. There are various human interface technologies, including immersive technologies, and one has concepts such as virtual reality (VR), augmented reality (AR). Many of these technologies have been developed for the games and entertainment industries. In particular, these technologies have been useful for exploring complex models and allowing humans to get an enhanced understanding of complex systems. These tools may prove useful in proving enhanced and more accurate situational awareness for the BT during incident handling.

AC takes many forms, and some of these will have interfaces directly to the brain [34, 39]. Such implements already exists, and over time these are certain to find uses with cybersecurity too. For our purpose, we shall be relatively agnostic as to *how* the AC system achieve its goals. We shall instead focus on the properties that would be useful for a BT to have.

1.3 Artificial Intelligence

Artificial Intelligence systems can help us with many decision making problems. Many of these problems are mundane and easily solved by humans. However, in decision making under duress, it is useful to offload mundane tasks to these system. Machine learning (ML) is recognized as a cybersecurity tool [19]. The combination of AC and AI/ML techniques has great potential for cybersecurity defenders. Advanced time-series analysis of events is but one area where an AC system with AI/ML capabilities would be of help.

1.4   Related Work

There is a substantial body of works on cyber security related to APT actors and the kill chain, and augmented cognition is a field to it own. Works on APT and APT defenses include [1,4,10,30,54], amongst many others.

However, the body of work related to cyber security and AC is much smaller. In [6], the authors presents a cognitive security model that integrates techno-logical solutions with the cognitive processes of security analysts. In [35], the authors presents a system for cognitive offloading that represents information in a knowledge graph. In [21], one presents the case for use of artificial intelligence (AI) and Cognitive Dynamic System (CDS) for cybersecurity. The paper is framed in the context of risk.

1.5   Paper Organization

Section 1 contains the introductory part of the paper. Section 2 gives an overview over the principal entities. Section 3 provides an outline of the basics of a kill chain. Section 4 outlines some of the problems that Blue Team is facing. Section 5 provides an analysis of some of the areas where augmented cognition may help derailing the kill chain. Section 6 briefly summarizes the paper and provide a short conclusion.

2   The Principal Entities

We have two categories of principal entities: The Blue Team and the APT actor.

2.1   The APT Actor

The kill chain is a model (set of models) outlining how an APT actor may act. The APT intruders are resourceful dedicated adversaries, maintaining an attacking campaign for long periods [1,4,10,30]. An APT campaign is a long-term game. The preparatory steps could take months to execute. The time between intrusion and detection (the "dwell-time") will vary, but is commonly more than half a year. Typically, the APT intruders are nation-state actors. Increasingly, organized crime and ransomeware actors also use APT methods.

MITRE has publish an overview over the APT groups in [33]. In [26], the security company Kaspersky has published an overview over methods used by APT groups (2020).

2.2   The Blue Team

The term **Blue Team** was coined in the US Department of Defense Directive 8570. A BT works with the system administrators to develop effective Computer Network Defense (CND) for the network/systems. According to DoDD 8570.1, a BT is: "A group of highly skilled individuals who conduct systematic examinations of IS or products to determine adequacy of security measures, to identify security deficiencies, to predict effectiveness of proposed security measures, and to confirm adequacy of such measures after implementation.". By now, the term has become established as a generic term for a group that handles incident response, operating system hardening, etc.

The BT is generally responsible for several proactive and reactive security measures. The proactive measures include operating system hardening, set-up of various perimeter defense measures, including traffic flow management, packet filtering, firewalls and intrusion detection systems. Event logging is a very important activity, as well as various digital forensics tasks. However, the main activities are focused on daily security operations management and so-called "incident response". Handling of cyber-security threat intelligence (CTI) is a large part of the daily operations. This includes exchange of updated threat landscape information, current trends in malware deployment, etc. between trusted partners. There is a long list of products, standards and tools in this area, and we are not going into any details concerning any of these. Suffice to say that a successful BT must be aware of these and use them effectively and efficiently.

An effective BT is a unit where the team aspects are highlighted. To defend against an APT will take a dedicated team, where all members must be prepared to stand in the front line.

3   The Kill Chain

There are several different kill chain models available. The Lockheed Martin (LM) model may be the original [25], but other similar models exists [40,45]. Basically, they outline a set of steps that an intruder probably will go through when executing APT attacks. The LM cyber kill chain steps:

1. Reconnaissance
2. Weaponization
3. Delivery
4. Exploitation
5. Installation
6. Command & Control (C2)
7. Actions on Objectives
8. Credential harvesting
9. Pivoting/Lateral movement
10. Defense Evasion

The kill chain steps are elaborated upon in the upcoming subsections. Steps 8–10 are not from the LM model per se. In reality, a kill chain will involve cycles and repeated steps, and some will be continuous activities.

3.1   Reconnaissance (Intelligence Gathering)

APT campaigns are well prepared and planned. This includes open-source intelligence (OSINT) gathering. All information that relates to the target may be of interest, and this includes information collection concerning employees, vendors, contractors, users and customers, etc. It also includes information gathered from network scanning and vulnerability scanning. The reconnaissances process can go on for long periods, and it is generally not possible to prevent it. The BT may be able to detect scanning activities and it is possible to have some level of information control pertaining to system architecture, key personnel, etc. Since the dwell time is long, the logs, etc. needs to be retained for a long time and regularly re-evaluated. Purpose-tailored ML tools should be useful here, and it may be combined with advanced visualization tools in an AC system. This *may* be of some help in detecting a pattern. Otherwise, the BT would need to utilize CTI information as best it can.

3.2   Weaponization (Preparing Exploits/Malware)

The intruders will need to find some vulnerability that they may exploit. This may include the use of malware or it may involve use of already installed tools (Living-off-the-Land) that may be used by the intruder [46]. We note that Living-of-the-Land tactics are harder to detect in that the tools are legitimately present in the system. The BT will need to stay alert and be prepared for new malware and new APT tactics. The "normal" system hardening tactics apply, as does usage of CTI information to actively bolster the defenses.

3.3   Delivery (Getting the Payload onto the Target System)

In the original LM Chain model, delivery was predominantly by email attachments, web-sites and USB devices [25]. BT countermeasures includes security awareness training to identity and prevent phising, unsavory use of web resources and USB devices. Additionally, one must deploy security controls concerning email attachments, control schemes for handling office-type of documents (with macros), browser hardening and blocking of black-listed web-sites, and implement security controls for USB devices to prevent automatic opening of devices, etc. All measures, security training of staff and technical security controls, must be kept updated and regularly revised.

3.4   Exploitation (Applying the Payload, Privilege Escalation)

The technically oriented controls will at this stage be to have security hardened system (no unnecessary software/tool, etc.), to have an updated system and to have proper access control systems in place (which in turn presumes a security policy). The BT tactics to counter this step would also involve system hardening to reduce the attack surface. For Living-off-the-Land tools, one could:

- Keep an updated inventory of tools (correlated with CTI information)
- Remove unused tools
- Restrict access to the tools (security policy, access control)
- Log tools usage, and develop associated monitoring and alerting functionality

Often, the delivered payloads will need some kind of user interaction to reach the "exploitation" stage. Thus, BT will depend on the behaviour of the legitimate users. However, errors will be made, and one better acknowledge that. A sound security culture will therefore be important. If there is a lot of stigma to report a security failure, then reporting will probably be late (if at all). This will delay BT responses. Effective "human sensors" can also react and help stop an intrusion before the APT can firmly establish itself. There will very likely be log entries from the exploitation phase, and use of adapted ML scanning of logs could provide hints. If the "hints" are ambiguous, a combined ML-AC system could highlight suggestions and proposal to the BT, and aid in the investigations of said events.

3.5   Installation (Installing Additional Malware/Tools)

This is an APT establishment stage. It is aligned with the exploitation stage, but the APT may choose to wait a while before executing this stage. An advanced visualization tools may be able to connect the dots and ignore the dwell-time between the events. To detect the connection of the dots will require advanced ML processing of event logs, and it will not always work. The "exploitation" defensive measures apply at this stage too.

3.6   Command and Control (C2) (Establishing Remote Control Channel)

The users will likely be unaware of C2 activities, but BT may be able to detect C2 communications by network access screening and logging. Nowadays, the C2 communication is likely encrypted and is likely camouflaged as maintenance activity or similar. Still, patterns may be detectable, and thus one should scan for these patterns. Tools such as Machine Learning (ML) and CTI will be needed to develop suitable scanning algorithms.

3.7   Actions on Objectives (Exfiltration, Lockdown, ...)

Nation-state actors will often want to steal information (espionage) and/or to develop capabilities to selectively cripple the infrastructure (cyber weapon). Exfiltration is likely to involve large, possibly encrypted, file transfers to rented cloud infrastructures. Critical infrastructures (of all sorts), high-tech companies, defence industry companies, etc. will be considered targets. Ransomeware actors will want to lockdown the infrastructure and demand ransom, but they will typically also exfiltrate data. Any target that is though to be willing to pay a ransom is a potential target. The actions-on-objectives will to some extent be visible in the system. The probable APT actions (end-goals) may be deducible, and will very often involve file system activities (file copy, modifications, etc.) and network activities (file transfers). BT should develop detection capabilities, including profiles for the most likely APT actions. The capabilities should include both real-time detection and after-the-fact detection (logs, etc.).

3.8 Credential Harvesting (Harvesting Additional User Account Info)

As an alternative to step 2 and 3, the intruder may also break into existing accounts. To do so, the intruder will need to harvest credentials and/or be able to bypass authentication. There may be purely technical attacking methods and there may be ways to achieve this by social manipulations. In either case, the end-result will be that the intruder will be able to log in on existing accounts. The BT should institute technical measures to detect anomalous login events, etc. There should also be user awareness of credential harvesting and suitable technical measures that makes this activity harder to execute and/or easier to detect.

3.9 Pivoting and Expanding (Lateral Movement)

This phase consists of spreading out and getting a better foothold in the target infrastructure. An intruder generally wants to establish itself in multiple ways. Additionally, the target system is likely to be segmented, and the intruder will want to be established across segments. The pivoting and expanding activity may involve all the earlier stages of the kill chain.

3.10 Defense Evasion (Deception, Hiding from Detection)

The APT will not want to be detected, or at least not until it chooses to. That means that the APT will seek to mask out its activities as legitimate activities when possible, and that it will be prepared to use a long period of time to achieve its goals. However, even highly sophisticated APT actors cannot entirely prevent leaving a footprint of its activities, and they do make occasional mistakes. There will also be some kind of pattern to their activities, even though it will be difficult to pick out signal from noise. Thus, the BT must be able to operate with partial information and must be able to use machine learning techniques and cyber threat intelligence information to fill in the blanks.

4 The Blue Team Conundrum

4.1 Blue Team Tasks

We shall focus on tasks related to incident response. We base these steps loosely on information derived from the NIST "Cybersecurity Framework" [36] and ENISA "Good Practice Guide for Incident Management" [17] The Blue Team will thus need to handle the following tasks:

1. **Preparation**
   To a large extent, this task is to know your own system, your assets, priorities, etc. It should also include an incident response plan, a business continuity plan, a disaster recover plan, etc. The plans will also need to be continually updated, and one will need to have incident response table top exercises amongst others.

2. **Identification**
   This is actions to verify that there is indeed an attack/incident. This includes information collection and internal surveillance to detect anomalies and attack patterns. It may also include actually identifying the APT group, even if this is not always possible.

3. **Containment**
   When an intrusion has been confirmed, one needs to investigate the extent of the intrusion. This includes uncovering when and where the intrusion occurred first, the number of compromised accounts, the number of infected servers/hosts, the integrity of the backups, etc. Then one wants to ensure that one has a reasonable understanding of the modus operandi of the intruder, and that one can prevent the intruder from gaining access to other parts of the systems (while not alerting the intruder).

4. **Eradication**
   This is the process to throw out the intruder. It includes rebuilding, reinstalling and reestablishing the infrastructure.

5. **Recovery**
   To throw out the intruder is not enough, and while a clean system is a good start, one needs to reestablish the system in an operational way. That is, one needs to be able use the system as intended again.

6. **Lessons learned**
   It is important to understand why and how the intrusion came about. In particular, one wants to be better prepared for the future, and mitigate or prevent similar future intrusion attempts. This includes both technical and organisational measures.

4.2 Attribution and Deterrence

For nation state APT actors, it is often the case that they do not want any attention. Of course, one may have offensive cyber-war attacks, like those carried out by Russia in Ukraina [20], where visibility is part of the game. That is, one may want plausible deniability, yet still allow a message to be sent. However, it is often the case that the APT actor does not want to be attributed. In those cases, attribution may actually become a goal for the BT, and it may serve as a deterrent in some cases.

The so-called "Diamond Model of Intrusion Analysis" may be useful here [11]. We believe that "Diamond Model"-related Machine Learning (ML) and AC tools could help the BT in this endeavour. Of course, for APT groups that do not want to be attributed, it is not uncommon to deliberately leave misleading evidence.

4.3 Handling Uncertainty

Cybersecurity defenders must be able to work under uncertainty for prolonged periods. This even relates to periods seemingly without any hostile actions, as one cannot necessarily know if there are attacks underway or not. Suffice to say that it is not a question of if one is going to be attacked, it is merely a question of when and how often.

There are different types of uncertainty, and some we will just have to endure [27]. We classically differentiate between epistemic and aleatoric uncertainty, but to the BT this may matter little. Aleatoric uncertainty covers "pure chance" uncertainty, where one simply have to accept the uncertainty. An AC system cannot alleviate this, and can at most ensure that the BT recognize the uncertainty. If the uncertainty is epistemic, it means that one could in principle resolve the uncertainty. Most problems in cybersecurity would likely fall in this category. Former US Secretary of Defense Donald Rumsfeld is well-known for his "There are known knowns" speech (12.02.2002, in the prelude to the second Iraq war). Although he was ridiculed for his statements, the categorization is useful:

- **KK: Known knowns**. Facts we know and are fully aware of.
- **KU: Known unknowns**. We know that there are facts to be known.
- **UK: Unknown knowns**. Known facts that we are unconscious of.
- **UU: Unknown unknowns**.We are unaware that we are unaware.

An AC system should obviously be able to highlight KK items. Given access to domain resources and being context aware, an AC system should also be able to highlight KU items. The category UK is interesting, and while a BT may be unconscious about this type of knowledge, an AC system may be able to highlight it. The combination of ML techniques and AC could prove potent for the UK category.

The UU category is to a large extent a failure of imagination. Some has likened this to Black Swan uncertainty [48], and there are similarities. However, while a Black Swan event *may* be initiated or orchestrated by humans, a kill chain event is invariably initiated by humans. An AC system may be of some help for UU related events too. But, it will be hard to find the needle in the haystack if you are unaware of haystacks and do not know that you are looking for a needle in the first place. Still, an AC system may help stimulate BT to envision and explore new forms of threats. As such, it may help alleviate the failure of imagination problem.

We note that while epistemic uncertainty may be resolved, there may be constraints that for practical purposes makes the resolution intractable. A BT will have limited resources and there will be temporal constraints. Some problems may yield with added resources, while others will remain infeasible to solve.

There may be active misleading from the APT to influence our perception of the problem [3]. An AC system may prove to be useful to mitigate the problem, and it could help the BT staying focused on the facts.

4.4   Information Handling: From Tiny Trickles to Virtual Torrents

The log files of a large system will consist of many GBytes of text-based information every day. Then there is the flow of CTI information and other source of news and tidbits that may be relevant. The number of alarms from the (Network) Intrusion Detection Systems (NIDS/IDS) can be quite high. Actors on the internet will routinely scan other networks, even if no attack is forthcoming. Amongst the alarms, there will be a certain number of "false positives". These are noise in the system, but needs to be handled seriously and cannot always be filtered out. There is a balancing act to filtering; if one filters out too many of the "false positives", then one will probably also filter out real events. The information flow in a Security Information and Event Management (SIEM) system will be high. An AC system cannot directly help with this, but together with ML algorithms and context-aware AC, one may be able to recognize significant events faster and respond better. The SIEM systems do have ML components these days, and some AC capabilities (at least context-aware visualizations).

4.5   Attention Overload and Fatigue

Attention overload is a well known concept and is recognized as a psychological condition. The overload may lead to fatigue, and an associated inability to take appropriate actions. The concept "security fatigue" is an established concept [18, 32,37,44]. An effective AC system will need to recognize when the BT collectively or individually is suffering from these conditions. Thus, the AC system should include sensors to monitor stress conditions. Should the condition only affect an individual, then the AC system may be able to let other BT members take over. Should the whole BT be affected, other actions may have to be taken.

We recommend that the tactics used by the AC system under such circumstances be discussed in the BT prior to any incident. During severe stress, people work best when the system (also the AC system) acts in a predictable fashion. In fact, it is explicitly recommended that these facets of the AC system be tested out in drills and exercises.

Another related aspect is human dysfunctionality caused by sleep depravation. During emergencies, the BT must be expected to work 24/7 for some time. The popular science book "Why We Sleep" [52] provides an broad account of how sleep depravation affects us. Since learning and other cognitive processes are deeply affected by sleep depravation, it stand to reason that the AC should be able to detect this condition in the BT. Also, the AC must be able to support the BT during times where the BT members suffer from this condition. Exactly how this is to be achieved is not clear, but suffice to say that awareness surely is a useful first step.

4.6   Overconfidence, Biases, Deceptions, and Self-deception

"Intelligence analysts should be self-conscious about their reasoning process. They should think about how they make judgments and reach conclusions, not just about the judgments and conclusions themselves." [23]

Overconfidence and Other Biases. The first line BT defenders may not be fully skilled security analysts. Human expertise is important when designing security defenses and when evaluating security risks. So, it is natural to ask if the security workers will be subject to the Dunning-Krueger effect [29]. That is, will the less skilled show sign of overconfidence?

The Dunning-Kruger effect is often misunderstood, and it is also criticized [42]. For our purpose, we only care that there is a tendency to misjudge one owns competence [24]. This can have repercussions in cybersecurity in the sense that one may arrive at the wrong precautions and countermeasures.

It has been shown that, under certain circumstance, scientist within political sciences can address their beliefs and biases to some degree [16]. That is, given suitable evidence, the scientists did at least partially change their minds. It is not immediately obvious that cybersecurity is vulnerable to the beliefs and biases affecting the political sciences, but all people are susceptible to such biases, and our BT members will be affected too.

We are also vulnerable with respect to our own though process and physiological aspects of our sensory organs and processing equipment (brain). The book "The Mind is Flat" elegantly illustrates some of these problems [13]. To recognize this is important, and we believe that an AC system for our BT should strive to help the BT group being aware of their own decision making. To this end, the AC must be able to recognize the decision making process and put BT attention to it. In the book "Pre-Suasion" [14], Cialdini gives a fascinating and thought-provoking account of how we are influenced, nudged and persuaded in general. Even without any deceptions played by the APT, we are certain to hold a number or more or less false beliefs, and this is dangerous for a BT. We are fooled by complexity, by randomness and number of other influences [47]. Thus, if an AC system can help us avoid at least some of these problems, the BT should benefit and be better at detecting and counter-acting APT activities.

Overconfidence can be problematic [5,31], in particular in an environment where the adversaries may deliberately want to mislead the defenders. In the lieu of this, AC may be a powerful tool to present information such that we can overcome biases. Reliably measuring "overconfidence" may be difficult, but over time an ML system may allow us to highlight signs of overconfidence. Other biases associated with emotional responses may also be detected. We recommend caution in using these cues, as interpretations of emotional state is highly personal. Still, if used with care and in a privacy-sensitive way, it may be very useful for the individual BT member to be alerted. It may also be useful as a high-level indicator to the BT group leader.

Deceptions and Self-deception. It is a given that the APT will try to deceive the BT and the users of the target system. Depending on circumstances and end-goals, the APT may use substantial resources to misdirect and confuse the legitimate users. This will range from social engineering tricks to credential harvesting and gaining unauthorized access to premises, etc. [9,28,38,53]. It will also include insiders behaving dishonestly. An AC system cannot directly alleviate these problems, but once there are log entries or other entries alluding to the problem, the AC system could be used to highlight the problem. Note that this would not be significantly different from other anomaly detection systems.

Self-deception is another interesting aspects that needs to be taken into account. On first sight, self-deception is a paradoxical concept. However, while remaining paradoxical, it also make sense in some situations. To some extent it seems that we have an innate ability to fool ourselves in some situations, and these situations is linked to biases and to an unwillingness to break with our existing belief-systems. That is, it appears that humans generally disregard facts that conflicts with our current beliefs. In some sense this can be attributed to a mismatch between our emotional state and the facts. This may lead to an avoidance, or disregard, of information that conflicts with what we want to be the case. Or, we may be too pre-occupied with what we fear, and let that influence us (effectively making us blind to other threats). Cyber threats, being a highly abstract concept, is susceptible to incorrect beliefs as our intuitions cannot readily be corrected by concrete (physical-world) experiences. Given that we deal mostly by internal mental models, it will be a mental and emotional cost to changing these models. Specifically, we are unlikely to look for facts and evidence that contradicts our beliefs and goals.

We should also note that if the BT, or indeed the system owner, has incentive systems or goals that would suffer in the face of an APT attack, then alerting to APT attacks would not necessarily be welcomed. A "shooting the messenger" culture is obviously detrimental to crisis handling, but even in a more modest form, it could delay a BT from reacting appropriately to an APT attack. There may be various forms of cognitive dissonance at play too. In [51], the authors gives a fairly broad overview of evolutionary aspects of self-deception. An even broader account is found in [50]. As with many aspects of psychology, there is some debate about what self-deception really is and how it affects us, etc. Whatever the background, false beliefs can clearly stand in the way of good and sound decision making. For our purpose, it matters little whether the self-deception is an evolutionary trait of not, we simply have to take it into account. It would therefore be highly useful if the AC is able to facilitate the decision making process in this area. Of course, it is possible to be too preoccupied with inconvenient truths, and to see attacks where there are none. Thus, one would also ideally have AC support to avoid cherry picking of unfavourable facts as well as favourable ones. This will of course be a very hard goal to attain.

4.7   Perception of Time and Volume

An APT campaign has a few features to do not match well with human perceptions. The human perception of time and our limited ability to both remember details from the past and be able to correlate it with current events, makes it hard to put events in the proper context. And, of course, the APT group will also try to play tricks on the BT and will use dwell time delays, etc. to try to deceive the BT. The relative inability for humans to perceive time correctly is investigated in the literature [2,7,15]. Our already mentioned book, "The Mind is Flat" also touches upon this [13]. The field itself consists of research in biology, neurosciences, cognitive linguistics and psychology.

Humans also have problems with perceptions of volume (as in size). While we generally have an ability to differentiate and compare relative sizes (larger than, equal, less than), this ability can be deceived. This may affect our abilities include color, shape, frequency and the fallibility of own memory. In particular, emotional aspects may seriously impact our ability to judge relative the importance of events. Thus, if we want to compare aspects of a previous incident (some time ago, but which affected us emotionally) with a current event, chances are we will get the comparison wrong. That, in turn, may affect of decision making. It should also be noted that humans tend to have problems when comparing abstract events, numerical sizes, etc. [22]. That is, we do it anyway, and we do it based on our own internal model of the problem. Cybersecurity incidents are of course abstract, and to usefully compare events one needs there to be good-enough correlation and correspondence of our internal model and the real-world events.

And, as exposed in [47], humans are generally not very well adept at comprehending randomness, and may see patterns where there are none. An AC system should be able to help out with the visualization part and the AC model should be able to take emotional state into account. The AC must be able to adapt to strong emotions, perhaps instigating a "time out" or otherwise let the BT member recover when needed.

4.8   Blue Team Risk Management

The BT must handle risk in a variety of ways. However, as strongly alluded to by Taleb [49], one must be cautions about existential threats. Thus, if an APT attacks is seen as potentially existential, then it is sound advise to be cautions. For companies, a full lockdown of the infrastructure could indeed become an existential threat. A treatise on risk analysis, with these aspects accounted for, is found in [8]. There are others risk handling aspects too, but we shall not focus on those in this paper.

5   Derailing the Kill Chain

5.1   Prerequisite: Trust in the AC System

We postulate that an effective AC system for BT work should include ways to measure stress, fatigue and emotional state. It may also be useful for the AC system to develop a psychological profile of how the individual BT members behave during incident handling. The more the AC system can take this into account, the better it can facilitate the BT. However, it is readily apparent that this kind of profiling is highly privacy sensitive. There needs to strong and robust consent processes, and the AC system needs to be designed with privacy in mind. The BT, both as a group and as individual members, needs to know what the AC system does with the data it collects about them.

One must also recognized that, invariably, BT groups will fail to effectively defend their system. There will be serious incidents and major compromises. Damage will be done, and there will be investigations of the incident handling. There could be substantial financial pressures, and there could very easily be blame-games to be played. The AC system must be designed such that it truly protects the BT members privacy, yet still be facilitating learning from whatever mistakes were made.

5.2 Improved Decision Making

The AC system can be designed to help with BT decision making in a number of ways. To fully realize its potential, the AC system should provide mechanisms to correlate and combine its efforts over the whole BT group. Thus, if one BT member is suffering from too much stress, then the AC system should be able to engage other BT members to overcome the difficulties. Specifically, the AC system should:

– *Capture signs of stress, fatigue, sleep depravation, physical exhaustion, etc.*
  The AC system needs to be context-aware. The system will need to learn and recognize specific types of situations and specific BT operator indications. Based on this, one can develop specific modalities for the context.
– *Capture indications of alterations of the emotional state.*
  This item is closely related to the above, but may occur without stress, fatigue, etc. The BT operators may provide explicit hints and other cues may be deduced indirectly. Otherwise, the AC system will need to learn and adapt to provide adequate and accurate responses to the BT members.
– *Decision support.*
  The AC should facilitate decision modes, in which the BT members get explicit support when making operational decisions. This should include ways for the BT members to indicate uncertainty and ways to test out hypothesises (possibly as a group effort). The situational awareness part of the AC system should include BT context awareness and "kill chain" state awareness. For important decisions, the AC system must enable group discussions and one-the-fly consequence analysis and logistics. The AC system must also take the BT group/member physiological and psychological state into consideration, and adjust accordingly. This may even include support and suggestions for time-outs and rest periods, when that seems to be needed or otherwise the best choice.
– *Provide interactive and fluent aid in interpreting data.*
  Based on the collected data (historic, current and immediate), the AC system should adaptively provide context-aware hints to the BT members. Advanced visualizations will help, but also ML-based projection of time-series data, CTI-based suggestions, etc. This may help reduce confusion and uncertainty.

– *Facilitate Learning.*
  The AC system should, whenever there is an opportunity, facilitate learning. The learning may be operational, in the active phase, but the AC system must also support retrospective learning. All incidents are learning opportunities, and the AC system would be remiss if this is goal is omitted. In fact, the AC system may be very well suited to recreate events and allow all BT members to catch up and have the same experience.
– *Facilitate the BT group and community.*
  The AC should enable building a team spirit in the BT group, and facilitate training and development of new methods, tactics, etc. To facilitate realistic training, with suitable rewards, should be a high priority. In particular, training which strengthens and emphasises cooperation amongst the BT members.

5.3   Context-Aware Specific Support for Kill Chain Events

We have been through the typical kill chain phases in Sect. 3. One may add concrete aspects from other kill chain models too, like for instance the unified kill chain [40] or from the MITRE ATT&CK model [45]. The AC system should be tailored to support the BT directly for each of the kill chain steps.

It should also provide direct support for the BT task as listed in Sect. 4.1. This will also encompass integration with SIEM system operation, and an ability to use AC methods to enable situational learning and to address real-time aspects (see the next subsection).

5.4   A Real-Time Operational Philosophy

In the recent book "Living in a Real-Time World" [43], Selman provides his experience as a professional IT leader. In the cyber world, things change fast, and this means that humans must be able to adapt to this increasingly impossible schedule. The book is set in the context of cyber-system development and operations, and the BT operates in this kind of context too.

It is not longer possible to have a solid and complete grasp of how a complex system works, and one must therefore seek an operational understanding that can be adapted to fast changing environments. Selman therefore advocates a strategy where one navigates the system without needing to understand everything. Specifically, Selman advocates development of six capabilities that one should strive to have. Roughly, these capabilities are:

1. **Accepting.** Stoically accepting the world as it shows up. Avoid resisting and do not fight lost fights. Move on in time.
2. **Being.** For humans, context is all-important. In a real-time world we need to be able to shift the context fast. This presumes context awareness.
3. **Listening.** Perceive and interpret. Moods shapes our thinking process. Be aware of our moods, and strive to modify them when needed.
4. **Communicating.** Effective communications is a learnable skill. Good communications skills will help us to continually choose our actions.

5. **Appropriating**. Situational learning. Learn fast and accept incomplete, disposable and ephemeral knowledge. Embrace group learning.
6. **Caring**. Adhere to and respect core values and ideals. These will outlast other aspects, and is fundamental to our own (and the groups) core identity.

In short, it is a system to preserve our mental and cognitive energy to the cases and context where it matters. Only then can we have any hope of mastering our cyber environment. It seems a worthy goal for an AC system to try to accommodate the six capabilities that Selman advocates as useful.

6 Summary and Conclusion

> "The question is, which is to be master — that's all."
> – Humpty Dumpty, in "Through the Looking Glass" [12]

The above Humpty Dumpty quote, although somewhat out of context, accurately summarizes the problem one faces. Will the APT's be the master or is it to be the Blue Team?

We have investigated the kill chain mode-of-operation models, to see if it is possible to use augmented cognition methods to tilt the battle in favour of the Blue Team. Augmented cognition methods could be of use in order to enhance the Blue Team capabilities. This pertains to most tasks, and to various levels and degrees.

To a large extent, this work has only identified the issues and the opportunities. The specifics on how an AC system may be used by the BT has rarely been touched upon. That is, we cannot claim to have solved any problem in this area, but we have hopefully shed some light on defining the problem. There is much work to be done in this area, and if nothing else, we hope that this paper may inspire future effort in this area.

References

1. Ahmad, A., Webb, J., Desouza, K.C., Boorman, J.: Strategically-motivated advanced persistent threat: definition, process, tactics and a disinformation model of counterattack. Comput. Secur. **86**, 402–418 (2019)
2. Allan, L.G.: The perception of time. Percept. Psychophys. **26**(5), 340–354 (1979)
3. Almeshekah, M.H., Spafford, E.H.: Planning and integrating deception into computer security defenses. In: Proceedings of the 2014 New Security Paradigms Workshop, pp. 127–138 (2014)
4. Alshamrani, A., Myneni, S., Chowdhary, A., Huang, D.: A survey on advanced persistent threats: techniques, solutions, challenges, and research opportunities. IEEE Commun. Surv. Tutor. **21**(2), 1851–1877 (2019)
5. Ament, C., Jaeger, L.: Unconscious on their own ignorance: over confidence in information security. In: PACIS, pp. 131 (2017)
6. Andrade, R.O., Yoo, S.G.: Cognitive security: a comprehensive study of cognitive science in cybersecurity. J. Inf. Secur. Appl. **48**, 102352 (2019)

7. Aschoff, J.: Human perception of short and long time intervals: its correlation with body temperature and the duration of wake time. J. Biol. Rhythms **13**(5), 437–442 (1998)
8. Aven, T.: The concept of antifragility and its implications for the practice of risk analysis. Risk Anal. **35**(3), 476–483 (2015)
9. Beckers, K., Krautsevich, L., Yautsiukhin, A.: Analysis of social engineering threats with attack graphs. In: Garcia-Alfaro, J., Herrera-Joancomartí, J., Lupu, E., Posegga, J., Aldini, A., Martinelli, F., Suri, N. (eds.) DPM/QASA/SETOP -2014. LNCS, vol. 8872, pp. 216–232. Springer, Cham (2015). https://doi.org/10.1007/978-3-319-17016-9_14
10. Bhatnagar, D., Som, S., Khatri, S.K.: Advance persistant threat and cyber spying-the big picture, its tools, attack vectors and countermeasures. In: 2019 Amity International Conference on Artificial Intelligence (AICAI), pp. 828–839. IEEE (2019)
11. Caltagirone, S., Pendergast, A., Betz, C.: The Diamond Model of Intrusion Analysis. Technical Report ADA586960, US Department of Defense, CENTER FOR CYBER INTELLIGENCE ANALYSIS AND THREAT RESEARCH HANOVER MD, July 2013
12. Carroll, L.: Through the Looking Glass and What Alice Found There. Penguin, New Yok (2010)
13. Chater, N.: The Mind is Flat: the Illusion of Mental Depth and the Improvised Mind. Yale University Press, London (2018)
14. Cialdini, R.: Pre-suasion: A Revolutionary Way to Influence and Persuade. Simon and Schuster, New York (2016)
15. Eagleman, D.M.: Human time perception and its illusions. Curr. Opin. Neurobiol. **18**(2), 131–136 (2008)
16. Eitan, O., et al.: Is research in social psychology politically biased? Systematic empirical tests and a forecasting survey to address the controversy. J. Exp. Soc. Psychol. **79**, 188–199 (2018)
17. ENISA: Good Practice Guide for Incident Management. ENISA, December 2010
18. Furnell, S., Thomson, K.L.: Recognising and addressing 'security fatigue'. Comput. Fraud Secur. **2009**(11), 7–11 (2009)
19. Ghafir, I., Hammoudeh, M., Prenosil, V., Han, L., Hegarty, R., Rabie, K., Aparicio-Navarro, F.J.: Detection of advanced persistent threat using machine-learning correlation analysis. Future Gener. Comput. Syst. **89**, 349–359 (2018)
20. Greenberg, A.: Sandworm: A New Era of Cyberwar and the Hunt for the Kremlin's Most Dangerous Hackers. Anchor, New York (2019)
21. Haykin, S.: Artificial intelligence communicates with cognitive dynamic system for cybersecurity. IEEE Trans. Cogn. Commun. Netw. **5**(3), 463–475 (2019)
22. Henik, A.: Continuous Issues in Numerical Cognition: How Many or How Much. Academic Press, Cambridge (2016)
23. Heuer, R.J.: Psychology of intelligence analysis. CIA, Center for the Study of Intelligence (1999)
24. Huang, S.: When peers are not peers and don't know it: The Dunning-Kruger effect and self-fulfilling prophecy in peer-review. Bioessays **35**(5), 414–416 (2013)
25. Hutchins, E.M., Cloppert, M.J., Amin, R.M., et al.: Intelligence-driven computer network defense informed by analysis of adversary campaigns and intrusion kill chains. Lead. Issues in Inf. Warfare Secur. Res. **1**(1), 80 (2011)
26. Kaspersky: APT annual review: What the world's threat actors got up to in 2020, December 2020. https://securelist.com/apt-annual-review-what-the-worlds-threat-actors-got-up-to-in-2020/99574/

27. King, M., Kay, J.: Radical Uncertainty: Decision-Making for an Unknowable Future. The Bridge Street Press, London (2020)
28. Krombholz, K., Hobel, H., Huber, M., Weippl, E.: Advanced social engineering attacks. J. Inf. Secur. Appl. **22**, 113–122 (2015)
29. Kruger, J., Dunning, D.: Unskilled and unaware of it: how difficulties in recognizing one's own incompetence lead to inflated self-assessments. J. Pers. Soc. Psychol. **77**(6), 1121 (1999)
30. Lemay, A., Calvet, J., Menet, F., Fernandez, J.M.: Survey of publicly available reports on advanced persistent threat actors. Comput. Secur. **72**, 26–59 (2018)
31. Malmendier, U., Taylor, T.: On the verges of overconfidence. J. Econo. Perspect. **29**(4), 3–8 (2015)
32. McGraw, G.: Security fatigue? Shift your paradigm. Computer **47**(3), 81–83 (2014)
33. MITRE: MITRE ATT&CK: APT Groups, February 2021. https://attack.mitre.org/groups/
34. Nam, C.S., Nijholt, A., Lotte, F.: Brain-Computer Interfaces Handbook: Technological and Theoretical Advances. CRC Press, Boca Raton (2018)
35. Narayanan, S., Ganesan, A., Joshi, K., Oates, T., Joshi, A., Finin, T.: Cognitive Techniques for Early Detection of Cybersecurity Events. arXiv preprint arXiv:1808.00116 (2018)
36. NIST: Framework for Improving Critical Infrastructure Cybersecurity. NIST, 1.1 edn., April 2018
37. Parkin, S., Krol, K., Becker, I., Sasse, M.A.: Applying cognitive control modes to identify security fatigue hotspots. In: Twelfth Symposium on Usable Privacy and Security (2016)
38. Peltier, T.R.: Social engineering: concepts and solutions. Inf. Secur. J. **15**(5), 13 (2006)
39. Poli, R., Valeriani, D., Cinel, C.: Brain-Computer Interfaces for Human Augmentation. MDPI, Basel (2019)
40. Pols, P., van den Berg, J.: The Unified Kill Chain. CSA Thesis, Hague, pp. 1–104 (2017)
41. Raisamo, R., Rakkolainen, I., Majaranta, P., Salminen, K., Rantala, J., Farooq, A.: Human augmentation: past, present and future. Int. J. Hum. Comput. Stud. **131**, 131–143 (2019)
42. Schlösser, T., Dunning, D., Johnson, K.L., Kruger, J.: How unaware are the unskilled? Empirical tests of the "signal extraction" counter explanation for the Dunning-Kruger effect in self-evaluation of performance. J. Econ. Psychol. **39**, 85–100 (2013)
43. Selman, J.: Living in a Real-Time World: 6 Capabilities to Prepare US for an Unimaginable Future. Independently published, January 2019
44. Stanton, B., Theofanos, M.F., Prettyman, S.S., Furman, S.: Security fatigue. IEEE Comput. Archit. Lett. **18**(05), 26–32 (2016)
45. Strom, B.E., Applebaum, A., Miller, D.P., Nickels, K.C., Pennington, A.G., Thomas, C.B.: MITRE ATT&CK: Design and Philosophy. Technical report (2018)
46. Symantec: Living off the Land; Turning Your Infrastructure Against You. White Paper, December 2019
47. Taleb, N.N.: Fooled by randomness: The hidden role of chance in life and in the markets. Random House Incorporated, New York (2005)
48. Taleb, N.N.: The Black Swan: the Impact of the Highly Improbable. Random house, New York (2007)
49. Taleb, N.N.: Antifragile: Things that Gain from Disorder. Random House Incorporated, New York (2012)

50. Trivers, R.: Deceit and Self-deception: Fooling Yourself the Better to Fool Others. Penguin, New York (2011)
51. Von Hippel, W., Trivers, R.: The evolution and psychology of self-deception. Behav. Brain Sci. **34**(1), 1–16 (2011)
52. Walker, M.: Why We Sleep: Unlocking the Power of Sleep and Dreams. Simon and Schuster, New York (2017)
53. Workman, M.: Wisecrackers: a theory-grounded investigation of phishing and pretext social engineering threats to information security. J. Am. Soc. Inf. Sci. Technol. **59**(4), 662–674 (2008)
54. Zhang, H., Liu, H., Liang, J., Li, T., Geng, L., Liu, Y., Chen, S.: Defense against advanced persistent threats: optimal network security hardening using multi-stage maze network game. In: 2020 IEEE Symposium on Computers and Communications (ISCC), pp. 1–6. IEEE (2020)

Location-Based Augmented Reality Games Through Immersive Experiences

Chutisant Kerdvibulvech(✉)

Graduate School of Communication Arts and Management Innovation,
National Institute of Development Administration, 118 SeriThai Rd, Klong-chan,
Bangkapi, Bangkok 10240, Thailand
chutisant.ker@nida.ac.th

Abstract. Augmented reality (AR) is an immersive experience of a physical world environment which is enhanced by virtual objects, offers interesting ways of human-computer interacting. Because location-based augmented reality allows people to enhance virtual information to geographical points of interest at specific predefined geolocations, it can help researchers to create amazing applications and augmented reality games in a different way. More recently, due to the technology's capacity and recent innovation, location-based augmented reality has been extremely popular by using geo-based features to create a new immersive experience. This paper presents a novel summary of pioneering location-based augmented reality systems and games through immersive experiences, including our own research, in an interdisciplinary augmented cognition perspective. To begin with, we explore location-based augmented reality researches, starting from non-game works such as SPIRIT and IntelligShop. Then, we discuss pioneering augmented reality games, particularly well-known games, since the early of the twentieth century until now, including Human Pacman, ARCarGame, Pokémon Go, and AR Mario Kart Live. We finally give a recommendation and predict a future scenario for location-based augmented reality systems and games.

Keywords: Location-based augmented reality · Augmented cognition · Human pacman · ARCarGame · Remote-controlled car · Pokémon go · AR Mario Kart live

1 Introduction

Due to rapid developments in mobile technology, augmented reality—an immersive experience of a physical world environment which is enhanced by virtual objects—has been a trending field of research in computer science and engineering for the past two decades. At the same time, cognitive augmented reality—a concept utilizing prior visual observation and learning of a complete manipulative workflow for making augmented reality content in each procedural task, as explained by Petersen and Stricker [1]—has become popular in human-computer interaction. More recently, this field has been even more a very popular trend when using geo-based or location-based features for augmented reality because of advancements in recent mobile and smartphone technology.

© Springer Nature Switzerland AG 2021
D. D. Schmorrow and C. M. Fidopiastis (Eds.): HCII 2021, LNAI 12776, pp. 452–461, 2021.
https://doi.org/10.1007/978-3-030-78114-9_31

We find a variety of location-based augmented reality used for different purposes. For instance, a museum tour guide mobile application is implemented by Tsai et al. [2] using location-based augmented reality experience. In this museum tour guide application, they design the content of the application using media richness theory for giving interactive information suggesting service, including entertainment and education functions, in real time. However, although there are various benefits in many aspects using location-based features for augmented reality, building a robust location-based augmented reality application, especially cognitive augmented reality, is not a trivial task. It has still so many challenges and difficulties, such as collecting data in location-based augmented reality, accurate tracking of objects in real time, and creating immersive environments and virtual avatars that are less side-effects for nausea, blurred vision, and headache. For example, studies of collecting authentic data in location-aware augmented reality learning experiences by Kyza et al. [3] and bridging locality and narrative in the context of augmented reality educational intervention for mobile by Georgiou and Kyza [4] give a broad overview of challenges in location-based augmented reality. The challenges include location-based augmented reality settings, collecting ecologically valid data, and applying head-mounted wearable cameras. Also, for building a robust location-based augmented reality application in many cases, it requires interdisciplinary technical expertise from various related fields, such as computer vision, deep machine learning, and computer graphics, to solve the common problems. To the best of our knowledge, even though there have been some works for summarizing augmented reality applications generally, such as an impact study of augmented reality applications on the students' learning motive in [5] by Khan et al., a summary for the development of modern augmented reality in the first two decades of the twenty-first century based on essential trends by Siriborvornratanakul [6], and a systematic landscape of augmented reality user studies for ten years of the twenty-first century (i.e., 2005–2014) by Dey et al. [7], only very little work exists that systematically and historically summarizes location-based augmented reality applications and games.

In this paper, our contribution is to propose a new summary of state-of-the-art location-based augmented reality systems and games through immersive experiences in an interdisciplinary augmented cognition perspective for the first two decades of the twenty-first century. The paper here is divided into two main parts: location-based augmented reality systems (Sect. 2) and location-based augmented reality games (Sect. 3). The first main part is to explore generally and broadly location-based systems using augmented reality. More specifically in games, the second main part focuses on the possibilities of utilizing location-based augmented reality to create games interactively both on tablets and smartphones. We discuss pioneering location-based augmented reality games, from Human Pacman and an interactive augmented reality ARCarGame for tracking a remote-controlled car, to recent location-based applications today, such as an augmented reality-based Pokémon Go and a very recent remote-controlled AR Mario Kart Live. Finally, in Sect. 4, we conclude the methods for location-based augmented reality in an interdisciplinary augmented cognition perspective and attempt to forecast the future of this field.

Fig. 1. The end-user experience using SPIRIT which interprets location-dependent augmented reality contexts for outdoor museums, presented by Kampa and Spierling [8].

2 Location-Based Augmented Reality Systems

This section will describe several examples of location-based systems using augmented reality, focusing on non-game researches. To begin with, a smart authoring work for location-based interactive digital storytelling experiences using augmented reality was presented by Kampa and Spierling [8] for outdoor museums. In their work, they create a research project, so called SPIRIT, which interprets location-dependent contexts using augmented reality and smartphone sensors, including Bluetooth, gyroscope, global positioning system (GPS) receiver, for tracking the device's location. A user can hold a tablet or smartphone and turn it to different directions, and then he/she can collect elements of a location-dependent story. With authored SPIRIT, this system can display a historic content interactively at the Saalburg Roman Fort in Bad Homburg, Germany, where they test the system. Figure 1 shows the end-user experience using this system. For this reason, this authoring system can be used by museum keepers for building location-dependent augmented reality storytelling experiences. Moreover, Adhikari et al. [9] built a location-based augmented reality system, called IntelligShop, for shopping experience via smartphones in a mall of Singapore. This system uses feature learning, so that it can support different smartphones in localization with cold start task. Sixteen locations are sampled for localization with six retailers. The retailers in malls can be recognized and the online reviews from both internet and social media sources can be fetched and shown via smartphones through location-based augmented reality. However, the IntelligShop system needs to collect wireless signals and the floor plan and layout of the mall for dealing with the indoor localization. In addition, Jimenez et al. [10] described a market potential and a commercialization strategy for a location-based assistive work using augmented reality to support the management of utilities. Although researches about location-based systems using augmented reality are popular, it may not clearly be commercialized significantly like location-based augmented reality games. In the next section, we will discuss about the games using location-based augmented reality technology in details.

Player walks across a cookie and it disappears.

Corresponding virtual world update in real time.

Fig. 2. Human Pacman, one of the pioneering researches in this field of location-based augmented reality game development, built by Cheok et al. [11] in 2004

3   Location-Based Augmented Reality Games

This section presents a new summary of state-of-the-art location-based augmented reality games through immersive experiences, including our own research, since the early of the twenty-first century until now. Due to the growing popularity of games, we explore well-known location-based augmented reality researches, particularly games, such as Human Pacman and an interactive augmented reality game for tracking a remote-controlled car, until recent location-based applications today, such as an augmented reality-based Pokémon Go and a remote-controlled AR Mario Kart Live. First, one of the pioneering researches about location-based augmented reality game is an interactive role-playing game, called Human Pacman, presented by Cheok et al. [11] at the beginning of the century in 2004. The name comes from the concept of Pac-Man, a classic maze arcade game. This game can bring the computer gaming experience by integrated with human-social and mobile-gaming. Virtual cookies are built and overlaid into the physical world which allows players to touch it virtually and provide interactive experiences of seamless transitions between virtual and physical worlds. This location-based augmented reality game uses in-built global positioning system receiver and sensorfusion with disaster risk management (DRM) for locating players accurately. Figure 2 illustrates an example of in-game screenshots when a player walks and collects virtual cookies in Human Pacman.

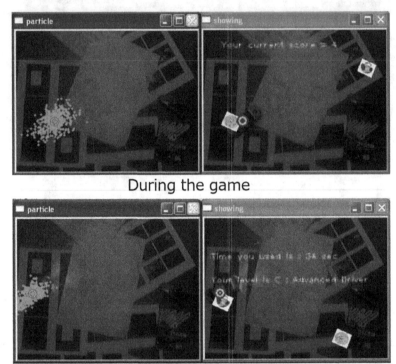

Fig. 3. ARCarGame, one of the pioneering researches in the field of location-based augmented reality game for remote-controlled car, developed by Kerdvibulvech [13] in 2010

Next, augmented reality is applied as an interactive game for tracking a physical remote-controlled car through immersive experiences, called ARCarGame, as proposed by Kerdvibulvech [12] in 2010 and later shortly in [13] for user evaluation in details. By using robust computer vision algorithms of extended particle filters and a Bayesian classifier, it accurately tracks the location and position of the color remote-controlled car to mainly consider the color feature in real time. Because the color is learnt online adaptively, it is also robust for extremely lighting changes while tracking the location. In this game, virtual items, such as coins and mushrooms, are augmented into the physical scene, which allows a player to control a car to collect the coins and the mushrooms interactively which each virtual item has a different score. If the coin is collected, a player gains just one point. On the other hand, if the mushroom is collected, points are double incremented. This means that each player must carefully control a car to collect items which have the highest possible points in the shortest period of time. More interestingly, a pioneering feature in ARCarGame is that it can give players feedback and the evaluation scores of each player automatically. In other words, a player scores according to the car control skills in a gamified way. In the end of the game, each player will be finally classified into three levels: a beginning driver (Level A), an intermediate driver (level B), and an advanced driver (level C). Figure 3 gives several examples of in-game screenshots from our location-based interactive ARCarGame with the feature of scoring according to the car control skills. To the best of our knowledge, we believe that this interactive augmented reality game for tracking a remote-controlled car with the feature of scoring was pioneering one of the newest forms of physical remote-controlled car gaming at that time.

Fig. 4. Pokémon Go, one of the world's most successful mobile games using location-based augmented reality with more than four billion USD in revenue, released by Niantic Inc. in 2016 [14]

Furthermore, similarly six years later in 2016, Niantic Inc. [14] developed an extremely popular location-based augmented reality game, called Pokémon Go. Virtual creatures (Pokémon) in the game are created and overlaid into the physical world, which forces each player to walk in the real world to battle each virtual creature and progress the game interactively. Figure 4 shows an example of Pokémon Go game in augmented reality mode. This game uses mobile devices with global positioning system to locate and battle many species of virtual creature by throwing a Poké ball. In terms of popularity and profit [15], Pokémon GO has over a billion downloads worldwide and commercially grossed more than four billion USD in revenue by early 2019. According to the Forbes source, Chamary has proclaimed that it is *"one of the most successful mobile games of all time"* [16], as it breaks many world records, such as the world's most-downloaded game in its first month of release and the fastest game to earn a hundred million USD in the world.

Fig. 5. An example of an outdoor mobile location-based augmented reality game, as presented by Santos et al. [17] in 2020, when searching augmented birds of prey

Four years after that period, in 2020, there are also many interesting location-based augmented reality games released in this year. For instance, Santos et al. [17] presented a mobile location-based game with augmented reality to create outdoor experiences for nature parks at the "Parque Biológico de Gaia" in Porto, Portugal. Their aim is to disseminate knowledge about the flora and fauna of the nature park using this location-based augmented reality game. In this game, it allows a player to find augmented objects, such as augmented birds of prey, using the smartphone camera, and then he/she can try to guess what the name of species is. Figure 5 displays an example of location-based augmented reality in-game screenshot which a player scores according to the answer of the name of species. Moreover, Schickler et al. [18] examined flexible framework and development of location-based games in the Augmented Reality Engine Application (AREA) project for mobile using augmented reality. In addition, similarly ten years later after our research about an interactive augmented reality ARCarGame for tracking a remote-controlled car has been proposed, a concept of using augmented reality for physical remote-controlled car game is again presented recently. A remote-controlled AR Mario Kart Live: Home Circuit was released by Nintendo [19] in October 2020 for celebrating the 35th anniversary of the Super Mario franchise and Nintendo Switch, the latest entry in the popular racing game series [20]. In this augmented reality game, players can race Mario at their own home on a customized virtual world through immersive experiences. The game is composed of a physical electronic remote-controlled car, called go-kart, that is topped with a small camera. This camera is used to capture the physical scene and respond to how the players play in-game. Then, AR Mario Kart Live: Home Circuit can create virtual objects, such as obstacles and opponents, with their own home as the background. As shown in Fig. 6, a virtual mushroom and virtual coins are augmented over a player's view of the physical world. Soon after the game's reveal, as suggested by Forbes' Tassi [21], the game is potentially nominated for the category of Best Family, together with other five games, at The Game Awards 2020. Also, this game sold more than seventy thousand copies within the first week of release in Japan in October 2020, so that it is the Japan's bestselling retail game of the week.

Fig. 6. AR Mario Kart Live: Home Circuit game and a Mario/Luigi kart, one of the latest augmented reality racing games using a physical remote-controlled car, released by Nintendo [20] in October 2020

4   Conclusion

This paper has presented a summary of state-of-the-art location-based augmented reality applications and games which is a popular issue for human-computer interaction through immersive experiences, including our own research, in an interdisciplinary augmented cognition perspective. We explore well-known location-based augmented reality researches for the last two decades, including SPIRIT, IntelligShop, Human Pacman, ARCarGame, Pokémon Go, and AR Mario Kart Live. We have briefly explained the technology behind each location-based augmented reality game. In general, computer vision and global positioning system are usually used for tracking the positions or/and providing geolocation. In this way, the robustness of its algorithms is still very important. Also, using an augmented cognition during physiological sensing of a user's cognitive state at the first place can help designing the location-based augmented reality game more systematically and user friendliness. In the future, due to the rapidly increasing volume and value of data in the next several years, we suggest that machine learning and deep machine learning based on artificial neural networks can be a great tool to help dealing with some critical problems. Therefore, it can enhance the robustness of location-based augmented reality applications and games effectively and efficiently. Besides, according to the Technavio [22], the global augmented reality market is possibly expected to reach 76.99 billion USD during 2020–2024. Due to mobile and broadband technology readiness and commercialization, we predict that the global market size of location-based augmented reality games will be dramatically increased in the next decade, especially when the 6G network is launched in the next step in the world of mobile connectivity.

Acknowledgments. This research presented herein was partially supported by a research grant from the Research Center, NIDA (National Institute of Development Administration).

References

1. Petersen, N., Stricker, D.: Cognitive augmented reality. Comput. Graph. **53**, 82–91 (2015)
2. Tsai, T.-H., Shen, C.-Y., Lin, Z.-S., Liu, H.-R., Chiou, W.-K.: Exploring location-based augmented reality experience in museums. In: Antona, M., Stephanidis, C. (eds.) UAHCI 2017. LNCS, vol. 10278, pp. 199–209. Springer, Cham (2017). https://doi.org/10.1007/978-3-319-58703-5_15
3. Kyza, E.A., Georgiou, Y., Souropetsis, M., Agesilaou, A.: Collecting ecologically valid data in location-aware augmented reality settings: a comparison of three data collection techniques. Int. J. Mob. Blended Learn. **11**(2), 78–95 (2019)
4. Georgiou, Y., Kyza, E.A.: Bridging narrative and locality in mobile-based augmented reality educational activities: effects of semantic coupling on students' immersion and learning gains. Int. J. Hum. Comput. Stud. **145**, 102546 (2021)
5. Khan, T., Johnston, K., Ophoff, J.: The impact of an augmented reality application on learning motivation of students. Adv. Hum. Comput. Interact. **2019**, 7208494:1-7208494 (2019)
6. Siriborvornratanakul, T.: Through the realities of augmented reality. In: Stephanidis, C. (ed.) HCII 2019. LNCS, vol. 11786, pp. 253–264. Springer, Cham (2019). https://doi.org/10.1007/978-3-030-30033-3_20
7. Dey, A., Billinghurst, M., Lindeman, R.W., Edward Swan, J.: A systematic review of 10 years of augmented reality usability studies: 2005 to 2014. Front. Robot. AI **5**, 37 (2018)
8. Kampa, A.: Ulrike spierling: smart authoring for location-based augmented reality storytelling applications. In: GI-Jahrestagung, pp. 915–922 (2017)
9. Adhikari, A., Zheng, V. W., Cao, H., Lin, M., Fang, Y., Chang, K. C.-C.: IntelligShop: enabling intelligent shopping in malls through location-based augmented reality. In: ICDM Workshops, pp. 1604–1607. IEEE Computer Society (2015). ISBN: 978-1-4673-8493-3
10. Perez Jimenez, R.J., Becerril, E.M., Nor, R.M., Smagas, K., Valari, E., Stylianidis, E.: Market potential for a location based and augmented reality system for utilities management. In: 2016 22nd International Conference on Virtual System and Multimedia (VSMM), pp. 1–4 (2016). https://doi.org/10.1109/VSMM.2016.7863171
11. Cheok, A.D., et al.:Human Pacman: a mobile, wide-area entertainment system based on physical, social, and ubiquitous computing. Pers. Ubiquitous Comput. **8**(2), 71–81 (2004)
12. Kerdvibulvech, C.: Real-time augmented reality application using color analysis. In: IEEE Southwest Symposium on Image Analysis and Interpretation (SSIAI), Austin, TX, USA, pp. 29–32. IEEE Computer Society, 23–25 May (2010)

13. Kerdvibulvech, C.: Markerless vision-based tracking for interactive augmented reality game. Int. J. Interact. Worlds (IJIW) **2010**, 14 (2010). Issue on Serious Games and Interactive Worlds, Article ID 751615

14. Pyae, A., Potter, L.E.: A player engagement model for an augmented reality game: a case of pokémon go. In: OZCHI 2016, pp. 11–15 (2016)

15. Liu, L., Wagner, C., Suh, A.: Understanding the success of Pokémon Go: impact of immersion on players' continuance intention. In: Schmorrow, D.D., Fidopiastis, C.M. (eds.) AC 2017. LNCS (LNAI), vol. 10285, pp. 514–523. Springer, Cham (2017). https://doi.org/10.1007/978-3-319-58625-0_37

16. Chamary, J.V.: Why 'Pokémon GO' Is The World's Most Important Game. Forbes, Science, 10 February 2018

17. Santos, L., Silva, N., Nóbrega, R., Almeida, R., Coelho, A.: An Interactive Application Framework for Natural Parks using Serious Location-based Games with Augmented Reality. In: VISIGRAPP (1: GRAPP) 2020, pp. 247–254 (2020)

18. Schickler, M., et al.: Flexible development of location-based mobile augmented reality applications with AREA. J. Ambient. Intell. Humaniz. Comput. **11**(12), 5809–5824 (2020). https://doi.org/10.1007/s12652-020-02094-9

19. Foxx, C., Live, M.K.: Mixed-reality karts race around the home, BBC Click, BBC News, Technology, 24 October 2020. https://www.bbc.com/news/av/technology-54663569. Accessed 20 Dec 2020

20. Nintendo, M.K.L.: Home Circuit. https://www.nintendo.co.uk/Games/Nintendo-Switch-download-software/Mario-Kart-Live-Home-Circuit-1832413.html. Accessed 20 Dec 2020

21. Tassi, P.: Here's The Game Awards 2020 Winners List With A Near-Total 'Last Of Us' Sweep. Forbes, Games, 11 December 2020

22. Technavio, Augmented Reality (AR) Market by Application and Geography - Forecast and Analysis 2020–2024, p. 148, SKU: IRTNTR40843, January 2020

Selecting and Training Young Cyber Talent: A European Cybersecurity Challenge Case Study

Muahmmad Mudassar Yamin[✉], Basel Katt, and Espen Torseth

Norwegian University of Science and Technology,
Teknologivegen 22, 2815 Gjøvik, Norway
{muhammad.m.yamin,basel.katt,espen.torseth}@ntnu.no

Abstract. With the increasing popularization of cybersecurity concepts due to ever increasing cybersecurity incidents, it is no secret that countries worldwide are investing heavily in cybersecurity education to build the necessary talent pool to cope with future cybersecurity challenges. At the same time, different cybersecurity competitions are being organized to identify leading countries in cybersecurity domains. One such competition is *European Cyber Security Challenge* in which countries across Europe participate annually to showcase their cyber capabilities. In this research, we present a first of a kind study that focused on identifying selection and training strategies of national cybersecurity teams for international cybersecurity competitions. In the study, we identified countries with major talent pools, their selection and training methodologies, and the training platforms they used.

Keywords: Cyber security · Education · Training · Team building

1 Introduction

ECSC (European Cyber Security Challenge) [1] is organized every year by ENISA (European Network and Security Agency) [2] since 2016. In ECSC countries across Europe participate to compete against each other to evaluate their cyber competence against cyber security curricula defined by ENISA. The curricula comprises of key skill and general domains like *Information/Crypto, Network, Operating Systems, Organizational and human factors* as well as specific domains like *Web, Mobile, IoT, Specific Operating Systems and Hardware Support, Privacy, surveillance and censorship, PKI in practice*. The curricula also focuses on cyber security approaches and methodology which contains *Reconnaissance, Cryptanalysis, Operations Security* and *Forensics/Malware Analysis*.

It can be seen that ENISA curricula cover a wide area of cybersecurity topics, though the target audience for ECSC is young individuals who are between 14 to 25 years old. The target audience is established to promote cybersecurity education from an early stage. However, this creates challenges in selecting and

D. D. Schmorrow and C. M. Fidopiastis (Eds.): HCII 2021, LNAI 12776, pp. 462–483, 2021.
https://doi.org/10.1007/978-3-030-78114-9_32

training individuals with variable age groups and variable skill sets. The cognitive capabilities, social skills, and previous experience of CTF (Capture the Flag) competitions are some of the different performance factors that affect individual and team performance. How to select and train teams with variable performance factors needed to be investigated and how to evaluate their performance based upon the received training.

Although the ENISA curricula provide clear guidelines on which skill set matrix a team performs needs to be evaluated, little or no research work is being carried out on how different countries train their teams and how it affects their performance. In this work, we are going to examine the selection and training strategies of various European countries for ECSC. First, we present the study's background and related work; after that, we share the methodology used to collect data systemically from different national teams during ECSC 2019. Following that, we present the selection, training strategies, and the training platforms employed by various European countries for ECSC. Continuing that, we present an analysis of the collected data and suggest key recommendations for training and selecting national teams. In the end, we share some of our planned future work and conclude the article.

2   Background and Related Work

The 2019 edition of ECSC was held in Bucharest, Romania, in which nearly 300 hundred participants from 20 European national teams participated. From Norway, a national squad of 17 participants participated in the competition, out of which 10 were the team members, 1 was a backup, 2 trainers, and 4 team officials. During the competition, the team officials investigated and analyzed the whole process of organizing such a mega event as Norway will host this mega international event in 2023. The team officials also investigated the training and selection methodologies of other countries to learn from their experience. The research activity yielded some interesting results which can be used to develop improved selection and training strategies for national cybersecurity teams. Some of the related work to the present research is presented as follows:

Dodge et al. [3] in 2003 focused on *Organization and training of a cybersecurity team*. The researchers first shared their experience in planning and executing CDX (Cyber Defence Exercise), an inter-service competition among different United States military academies. After that, they shared the challenges in building cybersecurity exercise infrastructure. The researchers identified that CDX provides an excellent platform for increasing the skill set and knowledge of participating teams and developing leadership qualities among individual participants. The researchers measured the team performance improvement during the exercise; however, there is no information on how the teams were trained before the exercise and how it affected the exercise outcome.

Manson et al. [4] in 2011 suggested developing a cyber league similar to national leagues for other sports like football, basketball, etc., for high school students. The researchers shared details of different cybersecurity competitions that were currently going on in the United States and stated that currently, the cybersecurity competitions are organized by different organizations according to their own needs. The researchers stated that a national level initiative from the high school level would help to develop a future cyber workforce more effectively. In ECSC, the competition rules ensure 50% of high school students in a national team, which is good for workforce development. However, it raises challenges with internal team dynamics like communication of juniors (14–20) with seniors (21–25) for better team performance, which is needed to be investigated.

Silva et al. [5] in 2014 focused on *Factors Impacting Performance in Competitive Cyber Exercises*. The researchers surveyed the participants of *Tracer Fire* cybersecurity exercise. *Tracer Fire* is a cybersecurity exercise that focuses on the training of *United States Department of Energy* employees. The researchers identified the most utilized tools and skill set in the exercise, Wireshark [6] and network analysis, respectively. However, they also focused on individual performance in the cybersecurity exercise. Team performance and factors impacting it were not investigated in the research.

3   Methodology

The researchers used a mixed-method approach [7] to gather qualitative and quantitative data. The team officials from Norway conducted one-to-one interviews with the coaches and team officials from other European countries. The research data is collected systemically in the form of a pre-structured questioner that the researchers carefully discussed and developed in their internal meetings. Most of the questions were open-ended, which were designed to gather qualitative data related to team selection and training strategies [8]. Some questions related to participation numbers and the number of training events they conducted before coming to the ECSC were asked to quantify the training and selection process.

The interview questions helped the researchers to collect the data related to the national teams' selection process's general idea. This is used to identify the technical and personal skill criteria of team member selection and identify their teamwork-related abilities that different countries employed. The questioner also identified the training strategies, training platform and future selection and training plans. A list of questions that were asked during the data collection process is given in Appendices A. A total of 20 countries participated in ECSC 2019, and team officials and coaches from 15 countries agreed to participate in the research activity. Details of countries that participated in the research activity regarding their ranking in ECSC 2019 are presented in Table 1.

Table 1. Participating countries with respect to their ranking in ECSC 2019

No	Country	ECSC ranking 2019	Participated in research
1	Romania [9]	1	✓
2	Italy [10]	2	✓
3	Austria [11]	3	✓
4	Germany [12]	4	✓
5	United Kingdom [13]	5	✓
6	Poland [14]	6	✓
7	France [15]	7	✓
8	Estonia [16]	8	✗
9	Denmark [17]	9	✗
10	Portugal [18]	10	✓
11	Czech Republic [19]	11	✓
12	Greece [20]	12	✓
13	Spain [21]	13	✓
14	Norway [22]	14	✓
15	Ireland [23]	15	✗
16	Netherlands [24]	16	✓
17	Switzerland [25]	17	✗
18	Cyprus [26]	18	✓
19	Liechtenstein [27]	19	✗
20	Luxembourg [28]	20	✓

4   Team Selection and Training Strategies

4.1   Romania

The Romanian team was the winner of ECSC 2019; they have 1 national qualifier in which 200 individuals participated, out of which they selected 25. After that, they organized two boot camps in which they arranged workshops and CTF for first selecting the top 16, and after that, they selected the top 10 team members and 1 backup for ECSC finals. The selection and training process of the Romanian national team is presented in Fig. 1.

4.2   Italy

The Italians have a very systematic and comprehensive model for selecting and training their national team. They have three rounds for selecting their national team. In first round, more than 3000 participants from 18 different national regions participated which were then assigned to 18 universities for 12 weeks of intensive training. After the training the second round was held in which each

Fig. 1. The Romanian national team for ECSC selection and training model

university organized a CTF in which top 4 performers from each university were selected. In the final round, an in house competition was conducted, which is more like a *king of the hill* [29] attack and defense competition in which the top 10 participants was selected for the national team. The selection and training process of the Italian national team is presented in Fig. 2.

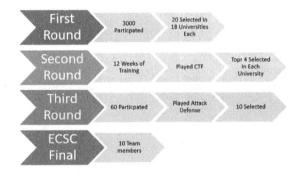

Fig. 2. The Italian national team for ECSC selection and training model

4.3 Austria

The Austrian national team selection and training model was similar to the Romanian model, in which they first conducted an online qualifier in which 600 participants participated. They invited the top 20 of the national qualifier for an in house CTF competition and then selected the top 10 for the national team. They organized two training boot camps for the national team's training before coming to ECSC in which they played different CTF competitions. The selection and training process of the Austrian national team is presented in Fig. 3.

4.4 Germany

The German training and selection model is a bit different from other countries. In Germany 5 seniors members of the teams were nominated by a selection

Fig. 3. The Austrian national team for ECSC selection and training model

committee based upon their skills and ranking in different online platforms. The senior members then decide which skills they lack and organize a CTF to select the 5 junior members. They then had 12 weeks of continuous training before coming to the ECSC. The selection and training process of the German national team is presented in Fig. 4.

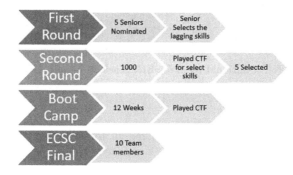

Fig. 4. The German national team for ECSC selection and training model .

4.5   United Kingdom

The United Kingdom process of training and selecting the national team is quite similar to Romania. They organized a national qualifier in which 42 individuals participated. They selected the top 20 individuals and then organized a boot camp in which they played CTF and selected the top 10 for the national team. They also organized a second boot camp in which they played CTF for training purposes. The selection and training process of the UK national team is presented in Fig. 5.

Fig. 5. The United Kingdom national team for ECSC selection and training model

Fig. 6. The Polish national team for ECSC selection and training model

4.6   Poland

Compare to other countries, the Polish model for selecting and training the national team was quite simple. They organized a CTF in which 77 people participated. They selected the top 10 and directly entered the competition without any training boot camp. The selection and training process of the Polish national team is presented in Fig. 6.

4.7   France

The French process of training and selecting the national team is quite similar to the British process. They organized a national qualifier in which 1200 individuals participated online. They selected the top 50 and then organized a final during a known event in which they played CTF and selected the top 10 individuals for the national team plus 4 substitutes. They also organized a second two days boot camp in which 1 day is used for training and the other day is for playing CTF. The selection and training process of the French national team is presented in Fig. 7.

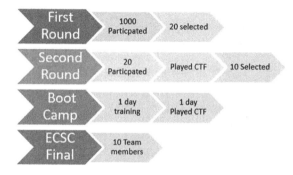

Fig. 7. The French national team for ECSC selection and training model

Fig. 8. The Portuguese national team for ECSC selection and training model

4.8   Portugal

The Portuguese model for selecting and training the national team was quite simple. They organized a CTF in which 30 people participated. They selected the top 10 and organized 1 boot camp in which they played CTF; they entered the competition after that. The selection and training process of the Portuguese national team is presented in Fig. 8.

4.9   Czech Republic

The Czech Republic team was selected after two national qualifiers and two boot camps. The first national qualifier has a general competition related to computer and IT technologies in which 3200 people of all age groups participated, out of which they selected the top 1500. In the second round, a cybersecurity challenge was created at the national level, which contained both theoretical and practical cybersecurity challenges. At the end of the second round, they selected the top 30 and invited them for an in-house training boot camp. They played CTF in the first boot camp and selected the top 15 from them. After that, they conducted a second training boot camp in which they also played CTF and selected the top 10 for the national team for ECSC. The selection and training process of the Czech Republic national team is presented in Fig. 9.

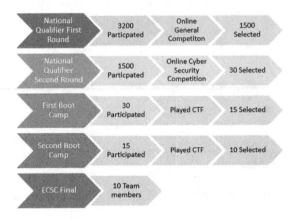

Fig. 9. The Czech Republic national team for ECSC selection and training model

4.10   Greece

The Greek team was selected after two main rounds in which first was an in house CTF competition, 40 individuals participated in that. They selected the top 25 from the 40 individuals and organized training camps for them. The training camps spanned over 8 months from March 2019 to October 2019 in which they paled CTF on every Saturday, excluding August due to holidays. At the end of the training camps, they selected the top 10 individuals with the best performance in the CTF for the ECSC final. The selection and training process of the Greek national team is presented in Fig. 10.

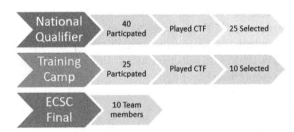

Fig. 10. The Greek national team for ECSC selection and training model

4.11   Spain

The Spanish team was selected after a two-round process; the first was an online qualifier, in which 1792 people of all age groups participated. They selected 168 top performers in the first round and invited them for face to face CTF challenges. In the second round, they selected the top 25 for the national team and invited them into a cyber camp in which they played CTF and conducted interviews. They selected 15 team members, 10 for ECSC final and 5 as a backup at the end of the cyber camp. The Spanish national team's selection and training process is presented in Fig. 11.

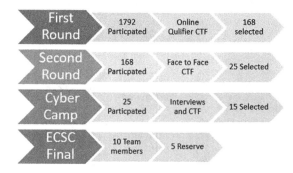

Fig. 11. The Spanish national team for ECSC selection and training model

4.12 Norway

The selection of the Norwegian national team was performed in two rounds of qualification. In the first round, an online CTF competition was organized in which 150 participants from all over Norway participated. The top 25 of the first round was selected based upon their ranking and was then invited for an in-house CTF challenge. In the in-house challenge, 10 + 2 participants were selected to be part of the national team based on their CTF performance and their personality analysis by an expert. For the national team training, two boot camps on weekends were organized in which two former national team members were assigned duties to train the national team. The trainers selected relevant CTF to the ECSC challenges and advised the national team to play the CTF for training. The selection and training process of the Norwegian national team is presented in Fig. 12.

4.13 Netherlands

The Netherlands has a straightforward selection method in which 13 teams were representing different educational institutions, which in total 100 players participated in a national final. Selection for ECSC was performed by selecting top senior and juniors from the highest-ranking teams. In the future, they are planning to add an extra layer in the selection process; they will be organizing a final with 200 players in more and smaller teams (maximum of 5 players) divided into junior and senior competitions. The best players from the top junior and senior teams (15 in each category) will be attending cybersecurity masterclasses for

Fig. 12. The Norwegian national team for ECSC selection and training model

approximately 2 weeks. From this 30 people long list, they will select the final 10 players. The selection and training process of the Netherlands national team is presented in Fig. 13.

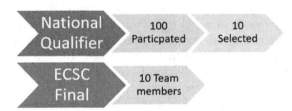

Fig. 13. The Netherlands national team for ECSC selection and training model

4.14 Cyprus

The selection of Cyprus national team was performed in two rounds of qualification. In the first round, an online 48-h CTF competition was organized in which 96 participants had initially registered, and 48 competed, including University students studying abroad. The Top 18 of the first round were selected based upon their ranking and were then invited for an in house/online personal meeting in order to identify their skills and personality. 10 + 4 participants were selected to be on the national team based upon their CTF performance, personality analysis, and ECSC age rules. For the national team's training, 9 seminars were organized in which mentors trained the national team. Also, the team participated in various CTF. The selection and training process of the Cyprus national team is presented in Fig. 14.

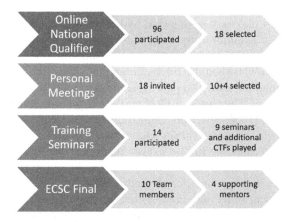

Fig. 14. The Cyprus national team for ECSC selection and training model

4.15   Luxembourg

Luxembourg's process for team selection and training was quite simple; for 6 months, online-challenges with about 150 registered participants were conducted. The ten best were selected and coached. They did not choose substitute players, so only 8 team members participated in ECSC finals. The selection and training process of the Luxembourg national team is presented in Fig. 15.

Fig. 15. The Luxembourg national team for ECSC selection and training model

5   Social and Teamwork Skills

The Romanians selected the individual team members that are technically adept and have good interpersonal skills. They conducted a separate team-building exercise, which helped the individuals to works as a team. On the other hand, the Italians focused only on selecting their national team's core technical skills. The Austrian conducted a personality evaluation on individuals to identify whether the individual is suitable for working in a team or not. For teamwork, the Austrian trainer emphasizes challenges that required teamwork for team building. The German team's juniors were selected by observing the CTF participants in the finals, how they communicate, talk, and collaborate, which was implicitly taken into account for their selection. For team building, the Germans focused on the team captain who should have team leading skills.

The United Kingdom team also performed a personality test before their final selection in the team. They used a Golf trip for a team-building exercise. On the other hand, the Polish selection team didn't consider social and teamwork related skills in their selection criteria. One senior volunteered to lead the team with an exceptional skill set in the Polish team and was respected by other team members. The French also considered the social and interpersonal skills of individuals before selecting them for the national team. The best French senior and junior in technical skills were not selected for the national team due to their bad communication skills. The Portuguese didn't account for any social and teamwork skills. They just selected the team members based upon their core technical skills.

The Czech focused on selecting individuals who have a good personality and can work with others. They also take into account how friendly and cooperative the individuals are in a team. In contrast, the Greeks selected individuals on core CTF skills only. Their team building was done in the training camps, and a team leader was selected based upon personal skills and previous experiences. The Spanish conducted interviews before selecting the final team for the competition. They used their training camps to teach soft skills that are required for the team's performance in the competition. The Norwegians also conducted a personality test before selecting individuals for the national team. They used *Blindfold Lego Build Challenge* as a team-building exercise. Netherlands and Luxembourg have a simple selection process, and they just used individual core CTF skills for selecting them in national teams. In contrast, the Cyprus selection committee used personal meeting before selecting individuals for the national team.

6   Training Platforms

Different countries employ a multitude of different training platforms for training purposes. Some are using more mainstream CTF platforms like HackThBox [30] and TheHackingLab [31] while others opted for different online CTF platforms. Most of these platforms are freely available for training purposes, while some have paid subscriptions for advance training. Such services' effectiveness is apparent from ECSC as 3 of the top 5 countries were using TheHackingLab [31]. Details of training platforms used by different countries are presented in Table 2.

Table 2. List of training platforms used by different countries

No	Country	Platforms
1	Romania	HacTheBox [30], Online CTF [32]
2	Italy	TheHackingLab [31]
3	Austria	TheHackingLab [31] , Google CTF [33], Custom CTF
4	Germany	TheHackingLab [31]
5	UK	HackTheBox [30], Online CTF [32]
6	Poland	hack.cert.pl [14]
7	France	Online CTF [32]
8	Portugal	Online CTF [32]
9	Czech Republic	Online CTF [32]
10	Greece	HackTheBox [30]
11	Spain	ihacklabs.com [34]
12	Norway	HacTheBox [30], Online CTF [32]
13	Netherlands	Online CTF [32]
14	Cyprus	CTFd [35], Cyber ranges, HacktheBox [30], Facebook CTF [36], Google CTF [33], Custom Platforms
15	Luxembourg	Online CTF [32]

7   Analysis and Results

During our analysis we identified that in term of participation number most countries are struggling to attract people for the competition with the exception of Czech republic, Italy, Spain, France and Germany as suggested in Fig. 16. In term of qualification rounds 5 of the participating countries have two qualifying rounds, 4 countries have 1 qualifying round, 3 countries have 3 qualifying rounds. And 1 country Czech have the most qualifying rounds in there selection process which is 4 as indicated in Fig. 17. In term of training Greeks have the most which is 24 weeks, after that Italian and German team have 12 Weeks of training, while Cyprus team have 9 weeks of training. Most other countries like Norwegian and Romanian team have two week of training each as presented in Fig. 18. It is an interesting finding that the Romanians were able to to win the competition with just 2 weeks of training, which indicates that the quality of given training is also play an important role in team performance. We also performed an additional analysis in which we compare the population size of participating country and the number of point obtained during ECSC. We identified that Norwegian team is on par with Austrian team which is presented in Fig. 19. It should be noted that countries with very small population were found as an big outlier in the analysis like Lichtenstein which obtained 0.06174 points/capita so its results are omitted from Fig. 19. Estonia on the other hand managed to get maximum points with respect to its population. This indicates that with better promotion of cyber security events large parts of the population can be attracted to participate in such competitions. The quantifiable data collected during the research is presented in Appendices B, C.

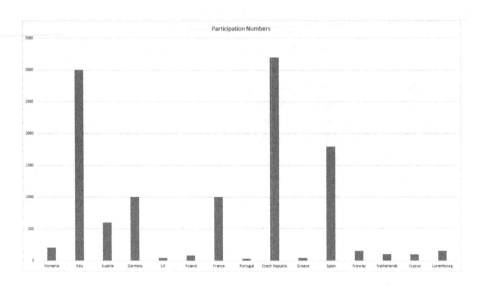

Fig. 16. Participation numbers with respect to analyzed countries

From the above analysis we can see that there is allot of variance identified in selection and training methodologies of different teams. However one common factor between 4 of the top 5 teams of the competitions is that they were using the same training platform as indicated in Table 2. Such training platforms are known as Cyber Ranges [37] and are used to develop new and unique cyber security exercise scenarios. Creating and modeling cyber security exercise scenarios is a difficult [38] and inefficient process [39]. While, work is currently being done on creating innovative cyber security exercises scenarios to reduce the overhead of cyber security exercise scenario creation process [40]. There is sill need to develop standardize training platforms for cyber security education [37]. The results of ECSC 2019 clearly indicated that countries that have access to top of the line cyber security training platforms are in clear advantage. But these training platforms are not freely accessible. During our discussion with German team we identified that they paid 40000 Euros for TheHackingLab [31] subscription. For some countries it is affordable while for others its not. It would be an interesting future work to identify the monetary investment in the national team and their corresponding position in competition final standing.

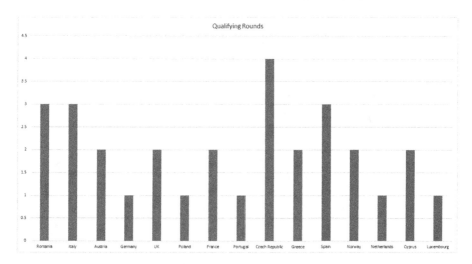

Fig. 17. Qualification rounds with respect to analyzed countries

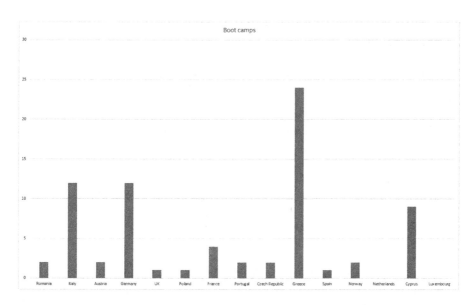

Fig. 18. Number of training boot camps with respect to analyzed countries

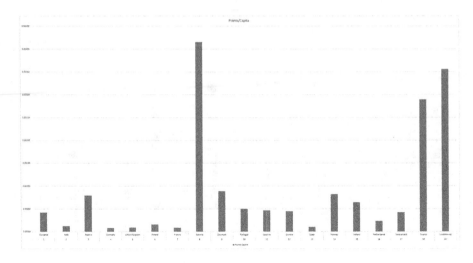

Fig. 19. Points to population ratio of a country in ECSC

8   Recommendations for Future Selection and Training Strategies

Based on our discussions with coaches and team officials of different participating countries, we recommend the following 5 steps for future team selection and training.

1. Good marketing for the national level competition is required to attract young talent. Placing posters in high school libraries, gaming arena, and prominent places can be a good strategy.
2. Corporation among regional universities for the selection and training of national teams can have a quantitative effect in increasing the talent pool and a qualitative effect due to regional competitions.
3. Minimum 12 weeks of intensive CTF training is recommended before sending the national team to ECSC as observed in Italy and Germany's training strategy.
4. Training platforms like HackTheBox [30] and TheHackingLab [31] are recommended for team training as they were used by the top 5 teams of ECSC 2019.
5. Focus on core technical skills in all domains of the competition curricula will develop a more robust team that will not be stuck in a challenge due to lack of particular skill set.

The proposed selection and training model based upon the above recommendation is presented in Fig. 20. We added marketing as the first phase of the selection and training model as it is very important to attract people to the competition. While most countries use digital marketing techniques nowadays, traditional marketing strategies can also play their role very well, as indicated by the youngest participant of the competition who stated that he saw a flyer related to the competition in school library's, which motivated him to participate in the competition. We divided the qualifiers into regional and national qualifiers, regional qualifiers will motivate people to participate from all regions of the country and expand the local talent pool. We consider that individual CTF and team-based attack defense exercise scenarios will help make local, regional teams. At the national level, we suggested the competition between regional teams in CTF and Attack Defense scenarios to check their effectiveness as a team.

Fig. 20. Proposed cybersecurity team selection and training model

We also recommend a king of the hill like competition at the national level to identify individual participants' excellence. The national team can be formed then by selecting the best team and best individuals combination for maximum effectiveness in the competition. We recommend multiple training workshops for the training in which experts can teach about the skill set required for the competition and then play CTF related to that skill set. Romania employs this training strategy, and we consider that this will ensure training quality for the participants. However, most countries consider social and teamwork skills as an important factor for team performance. However, countries like Italy, Germany, and Poland are focusing on core technical skill sets, which also yielded quite good results based upon their ranking in the competition. Yet, we added a team-building phase in the training of participants for creating a friendly atmosphere and better communication within a team.

9   Conclusion

In this research, we identified the selection and training process of different European teams in ECSC. We collected and presented valuable data to the best of our knowledge in a first of a kind research activity, highlighting that the Czech Republic and Italy have the largest cybersecurity talent pool. In contrast, Estonia has the most cyber security aware population if we ignore Lichtenstein as an outlier. On the other hand, Greece has the most trained team in the competition, followed by Italy and Germany. We also identified the parity between the point per capita of Austria, Denmark, and Norway, which can be attributed to their roughly similar sized populations. This research activity will help different countries to learn from each other experiences and increase their cyber competence. We suggested 5 basic steps to increase the talent pool, select and train the national team, and presented a model to implement those steps. In the future, we plan to continue the study while incorporating other factors like the amount of monetary investment in the national team and its effect on their ranking in the competition. We are also exploring research collaboration with ENISA to make such research activity more periodic to get information on new selection and training methodologies and their effectiveness employed by different countries.

A   Interview Questioner

1. What is the selection process for the national team?
2. Do you have a qualifying round?
3. How many qualifying rounds do an individual required to be the part of national team?
4. How many participants participated in first round and final round?
5. What technical traits you looked for individual selection?
6. What personal trait you looked for individual selection?
7. What team related skills you looked for the individual.
8. How you trained the selected team for the competition?
9. Any specific platform you used for the training?
10. What do you think can be improved in selection and training process?
11. Do you have hacking and CTF clubs in your country?

B   Collected Data

See Table 3.

Table 3. Quantitative data collected during the research activity

No	Country	Participation numbers	Qualifying rounds	Boot camps
1	Romania	200	3	2
2	Italy	3000	3	12
3	Austria	600	2	2
4	Germany	1000	1	12
5	UK	42	2	1
6	Poland	77	1	1
7	France	1000	2	4
8	Portugal	30	1	2
9	Czech Republic	3200	4	2
10	Greece	40	2	24
11	Spain	1792	3	1
12	Norway	150	2	2
13	Netherlands	100	1	0
14	Cyprus	96	2	9
15	Luxembourg	150	1	0

C   Points per Capita

See Table 4.

Table 4. Points obtained with respect to population size

Position	Country	Points	Capita (Wikipedia)	Points/Capita
1	Romania	8,188	19,401,658	0.00042
2	Italy	7,324	60,359,546	0.00012
3	Austria	7,036	8,857,960	0.00079
4	Germany	6,764	83,019,200	0.00008
5	United Kingdom	6,088	67,545,757	0.00009
6	Poland	6,040	38,433,600	0.00016
7	France	5,934	67,022,000	0.00009
8	Estonia	5,502	1,324,820	0.00415
9	Denmark	5,166	5,814,461	0.00089
10	Portugal	5,142	10,276,617	0.00050
11	Czech Republic	4,980	10,649,800	0.00047
12	Greece	4,854	10,768,477	0.00045
13	Spain	4,816	46,733,038	0.00010
14	Norway	4,362	5,328,212	0.00082
15	Ireland	4,206	6,572,728	0.00064
16	Netherlands	3,960	17,336,891	0.00023
17	Switzerland	3,626	8,570,146	0.00042
18	Cyprus	3,384	1,170,125	0.00289
19	Lichtenstein	2,380	38,547	0.06174
20	Luxembourg	2,184	613,894	0.00356

References

1. European cyber security challenge – ECSC. https://europeancybersecuritychall enge.eu/. Accessed 28 Feb 2021
2. Enisa. https://www.enisa.europa.eu/. Accessed 28 Feb 2021
3. Dodge, R.C., Ragsdale, D.J., Reynolds, C.: Organization and training of a cyber security team. In: SMC 2003 Conference Proceedings. 2003 IEEE International Conference on Systems, Man and Cybernetics. Conference Theme-System Security and Assurance (Cat. No. 03CH37483), vol. 5, pp. 4311–4316. IEEE (2003)
4. Manson, D., Carlin, A.: A league of our own: the future of cyber defense competitions. Commun. IIMA **11**(2), 1 (2011)
5. Silva, A.R., McClain, J.T., Anderson, B.R., Nauer, K.S., Abbott, R., Forsythe, J.C.: Factors impacting performance in competitive cyber exercises. Technical report, Sandia National Lab. (SNL-NM), Albuquerque, NM, USA (2014)
6. Wireshark · go deep
7. Newman, I., Benz, C.R., Ridenour, C.S.: Exploring the Interactive Continuum. Qualitative-Quantitative Research Methodology. SIU Press, Carbondale (1998)
8. Gill, P., Stewart, K., Treasure, E., Chadwick, B.: Methods of data collection in qualitative research: interviews and focus groups. Br. Dent. J. **204**(6), 291–295 (2008)
9. Cyber security challenge Romania. http://www.cybersecuritychallenge.ro/. Accessed 28 Feb 2021
10. Cyberchallenge.it. https://cyberchallenge.it/team. Accessed 28 Feb 2021
11. Cyber security Austria. https://www.cybersecurityaustria.at/. Accessed 28 Feb 2021
12. Die challenge—cyber security challenge Germany. https://www.cscg.de/cscg/challenge/. Accessed 28 Feb 2021
13. Ecsc: cyber security challenge UK (2019). https://www.cybersecuritychallenge.org.uk/what-we-do/ecsc-2019. Accessed 28 Feb 2021
14. hack.cert.pl-cert polska. https://hack.cert.pl/. Accessed 28 Feb 2021
15. Challenge européen de cybersécurité (ECSC)—agence nationale de la sécurité des systémes d'information (2019). https://www.ssi.gouv.fr/agence/cybersecurite/challenge-europeen-de-cybersecurite-ecsc-2019/. Accessed 28 Feb 2021
16. Ecsc eesti eelvoor. https://sites.google.com/view/kyberolympia/avaleht. Accessed 28 Feb 2021
17. Cyberlandshold. https://fe-ddis.dk/cyberlandsholdet/Pages/Cyberlandshold.aspx. Accessed 28 Feb 2021
18. Cyber security challenge PT 2020. https://cybersecuritychallenge.pt/. Accessed 28 Feb 2021
19. Kybernetická soutêž. https://www.kybersoutez.cz/. Accessed 28 Feb 2021
20. Ecsc 2019-gr team. https://www.ecsc.gr/. Accessed 28 Feb 2021
21. European cyber security challenge—cybercamp. https://cybercamp.es/en/ECSC-EN. Accessed 28 Feb 2021
22. Norwegian cyber security challenge - NCSC - NTNU. https://www.ntnu.no/ncsc. Accessed on 28 Feb 2021
23. Cybersecurity challenge Ireland - Ireland's team for the European cybersecurity challenge. https://cybersecuritychallenge.ie/. Accessed on 28 Feb 2021
24. Netherlands cyber security challenge. https://www.challengethecyber.nl/. Accessed on 28 Feb 2021

25. Swiss hacking challenge. https://www.swiss-hacking-challenge.ch/. Accessed 28 Feb 2021
26. Ccsc cyprus cyber security challenge. https://ccsc.org.cy/. Accessed 28 Feb 2021
27. Cybersecurity.li—cybersecurity Liechtenstein. https://cybersecurity.li/. Accessed 28 Feb 2021
28. Cybersecurity challenge Luxembourg. https://securitymadein.lu/news/cybersecurity-challenge-en/. Accessed 28 Feb 2021
29. Bock, K., Hughey, G., Levin, D.: King of the hill: a novel cybersecurity competition for teaching penetration testing. In: 2018 USENIX Workshop on Advances in Security Education (ASE 2018) (2018)
30. Hack the box: Penetration testing labs. https://www.hackthebox.eu/. Accessed 28 Feb 2021
31. Hacking-lab.com. https://www.hacking-lab.com/index.html. Accessed 28 Feb 2021
32. Ctftime.org/all about CTF (capture the flag). https://ctftime.org/. Accessed 28 Feb 2021
33. Google CTF. https://capturetheflag.withgoogle.com/. Accessed on 28 Feb 2021
34. ihacklabs - expertos en ciberseguridad, plataformas y capacitacion de profesionales. https://www.ihacklabs.com/en/. Accessed 28 Feb 2021
35. CTFd: The easiest capture the flag platform. https://ctfd.io/. Accessed on 28 Feb 2021
36. Facebook/FBCTF: Platform to host capture the flag competitions. https://github.com/facebook/fbctf. Accessed 28 Feb 2021
37. Yamin, M.M., Katt, B., Gkioulos, V.: Cyber ranges and security testbeds: scenarios, functions, tools and architecture. Comput. Secur. **88**, 101636 (2019)
38. Yamin, M.M., Katt, B.: Modeling attack and defense scenarios for cyber security exercises. In: 5th Inter Disciplinary Cyber Research Conference 2019, p. 7 (2019)
39. Yamin, M.M., Katt, B.: Inefficiencies in cyber-security exercises life-cycle: a position paper. In: Proceedings of the AAAI Symposium on Adversary-Aware Learning Techniques and Trends in Cybersecurity (ALEC 2018), pp. 41–43 (2018)
40. Yamin, M.M., Katt, B., Torseth, E., Gkioulos, V., Kowalski, S.J.: Make it and break it: an IoT smart home testbed case study. In: Proceedings of the 2nd International Symposium on Computer Science and Intelligent Control, pp. 1–6 (2018)

Author Index

Printed in the United States
by Baker & Taylor Publisher Services